WALES

BLUE GUIDE

WALES

AND THE MARCHES

Edited by
JOHN TOMES
C.B.E. B.A.

With Atlas, Maps, and Ground Plans

ERNEST BENN LIMITED
LONDON AND TONBRIDGE

RAND McNALLY & COMPANY
CHICAGO, NEW YORK, SAN FRANCISCO

FIRST EDITION 1922
SECOND EDITION 1926
THIRD EDITION 1936
FOURTH EDITION 1953
FIFTH EDITION (New format) 1969
SIXTH EDITION 1979

Published by Ernest Benn Limited
25 New Street Square, London EC4A 3JA
& Sovereign Way, Tonbridge, Kent

Rand McNally & Company
Chicago. New York. San Francisco

© Ernest Benn Limited 1979

Phototypesetting by Cold Composition Ltd.,
Tonbridge, Kent

Printed in Great Britain by
Tonbridge Printers Ltd., Tonbridge, Kent

ISBN *Hardcover* 0-510-01608-1   0-528-84631-0 (USA)
ISBN *Paperback* 0-510-01607-3   0-528-84630-2 (USA)

PREFACE

Easily accessible and long established as a holiday objective, Wales has during recent years seen an encouraging increase in the number of its visitors. This increase has been accompanied by an expansion of facilities of all kinds, this including not only the obvious fields such as travel, accommodation, and information, but also, to give only two examples, a growing emphasis on the countryside, through many admirable exhibition centres, the opening of country parks, and the waymarking of walks and trails; and an imaginative policy, already successful through specialized trails and a variety of technical and mining museums, for converting the industry of the past into a field of interest for today's visitor.

It thus seems appropriate that this sixth edition of the BLUE GUIDE to WALES should be a new book rather than a routine updating of its predecessor. The maps, town plans, and ground plans have been drawn by *Doug London* and are also entirely new. As in previous editions, the Marches, so closely if often violently associated with the story of Wales, are included in this book, and there are full descriptions of such border towns as Chester, Shrewsbury, and Hereford, and of the roads linking them and leading into Wales.

The editor, *John Tomes,* also edited the Blue Guides to Scotland, and to Belgium and Luxembourg, and assisted in the preparation of others.

Suggestions for the correction or improvement of the Guide will always be welcome and acknowledged.

Acknowledgements are due first to all who have contributed to the compilation and high reputation of this Guide since its first edition in 1922, special appreciation going to *Mr Harold Carter,* responsible for the bulk of the revision for the fifth edition, and to *Mr Stuart Rossiter,* M.A., editor of that edition and associated with Blue Guides since 1954 both as editor and writer. For this sixth edition, the editor is grateful to the many information centres of the Wales Tourist Board, and in particular to *Mr Roy Mason,* the Board's Publicity Manager, always a ready source of help and advice; to other information centres (of national parks, towns and cities, and elsewhere) throughout Wales and the Marches and too numerous to mention individually; to the Department of the Environment (Ancient Monuments) for cooperation in arranging special facilities for visits to sites in their care; to *Mr Hywel Rees* (Publications and Information Officer) and others at the National Museum of Wales, Cardiff, who took much trouble to ensure that the text on the museum was balanced and correct, and to the National Museum of Wales also for permission to base the plan in this book on that in the museum's own guide. Special thanks also go to *Mr W. R. Shotton* of the Mountaineering Club of North Wales, who checked many pages of text covering walks and climbs in North Wales; and to *Mrs Andrew Davison* for time-saving preparatory notes on museums and nature reserves.

6

Background Sources. Amongst many other publications, the editor has found the undermentioned valuable for reference and background. *Encyclopaedia Brittannica. Dictionary of National Biography. The Mabinogion,* translated by Gwyn Jones and Thomas Jones (Dent, Everyman's Library). Several publications of the Wales Tourist Board, notably *North Wales, Mid Wales,* and *South Wales.* Several H.M.S.O. publications, amongst these the official guides of the Department of the Environment, Ancient Monuments; *Snowdonia National Park,* edited by G. Rhys Edwards for the Countryside Commission; *Snowdonia Forest Park Guide,* edited by Herbert L. Edlin, B.Sc., Dip. For., Forestry Commission; *Ancient Monuments of Anglesey,* by O. E. Craster, M.A., F.S.A., Principal Inspector of Ancient Monuments. *The National Parks of Wales,* by Margaret Davies, M.A., PH.D. (Cardiff Naturalists' Society). *Pembrokeshire Coast National Park* (Dyfed County Council). *Isle of Anglesey Official Guide,* compiled and designed by Robert Williams and Jenny Steel (R. E. Jones and Bros., for Isle of Anglesey Tourist Association). *Chester, Heritage City* (Chester City Council). *City of Hereford,* edited and designed by Graham Roberts for Hereford City Council. *A Guide to Gower* (Gower Society). *South Wales Ports Handbook* (Ed. J. Burrow and Co. Ltd). *Welsh Coal Mines,* by Dr W. Gerwyn Thomas (National Museum of Wales). National Trust publications, especially *Plas Newydd, Penrhyn Castle, Croft Castle, Erddig,* and *Berrington Hall.*

CONTENTS

ROUTES

MAPS AND PLANS

MAPS

TOWN PLANS

GROUND PLANS

NOTES ON USING THE GUIDE

The Guide is in two parts. The first provides background and practical information, the main subjects being listed in the Contents. Intending visitors with no firm plans as to where to tour may be helped by the sections on the **Counties** and **National Parks** of Wales. The second part comprises 49 Routes, covering the Marches and Wales. The overall scheme of these Routes can be seen at a glance by referring to the **Plan of Routes** on p. 96.

Distances. The preamble to each Route gives its total distance. In both the preamble and text italicized distances are those between points along the basic Route, i.e. each italicized distance is the distance from the previous one. Other distances (e.g. to places to the side of the Route) are in Roman print. For a number of reasons (changing road alignments, by-passes, places lying off the main road) distances are only approximate.

Atlas and Index. Most places appearing in the *Atlas* are mentioned in the text. Since Routes often run close to one another or cross, it is advisable to use the atlas, and, by means of the *Index,* to look up places lying either side of the Route being travelled. This will ensure that places of interest within easy reach but described under other Routes are not missed.

Access to Sites. Opening times and other information are given on p. 88, this section being revised with each new printing of the Guide. In the Routes text the symbol (†) indicates sites for which access information is given.

Asterisks (*) draw attention to points of special interest or attraction.

Maps. There is a wide choice of maps covering Wales. The *Wales Tourist Map* (5 m. or 8 km. to one inch), published by the Wales Tourist Board, includes Wales and the Marches in one sheet and is useful for the broad planning of a tour. The reverse of this map carries general information, including small but clear plans of leading tourist towns, and lists of the Board's tourist information centres. A similar area, but without the S.E. corner, is within a single sheet of the *Bartholomew Grand Touring Series* (4 m. to one inch, or 2.5 km. to one cm.). Also useful for planning are the *Ordnance Survey 1:250,000* (quarter-inch) maps, which cover Wales and the Marches in two sheets. For motorists *Bartholomew's National Series* (1:100,000) includes in nine sheets all the Routes described in this Guide; each map has a brief description of the scenery and of the principal towns and other sites. For anyone wishing to explore minor roads and lanes and discover some of the remoter archaeological sites (some of the grid references of which are given in this Guide), the *Ordnance Survey 1:50,000* (1 km.= 2 cm., one grid square) is essential.

Abbreviations. In addition to generally accepted and self-explanatory abbreviations, the following occur in the Guide:-

A.D. = Anno Domini
A.M. = Inspectorate of Ancient Monuments
Attrib. = Attributed to
b. = born
B.C. = Before Christ
B.H. = Bank Holiday
c. = circa (about)
d. = died
Dec. = Decorated
E. = East
E.E. = Early English
F.C. = Forestry Commission
fl. = floruit (flourished)

H.M.S.O. = Her Majesty's Stationery Office
inhab. = inhabitants
km. = kilometre
m. = mile
M.C. = Military Cross
M.P. = Member of Parliament
N. = North
N.C. = Nature Conservancy
N.T. = National Trust
O.S. = Ordnance Survey
p. = page
Perp. = Perpendicular
pron. = pronounced
R.C. = Roman Catholic
Rev. = Reverend
R.N. = Royal Navy
R.N.L.I. = Royal National Lifeboat Institution
R.S.P.B. = Royal Society for the Protection of Birds
Rte = Route
S. = South
sq. = square
SS = Saints
V.C. = Victoria Cross
W. = West
W.T.B. = Wales Tourist Board

BACKGROUND INFORMATION

GENERAL DESCRIPTION OF WALES

Whatever the outcome of the devolution issue, Wales is and seems likely to remain an integral part of the United Kingdom. Nevertheless, whatever the constitutional position, nothing could be more mistaken than to regard Wales simply as a westward extension of England. Wales has a long history of its own, large parts of the land in the past enjoying prolonged periods of independence; most of the Welsh can claim a different origin (Brythonic Celt rather than Anglo-Saxon); and the separateness of Wales's identity will quickly impress itself on the visitor once he crosses the border and meets tongue-twisting Welsh names and signs, the distinctive and musical Welsh accent, the widespread use of the Welsh language, and the very real sense of a national homogeneity.

In shape Wales is roughly a rectangle (some 160 m. from N. to S., and some 50 m. from W. to E.), from which project Anglesey and the Lleyn at the N.W. and Pembroke at the S.W., between being the huge crescent of Cardigan Bay. The greater part of the country is hilly or mountainous, the principal ranges being magnficent Snowdonia and Cader Idris to the N.W., with the lesser Clwydian and Berwyn hills to the N.E.; the succession of Rheidol Forest, Plynlimon, and Towy Forest stretching N. to S. behind the coast between the Dyfi estuary and the valley of the Towy at Llandovery; and, across the S.E., the mountains of Brecon Beacons National Park, with, to their S., the high ground of the South Wales coalfield, broken by the series of largely industrialized valleys which slice in from the busy coast. The border lands are mainly undulating and pastoral country, broken here and there by upland moor, a description which applies also to much of the S.W., to the N.E. immediately behind the string of coastal resorts, and to Anglesey and parts of the Lleyn. Other scenic features of Wales are the many beautiful river valleys (e.g. Wye, Conwy, Teifi, Towy); lakes and reservoirs, frequently in lovely moorland or afforested settings; and cliff scenery, especially in the southwest. Indeed, apart from resort areas with their holiday camps and caravan sites and the industrial S.E., there are few parts of Wales which are not scenically attractive, and few also which do not offer almost limitless opportunities for walking.

But, leading attraction though it is, there is a lot more to Wales than its scenery, and a list of just some of the other things the country has to offer could include the choice of holiday resorts, whether the popular string along the N. coast or the many others elsewhere sought for their remoteness and quietness; several of the largest, most imposing, and most historic castles in Britain; great mansions, splendidly decorated and furnished and many owned by the National Trust; prehistoric sites, notably in Anglesey and on the Presely Hills; religious establishments, ranging from ruined abbeys, through great active cathedrals, to a wealth of interesting churches, many of them tiny and primitive; the famous little railways of Wales; museums and art galleries, descending from Cardiff's superb National Museum of Wales, with its nine specialized branch museums, down to modest but always interesting local collections; choirs, legend, weaving, and much else.

THE MARCHES. THE COUNTIES OF WALES

The MARCHES—now the western strip of the English counties of Cheshire, Salop, and Hereford and Worcester—are the border lands, subjugated by Norman adventurers who were made earls (of Chester, Shrewsbury, and Hereford) by William I and who, as Lords Marcher, for long acted as virtually independent rulers. Only with the Act of Union of 1536 did they lose their privileges, and the Council of the Marches in fact continued to function at Ludlow until 1689. Scenically the Marches are for the most part pleasant agricultural countryside, from which rise occasional high moorland or wooded hills, a distinctive feature being the many attractive black-and-white half-timbered houses. Embracing a wealth of historic or for other reasons interesting places, the Marches are in their own right an area of considerable tourist importance. For elsewhere in these counties, see the 'Blue Guide to England').

The following are only a few of the many places meriting a visit. **Cheshire:** *Chester,* for half-timbered houses, its famous 'rows', its cathedral and virtually complete town walls, and its 'heritage' museums. **Salop:** *Shrewsbury,* for half-timbered houses (notably Rowley's House Museum), and for the stained glass in St Mary's Church. *Haughmond Abbey.* The Romano-British town of *Viroconium. Stokesay Castle. Ludlow Castle.* **Hereford and Worcester:** *Hereford,* for its cathedral and various museums. The mansions of *Croft Castle* and *Berrington Hall. Goodrich Castle.* The beauty spot of *Symond's Yat Rock.*

Since the local government reorganization of 1974 Wales has been made up of eight counties instead of the previous thirteen. The main features of the counties are outlined below, reference at the same time being made to the former counties which have been embraced, most of these—possibly more familiar names to many travellers—becoming in whole or in part districts of the new counties. The new county and district names, and very generally indeed the areas they cover, often reflect early Welsh principalities and lordships.

CLWYD (County town, **Mold.** Former counties of **Flintshire** and most of **Denbighshire**) occupies the N.E. corner of Wales. Flintshire, although the smallest of the former counties, once ranked fifth in population because of the industrialization arising from the varied mineral wealth both here and in neighbouring Denbighshire; the name Flint is of uncertain origin, but is not derived from the stone. Geologically Clwyd is of considerable interest as nearly all formations between the Lower Silurian and Triassic are represented (*Geological Museum of North Wales* is at Bwlchgwyn). Of the county's five districts, that of Glyndwr recalls that this area was the home of Owen Glendower; for the district of Wrexham Maelor, see p. 132.

Within Clwyd are the part industrialized estuary of the Dee; Wales's N.E. coast, with its string of popular resorts, holiday camps, and caravan parks; the Vale of Clwyd, with to its E. the Clwydian Hills and to its W. the bleak upland of Mynydd Hiraethog with Clocaenog Forest below; the Vale of Llangollen (river Dee); and most of the range of the Berwyns. Among places of particular interest are *Chirk, Flint, Rhuddlan,* and *Denbigh* castles, the first still occupied, the others massive Edwardian ruins; the ruined abbeys of *Valle Crucis* and *Basingwerk;* the mansion of *Erddig* (Wrexham); the cathedral of *St Asaph;* and *Llyn Brenig* (on Mynydd Hiraethog) with its varied attractions. Churches, particularly in what was Denbighshire, are characterized by their parallel naves plan.

GWYNEDD (County town, **Caernarvon.** Former counties of **Anglesey, Caernarvonshire, Merioneth,** and part of **Denbighshire**) fills the N.W. of Wales, its inland boundaries running E. of the Vale of Conwy and to the S. generally following the course of the Dyfi to its mouth. The county includes the whole of *Snowdonia National Park* (see below), the most scenic and probably the most visited area of Wales. Other, if gentler scenic parts of the county are the Lleyn, with its mixture of mountain and pastoral land and choice of resorts, and the pleasant Vale of Conwy, lying just outside the National Park.

Anglesey is described as Rte 12. The former county of Caernarvon is now roughly divided into the districts of Dwyfor (Lleyn) and Arfon (S.E. of Menai Strait and including the Pass of Llanberis and most of Snowdon), while the district of Aberconwy straddles the length of the Conwy. Merioneth, now the district of Meirionnydd and forming the S. part of Gwynedd, was the Mervinia of the Romans and derives its name from Meirion, a grandson of the 5C Prince Cunedda.

Gwynedd is full of places of interest. On **Anglesey** are many prehistoric sites, notably *Bryn Celli Ddu* burial chamber, the hut circles on *Holyhead Island,* and the Iron Age village of *Din Lligwy; Plas Newydd,* with works by Rex Whistler, the magnificent Menai Strait home of the marquesses of Anglesey; and the great ruin of *Beaumaris Castle* overlooking the N. end of the strait. The resort of *Llandudno,* with *Great Orme's Head,* is in the district of **Aberconwy,** as is also *Conwy,* with its castle and town walls. In the district of **Arfon,** *Bangor* with its cathedral, and the mansion of *Penrhyn Castle,* are at the N. end of the Menai Strait, while at the S. end is *Caernarvon,* with castle and town walls and Roman *Segontium.* The Iron Age hillfort-village of *Tre'r Ceiri* and *Criccieth Castle* are both in the district of **Dwyfor** (Lleyn), while across the bay historic *Harlech Castle* stands high above the coast of **Meirionnydd.** In Meirionnydd too are the interesting *Tanygrisiau (pumped-storage) Power Station* near Blaenau Ffestiniog, and, between Dinas Mawddwy and Bala, *Bwlch-y-Groes* (1790 ft), the highest point on any motor road in Wales. Gwynedd is known also for its huge and mostly disused *Slate Quarries;* two near Blaenau Ffestiniog are open to visitors, and the *Quarrying Museum* is at Llanberis. Most of the *Little Railways* are also in Gwynedd (Snowdon, Llanberis Lake, Festiniog, Talyllyn, Fairbourne, Bala Lake).

POWYS (County town, **Llandrindod Wells.** Former counties of **Montgomeryshire, Radnorshire,** and **Breconshire**) lies entirely inland to the E. of Gwynedd's district of Meirionnydd and the county of Dyfed. The county's N. boundary is with Clwyd, its E. with England, and its S. with the counties of Gwent, Mid Glamorgan, and West Glamorgan, this last boundary being roughly the line followed by Rte 37B between

Brecon Beacons National Park and the uplands of the South Wales coalfield.

The former counties now form Powys's three districts, and it is convenient to describe the county under these. **Montgomery,** in the N. and roughly matching the ancient principality of Powys (*Powysland Museum* at Welshpool), is named after Roger de Montgomery, the Norman who subjugated these lands in c. 1090. Scenically the district is generally hilly, one of the most attractive places being Lake Vyrnwy in its wooded setting and with its mountain approaches from the direction of Bala. Another wild and attractive area is to the N.W. of Llanidloes, with Hafren Forest (below Plynlimon and source of the Severn and Wye) and the Mountain Road across to the valley of the Dyfi. The main place of interest is the mansion of *Powis Castle* (Welshpool). *Newtown* has some interesting museums, and the *Welshpool and Llanfair Railway* attracts many visitors.—**Radnor,** the central district, created by Henry VIII from the lands of the Lords Marcher and almost entirely English-speaking, perhaps traces its name to the Anglo-Saxon 'rade-nore' meaning 'land of hill tracks'. The district includes the high moorland of Radnor Forest, and in the N.W. near Rhayader the beautiful Elan Valley reservoirs. One of the loveliest stretches of the Wye provides the district's border between Rhayader and Hay-on-Wye. The scanty remains of *Cwmhir Abbey* are worth visiting for their pastoral setting and as possibly the resting place of Llewelyn the Last. Also of interest are *Old Radnor Church,* and *Llandrindod Wells Museum,* with finds from the nearby Roman fort of *Castell Collen.*—**Brecknock,** the southern of the three districts of Powys, is named from Brychan, a local prince of the 5C, and was earlier known as Brycheiniog. In the 11C the district was conquered by the Norman Bernard of Newmarch. Mountainous and hilly, Brecknock is largely made up of *Brecon Beacons National Park* (see below), while in the far N.W. of the district the uplands of Irfon and Towy forests provide another remote and scenic area. The city of *Brecon* has a historic cathedral, the outstanding Brecknock Museum, and (3 m. away) the Roman fort of *Y Gaer,* still with much of its stonework. *Tretower,* N. of Crickhowell, has a fine medieval manor house alongside a ruined castle with a circular tower, and in the S.W. corner of the district *Dan-yr-Ogof* caves are much visited.

DYFED (County town, **Carmarthen.** Former counties of **Cardiganshire, Carmarthenshire,** and **Pembrokeshire**) is a large county which administers all the southwest. The long coastline starts at the estuary of the Dyfi on Cardigan Bay, swings round the rugged Pembroke peninsula, and finishes at the estuary of the Loughor at the E. end of Carmarthen Bay. Because of the county's size it is convenient to describe it under the headings of the districts or groups of districts which make up the former counties. **Ceredigion** (Cardigan), with a coastline extending from the Dyfi to the Teifi estuary, is the N. district of Dyfed. Though largely agricultural, the district has the mountainous area of Plynlimon (with the scenic road past Nant-y-Moch reservoirs) at the north. Also in the N. is the Vale of Rheidol, up which the small *Vale of Rheidol Railway* runs from Aberystwyth to Devil's Bridge. The district's principal town is *Aberystwyth,* with a castle, the National Library of Wales, and the Ceredigion Museum. The ruins of the important abbey of *Strata Florida* are to the S. of Devil's Bridge, and those of the lesser abbey of *St Dogmaels* are near Cardigan town. The *West Wales Farm Park,* inland from New Quay, is an attraction of an unusual kind.—The districts of **Carmarthen** (W.), **Dinefwr** (N.E.), and **Llanelli** (S.E.) represent the former county of Carmarthen. Carmarthen was the chief centre of the Rebecca Riots in 1843-44; the county's story is illustrated in the *County Museum* at Abergwili (Carmarthen). Places of interest in the Carmarthen district include the *Museum of the Woollen Industry* and *Llanstephan Castle,* while *Kidwelly Castle* is the main site in Llanelli. The district of Dinefwr offers the Roman *Ogofau Goldmines* at Pumpsaint; and ruined *Talley Abbey* and *Dryslwyn* and *Carreg Cennan* castles, all near Llandeilo.—The districts of **Presely** and **South Pembrokeshire** make up what was the county of Pembrokeshire, noted for its coastal scenery, all now within *Pembrokeshire Coast National Park* (see below). Pembrokeshire was a part of the Demetia of the ancient chronicles, so called from the local tribe. There was extensive Flemish settlement in 1107 and South Pembrokeshire is sometimes called 'Little England beyond Wales', Flemish influence still being traceable in the local domestic architecture, e.g. at St Florence. A line drawn roughly E. and W. through Narberth and Haverfordwest divides the Welsh-speaking population on the N. from the English-speaking descendants of the Flemings on the south. Presely and South Pembrokeshire include a large number of places of outstanding tourist interest, among these being the large ruined castles of *Cilgerran, Llawhaden, Carew, Manorbier,* and *Pembroke; St David's,* with its historic cathedral and ruined bishop's palace; the attractive ruins of *Lamphey Bishop's Palace;* the *Presely Hills* with many prehistoric sites; little *St Govan's Chapel;* and the great anchorage of *Milford Haven* with its oil tankers and terminals.

The earldom of Pembroke was created in 1138. Gilbert de Clare, popularly known as Strongbow, being the first holder of the title and first of a long line of nobles who were amongst the most powerful and rapacious of the Lords Marcher. Families holding the title included the Marshals, De Valences, Hastings, and Tudors, one of these last being Jasper, uncle of Henry VII. In 1138 the Pembroke lands, mainly S. of Milford Haven, became a county palatine (independent of the national system of administration), the earls maintaining their local rights of sovereignty until the palatinate was abolished in 1536.

The former county of **Glamorganshire** is now the three counties of West, Mid, and South Glamorgan.

WEST GLAMORGAN (County town, **Swansea**) includes the Gower, with caves, popular beaches, important nature reserves, some prehistoric sites (notably *Parc le Breos*), and the ruined castles of *Oystermouth* and *Weobley.* Also of interest in the county are *Neath Abbey; Margam Park and Abbey; Port Talbot,* with its deep-water harbour and steelworks; and, leading N.E. from Port Talbot, the *Cwm Afan Scenic Route* with the *Welsh Miners Museum.*

MID GLAMORGAN (County offices, **Cardiff**) is the county of The Valleys (see Rte 41), slicing into the barren mountains of the N. part of the county. *Caerphilly Castle,* the largest and one of the most imposing ruins in Wales, is passed on the approach to Rhymney Valley. In the county's very different coastal zone either side of the Ogmore estuary are *Ogmore Castle* and *Ewenny Priory,* while the extensive remains of *Coity*

Castle are to the N.E. of the fast expanding industrial town of *Bridgend,* itself with a castle.

SOUTH GLAMORGAN (County offices, **Cardiff**) is made up of Cardiff and its environs (see Rte 40) and to the W. the largely rural Vale of Glamorgan. Sites here include prehistoric *Tinkinswood Cairn, Turner House Art Gallery* at Penarth, and the church at *Llantwit Major.*

GWENT (County town **Cwmbran**), forming the S.E. corner of Wales, was formerly **Monmouthshire,** lands which, though strongly Welsh in character, were removed from the jurisdiction of the Lords Marcher by Henry VIII and included among the English counties. Ecclesiastically though, Monmouthshire remained part of Wales, to which it returned under the local government reorganization of 1974. Today's name of Gwent, originally applying only to the region between the Usk and the Wye, derives from Venta Silurum (*Caerwent*), the Romano-Welsh town between Chepstow and Newport, the extensive remains of which are one of Gwent's more important sites. *Caerleon,* N. of Newport, is another important Roman site. *Newport* is visited for its cathedral; its good museum, with finds from Caerleon and Caerwent as well as more recent local material; and its curious Transporter Bridge. Topographically Gwent divides roughly into three N.-S. strips. To the W. are the mountains into which cut the industrialized Ebbw and Sirhowy valleys (Rte 41E.) In the centre, either side of the Usk, the country is undulating and agricultural, though to the N. of Abergavenny it rises to become the S. part of the Black Mountains; within this central strip the main sites are (N. to S.) *Llanthony Abbey,* and *Grosmont, Skenfrith, White,* and *Raglan* castles. The E. border of the county is the beautiful wooded Lower Wye Valley. Here *Monmouth* has a unique 13C fortified bridge and a local history centre; *Tintern Abbey* is one of the most visited sites in Wales; and impressively sited *Chepstow Castle* stands above the river's estuary, below being the huge but graceful *Severn Bridge.*

THE NATIONAL PARKS OF WALES

National Parks in England and Wales are designated primarily because of their outstanding scenic value; they receive central government financial backing. The movement for the preservation of, and access to, such countryside has its roots in the last century. The National Trust was incorporated in 1895, and the Commons Preservation Society and the National Footpaths Preservation Society merged in 1899. The Council for the Preservation of Rural England was founded in 1926, and its Welsh equivalent in 1928. Today's National Parks were set up by the National Parks Commission (since 1968 the Countryside Commission, see below) under the National Parks and Access to the Countryside Act of 1949, the purpose being both the positive preservation of natural beauty and also the promotion of public access and enjoyment. The parks however are neither true parks nor nationally owned, and most public access other than recognized rights of way has to be negotiated with private owners.

There are three other officially designated countryside areas. **Areas of Outstanding Natural Beauty,** generally smaller than national parks, are not subject to statutory administrative arrangements. In Wales such areas are the Anglesey coast, the Lleyn coast, and Gower. **Heritage Coasts** are lengths of unspoilt coastline, requiring protection by planning control and management. In Wales defined or potential heritage coasts are Great Orme's Head, parts of Anglesey, the Lleyn, Pembrokeshire, Gower, and the Vale of Glamorgan. **Country Parks** may be

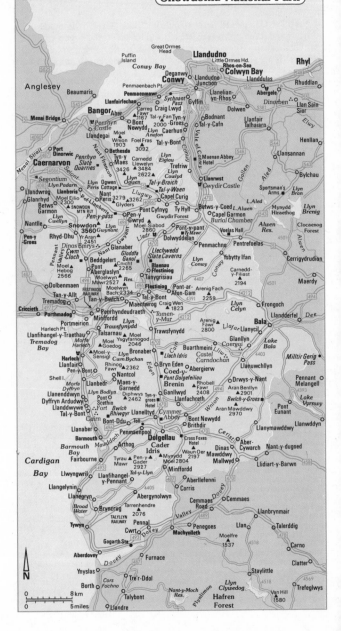

Snowdonia National Park

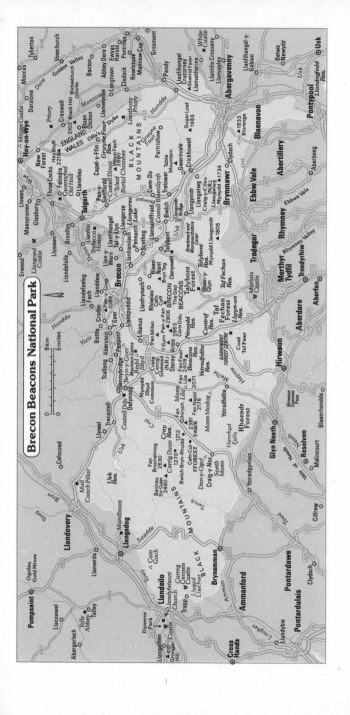

Brecon Beacons National Park

set up by local authorities or private owners. The purpose of such parks is to give townspeople access to countryside, without their having to travel far and without putting rural interests at risk. There are several such parks in Wales, the majority being mentioned in this Guide.

National Parks and other designated countryside areas are administered by planning committees of the counties in which they lie, or by other local authority committees. The Countryside Commission advises on designation, planning, and management, and provides financial help. One of the first acts of the original National Parks Commission was to draw up a *Country Code,* the ten points of which are: Guard against all risk of fire; Fasten all gates; Keep dogs under proper control; Keep to the paths across farmland; Avoid damaging fences, hedges, and walls; Leave no litter; Safeguard water supplies; Protect wildlife, plants, and trees; Go carefully on country roads; Respect the life of the countryside.

SNOWDONIA NATIONAL PARK (map, p. 20), designated in 1951, is the largest (845 sq.m.) and scenically most spectacular of Wales's three national parks, With mountains, lakes, forests, three estuaries and c. 30 m. of coast the park is scenically the most varied, as well as being the most generously provided with the picnic sites, information centres and exhibitions, waymarked and other trails and climbs, nature reserves, and other facilities that are essential features for wide public enjoyment.

Although the park is named for its highest and best known mountain group, Snowdon is geographically only one part of a park which includes several ranges as well as large areas of moorland and forest. The various areas merge into one another, but can conveniently be identified as below (roughly from N. to S.).

The **Carneddau Range,** much of it National Trust, extends N. from Llyn Ogwen and includes the great heights of *Carnedd Llewelyn* (3484 ft) and *Carnedd Dafydd* (3426 ft), after Snowdon the highest mountains in Wales. Farther N. is the high moorland between Conwy Bay and the Vale of Conwy, an area with some prehistoric sites, crossed by a Roman road, and popular with walkers. (Rtes 2C, 7B, 8, and 10).

Gwydir Forest, lying S.E. of the Carneddau, centres on Betws-y-Coed and to the N.W. merges into the wild country of mountain and lakes to the W. of Trefriw and Llanrwst. The forest is crossed by many waymarked walks, and there is a *Forest Centre* near Gwydir Castle (Llanrwst). (Rtes 7B and C, and 8).

Snowdon proper (*Y Wyddfa,* 3560 ft), the highest and most rugged section of the national park, towers as a mountain group above the narrow and steep-sided *Pass of Llanberis* on the N.E., beautiful *Nant Gwynant* on the S.E., and *Nant Colwyn* and *Llyn Cwellyn* on the southwest. (Snowdon and the Pass of Llanberis are described as Rte 9; Nant Gwynant under Rte 8; and Nant Colwyn under Rtes 8 and 11). A N.E. extension of Snowdon, the mass of the *Glyders* and other mountains, crossed by the Miners' Track and including Cwm Idwal Nature Reserve, fills the area between the Pass of Llanberis and Llyn Ogwen and steep Nant Ffrancon (Rte 10).

Moelwyns and Siabod Range. The *Moelwyns* (2527 ft) lie between Nant Gwynant and Blaenau Ffestiniog, between the two mountains being the great Stwlan dam and reservoir above Tanygrisiau (pumped-storage) Power Station. *Moel Siabod* (2860 ft), a solitary peak to the N. of the Moelwyns and S. of Capel Curig, is popular with walkers. (Rte 8).

The **Arenig Range** (2800 ft) is an isolated and barren range rising sharply to the S. of Llyn Celyn and dropping on the S. down to the lonely hillroad between Trawsfynydd and Bala Lake. (Rtes 17 and 19).

The **Rhinog Range** (2362 ft), rising to the E. of Harlech, is popular with walkers and includes the curious so-called *Roman Steps* and the narrow *Bwlch Drws Ardudwy*. (Rte 20B.).

Coed-y-Brenin, with an excellent forest centre, straddles the beautiful valley between Dolgellau and Trawsfynydd. The forest, with streams and cascades, is particularly well provided with waymarked walks. (Rte 19).

The twin **Arans** (2970 ft) stand above the E. of the road between Bala and Dolgellau. To the E. of the mountains there is a wild stretch of country reaching to Lake Vyrnwy (outside the national park) and crossed by a steep and narrow road which at *Bwlch-y-Groes* reaches the highest point (1790 ft) on any motor road in Wales. (Rte 25).

Cader Idris (2927 ft; Rte 18B), climbed by a choice of paths and second only to Snowdon in popularity, is the southernmost peak of the national park. The mountain's S. slopes drop to the lovely *Fathew* and *Dysynni* valleys, with the popular Talyllyn Railway and much else of interest. (Rte 26).

The **Coast** of Snowdonia National Park extends from Tremadog Bay in the N. to the Dyfi estuary in the S., a distance of c. 30 m. Scenically the stretch is largely one of coastal flats, sandy beaches, and estuaries, backed by high moorland and mountain (Rhinog Range and Cader Idris). Among places of interest down the coast are *Harlech Castle;* prehistoric sites between Harlech and Llanddwywe; *Mawddach Estuary;* and the *Talyllyn Railway.* (Rtes 20B and 26).

Tourist Information. Postal enquiries to Information Officer, Yr Hen Ysgol, Maentwrog, Blaenau Ffestiniog, Gwynedd, LL41 4HW. Centres, usually with exhibitions, at Llanrwst, Llanberis, Blaenau Ffestiniog, Harlech, Bala, Aberdovey, and Dolgellau. For F.C. centres see below.

The **Forestry Commission** (see below) is very active within the park, to the great benefit of visitors who enjoy many picnic sites, forest trails, information centres etc. Leaflets from centres or F.C. offices. *Snowdonia Forest Park,* comprising 9500 hectares of forest, moor, and water, includes Beddgelert and Gwydir forests. The former, to the N.W. of Beddgelert, has a caravan and camping site. Gwydir Forest (around Betws-y-Coed), which embraces the adjoining Lledr and Machno forests, has the *Gwydir Uchaf Information Centre,* across the Conwy from Llanrwst. For *Coed-y-Brenin,* also with an information centre, see above. For literature on the park's forests, see under Books below.

Nature Reserves. There is a large number of nature reserves within Snowdonia National Park. Perhaps the best known are *Snowdon-Y Wyddfa; Cader Idris; Coed Ganllwyd* (Coed-y-Brenin), for ferns, mosses etc.; *Coed Tremadog,* for woods, cliffs, and scree; *Cwm Idwal* at Llyn Ogwen, with important geological features and arctic-alpine flora; *Morfa Dyffryn,* for dunes; and *Morfa Harlech,* for dunes and salt marsh. Permits are required for Coed Tremadog, Morfa Dyffryn (parts), and Morfa Harlech. Information from Nature Conservancy (see below).

Trails and Walks traverse all parts of the park. The principal walking areas, and some walks and ascents, are indicated in this Guide, but walkers may obtain detailed leaflets from the Information Office at Maentwrog, information centres, the Forestry Commission, or Nature Conservancy (for addresses, see below).

Fishing licences and local permits are necessary. Apply Gwynedd River Division, Highfield, Caernarvon, LL55 1HR. See also 'Angling Guide to Wales' (W.T.B.).

The **Snowdon Sherpa Bus Service** enables Snowdon to be climbed by one route and descended by another. It can also be used if the popular but small car park at Pen-y-Pass is full.

Books. *Snowdonia National Park* (H.M.S.O.), edited by G. Rhys Edwards, covers a wide field including geology, flora, fauna, antiquities, the people, and recreation; the book also contains a bibliography. *Snowdonia Forest Park Guide* (H.M.S.O.), edited by Herbert L. Edlin, covers history; antiquities; geology;

Snowdon in literature; mountains, lakes, and rivers; forests; flora; fauna, with fish, birds, and butterflies; walks. *Gwydir Forest* (H.M.S.O.), by Donald L. Shaw, is a history of the forest, but contains also several informative appendices on the forest generally. *Snowdonia National Park Scenery* (National Museum of Wales), by D. Emlyn Evans, is a beautifully illustrated booklet describing the geology of Snowdonia.

BRECON BEACONS NATIONAL PARK (map, p. 21), designated in 1955, covers 519 sq.m., forming a rectangle some 45 m. long from W. to E. (Llandeilo to Abergavenny) and an average of 15 m. broad. The greater part of the park is above 1000 ft and there are many heights over 2000 ft. The park, especially Brecon Beacons and the Black Mountains, is very popular with walkers and pony trekkers. Within the park there are many prehistoric megalithic monuments; several of these are mentioned in this Guide, but visitors requiring more detail should get the Information Sheet 'Megalithic Monuments'. Although the park is named from its principal mountain group, situated at the centre, the Brecon Beacons are in fact only a small part of the whole, which conveniently divides into four distinct areas separated by valleys with main roads. Rather confusingly Black Mountain is at the W. end, while in the E. the park ends with the Black Mountains.

Black Mountain, between A40/A483 and A4067, and crossed by A4069, rises to a group of mountains at the E., the two main peaks being *Bannau Sir Gaer* (or the *Carmarthen Van,* 2460 ft) and *Fan Brycheiniog* (or the *Brecknock Van,* 2630 ft). The name Carmarthen Van is frequently applied to the group as a whole. To the W. Black Mountain drops to Llandeilo and strikingly sited Carreg Cennan Castle, while to the N. moor and forest stretch away to Usk Reservoir. To the E., and also near Usk Reservoir, there are standing stones. (Rtes 29, 34, and 37).

Fforest Fawr (several peaks over 2000 ft), between A4067 and A4059, was long a hunting preserve of the lords of Brecon and it was not until the early 19C that the district was enclosed. To the S. of the mountains is *Rhaeadr Forest,* with to its E. the Mellte and Hepste rivers, with waterfalls and cascades. A minor road, passing standing stones, runs N. to S. between the peaks of Fan Nedd (2176 ft) and Fan Llia (2071 ft). The *Mountain Centre* is on the N. foothills.

The **Brecon Beacons** (N.T.), immediately S. of Brecon (itself within the park, Rte 33A), culminate in a striking pair of peaks (2906 ft), which to the S. shade down to an area of beautiful forest and lakes (*Talybont* and *Taf Fechan* forests). The Beacons are one of the most popular walking districts in Wales. (Rte 33B, which includes walks and a motor circuit).

The **Black Mountains** (*Waun Fach,* 2660 ft) lie beyond the valley of the Usk, which is quite wide in the N. but narrows to the south. The mountains, the E. slopes of which cross the park boundary (here Offa's Dyke Path) and extend into England, are another area popular with walkers. (Rte 37A for the Black Mountains and walks. Rte 37B for the pleasant and interesting valleys of the southeast).

Another section of the park (c. 8 m. long by under 2 m. wide) runs S. from Abergavenny to Pontypool and includes a part of the *Brecknock and Monmouthshire Canal.* Dug in 1797-1812, and until 1932 used for commercial traffic, the canal now serves recreational needs.

Tourist Information. Postal enquiries to National Park Officer, Glamorgan Street, Brecon, Powys, LD3 7DP (please send large stamped addressed envelope).

Other information centres are at Abergavenny, Llandovery, and the Mountain Centre (p. 263). Also Garwnant Forest Centre (see below).

Forestry Commission. Forests within the park include *Cilgwyn*, S. of Llangadog in the W.; *Rhaeadr*, to the S. of Fforest Fawr; *Talybont-Taf Fechan-Coed Taf Fawr*, to the S. of Brecon Beacons; and *Mynydd Du*, on the S. slopes of the Black Mountains. Together these forests provide many picnic sites and trails. Information from *Garwnant Forest Centre* on A470 near Llwyn-On reservoir, or F.C. offices.

Nature Reserves. *Craig Cerrig-Gleisiad*, off A470 between Libanus and Storey Arms (p. 263; permit required). *Craig-y-Cilau*, W. of Crickhowell (p. 257). Information from Nature Conservancy (see below).

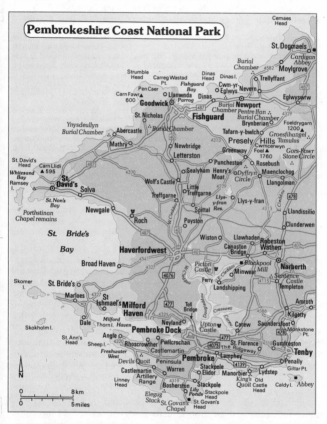

Fishing. A Water Authority licence and permission from the owner of the rights are necessary. See 'Angling Guide to Wales' (W.T.B.).

Pony Trekking. There is a concentration of pony trekking centres around the area of the Black Mountains. See leaflet 'Pony Trekking and Riding' (W.T.B.).

PEMBROKESHIRE COAST NATIONAL PARK (map above) covers 225 sq. m. and was designated in 1952. Rtes 45 to 49 all traverse parts of the park, which can conveniently be divided into four sections.

The **Coast,** much of it with fine cliff scenery, around which leads the

Coastal Path, opened in 1970. The path is 168 m. long, its ends being the estuary of the Teifi in the N. and Amroth on Carmarthen Bay in the south. Not always easy walking, the path for the most part follows the cliff-top, but some detours are unavoidable (e.g. Milford Haven, and the Castlemartin ranges); not all sections of the path are waymarked.

Islands. These include the monastic island of *Caldy,* and also *St Margaret's, Skokholm, Skomer, Grassholm,* and privately owned *Ramsey,* all nature reserves.

The **Presely Hills** in the N. are noted for their prehistoric remains and as the source of some of the stones of stonehenge.

Daugleddau is the tidal estuary of the Western and Eastern Cleddau.

Tourist Information. Postal enquiries to Information Officer, Pembrokeshire Coast National Park Department, County Offices, Haverfordwest, Dyfed. Information Centres at Tenby, Kilgetty, Pembroke, Haverfordwest, Broad Haven (Countryside Unit), St David's, and Fishguard.—The 'Official Guide Book of the Dyfed County Council', in addition to general information, includes a bibliography and sections on geology, climate, wildlife, and recreation. Among many pamphlets produced by the park authority may be mentioned 'Megalithic Monuments', 'Trails', 'Boat Trips', 'Islands', and 'The Presely Hills'.

Nature Reserves (Islands). For access, see 'Access to Sites'. Nature Reserve information on *St Margaret's, Skokholm,* and *Skomer* from West Wales Naturalists' Trust, 20A High Street, Haverfordwest. For *Grassholm,* information from Royal Society for the Protection of Birds, 18 High Street, Newtown, Powys.

Walking is encouraged throughout most of the national park, the Coastal Path and the Presely Hills being the most popular areas. Several leaflets, including some for self-guiding nature trails, are available. The National Park Information Service also organizes a programme of Guided Walks and Lectures ('Walks and Talks') covering such themes as archaeology, industrial archaeology, history, natural history, geology, marine biology etc.

ASPECTS OF WALES

The Flag (Red Dragon). The origin of Wales's flag, a red dragon on a green and white field, is lost in legend but may derive from Roman custom, a dragon having been the emblem of the cohort. In post-Roman times and legend warriors sometimes became known as 'dragons'. Arthur's father was Uther Pendragon, the 'chief dragon', and legend tells that he had a vision of a fiery dragon, interpreted by his seers as a sign that he would mount the throne. Legend (see below) tells too of the struggle between the red dragon of Wales and the white dragon of England, foretelling the victory of the former, a tradition that was fostered by the bards and made true by Henry Tudor whose standard was a red dragon. As Henry VII he incorporated the Welsh dragon in the Royal arms, where it remained until James I displaced it in favour of the Scottish unicorn. In 1801, however, the red dragon was officially recognized as the Royal badge of Wales, and in 1959 the Queen commanded that the red dragon on its green and white field should be the Welsh flag.—The leek, the national emblem, may well have been introduced into Britain by the Romans. Of many theories as to why it became the Welsh emblem the most popular is that in some ancient battle the Welsh wore leeks in their caps as an identification; the battle was won and thus the leek remained in favour.

Choirs. As long ago as the 12C Giraldus was writing of the Welsh love of music and of their gift for singing in harmony. However the development of today's choirs dates from the early 19C when the

Industrial Revolution brought crowded living conditions in the valleys, a boost for nonconformity, and the spread of chapels which became the focus of social life. Music was needed for the services, song schools were formed (music being more easily taught by the newly invented tonic-solfa method), and from these roots grew the choirs. Today many choirs welcome visitors to their rehearsals, the particulars of which are available from tourist information offices.

Bards. The bardic tradition is purely Celtic and in some aspects seems to have been associated with the Druids. Later—as prophets, exhortators, and as the guardians and tellers of tales—the bards filled the gap left by the Roman extermination of the Druids, playing a semi-political role in encouraging local pride and enjoying positions of honour at princely courts, where, needless to say, flattery of the prince and his line was an essential skill. As early as the 6C Gildas censures Maelgwn Gwynedd for being over-influenced by bardic flattery. Hywel Dda's codified legal system (10C) shows that by this date there had developed three grades of bard. Chief bards (who won their positions through competition, were awarded a chair of honour, and received a harp as symbol of office) ranked as senior officials. A chief bard's field of poetry, however, was limited to the lord and his family, God, and the saints. The second grade provided for the household what the chief bard did for the princely family, and was given more latitude of subject, in particular being allowed to sing of love and nature. The third grade (loosely called Minstrels) embraced a whole range of popular entertainers, restricted only in that they might not trespass on the metres or subjects of the upper grades. This third grade is important, because it was they who told the popular tales which later found written form as the 'Mabinogion'.

The above system survived into late medieval times, when the patronage of the princes began to be superseded by that of the gentry, and bards, no longer court officials, made regular circuits of patrons' halls. At the same time popular entertainers scarcely ranking as bards wandered around on unofficial begging circuits and, though at the time despised, were nonetheless important for their influence on folk-poetry. At the Caerwys eisteddfodau of 1523 and 1568, in an attempt to safeguard professional standards, a system was introduced by which apprentices progressed through three grades and were licensed to make a circuit of the halls of the gentry. Anybody unlicensed yet seeking patronage was officially classified as a vagabond.

Despite the above, however, the bardic system went into decline and the 17C saw the rise of poets independent of patronage and, more important, freed from ancient conservative poetic tradition.

Today's bardic system (with the *Gorsedd;* or Assembly, or Council), in some respects based on dubious foundations, was introduced in 1792 by Edward Williams (Iolo Morganwg), a self-taught scholar whose passion was ancient manuscripts bearing on Welsh history. His lead was followed up by enthusiasts who organized local eisteddfodau. In modern Wales a bard is a poet whose qualities have been recognized at an eisteddfod, and the Gorsedd has a defined role which includes the safeguarding of bardic custom and ceremony as well as much of the responsibility for the administration of the National Eisteddfod.

An **Eisteddfod** (plural, eisteddfodau) originally meant simply a meeting of bards, whether in poetic competition or simply to discuss professional problems. Although bards had for centuries won their positions through competition, the first recorded bardic contest is that of 1176 convened at Cardigan by Rhys ap Gruffydd. This, though the word eisteddfod was not used, had many eisteddfodic features, notably the fact that the festival was proclaimed a year and a day in advance, this being considered, as it still is today, essential to the achievement of high standards. The prizes, for both poetry and music, were miniature silver chairs, symbols of the chairs of honour of the chief bards. In 1450 the term eisteddfod was used for a festival at Carmarthen, important for having been the occasion when metrical rules were codified which even today apply to the principal or Chair Poem of the National Eisteddfod. Later important eisteddfodau were those of 1523 and 1568 at Caerwys when the licensing of bards was introduced.

During the 16 to 18C both bards and eisteddfodau sank to a local and largely impromptu level.

The conception of an eisteddfod as a major public occasion dates from the Corwen eisteddfod of 1789, an occasion which (under the patronage of the Gwyneddigion, a society of London Welshmen) marked both the start of a series of successful eisteddfodau and also a return to the custom of proclaiming the festival a year and a day in advance. Similar eisteddfodau flourished in the 19C, one noteworthy development being the inclusion of choral competitions as a result of the development of the chapel choirs.

The *National Eisteddfod of Wales* was established between 1861-80 as a means of achieving worthy national standards, of safeguarding the Welsh language, and of promoting Welsh culture. The governing body is the Court of the National Eisteddfod of Wales, and the festival is held alternately in North and South Wales annually during the first week of August. The National Eisteddfod (with details of the now wide-ranging competitions) is proclaimed by the Gorsedd at least a year and a day in advance, normally at a traditional ceremony within a Gorsedd Circle of Stones (itself laid out to a ritual pattern), the rites being to the accompaniment of harp music. These circles of stones will be found in many places at which the National Eisteddfod has been proclaimed.

Legend. Most of the legends of Wales spring from the 'Mabinogion', the creation of the bards of the Dark Ages, freely using material from their own imaginations, from romanticized historical or quasi-historical figures (e.g. Arthur and Macsen Wledig, the latter the Roman Magnus Maximus), and from folk tales and characters coeval perhaps with the earliest Celts. The earliest known written forms of the stories are in the 'White Book of Rhydderch' (1300-25; National Library of Wales) and the 'Red Book of Hergest' (1375-1425; Jesus College, Oxford). The 'Mabinogion' was translated by Lady Charlotte Guest in 1838, but the engaging stories, with their improbable heroes but many easily identified place names, are now available in modern and very readable form in the translation (1948; with an admirable interpretive introduction) by Gwyn Jones and Thomas Jones (Everyman's Library).

The hero Arthur figures prominently in the 'Mabinogion' and thus in Welsh legend. He slew a giant and was mortally wounded on Snowdon, and a number of burial chambers, older than Arthur by around 2000 years, bear his name. On the Presely Hills standing stones commemorate two of Arthur's sons, killed by a great boar.

Vortigern and Merlin are two other characters associated in legend with Wales, and since the legend refers to much visited places (Carmarthen and Dinas Emrys) and also relates to the Welsh Dragon flag, it is told below.

Vortigern, King of Britain during the 5C, invited the Saxons Hengist and Horsa to help him against the Picts and Scots, rewarding them with land. But Hengist and Horsa were not satisfied, and soon the British were at war with the Saxons, Vortigern having to flee both the Saxons and his own angry people. Reaching Wales, he was told by his wizards that he must build himself a strong tower, and after much searching Vortigern chose Dinas Emrys. However every time his masons started to build the foundations were swallowed by the earth, whereupon the wizards said that Vortigern must find a youth born of no earthly father, kill him, and sprinkle his blood on the mortar. Messengers were sent far and wide, until one, reaching Carmarthen, overheard a dispute between two youths, Dinabutius and Merlin, in which the former mocked Merlin for never having had a father. Brought to Vortigern and questioned, the mother (a king's daughter) admitted that a spirit in the shape of a man had lain with her, thereafter disappearing and leaving her pregnant. Merlin however mocked the wizards, telling Vortigern that his tower kept falling down because there was a pool below, the home of two sleeping dragons, one red and one white. Digging proved Merlin right, and when the awoken dragons started to fight and the red dragon killed the white dragon, Merlin interpreted this as the eventual victory of Wales over England. This theme became a favourite with the bards, leading to the adoption of the Red Dragon as the emblem of Wales and the realization of the prophecy through the accession of Henry VII.

Mining in Wales, once a vigorous national feature, has since the early years of this century experienced a steady and even dramatic decline, the reasons including exhaustion, alternative materials, foreign competition, and lack of demand. *Gold* was known in Wales in prehistoric times, but it was the Romans who started serious mining. Between then and the present day frequent ventures have been launched, but although gold is extracted the return has never justified continuing operations. There are a number of places where old workings can be explored, by far the best being the Roman and later Ogofau mines near Pumpsaint.—*Copper* was mined in Anglesey from Roman times until the late 19C, the opencast scars on bleak Parys Mountain remaining as reminders of this prosperous past. The copper mines around Snowdon carried on until about 1916, the remains of some of their buildings today being a feature of the Miners' Trail up the mountain.—*Lead* was mined in several places, notably on the plateau between Trefriw and Betws-y-Coed where between 1838 and the First World War there were as many as 19 mines, some producing over 2000 tons a year until defeated by competition from richer American deposits. Among other disused lead mines are those which rise beside the mountain road between Devil's Bridge and Rhayader.—*Slate* has been quarried and mined since the time of the Romans, but operations are now on a much diminished scale compared to the peak period of the late 19C. The principal survivor, still the largest opencast site in the world, is the Penrhyn quarry near Bethesda. Slate quarrying and mining has left scars which, though ugly, can at the same time because of their sheer size be awe-inspiring. Today some of these huge gashes into the mountains have been converted into imaginative tourist attractions (notably above Blaenau Ffestiniog), while the great disused quarries at Llanberis are becoming the site of one of the world's largest pumped-storage power stations.—*Coal* is still mined in both South and North Wales, but on a very small scale compared to the past. The South Wales field, with both deep and opencast mines, is known for its high-grade anthracite (between Glyn Neath and the Gwendraeth); its steam coals (beneath the Taff and Neath valleys); its top-quality coking coals (between Port Talbot and Blaenavon); and house coal (beneath the Ogmore and Garw valleys). In 1913 there were 620 mines and some 57 million tons were produced. Today there are some 50 collieries, producing around 9 million tons. Reserves however seem good and investment plans aim at considerably increased output. The Pembrokeshire sector, with 19 collieries in the 1850s, started to decline from 1900, the last colliery being closed in 1948. In the North Wales field the coal of the narrow Flintshire sector is nearly worked out, while in the Denbighshire sector the sharp increase in depth towards the E. imposes limits on development. One mine is still operating in each sector, total annual output being around 500,000 tons as compared to 3½ million in 1913.

Welsh Mountain Sheep, the native breed of the Welsh uplands, are one of the hardiest and most productive breeds in Britain. The sheep are small and normally white, though black and brown fleeces occur. The fleece is light in weight but of good quality, and Welsh mutton is renowned. Variants of the breed are Black Welsh Mountain and Badger-faced Welsh Mountain, the latter being rare and thought to be descendants of the original breed before the introduction of improvements.—Among other Welsh sheep, all named after their place of origin, are Beulah Speckle Face; Lleyn; Llanwenog, with brown hornless heads; and Kerry Hills, also hornless and with black spots on faces and legs.

Welsh Black Cattle will be seen in many parts of Wales, and since 1966 have been increasingly exported, especially to countries where their hardiness is much valued. The native cattle of Wales since pre-Roman times, the breed in its modern form derives from two strains, the compact Anglesey and the larger Pembrokeshire (Castlemartin). Though good milk providers and sucklers, Welsh Black are primarily beef cattle.

Woollen Industry. The Welsh woollen industry, known to have been well established before the Normans arrived, is perhaps the oldest such in Europe. By the 15C, if not considerably earlier, cloth fairs were a familiar feature of the Welsh and Borders scene, and the 16-18C saw a steady climb to prosperity until by the end of the 18C production of cloth had reached such a level as to be largely dependent on exports. Knitting was an important allied activity, particularly in Merioneth where, according to Pennant, the women had learnt to knit as soon as they could talk (see also p. 186). Stockings, gloves, and woollen caps (known as Welsh wigs) were among the popular articles offered to coach travellers and bought also by middlemen for resale in London and elsewhere in England.

In Wales spinning and weaving were essentially home crafts, side activities to farming and other occupations. However, because of the difference in cost between a spinning wheel and a loom, a separation developed between cottagers spinning yarn and the more prosperous owners of looms to whom they sold it. Frequently farmers, these latter insisted that their employees be as skilled at the loom as in the fields and in many cases found their cloth-selling to be more profitable than farming. All this ended with the Industrial Revolution, Wales showing herself loath to give up the traditional ways and slow to adopt machinery. The decline which then set in lasted through to the late 1960s when an upsurge in tourism brought with it a demand for traditional Welsh work, a demand which is now being met by a reborn and increasingly prosperous industry which is successfully adapting traditional designs to modern requirements. W.T.B.'s booklet *Crafts and Rural Industries* lists the many mills (most with shops) that can be visited.

Crafts. Although craft studios, workshops, and retail shops will be found all over Wales, there is no craft which is peculiar to the country. Many though (weaving, woodwork, slatework) are traditional. W.T.B.'s *Crafts and Rural Industries* lists the large number of craft establishments at which visitors are welcome. There are also many craftsmen whose workshops are not open. The Welsh Arts Council (53 Charles Street, Cardiff, CF1 4ED) keeps a register of craftsmen and can provide contacts for special requirements.

The W.T.B. booklet lists crafts under the following categories:

Textiles and Fabrics. See Woollen Industry above.

Wood, Cane, and Wickerwork includes the traditional local skills of bowl turning and spoon carving. 'Love-spoons', seen in a number of museums, were boy-to-girl courting tokens.

Corn Dollies, a pagan curiosity found over much of Europe and the Near East, were originally made from the last sheaf to be reaped. Kept in the house and planted in spring, dollies provided a winter home for the harvest spirits.

Slate and Stone. Slate sculpture makes an original souvenir of a craft which reached its peak with that of the huge quarries during the 19C.

Jewellery, with craftsmen often using local stones, and designs which reflect Celtic tradition.

Candles, of intricate design and varied colours, are often available with specially designed holders of local pottery.

Toys include dolls in traditional Welsh costume.

Wrought-Ironwork continues a tradition dating back to the firedog of the 1C B.C. found at Capel Garmon and which reached a peak with the 18C work of the Davies brothers.

Also *Pottery; Leatherwork;* and *Pictures, Etchings, Books, and Maps.*

PREHISTORIC WALES AND THE WELSH PEOPLE

By Professor H. J. FLEURE

Note: Except for very minor adjustments this article is reprinted as originally written (1953). Because of their greater geographic precision the old county names have been retained. For the relationship of the old counties to the new see pp. 15-19.

The beginnings of the human story of Wales are even more of a mystery than similar beginnings in many other lands, because finds are few and often raise as many problems as they solve. A generation ago, when it was believed that all stone knives or axes belonged to the ages before metal came into use, conclusions were sometimes over-hastily drawn as to Wales in the Stone Age, but now we realize that metal must have been scarce and precious in prehistoric times in many parts of such a land as Wales, and that even flint was obtainable only by trade from England or by collection on the Welsh beaches.

In the Ice Ages the Welsh plateau must at times have been almost all under ice, but the future may reveal traces of mankind from the age of retreat of the glaciers in the S. of Wales. So far we know only of caves such as that at Paviland in Gower, in which the remains of a male skeleton long known as the 'Lady of Paviland' were found. A somewhat lesser age has been claimed for remains from caves in the limestone district of N.E. Wales.

Shell heaps of unknown age have been described from Merionethshire, and there is some suggestion that, like the kitchen middens of the Iberian peninsula, etc., they may belong to the days when the ice was finally withdrawing, but this again is quite problematic.

At Aberystwyth, in Pembrokeshire, and elsewhere flint chipping-floors have been found, and it has often been noticed that the workmanship on the small flint implements is like that found among implements from French stations belonging to the Tardenoisian period following the retreat of the ice, but it would be very dangerous to argue as to the age of flint work merely from resemblances of style. Flints may have remained in widespread use till quite late prehistoric times considering the remoteness of Wales.

As the ice sheet and glaciers finally retreated from temperate Europe, a rise of sea level due to the melting of the ice allowed the water to penetrate into the river valleys of our islands and the adjacent parts of Europe. The valleys, still keeping many accumulations of glacial mud and boulders, were very wet and swampy, so the men of those days, still without metal tools, were forced to keep to the gorse and bracken heaths, the chalk and other grassy downs, and the coastal strips where the salt winds kept down the tree growth. Large numbers of flint weapons have been found in England, especially on the chalk lands, which are provisionally assigned to this period; they show advances in the art of tool-making. Wales was poor in flint, but, either during the period under discussion or later, the art of grinding stone was introduced and many beautiful tools were made out of blocks of the hard rocks of N.W. Wales and W. Pembrokeshire. Some of these, however, cannot but suggest some imitations of bronze tools, and the suggestion is reinforced because we find that some of these weapons, found for example in N. Cardiganshire, were made of stone from St David's Head, which, as we shall see in a moment, was probably a coastal station of sea-traders of the Bronze Age.

About the end of the third millennium before Christ there seem to have been considerable movements of peoples in Europe. To the N. of the Alps people with broad heads and stalwart frames seem to have moved N. along the S. part of the German plain to Bohemia and the Eastern Alps and Bosnia on the one hand, and to Denmark and the Low Countries on the other, still moving along lines fairly free from forest, showing that they had as yet no adequate means of tackling such country. From the E. shores of the North Sea, which may have been smaller than now, they reached East Britain, and are traced on our coast by their round barrows and their pottery, including especially drinking vessels now usually called 'beakers'.

Probably rather before this a coastwise maritime movement brought men northward along the W. coast of Europe, the Irish Sea and the Minch, the Pentland Firth, and the W. Baltic shores. Various groups apparently built different kinds of monuments with great unhewn stones, and in Wales these are notable in Anglesey, Caernarvonshire, W. Merionethshire, Pembrokeshire, Gower, and the coastlands of Glamorgan. Their positions in W. Caernarvonshire and Pembrokeshire suggest that some are on transpeninsular land routes avoiding the tide-races of headlands with offshore islets, so dangerous to small craft. The finest of these monuments in Wales is at Bryn Celli Ddu in Anglesey. Here a passage walled and roofed with great stones leads into a chamber similarly walled and roofed, and the whole is covered by a mound. Numerous other monuments may be more or less ruined examples of this type or simplifications of it; the commonest now show a chamber walled and roofed by great stones, the roof often being a single block. This type of monument has often been called a dolmen (Celtic for tablestone). One theory is that they were places of burial for portions of the body supposed to contain the spirit, and that the spirit thus awaited rebirth. Ritual in the hope of securing offspring has been practised near the analogous monuments in Brittany down to quite recent times. At Pentre Ifan (Pembrokeshire) a chamber, walled and roofed with great stones, shows remains of a forecourt partly outlined by standing stones. At Capel Garmon (Caernarvonshire) a chamber walled and roofed as usual shows special features allying it with rough stone monuments of the Cotswold area. On the Welsh moorlands, mostly away from the coast, there are some circles of standing stones (see also p. 36), but only very few of the chambered monuments. Standing stones (menhirs = long stones), solitary or grouped in some definite scheme, are another feature.

The late Dr Thomas of the Geological Survey found that the Blue Stones at Stonehenge must have been brought from the Preseli area of Pembrokeshire and that the so-called Altar Stone came from Cosheston near Haverfordwest. This was probably a transference of what was already a sacred monument, and it is of interest that Geoffrey of

Monmouth, writing in the middle of the 12C, refers to the tradition of the moving of sacred stones to Stonehenge. He supposed they came from Ireland; actually Pembrokeshire was on the route of prehistoric intercourse between Ireland and southern England.

Until the later phases of the Bronze Age, that is until bronze had spread far and wide, people still usually avoided the forested valleys, though they had long since begun to use the streams with their boats, as the distribution of finds of their tools shows us.

Let us try to picture the Welsh life of those days. The people live on the moorlands and have a struggle to get stone weapons for daily use; they doubtless move with the seasons from pasture to pasture, and are accustomed to tell those seasons from the perennial view of the valley woodlands below their homes (the old hut circles, often called Cytiau'r Gwyddelod, may be imaginatively allowed to represent their homes). In mid-May the woodland is bright in new living green and its upper edge is marked by a foaming crown of thorns and gorse in bloom. In mid-November the thorn leaves are red and yellow, and the woodland is ablaze with autumn tints. These two periods are marked in the traditional calendar as Calan Mai (May Calends, May Day) and Calan Gaeaf (Winter Calends, All Souls), subject to the eleven days' change that was made in the 18C. Calan Gaeaf and Clan Mai are still thought of as the traditional calendar dates in many parts of the Welsh hills rather than Y Dydd Cyntaf (the first day, Jan 1st) which is a relatively new term and everyone knows that the small boys' habit of burning Guy Fawkes is really a survival of the 'burning of the old year' as the custom is still called in the Channel Islands. In W. Wales, again, as in N. Lancashire, Scotland, etc., houses are often still rented from mid-November and mid-May. Probably these festivals were times of movement up to the higher pastures in May and down to the less chilly ones in November, and seasonal migration of this kind is still a feature of life in parts of the Balkan peninsula and the Alps. On the moorland hills are ridgeway roads which may well have been used in the olden time, and the pedestrian tourist will find their exploration an exhilarating pastime. The cattle may well have been of the breeds still in use. Whether much cultivation was done it is hard to say, but, if the folk-tales are any guide, the moorland people knew the secrets of the dairy and practised herbal medicine, the tradition of which, one tale says, was handed down to the physicians of Myddfai, of fairy descent, and so brought down to historic times. It is a tradition still by no means extinct. To the old moorland folk the forest was the abode of wolf and wild boar and wild cat, pine-martens, polecats, and eagles galore, a place of darkness and danger into which they occasionally penetrated, we may suppose, in bands heading down steep tracks, at times still preserved as hollow or deep-cut ways, to the streams, beating tom-toms and shouting to scare the wild beasts, though one cannot but figure them also hunting the pig by stealth, for their food supply must have been an anxious matter. The folk-tales let us into a secret tragedy, the high death-rate of infants and of women in childbirth.

In a late phase of the Bronze Age, men with better-hardened weapons and typically leaf-shaped swords seem to have spread from the Continent to Britain and westward into Wales, or N. Wales at least. Some students see in these invaders the earlier wave of Celtic-speaking peoples, the men of Goidelic speech, the language which has developed into Gaelic (in the Scottish Highlands and Ireland), and Manx; but others think these old languages are local modifications arising in Scotland, Ireland, and Man from contacts between Celtic invaders of the early Iron Age and people who spoke pre-Celtic tongues. Goidelic speech, in any case, has disappeared from Wales, if it ever existed there in prehistoric times, but there is reason to think it may have been brought in from Ireland in later Roman or post-Roman times to the coastal districts of N.W. and S.W. Wales.

Near the coast, in Anglesey, Caernarvon, Merioneth, and Pembroke at least, and some way in from the coast in Carmarthenshire (Carn Goch), are fortresses of rough stone without mortar, that on Yr Eifl being practically a city with its gateway and steps, its ramparts and its groups of dwellings. It has been thought that there was a sea trade in W. Europe in Iron Age times, and the few finds on these remarkable sites seem to connect the fortresses with this trade. Scattered over S.E. Britain are finds pointing to the occupation of its lower hillsides, and to the probable inauguration of better cultivation and perhaps village settlement, as well as undoubtedly to the making of roads used later as byways by the Romans. This development belongs to the last two or three centuries before the Roman invasion. Earthwork fortresses were features of this time, but those of eastern England differed in various respects from those of the west and of Wales. Men penetrating towards Wales along the valleys made clearings and developed farming, but all the while lived in awe of the other older civilization still lingering on the moorland. The folk-tales of Wales give us vivid pictures of the relations between the two civilizations. The valley folk try to marry fairy, i.e. moorland, women, who, however, must not come into contact with iron and must observe taboos, which in their new life they nearly always break with tragic results. Not only do they want women, the valley folk must have labourers, and the fairy wife knows their little ways and can manage them. Moreover, she knows the secrets of the dairy, so intimately related to little details of local climate and pasture; she knows the simples of the district and can minister to the sick; she is a valuable asset and a source of prosperity, and perhaps an intermediary in occasional more peaceable exchanges of cattle and sheep for corn and textiles with the moorland folk. The valley folk, then, raided for women, slaves and cattle. The moorland people raided for babies, and, one guesses, for corn and implements. One story tells of a fairy strike in a S. Wales valley against the introduction of the plough, another of the inveigling of a valley girl to the moorland to tend a fairy wife in childbirth, and many tell of disappearances of the fairies so easily to be understood by those who have felt the fascination of the eerie moorlands. In fact, the thought of these two civilizations, one belonging to the old moorland people probably under leaders derived from immigrants of the early Bronze Age, the other belonging to the people who spread up the valleys making clearings in the forest, helps us to understand the local folk-tales of Wales and to see their very unusual value. In the Mabinogion we have more sophisticated traditions, but some details are undoubtedly old and tell us of intercourse with Ireland; of days when the pig was just being domesticated, and so on. It is noteworthy that the places named in the simpler old folk-tales nearly all cluster around the smaller moorlands, especially in the fastnesses of the N.W.

The relation of the Romans to Wales is a subject that raises many problems, and for the present it will be best to be content with a few remarks supplemented by the indications here and there in the text of this guide. Very little more than military penetration seems to have occurred W. of the line from Chester to Caerleon in Monmouthshire, but there are numerous Roman sites indicating a penetration westward on the S. to Pembrokeshire beyond Carmarthen, and the using of the gold mines of Dolaucothi in the N. of Carmarthenshire. The Romans can be traced up into Cardiganshire past Loventium, but, in the far N. of that shire, they would seem to have been content to modify and adapt native tracks for their purposes. Besides leaving traces in Brecon and Radnor, the Romans occupied Caersws, and tradition has it that they came thence to Pennal near Machynlleth, while they had a small outpost on the wild Eisteddfa Gurig pass just south of Plynlumon. In the N. they certainly penetrated from Chester to Caernarvon (Segontium) where their site has been investigated. They are claimed to have spread thence S. into Merionethshire, at least, while towards the Welsh-English border the traces of them are abundant, and special mention should be made of valuable finds at Holt.

There is little doubt that Latin quite early exercised a considerable influence on the Welsh language, but the degree of the relationship between the Romans and Welsh life is still a matter of much doubt. With the weakening of Roman power the Welsh coast seems to have been attacked by raiders from Ireland and other more distant lands; but more important than these are the 'Saints' who preached Christianity, some spreading from Ireland, and especially from sacred places of the Wicklow Hills, to St David's, which thus became the sacred city of Wales as well as one of the chief centres of that country's prehistoric memories. At Llanilltyd Fawr (now Llantwit) in S. Glamorgan they had a seat of learning whence missionaries spread far and wide, as we read in the lives of the saints. The dedication of churches to these local apostles is highly characteristic of Celtic lands, and many are the venerated names of Wales of which the Roman calendar knows nothing. It is legitimate to think that during the wild times following the Roman retreat Welsh hillmen took their part in sacking Roman sites of the border country, and that the old seasonal movements up hill to the 'Hafod' or summer pasture, in May, and down hill to the 'Hendre' or permanent settlement in the valley, in or before November, became, or were already, important.

The reverence for ancient stone monuments, which early worried Christian missionaries in Spain and France, made the Celtic churchmen work by transmutation of pre-Christian into Christian sanctities, and we have many instances of this in Brittany and Ireland. In Wales a few can be traced, but a notable one is that of a rough stone monument, probably once a circle of standing stones, some of which survive in the wall of the churchyard with the church of St John at its centre at a place called Yspytty Cynfyn, i.e. the Hospitium of Cynfyn, in the days of the Monk's Bridge (at Devil's Bridge) and of the pilgrimages to the Cistercian abbey of Ystrad Fflur (Strata Florida).

There are many indications that not only in Pembrokeshire, Gower, and S. Glamorgan, which have lost their Welsh, but also in Cardiganshire, Llŷn, and Anglesey at least there has been settlement from the sea, settlement of Norsemen and Norse-Irishmen who have in these cases become as Welsh as their surroundings. There are traces also of the Flemings and Huguenot refugees and others, but to disentangle all this would be a task for a learned treatize rather than a popular article. The south coasts of Wales lay along the trade route between Bristol and Dublin and this was an important factor of the mixing of peoples here.

Many writers speak of the Welsh and Irish and Highland Scots as Celts and argue for or against a Celtic temperament which is supposed to be a racial inheritance. Celt in this sense means, primarily, 'British' but non-English; beyond that there is also a recognition that in the parts of the British Isles remote enough to retain Celtic speech there are retained also old modes of expression and old social standards. But nothing could be more fallacious than to suppose that a real race-difference separates English and Welsh. A large and increasing proportion of the people of England carries characteristics undoubtedly derived from ancient inhabitants of Britain who had established themselves in the country before the Roman conquest, and probably before Celtic speech was known in the land.

There are people with dark long heads and oval faces, short stature and usually slim build, who abound especially in South Wales where they are commonly supposed to be the representatives of the ancient Silures, that is of a conglomerate of prehistoric peoples dominating the southern moorlands. They are known to literary discussion by the name of Iberians, a tribute to the importance of prehistoric (Bronze Age) connections between Britain and Spain, but not a name of any special value for race purposes. These types occur in every parish in Wales and in most places in England, and include many sub-types of ancient date.

Here and there on the Welsh coasts, notably in W. Merionethshire and S. Caernarvonshire, are nests of dark-haired people with broad heads and often thick-set build. They occur also on coastal patches in S. Italy, N. Sardinia, Spain, Brittany, Devon and Cornwall, Ireland, the Hebrides, the Faröes, the Shetlands, and Norway, and are residual of some ancient drift of trade or migration which from its path we judge to be of the Bronze or pre-Roman Iron Age.

The Bala Cleft and some other through-ways in Wales possess people of the type of those whose remains are found interred with 'Beaker' pottery in E. Britain. We cannot, however, prove that this type came with its beakers to Wales; the Welsh through-ways may have received this element at a later date. The type is apt to be associated with independence of mind and leadership.

The Severn and Wye valleys have fair types in large numbers and these are commonly associated with the Iron Age movements, and so have perhaps as much right to the name Celtic, if not more, than any others. They give place to the older established dark type as we get to the hills.

The note on which we would then close is that the Welsh hills and remote valleys naturally preserve old treasures of thought and fancy, cherish an old language, and tell old folk-tales. Just as naturally they have been weak in political organization through difficulty of inter-communication, they have never had and are not likely to have an effective capital city, their law has disappeared for lack of an administrative centre, and their independence for lack of power of cohesion. Their nationalism is thus turned towards spiritual rather than purely political ends, and in this connection claims the special respect and sympathy of the other inhabitants of Britain.

HISTORY OF WALES

Prehistory

(B.C.)

See also preceding article 'Prehistoric Wales and the Welsh People' by Professor H. J. Fleure.

Much of Wales must have been under ice during the Ice Ages (until say 20-25,000 years ago) and man would first have made his way here as the glaciers retreated. The earliest trace is a skeleton found in Paviland Caves (Gower), radio-carbon dating placing this in the 17th millenium B.C. Other evidence of man's early presence is provided by remains found in the limestone caves of the N.E., and perhaps also by shell heaps, though these are of unknown age.

The ice was replaced by swampy valleys and pine forests, these features and the local lack of flint confining man to open upland or to the coast. During the third millenium (Neolithic, or New Stone Age) there was a general drift of peoples northwards following the European coast, this drift embracing Wales and bringing primitive agriculture, domesticated animals, and, later on, the first visible structures made by man. Around 1800 B.C., at the dawn of the Bronze Age, these early people seem to have been joined in the S. and N. by others who crossed the North Sea and drifted westwards; these are sometimes called the Beaker people, known for their round barrows and pottery and probably also responsible for many standing stones.

Other than hillforts the **Prehistoric Monuments** of Wales belong to the New Stone and Bronze Ages. There is a great deal of overlapping in both time and place, but roughly the monuments divide as below.

Burial Chambers or *Long Cairns* (2500 B.C. or earlier). Used for communal burials, these were megalithic structures, i.e. made of massive stones covered by a mound. Few signs of mounds survive, what remains now usually being the chamber capstone, frequently still resting on its uprights. In this Guide the term 'burial chamber' is normally used. Some maps and local names though may refer to these sites either as 'cromlechs' (curved stones), a term first used in the 16C, or as 'dolmens' (Breton for 'table stone'), a term invented by an 18C French archaeologist.

Standing Stones (c. 1800 B.C.) may have served a variety of purposes, including deity symbols, memorials, and boundary or route markers. They are sometimes called 'menhirs' (long stones).

Round Barrows (c. 1800 B.C.) are associated with the Beaker people who gave their dead individual burial.

Stone Circles and Alignments (1800-500 B.C.) probably marked places at which the people met for both ritual and secular purposes.

In the Dark Ages prehistoric sites were frequently associated with Arthur and other heroes, and were also protected under ancient law.

During the later Bronze Age (say 400-100 B.C.) there was continuing westward drift from the continent, now of men armed with metal weapons, by some authorities considered to be the first Celts.

Celts is the generic name for the ancient peoples who inhabited central Europe. During the last five centuries B.C. these people embarked on an expansion which took them into France, Spain, and Italy, down the Danube into the Balkans, and (by 300 B.C.) into Greece and Asia Minor, where later those who held on became the Galatians. Two sets of Celts, the Goidels and the Brythons (Britons) reached the British Isles. The Goidels crossed in the 4C B.C. directly to Ireland, and may also have been the metal-weaponed people who came to Wales; if these latter were Goidels, then their speech, later to become the Gaelic of Ireland and Scotland, took no permanent root in Wales either now or as the result of their invasions after the Roman withdrawal (see below). Rather later the Brythons crossed the Channel and spread through England and Wales.—**Druidism** was the Celtic religion up to the time of the Romans, the Druids themselves being not only priests but, more importantly, teachers, administrators, and judges exercising an authority which, backed by religion, crossed the many tribal boundaries. Druidism accepted many gods, preached immortality through rebirth, and sometimes practised human sacrifice. In Wales, Druidism was strongest in Anglesey.

It was thus the Brythonic Celts who in the Bronze-Iron Age centuries immediately preceding the Roman invasion provided the main influx into Wales (as also Cornwall and Cumbria) and whose language would become Welsh. These were the people who penetrated the valleys, made a start with land clearance, developed farming, and began to come together in villages. And it was these people who, now and later, built the drystone, wood, and earthwork hillforts (often referred to as British Camps), the remains of which are such a feature of the Borders and Welsh landscapes. At the same time, up on the moors, the earlier people and their ways lingered on.

Roman Period
(A.D. 61 to early 5C)

Suetonius Paulinus attacked northern Wales and Anglesey in 61, and between 74 and 78 Frontinus crushed much of the S. (the Silures and the Demetae). In 78 Agricola arrived in Britain, at once subduing the Ordovices in central Wales and also completing the conquest of the N.W. and Anglesey where the Druids were exterminated. Wales was held throughout the centuries of the Roman occupation of Britain, but, except to a limited extent along the S. coast, always as a military zone controlled by legions based on Deva (Chester) in the N. and on Isca (Caerleon) in the south. From these places roads penetrated westwards to stations such as Segontium (Caernarvon) and Maridunum (Carmarthen), with smaller forts even farther west. In the E. the linking road ran through Viroconium (Wroxeter) and Castra Magna (Kentchester). In the W. the N. to S. link was Sarn Helen (perhaps from the Welsh 'sarn heolen', a paved causeway) which ran from Caerhun through Tomen-y-Mur and Llania, beyond the latter bearing W. for Maridunum and E. and S. for Y Gaer (Brecon) and Nidum (Neath).

Thus Wales was never fully romanized, its inhabitants continuing to follow a more or less independent and uncouth existence in and around their hillforts. The Silures, transferred from their hillfort capital to Venta Silurum (Caerwent), were the exception. In the Borders Roman remains include walls and an amphitheatre at Chester, and the fine site of Viroconium. In Wales the outstanding sites are the amphitheatre at Caerleon, the extensive walls of Caerwent, and clearly defined forts such as Y Gaer near Brecon and Castell Collen near Llandrindod Wells.

Irish, Anglo-Saxons, and Norsemen
(*Dark Ages. Early 5C to 1066*)

The Romans were withdrawing early in the 5C and as their grip loosened the Welsh coast became open to the attacks of Irish (Goidelic) pirates, on their heels coming settlers in large numbers who established themselves particularly in what are now northwest Gwynedd (with Anglesey), and in the Pembroke peninsula. It is generally accepted that Goidelic became the language in these areas until the 7C, and it is known that there was an Irish dynasty of kings in the S.W. from the late 3 to the early 10C. Thus Wales became divided between the native Brythons and the Goidel invaders, the struggle between the two and the more or less simultaneous introduction and spread of Christianity now becoming the two main features of Welsh history.

The struggle between the Brythons and the Goidels, though obscure in its details, eventually resulted in complete victory for the former who, under the leadership of the northerner CUNEDDA, probably a romanized Northumbrian, forced the Goidels out of northern Wales, Cunedda's descendants becoming the rulers and establishing their headquarters at Deganwy on the Conwy estuary. The most notable of these descendants was MAELGWN GWYNEDD (Maglocunus, d. 547), known from the writings of his contemporary, the monk and chronicler Gildas, who while describing Maelgwn's court as licentious at the same time suggests that he was a Christian, at one time even eager to exchange his position as prince for that of a monk. Despite their defeat and absorption it was the Irish who brought Christianity to Wales, actively spreading the Faith and thus leaving their permanent legacy. These missionaries, named 'sancti' by Gildas (a word which soon became 'saint'), generally led the lives of hermits and often became known for their healing powers; hence the Holy Wells found throughout Wales, many of which date back to this time. One saint was Dewi, or David, later adopted as patron of Wales. Such was the influence of these saints that they before long achieved a status equal to that of the local lord, and it became the custom that the latter should grant the holy man a piece of land as a sacred enclosure ('llan'). In 546 St Dubricius (or Dyfrig), Bishop of all Wales, divided his see into three, appointing Deiniol to Gwynedd, Padarn to central Wales, and Teilo to the south.

Wales is rich in Early Christian monuments, such as inscribed stones, graveslabs, and crosses, dating from the 5C onwards. Many bear interesting Latin inscriptions; others bear Ogham characters, the oldest written form of Goidelic and thus of Gaelic (the writing takes the form of strokes or notches along a base line). The oldest known example of written Brythonic is on a stone of c. 650 in Tywyn church.

Towards the end of the 6C the Brythons had to face the onslaught of new invaders, the pagan Anglo-Saxon tribes who had swept across southern Britain, and there now started a struggle which would continue with little respite until Henry Tudor ascended the English throne as Henry VII some nine hundred years later.

The hero Arthur, if he ever existed at all, appears to date from about this time. Traditionally he was born at Tintagel in Cornwall, the son of Uther Pendragon and Ygrayne, and would have been a Christian chieftain (but not a king) who, as a military leader perhaps serving Ambrosius, a chief with Roman blood seeking to restore Roman law and order, led the Brythons against the Saxons. He is credited with victory at Mount Badon (? Liddingstone, near Swindon) and may have died in battle, reputedly being buried at Glastonbury. Arthur's association with Wales, as opposed to with the Brythons generally, is largely a matter of bardic legend.

In 577, after a victory at Deorham near Bath, the invaders reached the Bristol Channel, and in 613 Ethelfrid, the Anglian king of Northumbria, defeated an army of Brythons near Chester. It was these two battles which geographically determined the Wales of today, the first cutting off the Brythonic people of what is now known as the English West Country, and the second those of today's Cumbria. For the first time contained within their own frontiers, the still free Brythons of the mountainous west now began to call themselves 'Cymry' (fellow-countrymen) and the land 'Cymru' (whence Cambria). The name Wales derives from the Anglo-Saxon 'wealas' meaning 'foreigners'. The Brythons' hopes of reunion were finally shattered in 634 when Cadwaladr ap Cadfan, who had penetrated far to the E., was defeated S. of the Tyne, this enabling the Angles (or English as they would be called) to consolidate up to the foothills of the Welsh mountains. Only eight years later the Christian Oswald of Northumbria was killed by the pagan Penda of Mercia at Oswestry, this opening the way for the rise of that warlike people who inhabited England's Midlands and had their capital at Tamworth. In c. 784 Offa, the greatest of all the Mercian kings, constructed the long dyke which bears his name.

Offa's Dyke, built more as a line of demarcation than as a fortification, runs from the coast near Prestatyn southwards across the neck of Wales to Chepstow. Thus substantially the dyke still marks the border, the place names to the E. being English and those to the W. largely Welsh. Many sections of the dyke are still clearly visible and a waymarked path follows its 167 m. length.—**Wats Dyke,** possibly the work of the earlier Mercian king Aethelbald (716-57), is a shorter dyke (38 m.) running E. of Offa's Dyke between the Dee estuary and Oswestry.

By the middle of the 8C the Mercians became Christian, and it was also at about this time that the Welsh Church first submitted to the practices and ritual which later resulted in the absorption of the Celtic Church by the Roman; an important date was 768 when the Welsh accepted the Roman Easter, the date of which had long been a major cause of dispute between Augustinian and Welsh authorities.

Throughout the 9 and 10C Wales suffered under the savage raids of the Norse pirates (Vikings), who made their way round the N. of Scotland, settling there, in Ireland, and on the Isle of Man. That they did not to any lasting extent colonize Wales was due in large part to RHODRI MAWR (Roderick the Great of Gwynedd, d. 879), who became ruler of all Wales except the extreme S.E. and S.W., and also to the activities of Alfred the Great on whom the Welsh had to rely after Rhodri's death. The Norse presence survives in place names, particularly in Pembrokeshire, and in the intricately carved designs on stone monuments of the time. Rhodri Mawr's line continued as two branches, in the N. and in the S., his best known descendant being his grandson HYWEL DDA (Hywel the Good, d. 950), a member of the southern branch. Through marriage Hywel added Dyfed to his lands, and through force Gwynedd, but he is best remembered for the great assembly he convened at Whitland which succeeded in codifying the tribal customs of the various parts of Wales into a single legal system which remained in force until the arrival of Edward I. Meanwhile the Norse raids continued, St David's being sacked as late as 1088.

Although Hywel Dda's legal code survived, the political unity he had given to much of the country did not, and until just prior to the Norman invasion Wales became four distinct principalities, with borders more or less definitely fixed. Gwynedd was the dominant power in the north. To the S. of Gwynedd was Powys, corresponding roughly to the modern county but including also parts of Meirionnydd and Salop. The principality's ruling families, though often disunited, frequently sided with the English and continued to exert a powerful influence in the Marches until well into the Middle Ages. In the S. and S.W. ruled the princes of Deheubarth, comprising the earlier principalities of Dyfed (S.W.), Ceredigion (Cardigan), Ystrad Tywi (the Vale of Towy and Gower), and Brycheiniog (Brecon). Occupying the S.E. was the principality of Morgannwg (Glamorgan), which included the former principalities of Glwysing and Gwent. These Welsh princes continued to divide the country and quarrel for supremacy until just before the Norman Conquest when GRUFFYDD AP LLEWELYN (1039-63), an adventurer not of any royal house, succeeded in uniting the Welsh people and threatening the border. He was finally defeated and killed by Earl Harold Godwinson who, as King Harold, was to lose his own life three years later at Hastings.

Despite the splintering into principalities, the internal strife, and the fighting with the English, it would be wrong to picture the Welsh scene of the time simply as one of disorder. Wales still enjoyed Hywel Dda's legal code, with a defined system of administration. Each principality was divided into a number of cantrefs, roughly synonymous with the Anglo-Saxon hundred, and each cantref comprised several cymydau (commotes), each of these subdividing into trefs. There were no towns and scarcely any villages in Wales at this time, these trefs being no more than groups of farmsteads, each the property of a particular family. Each cantref was ruled by a lord, answerable to the prince. Status within the cantref depended upon birth, and certain distinct classes were recognized: royalty, noblemen, freemen, unfree persons, and slaves. The relations of these classes were legally defined, and courts existed for the redress of wrongs. Descendants of a common ancestor to the ninth degree, known as cenedl (kindred), were automatically bound together in a common, self-governing unit, and the law of gavelkind was observed, i.e. at the death of a father his land was divided equally among his sons, the division being made by the eldest and the choice starting from the youngest. This arrangement held good until the time of Henry VIII.

From the Normans to Edward I
(1066 to 1272)

Welsh Lords	English Kings
Rhys ap Tewdwr (Tudor) d. 1093	*William I (the Conqueror) 1066-87*
Gruffydd ap Cynan d. 1137	*William II (Rufus) 1087-1100*
Gruffydd ap Rhys d. 1137	*Henry I 1100-35*
Madoc ap Maredydd d. 1160	*Stephen 1135-54*
Owain Gwynedd d. 1170	*Henry II 1154-89*
Rhys ap Gruffydd	*Richard I 1189-99*
(Lord Rhys) d. 1197	*John 1199-1216*
Llewelyn ap Iorwerth	*Henry III 1216-72*
(the Great) d. 1240	*Edward I 1272-1307*
Llewelyn ap Gruffydd	
(the Last) d. 1282	

One of the results of the activities of Gruffydd ap Llewelyn was that the Normans, after William the Conqueror's victory at Hastings in 1066, regarded Wales as a danger. William, whose commitments elsewhere prevented him from giving Wales his personal attention, established three Marcher Lordships under earls of Chester, Shrewsbury, and Hereford. He encouraged these earls to extend their territories westwards at the expense of the Welsh, and to bring the Welsh leaders under Norman vassalage. The earls pursued the policy with vigour, but though some definite results were achieved (by 1098 Hugo d'Avranches, or Hugh Lupus, Earl of Chester, had virtually conquered Anglesey), the main objective of subjugating the entire peninsula was not realized.

Motte-and-bailey Castles were a Norman introduction, first appearing on the English side of the border c. 1055 when Edward the Confessor invited Norman knights to help him resist the inroads of the Welsh under Gruffydd ap Llewelyn. Old Radnor is one which dates from this time. After 1066 and the establishment of the Marcher Lordships such castles proliferated. The standard castle was a ditch (moat), usually dry, surrounding an earth mound (motte), the rim of which bore a palisade protecting an inner timber tower, or keep. (The basic word 'moat', or 'mote', or 'motte', came to be used loosely both for the ditch and for what had been heaped out of it). Annexed to the tower (sometimes within the main defence, sometimes extending outwards and with some defence of its own) was a flat area known as the bailey, used for all those activities which could not be contained within the tower, e.g. stabling. Remains of large numbers of these castles will be found in Wales, although in many cases only the motte and ditches are obvious, the bailey not being readily recognized. Only in the 12C were these primitive castles succeeded by stone keeps (later becoming full castles), often, when strength and space allowed, standing on the early mottes.

About 1081 GRUFFYDD AP CYNAN (d. 1137) came over from Ireland, whither his father had fled, to claim his patrimony in Gwynedd which he succeeded in freeing from Hugh Lupus. At about the same time RHYS AP TEWDWR (d. 1093), a descendant of Hywel Dda, returned from exile in Brittany to claim his lands in Deheubarth. Supported by Gruffydd ap Cynan he defeated his rivals, his rights were recognized by William I, and there followed twelve years of peace. At his death, however, his son GRUFFYDD AP RHYS (d. 1137) had to face the full weight of the Normans who now swept into the south. Gwent was overrun by William FitzOsbern, Earl of Hereford; Glwysing by Robert FitzHamon of Gloucester; Brycheiniog fell to Bernard of Newmarch, and Dyfed and Ceredigion to the house of Montgomery. Farther N., however, Roger de Montgomery, Earl of Shrewsbury, made little progress, and thus Powys and Gwynedd, still independent, became separated from the rest of Wales.

William II made expeditions into Wales in 1095 and 1097, penetrating as far as Meirionnydd, but by the time of his death in 1100 the Normans, especially in the S., were tending to contract marriages with the leading Welsh families, some of these Welsh-Norman lords even playing with ideas of independence. One such was Robert of Belesme, son of Roger de Montgomery, who tried to establish a western kingdom with Shrewsbury as his capital, but his plans were frustrated by the accession of Henry I, who was successful not only in checking both his own rebel barons and the Welsh but also in consolidating Norman gains. He also planted Flemish colonies in the Pembroke and Gower peninsulas, where their descendants still remain, speaking English and with traditions different to those of their Welsh neighbours.

The accession of Stephen (1135) and the consequent civil war in

England gave the Welsh an opportunity from which they profited, everywhere taking up arms and recovering much of their territory. OWAIN GWYNEDD (d. 1170) and his brother Cadwaladr, the sons of Gruffydd ap Cynan, had obtained control in Gwynedd and now harried the northern Marches, seizing the border fortress of Mold; Powys was united under MADOC AP MAREDYDD (d.1160), who took the castle of Oswestry. But Henry II acceded in 1154, soon turning his attention to Wales where he defeated Owain Gwynedd in 1157 and, in 1163, RHYS AP GRUFFYDD (Lord Rhys; d. 1197), the able and energetic son of Gruffydd ap Rhys. However these two princes rallied their armies, and, supported by Owain Cyfeiliog, Prince of Powys, and other leaders, in 1165 forced Henry to withdraw. After this his troubles with Becket occupied Henry's attention, and Rhys ap Gruffydd was able to extend his sway over South Wales so effectively that Henry, while on his way to Ireland in 1171, met and acknowledged him.

With varying fortune Rhys ap Gruffydd remained in power in the S. until his death in 1197, and the Wales of this time has been vividly recorded by Giraldus Cambrensis (Gerald of Barry; d.c. 1223), the son of a Norman settler in Dyfed, who became a noted scholar and churchman. In 1188 he made a tour in the train of Archbishop Baldwin who was seeking recruits for the crusades, and he recorded his reflections in two works, 'Itinerary through Wales' and 'Description of Wales'. His picture is of a frugal and poor people living in simple huts, yet bred to arms and having a bold individuality and courage. They seem to have been a pastoral people, with little inclination to trade. Of particular interest, and of course still true today, is the report that the Welsh had a love of poetry and music, this including a natural gift for singing in harmony.

Castles. It was Henry II who introduced stone keeps into England, as successors to the motte-and-bailey castles, and during the later 12C these began to appear also in Wales. One of the first, and still surviving, was that at Dolwyddelan.

Religious Houses. The 12C also saw the development in Wales of the Norman monastic system. The monastery in pre-Norman Wales had been of the usual Celtic type, with an abbot and a community of monks occupying individual cells. Such monasteries had however already begun to decline as far back as the 8C, and the Normans dissolved the surviving houses in favour of their own type. The Benedictine Order was the first to be introduced into Wales, houses being established at Brecon (late 11C), St Dogmaels (1118), and Ewenny (1141). The Savigniac Order founded abbeys at Neath (1130) and Basingwerk (1131), but in 1141 this order was merged with the Cistercian, because of its charity and simplicity by far the most popular in Wales. The first Cistercian houses were on the border at Tintern (1131) and in the heart of the country at Whitland (1140), and from these others were colonized (some under the patronage of native princes) at Cwmhir (1143), Margam (1147), Strata Florida (1164), Strata Marcella (c. 1170), Aberconwy (1186), Cymmer (1199), and Valle Crucis (1199). The Cistercians, of whom Rhys ap Gruffydd was a liberal patron, came to own large tracts of land and their farming methods had a marked influence on the native agriculture; indeed their successful sheep rearing set a pattern which persists today. The Premonstratensians established themselves at Talley (before 1197), and the Augustinians later at Penmon.

After the death of Owain Gwynedd in 1170, the power of Gwynedd was weakened by a struggle for supremacy among his sons. In the S., though the agreement between Rhys ap Gruffydd and Henry II stood until the latter's death in 1189, the absence of Richard I on crusades was the signal for disorder. Rhys ap Gruffydd reduced many of the Norman castles, but his deperate struggle to keep his independence was cut short by his death in 1197.

In 1194 LLEWELYN AP IORWERTH (d. 1240), grandson of Owain Gwynedd and later styled Llewelyn the Great, became Prince of Gwynedd. He was to become the most powerful ruler in Wales since the Norman invasion. First he had to overcome the rivalry of Gruffydd ap

Gwenwynwyn (d. 1216), a prince of southern Powys who, departing from the normal pro-English policy of his house, attempted to lead a national revival. Llewelyn succeeded in taking over the whole of Powys, the result being that under his rule all North Wales enjoyed almost complete independence. In 1204 he married Joan, a natural daughter of King John, but despite this in 1211 he had to face an attack by his father-in-law, who himself held lands in the Marches and feared Llewelyn's growing power. After this experience Llewelyn sided with the English barons and obtained rights for Wales under Magna Carta. In the same year he invaded South Wales, making himself overlord of the feeble successors of Rhys ap Gruffydd and forcing the Normans to surrender many castles. It was not only militarily and territorially that Wales prospered under Llewelyn; he was also a patron of the bards, he encouraged the study of the Welsh laws, and he gave generously to the monastic orders. In 1238 he entered the monastery of Aberconwy, where he died two years later.

Despite all he had achieved, and although he had his son Dafydd (d. 1246) recognized as ruler in Wales by the lesser princes, Llewelyn the Great had given Wales only a superficial unity. There was no central government; province was divided from province, commote from commote; and the system of gavelkind, with its continual division of property, was a constant weakness. Such unity as there was died with Dafydd. But only for ten years, for in 1255 LLEWELYN AP GRUFFYDD (Llewelyn the Last), grandson of Llewelyn the Great, overcame his brothers and began a campaign designed to clear the English out of Gwynedd and to establish his own authority throughout Wales. His opportunity was that of his grandfather, the strife between the English king and the barons, and Llewelyn was soon close to his objectives; the English were thrown back from Gwynedd, and Llewelyn, demanding the homage of the other chieftains, proclaimed himself Prince of Wales, a title which was recognized by Henry III in 1267 under the Treaty of Montgomery.

Edward I.   The Conquest of Wales
(1272 to 1307)

Only five years after the Treaty of Montgomery Edward I became king; his declared intention was to control his barons and to deal with unruly Wales and Scotland. Llewelyn the Last, seemingly unaware of the changed spirit in England, refused to pay homage and in 1277 Edward launched his attack and, by establishing a series of fortresses backed by the new weapon of sea-power, forced Llewelyn (Treaty of Conwy) to pay homage in London and to give up virtually everything except a part of Gwynedd reaching from the Conwy to the Dyfi and his now empty title. In 1282 Llewelyn's brother Dafydd rose against Edward, and Llewelyn, eager for revenge, joined him. Edward's reponse was shattering. He pushed through Gwynedd, extending his line of fortresses; took Anglesey, the granary of Wales; forced Llewelyn back into the fastnesses of Snowdon, whence he retreated southwards to be killed in a skirmish at Cilmeri; and finally disposed of the Welsh 'dynasty' by executing Dafydd. With these events ended—until the arrival of Owen Glendower on the scene a hundred years later—all serious hopes of establishing an independent Wales.

Edward remained in Wales for about three years to secure his position and establish the direct rule of the English Crown. He issued the Statute of Rhuddlan (1284; sometimes called the Statute of Wales), which provided for the government of the conquered principality; he divided Llewelyn's small remaining patrimony of western Gwynedd into the shires (counties) of Anglesey, Caernarvon, and Merioneth; he created the county of Flint as a buffer for that of Chester; he reorganized the administration of the provinces of Cardigan and Ystrad Tywi (Carmarthen); he suppressed the Welsh code of laws stemming from that of Hywel Dda, imposing instead the English system; finally, he embarked on a massive programme of castle construction, in the shadow of some of their walls creating 'English boroughs'.

Castles. The motte-and-bailey castle had been followed in the 12C by the stone keep. Now, a hundred years later, Edward built in Wales huge concentric fortresses of a type previously developed on the Continent and in the Near East, much of the work being in the hands of James of St George, an engineer whom Edward had brought back from France on his return from the last crusade. Detail depended on the site, but ideally the concentric castle consisted of two baileys or wards, square in shape and enclosed by strong buttressed walls. The inner ward, which contained the domestic buildings, was normally placed well within the outer, the whole being reinforced whenever possible by a moat. The castle was entered across a drawbridge and through an immensely strong gatehouse, which often also served as keep. If there could be a seaward protection, and perhaps a dock, so much the better.—Edward completed his castles at Flint, Rhuddlan, Builth, and Aberystwyth; he also built large new fortresses at Conwy, Caernarvon, Beaumaris, and Harlech, below these establishing 'English boroughs'; finally he took over and strengthened castles already built by the Welsh at Criccieth, Bere, Dolbadarn, Ewloe, and elsewhere. Other castles built by the Lords Marcher (Denbigh, Caerphilly etc.) were to a similar pattern as the King's, Caerphilly in fact actually preceding the royal castles in date.

English Boroughs, the nearest approach to anything like a town hitherto seen in Wales, were founded below the walls of the castles mentioned above and also of some of the castles taken over from the Welsh. They were granted charters, often before the castles themselves were complete, and English traders, who were expected also to form part of the garrison, were encouraged to settle, to the exclusion of the native Welsh, usually compensated with land in other districts. Each town, protected by walls, was laid out on a regular plan, with wide streets at right angles and a central market place. As the Welsh were forbidden to trade elsewhere than in these markets, the boroughs inevitably became the administrative centres for the regions surrounding them. Other similar ('royal') boroughs were later established at Newborough (Anglesey), Bala, and Pwllheli. (Comp. 'The Mediaeval Boroughs of Snowdonia', by E. A. Lewis.)

Efficient and orderly though Edward's measures may seem, it was no part of his plan to knit Wales into a unified nation. The largely self-governing lordships of Denbigh and Montgomery and those in southern Wales were left undisturbed, partly as a reward for their help in overcoming Llewelyn and partly no doubt because by this time the border lords had become so powerful that interference would have been both impolitic and difficult. Indeed the system of lordships was extended, so that others of Edward's helpers could have their share of the spoils, these including many Welsh lords who had had no wish to support Llewelyn; Powys and Deheubarth were amongst those who sided with Edward, and several leading families willingly provided him with administrators. The result was that much of Wales remained, as before, under the rule of numerous petty barons and outside the jurisdiction of the central courts in London.

Edward's measures inevitably led to rebellions, though none was effective and the last (by Madog ap Llewelyn) petered out in 1294.

However he remained well aware that he had to continue to guard against revolt as much by his own barons as by the Welsh, the two by now not always distinguishable, and in 1301, in a move designed both to gain Welsh sympathy and to confront the barons with a royal Welsh authority, he revived the title of Prince of Wales, conferring this on his son, born at Caernarvon in 1284. Edward I died in 1307.

Edward II to Henry Tudor (Henry VII)
(1307 to 1485)

Welsh Lords	English Kings	
	Edward II 1307-27	
	Edward III 1327-77	Plantagenets
	Richard II 1377-99	
Owain Glyndwr (Owen Glendower) d.c. 1416		
	Henry IV 1399-1413	
	Henry V 1413-22	Lancastrians
	Henry VI 1422-61	
	Edward IV 1461-83	
	Edward V 1483	Yorkists
	Richard III 1483-85	
Harri Tewdwr (Henry Tudor)	Henry VII (Harri Tewdwr) 1485-1509	

Note: *Henry VI, deposed in 1461, was murdered in 1471. Edward V, with his brother one of the boy 'princes in the tower', was declared illegitimate by Richard III and murdered; he was never crowned.*

Wales appeared to settle down and apart from minor rebellions during the reign of Edward II the 14C was a peaceful one, the country becoming more prosperous and ports such as Rhuddlan, Beaumaris, and Haverfordwest developing into trading centres; it was also the century in which Welsh poetry rose to perhaps its greatest heights with the work of Dafydd ap Gwilym. With the death of the strong Edward III, however, the Lords Marcher again began to stir and the royal officials to become increasingly rapacious. Revolt was in the air and came to a head in the person of OWEN GLENDOWER (Owain Glyndwr; d.c. 1416), an enigmatic figure who has been both lauded as a popular national hero and condemned as a bloodthirsty tyrant seeking his own aggrandizement.

As a descendant of the princes of northern Powys, and also, through his mother, as a representative of the royal line of Deheubarth, Glendower had claims to be regarded as a rightful Prince of Wales. Nevertheless he had been a courtier in London, had fought under the banner of Richard II, and had made no protest on the accession of Henry IV, so his revolt in 1400, sparked off by Henry's refusal of redress when Lord Grey of Ruthin seized some Glendower land, came as a surprise. Raising his standard on the Dee, Glendower soon laid waste the English settlements in northeast Wales, and what started as perhaps an act of personal pique became an excuse for Wales to unleash its resentment against the English and initiated a bitter struggle that lasted for nearly fourteen years and devastated much of Wales and the Marches.

At first Glendower had the advantage of facing a king who was insecure in his position (Henry was holding prisoner the young Earl of March, nephew of the powerful Marcher landowner Sir Edmund Mortimer and, as direct descendant of Edward III, a threat to the throne). Furthermore Henry underestimated the Welshman's personal qualities and the strength of the national sentiment to which, as a member of two princely houses, he could appeal. An early and important success was the battle at Pilleth; not only did Glendower for the first time decisively defeat a royal army and thus establish himself as a national leader, but here he also captured Sir Edmund Mortimer. Mortimer's position was of course equivocal, and it was not therefore surprising that he sided with Glendower, sealing the alliance by marrying one of Glendower's daughters.

Glendower was declared Prince of Wales and he held parliaments at Machynlleth, Dolgellau, and Harlech. He sought alliances with the Scots and Irish, and to secure French support he concluded a treaty with Charles VI for the provision of troops; he even entered into negotiations with the Pope at Avignon. He appointed bishops, issued pardons under his Great Seal, and mapped out a statesmanlike policy, demanding the independence of the Welsh Church from Canterbury and proposing the establishment of two Welsh universities. He also formed an alliance with the powerful Duke of Northumberland and his son Hotspur, at the start disastrous as, while Glendower was engaged in the S., Hotspur, coming to his aid, was intercepted by the royal forces near Shrewsbury and killed (1403). Later, in 1405, Glendower, Northumberland, and Mortimer signed the Tripartite Indenture by which England and Wales were to be divided among the three.

Glendower exercised great military skill, and though Henry made at least five expeditions against him, not one of them came within sight of crushing the revolt. Despite this, in the end Glendower failed. The French assistance proved insufficient, and, as the position of the House of Lancaster grew less precarious (Henry held the heir to the Scottish throne, and Northumberland was crushed in 1408), the King became able to turn his attention to Wales. Glendower had pressed into England as far as Worcester, but was thrown back by Prince Henry (later Henry V); in 1408 the prince took Aberystwyth and soon afterwards he captured Harlech, Glendower then being forced into outlawry, after 1412 disappearing from the scene and dying four years later in some unknown hiding-place. (In 1413 and again in 1415 Henry V offered a pardon, but Glendower never responded).

Wales was exhausted. Politically the country finished the long revolt virtually where it had started; still partly under English law, still partly ruled by barons. Economically the consequences were disastrous. The lords of the manor lost their rents and services, their houses and farm buildings had been destroyed and their lands neglected; Welshmen generally suffered heavy penalties, were barred from public life, and had every possible disability heaped upon them. Nevertheless the people had experienced a new upsurge of national feeling, and the old idea preached by the bards, that a prince of Brythonic blood should rule in Britain, was still kept alive. Despite repression and a huge burden of fines and debts the national spirit remained uncrushed, expressing itself by a flourishing of the arts, particularly in the field of literature; poets and prose writers abounded, old manuscripts were transcribed for the first time, and the intricate canons of Welsh verse were reduced to their final form.

The Wars of the Roses brought new unrest to Wales, years of strife which would however have a triumphant conclusion.

The **Wars of the Roses,** fought with great brutality by both sides, were between the house of Lancaster (red rose), whose representative, the simple Henry VI, was on the throne (though it was his wife, the indomitable Margaret of Anjou, who counted), and the Yorkists (white rose). The Yorkist claimant was Edward Mortimer Duke of York, great grandson of Edward III. The wars lasted from 1455 (first battle of St Albans) until 1485 (accession of Henry VII). In December 1460, at Wakefield, the Yorkists were defeated and the Duke of York killed; but in February 1461 his son Edward won a victory at what is now called Mortimer's Cross, soon entering London, dethroning Henry VI, and assuming the Crown. Although vicious fighting continued (Margaret was captured, and Henry VI's son Edward, Prince of Wales, was killed at Tewkesbury in 1471) the Yorkists remained on the throne until Richard III was defeated by Henry Tudor at Bosworth in 1485, the latter then becoming Henry VII.

So far as Wales was concerned York was represented by Edward IV, a Mortimer and as such chief of a family which by marriage and attainder had absorbed many of the Marcher lordships. Lancaster however held sway, not only by virtue of Henry VI's royal castles and Welsh estates, but also because of the backing of the Tewdwrs (Tudors), an old-established family whose prestige was on the ascendant. Owen ap Maredydd ap Tewdwr, an Anglesey landowner (executed by the Yorkists after Mortimer's Cross), had married Catherine of Valois, widow of Henry V, and his sons Edmund and Jasper had been created earls of Richmond and Pembroke. Edmund, who had married Margaret Beaufort, a descendant of John of Gaunt, died before the birth of their son Henry Tudor (Earl of Richmond). Between the ages of five and twelve this boy survived the seven-year-long siege of Harlech, but after Tewkesbury in 1471 he had to flee to exile in Brittany, because the death at Tewkesbury of Henry VI's son now made him the main claimant to the throne. His uncle Jasper proved a loyal and valuable Lancastrian supporter, and it was to a great extent due to his efforts that in 1485 Henry Tudor returned from exile, landing at Milford Haven on 7 August. On 21 August he won the Battle of Bosworth Field, Richard III was killed, and Henry became Henry VII. If for England Bosworth Field marked the final triumph of Lancaster over York, for the Welsh it meant the fulfilment of an ancient prophecy, and the fact that a Welshman (a Briton) now occupied the throne.

The Tudors
(Henry VII, 1485-1509, Henry VIII, 1509-47. Edward VI, 1547-53. Mary I, 1553-58. Elizabeth I, 1558-1603)

Two important acts were passed during the reign of Henry VIII. The Act of Union (1536) removed the privileges of the Lords Marcher, converting their lands into shires, and decreed that Welsh shires and boroughs should return members to the English parliament. The Act for Certain Ordinances (1542) reconstituted the Council of Wales and the Marches, first established by Edward IV, and enacted that courts of justice should sit twice a year in every county; at the same time all Welsh laws which were at variance with the laws of England were declared void, this including the damaging system of gavelkind which now gave way to primogeniture. Thus Wales now officially enjoyed the same liberties as across the border, and the ruling classes found new careers open to them in England. Welshmen entered the army and navy and the learned professions, making names for themselves in Church and State. Indeed in many ways the Tudor years, and especially the reign of Elizabeth I, were, outside the country, the most brilliant in Welsh history, one noteworthy example of Welsh intitiative in England being the foundation in 1571 of Jesus College, Oxford, by Hugh Price, treasurer of St David's.

Within Wales though the picture was greyer. For the upper class of country squires the Tudor succession might mean a break with the past and the abandonment of native traditions in favour of English custom. But the peasantry remained poor and Wales predominantly pastoral. The two principal exports remained cattle and cloth, and scarcely any effort was made to exploit the great mineral wealth of the country. The Dissolution of the Monasteries, though in Wales none of these was very wealthy, also brought the disruption of a cultural tradition, learning having been very largely under the care of the monks. Tithes and church lands too passed into the hands of laymen, usually the local gentry, the country clergy thus being reduced to an unbefitting state of poverty.

The Dissolution apart, the Reformation created remarkably little disturbance in Wales. Some of the finest scholars fled to the Continent, but others equally brilliant were content to accept the new religion, and the main stream of native Welsh history now began to assume a largely religious and educational character. In the years 1567 to 1588 three works, as remarkable for what they were as for what they achieved both for religion and for establishing a classical written Welsh, were written in Wales, though published in London. Richard Davies, Bishop of St David's and a leading spirit behind the moves for a national Church policy, worked together with his friend William Salesbury of Llanrwst, generally credited with being author of the first book printed in Welsh in c. 1545, the result of their joint labours at Abergwili being the publication in 1567 of Welsh versions of the Book of Common Prayer and of the New Testament. The Book of Common Prayer was mainly the work of Davies, while the New Testament (except for some epistles translated by Davies, and the Book of Revelation, contributed by Thomas Huet, precentor of St David's) was that of Salesbury. Then in 1588, after eight years of work, William Morgan, vicar of Llanrhaeadr-ym-Mochnant and later Bishop of Llandaff and St Asaph, saw his translation of the entire Bible issued by the royal press and distributed throughout the parishes of Wales; it would later be replaced in the reign of James I by the Authorized Version, translated by Bishop Parry of St Asaph, helped by Dr John Davies of Mallwyd, the first real Welsh lexicographer.

The Stuarts and the Commonwealth

*(James I, 1603-25. Charles I, 1625-49. Commonwealth, 1649-60.
Charles II, 1660-85. James II, 1685-88. William III and Mary II,
1688-94. William III, 1694-1702. Anne, 1702-14)*

With the accession of the Stuarts, the special favour enjoyed in England by Welshmen came to an end. In addition the Council of Wales and the Marches, for long a guardian of Welsh interests and an anchor for law and order, now declined in importance until it became little more than an intermediary between the local courts and the King's Council in London. It was abolished in 1689. Nevertheless the tradition of loyalty to the Crown continued under the early Stuarts, and the development of Puritanism in England at the start of the 17C was little felt in Wales. As a result Wales was predominantly Royalist during the Civil War.

Wales and the Marches suffered relatively little from the fighting. After raising his standard at Nottingham in August 1642, Charles I moved to Shrewsbury which he used as a base for recruiting and where he was soon joined by Prince Rupert. In South Wales Lord Hertford was in arms, but moved to Oxford as soon as Charles went there. In April 1643 the Parliamentarian Sir William Waller took Hereford, but soon had to retire back east. In 1645, after the decisive Royalist defeat at Naseby in June, the King and Rupert retired to South Wales to try to raise more infantry. They had little success, and when in August Rupert was defeated and surrendered at Bristol, Charles moved northwards; there was some skirmishing at Chester, then Charles, defeated at nearby Rowton Moor, withdrew temporarily to Denbigh. Chester held out for the King until starved into surrender by February 1646, Denbigh until August, and Harlech until March 1647. Except for Raglan, which did not surrender until August 1646, South Wales was overrun by the Parliamentarians by the end of 1645. What is sometimes called the Second Civil War (1648) started in Wales in March 1648 when Colonel Poyer, Parliamentarian governor of Pembroke, openly declared for the King, most of South Wales rising in support. But the rising was defeated in May at St Fagans, near Cardiff, and by 11 July Pembroke Castle had been battered into submission.

As has been noted, Puritanism had been slow to develop in Wales. Nevertheless the roots were there. In 1588 John Penry of Brecon sent two appeals to parliament urging a Puritan policy for Wales, while later Rhys Pritchard (1579-1644) of Llandovery became celebrated for his Puritan preaching and writing. William Wroth (d. 1642), another Puritan, in 1639 founded a community at Llanfaches, this now generally being accepted as the first dissenting chapel in Wales. The Civil War intervened, but with its close Cromwell, doubtless mindful of Welsh Royalist loyalties, was not slow to act. Within a month of the King's execution in 1649 he passed an Act for the Better Propagation and Preaching of the Gospel in Wales, which gave his 70 commissioners almost unlimited control over Welsh Church affairs. As a result huge numbers of incumbents were dismissed (330 out of 520 in St David's and Llandaff alone), their place being taken by carefully selected itinerant preachers. Not until the Restoration and the Act of Uniformity (1662) were the ejected clergy restored, several Puritans in their turn losing their positions.

The Eighteenth Century. Methodism and Education
(George I, 1714-27. George II, 1727-60. George III, 1760-1820)

Daniel Defoe, passing through Wales in 1722, described a scene of calm and apparent content. He found the Welsh gentry 'civil, hospitable, and kind' and that 'they valued themselves much upon their antiquity' and 'had preserved their families entire for many ages'; rural life, and the trade in cloth and cattle, was still carried on in the old way. But this calm was to a great extent illusory; beneath the surface was gathering the storm that broke over Wales in the shape of the Methodist Revival, a movement which, together with the closely allied educational movement, was to alter the life and thought of the Welsh people, which created new organizations, evolved new habits, and brought about a wholly changed social atmosphere.

It was the continued disregard of the problems of Wales both by the Welsh gentry and the English parliament that led inevitably to the great rupture in the Established Church, conservative, pro-English, and indifferent or even opposed to the particular needs of Wales. Directed from England, it was becoming increasingly out of touch with the people; all the bishops were English (no Welshman was elected to a Welsh see between the reign of Anne and 1870), and the majority were also non-resident, regarding the Welsh sees, without exception poor, merely as stepping stones to more remunerative positions; plurality was rampant, and such country clergy as did attend to their parishes were hampered by poverty and unfitted by education to administer to the spiritual needs of the people.

In such fertile ground the seeds of dissent were sown, at first unwittingly by men whose real concern was the education of a people the mass of whom at the opening of the century were illiterate. An early example was Stephen Hughes (1623-88), an ejected Puritan minister who published religious literature in Welsh. Later came Sir John Philipps of Picton (d. 1736), a wealthy Pembrokeshire landowner and one of the founders of the Society for the Promotion of Christian Knowledge, who issued devotional books and founded schools in which children were encouraged to read in their own language. Most influential of all perhaps was Griffith Jones (1683-1761), rector of Llanddowror, who, helped both by Sir John Philipps and Mrs Bridget Bevan of Laugharne, organized a system of itinerant teachers; so successful was Jones that by the date of his death nearly a third of the entire population of Wales could read the Bible.

Thus a basis of popular education was provided upon which the Nonconformist movement could at last develop. The first Nonconformist chapel had been founded (by William Wroth) as long before as 1639, and the Quakers (Society of Friends), Baptists, and Independents had all opened chapels in the 17C, but teaching, falling on illiterate and ignorant ground, had made little impression. Now all was changed, and for the first time since the Reformation an appeal could be made to the people themselves. There were a number of able and eloquent Methodists ready to seize this opportunity. One was Hywel Harris (1713-73) who at Trefecca in 1752 founded an institution for dissenters on a communal system similar to that of the Moravians; it survives today as a museum. Others were Daniel Rowlands (1713-90), curate of Llangeitho, who soon became one of the most popular preachers in Wales; William Williams (1717-91) of Pantycelyn, whose hymns have become part of Welsh literature; and Peter Williams (1722-96), who made a name as a Welsh Bible commentator. Towards the close of the century Methodism began to spread through North Wales, a leading influence here being Thomas Charles (1755-1814) of

Bala, one of the founders of the British and Foreign Bible Society.

At first the Methodists attempted to work within the framework of the Established Church—they had no intention of forming a separate denomination—but their departures from conventional discipline and the opposition this aroused among the bishops (all, it should be remembered, English) finally led to schism in 1811 when an independent, dissenting communion, known as the Calvinistic Methodists, was founded. The communion's adherents were mainly drawn from the farming and labouring classes, while the gentry remained faithful to the Established Church. After the death of John Wesley (1703-91), who generally had kept aloof from Wales, the Wesleyan Methodists began to infiltrate, and at the same time the Baptists and Independents increased their influence. But the Calvinistic Methodist Church remained independent, and is today usually known as the Presbyterian Church of Wales.

The 18C was also not without its cultural advances. The Morris brothers of Anglesey became widely known as men of letters and patrons of the arts. Lewis (1701-65) was a poet and scholar; Richard (1703-79) was also a patron of the arts, while William (1705-63) was founder in 1751 of the Cymmrodorion Society to encourage Welsh literature, science, and art. Goronwy Owen (1723-69), son of a tinker and also born in Anglesey, was inspired by Lewis Morris and became leader of a group of poets writing in a classical style still alive today. Other important events of the century were the eisteddfod at Corwen in 1789 which marked the rebirth of such festivals, and the introduction by Edward Williams in 1792 of what has become today's bardic tradition. At the same time, and given impetus by the growth in coach travel, cultivated Englishmen began to take a discerning interest in Welsh scenery and antiquities.

The Nineteenth and Twentieth Centuries
(*George IV, 1820-30. William IV, 1830-37. Victoria, 1837-1901. Edward VII, 1901-10. George V, 1910-36. Edward VIII, 1936. George VI, 1936-52. Elizabeth II.*)

The developments of the 19 and 20C can conveniently be recorded under headings.

Industry (see also the opening paragraphs of Rte 41). The Industrial Revolution had already exploded in South Wales by the later years of the 18C, its stimulus being the combination of iron ore and coal, the attendant metal industries, and the convenient ports. Over only a few years small market towns such as Merthyr Tydfil, Newport, and Cardiff became centres of industry, quiet valleys were torn apart for iron and coal, and a network of railways began to spread across the country. Such a change in a short time, while bringing prosperity to some, brought grinding hardship to the majority and with this came social unrest, the two best known occasions being the Chartist Riots of 1839 and the Rebecca Riots of 1843.

Chartist Riots. Largely as a result of the inadequate Reform Bill of 1832, a 'People's Charter' was drawn up in 1837 by the London Workingmen's Association, the charter's six points being equal electoral areas; universal suffrage; payment of M.P.s; no property qualification for voters; vote by ballot; and annual parliaments. This movement for social equality spread rapidly over much of

Britain, the Welsh miners being among the most militant groups. A petition signed by over 1¼ million people was rejected by parliament in July 1839, and in November rioting broke out in Lancashire, Yorkshire, and Wales, where an attack on Newport was led by the ex-mayor John Frost. The operation was poorly planned, the Chartists walked into a trap, and Frost and other leaders were sentenced to death, this later being reduced to transportation. In 1842 another petition, this time with nearly 3½ million signatures, was rejected. Chartism then went into decline, this being accelerated when the repeal of the corn laws in 1846 much bettered the lot of the working classes.

The **Rebecca Riots** were confined to South Wales. Though caused by the same economic circumstances as the Chartist troubles, the riots were in the first instance directed against tollgate charges (which hampered the small itinerant traders) and took their name from Genesis XXIV 60 'And they blessed Rebekah and said unto her, thou art our sister, be thou the mother of thousands of millions, and let thy seed possess the gate of those which hate them'. The rioters, often disguised as women and led by group leaders called 'Rebeccas', destroyed tollgates and their houses, and then, encouraged by success, demanded redress of other grievances. The disorders were quelled, but in South Wales tollgates disappeared.

In Wales, and especially in the S., the industrial upsurge did not last. The need for better quality ore for improved steel manufacturing processes, the depression, two wars, the replacement of coal by oil, and the drop in world demand for steel and slate, all combined to bring about an accelerating decline, underlined in the 1970s by the problems of British Steel Corporation and the attendant unemployment. But the lessons of over-dependance on one sector of industry appear to have been learnt, and diversification and trading estates are increasingly the pattern.

Politics. The conservative attitude of the Methodists, who felt interference with the supposed Divine Will to be sinful, and also of the older Dissenters who although maintaining the Whig tradition of liberty were disinclined to bring about reform through force, did not at first favour the rise of a representative political party. But the Industrial Revolution meant that the reign of the landowning classes, who had long monopolized parliamentary representation, was at an end, and at length a new party arose, the Liberal Party, which expressed the aspirations of a rising middle class whose wealth was based on industry. In the General Election of 1868 Wales returned 22 Liberal members out of a total of 30, and less than half a century later it would be a Welsh Liberal, David Lloyd George, who would lead the British in the First World War. Not long after the birth of the Liberals, the working classes too began slowly to find political expression, and the first Labour M.P. in Britain was returned for Merthyr Tydfil in 1900, since when Labour support in the industrial regions has been solid.

In recent years many factors, not the least being the hardships caused by the reorientation of industry, have led to increased pressure for more control of local affairs. Plaid Cymru, the Welsh National Party, has won seats in parliament; Cardiff was granted capital status in 1955; the Welsh flag was given royal approval in 1959; the post of Secretary of State for Wales was raised to cabinet rank in 1964; and during the 1970s devolution in some form or other has become a dominant issue.

Culture and Education. The cultural advances of the 18C, with the rebirth of eisteddfodau after the Corwen festival of 1789, have already been noted. The 19C saw the founding of the annual National Eisteddfod (see p. 28). The desire for national expression also entered the field of education. The first institution of university rank was established at Aberystwyth in 1872, this being followed by university colleges at Bangor and Cardiff (1883). In 1893 these were combined to form the University of Wales, to which a fourth college, at Swansea, was added in 1920, while in 1971 St David's College, Lampeter, became constituent. Charters for the establishment of a National Museum and a National Library were granted in 1907, and these institutions (at Cardiff and Aberystwyth respectively) are among the most valuable and influential in Wales.

Religion. In the sphere of orthodox religion there had been from the mid 19C a movement to break away from the domination of the Church of England, but it was not until 1920 that an Act for the Disestablishment of the Church in Wales was passed, and the four Welsh dioceses of St Asaph, Bangor, Llandaff, and St David's were combined into an independent and self-governing body, though still in communion with the Church of England. Its archbishop has no fixed see. A new diocese of Newport and Monmouth was formed in 1921 (St Woolos Church at Newport became a full cathedral in 1949), and another of Swansea and Brecon in 1923.

Conservation and the Countryside have become increasingly important themes during the present century, and especially so since the last war. This aspect of Wales is discussed under National Parks (p. 19) and under the various concerned organizations (pp. 72-74).

BIOGRAPHICAL NOTES

These notes identify and elaborate on selected personalities about whom users may like to know more. Well known names are not generally included, nor are people who are sufficiently identified in the History or Routes texts.

Abel, John (1577-1674). Architect of timber houses, including the old town halls of Hereford (demolished 1858) and Leominster (demolished 1861 but re-erected), and Old House in Hereford. When over the age of 90 he designed his own monument at Sarnesfield. With the Scots besieging Hereford in 1645 Abel much helped the town by building corn mills, this leading Charles I to grant him the title of 'King's Carpenter'.

Agricola, Gnaeus Julius (37-93). Roman general and governor of Britain, where he spent some seven years, conquering North Wales and Anglesey and southern Scotland. His daughter married the historian Tacitus. May have died of poisoning.

Anselm (c. 1033-1109). Saint. Born in Italy. Abbot of Bec in Normandy (1078), Bec soon becoming a leading seat of learning and Anselm laying the foundations of his reputation as a great philosophical and religious writer and thinker. While in England advising Hugh Lupus on the building of his abbey at Chester, William II made Anselm Archbishop of Canterbury (1093). There followed perpetual quarrels with William II and Henry I, largely over the issue of lay investiture. Canonized in 1494.

Ascham. Roger (c. 1515-68). Scholar and writer best known for his 'Toxophilus', a treatise on archery for which he received a small pension from Henry VIII. In this and in other writings he made a strong plea for increased literary use of English in place of Latin or Greek. From 1546-54 he was Public Orator of Cambridge, becoming known for his letters to the future Elizabeth I encouraging her with her studies. 'The Scholemaster', another well-known work, described as a treatise on the 'right order of teaching', included a plea against flogging and other school brutalities likely to discourage learning.

Baldwin (d. 1190). Archbishop of Canterbury. His visit to Wales in 1187 was the first ever by an archbishop. In 1188 he toured Wales with Giraldus (then archdeacon of St David's) preaching the Third Crusade. Professing himself appalled by the excesses of the crusaders, he died on reaching the Holy Land.

Benbow, John (1653-1702). Vice-Admiral. Son of a Shrewsbury tanner he ran away to sea, later owning his own frigate before joining the navy. 1670, Vice-Admiral. Best-known for the action (1702) against a French squadron in the West Indies when he was left unsupported by mutinous captains (largely on grounds of personal dislike). As a result he lost his leg and his life, but not before he had arranged courts martial by which several officers were shot or cashiered.

Birch. John (1619-91). Parliamentary commander who made his name by taking Hereford in 1645. Next year he took Goodrich Castle. His sympathies later changed and he was active in the preparations for the Restoration.

Bodley, George Frederick (1827-1907). Architect. Articled to Gilbert Scott and became a leading exponent of the Gothic revival and one of the principal ecclesiastical architects of his time. Among his buildings are All Saints in Cambridge, and in U.S.A. the cathedrals in Washington D.C. and San Francisco. He also made a name as a designer of furniture and domestic decoration (e.g. Powis Castle).

Bolingbroke, Henry (1367-1413) = Henry IV (1399). Son of John of Gaunt by Blanche of Lancaster. For several years he travelled and fought as an adventurer, but when on John of Gaunt's death in 1399 Richard II confiscated the estates of Lancaster Bolingbroke landed in Yorkshire and was joined by the Percys and other barons. Richard II, absent in Ireland and unpopular because of his arbitrary taxation, lost all support and soon surrendered at Flint. Richard died the following year, probably as the result of hardships of winter imprisonment rather than by murder as told by Shakespeare.

Borrow, George (1803-81). Philologist and linguist (he even translated the New Testament into Manchu). Travelled widely, acting as agent for the British and Foreign Bible Society. While in St Petersburg he published 'Targum', a series of translations from 30 languages and dialects. He became something of a tramp, wandering the roads of England and Wales, in the latter context being known for his 'Wild Wales' (1862), a description of a tour he made with his step-daughter. Very interested in gypsies, who provided material for several works.

Bradshaw, John (1602-59). Born at Presteigne. Lord President of the Parliamentary Commission which brought Charles I to trial, Bradshaw's signature headed the list of those who signed the death warrant. He refused to let the King speak in his own defence. Later he pronounced sentence of death on many Royalists.

Brown, Lancelot or 'Capability' (1715-83). Landscape gardener and architect. Founder of the English style as distinct from the French geometrical style (as at Versailles), Brown's aim was always to emphasize the natural lines of the landscape. The grounds of Blenheim and Kew, and in Wales and the Marches of Powis Castle and Berrington Hall, are examples of his work.

Brunel, Isambard Kingdom (1806-59). Engineer, mainly of docks, railways, and steamships. In 1833 Brunel was appointed engineer of the projected Great Western Railway, one of his early proposals being that the railway should be prolonged by a steamship ('Great Western', 1838) from Bristol to New York. He also designed the 'Great Britain' (1845) and the 'Great Eastern' (1859). Brunel's associations with Wales include the railway (see p. 362) and initial work on the docks at Milford Haven. His father (Sir Marc Isambard, 1769-1849), a refugee from revolutionary France, was also a distinguished engineer and inventor.

Burges, William (1827-81). Architect and decorator. His monuments in Wales are Cardiff Castle and Castell Coch. He is also associated with Salisbury chapter house, Brisbane and Cork cathedrals, and the College of Hartford, Conn.

Burne-Jones, Sir Edward (1833-98). Painter and designer. In 1862 Burne-Jones, William Morris, and D. G. Rossetti started a successful applied arts business. Burne-Jones most made his mark as a designer, and stained glass windows from his designs are widespread.

Burney, Charles (1726-1814). Musician, musical historian, and fashionable teacher. 'History of Music' was published in four volumes, the first in 1773. Perhaps best known as the father of the diarist Fanny Burney.

Bute, 3rd Marquess. John Patrick Crichton Stuart (1847-1900). Inherited from his father the 2nd Marquess (first builder of Cardiff docks) huge estates in Scotland and in and around Cardiff. In 1868 he became a Roman Catholic, an incident which may have suggested to Disraeli the plot for his novel 'Lothair'. The 3rd Marquess published several erudite works, largely on religious topics. In Wales he is best known for commissioning the work by Burges on Cardiff Castle and Castell Coch.

Butler, Samuel (1612-80). Poet and author. Best known for 'Hudibras', most of which was written in Ludlow Castle. The poem, 10,000 doggerel verses of contemporary satire and ridicule, was immensely popular.

Butler, Dr Samuel (1774-1839). Classical scholar and divine, noted for the high standard of scholarship achieved by Shrewsbury School while he was headmaster. At the same time he held various Church appointments, becoming Bishop of Lichfield in 1836. Father of Samuel Butler (d. 1902, see below).

Butler, Samuel (1835-1902). Author, painter, and musician. Educated at Shrewsbury and Cambridge, he emigrated to New Zealand but returned to England in 1864. Exhibited at the Royal Academy from 1868-76. The best known of his many writings are 'Erewhon', the story of an imaginary country and a satire on his times, and 'The Way of All Flesh', his autobiographical novel.

Caldecott, Randolph (1846-86). Artist. Born in Chester, died in Florida. Best known as an illustrator (books by Washington Irving and Mrs Comyns Carr).

Caractacus, or Caradog or Caratacus, was the British chief of the Catuvellauni tribe, and son of Cunobelinus, chief of the Trinobantes. He led the resistance against the Romans in 43-47, and after defeat at Wallingford on the Thames retreated into Wales, where a number of hillforts bear his name. He was finally defeated in 51 by Ostorius Scapula, most probably at the Caer Caradoc either near Church Stretton or between Clun and Knighton. He and his family were taken to Rome, where the emperor Claudius allowed them to live.

Carȍe, William Douglas (1857-1938). Architect. Son of the Danish consul in Liverpool. Carȍe's work was largely ecclesiastical, and he was consulting architect to several cathedrals (including Canterbury and Durham) and also to Malvern, Romsey, and Tewkesbury abbeys. In Wales he is known for his fine work at Brecon.

Churchyard, Thomas (c. 1520-1604). Author and soldier of fortune, born at Shrewsbury. As a soldier he fought in Ireland, Scotland, and the Netherlands. His writings are mainly autobiographical, describing with interesting contemporary detail the campaigns in which he fought.

Clifford, Rosamond. See Fair Rosamond.

Clive, Robert (1725-74). Founder of the British empire in India. Went to Madras as a clerk in the East India Company, but soon made a name in the fighting which marked the Anglo-French struggle for India. His defence of Arcot prompted Pitt to call him a 'heaven-sent general', and there followed his campaign against Suraj-ud-Dowlah (notorious for the Black Hole of Calcutta) which ended with Clive's victory at Plassey. In 1760 Clive returned to England, was made Baron Clive (Irish peerage) and became M.P. for Shrewsbury. Back in India in 1765-67 he pushed through many reforms and left Britain supreme. On his return to England attempts by jealous enemies to impeach him largely misfired, but nevertheless, in ill health and depressed at being treated 'like a sheep-stealer', he took his own life. His son acquired Powis Castle by marriage and became Earl of Powis.

Cobbe, Frances Power (1822-1904). Social writer and worker, and suffragist. Contributed to newspapers and reviews on such topics as vivisection (of which she was a strong opponent), destitution, women's rights, and divorce. Of her many works may be mentioned 'The Duties of Women' (1881) and her autobiography (1894). Buried at Llanelltyd.

Combermere, Stapleton Cotton (1773-1865). Viscount and Field Marshal. Home was Combermere Abbey, Cheshire, and his statue by Marochetti stands in front of Chester Castle. Saw service in the Cape, India, and Ireland, and commanded Wellington's cavalry in Portugal. Created Viscount after taking Bhurtpore in India (1826).

Cornwell, John Travers (1900-16). Boy Cornwell V.C., R.N. While serving on H.M.S. 'Chester' at the Battle of Jutland he was mortally wounded but remained at his post, with the others of the gun's crew all dead or wounded, because he 'felt he might be needed'.

Dafydd ap Gwilym (c. 1340-c. 1400). Poet and chief bard, described by Borrow, who translated some of his verses, as the Horace of Wales. Wrote nature poems, usually in the 'cywydd' form, a short ode with each line having the same number of syllables. Probably born at Broginin near Aberystwyth, he is said to have eloped with a princess of Anglesey. He may be buried at Talley.

Davies, John (c. 1570-1644). Welsh lexicographer. Rector of Mallwyd (1604). Assisted Parry with his Welsh bible of 1620. His own major work was 'Antiquae Linguae Britannicae Dictionarium Duplex' (1632), in Welsh-Latin and Latin-Welsh parts.

Dyer, John (1700-58). Welsh poet born at Aberglasney, which district he describes in his 'Grongar Hill'. His longest work is 'The Fleece', an epic in blank verse covering the subject of wool from the sheep through to the cloth trade.

Edward II (1284-1327). The irresponsible and probably homosexual son of Edward I. Born at Caernarvon Castle and made Prince of Wales in 1301 (see p. 159). Acceded in 1307. Notorious for his favourites and their influence over him. The first was Piers Gaveston, murdered by the barons in 1312. In 1308 Edward married Isabella of France. In 1314 he was ignominiously defeated by the Scots under Bruce at Bannockburn. In 1318 the Despensers (father and son, both Hugh) became Edward's favourites and effectively ruled England until 1326. In that year Isabella led a revolt against Edward, who found himself deserted. In Glamorgan he took refuge in the Despensers' Caerphilly Castle, but Isabella followed and, after an attempt to escape by sea from Chepstow, Edward was forced back into Cardiff. He and the younger Despenser were taken at Llantrisant Castle, both Despensers then being put to death while Edward was murdered the following year.

Evans, Christmas (1766-1838). Orphan son of a cobbler he became a

Baptist minister because the Presbyterians demanded an academic standard he did not have. After a period in the Lleyn, he was in Anglesey for over 30 years, becoming the centre of the Baptist movement and attracting huge crowds to his oratorical and emotional sermons.

Evans, Petty Officer. See under Scott, Robert Falcon.

Fair Rosamond (d.c. 1176). Daughter of Walter de Clifford and possibly born at Clifford Castle. She was probably mistress of Henry II secretly for several years, but was openly acknowledged only when Henry imprisoned his wife Eleanor of Aquitaine after she had incited her sons to rebellion. After her death Rosamond became the source of many stories, amongst these being that of the secret bower at Woodstock and also that she was poisoned by Eleanor.

Garrick, David (1717-79). Actor and theatre manager. Born in Hereford of a good family he was from an early age obsessed with the stage, making his name in 1741 as Richard III. In 1747 he and another bought Drury Lane, Garrick here producing and often acting in some 24 Shakespearean plays. After separating from his mistress, the actress Peg Woffington, he married (1749) Eva Maria Veigel (Violetta), a German dancer. Garrick acted little after 1766, but continued to manage Drury Lane. Although below average height he had a magnetic personality and there was virtually no part in which he did not triumph. The undisputed theatrical personality of his time he gave the theatre, hitherto a low haunt, an artistic and social status and a professionalism it had not hitherto known.

Gaveston, Piers (d. 1312). Son of a Gascon knight. Favourite of Edward II. Twice banished on the insistance of the barons, he each time was called back and was finally beheaded by his enemies.

Geoffrey of Monmouth (d. 1154). 'Historian' and churchman. Nephew of a bishop of Llandaff. Born at Monmouth, where he may also have been a monk. His best known work is his 'Historia Britonum' (c. 1139), claiming to be a translation from a Celtic source but today generally accepted as Geoffrey's own work and to be a mixture of ancient tradition, pure fiction, and only to a very small extent fact. Whatever it was it gained for its author a name for erudition and the appointments of Archdeacon of Llandaff (c. 1140) and Bishop of St Asaph (1151). He may also be the author of a 'Vita Merlini' (a life of Merlin) in Latin verse. The 'Historia Britonum' laid the written foundations of the Arthurian legend, and was widely accepted as history until as late as the 17C. It provided Shakespeare with the story of King Lear.

Germanus, Saint (?378-448). Bishop of Auxerre (418), of which he was a native. In 429 the British bishops asked the help of their colleagues in Gaul in their struggle against the Pelagian heresy. Germanus and Lupus of Troyes were sent to Britain, one event during their visit being the Alleluia Victory (p. 135). In 447 he again came to Britain, this time with Severus of Treves; a combination of miracles and vigorous preaching soon led to the decline of Pelagianism. Germanus was for some time in Wales, becoming the subject of several legends, amongst these that he cursed Vortigern for incest. He lives on in several place names.

Gibson, John (1790-1866). Sculptor, born at Conwy. First made his name in Rome, where he was befriended by Canova. Best known for his bas-reliefs, and as the first British sculptor to use colour.

Gildas (c. 516-570). Probably a monk, the earliest British historian. His main work was 'Gildae Sapientis de excidio et conquestu Britanniae', comprising a preface, a history, and an epistle. The history, which is cursory, reviews the history of Britain from the arrival of the Romans until the author's own time; the epistle is largely a condemnation of the vices of his countrymen.

Giraldus Cambrensis (c. 1146-c. 1223). Nobleman, churchman, scholar, and historian. Born at Manorbier of mixed Welsh-Norman parentage, then studied in Paris until 1172. Archdeacon of Brecon (1175) and of St David's (1180). Accompanied Prince John to Ireland and wrote a history of the conquest. In 1188 he accompanied Archbishop Baldwin through Wales preaching the Third Crusade, as a result of this writing his 'Itinerarium Cambrense' which gives a picture of Wales of the time. In 1198 he was proposed for the bishopric of St Davids, but Rome did not approve (see p. 354). His friendship with such men as Innocent III, Richard I, John, Stephen Langton, and others provided valuable background for his writings.

Gower, Bishop Henry (d. 1347). Member of a noble English-speaking Gower family. Best known for his benefactions and as an architect, in the latter capacity being the originator of an attractive and unusual local form of Dec. Gothic. In 1322-23 he was chancellor of Oxford University.

Greville, Fulke (1554-1628). Poet and author. Educated at Shrewsbury and Cambridge. Close friend of Philip Sidney whom he commemorated in his 'Life of the Renowned Sir Philip Sidney'. 1583, Secretary to the Principality of Wales. Later held various court positions, being made Baron Brooke in 1621 and receiving Warwick Castle. In 1746 Greville's descendant Francis Greville, 8th Baron Brooke, was created Earl of Warwick.

Grosvenors, The. Descendants of Hugh Lupus (Hugo d'Avranches), created Earl of Chester by William I. Granted title of Duke of Westminster in 1874.

Gwynne, John (d. 1786). Architect. Began his career as a carpenter, and as an architect was largely self-taught. Founder member (1768) of the Royal Academy. Prolific writer on architecture. Best known for his bridges, these including those at Atcham, Shrewsbury, and Worcester, and also Magdalen Bridge, Oxford.

Heber, Reginald (1783-1826). Bishop and hymn writer. 1812, Prebendary of St Asaph. 1823, Bishop of Calcutta, Heber dying in India three years later. Among his hymns were 'Holy, Holy, Holy, Lord God Almighty' and 'From Greenland's Icy Mountains'. In 1822 he edited the works of Jeremy Taylor.

Hemans, Mrs Felicia Dorothea (1793-1835). Poetess. Lived near St Asaph before her separation from her husband. Worked together with Sir Walter Scott who wrote an epilogue for her play 'The Vespers of Palermo'. Probably her best known lines are 'The boy stood on the burning deck, Whence all but he had fled'.

Henry IV. See Bolingbroke.

Herbert of Cherbury, Lord Edward (1583-1648). Diplomat, soldier, and writer. Brother of the poet George Herbert. 1610, fought in the Netherlands for the Prince of Orange. 1617-24, Ambassador in Paris. 1624, created Baron Cherbury. 1644, surrendered Montgomery Castle to Parliament. His written works include religious philosophy, poems, and an autobiography.

Herbert, George (1593-1633). Poet. Brother of above. His poems, in Latin and English, are largely of a metaphysical religious nature, and he also wrote hymns. Ordained priest in 1630.

Hopper, Thomas (1776-1856). Architect. First made his name through alterations for the Prince Regent to London's Carlton House, after this becoming fashionable with nobility and gentry. In Wales his monument is Penrhyn Castle. In London he was associated with the Royal Exchange, Houses of Parliament, and many other buildings.

Horton, Thomas (d. 1649). Parliament's commander who (with Philip Jones) defeated Poyer and Laugharne at St Fagans. Signed the King's death warrant. Died in Ireland, where he was accompanying Cromwell.

Hubert de Burgh (d. 1243). Served Richard I, John, and Henry III, under the latter two being Chief Justiciar, the king's closest adviser. He reached the height of his power when in 1227 he declared Henry III to be of age, and when, as the result of four marriages, he had acquired extensive lands. But Henry, with ambitious military plans, became impatient at Hubert's caution and in 1232 stripped him of his post, honours, and lands, including White, Skenfrith, and Grosmont castles. In 1234 he regained some favour and his earldom, but the position of justiciar declined in importance.

Hughes, Thomas (1822-96). Lawyer, author, and social reformer. As an M.P. (1865-74) he unsuccessfully introduced a trades unions bill. Author of 'Tom Brown's Schooldays', based on his school experiences at Rugby under Arnold.

Jeffreys, George (1648-89). Judge. Born at Acton (Wrexham) and educated at Shrewsbury and Cambridge. 1678, appointed Recorder of London. After the alleged Popish plot revelations of Titus Oates, Jeffreys was identified with the consequent series of state trials, siding with the Crown, becoming Lord Chief Justice, and being created Baron Jeffreys of Wem (near Chester) by James II. He gained notoriety through his mercilessness at the 'Bloody Assizes' which followed Monmouth's rebellion. When James II fled, Jeffreys (after an attempt at escape disguised as a woman) was held in the Tower where he soon died.

Johnson, Dr Samuel (1709-94). Writer, lexicographer, and conversationalist. Best known for his 'Dictionary' which, though highly individual in its definitions, won fame as a dictionary that could be read with pleasure. He achieved a prolific output of miscellaneous writing (including his popular 'Lives of the Poets'), enjoyed a wide circle of friends, and became renowned for his brilliant conversation and pronouncements. His name is inseparably linked with that of his friend and biographer James Boswell. See also Thrale, Hester Lynch.

Jones, Inigo (1573-1651). Architect. His patron was the Earl of Arundel who sent him to study in Italy where he admired the style of Palladio. He was so successful in Venice that he was invited by Christian IV to Denmark where he designed the palaces of Rosenborg and Frederiksborg. Through the influence of Anne of Denmark, wife of James I, he became architect to the English court (1605) and Surveyor of Royal Buildings (1612). He held the same posts under Charles I but was heavily fined after the Civil War and died in penury.

Jones, Philip (c. 1618-74). Born in Swansea, of which, as a Parliamentary supporter, he was made governor in 1645. In 1648, with Horton, he defeated Laugharne and Poyer at St Fagans, afterwards being made governor of Cardiff Castle. Throughout the Commonwealth he was a trusted adviser to Cromwell, but somehow he survived the Restoration, keeping his estates and in 1664 even acquiring Penmarc and Fonmon castles.

Kembles, The. Family of actors the father of which was Roger (1721-1802), a wandering player. Roger Kemble had 12 children, the best known of which were Sarah Siddons (1755-1831) and John Philip (1757-1823). In 1788 John Philip became manager of Drury Lane. Other actor children of Roger were Stephen (1757-1822). Charles (b. Brecon in 1755), and Elizabeth Whitlock (1761-1836). Fanny (1809-93), actress and writer, and Adelaide (1814-79), opera singer, were daughters of Charles Kemble.

Kent, William (1685-1748). Painter, architect, and landscape gardener. After studying in Italy he worked for the rest of his life under the patronage of Lord Burlington. It is as a landscape gardener that he is best known, being one of the first to stress the natural as opposed to the artificial and thus paving the way for 'Capability' Brown and Humphry Repton.

Landor, Walter Savage (1775-1864). Poet, prose writer, and idealist with republican sympathies. In 1808 he went to Spain and at his own expense raised a troop to fight Napoleon, a venture which failed and cost Landor a lot of money but provided the material for one of his finest poems, 'Count Julian'. There followed the Llanthony Priory affair (see p. 286), after which Landor lived on and off in Italy. His first great poem was 'Gebir' (1798) and among his best prose works was his series of 'Imaginary Conversations' (1824-46).

Laugharne, Rowland (d. after 1660). Home was at Laugharne. Successful Parliamentary commander in South Wales, taking Haverfordwest, Tenby, Carew, Cardigan, Picton, and Carmarthen. But Laugharne was dissatisfied with his rewards, complaining also that he had had no refund for personal moneys paid on Parliament's behalf and that for two years he had had to pay his soldiers out of his own pocket. He then joined Poyer's revolt, with him being defeated by Horton and Jones at St Fagans. Laugharne, Poyer, and a Colonel Powell were sentenced to death, but Cromwell decided that only one should be executed, the choice being made by lot. Poyer was the loser.

Lawes, William (d. 1645). Composer. Wrote 'Gather ye rosebuds while ye may'. Killed on the walls of Chester while fighting for the King. He was brother of the rather better known composer Henry Lawes who wrote the music for Milton's 'Comus'.

Lloyd, William (1627-1717). Successively Bishop of St Asaph, Lichfield and Coventry, and Worcester. Noted as an opponent of the Roman Catholic leanings of James II and was one of the seven bishops tried for refusing to have the Declaration of Indulgence read in their dioceses.

Luxmoore, Charles (1794-1854). Helped by his father John Luxmoore, who was successively Bishop of Bristol, Hereford, and St Asaph, Charles held at the same time the deanery of St Asaph, the chancellorship of St Asaph, the position of prebend of Hereford, and three rectories.

Magnus Maximus (d. 387). Roman commander. While in Britain he was proclaimed emperor by disaffected local troops, on this denuding Britain of troops and crossing to Gaul where he killed Gratian, co-emperor with Theodosius I. Theodosius then recognized Magnus as emperor in Gaul, Spain, and Britain. In 387 the ambitious Magnus crossed the Alps, but was defeated and beheaded. He passed into Welsh legend ('Mabinogion') under the name of Macsen Wledig.

Margaret of Beaufort (1443-1509). Countess of Richmond and Derby and mother of Henry VII. After her husband Edmund Tudor's death she married in succession the son (d. 1482) of the Duke of Buckingham, and Thomas Stanley, later Earl of Derby. Throughout his exile in Brittany she and Stanley were in constant communication with her son, Stanley doing much to help his cause. Margaret became known for her many foundations, these including Christ's and St John's colleges at Cambridge, and chairs of Divinity at Oxford and Cambridge. In Wales she is associated with the chapel at Holywell.

Marten, Henry (1602-80). As an M.P. Marten was always outspoken against Charles I. Although he played no significant part in the Civil War, he was one of the King's judges and signed the death warrant. At the Restoration he was imprisoned in Chepstow Castle where he died 10 years later. Although a Puritan he kept a mistress, and while in Chepstow he published 'Henry Marten's Familiar Letters to his Lady of Delight'.

Merlin. Wizard of Arthurian romance who may possibly derive from an early bard. Traditionally he had a spirit father and a human mother (for this, as also for Merlin and Vortigern, see p. 29). An ancient 'Vita Merlini', which associates Merlin with Scottish legend, may be the work of Geoffrey of Monmouth. Geoffrey also collects the legends of Merlin and Arthur in his 'Historia Britonum'.

Morris, William (1834-96). Poet and artist. In 1862 Morris, Burne-Jones, Rossetti, and others started an applied arts business. Stained glass windows and other decoration from his designs are often met in England and Wales, and in later years he became interested in printing, acquiring a private press. He founded the Society for the Protection of Ancient Buildings, largely because of his disapproval of the restoration work of Sir George Gilbert Scott.

Myddelton, Sir Hugh (d. 1631). Engineer. Born near Denbigh. He is known for London's New River (1609-13), a 40 m. long aqueduct bringing water from springs near Ware in Hertfordshire to a reservoir at Clerk's Well (Clerkenwell).

Mytton, Thomas (c. 1597-1656). Parliamentary leader and commander. Native of Halston, Salop. His many Civil War successes included the taking of Wem, Ellesmere, Oswestry, and Shrewsbury. In 1645 he was appointed commander for North Wales, further successes including Ruthin, Caernarvon, Beaumaris, Conwy, Denbigh, and Harlech. Buried in St Chad's, Shrewsbury.

Nash, John (1752-1835). Architect. Possibly born at Cardigan. Becoming fashionable with royalty and the nobility, his name is mainly associated with the part he played in the improvement of London

(Regent Street, Regent's Park surrounds, reconstruction of Buckingham Palace).

Nash, Richard (1674-1762). Beau Nash, the dandy. Born at Swansea. In 1705 he became Master of Ceremonies at Bath, soon introducing sweeping reforms and making Bath England's leading centre of fashion.

Ordericus Vitalis (1075-c. 1142). Chronicler. Born at Shrewsbury, son of a French priest, he went to Normandy and at the age of 11 entered the monastery of St Evroul, remaining closely associated with it for the rest of his life. The monastery was a focus for retired knights and visitors from all over Europe, and Ordericus profited from listening to these people. His 'Historia Ecclesiastica', a history of his times, is in particular a source of information on William II and Henry I.

Owen, Daniel (1836-95). Welsh novelist and short story writer, whose trade was that of tailor. A native of Mold (museum). Sometimes described as the Welsh Dickens, his writings are among the more important records of the era of the arrival of the railways and of the spread of religious revivalism.

Owen, Sir Hugh (1804-81). Born in Anglesey. Promotor of Welsh education, his main achievement being the establishment of the University College of Wales at Aberystwyth. He also played a large part in the reforms of the National Eisteddfod, and was concerned in the revival (1873) of the Society of Cymmrodorion which had died in 1843. Also did much philanthropic work (London-Welsh Charitable Aid Society. London Fever Hospital. National Temperance League). Knighted in 1881 for services to Welsh education.

Owen, Sir John (1600-66). Royalist commander. Born in Caernarvonshire. Knighted in 1644 by Charles I, at which time he was governor of Harlech. In 1648, at Caernarvon, he attempted a last uprising for Charles I but was defeated at Llandegai. He retired to Anglesey, where in 1659 he headed another uprising.

Owen, Robert (1771-1858). Social reformer born at Newtown (museum). He early made his name as an efficient yet humane cotton mill manager, and is most associated with the New Lanark mills in Scotland of which he became manager and part owner. Here, for a labour force of 2000 including 500 children, he built improved housing, opened a cost price store, and started the first infant school in Britain. Later (1825), impatient over government lack of support for his plans for industrial reform and for self-contained communities, he founded New Harmony in Indiana U.S.A., but this failed and Owen lost most of his money. On his return to England he was accepted as the workers' leader and became much involved in the growth of trade unionism, as also in such fields as education and marriage law reform. His four sons all settled in America, the eldest sitting in Congress and achieving many social reforms. Buried at Newtown.

Patti, Adelina Juana Marina (1843-1919). American singer. She made her first appearance in 1859 in New York as Lucia in 'Lucia di Lammermoor'. Sang at Covent Garden in 1861, soon becoming world famous. Her marriage at Brecon in 1898, her third, was to the Swedish Baron Cederström. She bought her home at Craig-y-Nos in 1878.

Pelagius (c. 360-c. 420). British theologian who may have spent his early years at the monastery at Bangor-is-Coed. For the rest of his life he was in Rome, Africa, and Palestine. The main plank of his philosophy was the freedom of the human will, as opposed to the current official doctrine of original sin. His views were spread largely through the enthusiasm of his younger and bolder Italian friend Coelestius. In 429 St Germanus, Bishop of Auxerre, was sent to Britain to combat the heresy, which later was also a source of worry to St David.

Pennant, Thomas (1726-98). Traveller, naturalist, and prolific writer. Native of Downing, near Holywell, his first publication (1750) being an account of an earthquake felt here. In 1767 he was elected a Fellow of the Royal Society, and in 1771 he published 'Synopsis of Quadrupeds'. He made tours of Scotland in 1769 and 1772, as a result publishing 'Tour in Scotland' and 'Flora Scotica'. His 'Tour in Wales', written as the result of several journeys, was published in 1778. Amongst other works his 'British Zoology' and 'History of Quadrupeds' are classics of their time.

Philips, Katharine (1631-64), Poetess. She made her home (The Priory, Cardigan) a centre of a Society of Friendship, the members of which addressed one another by romantic names, she being Orinda, to which her admirers prefixed 'matchless'. It was she who pressed Jeremy Taylor to write his discourse on friendship.

Poyer, John (d. 1649). In 1642, as mayor of Pembroke, he sided with Parliament. In 1648, alleging that Parliament had not repaid moneys he had disbursed on its behalf and that he had had to pay his soldiers out of his own pocket, he declared for the King and was joined by Laugharne who had similar grievances. The pair were defeated at St Fagans and Cromwell battered Pembroke into surrender. In 1649 Poyer, Laugharne, and a Colonel Powell were sentenced to death, but Cromwell decided that only one of the trio, to be chosen by lot, should die. Poyer lost, and was shot in London's Covent Garden.

Prynne, William (1600-69). Extremist Puritan. In his 'Histriomastix' he made a violent attack on the threatre and particularly on royalty who patronized it. As the Queen happened at the time to be taking part in theatricals. Prynne spent a year in the Tower and had his ears cut off. In 1637, after an attack on bishops, he lost what was left of his ears and was imprisoned in Caernarvon. Freed in 1640 he continued his campaign against personal freedom in religion. He opposed the execution of Charles I and was later several times imprisoned, generally because he refused to pay taxes he considered illegal.

Rees, Abraham (1743-1825). Encyclopaedist. Between 1778-88 he published a revised and expanded edition of Ephraim Chambers's 'Cyclopaedia' (shortened title), claiming to have added over 4400 new articles.

Repton, Humphry (1752-1818). Landscape gardener. Although a follower of 'Capability' Brown, he was far less rigid in his attitude, maintaining that the house must always be the principal factor in a design and that the gardens should be subordinate. Repton is known for his 'Red Books', these being reports in red covers giving details of each of his more important undertakings and including sketches showing what the effect would be as the trees reached maturity.

Richard II. See under Bolingbroke.

Richard, Henry (1812-88). Native of Tregaron. His lifelong theme was the need for arbitration in international disputes, these principles first being made public in a speech in London in 1845. From 1845-88 he was secretary of the Peace Society, as such attending a series of international conferences. He also did much for Wales, serving as M.P. for Merthyr and becoming known as the 'member for Wales'.

Roberts, Samuel (1800-85). Social and political reformer, and leader of Nonconformist opinion. Advocate of free trade, franchise extension, Catholic emancipation, and temperance. He was also active in fighting for special railway routes through Wales. In 1827 he advocated a system of inland penny post, and in 1883 his efforts at general postal reform were recognized by an official testimonial and award. Between 1857-67 he was in America, with his brother Richard, preaching racial equality.

Rodney, George Bridges (1718-92). Admiral. Rodney's crowning achievement was off Domenica in the West Indies when the French were supporting the American colonists. By defeating the French admiral the Comte de Grasse he saved Jamaica and dealt a severe blow to French naval prestige. After the battle he was created Baron Rodney. See also p. 253.

Rolfe, Frederick (1860-1904). Artist, scholar, and writer. Twice attempted to become a R.C. priest, but was turned down as unsuitable, this leading him to a hatred of Roman Catholicism. Styled himself Baron Corvo, and led a drifting life as an artist and photographer. Commissioned (1895) to paint banners for Holywell, but this venture ended in a financial row (but banners can be seen at R.C. church). Best known as author of the novel 'Hadrian the Seventh'.

Rowlands, John. See Stanley, H.M.

Rupert, Prince (1619-82). Count Palatine of the Rhine and Duke of Bavaria. Third son of Frederick V, 'winter king' of Bohemia and of Elizabeth, daughter of James I. Came to England and during the Civil War was his uncle Charles I's dashing cavalry commander and, later, army commander. Later again, becoming doubtful about both the rightness and the outcome of the King's cause, Rupert surrendered Bristol and left England. He returned at the Restoration and became a successful admiral. Rupert was also an artist and inventor, being a distinguished mezzotinter and inventor of a form of brass for guns known as 'prince's metal'.

Savage, Richard (d. 1743). Poet. He claimed to be natural son of Richard Savage, 4th Earl Rivers, and of Lady Macclesfield, a claim rejected by the latter, now Mrs Brett. However Savage blackmailed so successfully ('The Bastard' was published in 1728) that he was bought off with a pension from Mrs Brett's nephew, Viscount Tyrconnel. When as the result of a quarrel this pension was stopped, Savage was reduced to penury and his always faithful friend Pope gave him a small allowance and sent him to Swansea to escape his creditors. But impatient at the conditions imposed by Pope and others who had helped, Savage unwisely moved to Bristol where he died in the debtors' prison. As a writer he is best known as a satirist.

Scott, George Gilbert (1811-78). Architect. Among his achievements are the Martyrs' Memorial, Oxford (1840); the restoration of Ely Cathedral (1847), and later of Hereford, Lichfield, Salisbury, and Ripon cathedrals; several government buildings around Whitehall, these being the subject of much conflict between the Gothic and the Classical schools, the latter in the end winning; St Pancras station and hotel (1865); and the Albert Memorial (1872). The criticism was made of him that he remodelled rather than restored, and it is ironic that it was his work that to a great extent led to the founding (by William Morris) of the Society for the Protection of Ancient Buildings (1877).—His sons George (1839-1907) and J. Oldrid (1842-1913) and his grandson Giles (1880-1960) were all distinguished architects.

Scott, Robert Falcon (1868-1912). Leader of Antarctic expeditions in 1900-04 and 1909-12, on the latter occasion reaching the South Pole, only to find that he had been forestalled by Amundsen. He and his companions all died during the return sledge journey. His companions included Petty Officer Evans, whose home was Rhossili on Gower.

Shelley, Percy Bysshe (1792-1822), Poet. Shelley was in Wales on and off between 1811-13. The first occasion was a visit to his cousin Thomas Grove at Cwm Elan near Rhayader, following his expulsion from Oxford because of his pamphlet 'The Necessity of Atheism'. Soon after, he eloped with the schoolgirl Harriet Westbrook, marrying her in Scotland. In Wales the pair first stayed at Nant Gwyllt (April-June 1812) near Cwm Elan. Both places are now submerged below the Elan reservoirs. Later Shelley and Harriet moved to Tan-yr-Allt, scene of the Tremadog incident (see p. 162). After this they were briefly at Gwynfryn near Criccieth. In 1814 Shelley virtually deserted Harriet when he fell in love with Mary Godwin, and in 1817 Harriet drowned herself in London's Serpentine. Shelley then married Mary Godwin, but in 1822 he too died by drowning in a storm at sea off Italy.

Siddal, Elizabeth (d. 1862). Wife of D. G. Rossetti. A great beauty, she was painted by Holman Hunt and Millais and several times by Rossetti, who married her in 1860 when she was already dying of tuberculosis.

Siddons, Sarah (1755-1831). Actress. Born at Brecon, daughter of the player Roger Kemble, she is said to have made her first appearance at Kington in 1772 or 73. But it was her performance as Belvidera (in Otway's 'Venice Preserved') in 1774 at Cheltenham that prompted Garrick to engage her for Drury Lane. From then on her career was a series of triumphs, Lady Macbeth probably being her most famous role. She was a close friend of Dr Johnson.

Simon de Montfort (c. 1200-65). Born in France, youngest son of Simon IV de Montfort, leader of the Albigensian Crusade. Came to England in 1230, attached himself to Henry III, and was made Earl of Leicester. There followed constant quarrels with Henry, Simon on more than one occasion returning to France. When Henry accepted the crown of Sicily for his son and pledged England's credit to the Pope for the conquest of the island, Simon and the barons forced upon the King the Provisions of Oxford (1258), placing the government in the hands of a feudal oligarchy which strictly controlled expenditure. Henry submitted, but soon obtained papal absolution from his promises. In 1263 Simon led a rebellion, at Lewes defeating and capturing Henry and his son (the future Edward I). Simon then set up a parliamentary system, a feature of which was to be parliamentary control over the government. However Edward escaped from captivity in Hereford (see p. 280) and soon defeated and killed Simon de Montfort at Evesham.

Smith, John 'Warwick' (1749-1831). Painter. His patron was the Earl of Warwick (hence his nickname) with whom he toured Italy. He was a major contributor to the exhibitions of the Watercolour Society.

Southey, Robert (1774-1843), Poet and miscellaneous writer who in

1813 became Poet Laureate. Today best known for ballads such as 'The Inchcape Rock' and 'The Battle of Blenheim'. He came to Wales to visit his patron Sir W. Williams Wynne of Llangedwyn Hall.

Stanhope, Lady Hester (1776-1839). Eldest child of the 3rd Earl of Stanhope and Lady Hester Pitt, she was niece of William Pitt. She was endowed with great energy and considerable business acumen, and from time to time acted as the statesman's private secretary. In 1810 she suddenly left England and settled on Mount Lebanon, where through a combination of sheer personality and careful fostering of the local belief that she had the gift of divination, she achieved a position of almost absolute authority over the Druse tribe.

Stanley, Sir Henry Morton (1841-1904). African explorer. Born John Rowlands at Denbigh, he was placed in St Asaph workhouse at the age of six. Nine years later he ran away and sailed as a cabin boy to America where he was adopted by Henry Morton Stanley. During the American Civil War he served in the Confederate army, later travelling across America and becoming a recognized descriptive writer. After travels in Asia Minor and Tibet, and after being first with the news of the fall of Magdala in Abyssinia, he was commissioned by Gordon Bennet of the New York Herald to go to Africa to find David Livingstone. In this he succeeded in 1871. On his second African journey (1874-77), undertaken on behalf of Leopold II of Belgium, he traced the course of the Congo, remaining in what became the Congo State until 1884. On his third journey, a half political and half military expedition marked by appalling hardships, he discovered the Mountains of the Moon. He was knighted in 1899.

Steele, Sir Richard (1672-1729). Irish man of letters. Editor of the 'Gazette', the 'Tatler', and the 'Spectator', he achieved wide recognition through his many essays in the last two. Lived and died at Carmarthen.

Stephen, King (?1097-1154). Grandson of William I and nephew of Henry I. His reign was marked by civil war arising from the rival claim to the throne made by Matilda, daughter of Henry I and widow of the emperor Henry V. Although in 1126 Henry I compelled Stephen and the barons to recognize Matilda as his successor, on his death in 1135 Matilda was out of the country and the barons, unwilling to accept a woman sovereign, proclaimed Stephen. Civil war followed, during which Stephen was captured and Matilda ruled for a while as Lady of England. But Matilda's arrogance soon alienated her supporters, and after defeat at Winchester she had to release Stephen. Matilda retired to Normandy, and eventually Stephen recognized her son (the future Henry II) as his heir.

Stephenson, Robert (1803-59). Engineer. Surveyed the Stockton and Darlington railways. His monument in Wales is the Conwy tubular railway bridge. His similar bridge across Menai Strait was burnt in 1970.

Street, George Edmund (1824-81). Architect and architectural writer. His preference was the Gothic style and he specialized in ecclesiastical buildings. He also designed London's Law Courts, though the building was completed after his death by Blomfield and Street's son. Among his written works are 'The Brick and Marble Architecture of Northern Italy' and 'The Gothic Architecture of Spain'.

Taylor, Jeremy (1613-67). Divine, writer, and Royalist. As a Royalist he lost his rectorship of Uppingham and was later captured at Cardigan.

After this he found refuge as private chaplain to Richard Vaughan, 2nd Earl of Carbery, at the latter's mansion of Golden Grove near Llandeilo. Taylor's perhaps best known work is 'Golden Grove; or a Manuall of daily prayers and letanies' (1655). His 'Discours of the Nature, Offices, and Measures of Friendship' (1657) was written on the prompting of Katharine Philips ('matchless Orinda') of Cardigan. Taylor was imprisoned in 1654-55, a second time in 1655 at Chepstow, and in the Tower in 1657-58, on all occasions apparently because of his episcopal views rather than simply as a Royalist. At the Restoration he was made Bishop of Down, Connor and Dromore (in Ireland) and also Vice Chancellor of the university of Dublin. His second wife, Joanna Bridges, born at Mandinam, was said to have been a natural child of Charles I.

Telford, Thomas (1757-1834). Scottish civil engineer, specially known for his canals (Caledonian in Scotland), roads, and many still surviving bridges. In Wales his main achievements were what is now the A5 road, the Menai and Conwy bridges, and the Pont-y-Cysylltau aqueduct.

Thrale, Hester Lynch (1741-1821). Writer and social figure. Born near Pwllheli. Best known as the friend of Dr Johnson, a frequent resident of her house at Streatham, London, which became a regular meeting place for many distinguished people of the time. After her husband's death (he was a Southwark brewer) she married Gabriele Piozzi, an Italian musician, living at Brynbella near St Asaph where Piozzi died. His widow then retired to Bath where she died soon after celebrating her 80th birthday with a ball for over 600 people. She wrote poems, essays, letters etc., and also much about Johnson, including 'Anecdotes of the late Samuel Johnson'.

Traherne, Thomas (c. 1637-74). Poet. Son of a Hereford cobbler, he became a priest, being rector of Credenhill and chaplain to his patron Sir Orlando Bridgeman, Lord Keeper of the Seals. His poems, which he left in manuscript, were only found (on a bookseller's cart) in 1897. At first ascribed to Henry Vaughan, they were later recognized as Traherne's and published in 1906.

Trevithick, Richard (1771-1833). Engineer and inventor. In 1801 his road locomotive became the first ever to pull a load of passengers by steam, and in 1804 he was active in Wales with tramroad steam locomotives. In 1808 he operated a circular railway at London's Euston Square. Later he built mining engines for Peru.

Vaughan, Henry (1622-95). Poet and mystic. Self-styled 'The Silurist' because the tribe of the Silures had inhabited the part of Wales in which he lived (Brecon area). A Royalist, he fought at Rowton Moor. As a poet he is known for his mystical view of nature and his works are thought to have influenced Wordsworth. Henry Vaughan's twin brother was Thomas, who gained some repute as an alchemist and poisoned himself with fumes of mercury.

Waller, Sir William (c. 1597-1668). Parliamentary commander and M.P. Was the originator of the idea of the New Model Army, but lost his own command under the Self Denying Ordinance. Later he changed allegiance and was active in the negotiations for the Restoration.

Wesley, John (1703-91). Founder (with his brother Charles) of Methodism, this originating in meetings of a group of Oxford students. In Wesley's words the purpose of Methodism was to 'spread scriptural holiness over the land'; it was not to form a separate Church group.

From 1735-38 he was in Georgia. Back in London he founded his Societies, and in 1743 he started his main itinerant work, travelling 5000 miles a year and preaching 15 sermons a week. Wesley is known too for his writings (hymns, philosophical works, and his 'Journal') and as a social reformer.

Whistler, Rex (1905-44). Painter, decorator, and stage designer. Killed in action in Normandy while serving in the Welsh Guards. Among his works are the decorations in the restaurant of London's Tate Gallery (1926-27) and those at Plas Newydd (1937). He did stage designs for Covent Garden, Sadler's Wells, and C. B. Cochran revues.

Williams, John (1582-1650). Archbishop of York. Native of Conwy. During the Civil War he held Conwy for the King whom he afterwards joined at Oxford. Later, on discovering that Sir John Owen, now at Conwy, had on the King's orders seized some property which had been entrusted to his care, Williams went over to Parliament and helped Mytton to take Conwy in 1646.

Williams, William Charles (d. 1915). Able Seaman, V.C. Native of Chepstow (memorial). In the Dardanelles, while helping to move lighters to the shore, he stood firm under continuous fire holding on to a vital line until he was killed. Described by his commander as 'the bravest sailor I have ever met'.

Williams-Ellis, Sir Clough (1883-1978). Welsh architect and landscape designer, best known for his creation of Portmeirion. Won Military Cross during First World War. Chairman of Stevenage New Town Corporation. Knighted in 1972. His style is generally Classical and Georgian. A vigorous conservationist, he wrote several books.

Wilson, Richard (1714-82). Welsh-born landscape painter. An original member of the Royal Academy where he exhibited until 1780. His work was not appreciated until after his death and he lived in London in some poverty until his brother's death brought him a small property near Mold (Plas Colomendy).

Winde, William (d. 1722). Architect. Born in Holland, son of a refugee Royalist, he came to England at the Restoration. He followed a military career (fighting at Sedgemoor) until 1688 when he changed to architecture. One of his buildings in London was Buckingham House (1705), later incorporated by John Nash into Buckingham Palace.

Wood, John (c. 1705-54). Architect. Follower of the Palladian style. Best known for his work in Bath. In Wales he is known for his 'restoration' of Llandaff Cathedral by means of an Italianate temple, removed a few years later.

Wyatt, James (1746-1813). Architect, known as a reviver of Gothic. In 1776, appointed Surveyor of Westminster Abbey. He 'restored' several cathedrals, including rebuilding the nave of Hereford, his work earning him the title of the Destroyer from his contemporaries.

Yale, Elihu (1649-1721). Born near Boston, Mass. In 1672 he went to India, becoming governor of Madras. On his return to England he became known for the generosity with which he gave away the books, etc, he had collected. After being invited to help a struggling college in America, Yale sent off a cargo of books, pictures, etc., the sale of which raised so much that it was decided to give his name to the new college building at Newhaven. In 1745 the whole institution became Yale University. Buried at Wrexham, the family home.

PRACTICAL INFORMATION

This section is concerned principally with information special to Wales. For practical information regarding the Marches please see the *Blue Guide to England,* many of the sections of which apply equally to Wales.

Publications. Several publications are mentioned below. Unless otherwise stated these are priced. Priced publications can be bought at information centres and at leading booksellers. Free publications can be obtained at information centres or by written application to the organizations concerned. Written applications should be accompanied by a sensibly sized stamped addressed envelope.

ORGANIZATIONS

Wales Tourist Board. The Board has information centres throughout Wales, several of which are open all year and all of which are open from Easter to September or October. Several centres operate a bed booking and room reservation service. The board publishes a tourist map (see p. 12) and several booklets, a number of which are recommended elsewhere in this Guide. In London and outside the United Kingdom the Board is represented by the **British Tourist Authority,** 64 St James's Street, London, S.W.1., with a worldwide network of branches and agents. The Authority publishes a monthly journal *In Britain*, with announcements of coming events, including events in Wales

Wales Tourist Board, P.O. Box 151, W.D.O. Cardiff, CF5 1XS.
North Wales Tourism Council, Glan-y-Don Hall, Civic Centre, Colwyn Bay, Clwyd.
Mid Wales Tourism Council, Owain Glyndwr Institute, Maengwyn Street, Machynlleth, Powys.
South Wales Tourism Council, Darkgate, Carmarthen, Dyfed.

The **Welsh Inspectorate of Ancient Monuments** (A.M.) is responsible for all officially designated Ancient Monuments. A fee is charged at sites where there is a custodian, and a season ticket giving access to all A.M. sites in Britain can be a considerable saving. Season tickets, valid for a year, can be bought at most sites; at H.M.S.O. bookshops; from Department of the Environment (A.M.), 25, Savile Row, London, W1X 2BT; or from Welsh Inspectorate of Ancient Monuments, Ty Glas, Llanishen, Cardiff.—At most sites excellent ground plans can be bought for a few pence.

The **Forestry Commission** (F.C.), set up in 1919, is in evidence throughout most of Wales, an important if secondary part of its work being the provision of information and recreational facilities. These take the form of information centres, picnic sites, forest drives, forest trails, and camping and caravan sites. Trails, of varying length (2 m. is about average), usually start from parking and picnic sites and make a round. For many trails leaflets are available, but not necessarily at the site itself (although 'honesty boxes' are being increasingly installed), and visitors planning to enjoy F.C. facilities are advised to start by going to the nearest information centre. A leaflet *See your Forests—Wales* can be obtained from the F.C. offices at Churchill House, Churchill Way, Cardiff, CF1 4TU, or Victoria House, Victoria Terrace, Aberystwyth, Dyfed, SY23 2DA. This leaflet (free), with small maps, locates all forests and summarizes their facilities. Also free are *Camping and Caravan Sites, Cabins and Holiday Houses, Conservation,* and *Recreation in your Forests.*

The Commission also issues a wide range of priced publications, a free catalogue of which can be obtained from the above addresses. Publications are available at H.M.S.O. bookshops, leading booksellers, and at F.C. information centres. The Commission's *Forest Guides,* containing a wealth of information and written in readable non-technical style, can be recommended.

The **National Trust** (N.T.) was founded in 1895 by a group of people who foresaw the threats arising from increasing population, spreading industry, and inadequate planning. The group's aim was to set up a body of private citizens willing to act as trustees for the nation in the acquisition and ownership of land and buildings worthy of permanent preservation. Only 12 years later, under the National Trust Act of 1907, Parliament gave the Trust the right to declare its land inalienable, this meaning that today the majority of the Trust's properties cannot be sold or compulsorily acquired. The Trust is in no way a government department, but a charity supported mainly by the subscriptions of its members and by the contributions of visitors to Trust properties. Members have free access to all properties including those of the National Trust for Scotland. In Wales and the Marches the Trust owns or protects many and often extensive areas of countryside, to most of which there is free public access. It also owns several both small and large buildings, the latter including a number of great houses, complete with their original decoration, furniture, and pictures.

The Trust may be joined at many of its properties, or by application to the *Membership Department,* P.O. Box 30, Beckenham, Kent, BR3 4TL. Other addresses:—*Headquarters:* 42 Queen Anne's Gate, London, SW1H 9AS. *North Wales:* Dinas, Betws-y-Coed, Gwynedd, LL24 0HG. *South Wales:* 22 Alan Road, Llandeilo, Dyfed, SA19 6HU.

The **Nature Conservancy Council** (N.C.) was established by the Nature Conservancy Council Act 1973 'for the purpose of nature conservation and fostering the understanding thereof'. Among a number of statutory functions the one most apparent to the general public is 'the establishment, maintenance, and management of nature reserves'. Although responsible for such reserves, Nature Conservancy does not necessarily own them, and also in some cases leases them to local Naturalists' Trusts. A number of the more important reserves in Wales are mentioned in this Guide. In several cases access is only by permit, and for many reserves there are interpretive booklets and nature trail leaflets, unlikely however to be obtainable at the reserve itself. Booklets and leaflets will often be found at local information centres, but anyone wishing to visit reserves is advised to write in advance to the appropriate N.C. regional office, i.e. *North Wales:* Ffordd Penrhos, Bangor, Gwynedd, LL57 2LQ. *Dyfed/Powys:* Plas Gogerddan, Aberystwyth, Dyfed, SY23 3EB. *South Wales:* 44 The Parade, Roath, Cardiff, CF2 3AB.

The **Countryside Commission** is an independent statutory body with powers defined under the National Parks and Access to the Countryside Act of 1949; the Countryside Act 1968, under which the Commission replaced the National Parks Commission; and the Local Government Act of 1974. In broad terms the Commission's task is 'to keep under review matters relating to the conservation and enhancement of landscape beauty in England and Wales, and to the provision and improvement of facilities for enjoyment of the countryside, including the need to secure access for open-air recreation'. More specifically the Commission has responsibilities (designation; advice on planning and management) for National Parks, Areas of Outstanding Natural Beauty, Country Parks, and Heritage Coasts, for all of which see p. 19. Long-distance footpaths and bridleways, picnic sites, and car parks at viewpoints are among other concerns of the Commission.— Countryside Commission, John Dower House, Crescent Place, Cheltenham, Glos, GL50 3RA. *Welsh Office:* 8 Broad Street, Newtown, Powys, SY16 2LU.

The **Welsh Development Agency,** set up in 1976, undertakes the interrelated functions of land reclamation, environmental improvement, the provision of industrial estates, and financial backing for industry. To the visitor the Agency's work will be most apparent in the measures designed to treat the industrial scars of the past, this particularly applying to The Valleys (see beginning of Rte 41). For further information, write to the Welsh Development Agency, Treforest Industrial Estate, Pontypridd, Mid Glamorgan, CF37 5UT.

The **National Gardens Scheme** operates in England and Wales. It originated in 1927 (after the death of Queen Alexandra, who had done so much for nursing, particularly as patron of the Queen's Institute of District Nursing), many owners of gardens opening these to the public and charging a small fee which went to the Queen's Institute. Proceeds today go principally to nurses' general welfare, and a proportion to the National Trust to help in preserving gardens of national and historic importance. The Scheme publishes annually an illustrated guide of gardens open to visitors on certain days throughout the year. This can be bought, from about March onwards, from principal booksellers. The Scheme's address is 57 Lower Belgrave Street, London, SW1W 0LR.

TRAVEL, ACCOMMODATION, FOOD AND DRINK

WEATHER AND SEASON. In general the weather in Wales is much as in England—that is, changeable with only very rare extremes of hot and cold—but because of the hilly geography Wales tends to get more rain. The N.E. coast has a reputation for being sheltered from rain, and the S. and W. coasts, especially Gower and Pembroke, for mildness and sunshine. Snow is never sufficient to guarantee winter sports.

The tourist season lasts from Easter to the end of September, although a number of sites which open at Easter close again until a few weeks later. July and August are very crowded months which should be avoided by anybody wishing to visit the more popular areas; nevertheless even during these months it is possible to enjoy many out-of-the-way roads and districts. From most points of view May, June, and September are the best months for touring.

ROAD TRAVEL. The main road approaches to Wales are, in the *North,* A55 from Chester, running across the N. of the country to Bangor on Menai Strait: in the *Centre,* Telford's A5 from Shrewsbury across Menai Strait to Holyhead; or A458 from Shrewsbury to Dolgellau and Machynlleth near the W. coast; or A44 from Leominster to Aberystwyth; or, towards the S., M50 and A40 from Tewkesbury through Monmouth, Brecon, and Carmarthen into the Pembroke peninsula: in the *South,* M4 across the Severn Bridge and continuing along the S. coast. Between the above there is a continual choice of other roads.

Within Wales there is only one motorway (M4) running along the S. coast. Other roads are of average British Isles standard, if often hilly and twisting, but there are few dual carriageway stretches. Main road passes such as Llanberis (1169 ft) or Bwlch Oerddrws (1178 ft) should present no problems, but the road across Bwlch-y-Groes (1790 ft) is narrow and steep. A number of the places mentioned in this Guide are accessible only by narrow lanes sometimes not suitable for larger cars.

Automobile Association, West and Wales Region, Fanum House, Park Row, Bristol, BS1 5LY (Bristol 297272).
Automobile Association Service Centre, 7 Wood Street, Cardiff (Cardiff 394111).

Automobile Association road conditions information, ring Cardiff 8021.
Royal Automobile Club, 205 Newport Road, Cardiff CF2 1YR (Cardiff 35544).
Express Coach Services. There are daily express coach services from all over England and from Glasgow and Edinburgh to most principal Welsh centres. From London the Red Dragon service leaves Victoria Terminal roughly every two hours, reaching Cardiff in 3½ hours and Swansea in another 1½ hours. Within Wales there is a comprehensive network of express services. All services to and within Wales are operated by National Bus Company or its subsidiaries. 'Coachmaster' tickets, valid for periods of between one and four weeks and offering unlimited travel, are available only to overseas visitors. On many routes Sunday services are limited or non-existent.
National Travel Ltd., Victoria Coach Station, London SW1W 9TP. (01-730 3466).
South Wales Transport Co. Ltd (subsidiary for Southwest Wales), 31 Russell Street, Swansea, SA1 4HP.
National Welsh Services Ltd: Jones Omnibus Service Ltd (subsidiaries for Southeast Wales), 253 Cowbridge Road West, Ely, Cardiff, CF5 5XX.
Crosville Motor Services Ltd (subsidiary for the rest of Wales and Cheshire), Crane Wharf, Chester, CH1 3SQ.
Cycling. Being so hilly Wales is not an ideal country for the cyclist. Nevertheless the Cyclists Touring Club issues cyclists' routes. For membership apply, Cyclists Touring Club, 69 Meadrow, Godalming, Surrey.

RAIL TRAVEL. The main line for **North Wales** is from London (Euston) via Crewe and Chester (northern connections at both places). The line then follows the N. coast and crosses the Menai Strait for Holyhead (for Dublin). There are about four through services daily, the journey times from London being 2¾ hours to Chester; 4½ hours to Bangor; and 5 hours to Holyhead.—Off this line there are branch lines from Hawarden to Wrexham, and from Llandudno Junction to Betws-y-Coed and Blaenau Ffestiniog.

The main line for **South Wales** is from London (Paddington) through the Severn Tunnel to Cardiff, Swansea, and Fishguard (for Rosslare). There are roughly hourly daytime services to Cardiff and Swansea, and two services a day to Fishguard, the journey times from London being 2 hours to Cardiff, 3 hours to Swansea, and 5½ hours to Fishguard.—Off this line there are branch lines from Newport to Hereford; from Cardiff to Penarth and Barry, and up The Valleys to Pontypridd, Treherbert, Merthyr Tydfil, and Rhymney; from Whitland to Pembroke Dock; and from Clarbeston Road to Milford Haven.

There are also main line services from London to Hereford (3¼ hours) and Shrewsbury (2½ hours).

In addition to the above N. and S. routes, there are two other principal lines within Wales. The Cambrian Coast and Mid Wales line runs from Shrewsbury to Dovey Junction; thence either S. to Aberystwyth, or N. along the coast viâ Harlech to Pwllheli. The other internal line connects Shrewsbury via Llandrindod Wells to Swansea.

Summer only **Motorail** from London to Fishguard.

British Rail offer a range of special tickets at reduced fares. Particulars from British Rail, Stoke-on-Trent (Tel: 48261) for the North Wales area; or from British Rail, Brunel House, Cardiff (Tel: 499811) for the remainder of Wales. Information also available at most stations.

Little Trains. Particulars of 'Little Trains' will be found under Routes as follows:— Rte 9A *Llanberis Lake;* Rte 9B *Snowdon;* Rte 16 *Bala Lake;* Rte 17 *Festiniog;* Rte 22B *Welshpool and Llanfair;* Rte 26 *Talyllyn* and *Fairbourne;* Rte 27 *Vale of Rheidol.*

SEA SERVICES. There are three sea services to Wales:

Dún Laoghaire (Dublin) to Holyhead. Crossing 3¼ hours. Information from British Rail.

Rosslare to Fishguard. Crossing 3¼ hours. Information from British Rail.

Cork to Swansea. Crossing 9½ hours. Information from British and Irish Steampacket Co. Ltd., 155 Regent Street, London W1.

AIR SERVICES. There are no direct inter-continental services to Wales. From *Cardiff (Rhoose)* there is a variety of seasonal short-haul services to English centres, and to Eire, Northern Ireland, Scotland, Holland, France, and the Channel Islands. Operators are British Airways, Dan Air, Aer Lingus, and Air Wales. From *Swansea (Fairwood Common)* there are short-haul summer services (Air Anglia).

ACCOMMODATION. W.T.B.'s annual booklet *Where to stay in Wales* is a very comprehensive guide, listing accommodation under five main categories:— Hotels, Motels, Inns, and Guest Houses; Farmhouses; Furnished (self-catering) Accommodation; Caravan and Camping Sites; Special Interest Holidays. This last category includes, to name only a few, such interests as pony trekking; painting and crafts; sailing and canoeing; canal cruising; pottery; field studies; hang gliding; walking and climbing; and natural history. With the exception of the special interests category, by its nature a special case, all establishments listed have made a declaration that the accommodation and facilities offered conform to the minimum standards set by W.T.B. and listed for each category in their booklet.

Reservations. Accommodation of all kinds is much in demand during the summer season, especially in July and August, and intending visitors with fixed plans are advised to book in advance. Others may use W.T.B.'s *Accommodation Booking Service* (small charge), available at most information centres.

Camping and Caravanning. In addition to the list of sites given in the W.T.B. booklet, campers and caravanners may use lists provided by the Forestry Commission, motoring associations, and camping and caravanning clubs. It is worth noting that there is a large municipal site close to Cardiff city centre, and that there are racecourse sites, also close to the town centres, at Chepstow and Chester, the latter for caravans only.

Youth Hostels. The Youth Hostels Association owns a large number of hostels in Wales and the Borders. For membership apply Y.H.A. National Office, St Alban's Herts, AL1 2DY; Y.H.A. Services, Southampton Street, London, W.C.2; or at either of the Regional Group offices. The Association's annual handbook lists all hostels.—*North Wales Regional Group:* Merseyside Youth Hostels Ltd., 40 Hamilton Square, Birkenhead, Merseyside L41 5BA. *South Wales Regional Group:* 131 Woodville Road, Cardiff, CF2 4DZ.

FOOD AND DRINK. Welsh mutton is famous, many visitors will enjoy local salmon and trout, and others perhaps may try the seaweed preparation called 'laver bread', but, these apart, there are no widely known Welsh specialities. Recently however there has been increasing interest in traditional Welsh recipes and a number of books have been published, while the Welsh Folk Museum has been researching and collecting recipes. W.T.B. booklet *Try a Taste of Wales* (free) lists establishments where traditional dishes may be served or which place emphasis on local fresh produce.—**Licensing Hours** vary from district to district but apart from Sundays are generally the same as in England (about 11.00 to 15.00 and 18.00 to 22.30). As to Sundays, Wales holds a referendum every seven years to decide whether licensed premises should open, the result of the 1975 referendum being that Arfon, Carmarthen, Ceredigion, Dwyfor, Meirionnydd, and Anglesey are dry. However residents can buy drinks for themselves and their guests.

OUTDOOR PURSUITS

Walking. Whether along waymarked trails or following long-distance ways across remote mountain moorland walking is one of the most popular outdoor holiday pursuits in Wales. The better-known walking areas, and many walks within them, are indicated in this Guide, but it has only been possible to touch the fringe of an activity which in its own right is the subject of a mass of literature. A useful introductory booklet is W.T.B.'s *Walking* (with maps) which lists over 150 waymarked walks and over 300 unwaymarked. The first list includes, for each walk, details on location, the organizers, publications available, parking facilities, public transport access, length, time required, and a 'suitability grading'. The booklet also includes a bibliography relating to walking in Wales. Leaflets for walks may be obtained from information centres, in some cases from 'honesty boxes' at the start of the walk, or by writing (enclose stamped addressed envelope) to the organizing authority.

It is emphasized that not all mountain, moorland, and coastal walks are for the inexperienced, especially if there is any doubt about the weather, and that correct clothing, food and equipment, a good map, and a compass are essential.

There are three **Long-Distance Paths** in Wales and the Borders.
Offa's Dyke Path. Prestatyn (Clwyd) to Chepstow (Gwent). 167 m., made up of many shorter excursions.
Pembrokeshire Coast Path. 168 m. See p. 25.
Coed Morgannwg Way. Hirwaun to Margam Park. 23-25 m. See p. 307.

Pony Trekking. Much of Wales is ideal country for pony trekking, an activity which is becoming increasingly popular, whether simply for a half day or for a week or longer. The Pony Trekking and Riding Society of Wales (Maerdy, Taliaris, Llandeilo, Dyfed) is concerned with the standards of centres, an approved list of which is contained in W.T.B.'s leaflet *Pony Trekking and Riding* (free).

Angling and Fishing. With its long and varied coast and many rivers and lakes, Wales attracts angling and fishing enthusiasts of many kinds. W.T.B.'s *Angling Guide to Wales* (illustrated and with maps) includes a wealth of detail under the three main chapter headings of Sea Angling, Game Fishing, and Coarse Fishing.

Beaches and Bathing. With some 750 m. of varied coastline facing N., W., and S., Wales can offer virtually every kind of beach and beach background, ranging from the sands of the popular resorts to remote open sweeps, hidden coves, and beaches below towering cliffs. W.T.B.'s three *Regional Guides* (North, Mid, and South Wales) contain special sections on beaches, with notes on their characteristics (sand or shingle), safety, facilities, etc.

Other Pursuits. For the many other outdoor pursuits for which facilities are available (Golf; mountaineering and rock climbing; hang gliding; water sports; canal cruising etc.), see the Special Interest Holidays section of W.T.B.'s *Where to stay in Wales.*

THE WELSH LANGUAGE

By the late Professor T. GWYNN JONES

(With minor changes and an expanded glossary)

The Welsh Language belongs to the Celtic branch of the Indo-European family. A Goidelic development of Celtic is represented by Gaelic (Irish and Scottish) and Manx; a Brythonic form by Welsh, Breton, and Cornish. It is probable that Welsh was already spoken in the 6C, when the emigration to Brittany occurred, and the earlier verse-material found in Welsh may contain 6C elements, afterwards modified. A few glosses of the 9-11C are known, and some poems which probably belong to the same period. The tales usually called 'Mabinogion' are known in 12 and 13C redactions, but there were certainly much earlier forms. The works of the many bards of the 12C, with a few compositions going back perhaps to the 9C, have been preserved, and from that time to this a vast amount of literature has been produced.

The language is phonetically written, so that, without some acquaintance with the principle of mutation, some difficulty is experienced. If an English colloquial form, such as 'Lunnon'(=London), be considered, it will be seen that the second *n* represents a natural mutation of the *d*, induced by the preceding *n*. In Welsh this kind of sound-change takes place medially and initially. If 'Caernarvon', say, be preceded by *yn*, the Welsh equivalent of the preposition *in*, the combination is written 'yng Nghaernarvon', which appears difficult to those unacquainted with the principle involved. As a matter of fact it is simply natural avoidance of the effort necessary to produce the combination -*nk*-. The English word spelt *ink* is pronounced *ingk*, not *in-k*, the *k* sound converting the *n* into *ng*. That would only give us 'yng Caernarvon', but in Welsh a further step is taken, which is the weakening of the *C*, so that it becomes a mere breathing. Hence the sound nearly is 'yng Haernarvon'. As this to some extent obscures the derivation and is perhaps not quite an exact record, the notation 'yng Nghaernarvon' is adopted. The principle here explained is characteristic of all the Celtic languages and is found in Sanskrit.

In Welsh there are Soft, Nasal, and Spirant Mutations. The Soft Mutation occurs, for instance, when an original hard sound (*c, p,* or *t*) comes between two vowels, and is softened into *g, b,* or *d*. In turn original *g, b* and *d* in the same position become * (no sound), *f*(=*v*), and *dd* (=*th* in English *the*): thus *pen, o ben; tad, am dad; coed, i goed.* It will be noted that *am* does not end in a vowel, so that, when it is prefixed to *tad*, the *t* is not intervocalic; but formerly *am* ended in a vowel (cp. Lat. *ambi*, Greek ἀμφί), and the mutation of the *t* goes back to that period. The Nasal Mutation occurs when the mutable sound is preceded by a nasal. The nasal affects the following sound, as illustrated in *ink* above. The Spirant Mutation occurs when an aspiration is caused, converting *pp, tt, kk* into *ff, th, ch.* Vowels also undergo changes analogous to that found, for instance, in the English form *men*, pl. of *man*, *geese*, pl. of *goose*, etc. Thus, in using a dictionary, words beginning with mutated sounds should be looked for under their radical forms. For instance, in *Gelli*, a form common in place-names, the initial *g* is due to the article *y*, which may have been lost. The unmutated form is *celli* (Welsh *c* = English *k*, always). Forms in composition beginning with *g*, *b*, *d* should therefore be looked for in the dictionary under *c*, *p*, *t*, and forms beginning *, *f*, *dd* under *g*, *b*, *d*. Compound elements beginning with *l*, *r*, and *f* may be looked for under *ll*, *rh*, and *m* (or *b*).

VOWELS. The vowels *a*, *e*, *i*, *o* when long are pronounced as in the vowel-sounds in *far*, *glare*, *meet*, *more;* when short as in *cat*, *get*, *pin*, *hot;* *u* and *y* long resemble the *i* in *is*, or the French *u* sound but produced with rounded lips; *w* is *oo;* *y* short is like *u* in *fun*.

CONSONANTS. Most consonants are pronounced as in English, but *c* and *g* are always hard (as in *cat*, *gun*); *ch* as in the Scottish loch or German *nacht;* *dd* as *th* in *the;* *f* as *v;* *ff* as *f;* *th* as *th* in *sympathy*. There is no exact equivalent for *ll*, but the *l* in Northern English *tl* (as in Bentley, Pentland) is very near. The letters *j*, *k*, *q*, *v*, *x* and *z* are absent from the Welsh alphabet, while *w* occurs as a consonant only in conjunction with *g* (as in *gwyn*).

The ACCENT falls regularly on the penultimate, except in the case of contractions, where it comes on the ultimate syllable, and is sometimes denoted by the acute (*caniatáu*) or the circumflex (*caniatâd*) sign. In the dialects, simplification of diphthongs occurs in unaccented positions especially.

PLURAL TERMINATIONS are: *au; on, ion; i, ydd, oedd, edd; ed, od; ant, aint; er, yr*. Plurals are made also by internal vowel change, e.g. *bardd* (*bard*), pl. *beirdd; ffon* (stick), pl. *ffyn;* or by internal vowel change and addition, e.g. *dar* (oak), pl. *deri; adain* (wing), pl. *adanedd; gwaith* (work), pl. *gweithydd; câr* (relative), pl. *ceraint; brawd* (brother), pl. *brodyr*.

CHIEF ADJECTIVAL TERMINATIONS: *aid* (*euraid*, golden); *aidd* (*peraidd*, sweet); *ain* (*cywrain*, skilful); *ig* (*mynyddig*, mountainous); *in* (*gerwin*, from *garw*, rough); *og*, *iog* (*enwog*, from *enw*, name, i.e. famous); *ol* (*amserol*, timely); *us* (*deallus*, intelligent); *wy* (*ofnadwy*, fearful); *ys* (melys, sweet).

REGULAR COMPARISON OF ADJECTIVES. Positive, *glan* (holy, clean); equative, *glaned;* comparative, *glanach;* superlative, *glanaf*.

Glossary of words associated with place names

pl.= plural   sg.= singular   *= dropped;   no sound   masc.= masculine   fem.=
feminine   adj.= adjective   dim.= diminutive

Aber	Fall of one water into a greater, or of a river into the sea. Mouth
Adar. sg. *aderyn, ederyn*	Birds
Adwy	Gap. Pass
Ael	Brow. Headland
Aeron	Fruits
Afanc	Beaver. Monster
Afon	River
Allt	Wooded hill or cliff
Am	Around. About (in compounds)
Ar	Bordering on. Upon
Aran	High place. Mountain

Mutations of B *are* F *and* M

Bach	Corner. Retreat. Small
Bala	Efflux of a river from a lake
Ban. pl. *bannau*	Height. Mountain. Lofty
Banc	Bank. Hill
Banw	A sow
Bedd	Grave
Beddrod	Grave enclosure
Bedw	Birch
Bedwas	Place of birches
Berr (fem.)	Short
Betws	Bede house; probably from Anglo-Saxon *bed* (prayer) and house
Blaen	Source. Point. Head of a valley
Boch	Cheek
Bod	Abode. Dwelling
Bon	Stem. Lower end
Bont	Bridge
Braich	Arm
Braith (fem.)	Speckled
Bran. pl. *brain*	Crow
Bras	Fat. Productive. Great
Bre	Hill
Brig	Summit
Brith (masc.)	Speckled
Bro	Vale. Plain
Broch	Badger
Bron	Breast or slope of a hill
Brwyn. sg. *brwynen*	Rushes
Brych	Speckled. Variegated
Bryn	Hill
Bu	Ox
Buarth	Cattle enclosure
Buwch. pl. *buchod*	Cow
Bwch. pl. *bychod*	Buck
Bwlch. pl. *bylchau*	Defile. Pass
Bychan	Small
Byrr (masc.)	Short

Mutations of C *are* G *and* Ch

Caban	Cabin
Cad	Host. Battle
Cadair. Cader	Chair. Seat. Stronghold
Cadarn. pl. *cedyrn*	Mighty
Cadno. Cadnaw	Fox
Cae	Field
Caer	Fort. Entrenchment. City
Cafn	Trough
Cail	Sheep-fold or pen
Cain	Bright. Beautiful

Calch	Lime
Cam	Crooked. Bent
Camlas	Canal
Canol	Middle. Centre
Cant	One hundred. Rim. Circle
Cantref	A division of land. A Hundred
Capel	Chapel
Carn	Cairn. Heap of stones
Carnedd. pl. *carneddau,* *carneddi*	Cairn (usually on a high place)
Carreg. pl. *cerrig*	Stone
Carrog	Stream
Cas	Castle
Caseg. pl. *cesig*	Mare
Castell. pl. *cestyll*	Castle
Cawr	Giant
Ceann	Head. Top
Ced	Gift
Cefn	Back. Ridge
Cegid	Hemlock
Celli	Grove
Celyn	Holly
Cemaes or *Cemais*	Bend (of coast, river)
Cesail	Nook
Ceunant	Ravine
Chwech	Six
Chwith	Left
Ci. pl. *cwn*	Dog
Cil. pl. *ciliau*	Retreat. Nook. Church
Claf	Sick
Clafdy	Hospital
Clawdd. pl. *cloddiau*	Ditch. Hedge
Cleddau. Cleddyf	Sword
Clegyr	Rocks. Stones
Cloch. pl. *clychau*	Bell
Clogwyn	Cliff. Precipice
Clos	Close. Small field
Clun	Meadow
Clwyd	Gate. Perch
Clyd	Cosy
Clyder	Sheltered valley
Cob	Dyke
Coch	Red
Coed. sg. *coeden*	Trees. Forest or woodland
Coes	Leg. Limb
Coetan	Quoit (often used for burial chambers)
Coll. pl. *cyll*	Hazel
Coll. Colled	Loss. Slaughter
Cop. Copa	Summit
Cor	Choir. Cowhouse
Corn	Horn
Cornel	Corner
Cors. pl. *corsydd*	Bog
Craig. pl. *cregiau* or *creigydd*	Rock
Crib. pl. *cribau*	Ridge
Croes	Cross. Crosswise
Croesffordd	Crossroads
Crog	Cross. Hanging or overhanging
Crom (fem.)	Crooked. Bent
Cron (fem.)	Round
Crud	Cradle
Crug. pl. *crugiau*	Mound
Crwm (masc.)	Crooked. Bent
Crwn (masc.)	Round
Crwth	Kind of musical instrument. Concave vessel

Crythor	Minstrel (player on the crwth)
Cul	Narrow
Cut. pl. *cutiau, cwt,* or *cytiau*	Hut
Cwm. pl. *cymoedd, cymau*	Valley. Cirque
Cwn. sg. *ci*	Dogs
Cwymp	Fall. Slope
Cwys	Furrow
Cymer. Cymmer	Confluence
Cyrn	Peak

Mutations of D are Dd and N

Dan	Under. Below
Dar. pl. *deri*	Oak
Dau (masc.) *Deu* (in composition)	Two
Deheu. De	South. Right
Derw. sg. *derwen*	Oaks
Diffwys	Precipice
Din. Dinas	Fortification. City
Dol. pl. *dolydd, dolau*	Meadow
Dor. pl. *dorau*	Door
Dre	Homestead
Drem	Sight. View
Drud. pl. *drudion*	Brave. Mighty
Drum	Ridge
Drws. pl. *drysau*	Pass. Door
Du. Ddu. pl. *duon*	Black
Duw	God
Dwfr. Dwr. pl. *dyfroedd*	Water
Dwy (fem.)	Two
Dwyf. Dwy	God
Dwyrain	East
Dyffryn. pl. *dyffrynnoedd*	Valley
Dyserth, or *Diserth*	A retreat. Place apart

Eglwys. pl. *eglwysi, eglwysau, eglwysydd*	Church
Eligug	Guillemot
Epynt	Horse track
Erch	Pale colour. Terrible
Erw	Acre
Esgair	Long ridge. Escarpment

Mutations of F are B and M

Fach	Small
Fal. Fali	Valley
Fan	High place
Fawn	Peat
Fawr	Large. Great. Extensive
Fechan	Small
Felindre	Mill
Ffair	Fair
Ffin	Border. Limit
Fflur	Flowers. Blossom
Ffordd. pl. *ffyrd*	Road
Ffos. pl. *ffosydd*	Ditch. Embankment
Ffraw	Rapid. Violent
Ffridd. Ffrith	Moorland. Meadows
Ffrwd. pl. *ffrydiau*	Stream
Ffynnon	Well
Foel	Bare hill
Fychan	Small

*Mutated forms of G are C, Ng, or * (dropped)*

Gafr. pl. *geifr*	Goat
Gallt	Wooded hill or cliff
Gam	Crooked. Bent

Gardd	Garden
Garth	Hill. Promontory
Gast	Bitch
Gefail	Smithy
Gelyn	Enemy
Ger	Near. By
Glan	Edge. Brink. Shore
Glas	Green. Blue
Glo	Coal
Glyder	Sheltered valley
Glyn	Valley. Glen
Godre	Foot of a hill. Edge
Gogledd	North
Gogof	Cavern
Gorllewin	West
Gris. pl. *grisiau*	Step
Gro	Gravel
Grug	Heather
Gwair	Hay
Gwastad	Level area. Smooth. Even
Gwaun. pl. *gweunydd*	Moorland field. Downland
Gwern	Alder tree. Damp meadow
Gwig	Haven. Woodland
Gwrych	Shrubs. Hedge. Bristles
Gwydd	Trees
Gwydd	Goose. adj. Wild
Gwyddfa	A wild place
Gwyn	White
Gwynt	Wind
Gwyrdd	Green
Gwyryddon. Gwyryfon	Maidens
Hafod	Summer residence
Heli	Brine
Hen	Old
Hendre	Winter residence
Heol	Paved way
Hir	Long. Tall. Tedious
Hiraeth	Longing
Hwylfa	Path. Entry
Hydd	Stag
Hyll	Ugly
Isel, is, isaf	Lower, lower, lowest
Kil (Gaelic)	Retreat

For mutated forms beginning with L, *see also under* G *and* Ll
(e.g. *glan*, *lan; *llan*, *lan)

Llaeth	Milk
Llain	Blade. A stretch of anything
Llaith	Damp. Wet. Disease
Llam	Leap
Llan	Enclosed place. Church. Hence village or town
Llanerch	Clearing
Llaw	Hand
Llawnt	Lawn
Llawr	Floor
Llech	Slate. Flagstone
Llechwedd	Slate slope
Lled	Width
Lleng	Legion
Llethr	Slope
Llew	Lion
Llif	Flood
Llith	Bait. Lesson

Lliw	Colour
Llog	Interest payment. Part of a monastery
Llong	Ship Damp (fem.)
Llwng	Damp (masc.)
Llwyd	Grey
Llwyn	Grove
Llwynog	Fox
Llyn. pl. *llynnoedd, llynnau*	Lake
Llys	Place. Court. Enclosure
Llyw	Rudder. Ruler
Llywarn. pl. *llewyrn*	Fox

Mutation of M *is* F

Ma. In compounds *Fa*	Place. Plain
Mab. pl. *meibion*	Son
Maen. pl. *meini, main*	Stone
Maes. pl. *meysydd*	Field
Mall	Rotten. Evil
Mam	Mother
Man	High place
March. pl. *meirch*	Steed
Marian	Beach
Mawn	Peat
Mawr	Great. Big. Extensive
Melin	Mill
Melyn	Yellow
Merch. pl. *merched*	Woman. Daughter
Mign	Bog
Mil	Thousand. Beast
Min	Edge. Border
Moch. sg. *mochyn*	Pigs. Rapid (adj.)
Moel	Bare or rounded mountain
Mor	Sea
Morfa	Coastal marsh
Mur	Wall
Murddyn	Ruin
Mynach	Monk
Mynydd	Mountain

Nant. pl. *naint, nentydd, nannau*	Brook. Valley
Naw	Nine
Neuadd	Hall
Newydd	New
Nos	Night

Ochr	Side. Slope
Od	Snow
Oer	Cold
Og	Harrow
Ogo. Ogof	Caves
Onn. pl. *ynn*	Ash
Or	Border. Rim. Edge

Mutations of P *are* B, Mh, Ph

Pant	Hollow ground
Parc	Field
Pedwar	Four
Pell	Far
Pellaf	Farthest
Pen	Head. Top
Penmaen	Rocky headland
Pennant	Upper reaches of a valley
Pentref	Village. Hamlet
Pig. dim. *pigyn*	Point. Summit
Pistyll	Cataract

Plas	Hall. Place
Poeth	Hot. Burnt
Pont. pl. *pontydd*	Bridge
Porth. pl. *pyrth*	Landing place
Pren	Tree. Timber
Pridd	Soil
Prys. Prysg	Shrubs
Pump	Five
Pwll	Pool
Rhaeadr. Rhaiadr.	Waterfall
Rhayader (English spelling)	
Rhewyn	Pool. Gutter. Drain
Rhiw	Hill
Rhod	Circle. Wheel
Rhodwydd	Embankment. Earthworks
Rhos	Moorland. Rose
Rhudd	Red. Ruddy
Rhwth	Open. Glaring
Rhyd	Ford
Rhydd	Free
Rhyn	Headland
Saeth	Arrow
Saith	Seven
Sarn	Causeway
Sych	Dry

Mutations of T *are* D, Nh, Th

Tafarn	Tavern
Tal	Front. Forehead, End. Tall
Tan	Under. Beneath. Fire
Tarw. pl. *teirw*	Bull
Teg	Fair
Telyn	Harp
Telynor	Harpist
Tir. pl. *tiroedd*	Land
Tomen	Mound
Ton	Wave. Surface. Green. Lay land
Torr	Flank
Traeth	Shore
Traws	Across
Tre. Tref	Habitation. Village
Trem	Sight. View
Tri	Three
Tro	Turn. Bend
Troed. pl. *traed*	Foot
Tros	Over
Trowthwy	Threshold
Trum	Ridge
Tud	People. Country
Twle. Twlch	Knoll
Twll	Hollow
Twmp	Tump
Twr. pl. *tyrau, tyroedd*	Tower
Twrch	Pig. Boar
Twrch daear	Mole
Ty. pl. *tai*	House
Tyddyn	Farmstead
Tylwyth Teg	Fairies
Tyn	Small farm
Tywarch. pl. *tyweirch*	Sod
Tywyll	Dark
Tywyn	Shore
Uchel, uch, uchaf	High, higher, highest
Udd	Lord
Un	One

Velindre (incorrect; properly *Felindre*)	Mill
Wen	White
Wern	Alder
Wrth	Near. By
Wyth	Eight
Y (before consonants). *Yr* (before vowels)	The
Ych. pl. *ychen*	Ox
Yd	Corn
Yn (*Ym* before m; *yng* before c)	In
Ynys	Island
Ysbyty. Yspytty	Hospice
Ysgal. sg. *ysgallen*	Thistles
Ysgol	School. Ladder
Ysgor	Rampart. Defence
Ysgubor	Barn
Ystrad	Valley. Strath
Ystryd. pl. *ystrydoedd*	Street
Ystum	Shape. Curve
Ystwyth	Pliable. Agile. Winding

ACCESS TO SITES

Opening times of sites are corrected with each printing of this Guide. Nevertheless the caution must be given that times may be changed at short notice.

Because of theft and vandalism churches may often be found to be locked. Sometimes a notice states where the key can be found; otherwise application may be made to the vicarage.

The opening times of principal sites under the care of the Inspectorate of Ancient Monuments are standard, and there is normally an entrance fee. For these sites the entry 'Standard' is used below. The standard times are:

	Weekdays	Sundays
March-April	09.30 to 17.30	14.00 to 17.30
May-Sept.	09.30 to 19.00	14.00 to 19.00
Oct.	09.30 to 17.30	14.00 to 17.30
Nov.-Feb.	09.30 to 16.00	14.00 to 16.00

Times etc. are normally inclusive, i.e. April-Sept.= 1 April-30 Sept. The last time given is that at which the site closes; not that of last admission.

Route 1. *Offical guided tours:* All year except Dec. and Jan. Mon.-Sat., 11.00 and 14.30. Fee.—*Chester Heritage Centre:* April-Sept., Tues.-Sat., 10.00 to 17.00. Sun., 14.00 to 17.00. Oct.-March, Tues.-Fri., 10.00 to 13.00. Sat., 10.00 to 16.30. Fee.—*Agricola Tower.* Summer only. Mon.-Sat., 09.30 to 19.00. Fee.—*Museum of the Cheshire Regiment:* 09.30 (Sun. 12.00) to 18.00 (17.00 Oct.-March). Fee.—*Grosvenor Museum:* Mon.-Sat., 10.00 to 17.00.—*Stanley Palace:* Mon.-Sat., 10.00 to 12.00. 14.00 to 17.00. Closed Thurs.—*Guildhall:* June-mid.-Sept., 14.00 to 16.00. Closed Wed. and Sun. Fee.—*Civil War Museum* and *Water Tower:* Easter period. May-Sept., Mon.-Sat., 10.00 to 17.15. Sun., 14.00 to 18.00. Fee.—*British Heritage:* 09.00 to 17.00. Fee.—*Upton Zoological Gardens:* 09.00 to dusk. Fee.—*Mouldsworth Motor Museum:* First Sun. in each month 12.00 to 18.00 (summer) or 16.00 (winter). Fee.

Route 2A. *Gwrych Castle:* Easter-Sept., from 10.00. Fee.—*New Colwyn Gallery:* Mon.-Sat., 10.00 to 13.00. 14.30 to 17.00 Closed Wed. and B.H.—*Welsh Mountain Zoo:* All year. Daily. Fee. Arrival before 14.30 advised for eagle etc. free flying displays.

Route 2B. *Hawarden Old Castle:* Easter-Sept., Sat., Sun., B.H., 14.00 to 17.30. Fee.—*St Winefride's Chapel:* Fri. and Sat., 11.00 to 19.00.—*Bodrhyddon Hall:* June-Sept., Tues. and Thurs., 14.00 to 17.30. Fee.—*Rhuddlan Castle:* Standard.—*Conwy Castle:* Standard.—*Plas Mawr:* Summer, 10.00 to 17.30, Winter, Mon.-Sat., 10.00 to 16.30. Fee.—*Aberconwy:* (N.T.). Easter-Sept., Mon.-Sat., 10.00 to 12.30. 14.00 to 17.30. Fee.

Route 3. *Rapallo House:* April-Nov., Mon.-Fri., 10.00 to 12.45. 14.00 to 17.00 or 16.00. Also by appointment.—*Doll and Model Railway Museum:* Easter-Sept., Mon.-Sat., 10.00 to 13.00. 14.00 to 17.30. Sun., 14.00 to 17.30. Winter, by appointment. Fee.

Route 4. *Museum of Welsh Antiquities:* Mon.-Sat., excl. B.H., 10.30 to 16.30.—*Oriel Bangor:* During exhibitions, Mon.-Sat. excl. B.H., 10.30 to 17.00.—*Penmachno Stones:* Apply Gwynedd Archaeological Trust, Ffordd Deiniol (Tel. 52535). See also p. 185.—*Penrhyn Castle:* (N.T.). April-Oct., daily at the following times. April, May, Oct., and all Sats. and Suns., 14.00 to 17.00. June-Sept., Mon.-Fri., 11.00 to 17.00. B.H. Mon., 11.00 to 17.00. Grounds close at 18.00. Fee.

Route 5. *Wrexham Dolls' House:* Mon.-Sat., 10.30 to 18.00. Sun., 14.00 to 18.00. Fee.—*Erddig:* (N.T.). July-Oct., daily except Mon. (but open B.H.). 12.00 to 17.30, but last adm. to house 16.30. Fee.—*Daniel Owen Centre:* Mon.-Fri., 09.30 to 19.00. Sat., 09.30 to 12.30. Closed B.H.—*Llyn Brenig Information Centre:* Mon.-Fri., 14.00 to 17.00. Sat. and Sun. (if staff available), 13.00 to 19.00.

Route 6. *Denbigh Castle:* Standard.—*Denbigh Town Walls:* Standard. Parties of four or more. Key from castle.

Route 7A. *Bodnant Garden:* (N.T.). April-Oct., Mon., Tues., Wed., Thurs., Sat. 13.30 to 16.45. Also some Suns. Fee.—*Encounter, Museum of Wildlife:* Summer, Mon.-Sat., 09.30 to 18.30. Sun., 10.30 to 18.30. Winter, Mon.-Fri., 10.30 to 16.00. Fee.

Route 7B. *Gilfach Garden:* April-Sept., Mon.-Sat., from 10.00. Fee.—*Trefriw Wells:* Easter-Sept., 10.30 to 16.30. Fee.—*Gwydir Castle:* Easter-mid. Oct., 10.30 to 17.00. Closed Sat. Fee.—*Gwydir Uchaf Chapel:* Easter-Oct., 10.00 to 17.00. Key from adjacent F.C. offices.—*Gwydir Forest Exhibition:* Easter-Oct., 10.00 to 17.00.

Route 7C. *Conwy Valley Railway Museum:* Easter-mid Oct., 10.30 to 18.00. Fee.—*Ty Mawr:* (N.T.). Easter-Oct., 10.00 to 18.00. Fee.—*Dolwyddelan Castle:* Standard.—*Gloddfa Ganol:* 10.00 to 17.30. Fee.—*Llechwedd Slate Caverns:* March-Oct., 10.00 to 18.00. Last tram 17.15. Fee.—*Tanygrisiau Power Station.* Easter, and Whitsun-Oct. Guided tours daily at regular intervals 09.00 to 18.00. Fee.—*Stwlan Dam:* In summer coach service from Tanygrisiau Reception Centre at half-hourly intervals 10.30 to 16.30. Fee.

Route 9A. *Dolbadarn Castle:* Standard.—*North Wales Quarrying Museum:* Easter-Sept., 09.30 to 19.00. Fee.—*Llanberis Lake Railway:* Easter, and throughout summer.

Route 9B. *Snowdon Mountain Railway:* Easter-early Oct., Mon.-Fri. Reduced service Sat. and Sun. Departures half-hourly, 09.00 to 17.00 or 15.30. Certain trains may be booked for coach parties (09.00 to 10.30). Service subject to weather and number of passengers (min. 25). Long waits likely in season.

Route 10. *Penrhyn Quarries:* April-Sept. Groups only (by arrangement).

Route 11. *Caernarvon Castle:* Standard.—*Museum of Royal Welch Fusiliers:* As for castle. No additional fee.—*Segontium:* Standard.

Route 12A. *Museum of Childhood:* Easter-Oct., Mon.-Sat., 10.00 to 18.00. Sun., 13.00 to 17.00. Winter, by arrangement. Fee.—*Tegfryn Art Gallery:* 10.00 to 18.00.—*Penrhos Nature Reserve:* Access to specialist sections is restricted. For permit and leaflet phone Holyhead 2522.—*South Stack Lighthouse:* May-mid July.

Route 12B. *Plas Newydd:* (N.T.). Easter Sun.-Oct., 12.30 to 17.30. Last adm. 17.00. Closed Sat. Fee.—*Wylfa Power Station:* May-Sept., 10.00 to 20.00. Oct.-April, 10.00 to 16.00.—*Beaumaris Castle:*

Standard.—*Beaumaris Gaol:* July-Sept., 11.00 to 18.00. Fee.—*Trwyn Du:* Fee for cars.

Route 13. *Fort Belan:* May-Sept., 10.00 to 18.00. Fee.—*Bardsey Island:* Boats in summer from Aberdaron, Abersoch, and Pwllheli, Fee.—*Bird and Field Observatory:* Visits usually of one week. Apply Mrs Helen Bond, 21 Gestridge Road, Kingsteignton, Newton Abbot, Devon.—*Plas Yn Rhiw:* By appointment (Tel: 075 888 219).—*Lloyd-George Museum:* May-Sept., Mon.-Fri., 10.00 to 17.00. Fee.—*Criccieth Castle:* Standard.

Route 14. *Chirk Castle:* Easter Sat. and Sun. Then Tues., Thurs., Sat., Sun. to end Sept. 14.00 to 17.00. Easter Mon., May, Spring, and Aug. B.H., 11.00 to 17.00. Fee. Smaller fee to drive through grounds.—*Plas Newydd:* May-Sept., Mon.-Sat., 10.00 to 19.30. Sun., 11.00 to 16.00. Fee.—*Canal Exhibition Centre:* Easter-Sept., 11.00 to 17.00. Fee. Boat trips, April-Sept., Sat. and Sun. afternoons. July and Aug., every afternoon.—*Valle Crucis Abbey:* Standard.

Route 15. *Voelas Hall:* Brachmael Stone shown on written application.—*Penmachno Stones:* Apply Gwynedd Archaeological Trust, Ffordd Deiniol, Bangor (Tel. 0248 52535).

Route 16. *Geological Museum:* Mon.-Fri., 09.00 to 17.00. Sat., 10.30 or 11.00 to 17.30. Sun. and B.H. (Easter-Oct. only) 11.30 to 17.30. Fee.—*Bala Lake Railway:* Easter-late Oct.—*Penmaenpool Nature Information Centre:* Spring B.H. Roughly June-Sept., 12.00 to 18.00.

Route 17. *Portmeirion:* April-Oct., 09.00 to 18.30. Fee.—*Porthmadog Marine Museum:* April-Sept., 10.00 to 18.00. Fee.—*Festiniog Railway:* Mid Feb.—mid Nov., but limited service outside holiday period. Return journey 2¼ hours.

Route 19. *Coed-y-Brenin Visitor Centre:* Easter-Oct., 10.00 to 17.00 (to 19.00 in July and Aug.).—*Trawsfynydd Power Station:* Approved parties by arrangement.

Route 20A. *R.N.L.I. Museum:* Easter. Spring B.H.-mid Sept., Mon.-Sat., 11.00 to 13.00. 14.00 to 16.00. 19.00 to 21.00. Sun., afternoon and evenings only. Winter, by arrangement. Donation.

Route 20B. *Old Llanfair Quarry:* Easter-Oct., 10.00 to 17.30. Fee.—*Harlech Castle:* Standard.—*Colleg Harlech:* Exhibitions, Mon.-Sat., 10.00 to 17.00.

Route 21. *Castle:* Mon.-Sat., 10.00 to 17.00 or 16.00. Fee.—*Clive House Museum:* Mon., 12.00 to 13.00. 14.00 to 18.00. Tues.-Sat., 10.00 to 13.00. 14.00 to 18.00. In winter, closes 16.30. (Coleham Beam Engines: Wed. and Fri., 14.00 to 17.00).—*Rowley's House Museum:* Mon.-Sat., 10.00 to 13.00. 14.00 to 17.00.—*Abbey Church:* Easter-Oct., 10.00 to 12.00. 14.00 to 16.00 Only opened if staff available.—*Haughmond Abbey:* Standard.—*Attingham:* (N.T.). Easter-Sept., Tues., Wed., Thurs., Sun., B.H. Mon., 14.00 to 17.30. Fee.—*Viroconium:* Standard.

Route 22A. *Powysland Museum:* Mon.-Fri., 11.00 to 13.00. 14.00 to 17.00. Sat., 14.00 to 16.30. Closed Wed. in winter.—*Powis Castle:* (N.T.). Easter Sat.-Mon., 14.00 to 18.00. May-mid Sept., daily except Mon. and Tues., 14.00 to 18.00. Also open Spring and Aug. B.H., 11.30 to 18.00. Gardens as above, and also in July and Aug. open from 11.30 on Wed. and Sun. Last adm. 17.30. Fee.—*Robert Owen Memorial Museum:* May-Sept., 14.30 to 16.30—*Textile Museum:* April or Easter,

whichever earlier, to Oct. Tues.-Sat., 14.00 to 16.30. Donation.—
Gregynog Hall: Hall by appointment. Visitors may walk but not drive around the grounds (parking at the hall).—*Llanidloes Museum:* Easter. Spring B.H.-Sept., Mon.-Sat., 11.00 to 13.00. 14.00 to 17.00.—*Hen Gapel Museum:* April-Sept., Mon.-Sat., 10.00 to 17.00.

Route 22B. *Welshpool and Llanfair Railway:* Easter-mid. Oct. Also limited spring and autum service.

Route 25A. *Centre for Alternative Technology:* 10.00 to 17.00 or dusk. Closed Christmas Day. Fee.—*Corris Railway Museum:* Mid July-Aug., Tues.-Fri., 13.00 to 17.30. Also open all B.H. except Christmas and New Year days. Donation.

Route 26. *Outward Bound Sailing Museum:* Summer, Mon.-Fri., 09.30 to 12.00. Donation.—*Talyllyn Railway:* Easter-early Oct.—*Talyllyn Railway Museum:* April-Oct., 10.00 to 17.00. Nov.-March, by arrangement. Fee.—*Abergynolwyn Museum:* Summer, Mon.-Sat., 11.00 to 18.00. Donation.—*Fairbourne Railway:* Easter-Sept. Restricted service in spring and autumn.

Route 27. *Cliff Railway:* Easter-Oct., 10.00 to 19.00. Every 10 min.—*Aberystwyth Yesterday:* Midsummer, Mon.-Sat., 11.00 to 20.00. Victorian shop open afternoons only. Fee.—*Ceredigion Museum:* Mon.-Sat., 14.00 to 18.00. Closed Good Friday, Christmas and Boxing days. Donation.—*University College: New Campus* conducted tours, July-Sept., Mon.-Fri., at 14.15. Fee.—*Arts Centre:* Mon.-Sat., 10.00 to 17.00. Closed on days required for university purposes.—*National Library, Readers' Room:* Open to holders of readers' tickets, obtainable on written application. Mon.-Sat., 09.30 to 18.00 (17.00 on Sat.).—*National Library, Gregynog Gallery and Central Hall Exhibitions:* Mon.-Sat., 09.30 to 18.00 (17.00 on Sat.).—*Vale of Rheidol Railway:* Easter-early Oct.

Route 28A. *Rheidol Power Station:* Easter-Sept. Guided tours at intervals from 11.00 to 16.30. Fee.—*Llywernog Mine:* Easter-Oct., 10.00 to 17.30 (to 16.30 in Sept. and Oct.). Winter, by arrangement. Fee.

Route 28B. *Nanteos:* June-Sept., 13.00 to 17.30. Fee.

Route 29. *Llandrindod Wells Museum:* Mon.-Fri., 10.00 to 12.30. 14.00 to 17.00.—*Talley Abbey:* Standard.—*Carreg Cennen Castle:* Standard.

Route 30A. *Hergest Court Gardens:* Easter. May-Aug., 11.00 to 19.00. Also open first half of Oct. (for autumn colours). Fee.—*Burton Court:* Spring B.H. to mid Sept. Wed., Thurs., Sat., Sun., 14.30 to 18.00. Fee.

Route 30B. *Croft Castle:* (N.T.). First Wed. in April or Easter Sat., whichever earlier, to Sept. Wed., Thurs., Sat., Sun., B.H. Mon. In Oct., Sat. and Sun. 14.15 to 18.00. Fee. In winter, by written arrangement.

Route 31. *Condover Hall:* Summer, Mon.-Fri., 10.00 to 16.00.—*Langley Chapel:* Fri., Sat., Sun., 14.00 to 19.00 (or 16.00 out of season).—*Acton Scott Farm Museum:* April-Sept. or later. Mon.-Sat., 13.00 to 17.00. Sun. and B.H., 10.00 to 18.00. Last adm. 30 min. before closing time. Picnic area (free) open from 12.00. Fee.—*Stokesay Castle:* 10.00 to 18.00 (16.30 in winter). Closed Tues. Last adm. 30 min. before closing time. Fee.—*Ludlow Museum:* Easter-Sept., Mon.-Sat., 10.30 to 12.30. 14.00 to 17.00. Sun. (July and Aug. only), 10.30 to 13.00. 14.00 to 18.00. Oct.-mid Dec., Mon.-Fri., 14.00 to 17.00. Sat., 10.30 to 12.30.

14.00 to 17.00. Fee.—*Ludlow Castle:* April-Sept., 10.30 to 19.30. Oct.-March, Mon.-Sat., 10.30 to 16.30. Fee.—*Mortimer Forest Museum:* Mon.-Fri., 09.00 to 16.00.—*Berrington Hall:* (N.T.). First Wed. in April, or Easter Sat. if earlier, to Sept. Wed., Sat., B.H. Mon., 14.00 to 18.00 or sunset if earlier. Fee.—*Eye Manor:* Easter-June. Wed., Thurs., Sat., Sun. July-Sept. daily. Also Easter and Spring B.H. 14.30 to 17.30. Fee.—*Leominster Museum:* April-Sept., Mon.-Sat., 10.00 to 13.00. 14.00 to 17.00. Sun., 14.00 to 17.00. Oct.-April, Fri. and Sat. at above times.—*Dinmore Manor:* 10.00 to 18.00. Closed Christmas and Boxing days. Fee.

Route 32A. *Trefecca House:* Mon.-Fri., 11.00 to 17.00—*Tretower Court and Castle:* Standard.

Route 33A. *Brecknock Museum:* Mon.-Sat., 10.00 to 17.00.—*South Wales Borderers Museum:* April-Sept., daily. Oct.-March, Mon.-Fri. 09.00 to 12.30. 14.00 to 17.00.—*Christ College:* On application.—*Salmon Hatchery:* Mon.-Fri., 10.00 to 12.00. 14.00 to 16.00.

Route 33B. *Mountain Centre:* 09.30 to dusk. Closed Christmas.—*Garwnant Forest Centre:* Easter-Sept., Mon.-Fri., 09.00 to 16.00. Also, in July and Aug., Wed. and Thurs., 18.00 to 20.00. B.H., 12.00 to 18.00. Sat. and Sun. times are 13.00 to 18.00 (July, Aug.), 14.00 to 16.00 (April and Sept.), 14.00 to 17.00 (May), 14.00 to 18.00 (June).

Route 35A. *Brecon Beacons National Park Exhibition:* Easter-Sept., Mon.-Sat.—*Abergavenny Museum:* March-Oct., Mon.-Sat., 11.00 to 13.00. 14.00 to 17.00. Sun., 14.30 to 17.00. Nov.-Feb., Tues., Thurs., Fri., Sat., 11.00 to 13.00. 14.00 to 16.00. Fee.

Route 35B. *White Castle:* Standard.—*Rural Crafts Museum:* Summer, Sun. and B.H. 15.00 to 18.00. Fee.

Route 35C. *Raglan Castle:* Standard.

Route 35D. *Usk Castle:* On written application.—*Caerleon Amphitheatre:* Standard.—*Caerleon Legionary Museum:* Standard.

Route 36. *Old House:* April-Sept., Mon.-Sat., 10.00 to 13.00. 14.00 to 17.30. Sun., 14.00 to 17.00. Oct.-March, Mon.-Fri., 10.00 to 13.00. 14.00 to 17.30. Sat., 10.00 to 13.00. Fee.—*City Museum and Art Gallery:* Mon.-Fri., 10.00 to 18.00 (17.00 on Thurs.). Sat., 10.00 to 17.00 (16.00 in Oct.-March).—*Chained Library:* Easter-Sept., Mon.-Sat., 10.30 to 12.30. 14.00 to 16.00. Oct.-Easter, by prior application. Fee.—*Waterworks Museum:* April-Sept., first Sun. in each month. 11.00 to 17.00. Fee.—*Railway Centre:* Enquire at Tourist Information for dates of static displays and steam open days. Fee.—*Coningsby Hospital:* Easter-Sept., daily except Mon. and Fri., 14.00 to 17.00. Fee.—*Churchill Gardens Museum:* 14.00 to 17.00. Fee.—*Regimental Museum:* Mon.-Fri., 09.00 to 12.30. 14.00 to 17.00.

Route 37A. *Moccas Court:* April-Sept., Thurs., 14.00 to 18.00. Fee.—*Dan-yr-Ogof:* Easter-Oct., 10.00 to c. 18.00. Fee.

Route 37B. *Kentchurch Court:* May-Sept., by appointment. Fee.—*Llanfihangel Court:* Easter, and certain Suns. in June-Aug. 14.30 to 18.00. Fee.—*Cyfarthfa Castle (museum):* April-Oct., 10.00 to 13.00. 14.00 to 18.30 (17.00 in April and Oct.). Fee on Sun. and B.H.—*Penseynor Wildlife Park:* 10.00 to dusk. Fee.—*Neath Abbey:* Standard.

Route 38. *Goodrich Castle:* Standard.—*Monmouth Local History Centre:* Mon.-Fri., 09.00 to 17.30. Sat., 09.00 to 12.30. Fee.—*Nelson Collection:* March-Oct., Mon.-Sat. Times are: 10.30 to 13.00. 14.15 to

17.15 (April-June. Sept. and Oct.). 10.00 to 18.00 (July and Aug.). Also Sun. at Easter, Whitsun, and in July and Aug., 14.30 to 17.30. Fee.—*Wolves Newton Museum:* Mon.-Sat., 09.30 to 18.00. Fee.—*Tintern Abbey:* Standard.—*Chepstow Castle:* Standard.—*Chepstow Museum:* Summer, 14.00 to 17.00. Fee.

Route 39. *Caldicot Castle:* March-Oct., Mon.-Fri., 13.30 to 17.00. Sat., Sun., B.H., 14.30 to 19.00. Fee.—*Penhow Castle:* Good Friday-Oct., Wed.-Sun. and B.H., 10.00 to 18.00. Fee.—*Newport Museum:* Mon.-Sat., 10.00 to 17.30. Closed B.H.—*Dyffryn House Gardens:* Summer afternoons. Fee.—*Turner House Gallery:* Tues.-Sat. and B.H. Mon., 11.00 to 12.45. 14.00 to 17.00. Sun., 14.00 to 17.00. Closed Christmas Eve; Christmas, Boxing, and New Year's days; Good Friday.—*Merthyr Mawr House (Stones):* Wed. afternoons in summer. Fee.—*Bridgend Castle:* Standard.—*Coity Castle:* Standard.—*Margam Park:* May-Sept., Tues.-Sun. and B.H., 10.30 to 20.00. Last entry 18.30. Fee.—*Margam Abbey Museum:* Wed., Sat., Sun., B.H., 14.00 to 17.00 (16.00 in Nov.-Feb.). Fee.—*Afan Argoed (Countryside Centre and Miners Museum):* Easter-Sept., 10.30 to 18.00. Oct.-Easter, Sat. and Sun., 12.00 to 17.00.—*Llanelli Public Library Exhibition Gallery:* Mon.-Sat., 09.30 to 18.00. Closed B.H.—*Parc Howard:* Summer, Mon.-Sat., 10.00 to 20.00. Winter, Mon.-Sat., 10.00 to 16.30.—*Kidwelly Castle:* Standard.

Route 40. *Castle:* Conducted tours of interior: March, April, and Oct.; Mon.-Sat., tours at half-hourly intervals between 10.00 to 12.30 and 13.30 to 16.00. Sun., tours at 10.00, 12.00, 14.00, 15.00, 16.00. May-Sept; Mon.-Sat., tours at 20 min. intervals between 10.00 to 12.40 and 13.40 to 18.20. Sun., tours at half-hourly intervals between 10.00 to 12.30 and 14.00 to 18.00. Nov.-Feb.; Mon.-Sat., tours at 11.00, 12.00, 14.00, 15.00. Sun., tours at 11.00, 12.00, 15.00. The Castle Green, Roman Wall, and Keep are open daily from 10.00 to 19.00 (to 17.00 Oct.-April). Castle is closed on Christmas and New Year B.H. Fee.—*Museum of the Welch Regiment:* 10.00 to 19.00 (to 17.00 Oct.-April). Fee.—*Chapter Workshops and Centre for the Arts:* Mon.-Sat., 10.00 to 22.00. Gallery open Mon.-Fri., 12.00 to 22.00. Sat., 14.00 to 20.00. All closed for 10 days over Christmas.—*Oriel:* Mon.-Fri., 09.30 to 18.30. Sat., 09.30 to 17.30.—*Sherman Theatre Gallery:* Mon.-Sat., 10.00 to 22.00. Closed Aug.—*National Museum of Wales* and *Industrial and Maritime Museum:* Mon.-Sat., 10.00 to 18.00 (17.00 Oct.-March). Sun., 14.30 to 17.00. Also open to 18.00 on B.H. Mon. and following Tues. Closed Christmas Eve, Christmas Day, Boxing Day, New Year's Day, Good Griday.—*Welsh Folk Museum:* Mon.-Sat., 10.00 to 18.00 (17.00 Oct.-March). Sun., 14.30 to 18.00 (17.00 Oct.-March). Closed Christmas Eve, Christmas Day, Boxing Day, New Year's Day. Fee.

Route 41A. *Castell Coch:* Standard.

Route 41D. *Caerphilly Castle:* Standard.

Route 41E. *Cwmcarn Forest Drive:* Easter-Aug., 11.00 to 20.00. Sept. and Oct., 11.00 to 18.00. Fee.—*Abertillery Museum:* Tues. and Thurs., 14.00 to 16.30. Sat., 09.30 to 13.00. 14.00 to 16.30.

Route 42A. *Glyn Vivian Art Gallery:* Mon.-Sat., 10.30 to 17.30. Closed Christmas, Boxing, and New Year's days.—*Royal Institution Museum:* Mon-Sat., 10.00 to 17.00. Fee.—*Maritime and Industrial Museum:* Mon.-Sat., 10.30 to 17.30. Closed Christmas, Boxing and

New Year's days.—*Brangwyn Hall:* Mon.-Fri., 10.00 to 12.30. 14.30 to 16.30. Closed B.H.—*University College Exhibition Gallery:* In term (Oct.-June). Mon.-Fri., 09.00 to 17.00. Sat., 09.00 to 12.00. Closed B.H.—*University College Wellcome Collection:* By arrangement during term (Oct.-June). Apply Assistant Registrar, Information Services.

Route 42B. *Oystermouth Castle:* Mon.-Fri., 11.00 to 15.30. Fee.—*Weobley Castle:* Standard.

Route 43. *Carmathen County Museum:* Mon.-Fri., 10.00 to 16.30.

Route 44A. *Bryn-Eithyn Museum:* 10.00 to 22.00. Fee.

Route 44B. *Yr Oriel,* Tregaron: Mon.-Sat., 09.30 to 13.00. 14.00 to 18.00.—*Cors Tregaron:* Permit holders only. Apply Nature Conservancy, Plas Gogerddan, Aberystwyth. Tel: 097 087 551.—*Strata Florida Abbey:* Standard.

Route 45. *Museum of the Woollen Industry:* April to Oct., Mon.-Sat., 10.00 to 17.00.—*St David's Chapter Library:* Thurs., 14.30 to 16.30. Fee.—*Bishop's Palace:* Standard.

Route 46. *Blackpool Mill:* Easter-Sept., 11.00 to 18.00. Fee.—*Picton Castle:* No adm. to castle. Gardens: Easter-Sept., daily except Mon. and Fri., 11.00 to 13.00. 14.00 to 18.00. Graham Sutherland Gallery: April-Sept., daily except Mon. and Fri., 11.00 to 13.00. 14.00 to 18.00. Oct.-March., Sat. and Sun., 14.00 to 17.00. Other times by appointment. Parking fee.—*Haverfordwest Museum and Art Gallery:* Mon.-Sat., 10.00 to 18.00 (summer) or 11.00 to 16.00 (winter). Closed Good Friday, and Christmas, Boxing, and New Year's days.—*Haverfordwest Regional Library:* Mon.-Sat., 10.00 to 17.00.—*Nant-y-Coy Mill:* June-Aug., 10.00 to 17.00. Fee.—*Triffleton Waterfowl Collection:* 10.30 to 18.30 or dusk. Daily July-Sept.; closed Mon. in other months. Fee.

Route 47A. *Avondale Glass:* Mon.-Fri., 07.30 to 15.00 (13.00 on Wed.).—*Carew Castle:* April-Sept., Mon.-Sat., 10.00 to 18.00. Sun. in Aug., 14.30 to 17.30. Oct.-March, Wed. and Sat., 10.00 to 16.00. Fee.—*French Mill:* April-Sept., Mon.-Sat., 10.00 to 18.00. Sun., 14.00 to 18.00. Fee.—*Upton Castle Grounds:* Feb.-Oct., Tues., Wed., Thurs., Fri., and B.H., 10.00 to 16.30.—*Pembroke Castle:* Easter-Sept., Mon.-Fri., 10.00 to 19.00. Sat., 10.00 to 18.00. Sun., 11.00 to 19.00. Oct.-Easter., 10.30 to 16.00 or 17.00. Fee.—*Pembrokeshire Motor Museum:* Easter-Sept., Sun.-Fri., 10.00 to 18.00. Fee.—*Skomer:* Boats from St Martin's Haven or Dale. Easter, and Whitsun-c. Sept. From 10.30 depending on demand. Not Mon. unless B.H. Fees for boat and for landing. Visiting also by National Park guided walk.—*Skokholm:* Only by National Park guided walk.—*Grassholm:* Boats from Dale or Solva by arrangement.

Addresses for visits to Skomer, Skokholm, and Grassholm: West Wales Naturalists' Trust, 20A High Street, Haverfordwest, Dyfed. Dale Sailing Co., Dale, Haverfordwest, Dyfed. Pembrokeshire Coast National Park (Guided Walks Bookings), Information Centre, Kilgetty, Dyfed.

Route 47B. *Tudor Merchant's House:* (N.T.). Easter-Sept., Mon.-Fri., 10.00 to 13.00. 14.30 to 18.00. Sun., 14.00 to 18.00. Fee.—*Tenby Museum:* April-Sept., 10.00 to 18.00. Oct.-March, Mon.-Sat., 10.00 to 13.00. 14.00 to 16.00. Fee.—*Caldy Island:* Several boats from Tenby during summer, Mon.-Fri. First dep. 09.45 and last return 18.00, but these times dependent on tide and demand. Also some Sat. afternoons in July and Aug. Queues must be expected.—*Manorbier Castle:* Easter, and May-Sept., 11.00 to 18.00. Fee.—*Manor House Park:* Easter-Oct., 10.00 to 18.00. Fee.—*Lamphey Bishop's Palace:* Standard.

Route 49. *Cilgerran Castle:* Standard.—*West Wales Farm Park:* Mid May-Sept., 10.00 to 18.00. Fee.

The Skerries
Amlwch
Anglesey
Holyhead Valley
Beaumaris
Menai Br
Rhosneigr
Newborough
Caernarfon
Clynnog Fawr
Nefyn
Porthmadog
Aberdaron
Pwllheli
Abersoch
Bardsey I.
Llanenddwyn
Barmouth

12B
12B
12A
11
10
9B
11
13
13

Llandudno 3
Conwy
Colwyn Bay
Prestatyn
Rhyl
St. Asaph
Holywell
Flint
Chester 1
2A
2B
2C
Bangor
Bodnant
Bwlch y
Bychau
Denbigh
Mold
Capel
Curig
Llanrwst
Betws-y-Coed
Pentrefoelas
Ruthin
Bwlchgwyn
Wrexham
Snowdon
Beddgelert
Maerdy
Llangollen
Chirk
Whitchurch
Ffestiniog
Bala
Corwen
14
Oswestry
23
Whittington
Llynclys
Nesscliff
Shrewsbury
Penrhyndeudraeth
Bronaber
Harlech
Bwlch-y-
Groes
Penybontfawr
24B
24C
24A
Llanwddyn
Buttington
Welshpool
Bayston
Hill
Church
Stretton
Dinas Mawddwy
Llwyngwril
Cemmaes
Rd.
Neuadd
Talerddig
Chirbury
29
31
Tywyn
Aberdovey
Talybont
Machynlleth
Staylittle
Caersws
Newtown
Lydham
Ludlow
31
Aberystwyth
Ponterwyd
Llanidloes
Llangurig
Clun
Knighton
29
Mortimer's
Cross
Llanfarian
Devil's
Bridge
Pontrhydfendigaid
Rhayader
Cross
Gates
30
Walton
30B
Leominster
31
Aberaeron
Tregaron
Beulah
Kington
30A
Willersley
Synod Inn
Sarnau
Lampeter
Llanwrtyd
Wells
Builth Wells
32A
Hay-on-Wye
Hereford
36
Cardigan
Newport
Crymych
Newcastle
Emlyn
Llandysul
Pumpsaint
Llandovery
Erwood
Bronllys
Madley
Ross-
on-Wye
Fishguard
Pont-ar-Sais
Llanwrda
Brecon
37A
Tretower
37B
St.
David's
Haverfordwest
Milford
Haven
Narberth
St. Clears
Carmarthen
Llandeilo
Sennybridge
Craig-y-nos
Brynmawr
Abergavenny
35
Monmouth
Pembroke
Tenby
Cross
Hands
Llanelli
Merthyr Tydfil
Ebbw
Vale
Usk
38
Swansea
Gower
Neath
Hirwaun
Aberdare
Pontypool
Chepstow
39
Port
Talbot
Tonypandy
Pontypridd
Bridgend
Caerphilly
Newport
Porthcawl
Cowbridge
Cardiff
Southerndown
Barry
Llantwit
Major

River Severn

Cardigan
Bay

Bristol Channel

44A
49
45
46
46
47
47A
48
46
49
47A
47B
49
43
42A
42B
41A
41B
41C
41D
41E
40
39
39
39
38
35C
35D
35E
35B
37B
33B
32
32B
33A
34
29
34
33
34
32A
37A
29
44B
44
45
28
28A
28B
44B
30
29
29
31
22A
22A
22B
25A
25B
25B
18B
26
20A
19
18A
20B
16
15
15
16
16
14
24
24A
23
22
21
17
16
15
16
15
13
9B
8
7A
7B
6
6
5
2B
2B
4
5

1 CHESTER AND ENVIRONS

CHESTER (district of Chester, 117,000 inhab.), the county town of the English county of Cheshire, is situated on the right bank of the Dee, 7 m. above its estuary. With its complete circuit of well-preserved Roman and later walls, its famous and picturesque 'rows', its timber houses, and fine cathedral, the city retains much of its medieval appearance. Restoration and conservation by the Victorians, continued by later generations, received new impetus in 1975 when Chester was nominated as one of the Council of Europe's pilot projects for European Architectural Heritage Year. The Chester Heritage and British Heritage exhibitions respectively provide admirable background to the city's buildings and general history.

Tourist Information. Town Hall. Guided tours.†
Parking. Rear of Town Hall. Little Roodee (S. of castle). Below Watergate. Shopping Precinct.
Caravan Site. Racecourse.
Railway Station. General, City Road (¾ m. N.E. of centre).
Main Post Office. 2 St John Street.
Early Closing. Wednesday (some shops, and market).
Bus Services. *Chester City Transport* services from Town Hall Square, Eastgate Street, Foregate Street, and Railway Station. *Crosville* local services from Town Hall Square. *Long Distance* services from Delamere Street.
Motor Launches. In summer, river excursions from The Groves (Chester 25394).
Horse-drawn Boat. In summer, canal excursions (Chester 21519).
Theatre. Gateway, Hamilton Place.
History. Chester, the Roman Deva or Castra Devana, the camp on the Dee, was founded c. A.D. 48, later becoming, and for centuries remaining, the headquarters of the famous 20th Legion. It was also known as Castra Legionum, from which the Welsh name Caerleon and the Anglo-Saxon Legaceaster, shortened to Ceaster, were derived. After the departure of the Romans (c. 380) the town which had grown up around the camp was successively in the hands of the British, the Saxons, and the Danes, being largely destroyed c. 614. In 907 the town was rebuilt and the Roman walls extended S. and W. by Ethelfleda ('Lady of the Mercians', the doughty daughter of Alfred the Great and wife of Ethelred, Earl of Mercia), largely as a defence against the Norsemen, now settling in Wirral. Soon after this the relics of St Werburgh (see below under Cathedral) were brought here. In 973 Edgar, crowned King of England, came to Chester to receive the homage of eight subject kings who, the story goes, demonstrated their allegiance by rowing him on the Dee. Chester held out longer than any other English city against William the Conqueror, but in 1070 was granted, with surrounding lands, to his nephew Hugh Lupus (Hugo d'Avranches), created Earl of Chester and ruling a virtually independent territory. The earldom reverted to the Crown in 1237, and in 1254 Henry III granted it to his son, since when (apart from 1264-65 when it was held by Simon de Montfort) the earldom has always been one of the titles of the eldest son of the sovereign. The Benedictine abbey was founded in 1093, one result being centuries of friction between the abbey and the citizens, largely on trade matters. Nevertheless, due largely to its port, the town's prosperity grew throughout the Middle Ages, until, as the river began to silt up, trade gradually shifted to Liverpool. During the Civil War Chester held out stoutly for Charles I, but after his defeat at Rowton Moor (Sept. 1645), fought about 3 m. S.E., it was starved into submission on 3 Feb. 1646. William Lawes, the composer, was killed during the siege. In Victorian times prosperity returned as communications improved with the opening of Grosvenor Bridge and the spread of the railways. In 1888 Chester became a County Borough, a status which continued until 1974 when the new district of Chester was formed, the principal of the eight districts making up the county of Cheshire.

Chester had until 1962 the only original Assay Office in England, outside London, for the hallmarking of gold and silver.

Mystery Plays. From the 14 to the 17 C Chester was famed for its Mystery Plays.

today sometimes revived on television and elsewhere. These were Bible stories turned into plays, some by the Benedictine monks, and acted by members of the guilds. The plays were performed, usually at Whitsun, at the Abbey Gateway, then repeated around the city, with carts serving as stages.

Within the Walls

The city centre is the **Cross**, at the junction of Northgate, Bridge, Eastgate, and Watergate streets. The Cross was destroyed by Parliament in 1646; reconstructed, but including some original fragments, it was restored to its original position in 1975 as an Architectural Heritage Year project. *St Peter's Church*, at the Cross, stands on the S. part of the Roman Praetorium (headquarters); most of the building is restoration, but the lower part of the tower is work of the 14C. The main feature of central Chester are the unique and attractive ***Rows**; arcades, and galleries forming continuous passages along the first floors of the houses and shops. Why this curious arrangement developed, probably in the late 13C, is uncertain, but the most accepted explanation is that the solid Roman ruins forced the later inhabitants to build both above and in front of this obstacle. Some of the shops preserve medieval crypts.

The description below is in four sections; N., S., W., and E. from the Cross.

NORTH FROM THE CROSS. In Northgate Street (Via Decumana) important remains of the Roman Praetorium survive in the basement of No 23 (shown on request). Beyond, off the same side, a window in Hamilton Place allows a view of the Roman strongroom. Just beyond, still on the W. of Northgate Street, are the Forum Precinct, *Tourist Information*, and the **Town Hall** (1869), where visitors may see the Assembly Room and Council Chamber; it was here in 1890 that there was given the earliest recorded public showing of a moving-picture film. Opposite the town hall, on the site of the abbot's lodging, a building (Arthur Blomfield, 1876), formerly the King's School and now occupied by a bank, partly masks the W. front of the cathedral. Near here, in Music Hall Passage off the W. of St Werburgh's Street, are the remains of a chapel, originally built c. 1280 for the parish of St Oswald and serving later as a wool hall, and after 1773 as the Theatre Royal.

Northgate Street continues N., passing (E.) the *Abbey Gateway* (14-15 C), leading into the Abbey Square with pleasant Georgian houses (see below at the end of the description of the cathedral). Beyond, off the same side of Northgate Street, there survives an arch of *Little Abbey Gate*, while, across the road, stands the *Pied Bull Hotel*, claiming to be the oldest inn in Chester; the exterior is late 18C, but the interior has panelling, a fireplace, and a staircase, all 16-17C. Just beyond stood the *Blue Bell Inn* (now a small shop), a 15C timber, wattle-and-daub building.

The ***Cathedral**, as an ancient foundation, as an abbey church until the Reformation, and as a cathedral since 1541, is a building of outstanding interest. Built of red sandstone, it enjoys a variety of architectural styles ranging from Norman to late Perpendicular.

History. The site of the cathedral was formerly occupied by a college of secular canons, dedicated to St Werburgh (d.c. 700), a Mercian princess active in founding religious houses; her relics were brought here in the early 10C. In 1092 Hugh Lupus, assisted by St Anselm, who had come over from his own abbey of Bec in

Normandy, transformed the place into an abbey. The chief remains of this Norman abbey church are to be found on the N. side. The rest of the cathedral, beginning with the Lady Chapel (1250-75), reflects all periods up to the 19C. The choir, the work of Edward I's military engineer, Richard of Chester, dates from the turn of the 13 and 14C; the arcades of the S. transept and the S. arcade of the nave from the mid 14C; the rest of the nave, the clerestory of the S. transept, and the top stages of the tower, from the end of the 15C. The S.W. porch, with its upper chamber, is Tudor. The S. front of the S. transept is the work (1819-20) of the Chester architect, Thomas Harrison. Between 1868-76 Sir Gilbert Scott carried out a major restoration affecting much of both the exterior and interior; his work includes the turrets on the central tower and W. front, the pinnacles at the E. end of the Lady Chapel, and the flying buttresses on the S. side.

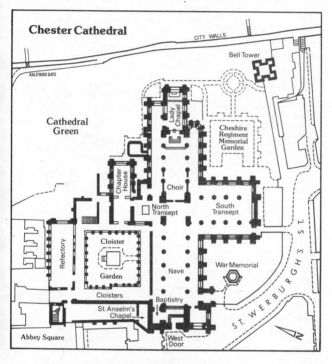

At the Reformation St Werburgh's, unlike most abbeys, escaped lapsing into ruin, instead in 1541 being declared the cathedral of the new diocese of Chester, with the last abbot becoming the first dean. The fact that the title 'Bishop of Chester' frequently occurs at an earlier date is because the Mercian see of Lichfield was in the 11C for a few years transferred to Chester (see St John's Church, p. 107).

In 1974 the cathedral was given a detached Bell-Tower in the S.E. corner of the precinct; it is built of concrete, faced with slate.

Entrance is normally either into the large S. transept, or from Abbey Square and through the cloister. The description below starts at the W. end of the nave.

NAVE. From the W. end, raised a few steps, the vista is one of simplicity and beauty, enhanced by the warm red of the stone. The glass in the W. window (1961) is by W. T. Carter Shapland. At the W. end of

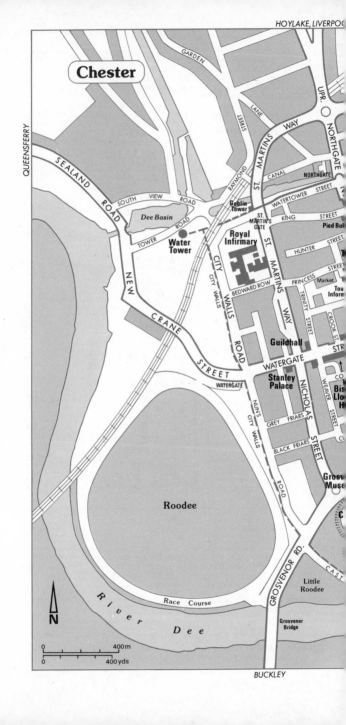

Chester

HOYLAKE, LIVERPOOL

QUEENSFERRY

GARDEN LANE

UPR.

NORTHGATE

ST. MARTINS WAY

CANAL

NORTHGATE

SEALAND ROAD

SOUTH VIEW ROAD

RAYMOND STREET

WATERTOWER STREET

Dee Basin

TOWER ROAD

Goblin Tower

ST. MARTIN'S GATE

KING STREET

Pied Bul

Water Tower

CITY WALLS ROAD

Royal Infirmary

ST. MARTINS WAY

HUNTER STREET

STREET

NEW

PRINCESS

Market

Tou Inform

BEDWARD ROW

TRINITY STREET

CROOK ST.

CRANE STREET

Guildhall

STR

WATERGATE

WATERGATE

Stanley Palace

NICHOLAS STREET

WEAVER STREET

CO

Bis Llo H

NUNS' CITY WALLS

GREY FRIARS

BLACK FRIARS

ROAD

Gros Muse

CAST

Roodee

Little Roodee

GROSVENOR RD.

Race Course

Grosvenor Bridge

N

River Dee

BUCKLEY

0 — 400m
0 — 400yds

General Station

Leisure Centre

ST. ANNE STREET

STATION ST.

BROOK ST.

HOOLE WAY

BROOK STREET

EGERTON STREET

ROAD

ST. OSWALD'S WAY

STREET

King Charles's Tower

Bishop's House

KALEYARD GATE

ABBEY STREET

KALE YARD

Shropshire Union Canal

CITY ROAD

ST. OSWALD'S WAY

FRODSHAM STREET

QUEEN STREET

YORK ST.

THE BARS

Cathedral

CITY WALLS

FOREGATE STREET

GROSVENOR PK. RD.

BATH ST.

DEE LANE

ST. WERBURGH'S ST.

EASTGATE ST.

St. Peter's

THE CROSS

ROWS

EASTGATE ST.

ST. JOHN'S ST.

G.P.O.

LOVE ST.

UNION ST.

Grosvenor Park

BRIDGE STREET

Shopping Precinct

NEWGATE ST.

Library

British Heritage

VICARS LA.

ROAD

St. Michael's

WOLFE GATE

NEWGATE

LT. ST. JOHN'S ST.

Roman Amphitheatre

St. John's

THE GROVES

GROVES

River Dee

PEPPER STREET

Heritage Centre

ALBION ST.

Roman Gar.

SOUTER'S LANE

Queen's Park Bridge

Old King's Head

LOWER BRIDGE STREET

DUKE STREET

THE GROVES

LOWER PARK ROAD

ROAD

ST. MARY'S HILL

Bear & Billet

Wishing Steps

ST. MARY'S

BRIDGEGATE

Recorder's Steps

nty Jr

DRIVE

Dee Bridge

Site of Dee Mills

VICTORIA CRES.

ST. JOHN CRES.

Edgar's Field

HANDBRIDGE

PARK ROAD

QUEEN'S ROAD

LANE

St Mary's

MEADOW

the S. aisle, in the base of an unfinished tower of c. 1508, is the Consistory Court, with furniture of 1636. The wall of the N. aisle, basically Norman, is covered by mosaics of scriptural scenes (J. R. Clayton, 1886). At the aisle's W. end (c. 1140) is the Baptistery, with a Venetian font of 1885. From both ends of this aisle, doors (the E. one Norman of c. 1100) lead into the cloisters (see below).—The small NORTH TRANSEPT was part of the original Norman church and is thus the oldest part of the cathedral. In the centre is a monument (Blomfield, 1863) to Bishop Pearson (1673-83), author of the 'Exposition of the Creed', and a mural tablet commemorates Randolph Caldecott, the artist (1846-86), a native of Chester. A Norman archway on the E. side opens into the Sacristy, in Transitional style, which replaces a Norman apse. Above is a small row of triforium arches of the earliest period.— The SOUTH TRANSEPT is remarkable for its huge size; including two aisles it is as large as the choir and nearly as large as the nave. The reason is that the monks of the 14C wished to extend their church, but could not touch the N. transept without destroying their domestic buildings. From the early 16C this S. transept was used as the parish church of St Oswald. There are four chapels along the E. wall, the one at the S.E. end being that of SS Nicholas and Leonard; here colours of the Cheshire Regiment once covered Wolfe's coffin at Quebec. The altars in this chapel, and in the adjoining Chapel of St George (that of the Cheshire Regiment), were both designed by Giles Scott (1917, 1921). The Royal Air Force Memorial, with a wooden propeller, is on the W. wall of the transept, and in a case against the N.W. pier are the two flags flown by H.M.S. Chester at Jutland (1916), the ship in which Boy Cornwell won his Victoria Cross. On the E. side of the pier is the attractive monument to Thomas Greene (d. 1602), Mayor of Chester, and his two wives.— Above the entrance to the CHOIR is a large Rood (1913), designed by Giles Scott. The choir was built in the 13 and 14C, principally by Richard of Chester; above is a beautiful triforium. The *Stalls* (c. 1380), with their spired canopies and misericords, are perhaps the chief treasure of the cathedral; particularly noteworthy are the carvings on the misericords, and the Tree of Jesse which decorates the end of the Dean's Stall. The Bishop's Throne (1876) was designed by Gilbert Scott. The S. choir aisle was lengthened to the E. about 1500, but the apsidal termination, the quaint conical roof of which is a feature of the cathedral exterior as seen from the city wall, was the work of Gilbert Scott, modelled, from the evidence of old masonry, on a similar 14C roof. Buried in this aisle is Ranulf Higden, a monk here at the beginning of the 14C. Author of many books describing his life and times, he is best known for his 'Polychronicon', a history of the world from the Creation to 1352; a facsimile of a page is displayed in the chapter house off the cloisters. In the N. choir aisle can be seen the base of a Norman column, and, alongside, a capital which has been turned over and used as a foundation for the later building. A band of dark marble in the pavement marks the line of the Norman apse. This choir aisle still retains its prolongation of c. 1500, now St Werburgh's Chapel.—The LADY CHAPEL (c. 1275-80), reached from the N. choir aisle, contains the shrine of St Werburgh (c. 1330), which until the Reformation contained her relics. Noteworthy in this chapel are the three ceiling *Bosses* (recoloured 1960), particularly the delightful Madonna and Child which forms the central boss.

The CLOISTERS AND DOMESTIC BUILDINGS are reached through either of two doors from the nave N. aisle. The cloisters were rebuilt c. 1526 and restored by Giles Scott in 1911-13; thus they are considerably more recent than the domestic rooms which open off them. The windows on to the garden date from 1921-27 (A. K. Nicholson and F. C. Eden); they illustrate the calendar of the Church of England Prayer Book. Off the E. walk, a Vestibule leads into the *Chapter House*. Both are good 13C work, the graceful way in which the mouldings in the vestibule run up into the vaulting without capitals being a particularly pleasing feature. The chapter house now contains cathedral books, and a notable 13C cupboard. Also off the E. walk are a slype, a passage probably leading to the infirmary, and, lit by a 13C quatrefoil window, the remains of the stair to the dormitory which would have run the length of the E. upper floor; in this corner too is a vaulted room (no adm.), probably a common room for the monks and now used for choir practice. The S. walk wall is part Norman. The double arcade on the garden side in this walk, and in part of the W. walk, marks the position of compartments to which the monks retired for study. From the W. walk doors lead to the cellar (12C), or abbey storeroom, which runs the length of this walk. Part (no adm.) is now used as the cathedral workshop, and part serves as the bookstall; above was the guest house. Behind the N. walk stretches the large *Refectory* (13C, but with 15C windows), still used for the serving of refreshments. Here the lector's pulpit, with a staircase in the wall, is one of the only two surviving in England, the other being at Beaulieu.—In the centre of the garden was the water tank, supplied by pipe from Christleton, 2 m. south-east.

From the cloister N.W. corner there is an exit into **Abbey Square**. Here *Abbey Gateway* (W.) dates from the 14C, but is flanked by 19C houses, that on the S. side being by Arthur Blomfield. At the S.E. of the square are two small houses, built in 1626 for lay clerks. The remaining buildings in the square date from c. 1760. *St Anselm's Chapel* (adm. on request), reached from Abbey Square, dates from the 12C and was the chapel of the abbot's lodging; the chapel's most notable feature is the fine plaster ceiling from the time of Charles I.

SOUTH FROM THE CROSS. Bridge Street has 'rows' on both sides. At No 12 there is a vaulted crypt, and at No 39 the remains of a Roman bath, consisting of a hypocaust and tank (adm. to both on request). On the W. side, near the corner of Commonhall Street, the *Dutch Houses* (restored 1974) date mainly from the 17C but have 13 or 14C fragments. In Whitefriars (W.) No. 1 is an attractive house with a gable of 1658. Opposite Whitefriars the former St Michael's Church (mainly 19C., but mentioned in 1172 and with early wood vaulting) now serves as the **Chester Heritage Centre†**, an exhibition illustrating Chester's history as seen through its architecture, and explaining much about both the skills and the administration of conservation. The exhibition includes an audio-visual presentation.

Lower Bridge Street offers several fine old houses. The *Falcon*, diagonally across from the Heritage Centre, dates mainly from 1626; once the town home of the Grosvenor family, it later became an inn where Handel stayed in 1741. *Tudor House* (E.) is late 16C or early 17C. *Ye Olde King's Head* (W.), mainly early 17C, was the home of Randle Holme, mayor in 1633-34. *Gamul House* (W.) was where Charles I stayed in 1645, and the *Bear and Billet Inn* (W. at the foot of the street), dating from 1664, was until 1867 the town house of the earls of Shrewsbury.

The **Castle**, 150 yards W. of the foot of Lower Bridge Street, is today a group of Classical buildings (1793-1820) by Thomas Harrison, serving as assize courts, county records office etc. The original castle, built c. 1070 by Hugh Lupus, stood here as a typical medieval fortress until 1879, but today the only surviving ancient part is the early 13C *Agricola Tower*† with, on its first floor, the vaulted chapel of St Mary de Castro. The castle precincts were long outside the jurisdiction of the civic authority, and in the 18C provided John Wesley with a refuge. At the N. corner of the castle is the *Museum of the Cheshire Regiment*†, covering over 250 years of service.

The church of *St Mary-on-the-Hill* (closed as a church in 1973), behind the regimental museum, has a 12C foundation but belongs mainly to the 15 and 16C. The nave has a medieval timber roof, said to have come from Basingwerk Abbey.—The bronze equestrian statue of Field Marshal Viscount Combermere (d. 1865), in front of the castle, is by Marochetti.

From the castle Grosvenor Street angles back to the city centre. The **Grosvenor Museum**† is on the right at the castle end of the street.

GROUND FLOOR. Temporary exhibitions. *Newstead Gallery:* Roman coins, pottery, tools, building materials, and domestic equipment. A model of Deva (Chester fort). **Roman Stones Gallery*, with an outstanding if local collection of inscribed stones, all fully described. *Period Rooms:* Georgian and Victorian rooms: also old prints, and cases containing material of these periods.—FIRST FLOOR. Natural History.—UPPER FLOOR. *Art Gallery*, with changing exhibitions from the museum's permanent collection.

WEST FROM THE CROSS. Watergate Street, once the main street to the now vanished port, has 'rows' on both sides and, all on the S. side, some of Chester's finest timbered houses. *God's Providence House* is a reconstruction of 1862. The beam with the Puritan text is original (1652), and the text is said to refer to the fact that the house remained free of the plague. No 11 has the finest medieval crypt in the city (adm. on request, if convenient). *Leche House* (16C. with later additions) belonged to the Leche family, one of whose ancestors was John Leche, surgeon (leech) to Edward III; the house has a fine hall, which is normally shown on request. *Bishop Lloyd's House*, built in 1615, is the most richly carved house in Chester, the subjects being mainly scriptural. Bishop Lloyd was Bishop of Chester from 1604-15. His eldest daughter married twice, both her husbands being associated with the early colonization of America. Her first husband was Thomas Yale, grandfather of Elihu Yale; her second, Theophilus Eaton who in 1639 founded the settlement of New Haven. The *Old Custom House Inn*, on the corner of Watergate and Weaver streets, is of 1637. Below is the *Stanley Palace*† (1591), until 1931 a residence of the Stanleys, earls of Derby, and now occupied by the English Speaking Union. From here the earls controlled the Water Gate from the port, exacting a toll on all goods entering the city. *Guildhall*†, roughly opposite, occupies the former Trinity Church; documents, regalia, silver etc. of the city guilds may be seen.

EAST FROM THE CROSS. Eastgate Street (Via Principalis), with 'rows' on the S. side, is still Chester's principal street. The shop, Browns of Chester, uses a 13 C vaulted crypt as one of its departments. Roughly opposite, *Ye Olde Boot Inn* was established in 1643. The **Eastgate**, straddling the street, dates in its present form from 1769 when the previous narrow medieval gate was demolished; the clock commemorates Queen Victoria's Diamond Jubilee of 1897. Just S.W. of the gate is the *Shopping Precinct.*—For places E. of Eastgate (Roman amphitheatre. British Heritage. St John's Church) see p. 107.

Around and Outside the Walls

The ancient *City Walls were first built by the Romans who threw up a turf rampart some 16 feet high and 20 feet thick, the gates of this enclosure being of timber. When later the decision was taken to make Deva a permanent fortress the old rampart gave way to a stone wall linking twenty-six towers and four gates. The main extension to this system was that by Ethelfleda to the W. and S. in c. 907. More towers, many of which have now disappeared, were added in the 13 and 14C. Today's walls, of red sandstone and some 2 m. in circuit, are mainly medieval, though on the E. and N. sides where they follow the Roman line something of the Roman work can be seen. The complete circuit offers much of interest, but visitors not wishing to walk so far should at least cover from Eastgate to Newgate and Roman Gardens (250 yards) and Eastgate to Northgate (600 yards). The principal places of interest outside the walls (all near Newgate) are the Roman amphitheatre, the British Heritage exhibition, and St John's Church, all described below as part of a circuit running anti-clockwise from Eastgate.

From **Eastgate** (see above) the walk northwards passes the modern grey detached bell-tower and then affords a view of the cathedral. *Kaleyard Gate,* a postern at the end of Abbey Street, gave access to the abbot's kitchen gardens. Here it is worth descending and going through the gate to view (to the S.) some courses of the Roman wall and the foundations of a 13C drum-tower. The walk next rounds the choir school playing fields, at the N.E. corner being **King Charles's Tower** (restored 1658), also known as the Phoenix Tower from the crest of the Painters', Glaziers', Embroiderers', and Stationers' Guild who once occupied it. Traditionally it was from here that Charles I watched the defeat of his troops at Rowton Moor, and the tower contains a small *Civil War Museum†.* The N. wall, part of which may be Norman work, and which also has lengths of Roman stone, is skirted by the Shropshire Union Canal on the site of the former moat; beyond the canal stands the *Northgate Arena* sports centre, (swimming, squash, gymnastics etc). **Northgate** was rebuilt in 1808 by Thomas Harrison. The earlier gate was a prison with a dungeon, and condemned prisoners were taken to a final service in a chapel just outside the gate. So frequent, however, were the rescue attempts that a footbridge was built to give direct communication between prison and chapel. It is worth descending to Northgate Bridge to see this prison bridge, and also, particularly to the W., the Roman walling.

Next comes a square tower overlooking a flight of canal locks and commanding a view of the Welsh hills; known as *Morgan's Mount,* this tower was the victim of particularly heavy bombardment during the Civil War siege. The walk now crosses *St Martin's Gate* (1966), above the St Nicholas Street viaduct, to reach the *Goblin Tower* (rebuilt in 1702 and 1894), with an inscription recording the restoration of the city walls in 1701-08; this tower was long known as Pemberton's Parlour, after a ropemaker whose custom it was to sit here and supervise his men working below. To the S. is the *Royal Infirmary*, one wing of which stands on Infirmary Field, first a Roman cemetery and later the resting place of those who died of the plague. The N.W. corner of the walls is cut by the railway, just beyond which is *Bonewaldesthorne Tower*, connected by a projecting wall with the **Water Tower**† in which there is an exhibition on medieval Chester. Built in 1322 and little altered, the tower, once surrounded by water, was intended to defend the port.

The walk now turns S., passing the Royal Infirmary and reaching **Watergate** (rebuilt 1788), a profitable source of toll-income for the earls of Derby whose house (Stanley Palace) is a short way east. Nun's Road, below the wall here, recalls a 12C priory, dissolved at the Reformation. To the W. now stretches the **Roodee**, a large public open space surrounded by the racecourse, site of the Chester Races since 1540. The curious name stems from 'rood eye', or 'cross island', though whether any cross ever stood on an island here is obscure; the stump in the S.E. part of the space, while traditionally a part of the rood, seems more likely to have been a medieval parish boundary marker. The Roodee was the Roman and later harbour, becoming reclaimed land as the Dee silted and changed course; a part of the Roman quay wall can be seen below the present wall at the S. end of the racecourse stands. The modern police building, on the site of the priory mentioned just above, is passed (E.), just beyond being **Grosvenor Bridge** (Thomas Harrison, 1831); the single stone arch of 200 ft was at the time the world's largest.

After crossing Grosvenor Road, the walls skirt the castle, turning N.E. and at *Bridgegate* (1782) running above **Dee Bridge**, until the building of Grosvenor Bridge in 1831 Chester's only bridge. The bridge (1280, but very likely successor to Roman and Norman bridges) has many times been rebuilt and in 1826 was widened by the provision of a footpath. The song 'The jolly miller of Dee' recalls the mills which from Norman times until their destruction by fire in 1895 stood at the N. end of the bridge. Today salmon fisheries extend downstream from the weir, said to have been built by Hugh Lupus to provide power for the mills. Across the river, immediately S.W. of the bridge, *Edgar's Field* is traditionally the site of that king's castle.

Soon turning N., the walls pass the *Recorder's Steps* (1700), built for the then recorder of Chester whose house stood nearby. Beyond come the *Wishing Steps* (1785), a series of short flights where anybody who can run up and down, and up again, without drawing breath will have his wish granted. Below (inside) are the *Nine Houses* (now six), a 17C timbered terrace restored in 1969. Below (outside) are the *Roman Gardens,* containing a reconstructed hypocaust and some Roman columns (none in situ). **Newgate** (Walter Tapper, 1938) replaced the narrow *Wolfe Gate*, which survives immediately to the north.

Eastgate, beyond ruined *Thimbleby's Tower* (14C; also known as Wolfe Tower), is 150 yards N., but visitors should leave the walls at Newgate to reach places of interest a short way east. Newgate itself bears heraldic decoration; the arms of the city, of the Prince of Wales, and of the Grosvenors, Stanleys, and Egertons. This is the point where the medieval walls meet the Roman walls (the S. line of which here turned

W.), and immediately outside Newgate there survives something of the Roman wall and of its angle-tower. The ***Roman Amphitheatre**, discovered in 1929, dates from c. 100 but covers an older wooden site. The largest discovered in Britain (though only the northern part has been excavated), the amphitheatre measured 314ft by 286ft and would have seated some 9000 people; it is unusual in having a small temple to Nemesis, immediately W. of the N. entrance. The site contains a particularly good explanation and diagrams.

In St John's Street, just N., a plaque recalls that in 1752 John Wesley here first preached in Chester.

British Heritage†, just beyond the amphitheatre, brings to life the history of Chester. The main features are an excellent mock-up of the 'rows' as they would have been c. 1850; a room with models of Roman, medieval, and modern Chester, and a console enabling places to be pinpointed by lights; and an audio-visual presentation.

St John's Church has an ancient and interesting history. Its interior is a fine example of stately Norman architecture.

History. Standing on the site of a Saxon foundation of c. 690, the present church was started in 1075 by Bishop Peter of Mercia, who moved here from Lichfield when the Normans decreed that bishops had to reside in nominated important towns; hence early references to a bishopric of Chester some 500 years before the declaration in 1541 that St Werburgh's was to be a cathedral. On Bishop Peter's death in 1085, by which time he had completed the arches of a central tower and nave, his successor moved to Coventry and St John's ceased to be a cathedral, remaining in fact roofless until c. 1190, when building was resumed, and the church became collegiate. In 1573 the N.W. tower collapsed, destroying the W. end of the church. Eight years later Queen Elizabeth gave what was left to the parishioners, in return for some of the lead which she needed for shot; then, to give themselves a manageable church, the parishioners built an E. wall and left everything beyond as ruin. Further damage was suffered in 1645 when the Parliamentary army used the church as a barracks and a base for its attack on Wolfe Gate. After the Restoration St John's resumed as parish church, in 1881 again being damaged when the lofty, detached belfry, erected on the site of the collapsed N.W. tower, also fell, crushing the N. porch.

The present building is little more than the crossing and part of the nave of the Norman collegiate church. On the exterior (E.) are the ruins of the choir and Lady Chapel, with good Norman Transitional work. The vaulted 'crypt', perhaps the chapter house, at one time served as kitchen for a house above in which De Quincey lived as a boy. At the W. end exterior can be seen the ruins of the collapsed belfry. The belfry was replaced by the incongruous structure on the N.E.; today's N. porch is a restoration of the original.

In the nave the four round arches and their massive pillars date from Bishop Peter's time. The triforium of four arches to each bay and the aisles are Transitional (c. 1200), while the Early English clerestory dates from rather later. On the S. side is the Warburton Chapel, with a memorial to Lady Warburton by Edward Pierce, a pupil of Sir Christopher Wren. In the N.W. corner of the church are Saxon crosses, medieval graveslabs, and effigies (13 and 14C). Also of interest are the W. window, the glass (Edward Frampton, 1860-66) portraying incidents in the life of the church; the organ, used in Westminster Abbey at the coronation of Queen Victoria; a 14C mural on a nave pillar; and a plaque commemorating Thomas Hughes, author of 'Tom Brown's Schooldays', who lived near here from 1885-96.

The *Hermitage*, below the S. wall of the churchyard, is an 18C building with some medieval stonework. It stands on the site of an anchorite's cell (mentioned in 1363), and during the 18C served as meeting house for the Weavers' Guild.

Below St John's, on the river bank, are *The Groves*, Chester's shady riverfront with boat landing stages. To the E. extends *Grosvenor Park*, in the lower part of which has been re-erected the 13C Shipgate, which stood near Bridgegate. Thomas Hughes (see just above) lived at 16 Dee Hills Park, immediately E. of Grosvenor Park.

Environs of Chester

Upton Zoological Gardens†, 2 m. N., can be reached by C 40 bus. First opened in 1931, today the Zoo estate covers some 600 acres, this enabling many of the animals to be kept in something like natural surroundings. The gardens have fine floral displays, and the Zoo waterbus is a popular feature.

Mouldsworth, 6 m. N.E., has a *Motor Museum.†*

Christleton is a village 2 m. southeast. From a well here, now a pond, water was once piped to the tank in the Chester Abbey cloisters. In the village there are three packhorse bridges. *Rowton Moor*, immediately S. between Christleton and Rowton, was where Charles I was defeated in Sept. 1645.

Eccleston, 3 m. S., may be reached by the Roman Watling Street from Dee Bridge, or by river boat. *Eaton Hall* (1869-82), just S., has since Norman times been the home of the Grosvenors; in front stands a bronze figure, by G. F. Watts, of Hugh Lupus, a Grosvenor ancestor. The gardens, chapel, and coach collection are sometimes open.

For other places in England, see 'Blue Guide to England'.
For Chester to *Bangor*, see Rte 2; to *Bala*, see Rte 16. For *Wrexham, Caergwrle,* and *Mold*, see Rte 5.

2   CHESTER TO BANGOR

As far as Llandudno Junction, just E. of Conwy, there is a choice of roads, one following the coast (Rte 2A), the other running a short distance inland (Rte 2B). The coast is not scenic, and between Mostyn, which is mainly industrial, and Colwyn Bay is a stretch largely of crowded resorts, caravan parks, holiday camps, and in places shoddy building. The inland road is both pleasanter scenically and more interesting; places of interest between the two are included under this latter Route. Conwy to Bangor is described as Rte 2C, and Llandudno as a separate Route (Rte 3). The total distance from Chester to Bangor is c. 60 m.

A Coastal Road to Conwy

A548 to Abergele: A55 to Conwy. 43 miles.—*8 m.* **Shotton.**—*5 m.* **Flint.**—*4 m.* *Greenfield.*—*3 m. Mostyn.*—*6 m.* **Prestatyn.**—*3 m.* **Rhyl.**—*4 m.* **Abergele.**—*6 m.* **Colwyn Bay.**—*4 m.* **Conwy.**

Chester, see Rte 1.

A548, on the N. side of the Dee and entering Wales in about 2 m., crosses land reclaimed by the embankment of the river in 1732. Three miles beyond the border the road turns S. to cross the canalized Dee at *Queensferry,* now with two bridges. The large Deeside Leisure Centre

(sports complex) here was opened in 1971.—*8m.* (from Chester)
Shotton has important steelworks.

Shotton Steelworks originated at Stalybridge in Cheshire, where John Summers
rolled puddled iron into steel strips from which to make nails for clogs. In the early
1890s his sons acquired reclaimed land on the Dee estuary for new works, and by
the turn of the century there were 30 rolling mills in operation. Open hearth
furnaces and a bar mill were soon added, and by 1908 Shotton had replaced
Stalybridge as the firm's headquarters. Hot and cold continuous rolling mills were
commissioned in 1939. Nationalization came in 1967, but the works now face an
uncertain future under British Steel Corporation's rationalization plans.

2m. Connah's Quay, no longer a port of any significance, is said to
derive its name from a local publican. A bird sanctuary is associated
with the power station (for visits telephone 0244 816061).

3m. **Flint** (15,000 inhab.), once the centre of a mining district and also
a port, is now mainly concerned with rayon production. The town's
early story is that of its *Castle,* built on a low rock on the shore.

History. Flint, begun in 1277 and completed by James of St George c.1281, was
the first of Edward I's Welsh fortresses. The associated borough was also the first,
receiving its charter in 1284. In 1312 the castle was the scene of the meeting between
Edward II and Piers Gaveston on the latter's return from exile. In 1399, coming
from Conwy, Richard II met Bolingbroke (soon to be Henry IV) here, virtually
becoming the latter's prisoner, In Shakespeare's 'Richard II' Richard says 'What
you will have, I'll give, and willing too; For do we must what force will have us do',
and Froissart describes how Richard's favourite greyhound deserted him to fawn
upon the upstart conqueror. During the Civil War the castle was held for the King
by Sir Roger Mostyn, but was taken by General Mytton in 1647 and slighted.

The castle's plan is roughly a square with a three-quarter drum-tower
at each of three angles. At the S.E. angle, outside the main enclosure and
separated from it by a moat, is a larger circular tower consisting of two
concentric walls, divided by two stages of barrel-vaulted annular
passages. This, with its own well, both served as a keep and commanded
the entrance of the inner ward. The connection with the inner ward was a
rampart walk on a wall across the moat. This defensive plan is unique in
Britain, but has a parallel in the Tour de Constance at Aigues Mortes in
southern France. The castle would have been considerably larger than is
immediately apparent today, as can be judged from the remains on the
S. side of an extensive outer ward, separated from the inner castle, as
also from the town, by moats.

The road continues parallel with the railway along the *Sands of Dee,*
at low tide a depressing expanse of sand and mud. Giraldus records that
he crossed the quicksands near Bagillt in 1188 'not without some degree
of apprehension'; and in 1637 Edward King, Milton's friend at
Cambridge, was shipwrecked and drowned here, 'Lycidas' being the
poet's contribution to a collection of memorial verses.—*4m. Greenfield.*
For *Basingwerk* and *Holywell,* both just inland, see pp. 112-13.—*3m.*
Mostyn is an industrial strip, the road running beside the railway and
docks. The manor of Mostyn was granted in 1295 to James of St George,
and he probably died there in 1308. Mostyn Hall, in part dating from the
time of Henry VI though mostly modern, was where Henry VII, then
Earl of Richmond, escaped from the soldiers of Richard III by leaping
from a window. At Ffynnongroew, beyond Mostyn, is the *Point of Ayr
Colliery,* dating back to 1873. A second shaft was sunk between 1950-57.
About 75% of the output goes to Connah's Quay power station and to
Fiddler's Ferry power station in Lancashire. Annual output is over

340,000 tons and some 650 men are employed.—*3 m. Talacre.* To the N., Point of Ayr marks the W. end of the Dee estuary.

3 m. **Prestatyn** and, *3 m.* farther, **Rhyl** (combined pop. c. 47,000, but vastly increased in summer) form two virtually linked parts of the borough of Rhuddlan. Both are very popular resorts with miles of sands and virtually nonstop entertainment to suit most visitors' tastes.

Prestatyn *(Tourist Information,* Nant Hall Road, S. of the station), at the N. end of Offa's Dyke, is cut by the railway, the main town being to the S. and the Promenade about ½ m. away. There are two large holiday camps. *Ffrith Beach* (W.) offers patrolled bathing, minigolf, and a children's area. At Central Beach is the *Royal Lido Entertainment Centre,* with a heated outdoor swimming pool, music hall, concerts, ballroom etc. *Barkby Beach* (E.) has a boat park and launching facilities, and is backed by a golf course (18 holes). On the S. edge of the town, above St Melwyd Golf Course is *Bishopwood Nature Trail* (2 m.).

Rhyl *(Tourist Information,* Town Hall; also Promenade), on the E. side of the mouth of the Clwyd, has a Parade over 2 m. in length. At the W. end the river is crossed by the *Foryd Bridge* by which is the small harbour. From the bridge there is a view up the Vale of Clwyd (see Rte 6), with Rhuddlan Castle, the tower of St Asaph Cathedral, and the white steeple of Bodelwyddan. Just S. of West Parade are *Ocean Beach Park* and *Marine Lake* (boating; amusement park). Along the seaward side of Promenade, the stretch between West Parade and East Parade, come attractions such as the children's paddling pool, the roller skating rink, the children's cycle track, the bandstand, the open air swimming pool, and the *Royal Floral Hall,* known for its magnificent displays. On East Parade, *Suncentre* has a surfing and other pools, restaurant etc. Beyond, Marine Drive leads to the golf links (18 holes). Entertainment will be found at the Coliseum and Gaiety theatres, both on the waterfront. In the S.E. part of the town the *Botanical Gardens* offer not only gardens but also putting, bowls, tennis, and an aviary and aquarium.

Rhyl is left by Foryd Bridge, to the S. now being the reclaimed marshland of *Morfa Rhuddlan,* where in 795 the Welsh under Caradoc were routed by Offa of Mercia. The road between Rhyl and Abergele threads a succession of huge caravan sites and holiday camps.

4 m. **Abergele** (14,500 inhab., resident), itself an inland market town, forms with *Pensarn* (1 m. N. on the coast, and with many caravan sites) a joint modest resort. The beach is pebble, but with sand as the tide recedes, and there is a golf course (18 holes). In Abergele the twin-nave 16C church is successor to one of c. 800. It contains a 13C floor cross, a pre-Reformation screen (1511), a dugout chest, and in the vestry fragments of 15 or 16C glass. In the churchyard monuments recall disasters to the 'Ocean Monarch' (1848) and the Irish mail train (1868). The busy livestock market (Mon.) is a local attraction.

Gwrych Castle† (1 m. W.) is a huge mock medieval castle put up in 1815. It is now an amusement centre, with jousting, miniature railway, crafts etc. Mrs Hemans spent part of her early life in *Hen Wrych,* the former hall.—*Castell Cawr* (Giant's Castle), on a low wooded hill ¾ m. S. of Abergele, and *Penycorddyn,* 1 m. farther W., are hillforts. Nearby there are traces of Roman lead mining. *Cefn-yr-Ogof* (670 ft), ½ m. N. of Penycorddyn, has a large, shallow cave.

A55 runs below Gwrych Castle.—*2 m. Llanddulas,* at the mouth of the Dulas, is traditionally the place where in 1399 the Earl of Northumberland betrayed Richard II into the hands of Bolingbroke. The church here was designed by Street.—The road ascends over the headland of *Penmaen Rhos;* of the original road Dr Johnson wrote that it was so narrow and unprotected that few persons dared 'trust themselves upon their horses' here.

4 m. **Colwyn Bay** (26,000 inhab., resident), until the end of the last war no more than a village, is now a large resort with good sands which has

filled the gap between the former villages of *Old Colwyn* (E.) and
Llandrillo-yn-Rhos (W.), the latter now on the edge of the resort of
Rhos-on-Sea. Tourist Information is at the Prince of Wales Theatre,
Abergele Road. A promenade c. 3 m. long covers most of the stretch,
and visitors will find all the expected attractions. *Eirias Park,* (50 acres),
running S. from the Promenade, offers boating, bowls and tennis, a
sports arena, picnic area etc. Southeast from here is the golf course (18
holes). The *Pier* has a pavilion, and entertainment will also be found at
the Prince of Wales Theatre, while *New Colwyn Gallery*†, at 26A
Penrhyn Road, holds monthly exhibitions by local artists. In the S.W. of
the town is the *Welsh Mountain Zoo*† (frequent bus in summer from the
pier), founded in 1963 in a 37 acre estate overlooking the bay. The
animals are kept as far as possible in natural surroundings. The
collection of birds of prey is outstanding, and, weather permitting, there
are daily early afternoon free-flying displays by eagles, falcons, and
other birds. A feature of the zoo is the Safari Restaurant, with a balcony
above the lion compound.—**Rhos-on-Sea,** with a pebble foreshore, has
a large open air swimming pool, a golf course (18 holes), and the
Harlequin Puppet Theatre. There was an abbey here (12C) and a plaque
recalls the fish trap operated by the monks. On the foreshore stands *St
Trillo's Chapel,* built over an ancient holy well and of unknown age. The
chapel is tiny (11 ft by 8 ft) and services are held outside.

Llandrillo-yn-Rhos, the old village of Rhos, has a 13-15C church with a 13C
font. Traditionally it was from here that Madoc ap Owain Gwynedd (1150-80)
sailed with 10 ships and 300 men into the Atlantic but never returned.—*Bryn
Euryn Scenic Trail* (1½ m.) is a walk a short way S. of Llandrillo. Lys Euryn ruins
are probably those of a 15C manor house.

2 m. Llandudno Junction and *2 m.* farther, **Conwy.** For both, and
Conwy estuary, see Rte 2B. For **Llandudno,** see Rte 3.

B   Inland Road to Conwy

A55 to Gorsedd; A5151 to Rhuddlan: A525 to St Asaph: B5381 to Llandudno
Junction: A55 to Conwy. 48 miles.—*7 m.* **Hawarden.**—*2 m. Ewloe Castle.—3 m.
Northop.—6 m.* **Holywell.—***3 m. Gorsedd.—4 m. Trelawnyd.—2 m. Dyserth.—
2 m. **Rhuddlan.**—*2 m.* **St Asaph.**—*15 m. Llandudno Junction.—2 m.* **Conwy.**

Chester, see Rte 1.

7 m. **Hawarden** (pron. Harden) is a small town perhaps best known as
the home for some sixty years of W. E. Gladstone, the 19C statesman,
who marrried the daughter of Sir Stephen Glynne, whose family had
acquired the estate after the Civil War. *Hawarden Castle* (no adm.), in
which Gladstone lived, was started in 1750 and added to and castellated
in 1809 by Sir Stephen. In the park are the ruins of the *Old Castle*†. First
a British fort, then in 1264 the scene of a meeting between Simon de
Montfort and Llewelyn the Last, the earliest stone structure dates
probably from c. 1280 and was briefly held in 1282 by Llewelyn's son
Dafydd. There was considerable extension 200 years later, but the castle
was destroyed by Parliament in 1646. The chief ruins are the large
circular keep and the hall, the whole surrounded by a double earthwork
defence. The parish *Church* has a W. window by Burne-Jones, and a
Gladstone Memorial Chapel with marble recumbent figures of

Gladstone and his wife by W. B. Richmond; the couple in fact rest in Westminster Abbey. The Holy Rood above the choir arch is by Giles Scott. The parish is interesting for being a 'peculiar', that is exempt in some respects from the control of a bishop; this position, which is pre-Reformation, was legally confirmed in 1953. Beside the church is *St Deiniol's Residential Library,* founded by Gladstone in 1895; it is a unique foundation (with board residence), housing a mainly theological library of around one hundred thousand books and pamphlets. The library is open throughout the year at moderate charges to all who wish to study (apply to Warden).—*2m.* Ewloe Castle (A.M. sign on A55 W. of village) is the extensive ruin of a stronghold of Llewelyn the Last. The most interesting feature is the well-preserved D-shaped tower (c. 1210) in the centre of the upper ward. The rest of the building, including the circular W. tower, dates from c. 1257.—At (*3m*) *Northop* the church, with an early 16C tower, 98ft high, is said to have been a foundation of 'Lady Margaret' Beaufort (see below under Holywell).

Beyond Northop, to the W., is the long ridge of *Halkin Mountain* (943ft), much scarred by quarries and lead mines. The latter were worked by the Romans, whose Via Antonina from Deva (Chester) to Kanovium (Caerhun) is thought to have followed the ridge. Cornish miners were attracted to this district during the 18C and 19C.—*Coleshill* (N.E. of A55 2m. short of Holywell) was the site of a battle of 1156 in which Owain Gwynedd defeated Henry II.

6m. **Holywell** (8900 inhab.) is named after its well which for centuries up to the Reformation was one of Christendom's principal places of pilgrimage. The well, St Winefride's Chapel (or the Beaufort Chapel), and the parish church form a pleasant compact group below the main town on the road to the coast.

History and Legend. In the 7C St Beuno built a chapel, probably on the site of today's parish church. Legend has that soon afterwards Caradoc, a prince from Hawarden, tried to seduce Winefride, a local princess and Beuno's niece or sister. She ran towards Beuno's chapel, but failed to reach sanctuary before the thwarted Caradoc slashed off her head. Where the head fell there gushed a spring. Beuno emerged from the church, replaced Winefride's head, and the lady lived on to become an abbess. Caradoc however was swallowed up by the ground. From this moment until the Reformation the well became a place of pilgrimage. Indeed, in such high regard was the saint held, that in 1415 Henry V invoked her aid before Agincourt, after the battle making a visit of gratitude. At this time, in fact from 1240 to 1537, the well was in the care of the Cistercians of nearby Basingwerk (see below). When c. 1490 it was decided to build a chapel above the well, a principal benefactor was Margaret Beaufort (1441-1509), mother of Henry VII and the 'Lady Margaret' of many learned and holy foundations. Many would-be pilgrims suffered martyrdom after the Reformation, but in the 18C pilgrimage resumed and is still made today. A hospice for poor pilgrims was erected in 1870 and is still used. Once an unfailing spring, the well was greatly affected by mining in the hills above, until in 1917 the flow ceased, since when water has been provided by a reservoir.

The *Well* (small fee) is in a polygonal basin in what now forms the crypt of the chapel, beside it being a medieval bath with steps at either end. Pilgrims generally enter the bath, then kneel in prayer on the submerged stone of St Beuno. Though much weathered some of the ceiling carving merits attention, notably the heads of Margaret Beaufort and her husband; a figure of St Winefride, seated with a staff in her hand; and a small effigy of St Beuno.

St Winefride's (Beaufort) Chapel† (c. 1490; restored 1966) is a notable example of Perp. work; it contains much stone and wood carving, and bears an external frieze of real and mythical animals. The parish *Church of St James* was built in 1770 (tower 14C), as successor to a medieval predecessor dedicated to St Winefride. A curiosity inside the church is the 'gloch bach', a bell in use from 1714 to 1857; hung from the waist it struck against the padded knee of a man known as the 'walking steeple', who perambulated the town, in parts of which the bell of the low-lying church could not be heard.

Above the parish church stands the 19C *St Winefride's R.C. Church and Hospice*. The church possesses banners designed by Frederick Rolfe (shown on request).

Holywell *Textile Mills,* established in 1874, specialize in Tweed made with wool from Jacob's sheep, sheep with four horns and a spotted or striped coat.

Pantasaph, 2 m. W. of Holywell, is a Roman Catholic community founded by the Earl and Countess of Denbigh in 1852. The buildings include the church with the tomb of the Earl of Denbigh (d. 1892); a Franciscan monastery; a school, with an orphanage, controlled by a Dutch order of Sisters of Mercy; and a pilgrimage path with Stations of the Cross.

Basingwerk Abbey, c. 1 m. N. of Holywell and standing on a pre-Norman fortified site, was founded in 1131 by Randulf, Earl of Chester, as a house of the Savigniac Order, and received into the Cistercian Order in 1147. At the Reformation the buildings were dismantled and sold, the timber roof of the choir going to St Mary-on-the-Hill at Chester, that of the refectory possibly to Cilcain, and stained glass to Llanasa, and, possibly, Dyserth. The few remains of the church comprise the W. and S. walls, some pier bases, and something of the transepts. Immediately S. of the church the open space formed the cloister, with (along the E. side, from N. to S.) the sacristy, the chapter house (with traces of the bench around the walls), the parlour, and the novices' lodging and warming house extending south. The large room to the W. of the warming house is the refectory; it has internal arcading on its W. wall, and traces of the hatch to the kitchen can be seen. Of the kitchen, against the S.W. corner of the cloister, little remains, though the base of the fireplace is visible against the S. wall.

3m. (from Holywell) *Gorsedd.* Here there is a choice of roads, the direct road to St Asaph being A55. This Route bears right on A5151.

Thomas Pennant (1726-98), author of 'Tours in Wales', is buried in the church at *Whitford,* a mile N. of the road fork; he lived nearby, but the house (Downing) was burnt down in 1920.

A crossroads is reached 1½ m. after the Gorsedd fork. Here a diversion may be made (1 m. N.) to see the *Maen Achwynfan,* a well-preserved free-standing cross (10 or 11C), nearly 11 ft high and the tallest of its type in Britain. For a short distance A5151 follows Offa's Dyke.— *4m.* (from Gorsedd) *Trelawnyd,* sometimes called Newmarket, has a well-known male choir, whose rehearsals visitors may attend. On the hill above the W. end of the village stands an exceptionally large tumulus. The church at *Llanasa* (1½ m. N.E.) contains stained glass from Basingwerk.—*2m.* **Dyserth,** a small town at the foot of a limestone hill, has a picturesque cascade. The church contains a 15C Jesse window, possibly from Basingwerk, and a badly damaged 12-13C cross. Earthworks on the hill above mark the site of a castle built by Henry III in 1241 and destroyed in 1263 by Llewelyn the Last. Above is *Craig Fawr,* a National Trust property (since 1973) of over 60 acres, of special geological and botanical interest, and including a viewpoint.

Bodrhyddan Hall†, halfway between Dyserth and Rhuddlan, is a 17C manor house, the home of Lord Langford. The house contains a collection of armour, furniture, pictures etc. In the gardens there is a wishing well, said to have been designed by Inigo Jones.

2m. **Rhuddlan,** visited for its great castle, is a name notorious in Welsh history, since it was from here in 1284 that Edward I issued his statute providing for the government of the conquered principality. Traditionally the statute was enacted on the site now occupied by *Parliament House* (tablet) in the main street of today's small town; the wording of the tablet implies that the statute assured the rights and independence of Wales, rather than laying down the terms of the country's subjection. Until the Civil War the town's story was that of its *Castle†*.

History. The first castle here, a primitive native fort, was succeeded by a motte-and-bailey of 1073, the builder being one Robert of Rhuddlan, a kinsman of Hugh Lupus and known as 'the terror of North Wales'. Giraldus received hospitality here in 1188, apparently being impressed by the 'noble castle' which survives today as Twt Hill (see below). In 1277 the victorious Edward I started work on today's castle, the architect being James of St George and the castle Edward's second in Wales (Flint was the first). By 1282 the castle had been completed, as had also the task of diverting and canalizing the Clwyd, the mouth of which was 2m. away, Edward thus being able to supply himself by sea; Rhuddlan continued as a port until about a century ago. In 1282 Edward's queen gave birth here to her daugther Elizabeth; the year 1284 saw the Statute of Rhuddlan, and 1292 the founding of a Dominican priory (see below). Prior to the building of the castle Rhuddlan would have been a settlement around the motte-and-bailey; now Edward created one of his boroughs, and it was from this that modern Rhuddlan developed. In 1399 Richard II was here, virtually as a prisoner, on his way to Flint. In the Civil War the castle fell (July 1646) to General Mytton, two years later being slighted and for the next 300 years serving as a ready source of building material.

The rectangular castle was designed on a concentric plan, a walled inner ward standing within and above an outer curtain defence of walls and towers; a plan which enabled both outer and inner bowmen to shoot at the same time. It was guarded on the S.W. by the river, on the other sides by a moat filled by tidal and river water. There were diagonal E. and W. gates, each protected by flanking towers, four storeys high and with seven-sided rooms above a circular base. Around the outer ward perhaps the most interesting feature is the dock gate and moat inlet at the angle nearest the river.— *Twt Hill,* the Norman motte, is 300 yards S.E. by footpath. The remains (S. cloister range) of the priory are part of the outbuildings of *Abbey Farm,* (also called Plas Newydd), about the same distance farther southeast. The *Church,* of the local twin-nave type, dates from the 13C and contains graveslabs, probably from the priory; Edward's daughter was christened here. The piers and arches of the *Bridge* are of 1595.

2m. **St Asaph** (3400 inhab.), on a ridge between the Clwyd (E.) and the Elwy (W.), is mainly visited for its *Cathedral,* which gives this small town the official status of city. Both city and cathedral are in fact the smallest in Britain, the latter measuring only 182ft by 65ft, or 108ft across the transepts. Nevertheless, with its plain exterior and solid central tower, the cathedral achieves a quiet dignity. In front stands a monument to Bishop Morgan, buried in the cathedral, and to his fellow translators of the Bible into Welsh.

History. There is some evidence that this may have been the site of the Roman station of Varae, mentioned in the Antonine Itinerary. More certain is that the town grew as the result of the founding of the cathedral in 560 by St Kentigern (also known as St Mungo; d. 603), who earlier had founded the first church on the site of today's Glasgow cathedral. His successor in 573 was Asaph, holder of an administrative post at the local monastery. At this time the place was known only by its Welsh name of Llanelwy (the holy enclosure beside the Elwy), the English name of St Asaph not being recorded before 1100. There is no definite record of any bishop between St Asaph and 1143, though possibly the succession was continuous. Among distinguished later bishops were Dr Morgan (1601-04, see above); William Lloyd (1680-92), one of the 'seven bishops'; and Samuel Horsley (1802-06), the opponent of Priestley in the Trinitarian controversy. John Luxmoore, father of the notorious pluralist Charles Luxmoore, held the see from 1815-30. The cathedral, described by Giraldus in 1188 as 'paupercula sedis Laneluensis ecclesia', was destroyed by the English in 1282. Edward I then wished to rebuild at Rhuddlan, but Bishop Anian II (1268-93) insisted that the new cathedral be at St Asaph and got his way, such was the power of the Church even against a conqueror like Edward I. Today's building was therefore started by Bishop Anian II, and completed by his two successors. The woodwork was burnt in 1402, but the church was reroofed and restored by Bishop Redman (1471-96). The tower was rebuilt in 1715, after its destruction in a storm, and the choir was remodelled c. 1780. There was major restoration by Gilbert Scott in 1869-75, and further restoration in 1929-32. In 1920, Dr A. G. Edwards, bishop since 1889, was enthroned as the first archbishop of the newly constituted Church in Wales.

Inside the cathedral the roof painting and gilding (1967) celebrate the investiture of Prince Charles as Prince of Wales. The Dec. Nave, begun by Bishop Anian II, has 14C arcades with continuous mouldings and a good 15C clerestory. The SOUTH AISLE contains a recumbent effigy of a bishop, virtually certainly Anian II; also the curious Greyhound Stone, bearing unexplained heraldic decoration. In this aisle, too, are tablets to Mrs Hemans (d. 1835), the poetess, who lived for several years near St Asaph; and to H. M. Stanley (d. 1904), of African fame. Stanley, then John Rowlands, was as a youth an inmate of the St Asaph workhouse; the tablet was put up in 1977. The Transepts are contemporary with the nave, and something of Bishop Redman's 15C roof has survived. The SOUTH TRANSEPT now serves as a chantry chapel, the gift in 1957 of the Guild of All Souls; here there is an exquisite little 16C Spanish ivory Madonna, said to have come from a wrecked Armada galleon. The aisleless CHOIR was mostly rebuilt by Scott in the style of the 13C, but incorporates some genuine work of that period which escaped the damage of 1282. The stalls, with their carved elbows, date from the restoration by Bishop Redman; the sedilia and the E. window, with glass of 1968, are 14C (restored). The Victorian bishop's throne stands over Bishop Morgan's tomb.—The CHAPTER MUSEUM, below the Diocesan Registry, is shown on request (not Sun.). It houses a collection of early bibles and prayer books. The collection includes three copies of the first prayer book of Edward VI (1549), one of which belonged to Roger Ascham, the 16C scholar, and has notes in his own handwriting; a copy of the rare 'sealed' prayer book (1662); the first Welsh New Testament (1567); Bishop Morgan's Bible (1558), used at the investiture of Prince Charles; the second and third editions of the Welsh Prayer Book (1586, 1599); and Middleton's and Archdeacon Prys's Metrical Psalms in Welsh (1603, 1621). Also in the museum are a hornbook (unique in Wales; early 17C); the Triglot Dictionary (Welsh, Greek, and Hebrew) of Dic Aberdaron, a local self-taught genius, buried in the parish church churchyard; prehistoric and Roman material; a copy of the newspaper 'Commonwealth Mercury', announcing the death of Oliver Cromwell; church plate (mainly 16 and 17C); a collection of autographs, including those of the Prince Consort, Charles Dickens, Charles Darwin, W. M. Thackeray, Holman Hunt, and Florence Nightingale.

For St Asaph to *Denbigh, Ruthin,* and *Corwen,* see Rte 6.

A55 leads direct to Abergele, in 2 m. passing *Bodelwyddan,* with its 'marble' church built in 1856-60 by Lady Willoughby de Broke as a memorial to her husband. The arcades are of marble, but the exterior is white limestone. The design was by John Gibson; the font is by Hollings of Birmingham, the curious lectern by Kendal of Warwick, and the bust of Lady Willoughby by M. Noble. The graceful spire is 200 ft high. To the S. of the choir are the graves of Canadian soldiers who died during the First World War at nearby Kinmel Park Camp, now a girls' school.—The village of *Llan Sain Sior* (St George), 2 m. farther N.W., is where by local repute St George slew the dragon. Above and S. of the village is the hillfort of *Dinorben,* approached by climbing the hill by the quarry; the fort seems to have been occupied from 500 B.C. to A.D. 700.

This Route continues along B5381.—*6 m.* from St Asaph A548 is crossed, 2 m. S. down which is *Llanfair Talhaiarn,* the burial place of John Jones ('Talhaiarn', 1810-69), a poet sometimes described as the Welsh Burns.—*3 m. Dolwen,* 2 m. N.W. of which, in the church of *Llanelian-yn-Rhos,* is preserved the graveslab of Ednyfed Fechan, minister of Llewelyn the Great.—*6 m. Llandudno Junction* (station for Conwy), where the Conwy estuary is reached and this Route is joined by Rte 2A.

The **Conwy Estuary** is known for its mussels, alluded to by Tacitus and praised in verse by Drayton and Spenser. These, as also normal fishing (dabs in particular), still support a fishing population. *Deganwy* (Dinas Conwy, the fort on the Conwy), with its sandy beach and small harbour today a popular holiday resort and sailing centre, guarded the N. entrance to the estuary. Slight remains of the castle survive above the small town. Frequently mentioned in Welsh history, the castle is said to have been a favourite seat of Maelgwn Gwynedd as early as the 6C, and it may have been here that he received Gildas, who later wrote so maliciously about him. The first castle in the modern sense was probably erected soon after the Norman Conquest, perhaps by Hugh Lupus, but the existing ruins are those of a fortress built by the Earl of Chester in 1211. Henry III was besieged here by the Welsh, and the castle was finally destroyed by Llewelyn the Last in 1263.—Three adjacent bridges cross to Conwy. The road bridge was opened in 1958, superseding the graceful suspension bridge (N.T.) erected by Telford in 1824-26 in the same style as his slightly earlier Menai Bridge, except that the towers are copied from those of Conwy Castle. The third bridge, carrying the railway, is a tubular one built by Robert Stephenson in 1846-48.

CONWY (greater Conwy 12,100 inhab.), or **Conway,** pleasantly situated on the estuary below wooded hills, and with its great castle and circuit of high town walls complete with twenty-one towers, is the most historic and exciting place along the Welsh N. coast. It is also a popular holiday and yachting centre.

Tourist Information. Castle Street. *National Trust* at Telford's bridge.

Parking. *Castle Square* (limited). Also convenient for the castle are *Conwy Quay, Rose Hill Street* (within the walls), and *Morfa Bach* (reached by a bridge under the railway immediately W. of the castle). This last offers a good view of the twelve lavatories built on to the walls (see below under Town Walls). *Mount Pleasant* (outside the walls at the W. end of the town).

Camping and Caravans. Municipal site at Conwy Morfa.

Railway Station. Llandudno Junction, on the E. side of the estuary.

Post Office. Bangor Road.

Early Closing. Wednesday.

River Trips. In summer, launches upriver to *Tal-y-Cafn* and *Trefriw* (round trip c. 3½ hours). The excursion is through the pleasant wooded and pastoral Vale of Conwy (see Rte 7). Near Glan Conwy a burial chamber is passed, and, beyond Tal-y-Cafn on the l. bank below the church of Caerhun, the scanty earthworks of the Roman fort of Kanovium.

Early History (town). There would probably have been a settlement around the Norman motte-and-bailey which stood on the site of today's castle, but the early history of the town is more that of the Cistercian abbey of Aberconwy, started in 1172 and completed in 1187. In 1198 Llewelyn the Great granted a charter to the abbey, which became renowned for its library; he took the habit here in 1238 and died here two years later. In 1245 Henry III plundered the abbey, and in 1283 Edward I, requiring the site for his castle and borough, removed it to Maenan. Parts of St Mary's Church are all that remain. From now on the history of Conwy becomes that of the castle.

The **Castle**†, though smaller than some, is among the most picturesque of Welsh fortresses. The ground plan is an irregular oblong with its greatest length (400 ft) from E. to west. The curtain walls are 15 ft thick and enfiladed externally by eight cylindrical towers, of which the

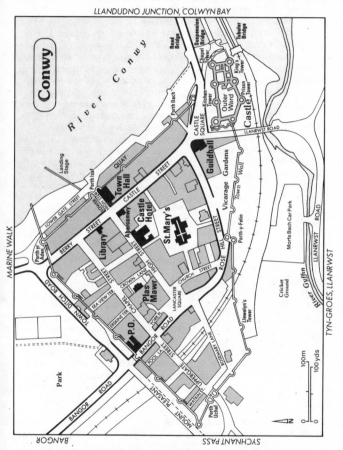

four on the E. are crowned by smaller, circular turrets. The rampart walk is carried round the flattened inner face of the towers by corbelled-out galleries. Of the two wards the W. (outer) and larger is the castle proper, while the smaller E. (inner) ward served really as a royal palace.

History. Originally a Norman motte-and-bailey stood here. The present castle was begun by Edward I in 1283, the work being largely that of James of St George, and completed a little over four years later, together with the associated borough which received a charter as early as 1284. In 1294 Edward was besieged here (nearly having to surrender through famine) during a Welsh uprising, the castle being in part garrisoned, in accordance with the terms of the charter, by the Anglo-Norman settlers who were the borough's first citizens. In 1399 Richard II sought refuge here on his return from his ill-timed visit to Ireland and just before his surrender to Bolingbroke (Henry IV) at Flint. In 1401 Owen Glendower's supporters took the town and castle. During the Civil War the castle was held for Charles by Archbishop Williams of York, a native of Conwy, and afterwards by Sir John Owen, but was taken for Parliament by General Mytton in 1646. It was finally dismantled in 1665. Important though the castle was from time to time, the town's growth seems to have been slow. A mere sixty houses are recorded in Elizabethan times, and Pennant writing in the 18C remarks on the few inhabitants. The growth of modern Conwy dates largely from the arrival of the railway in the 19C.

The modern entrance (N.W. corner) is into a projecting barbican, formerly reached by a steep ramp and drawbridge; remains of the ramp and portcullis can be seen. Immediately S. of this projecting barbican was a small fortified terrace or inner barbican, from which the main gateway leads into the outer ward. The absence of a definite gatehouse is unusual in a castle of this date; its place is here taken to some extent by the exceptionally strong barbican and by the abrupt right-angle turn immediately beneath two towers. The OUTER WARD has along its S. side the Great Hall (125 ft by 38 ft), its irregular shape dictated by that of the outer curtain wall. The wooden roof of the hall was supported, rather unusually, by stone arches, of which one (restored) remains. The kitchens were on the opposite side of the ward, below the Kitchen Tower, while on the E. side, sunk in the solid rock, is the great water-tank, made necessary by the absence of a well. Here the INNER WARD or PALACE is entered. On the S. side (first floor) is the King's Banqueting Hall, with his withdrawing-room to the E. and what was probably his bedchamber in the S.E. (King's Tower). The Queen's Banqueting Hall occupied the first floor on the E. side of the ward; on the same floor, opening out of the N.E. tower (Chapel Tower), is a lovely small *Oratory,* the most delicately finished part of the whole castle, with polygonal apse, vaulted roof, and mutilated wall arcades. A gateway under the Queen's Hall leads on to the EAST BARBICAN, flanking the whole E. end of the castle; this may once have been a garden for the queen, and at its N.E. corner are the remains of the original watergate stairs.—Of the TOWERS, the King's Tower (S.E.) and Chapel Tower (N.E.) have already been mentioned. The other towers along the S. side from E. to W. are Bakehouse Tower, with a large oven in the basement; the Prison Tower, with dungeon; and the Southwest Tower. Along the N. side, also from E. to W., are the Stockhouse Tower, where criminals suffered in the stocks; the Kitchen Tower; and the Northwest Tower. The walls, towers, and turrets offer good impressions of the castle interior as a whole, as well as views of the town and its walls, the three bridges, and the estuary.

The *Town Walls,* c. 1400 yards long, with an average height of 30 ft, and built at the same time as the castle, are the best example in Britain of the defence works introduced by Edward I. The castle's defence and that of the town is one integral scheme, the walls protecting both and the town growing up in what is in effect an outflung ward of the castle. The walls are remarkable for their great height, the prominence of twenty-one towers, and the hilly nature of the area enclosed.

From the castle the walk is along the busy *Quay* (1831) to *Porth Isaf* (Lower Gate) at the foot of High Street, the least important gate from a defence point of view since it was on the water. From the N. corner (*Porth-yr-Aden*), a spur, once ending in a tower, runs out to the water to protect the N. entrance to the harbour. From Porth-yr-Aden the wall runs S.W., climbing to its highest point to reach *Porth Uchaf* (Upper Gate). This is the most elaborate of the three main gateways, with both outer and inner barbicans. The wall now bears roughly E., passing Llewelyn's Tower to reach *Porth-y-Felin* (Mill Gate), set in an odd angle. This eastern entrance to the town would probably have been associated with a ferry across the Afon Gyffin. Beyond Porth-y-Felin the top of the wall has twelve lavatories, two still roofed, said to have been reserved for the royal clerks.

Within the walls there are three main places of interest, all close to High Street. **Plas Mawr†**, the 'Great Mansion', built by Robert Wynne of Gwydir in 1577-80, is a picturesque and interesting example of an Elizabethan house, with courtyards, crow-stepped gables and octagonal watchtower. The chief façade is in Crown Lane, but the entrance is in High Street. Of interest inside are the elaborate plaster ceilings (copied from the parent house, Gwydir Castle, see p. 143), the chimneypieces, and the curious bread-safe and turkey-cooker. In the Queen's Parlour the chimneypiece bears the initials of Elizabeth, and the royal arms supported by the lion and the Tudor dragon. The house is now occupied by the *Royal Cambrian Academy of Art* (annual summer exhibition, June-Sept.).—**St Mary's Church,** the other side of High Street, occupies the site of the early Cistercian abbey (see early history of the town). The E. and W. buttresses and parts of the walls, particularly on the N. side, are survivals from the original abbey church which, after the removal of the abbey to Maenan in 1283, became the parish church. The striking though mutilated W. doorway is probably that of the chapter house; at the W. end of the nave hangs a picture showing the W. face of the church as it may well have appeared in Cistercian times. To the 14C belong the lower stages of the tower, the south transept, and the porches; to the 15C the upper part of the tower, the very fine rood-screen (now without its loft, though something of the stair can be seen), and the font, at which John Williams, later Archbishop of York and defender of Conwy for Charles I, was christened. In the 16C the aisle roofs were raised, and in 1872 that of the nave as part of a restoration by Gilbert Scott. On the choir floor is the worn graveslab of one Nicholas Hookes (d. 1637), the forty-first child of his father and himself the father of twenty-seven. In the S. aisle are a bust by Theed of John Gibson, a local sculptor, christened here in 1790, and an effigy of Mary (d. 1585), mother of John Williams. The *Parish Museum* in the church is opened on request. It contains beautiful squares of lace (c. 1450); copper collecting boxes; a processional cross from Monza, Italy, of early Byzantine workmanship (?7C); interesting old pictures of the church in the past, and a benefactions board.—Farther N., on the corner of High Street and Castle Street, is a stone and timber building of c. 1500 (much restored) called **Aberconwy†**, interesting, both externally and internally, for illustrating how the majority of the better houses in Conwy looked at this time.

Immediate Environs of Conwy. *Conwy Mountain* (808ft). 1m. W., has hut circles and the remains of a hillfort (Caer Leion) on its summit. From here there are footpaths in most directions, including S. to *Sychnant Pass* (550ft), the old road pass connecting Conwy with Penmaenmawr. In summer a minibus service operates across the pass.—*Llangelynin Church* (4m. S.) can be reached by lane. At over 900ft this is one of the highest parish churches in Wales, as well as being a virtually untouched example (13-15C), even to the earthern floor of its N. transept. of the ruder Welsh type. Noteworthy are the roofs and porch, the primitive font. the sawn-off ends of the rood beam, and an old bier.—*Gyffin*, a village just S. or the Trefriw road, was the birthplace of Richard Davies, Bishop of St David's and translator (1567) of the Book of Common Prayer into Welsh. The church has a 13C door and a painted barrel ceiling (15-16C, restored), with panels over the altar.

For Conwy to *Betws-y-Coed* and *Ffestiniog,* see Rte 7.

C   Conwy to Bangor

A55. 15 miles.—*5 m.* **Penmaenmawr.**—*3 m.* **Llanfairfechan.**—*2 m.* **Aber.** -*5 m.* **Bangor.**

This stretch of the Route is scenically more interesting, with views across Conwy Bay to Great Orme's Head and Anglesey, and, inland, high ground, crossed by many paths and popular with walkers—*Sychnant Pass* (see above) to Penmaenmawr offers an alternative to the main road.

Beyond Conwy the road rounds *Conwy Mountain* and there is a view across to Great Orme's Head before the curved tunnel (1932; 565 ft long) below Penmaenbach Point (Little Stone Point) is entered. After the tunnel Puffin Island and Anglesey come into view.—*5 m.* **Penmaenmawr** (4000 inhab.), on the hillside between the headlands of Penmaenbach and Penmaenmawr, takes its name from the latter (1550 ft). It is a small resort with a 3 m. stretch of sand and all the usual facilities. Prehistoric man was active here, using the local stone to fashion his tools, and an 'axe factory' was discovered in 1919 on the slopes above Craig Lwyd (½ m. S.E.). Granite is still quarried, and shipped from the town's small quay.

Walks from Penmaenmawr. The high upland behind the town offers a variety of walks. Three, easily combined into one, are suggested. 1. The principal walk is the *History Trail* (3½ m.). The path, signed 'Druids' Circle', starts from Craig Lwyd (see above) and climbs to the stones at about 1200 ft. on the N.E. slope of Moelfre (1422 ft). The stones are the remains of two circles, long associated with the worship of two sinister goddesses, Andras and Ceridwen, whose names still survive in Welsh oaths. A trail leaflet is available at local shops. 2. *Fairy Glen* and *Jubilee Walk*. The approach is through Dwygyfylchi, 1½ m. northeast. Fairy Glen has pretty cascades; Jubilee Walk (1887) makes the round of Foel Lus (1100 ft). Total distance c. 4 m. 3. *Penmaenmawr* (1550 ft) is a mass of green felspathic porphyry, now much scarred by quarries. A path starts just W. of the town and reaches the summit in 2 m.—Paths from these uplands lead from Tyn-y-ffridd farm between Foel Lus and the Druids' Circle to *Llangelynin* (p. 119); and to *Tal-y-fan* (2000 ft), 2½ m. S. of Penmaenmawr town, and thence to the Conwy valley near Caerhun.

Today's road past Penmaenmawr headland is a modern highway with tunnels and walls, but formerly the mountain was a formidable obstacle to travellers. In 1685 Lord Clarendon, Lord Lieutenant of Ireland, found the path at this point impassable except on foot, and indeed many people preferred to use the sands at low tide. The first road, as opposed to bridlepath, was made in 1772; but Dr Johnson traversed it with some anxiety in 1774. Public houses stood at either end of the 'pass' to nerve travellers at the start and comfort them on arrival.

3 m. **Llanfairfechan** (4000 inhab.), the name meaning Holy Enclosure of St Mary the Less, lies at the W. base of Penmaenmawr; through the little town tumbles a stream which in its length of 3 m. falls about 2000 ft. This is a quiet and modest resort, as popular for its beach, sailing etc. as for the walks that may be enjoyed on the high ground behind, for which there is a special local map.

Walks from Llanfairfechan. 1. *Penmaenmawr* (see above) and *Carreg Fawr* (1167 ft), 1½ m. respectively N.E. and S., are two local climbs, both with paths. 2. *History Trail* (6 m.; local leaflet). Starting at Three Streams car park and picnic site (1 m. S.E.) the trail includes the Aber to Kanovium Roman road, hut circles, and, on the Bwlch-y-Ddeufaen (Pass of the Two Stones; 1403 ft), two standing stones. The eighth Roman milestone from Kanovium (replica on site) is now in the British Museum. The return may be made to Llanfairfechan; alternatively the track, passing a burial chamber, continues down to the Conwy valley at Ro-wen, c. 7 m. from the coast. 3. *Llyn Anafon*, on N.T. land 4 m. S. and also known as Aber Lake, is Llanfairfechan's water supply. It may be reached by a track rounding Carreg Fawr, then heading S.E. round Yr Orsedd. From the lake a track follows Afon Anafon down to Aber and the coast. 4. *Carnedd Llewelyn*, 9 m. S., see below.

2 m. **Aber,** a little town about ½ m. from the sea, has never become a coast resort and is better known as a centre from which to explore the hilly country inland, including, close to Aber, the beautiful Coedydd Aber glen (nature reserve) and the Aber falls. Aber has its place in history, the *Mwd* being the site of the motte-and-bailey castle built by Llewelyn the Great; it was here in 1282 that Llewelyn the Last received and rejected Edward I's demand that he should acknowledge his sovereignty, a rejection which quickly led to Edward's conquest of Wales. Off the coast are the *Lavan Sands,* across which, before the building of the Menai Bridge, travellers rode to the ferry for Beaumaris, a bell in Aber church tolling to guide them in foggy weather. Welsh tradition associates these sands, and indeed the whole of this coastline, with drowned towns and fertile valleys.

Walks from Aber. 1. *Coedydd Aber Nature Reserve* is a lovely glen which opens just S. of Aber between Maes-y-Gaer (730 ft; hillfort) to the E. and Ffridd Ddu (1187 ft) to the west. A curious fact about the former is that from the early 18C until 1899 it operated as a rabbit warren with a resident keeper. Cars may be parked at Bont Newydd, ¾ m. from Aber; from here there is a nature trail (N.C.) which, rising some 500 ft, climbs the glen for 1½ m., on the way passing a cottage which has been converted to a display centre. At the glen's head are two falls; Rhaeadr Mawr (120 ft) is more or less vertical, while ¼ m. to the W. the Afon Bach comes down in a series of broken cataracts.—The falls are on the N. edge of the large N.T. territory of *Carnedd,* which reaches some 7 m. S. to beyond Llyn Ogwen (p. 156) and averages 2 to 3 m. in breadth. Carnedd is crossed by several paths, two of which are suggested below.—2. From the falls the smooth top of *Moel Wnion* (1903 ft) is 1½ m. west. From the summit paths descend to either Aber (2 m.) or S. to Bethesda (3 m.). 3. *Carnedd Llewelyn* (3484 ft), the second highest summit in Wales, is 6 m. S.E. of Aber as the crow flies. There are three approaches from Aber, but all involve a long mountain walk, not to be attempted by the inexperienced or in poor weather; the descent may be made to Bethesda, Llyn Ogwen, or Capel Curig. The most direct ascent is from the Aber falls, but this is in part steep and dangerous. There are two alternatives. One is to follow the lane leading E. from Bont Newydd on to the open hillside, thence taking the track up the valley to *Llyn Anafon*. From here there is a steep ascent to the ridge between Drum (2528 ft) and the level summit of Foel Fras (3091 ft), from where a walk of 2¾ m. in a generally S.S.W. direction, keeping ½ m. E. of Yr Aryg (2875 ft) and crossing Foel Grach (3195 ft), arrives at the summit of Carnedd Llewelyn. Another route from Aber is to follow a track along the N. and E. slope of Moel Wnion to the head of the short glen rising from Aber falls; from the shoulder the track leads roughly S.E. over Drosgl and Yr Aryg. Thence, as above, via Foel Grach.

4 m. **Llandegai** is the modern development of the model village built in the 19C for Lord Penrhyn's estate workers. The name derives from St Tegai, who is said to have had a cell here in perhaps the 5C. The present church, early 16C and of the cruciform type uncommon in Wales, is approached by an avenue of yews, probably nearly twice as old as the church. Inside are monuments to Archbishop Williams of York (d. 1650), with his helmet and spurs hanging above, and (by Westmacott) to the first Baron and Lady Penrhyn. Llandegai was where in 1648 Sir John Owen was defeated by Parliamentary troops under Colonel Thistleton. Rte 10 is joined here, opposite being the entrance to *Penrhyn Castle* (p. 130).—1 m. **Bangor,** see Rte 4.

3   LLANDUDNO AND ENVIRONS

LLANDUDNO (pron. Chlandidno) has a resident population of some 19,000, but this is enormously increased in summer, a large number of these visitors coming from the north of England and the Midlands. Though animated and crowded, and offering all the attractions and facilities the visitor expects, the town tends to be conservative, retaining something of its Victorian dignity and elegance and avoiding the more vulgar forms of commercialism. It straddles the neck of the Great Orme (a tourist attraction in its own right), the main town being on the N.E. side, its broad 2 m. long promenade following the curve of Orme's Bay (or Llandudno Bay) with its fine sands.

Tourist Information. All year in *Chapel Street.* Also, from spring to end Sept., opposite *Pier Gates* and at *Arcadia Theatre,* both on the Promenade.

Parking. *Promenade* (seaward side). *Happy Valley* (N.E. corner), for pier and Great Orme cabin lift. Several other place near town centre, e.g., Gloddaeth Street.

Main Shopping Street. Mostyn Street.

Railway Station. Augusta Street, in town centre.

Bus and Coach Services. General Inquiries, Clonmel Street, (76201). Coaches for local tours and Marine Drive leave from Promenade (Prince Edward Square). Bus to Great Orme and Church of St Tudno from opposite Town Hall.

Main Post Office. Vaughan Street.

Early Closing. Wednesday.

Steamers from pier. Day excursions to Isle of Man (coach tour), Puffin Island, Red Wharf Bay (Anglesey).—Local cruises in smaller boats from jetty near pier. Popular trips are to the cliffs and caves of Great and Little Orme.

Amusements. Summer shows at *Pier Pavilion, Arcadia Theatre,* and *Happy Valley Open Air Theatre.* Repertory at *Grand Theatre.* Concerts at *Pier Head Pavilion* and *Astra Theatre.* Evening concerts by Llandudno Town Band at Promenade bandstand.—*Welsh Choirs* at St John's Church, Mostyn Street (summer Sun., 20.00).

History. Llandudno has its roots on Great Orme, home of prehistoric man and chosen in the 6C by St Tudno as the site of the cell from which he preached. Hence the town's name, meaning Holy Enclosure of St Tudno. In probably the 12C a church was built here and became parish church. In 1850 Llandudno was no more than a village, but after this date, and particularly with the development of the railway, growth as a leading resort was rapid.

The town centre is a gently curving rectangle bounded on the N. and S. by the Promenade and Mostyn Street, and on the E. and W. by Vaughan Street and the park of Happy Valley.

The PROMENADE, a crescent nearly 2 m. long, for the most part late Victorian, sweeps round the curve of beach and bay, guarded at the E. end by Little Orme and at the W. by Great Orme. Bowls, tennis, and children's playground and paddling pool are in the eastern part. The *Bandstand* is on the seaward side roughly opposite Vaughan Street. Farther W., beyond the war memorial and Prince Edward Square (starting place for town and Marine Drive tours) and at the foot of Great Orme, is the *Pier Pavilion,* by the base of the **Pier,** 2296 ft long and a fine example of a typical Victorian pier; it has a landing stage for steamers and a pierhead concert hall. **Happy Valley,** just W. of the pier, is a public park with a children's playground, rock gardens, and an open air theatre. From the park start the Great Orme cabin lift and the nature trail (see below).—The wooded hill, c. ¼ m. W. of the park, is *Pen-y-Dinas* with a hillfort; on the N.W. there are traces of ramparts, and the area includes hut circles. Here too is *St Tudno's Cradle,* a stone which once rocked and may have been associated with prehistoric ritual.

Parallel to the Promenade run, in succession from E. to W., Mostyn Avenue, Mostyn Broadway, and MOSTYN STREET, this last the broad, pleasantly tree-lined main shopping street.

In Ffan Bach Road, about 500 yards S. of Mostyn Avenue and over a mile from the town centre, is *Rapallo House*†, a museum and art centre. Exhibits, which include material on loan from the National Museum of Wales, include Roman finds from Kanovium, a replica of a typical old Welsh kitchen, porcelain, sculpture, and pictures.

Vaughan Street, with the post office on its corner, leads to the station. In Mostyn Street, beyond the crossing of Trinity Square and Clonmel Street (bus information), are the *Public Library* (S.) and, opposite, *St John's Church*, where on Sundays in summer Welsh choirs may be heard. Mostyn Street crosses the end of Lloyd Street, with the *Town Hall* (starting place for buses to Great Orme and St Tudno's church) and, beyond in Chapel Street, the principal *Tourist Information* office. From Prince Edward Square, Gloddaeth Street and Avenue end at West Parade on the W. shore. Across Gloddaeth Street from Mostyn Street (in Masonic Street) is the *Doll and Model Railway Museum*†. Mostyn Street is continued N.W. by Upper Mostyn Street which runs into Church Walks. Here (S.W.) are the station of the *Great Orme Tramway* and, beyond, terraced *Haulfre Gardens*.

The WEST SHORE (bus from Mostyn Street), with dunes and beach, offers a quieter alternative to the often crowded main beaches and also commands a view of Snowdonia. Below the West Parade there is a large *Model Yacht Pond*, N. of this being *Gogarth Abbey Hotel*, successor to a residence of Dean Liddell often visited by Charles Dodgson (Lewis Carroll), whose walks here with the dean's little daughter inspired him to write 'Alice in Wonderland'. A memorial (replica) by F. W. Forrester, portraying the White Rabbit, was unveiled in 1933 by Lloyd George.

Great Orme's Head

Great Orme's Head is a mass of white carboniferous limestone rising steeply to the immediate N.W. of Llandudno. The headland, within which are a number of minor antiquities, may be visited by boat, tramway, cabin lift, road, on foot, or by various combinations (for instance the second half of the nature trail is along Marine Drive). The summit (679 ft) commands magnificent views, including the mountains to the S.W. (with Carnedd Llewelyn as the highest point visible), Anglesey, and, in very clear weather, the Cumberland mountains and the Isle of Man.

BOAT is the best way to see the cliffs and caves. Steamers and boats from Llandudno pier and jetty.

The GREAT ORME TRAMWAY celebrated its 75th anniversary in 1977. In summer there is a continuous daily service from Church Walks to the summit.

The CABIN LIFT (1 m.) is the longest passenger cable car system in Britain. In summer continuous daily service from Happy Valley to the summit.

ROAD. Bus service from opposite the Town Hall. Marine Drive tour coaches leave from Prince Edward Square.

A network of roads covers the town end, the summit being reached either by Ty-Gwyn Road from Church Walks, or past the church of St Tudno from Marine Drive. *Marine Drive (fee), opened in 1878 and over 4 m. long, encircles the base of the headland. The start is near Happy Valley, from where the road gradually ascends, skirting the cliffs, to *Pen Trwyn* at the N.E. angle. Bearing W. the road passes above caves

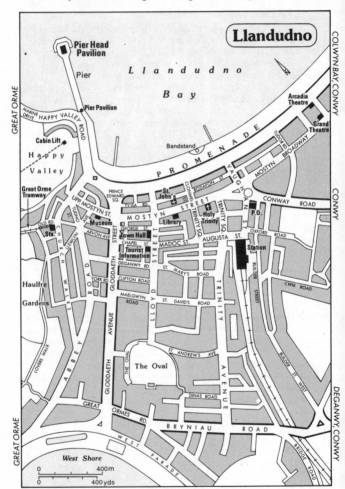

(accessible only by boat) and reaches the turn up to the summit, passing *St Tudno's Church*.

As noted above (History) it was on this site that in the 6C St Tudno built and preached from his cell, this being followed centuries later by the church that became the parish church of Llandudno. To-day's church is a primitive little building, the oldest part of which (N. wall) dates from the 12 or 13C; the remainder is mostly 15C. In 1839 the roof was destroyed in a storm, the church then being abandoned until restored in 1855. Inside are some 13C graveslabs and an 11 or 12C font. In summer, weather permitting, open air services are held on Sunday mornings.

Marine Drive continues W. to *Great Orme's Head Lighthouse* at the N. tip of the headland, then bears S.W., passing above the *Llech Cave* (Hiding Cave), said to have been used as a summer house by a 16C member of the Mostyn family, and *Hornsby Cave*, named after a brig wrecked here in 1824. The old road (followed by the nature trail) comes in from the E., within the angle of the junction being a group of hut circles. Where the road rounds the W. point there is a fine view of the Conwy estuary, with Conwy Castle backed by mountains, while more to the W. are Puffin Island and Anglesey. Wild goats may be seen below the road here. Descending, the road passes above the ruins of *Gogarth Abbey,* misnamed because this was in fact a palace of the bishops of Bangor, said to have been given by Edward I to the then bishop in appreciation for his having christened the son whom Edward later proclaimed Prince of Wales. The 'abbey' was destroyed by Owen Glendower. The track which here joins Marine Drive from the N.W. is known as the Monks' Path, the path between the 'abbey' and the church of St Tudno. Marine Drive ends close to Gogarth Abbey Hotel (see above).

NATURE TRAIL The **Great Orme Nature Trail** (5 m.; waymarked) passes close to most places of interest on Great Orme. A booklet, obtainable from Tourist Information, explains in detail the geology, flora, fauna (which includes wild goats), and other features along the trail, generally and at each of its 18 stations. Between the start in Happy Valley and the summit the trail leads past the long huts and other traces of what was probably a medieval settlement; a farmstead, in part 17C; a burial chamber (cromlech); the disused shafts of copper mines, started by the Romans and in use until the 19C; and Bishop's Quarry, where fossils may be found. From the summit the trail continues N.W., soon reaching an angle of a stone wall where there are further traces of long huts; of four outlines, the largest is 75 ft by 15 ft. Below lies the church of St Tudno, and just S. of the cemetery there are more traces of a hut settlement. Farther along, in the wall, is the Roman Well, the spring of which was possibly used by the Romans to wash their copper ore. Beyond, the trail reaches Marine Drive, at a point where there are hut circles, and returns to Llandudno along the road.

Eastern Environs of Llandudno

Little Orme's Head, the limestone headland at the E. end of Llandudno's bay, has even finer and steeper cliffs (400 ft in places) than Great Orme, and its summit (463 ft), reached by a path starting a short distance beyond the Craigside Hydro, commands a wide view. A walk is also possible round the foot of the headland where there are several caves. In one cave, in 1587, there was found a secret Roman Catholic printing press, possibly the first press in Wales.

For **Deganwy**, on the S. side of the peninsula, see p. 116. The castle here is said to have been a favourite seat of Maelgwn Gwynedd, said also to have died of plague in 547 in the church at *Llanrhos* (or Eglwys Rhos), a mile N. of Deganwy. Today's small church, in part 13C but much restored, contains an Early Christian inscribed stone (?6C), some fragments of old glass, and monuments of the Mostyn family. Perhaps confirming the tradition about Maelgwn, the hill above the church bears his name.—*Bodysgallen Hall* (½ m. S.E. of Llanrhos), now a hotel, also has ancient associations, the name meaning Abode of Gallen and the site thought to have been the home of a prince of that name in 446. The tower, in part 13C., may have been an outpost of the castle at ·Deganwy.—*Gloddaeth Hall* (½ m. N.E. of Llanrhos), now a school, was a seat of the Mostyns and also the last home of Archbishop Williams (d. 1650) who held Conwy for Charles I.

4   BANGOR
(Including Penrhyn Castle)

BANGOR (16,750 inhab.), the central part of which lies either side of a steep valley just S. of the Menai Strait, is visited for its cathedral and for Penrhyn Castle, 2 m. E. of the city centre. The prominent University College of North Wales gives Bangor academic importance, while facilities such as a pedestrians-only High Street nearly 1 m. long have made the city the shopping centre for a wide district.

Tourist Information. Town Hall.
Parking. Off W. side of Glanrafon, opposite cathedral. Wellfield Shopping Centre. Both these are convenient for the cathedral and museums.
Main Shopping Area. High Street. Wellfield Shopping Centre. Dean Street Market (Fri.). *Early closing*. Wednesday.
Main Post Office. Corner of Deiniol Road and Ffordd Gwynedd.
Railway Station. W. end of Deiniol Road.
Bus Station. Garth Road, near Town Clock.
Theatre. Gwynedd, Deiniol Road.
Menai Strait Ferry. Garth Jetty to Menai Bridge and Beaumaris (summer only).
History. Bangor owes its origin to St Deiniol, a nobleman contemporary of Maelgwn Gwynedd, who founded his monastic community here in 525; the word Bangor derives from the wattle fence which surrounded St Deiniol's primitive enclosure ('bangori' is still used in parts of Wales to describe the plaiting of twigs in a hedge). In 546 St Dubricius (or Dyfrig), Bishop of all Wales, divided his see into three, consecrating St Deiniol as the bishop responsible for Gwynedd (St Padarn got central Wales, and St Teilo the south). Thenceforward for nearly 13 centuries Bangor's story is that of its bishopric (see below), change only coming with the commercial activities of the early 19C. In succession then came the opening of the Penrhyn quarries, the development of a port (Penrhyn), the construction of Telford's road (now A5) in 1815-30 and of his suspension bridge (1819-26), and the arrival in 1848 of the railway, with the building of Stephenson's tubular bridge two years later. Bangor was given official municipal status in 1883, and the establishment of the University College of North Wales the same year ensured that the city would be an educational as well as a commercial centre.

The broad Deiniol Road runs roughly E.-W. along the floor of the valley, the cathedral and main town being to the S., and Upper Bangor, with the University College of North Wales, on the northern side.

SOUTH OF DEINIOL ROAD. The **Cathedral**, an unpretentious building on the lower slope of the valley, is probably the oldest in Britain in continuous use as such.

History. The history of the see is virtually blank from St Deiniol's time until 1071, when William II attempted to force on it as bishop a certain Hervé, a Breton; an unwelcome symbol of Norman power, he was in constant strife with his flock and soon departed. Between 1120-39 Bishop David, who is known to have ministered to the dying Gruffydd ap Cynan (d. 1137), built the Norman cathedral, and it would have been here that Archbishop Baldwin preached the Crusade in 1188. In 1211, and again during the wars of Edward I, the cathedral was much damaged, but rebuilding was begun before 1291 by Bishop Anian I (1267-1305), who was responsible for a central tower (burnt c. 1308), the Lady Chapel, and an enlarged S. transept. Building continued through the Dec. period until c. 1350, Bishop Anian II (1309-28) probably being responsible for the N. transept and nave.

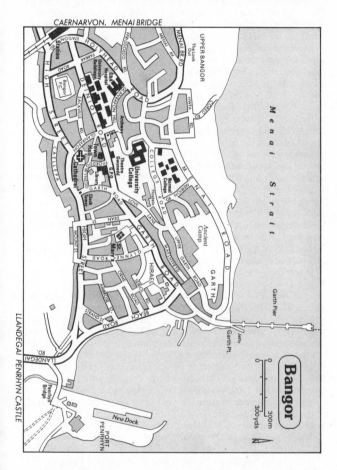

Disaster came in 1402 when the cathedral was badly damaged by the followers of Owen Glendower, the ruins lying virtually untouched for nearly a century. Bishop Deane (1494-1500) largely rebuilt the choir, including the E. window, and Bishop Skeffington (1509-34) added a nave clerestory and W. tower. During the Civil War and the two centuries that followed, the cathedral again suffered damage and neglect. A bishop during this period was Hoadly (1715-21), whose sermon on the 'Nature of the Kingdom or Church of Christ' gave rise to a pamphleteering war known as the Bangorian Controversy (1717-21). Between 1868-84 Sir Gilbert Scott carried out a drastic but successful restoration. His plans envisaged a lofty central tower and spire, but subsidence made this impracticable and in 1967-71 the tower was battlemented at its present height and given its small cap spire.—Four bishops of Bangor became archbishops of Canterbury: Henry Deane (1501), Thomas Herring (1747), Matthew Hutton (1757), and John Moore (1783). Bishop Green (1934) and Bishop William (1971) became archbishops of Wales.

Points to be noticed around the EXTERIOR are a blocked window and plain buttress (both S. wall of choir), the sole surviving visible evidence of the Norman cathedral; the inscription of 1532 over the W. doorway recording the building of the tower; the unusually thin buttresses of the N. aisle; and the late Dec. windows (?1350) of the aisles, the side walls of which survived the damage of 1402 by Owen Glendower. The transept ends were rebuilt by Scott in what is probably, from the indications afforded by fragments discovered in the 16C walls, the original design. The fine buttresses on the end of the S. transept, including the curious dwarf example in the middle, also escaped destruction in 1402. On the E. of the S. transept are traces of former chapels, probably demolished in the 15-16C and their stone used in the repair of the transept walls.

INTERIOR. On the right, on entering by the N.W. doorway, are various ancient stones, including the 14C slab of 'Eva, wife of Anwel'. The tiles on the floor are probably early 14C and were discovered under the floor of the choir during the 19C restoration. Here too are dog tongs, used to remove unruly dogs from the church; a 15 C miserere; and some 16C Flemish wooden figures. On a nearby *Nave* pier hangs the *Mostyn Christ of 1518, thought to have been concealed by the Mostyn family at the Reformation; Christ, bound and wearing a crown of thorns, is seated on a rock. All the woodwork in the nave is modern. The nave altar frontal (1975), the main motif of which is the Celtic Cross, is the design of Iris Martin and the work of Celtic Studios of Swansea. In the *South Transept* the arched tomb in the S. wall was once thought to be that of Prince Owain Gwynedd (d. 1170), originally buried before the high altar. However since the tomb is 13C, it is now thought that it may have been prepared for Bishop Anian I. As to where Owain Gwynedd lies, one account relates that, since he died under excommunication, his remains were secretly removed at the behest of Archbishop Baldwin and interred in the churchyard. Also in the S. transept are a wallpainting (1955, Brian Thomas); a memorial to Edmond Prys (1544-1623), author of Welsh metrical psalms; and a tablet to Goronwy Owen (1723-69), the poet. In the *Choir* the stonework of the large Perp. windows in the E. and S. walls dates from 1494-1500; the glass is 19C. The stalls are 1868-79 and 1908, that of the Precentor bearing the arms of Gruffydd ap Cynan, and that of the Canon in Residence those of Owain Gwynedd; the bishop's throne is 1879; the reredos of 1881 was designed by J. Oldrid Scott.

The former close, just N. of the cathedral, is now the *Bishop's Garden*, with a Biblical Garden. The S. side of the path is planted with flowers and shrubs traditionally associated with the medieval Church, while on the N. side are examples of all trees, shrubs, and plants mentioned in the Bible and able to survive the local climate. Planted chronologically according to mention, each plant is labelled (handbook from town hall). The *Town Hall*, between the garden and Deiniol Road, dates from the 16-17C with 18 and 19C additions to the N. and east. Until 1899 it was the residence of the bishops.

The **Museum of Welsh Antiquities**†, housed in the Old Canonry

(1862) in Ffordd Gwynedd in the town centre, contains primarily the collections of the University College, with also material from the former Bangor City Museum. Exhibits include prehistoric stone and bronze implements, and burial urns; Roman material; Early Christian and medieval graveslabs, and fine examples of medieval woodcarving; Welsh furniture of various periods; and Welsh costumes (mainly Victorian). There is also material on the Menai suspension and tubular bridges, including a brass model (1875) of the former. One room has been arranged as an old Welsh kitchen, and another contains relics of old Bangor.—*Oriel Bangor*† (Art Gallery), run by the University College and also in the Old Canonry, holds 12 exhibitions a year of differing content.—For the *Penmachno Stones*†, see p. 185.

To the S. of the cathedral the pedestrians-only High Street runs E.-West. To the S. of this is *Bangor Mountain*, a ridge a mile in length and 300 ft. high, covered in gorse and bracken and fringed by pine woods; the golf course is at the E. end.

NORTH OF DEINIOL ROAD. On the corner of Deiniol Road and Glanrafon Hill stands the *North Wales Heroes' Memorial Archway* (1923, D. W. Thomas), which, with a number of bursaries tenable at the University College, commemorates the men of 'Gwynedd and Powis' who fell in the First World War. *Theatre Gwynedd*, farther E., is the county of Gwynedd's centre for live artistic entertainment, as also for films.

The main buildings of the **University College of North Wales** occupy a commanding position above the valley, and are approached viâ Glanrafon and College roads, or by the footpath from the memorial archway. This older part of the College is open throughout the year (except Sun., and the weeks of Christmas and Easter) and may be visited on application to the head porter.

The College, founded in 1883, is one of the five constituent colleges of the University of Wales (established in 1893), the other four being at Aberystwyth, Cardiff, Swansea, and Lampeter. There are c. 3000 students, a teaching staff of c. 300, faculties of Arts and Science, and departments ranging from Linguistics to Physical Oceanography. The original home of the College was a building previously known as the Penrhyn Arms Hotel (now demolished) near Port Penrhyn. Here William Smith O'Brien, the Irish patriot, died in 1864.

The main buildings, completed in 1910 from the designs of H. T. Hare in a kind of Renaissance-Jacobean style, are grouped round a quadrangle, with a plain but effective tower bearing statues of St David and Owen Glendower. Among the rooms of special interest are the *Prichard Jones Hall*; the *Council Chamber*, with a few portraits; the *Library* (400,000 volumes), rich in Welsh topography, and with newspapers and pamphlets, a complete collection of early translations of the Bible into Welsh, a copy of the first Welsh dictionary (1547), and an interesting collection of ballads sold at fairs (1698-1800); and the small *Powis Hall*. In the upper corridor is a good collection of glass and china. Fine views are obtained from the terrace.—The *Science Departments* are mostly housed in a group of buildings along Deiniol Road. The *School of Electronic Engineering* is in Dean Street, and the *Marine Science Laboratories* (including the departments of Marine Biology and Physical Oceanography) are in Menai Bridge on Anglesey.

Some departments are willing (on prior arrangement) to permit visits. The Department of Zoology has its own museum.

Views of Menai Strait, the bridges, and Anglesey can be obtained from the *Look Out* (Menai Bridge Road, c. 1 m. N.W. of town hall), and from *Garth Point* at the N.E. corner of the town, also c. 1 m. from the town hall. Behind the latter is the *Ancient Camp,* natural grounds with paths and a viewpoint.

Penrhyn Castle†

Penrhyn Castle (Thomas Hopper, 1827-37), about 2 m. E. of Bangor at the junction of A5 and A55, is, outside and in, a huge example of ostentatious Victorian Neo-Norman, worth visiting both as such and for the slate craftsmanship of the interior. Additionally the castle contains a collection of dolls and an industrial railway museum.

History. The estate. dating back to the time of Llewelyn the Great, in the 17C passed into the ownership of John Williams, Archbishop of York. Later, by marriage, it came in 1765 to Richard Pennant, who developed the Penrhyn Slate Quarries above Bethesda and was in 1783 created Baron Penrhyn of Penrhyn, in the peerage of Ireland. His successor, through the female line, was George Dawkins, who took the name of Pennant and commissioned Thomas Hopper to rebuild the Neo-Gothic mansion he had inherited, the outcome being the present castle. Features of the construction are a hot air heating system and water closets. His successor, again through the female line and again taking the name of Pennant, was Gordon Douglas Pennant; he entertained Queen Victoria and the Prince Consort in 1859 and in 1866 was created Baron Penrhyn of Llandegai. In 1949, on the death of the 4th Baron, the estate passed to his niece, Lady Janet Douglas Pennant, who in 1951 conveyed the castle and immediately surrounding grounds (40 acres) through the Treasury to the National Trust.

In the *Great Hall* the grills in the floor are part of the heating system. Note also the 'Norman' octagonal centre table; the marble side tables, one with entwined dolphin supports of slate; and the Zodiac windows by Thomas Willement. The *Library* well illustrates Hopper's richness of design in the carving on the walls, the plaster decoration in the arches, and the ribbed and bossed ceiling. The billiard table is mostly of slate. In the *Drawing Room* the 'Norman' motif is represented by the huge pillars of the window surrounds and the two large candelabra. By the door to the next room survives the spiral staircase of the 15C mansion. The sombre *Ebony Room* contains ebony furniture, while the arched surrounds of the fireplace and the doorways are of plaster painted to match. It was in here that the coffin always rested before family funerals. The *Chapel* was the scene of daily compulsory services for the whole household, the family and guests occupying the balcony, and the staff, segregated by sexes, the pews. *Lady Penrhyn's Bedroom Suite* contains the *Doll Collection*, which has no connection with the castle but started with the presentation to the National Trust of a doll in Welsh costume. The dolls (about 1000) cover from the early 19C to the present day and come from many parts of the world. The room also contains toys, and three paintings by Graham Robertson.

The visitors' route next leads to the keep. The *King's Bed*, elaborately worked in brass with a crown on top, was made for the visit of the Prince and Princess of Wales in 1894. The hangings of the bed, as also the wallpaper, were designed by William Morris. The *Slate Bed* weighs nearly one ton. Here also the hangings and wallpaper are by Morris. The blue china set is Spode. The *Dressing Room*, with wallpaper by Morris, contains a magnificent wardrobe.

From the keep the route returns along the gallery overlooking the Great Hall, passes the Chapel, and ascends to the *Natural History Collection*, most of the exhibits being native to Snowdonia. Beyond is the *State Bedroom* where in 1859 Queen Victoria slept in the huge carved oak bed, designed by Hopper. The *Grand Staircase* has a plaster ceiling in the form of a fan vault with Norman motifs. The staircase, in riotously carved slate, required 10 years of work after the completion of the rest of the castle. The *Dining Room* has a fireplace, three sideboards, and curtain pole, all in polished slate. The original hand-painted decoration of the walls (c. 1838) was only revealed in 1974 after the removal of the five coats of distemper which had covered it for perhaps 70 years. The dinner service is a Minton copy of a Sèvres service made for the Empress Catharine of Russia in 1778. In the *Breakfast Room* hang paintings of all the owners of the present castle. Beyond is the *Domestic Area*. A tea room occupies the former Housekeeper's Room, and the National Trust shop is in the kitchen.

The *Industrial Railway Museum* occupies the stable yard. The museum contains models; railway equipment; tickets; several old engines, including the Fire Queen (1848) and Haydock (1879; a smart saloon coach (1896); and the original Llanfair P. G. platform sign. Also of outstanding interest are the industrial prints and a collection of examples of slate craftsmanship.

The **Grounds** contain, near the car park, a Californian Big Tree planted by Queen Victoria in 1859, and a Turkey Oak planted by the Prince of Wales in 1894. The *Walled Garden* is terraced in three areas—the upper with formal beds; the middle with trees and shrubs, where something is in flower all year; the lower a wild garden.

For *Menai Strait* and its bridges, and *Anglesey*, see Rte 12. From Bangor to *Chester*, see Rte 2; to *Capel Curig*, see Rte 10; to *Caernarvon* and *Porthmadog*, see Rte 11.

5   WHITCHURCH TO BETWS-Y-COED VIA DENBIGH

A525 to Wrexham: A541 to Denbigh: A543 to Pentrefoelas: A5 to Betws-y-Coed.   60 miles.—*10m.* **Bangor-is-Coed.**—*4m.* **Wrexham (Erddig).**—*10m.* **Mold.**—*15m.* **Denbigh.**—*14m.* **Pentrefoelas.**—*7m.* **Betws-y-Coed.**
At first rolling pastoral country; after Denbigh becoming high open moorland with wide mountain vistas.

Whitchurch (8000 inhab.), known in the 12C as Blancminster, is a Salop market town. In the *Church of St Alkmund,* rebuilt in a Grecian style in 1713, is the canopied tomb, with an effigy in full armour, of the first Earl of Shrewsbury (1388-1453), Shakespeare's Old John Talbot (Henry VI, Part I), the doughty fighter who, with his son, died in battle at Castillon near Bordeaux. His heart, discovered during the rebuilding of the church, was reburied in the S. porch. Another monument is to John Talbot (d. 1550), founder of the Grammar School. Sir Edward German (E. G. Jones; 1862-1936), the composer, was born here.

After just under *2 m*. A525 enters a tongue of Wales, since 1974 part of the district of Wrexham Maelor but historically known as Maelor Saesneg (Saxon Maelor), or the Hundred of Maelor, a detached part of Flintshire incorporated into that county under Edward I's arrangements of 1284 despite being some 8 m. away. Just beyond the border Rte 23 bears southwest.—*3 m. Hanmer* (1 m. S. of A525) is where Owen Glendower and Margaret, daughter of Sir David Hanmer, are believed to have been married in the church that preceded the present beautiful but much restored Tudor building.—*5 m.* **Bangor-is-Coed** (Enclosure in the Wood), also known as Bangor on Dee, probably occupies the site of the Roman Bovium. The picturesque 17C bridge is said to have been the work of Inigo Jones. The village was the site of the oldest monastery in Britain, founded c. 180. Here the heretic Pelagius (a Greek form of the Welsh name Morgan, meaning sea-born) is said to have lived in the 4C, though not as a monk. The monastery was destroyed in 607 by Ethelfrid of Northumbria, in the last great battle of Saxon heathendom over British Christianity, when 1200 monks were slain, Ethelfrid maintaining that by praying against him they were fighting against him. Some survivors are said to have fled to Bardsey. *Overton* (3 m. S.W.) has a 13C church with, in its churchyard, twenty-one ancient yews.

4 m. **Wrexham** (39,600 inhab.) is an important industrial centre, to the tourist best known for its *Church of St Giles*, with the grave of Elihu Yale (1648-1721), the benefactor of Yale University. EXTERIOR. The wrought-iron churchyard gates are by Robert and John Davies; erected in 1720, they replaced a wooden lychgate. The tomb of Elihu Yale is in the churchyard W. of the tower, a site chosen by himself. The last two lines of the quaint rhymed epitaph are adapted from the funeral hymn for Ajax by James Shirley (1659). The tomb was restored in 1968 by members of Yale University to mark the 250th anniversary of the benefaction. A stone on the tower replaces one removed to form part of a replica of the tower built at Yale. The richly decorated * *Tower* (136 ft), surmounted by four graceful hexagonal turrets, was begun in 1506. Some of the existing sculptures are medieval; those of St Giles, of which there are several, can be recognized by his attributes of an arrow and a deer. The N. porch was restored by graduates of Yale in 1901 on the occasion of the bicentenary of their university (tablet inside).— INTERIOR. Inside the N. porch a figure of St Giles decorates the central ceiling boss. The church was originally of the aisled chapel plan, but the E. window was soon converted into an arch (note remnants of tracery), when a short choir with a three-sided apse was added. The *Nave* has interesting roof carving. The lectern is of 1524. Near it and the pulpit are the heads of the Earl of Derby and his wife Lady Margaret Beaufort, and over the choir arch are traces of a wallpainting of the Last Judgement. In the *North Aisle* there are medieval carvings on the corbels; a monument by Louis Roubiliac to Mary Myddleton (d. 1747) of Chirk Castle; in an adjacent window the words from 'From Greenland's icy mountains', the famous hymn written in 1819 by Reginald Heber, later Bishop of Calcutta, on the occasion of a missionary service in the church held while he was staying with his father-in-law, the vicar; and, at the E. end, the War Memorial Chapel, with, appropriately, the effigy of a 14C Welsh soldier. In the *South Aisle* there is a monument to Sir Richard Lloyd (d. 1676) who defended Holt Castle for Charles I.

The *Wrexham-Maelor Library and Arts Centre*, in Rhosddu Road, receives, roughly quarterly, touring exhibitions from the Welsh Arts Council, Victoria and Albert Museum, Council of Museums in Wales etc. The *Dolls' House*† (Ruabon Road) has a collection of Georgian and Victorian dolls and toys and other small material of the same periods.

Acton Park, in the N. of the town, was the birthplace of Judge Jeffreys (1648-89). The house was demolished in 1956.

Bersham (2 m. S.W.) was the home of the Davies brothers, famous for their fine ironwork, including Wrexham's churchyard gates. A plaque at Croesfoel (½ m.S.) marks the site of the brothers' smithy. Bersham colliery has two shafts, both sunk in 1868. Over 90% of the output is taken by the steelworks at Shotton. Annual output is around 155,000 tons and some 550 men are employed.

For Wrexham to *Corwen*, viâ *Bwlchgwyn* (North Wales Geological Museum) and places connected with the Yale family, see Rte 16; to *Chester*, see Rte 16; to *Oswestry* and *Shrewsbury*, see Rte 14.

---

*Erddig†

Erddig, 1 m. S. of Wrexham and standing within grounds of nearly 2000 acres, is a late 17C mansion with 18C additions. One of the National Trust's more important properties, a feature of particular interest is the complete range of outbuildings and domestic offices, equipped as they once were and including a remarkable collection of portraits of the staff. The main rooms, although rather cramped and gloomy, nevertheless contain outstandingly good 18 C furniture. The gardens have been restored to their formal 18C plan.

History. The original house (the present central bays) was built between 1684-87 and soon turned out to be a financial disaster for the owner, Joshua Edisbury, High Sheriff of Denbighshire. Unable to meet his debts (one of those from whom he had borrowed was Elihu Yale), he fled to London before the house was even completed and died there c. 1715. The following year John Meller, a London lawyer, acquired the property. To the original house Meller added two wings between 1721-24., and it was he too who collected the fine furniture which fills Erddig today. In this he was helped by his nephew Simon Yorke, to whom the property passed in 1733, remaining by direct line in the family (all called Simon or Philip) until given to the National Trust in 1973. Care for the staff was always a family tradition, one aspect of this being staff portraits, accompanied by verses by the various Philips and Simons. The first Philip completed (1774) new domestic offices to the S. of the house. During the present century the house has suffered considerable damage from mining subsidence.

The tour starts with the OUTBUILDINGS and DOMESTIC OFFICES. The *Estate Yard* is surrounded by buildings dating mainly from the early 19C and still in use today. These include joiner's workshop, sawpit, blacksmith's workshop, and wagon shed. The dovecot, just outside the yard, is early 18C. Off the *Limeyard* are the dog yard and the sawmill, the latter today containing pictures of family and staff. In the *Outer Yard* the central enclosure was the midden where straw and dung from the stables was collected. The *Stableyard* was completed in 1774. Today it contains carriages, old cars, and bicycles. In an adjacent room is an exhibition of the restoration work undertaken by the National Trust. The *Laundry Yard* and associated buildings was completed c. 1773. Noteworthy are the stone-filled box mangle (possibly part of the original equipment) and the goffering irons used for crimping starched collars. The *Bakehouse* has scuffle ovens, from which the ashes were raked or scuffled before the dough was slid in. The *New Kitchen*, with a Venetian window, is a particularly fine room, dating from 1772 when, possibly because of the danger of fire, the decision was taken to move the kitchen out of the main house. At this time it was completely detached, and the linking passage was not built until the 19C. In the basement passage hang photographs of the staff, one being a copy of a daguerrotype of 1852. The *Servants' Hall* contains Erddig's notable *Series of 18 and 19C portraits of the staff. The subjects range from John Meller's negro coachboy (early 18C; verses added c. 1795) to portraits of 1830 of the carpenter, woodman, and gardener. The principal artist of the series was John Walters of Denbigh.

FAMILY ROOMS. The Neo-Classical *Dining Room* (1826), the design of Thomas Hopper, was formerly the state bedroom and dressing room. It is hung with family portraits, among the artists being Gainsborough and Cotes. There is also a Still Life by Frans Snyders. Until 1770 the *Saloon* was two rooms, the N. end being a smaller saloon and the S. end a withdrawing room off the state bedroom and dressing room which now form the dining room. The early 18C furniture includes walnut chairs; a Boulle dressing table (c. 1700); a plaster gilt side table; and gilt pier glasses (1723 and 1726). There is also porcelain and glass of the 16 to 18C. In the *Tapestry Room* the tapestry is early 18C Soho. The chairs, settee, and pier glass are also early 18C. In the *Chinese Room* are painted scenes, part Chinese and part English imitation, attractively illustrating ways of earning a living. The *Library* contains John Meller's legal library; also, added by 'Philip (d. 1804), antiquarian books and copies of his own work of 1799, 'The Royal tribes of Wales'. The pictures in the *Entrance Hall* include three works by Kneller, one being of Judge Jeffreys. The hall also contains a collection of 18 and 19C musical instruments. In the *Drawing Room* the furniture includes armchairs and a settee, possibly of 1770 and by John Cobb, cabinet maker to the royal family. Among the pictures is a small landscape by Jan van Goyen.

BEDROOMS. In the *Red Bedroom* the ingenious lifting device of the bed may have been designed for the easier nursing of Anne Yorke, who died of consumption in 1770. The *Gallery* contains mother-of-pearl models (1765-80) made by Elizabeth Ratcliffe, daughter of a Chester clockmaker and companion to the then Mrs Yorke. The pictures include portraits of the royal family of Bohemia. Amongst the furniture are gilt pier tables with mother-of-pearl tops by Elizabeth Ratcliffe. In the *North Landing* there is a clock, signed by John Ratcliffe, father of Elizabeth. The bed in the *State Bedroom* is of 1720. Damaged by rain, leaking in as the the result of subsidence, the bed was restored in 1968-70 by the Victoria and Albert Museum. The Chinese screen is thought to have been a gift (1682) from Elihu Yale. The *Blue Bedroom* has a bed dating from before 1726. The mezzotints are by Thomas Frye (1760-62).

Also to be seen are the *Chapel* (1721-4); the *Tribes' Room*, so called from Philip Yorke's book, now housing an exhibition of family documents; the *Butler's Pantry*, with 17 and 18C silver; and the *Family Museum*.

Wrexham is left by A541.—*5 m.* **Caergwrle** was a Roman station, occupied as an outpost of Chester by the 20th Legion. The *Castle*, on a high ridge, vulnerable on one side only and there protected by a deep ditch, probably started as a British hillfort. The present castle dates from 1282 and was given by Edward I to his queen, Eleanor. The ruins indicate a simple polygonal enclosure, with drum-towers at the angles. A fine gold-decorated bowl of c. 800 B.C., now in the National Museum of

Wales, was found near here in 1820. Remains of *Wats Dyke*, which here generally followed the 400 ft contour, can be found 1½ m. N. beyond *Hope*, between A550 and the railway.—*3 m. Leeswood*. Leeswood Hall (1½ m. N.W. of the village) has iron gates (1726) by the Davies brothers. *Tower* (1 m. N.W. of Leeswood Hall) is an early 15C battlemented house, to the S. side of which a Queen Anne mansion has been joined. Here in c. 1470 a Welsh chieftain hanged the mayor of Chester and then burnt alive 400 citizens who tried to take him.

2 m. **Mold** (8700 inhab.), the Welsh Y Wyddgrug, is the pleasant small county town of Clwyd.

History. An important battle was fought near here as long ago as c. 430 (see below). But it was some 700 years later that Mold took roots under the protection of the early Norman motte and double bailey castle, now Bailey Hill within the road fork at the upper end of High Street. This was probably erected by Robert de Montalt (Mont haut), the town's name almost certainly being a corruption of this. In 1147 the castle was taken by Owain Gwynedd. In more modern history Mold has become known as the birthplace (1836) of Daniel Owen, the novelist (statue and museum).

The large *Church*, mainly late 15C., has a tower of 1773. The apsidal choir was added in 1856. Of interest inside are the decorated spandrels of the nave arcades, the carved capitals, and the friezes of animals. There is some good stained glass (15 and 16C): the Elizabethan window (N. aisle) illustrates the Legs of Man and the Eagle and Child of the Stanleys, once lords of Man. The adjacent window commemorates Richard Wilson (1714-82), the landscape painter, who died near Mold and is buried in the churchyard near the N. door. In Earl Road, the *Daniel Owen Centre*† contains a small museum with original manuscripts and personal items, including tools Owen used in his trade as a tailor.

Maes Garmon (Field of Germanus; 1 m. N.W. of Mold on the Gwernaffield road) is traditionally the site of the 'Alleluia Victory' of 430, when the native Christians under Germanus, Bishop of Auxerre, who had been sent to Britain to combat the Pelagian heresy, decisively defeated the heathen Picts and Scots. Terror-stricken by the simultaneous shout by the Christians, the pagans fled without striking a blow. The site is marked by an obelisk (1736) beside and above the road.
    FROM MOLD TO RUTHIN (A494. 11 m.; a pleasant run over the Clwydian Hills). Beyond *Gwern-y-Mynydd* the road drops into the upper valley of the Alyn (country park) at the *Three Loggerheads Inn*, which has a sign, showing two loggerheads, painted by Richard Wilson, who spent his last days at nearby Plas Colomendy, now a school. At *Tafarn-y-Gelyn* (4 m. from Mold) the old road to Ruthin, now a track, diverges and leads over the *Bwlch Pen-Barras* (1100 ft; 2 m.), whence the summit of *Moel Fammau* (1820 ft), a designated country park, is easily reached in 1½ m. On the top is the stump of a tower erected in 1820 in honour of George III's jubilee, blown down in 1862, and restored in 1970. The view can include Snowdonia, Cader Idris, Cumberland, and the Isle of Man. A494 continues to *Llanferres*, just beyond which B5430 leads S.E. to (2 m.) *Llanarmon*, where the church (of St Germanus) has two unequal naves divided by an 18C wooden arcade. Inside are the recumbent effigies of Gruffydd ap Llewelyn ap Ynyr (late 13C and very well preserved) and of a vested priest; the monument of Evan Lloyd (d. 1639); and a medieval bronze chandelier, with a small statue of the Virgin.—The *Moel Fammau Forest Trail*, starting from a F.C. picnic site just W. of the junction with B5430, makes a round of 3½ m which includes a burial mound and the summit of Moel Fammau.

A541 out of Mold in *2 m.* reaches *Rhyd-y-Mwyn*, where the Leet Nature Trail (3¾ m.), mainly with limestone gorge features, leads S.W. up the Leet. *Cilcain* (2 m. S.W.) has a 14C church (restored 1888) with two unequal naves, the N. and smaller of which serves as vestry. The chief feature of the church is the hammer-beam *Roof (restored), reputed to have come from the refectory of Basingwerk Abbey; the figures merit study. The 15C glass in the E. window may also have come from Basingwerk. On the floor at the W. end of the S. nave is a Norman font with interlaced ornamentation on the exterior and a conical interior.—*4 m.* *Nannerch* is just beyond the saddle connecting Halkin Mountain with the Clwydian Hills.—*3 m.* **Caerwys,** N. of the road, was, as its name suggests, a Roman station. Later it received a charter from Henry III. But the village is best known for its long association with the eisteddfod, the first of which is said to have been called here in 1100 by Gruffydd ap Cynan. There was another meeting in 1523, and in 1568 Queen Elizabeth granted permission for the bards and minstrels of Wales to be called together 'in a competitive festival'. This last occasion is commemorated by a window in the church.—*3 m.* *Bodfari,* just beyond Offa's Dyke, is where the road leaves the hills for the Vale of Clwyd. *Tremeirchion* (2 m. N.) has a 13C church. Inside is a good 14C tomb-niche with the effigy of a vested priest. In the chancel (N.) a tablet commemorates Hester Lynch Piozzi (1741-1821), Dr Johnson's Mrs Thrale, who lies here; she lived at Brynbella, a mansion just to the south. Just N. (1 m.) of Tremeirchion is *St Beuno's College* (1848), a Jesuit seminary, with in the grounds a chapel (1866) perched on a crag.—*3 m.* **Denbigh,** see p. 137.

Beyond Denbigh A543 ascends steadily through pleasant, wooded country to reach high open moor.—*5 m.* *Bylchau,*—*2 m.* *Llyn Bran* is a small lake S. of the road. Here a road branches S.E., in just over 1 m. reaching *Llyn Brenig, a reservoir c. 2½ m. long by 1 m. broad, opened in 1976 by the Prince of Wales; in conjunction with Lake Bala and Llyn Celyn, Brenig, dammed at its S. end, regulates the flow of the river Dee. More important for the visitor, the reservoir, with its surrounds of pasture, forest, and moor, forms an accessible yet unspoilt large natural environment, with a nature reserve, bird sanctuary, picnic areas, fishing and sailing facilities, and walks which include nature and archaeological trails.

At the S.W. corner of the reservoir, near the dam, there is an **Information Centre**†, telling the story of Brenig and describing its varied modern uses.—The **Nature Reserve,** with a bird sanctuary, is an area of moor and marsh of notable botanical interest around the reservoir's northern finger. Public access, with car parking, has been arranged to parts of the reserve.—To the E. of the northern finger there are two **Archaeological Trails** with a number of sites which have been restored by the Welsh Water Authority (leaflet from Information Centre); the starting point and car park are reached by a road off B4501. The short trail is some 600 yards long; the long trail, an extension, covers about 2 m. From the car park the trail, heading S., passes *Boncyn Arian,* a Bronze Age burial mound which contained first a central grave, and later six cremation burials. From this point three more mounds may be seen across the water. Near Boncyn Arian a stone marks the site of a Middle Stone Age camp (c. 5700 B.C.), possibly used by the first men to enter the valley after the ice retreated. Immediately S. there is a Bronze Age ring cairn, initially apparently a ritual monument and only later used for cremation burials. The remains of three individuals were found here, together with minor grave goods. A curious feature is the small semicircular cairn within the ring (N.W. corner). The trail leads N.E. to *Hafotai* (summer houses), the remains of a 16C settlement used when sheep and cattle were brought to graze on the moor. A circle of post-holes found near one of the huts may indicate prehistoric occupation. From here the short trail returns to the car park, while the long trail runs S. along the slope of the hill, in about 900 yards reaching a cairn known as the *Platform Cairn,* interesting because, from the evidence of charcoal and sherds found at the S.W. corner, the cairn seems to have been built on top of an earlier hut site. The original cairn was a ring with an open centre and contained two cremated burials, one (an adult and child) being within the S. arc of the outer ring, and the other within the inner ring. Later the centre was filled in to form a low platform, and later again a small semicircular cairn was added to the external outer ring (N.E. corner). Today's reconstruction shows the original open centre. Below the platform cairn is a site known as *Hen Ddinbych*, thought to be a medieval farm, and 400 yards E. of this is *Kerb Cairn*, so called from its distinctive kerb stones. The cairn covered a cremation burial, and wooden posts mark post-holes which suggest that earlier this may have been a hut site. *Maen Cleddau*, 200 yards S.W., is a glacial erratic. The name (Sword Stone) stems from a legend that a giant sliced off a piece. The trail returns past Hen Ddinbych, bearing left to pass another kerb cairn, covering a cremation burial, and a relatively modern square enclosure, to reach *Hafotty Sion Llwyd*, a house (rebuilt 1881) used by shepherds. Thence the trail returns to the car park.

   Alwen Reservoir, 1 m. S.W. of Llyn Brenig, was built at the beginning of the century as a water supply for Birkenhead. Some 3 m. long and attractively situated, the reservoir offers car parking, picnic site, and walks.

Beyond the little Llyn Bran, A543 passes the *Sportsman's Arms*, claiming to be the highest inn in Wales, and reaches summit level (1523 ft) on the desolate *Mynydd Hiraethog*, with a fine mountain vista. Soon the little Alwen stream is crossed, coming from Llyn Alwen (1251 ft; 1 m. W.) and descending in ½ m. to *Alwen Reservoir* (see above).—*7 m.* (from Llyn Bran) *Pentrefoelas*, and thence (*7 m.*) **Betws-y-Coed**, see Rte 15.

6 RHYL TO CORWEN

The Vale of Clwyd

A525 to Ruthin: A494 to Corwen. 30 miles.—*2 m.* **Rhuddlan.**—*3 m.* **St Asaph.**— *6 m.* **Denbigh.**—*7 m.* **Ruthin.**—*12 m.* **Corwen.**

This Route ascends the pleasant **Vale of Clwyd**, over 20 m. in length and narrowing gradually from a width of 8 m. at its mouth to 4 m. at Denbigh. The river is insignificant compared to the width of its valley. On the W. the hills rise to the bleak, high moorland of *Mynydd Hiraethog*, crossed by the road from Denbigh S.W. to Betws-y-Coed (Rte 5). Along the E. runs the more definite line of the generally fertile *Clwydian Hills*, ending in the S. at the mass of Llantysilio and Eglwyseg mountains overlooking Llangollen and the valley of the Dee. The hills are divided into short isolated ridges and rounded summits by a series of passes, possibly ancient breaches made by the sea. The highest point is *Moel Fammau* (1820 ft; see p. 135). From Roman times the hills were a line of British resistance, and earthwork traces will be found on the following hills: *Moel Hiraddug* (867 ft), just S. of Dyserth; *Moel-y-Gaer* (600 ft), N. of Bodfari; *Pen-y-Cloddiau* (1442 ft), S.E. of Bodfari, the largest of the hillforts; *Moel Arthur* (1494 ft), a designated country park 1½ m. S.E. of Pen-y-Cloddiau; a second *Moel-y-Gaer* (1092 ft) and *Moel Fenlli* (1676 ft), respectively roughly N.E. and E. of Ruthin.

For **Rhyl**, see Rte 2A. For (*2 m.*) **Rhuddlan** and (*3 m.* farther) **St Asaph**, see Rte 2B.

The main Route follows A525. An alternative is to take B5381 westwards out of St Asaph, almost immediately branching S.W. on a minor road which in 3½ m. reaches *Cefn Caves* (summer only), of little merit as caves but interesting for the human and animal bones (bison, bear etc.) found here. The caves are only one of a series of prehistoric settlements found on this ridge. Others are at *Bontnewydd* ¾ m. higher up the river, where implements of the Mousterian (mid Palaeolithic) period have been discovered, and *Plas Heaton* across the river.

2 m. **Llanerch** where the manor house has a large pleasure park with deer.

4 m. **DENBIGH** (8000 inhab.) is an old borough on the brow of a hill overlooking the Vale of Clwyd from the west. Distinguished natives are

H. M. Stanley, born here as John Rowlands in 1841; Humphrey Lloyd (d. 1568), antiquary and historian; Sir Hugh Myddelton (d. 1631), the engineer, thought to have been born at Gwenynog (see below), and brought up, with his brother Thomas, later Lord Mayor of London, at Galch Hill, a short way S.W. of the castle: and Thomas Gee (b. 1815), printer, publisher, Nonconformist preacher, and leader of Welsh political thought. The town is mainly visited for its **Castle**†.

History. The first castle (on an unidentified site) was that of Dafydd, brother of Llewelyn the Last. Denbigh was a centre of resistance to Edward I, who, after his victory, entrusted the occupation of the district to Henry de Lacy, Earl of Lincoln, who started to build the present castle in 1282. In 1294 it was taken and briefly held by the Welsh. De Lacy died in 1311 and the work was finished in 1322 by Thomas, Earl of Lancaster, the castle being modelled to some extent on the fortresses of Edward I, with the outer wall enclosing both castle and town. In 1399 the castle became the headquarters of Henry Percy (Hotspur). The town was burnt in 1402 by Owen Glendower and again in 1468 by Jasper Tudor, after which the rebuilding was outside the walls. Queen Elizabeth gave the castle to Dudley, Earl of Leicester, who entertained his sovereign here in sumptuous fashion. In 1645 Charles I took refuge here after his defeat at Rowton Moor, and, after a siege of nearly 11 months, Denbigh was one of the last fortresses to surrender to the Parliamentarians, by whom it was slighted.

The plan of the castle is a single ward in the shape of an irregular pentagon. Though much ruined it still has its large and beautiful *Gatehouse* on the N.E., the archway spanning the entrance passage bearing a mutilated statue, probably Edward I but possibly Henry de Lacy. The defensive system is ingenious; a passage between two octagonal towers leads to a large central octagonal chamber, supported at the back by a somewhat smaller octagon, and the exit to the ward involves a turn to the right. Another interesting defensive feature is the *Postern* (rebuilt after 1294) on the S. side of the ward; it was defended by three rectangular turns, two drawbridges, and an outer barbican, of which little survives. The postern tower, and the three towers to the W., originally formed part of the town walls, a section of which still extends E. from the postern. To the W. are the remains of the *Mantlet*, an additional defence work on the S. and W. sides. Within the ward the buildings are little more than foundations. Tradition has that the eldest son of De Lacy was drowned in the well.—The small castle *Museum* includes a model of the nearby birthplace (now demolished) of H. M. Stanley.

To the N. of the castle entrance stands the tower of *St Hilary's Church* (1334), the 'chapel within the walls'; the rest of the church was demolished in 1923. Just N.E. of this, in the grounds of Castle House and visible over a wall, are the outer walls of *Leicester's Church*, a large building begun by the Earl of Leicester in 1579, and perhaps intended to supersede St Asaph, but never completed. Just N. again, a door admits to the E. portion of the *Town Walls*†, begun before the castle after the capture from the Welsh of Denbigh in 1282, and greatly strengthened after the incident of 1294.

Environs of Denbigh. At the N. exit from the town are the remains of *Denbigh Friary*, a Carmelite house founded in 1284 by Sir John Salusbury, a crusader, buried here in 1289. The friary was restored in 1954, the chief surviving remnant of the old friary being the somewhat later chapel.

The church of *Eglwys Wen* (or Whitchurch), rather over 1 m. E. of Denbigh, dates from the 15-16C and is of the typical local double-nave type. In the S. choir is the alabaster Renaissance altar-tomb of Sir John Salusbury (d. 1578), with recumbent figures of Sir John and his wife: and in the N. choir a brass monument commemorates Richard Myddelton (d. 1575), father of Sir Hugh. There are wall memorials to Humphrey Lloyd, and to Thomas Edwards ('Twm o'r Nant', d. 1810), bard and author of Welsh interludes, popular at fairs and on holiday occasions until the Methodist revival in the 19C; Edwards is buried in the churchyard.

A pleasant walk (c. 2 m.) may be made to the S.W. of Denbigh, generally skirting *Gwenynog Park*. B4501 is taken out of the town and, just before reaching a bridge over the Ystrad, a footpath follows the stream through woods to the ruin of *Dr Johnson's Cottage*, where the doctor is said to have stayed in 1774; the lines over the door are attributed to Johnson. Just beyond is *Johnson's Monument*, with a Grecian urn placed here by Mr Myddelton of Gwenynog. The return to Denbigh may be made N.E. through the park, then either E. past *Galch Hill* or W. joining A543.

Henllan (2 m. N.W.), reached by B5382, the old coach mail route from Chester to Conwy, has a church with a detached tower. *Plas Clough*, 1 m. E. of Henllan, recalls Sir Richard Clough, associated with Sir Thomas Gresham in founding London's Royal Exchange.

For Denbigh N.E. to *Mold* and S.W. to *Pentrefoelas*, see Rte 5.

3 m. **Llanrhaeadr**, where the *Church of St Dyfnog* is successor to one founded here in the 6C by the saint beside a holy well. The present church has a 13C tower, but otherwise is mainly 15C (restored 1880). Grooves on the stones of the entrance archway are said to be due to arrow sharpening, recalling the days when the churchyard was used for archery practice. The treasure of the church interior is the *Jesse Window (1533), a remarkable survival since it was removed during the Civil War and buried until the Restoration. The W. window (15C) is similarly interesting, the glass having been found c. 1845 in a shattered heap in a cottage and then reassembled. Also noteworthy in the church are the hammer-beam roofs, and the ancient oak chest of two compartments (one for papers, the other for plate) and an attached alms box; keys to the three locks were held each by the vicar and two churchwardens.

There are two other interesting churches close to Llanrhaeadr, both reached by the small road leading E. from *Pentre* just to the south. At *Llandyrnog* (2 m. N.E. of Pentre) the rebuilt church has considerable remains of 15C glass, representing a Crucifixion and several saints. At *Llanynys* (2 m. S. of Llandyrnog) the 16C church has good hammer-beam roofs and quaint 18C wooden chandeliers.

4 m. **Ruthin** (4800 inhab.), on a hill overlooking the Clwyd, was originally called Rhudd-din, meaning Red Fortress, and the town's early history is that of its castle. Since the 11C the curfew has been rung here every night. In St Peter's Square there are two particularly attractive old houses. The former *Court House* (S.), now a bank, dates from 1401 and conveniently served both as law court and prison, even having the gallows attached to the building; a short length of the beam still projects from below the eaves. On the W. side stands *Exmewe Hall*, also now a bank, with in front Maen Huail, a stone on which King Arthur is said to have beheaded Huail, a rival in a love affair. The house was built c. 1500 by Thomas Exmewe, later Lord Mayor of London, and at one time was the home of Gabriel Goodman (see below). At the N.E. corner of the square is the *Church of St Peter*. Made collegiate in 1310 by Lord Grey of Ruthin, the church still styles its incumbent as Warden. The building is generally 14C; the choir was destroyed in 1663, and the spire (180 ft) was put up in 1859. The churchyard gates are by the Davies brothers. The most striking feature of the interior is the magnificent oak *Roof of the N. aisle (the original nave), with 500 elaborately carved panels, each one different, presented by Henry VII to all the men of Wales who had helped him mount the English throne. The church contains a bust (N. wall of choir) of Gabriel Goodman (d. 1601), a benefactor of the town, Dean of Westminster, and one of the translators of the New Testament. In the N. aisle there are also Goodman family brasses. The *Cloisters*, N. of the church, formed part of the original college; dating in origin from the 13-14C, they are now the residence of the Warden. The *Old Grammar School* (now a community centre), N. of the cloisters, and *Christ's Hospital Almshouses*, to the E., were founded by Dean Goodman; both are much restored. In Castle Street *Nantclwyd House*, in part 14C, has a fine half-timbered front, only revealed in 1928.

A hotel has been grafted on to the remains of the *Castle* (adm. only for guests), and medieval banquets are now held in the reconstructed hall.

History. The first castle was probably early Norman, perhaps built by Hugh Lupus soon after the Conquest. In 1277, under the Treaty of Conwy, Edward I granted the site to Dafydd, brother of Llewelyn the Last. Some building would have been carried out by Dafydd, but when in 1282 he supported his brother's uprising Ruthin was taken for Edward I by Reginald de Grey, who between 1282 and c. 1296 built the the rectangular fortress which survives as today's ruin. In 1400 the then Lord Grey seized some Glendower land, an act which sparked Owen Glendower's revolt, one of the first incidents of which was Glendower's unsuccessful attack on Ruthin. In the Civil War the castle was garrisoned for Charles I, but taken by General Mytton and dismantled in 1647.

Llanrhydd (1 m. S.E.) was the home of Stanley Weyman (1855-1928), the novelist, who died here. The church has a 15C rood screen and a 17C W. gallery.

RUTHIN TO CERRIGYDRUDION (B5105, 13 m.). The road runs through the southern part of **Clocaenog Forest**, a Forestry Commission district of over 15,000 acres, reaching N.W. towards Llyn Brenig. On the E. side of the forest there are recognized walks starting from *Clocaenog* (3 m. walk) and *Gyffylliog* (walks of 4 m. and 8 m.). Near Clocaenog once stood the Similinus Stone, now in the National Museum, a memorial (c. 450-600) inscribed 'Similini Tovisoci' and probably commemorating one of the many princes who gained local power after the departure of the Romans. From near *Pont Petryal* (7 m. from Ruthin) there are several forest walks starting from the F.C. picnic site, with an information board.

For Ruthin to *Mold*, see Rte 5.

From Ruthin A494 leads S., in 2 m. passing between (E.) *Llanfair-Dyffryn-Clwyd*, with a 15C church containing a 17C Communion table and a mosaic window of 15C glass, and (W.) *Efenechdyd*, where the small church has an unusual wooden tub-font, dating from early Norman and possibly even Saxon times.—*7 m.* (from Ruthin) *Derwen* is 1 m. N. of the main road. The 13C church contains a 15C rood screen and loft, and in the churchyard there is a good Celtic cross. The road now leaves the Clwyd, bearing S. through *Gwyddelwern*. Beyond, on the W. of the road just before the junction with A5, are the grounds of *Rug*, once a home of Owen Glendower and later the seat of the Vaughan family. The ancient but much restored chapel, seen from the road, was erected by William Salesbury in 1634; it has 17C woodwork and wallpainting (apply Estate Office, near road junction).—*5 m.* **Corwen**, see p. 184.

7   CONWY TO BETWS-Y-COED AND FFESTINIOG

As far as Betws-y-Coed this Route follows the Vale of Conwy, a fertile valley with wood and moor rising on both sides. The valley generally marks the E. boundary of Snowdonia National Park. There is a choice of roads, along the E. bank (Rte 7A) or along the W. bank (Rte 7B). Distances are 18 (E.) or 14 (W.) miles, and scenically there is little difference. The W. bank road passes more places of interest and offers access to the high moor between the Conwy and the coast (for walks, see Rte 2C). On the E. bank Bodnant Garden and Llanrwst, the two principal places, are both only a short way across bridges. The total distance from Conwy to Ffestiniog is c. 29 miles.

A   East Bank of the Conwy

A55 to Llandudno Junction: A470 to Betws-y-Coed. 18 miles.—*1 m. Llandudno Junction.*—*4 m.* **Bodnant Garden.**—*7 m.* **Llanrwst.**—*6 m.* **Betws-y-Coed.**

From **Conwy** (see Rte 2B) the estuary is crossed to *Llandudno Junction,* just beyond which A470 bears south.—*5 m.* ***Bodnant Garden**†, the garden of Bodnant Hall (c. 1790; enlarged later), was laid out in 1875 by Henry Pochin (a Lancashire industrialist with a passion for trees) and later extended by his daughter (who married the first Lord Aberconwy) and grandson, the 2nd Lord Aberconwy, who gave the greater part to the National Trust in 1949. Later the Trust acquired further land by purchase, and by gift from the 3rd Lord Aberconwy. Covering some 70 acres, and enjoying fine views of Snowdonia, the garden, with both formal and informal areas, is among the finest in Britain.

Less than 1 m. S., *Tal-y-Cafn Bridge* crosses the river for *Caerhun* (see West Bank).—*4 m.* (from Bodnant) *Cadair Ifan Goch* (672 ft), approached by a road running E. from Maenan Abbey Hotel and a footpath, is a National Trust property commanding a wide view. The name means Seat of Red Ifan, a giant who stood with one foot here and the other on Pen-y-Gaer the other side of the river. The name Maenan Abbey recalls the site to which the Cistercian monks of Conwy were moved by Edward I in 1283, and where they remained until the Dissolution.

3 m. **Llanrwst** (2700 inhab.) is a market and general centre serving a wide district.

History. The town's name derives from St Grwst (Restitutus), a 6C missionary to whom the church has long been dedicated. The settlement was destroyed in a battle of 954, when the sons of Hywel Dda invaded Gwynedd and here fought and lost to the princes of the north; again during Owen Glendower's revolt, after which the place was virtually abandoned for several decades; and yet again during the Wars of the Roses, when there was continual fighting between the Lancastrians of the Conwy valley and the Yorkists of Clwyd. With more settled times Llanrwst became modestly properous, its story during the 16 and 17C being associated with the Wynne family of Gwydir Castle across the river. By the mid 19C the town had almost twice today's population, its main activities being wool, malting, tanning, and the manufacture of harps. William Salesbury, who in 1567 first translated the New Testament into Welsh, lived here.

From the town square a short narrow road leads past *Jesus Hospital Almshouses,* founded in 1610 by Sir John Wynne 'for 11 old men and an old woman for their bedmaker', to the *Church of St Grwst,* dating from 1470 (tower and N. aisle 19C) and successor to a thatched building of 1170 destroyed in the fighting of 1468. The fine rood screen and loft came from Maenan Abbey. Adjoining the church is the **Gwydir Chapel,* built in 1633 (restored 1965) by Sir Richard Wynne (who was treasurer to Henrietta Maria, wife of Charles I), it is said to a design by Inigo Jones. The elaborate roof, the panelling and screens, and the various Wynne monuments are noteworthy, these last including several remarkable 17C brasses. The huge stone coffin is said to be that of Llewelyn the Great (d. 1240), whose remains the monks brought with them from Conwy to Maenan, the coffin coming here at the Dissolution. Beside this is the recumbent effigy of Howel Coetmor, an early owner of Gwydir Castle, who fought at Poitiers in 1356 and was killed in Flanders in 1388. In the churchyard a stone in the wall (r. on entering), bearing the Lamb and Flag, is said to have come from Yspytty Ifan.—The graceful, though for traffic inconvenient, *Old Bridge* was built in 1636 by Inigo Jones and modified in 1703 when a part was carried away; traditionally it could formerly be shaken by a person bumping his back against the parapet of the centre arch. At the bridge's W. end is *Tu Hwnt i'r Bont* (The House over the Bridge), a 15C stone building once used as a courthouse but later divided into two cottages. Owned by the National Trust, the house is now let as a café; within can be seen Welsh furniture and bygones. The *Gorsedd Stones* in the recreation ground opposite commemorate the National Eisteddfod held in Llanrwst in 1951. On the E. bank, just upstream of the bridge, is the *Snowdonia National Park Information Centre;* the exhibits include models of Capel Garmon burial chamber and of Roman Kanovium. A short way N.E. of here, off School Bank Road, is *Encounter Museum of Wildlife†.*

B5427/5113, with extensive views, leads S.E. to *Pentrefoelas* (8 m.) on Rte 15.

Betws-y-Coed is reached either by A470 in *6 m.,* with, in 1½ m., a small road ascending S. to *Capel Garmon Burial Chamber* (p. 185); or in *4 m.* by crossing the river to join the W. bank road at Gwydir Castle.

B   West Bank of the Conwy

B5106. 14 miles.—*4 m.* **Tyn-y-Groes.**—*1 m.* **Caerhun Church.**—*4 m.* **Trefriw.**—*2 m.* **Gwydir Castle.**—*3 m.* **Betws-y-Coed.**

Conwy (see Rte 2B.) is left through *Gyffin* (p. 119)—*4 m.* **Tyn-y-Groes.** To the E. is *Tal-y-Cafn Bridge,* for Bodnant Garden. To the W. at *Ro-wen, Gilfach†* is a garden of botanical interest. From Ro-wen walkers can follow the Roman road and other paths across high moor to the coast (see Rte 2C.)—*1 m.* **Caerhun Church,** reached by a lane towards the river, dates from the 13-14C, the nave N. and S. walls being the oldest part. The churchyard occupies the site of Roman *Kanovium,* a fort on the road between Deva (Chester) and Segontium (Caernarvon). Excavation has shown that the fort was abandoned about the middle of the 2C, but reoccupied in the 4C. The Welsh name derives from Rhun, a warrior son of Maelgwn Gwynedd. Virtually nothing visible now remains, but the clump of trees some 50 yards N.E. below the churchyard wall marks the site of the baths. Finds from here can be seen at Rapallo House, Llandudno, and there is a model at the Snowdonia National Park Information Centre at Llanrwst. —*1 m. Tal-y-Bont*, 1 m. N.W. of which *Pen-y-Gaer* (1225 ft) is a hillfort associated in legend with Cadair Ifan Goch on the E. bank. The fort comprises an internal area of nearly five acres, with hut circles, and on the vulnerable S. and W. slopes there was a 14 ft thick rubble rampart, below this being four ditches and earthworks. Defence was also strengthened by pointed stones set in the ground. From Tal-y-Bont a lane and path lead S.W. (4 m.) to the reservoir of *Llyn Eigiau* (1219 ft).—*2 m. Trefriw Wells†* is a 19C pumproom. The chalybeate water here was first found by the Romans in a cave. A bath-house was built in 1745, and the pumproom, built as a commercial concern in 1873, functioned as such until 1952. The present owner has restored the property, and visitors can now see the Roman cave, with some paving, and the bath-house, and also try the water.— *1 m.* **Trefriw** is a small town associated with Llewelyn the Great, who had a house here and who is also said to have built a church here to please his wife who refused to climb to the church at Llanrhychwyn (see below). Today's church has a medieval timbered roof and an elaborate pulpit of 1633. Trefriw's chief attraction is its wool mill (with shop), where visitors are welcome. The mill dates from c. 1830, and until 1900, when electricity was installed, used water wheels driven by the Crafnant river

In addition to Llyn Eigiau, mentioned above, there are other reservoirs in the wild country to the W. of Trefriw. *Llyn Cowlyd*, the largest, is reached by a path which crosses the bleak ridge of *Cefn Cyfarwydd* (1407 ft); it supplies Colwyn Bay and a power station at Dolgarrog, and is linked by an open channel with Llugwy Reservoir to the S. and by tunnel with Eigiau. The bursting of a dam below Cowlyd in 1925 caused a disastrous flood.—*Llyn Crafnant* (603 ft; ¾ m. long) is reservoir for Trefriw, whence it may be reached by a narrow lane.—*Llyn Geirionnydd* (616 ft; ¾ m. long) is the closest and most accessible. It can be reached by roads from Trefriw, Llanrwst, or from the Betws-y-Coed to Capel Curig road a short way W. of Swallow Falls. All these roads are narrow and steep, especially that from Trefriw which is a lane not suitable for larger cars. This last approach, however, passes the remote little mountain church of *Llanrhychwyn*, said to have been the place of worship of Llewelyn the Great, at least until, at his wife's insistence, he built a more accessible church at Trefriw. The quaint and simple church has a double nave (13-16C), a 12C font, and fragments of medieval glass. The reservoir, on the N.W. corner of Gwydir Forest (F.C.), has a picnic site from which starts a ¾ m. long waymarked trail. The trail passes lead mine workings (1840-1914), the levels of which are dangerous and should not be entered, the ruin of the mine explosives store, and the old tramway. At the N. end of the lake there is a monument to Taliesin, the 6C bard, who however had no known association with this district (see also p. 216).

2 m. **Gwydir Castle†** is a 16 and 19C mansion built around a 14C hall. There was already a fortification here in the 7C, and in the early 14C Howel Coetmor, whose effigy can be seen at Llanrwst, built a tower. Later the property was acquired by Maredudd ap Ievan of Dolwyddelan (d. 1525), who built the hall. John Wynne (d. 1559), one of Maredudd's 26 children, enlarged the house which remained in the family until 1674; the family had a close association with Charles I and his queen, Henrietta Maria. After various owners and several fires, the house was bought in 1944 by the late Arthur Clegg, who, with his son, the present owner, restored and furnished Gwydir. The furniture includes a magnificent bed of 1570, with carved panels representing passages from the Bible, and ornate chairs used at the wedding of Charles I. Some of the roof timbers were part of the monastery at Conwy, being later used in the construction of Maenan, and finally incorporated in Gwydir after the Dissolution. The gardens include cedars planted to commemorate the wedding of Charles I, an arch marking the end of the Wars of the Roses, and a yew over 700 years old. There are over 50 peacocks, including some of the rare white type.

Gwydir Uchaf Chapel and Gwydir Forest Exhibition are adjacent to one another W. of the road and a few yards S. of Gwydir Castle.— *Gwydir Uchaf Chapel*†, not to be confused with Gwydir Chapel in Llanrwst, was built by Sir Richard Wynne in 1673, primarily as the chapel of Gwydir Uchaf House, now the Forestry Commission offices and exhibition. The chapel retains many of its contemporary fittings, but the outstanding feature is the *Painted Ceiling, one of the most remarkable examples in Britain of this class of 17C art. Among the themes portrayed are the Creation, the Trinity, and The Day of Judgement.—The Forestry Commission offices, with the *Gwydir Forest Exhibition*†, occupy the much altered 17C Gwydir Uchaf House, which the family generally seem to have preferred to the larger castle below. Gwydir Forest, on the W. side of the Conwy valley, covers a forest and agricultural area of over 20,000 acres extending from roughly Llyn Geirionnydd in the N., across A5 and A470, to the Machno valley in the south. A waymarked trail (Lady Mary's walk, 1 m.) makes a round from the exhibition, and another trail (Drws Gwyn, 3 m.; see p. 145) runs to Betws-y-Coed. For other walks, see under Betws-y-Coed.—*3 m.* **Betws-y-Coed.**

C   Betws-y-Coed to Ffestiniog

A470. 13 miles.—*6 m.* **Dolwyddelan Castle.**—*4 m.* **Blaenau Ffestiniog.**—*3 m.* **Ffestiniog.**

Betws-y-Coed (800 inhab., but many more in summer) is a sprawling overgrown village, mainly on the Llugwy just above its confluence with the Conwy, and 1½ m. below the meeting of the Conwy and Lledr. With these three valleys of glen and river scenery, all part of Snowdonia National Park and of beautiful Gwydir Forest, and situated on the main A5 approach to Snowdonia proper, Betws-y-Coed is a busy holiday centre, liable to be overcrowded and a traffic bottleneck in summer. *Tourist Information* is at the Waterloo Complex (Motel etc.) at the S. edge of the town near *Waterloo Bridge* (Telford, 1815), a graceful iron bridge over the Conwy. At the station, N. of the complex and between A5 and the Conwy, is the *Conwy Valley Railway Museum*†. Just E. of the station the *Old Church*, the Bede or Prayer House, gives Betws-y-Coed its name (Prayer House in the Forest). In use from the 14C or earlier until the construction of the town's new church in the 19C, the old church has a 14C nave and choir and a 19C single transept. The font is 12C, there are some remains of 15 or 16C glass, and the pulpit is made up of 15-17C fragments. An effigy in unusual studded armour is that of Dafydd Goch (c. 1380), grandson of the Prince Dafydd who was executed by Edward I in 1283; his home was Fedw Deg, on the hill within the junction of the Conwy and Lledr. In the N. part of the town the bridge across the Llugwy, *Pont-y-Pair* (Bridge of the Cauldron), may date from 1470.

Walks near Betws-y-Coed. Several walks have been waymarked (yellow, with numbers) by the Forestry Commission. These are outlined below, but detailed descriptions, with plans and notes about the various trees, will be found in the Commission's booklet 'Walks in Gwydir Forest'. The warning is given that there are dangerous disused mineshafts (lead mines) close to some of the walks. Some walks are close to others with which they may be combined.

Forest Trail (3 m.). This walk is not included in the F.C. booklet but is the subject of a separate guide. The walk, above the N. bank of the Llugwy, is between Ty Hyll (Ugly House), on A5 2 m. W. of Betws-y-Coed, and Miners' Bridge (½ m. above the town), a picturesque footbridge, used by generations of miners, 50 yards above a ford where the Roman Sarn Helen crossed the river. Six stages illustrate reafforestation.

1. *Church Walk* (¾ m.). From St Mary's Church on A5 opposite the station to A5 N. of Pont-y-Pair. Mixed woodland.—2. *Cyrau* (2 m.) Starts and finishes at Pont-y-Pair (N.) car park. The walk is a climb through open woodland below the Cyrau rocks to c. 650 ft. Views across Conwy valley.—3. *Llugwy Gorge* (c. 4½ m. return). From Pont-y-Pair (N.) car park. The walk follows the road up the N. bank of the river for ¾ m., then forest track past some of the tallest and oldest trees in the forest; it then leads through the gorge below Swallow Falls (see p. 147). After the gorge there is a choice of return routes, by road either side of the river or by following Forest Trail; this last will add about an hour to the times.—4. *Plateau* (3½ m.) starts and ends at Pont-y-Pair (N.) car park. Mainly forest tracks with upland views.—5. *Drws Gwyn* (3 m.).From Pont-y-Pair (N.) car park to Gwydir Castle, Gwydir Uchaf Chapel and the Forest Exhibition. Mainly along paths and forest roads, this walk leads through Aberllyn Ravine to Llyn Parc (700 ft), a lake which was artificially deepened by a dam in order to supply the now disused Aberllyn mine. Drws Gwyn means White Door and recalls a wall, parts of which can be seen, built by the French prisoners during the Napoleonic War around Gwydir Uchaf, Drws Gwyn being one of the entrances. A cave above the track down was the hiding place of Dafydd ap Siencyn, an outlaw and local Lancastrian supporter during the Wars of the Roses.—6. *Llyn Sarnau* (5 m.). Starts and finishes an Pont-y-Pair (N.) car park. Forest roads and tracks, with upland scenery and some mountain views. Through Aberllyn Ravine to Llyn Parc is the same as No. 5. Llyn Sarnau is shallow and in summer sometimes dries. The picnic site beyond is near the old mine of Cyffty (see also No. 8).—7. *Craig Forys* (1½ m.). Starts and finishes at picnic site on A5, 400 yards W. of Swallow Falls. Forest road past the F.C. arboretum (started 1950), with more than 40 tree species. The forest road drops down to the old Capel Curig road along the S. bank of the Llugwy (for Roman Caer Llugwy, 500 yards W. see p. 147) and the walk returns along A5.—8. *Llyn Glangors* (2¼ m.). Starts and finishes at Cyffty picnic site (see No. 6) on the small road between Ty Hyll and Gwydir Castle, at the junction of the road from Llyn Geirionnydd. Forest road offering extensive views of Snowdonia. Llyn Glangors was reservoir for a now disused lead mine. The return is by the same route.—9. *Artists' Wood* (1½ m.). Starts and finishes at Miners' Bridge (see Forest Trail). The S. bank of the Llugwy is followed W. to an old mine building, once housing ore crushing machinery. A5 is then crossed to reach Artists' Wood, so called from its popularity with 19C artists such as David Cox and Turner.—10. *Chapel* (¾ m.). Starts and finishes at Llyn Sarnau car park (see also No. 6). Track and forest road with a viewpoint towards Conwy valley. The chapel, first used in 1863, was built out of contributions by the local scattered community of smallholders, shepherds, and miners.

A list of several other walks can be obtained from Tourist Information. These include *Jubilee Path* to *Llyn Elsi* (1 m. S.), reservoir for Betws-y-Coed; *Llanerch-Elsi Loop*, beyond; and *Fairy Glen* and the *Lledr Valley* (see below).

For Betws-y-Coed to *Bangor*, see Rtes 8 and 10; to *Llanberis*, see Rtes 8 and 9; to *Beddgelert* and *Penrhyndeudraeth*, see Rte 8; to *Corwen*, see Rte 15; to *Denbigh*, see Rtes 15 and 5.

From the E. side of Waterloo Bridge the lower road S. soon recrosses the Conwy, just before this crossing being a sign to *Fairy Glen*, where the Conwy flows through a narrow wooded gorge. The road ascends the beautiful *Valley of the Lledr*, at first green and pastoral but soon becoming rocky and wilder. To the S. opens the valley of the Gwibernant, up which a road leads in 1½ m. to *Ty Mawr*†, farmhouse birthplace of Bishop Morgan, translator of the Bible into Welsh.—*4 m.* (from Betws-y-Coed) *Pont-y-Pant*, crossing place of the Roman Sarn Helen from Tomen-y-Mur to Kanovium.

2m. **Dolwyddelan Castle**† is a square, isolated keep standing on a ridge above the road.

History. The castle was built c. 1170, possibly by Iorwerth, father of Llewelyn the Great who may have been born here in 1173 and who later certainly used Dolwyddelan as a residence. In 1281 Llewelyn the Last was here, but two years later the castle was taken by Edward I and strengthened. In 1488 the place was acquired by Maredudd ap Ievan (see Gwydir Castle), who built the village church in which his kneeling effigy in brass can be seen. After Maredudd the place fell into ruin, The modern roof and battlements were added in the 19C.

The ruins comprise a small ward, with a keep and W. tower. The keep (12C) is the oldest part, its most interesting feature being its curious defensive entrance. This was at the first floor and was covered by a small barbican, now very ruined, reached from outside by steps along the face of the keep; inside the barbican was a pit, covered by a drawbridge. Inside the keep the main room was originally covered by a gabled roof which was nevertheless still enclosed by the keep walls which rose above it. Traces of this can still be seen. In the 15C this was replaced, probably by Maredudd, by a flat roof and upper room. The curtain wall is early 13C, but the inner walls of the W. tower date from the end of that century.

To the N. of Dolwyddelan rises *Moel Siabod* (2860 ft). The road crosses the river at *Roman Bridge,* which has in fact no clear Roman association, then passes over bleak hills by the *Crimea Pass* (1263 ft); the name recalls that of a now vanished inn. On the descent which follows two unusually interesting slate mines can be visited. The first is **Gloddfa Ganol**† (Mountain Tourist Centre), on the impressive site of what was the world's largest slate mine. The site includes machinery; panorama walks above the quarry workings 350 ft below; three cottages of c. 1840, furnished in the styles of the late 1800s, 1914-18, and as used until the late 1960s; and a museum telling the story of the slate mining industry. A miner at the museum demonstrates slate-splitting and other skills. By arrangement there are conducted tours of mine tunnels.—**Llechwedd Slate Caverns**† are a short way farther down the hill. Here the visitor can take a tram-ride along the miners' tramway through a network of tunnels and underground quarries of 1846. Some of the caverns have been left untouched, while in others Victorian mining conditions have been recreated. In the slate mill, with old machinery, slate-splitting is demonstrated.

4m. (from Dolwyddelan) **Blaenau Ffestiniog** (5500 inhab.), largely industrialized, lies below hills scarred by quarrying. In the main street is a *Snowdonia National Park Information Centre. Tanygrisiau Power Station*†, 2 m. S.W., is one of the largest pumped storage systems in the world, electricity being generated at peak periods and water pumped back to the upper reservoir at other periods. The lower reservoir (stocked with fish from the hatcheries at Trawsfynydd) has been formed by damming the river Ystradau, and the power station has a Reception Centre and Exhibition. The upper reservoir's *Stwlan Dam*† (1963) can be seen from many miles away. Visits are by coach service from the reception centre. For the *Festiniog Railway,* see Rte 17.—*Manod,* the straggling S. extension of Blaenau Ffestiniog, has huge underground quarries which, air-conditioned and fitted with brick chambers, housed most of the National Gallery's paintings from 1940-45.—*3m.* **Ffestiniog,** see p. 189.

8. BETWS-Y-COED TO BEDDGELERT
AND PENRHYNDEUDRAETH

A5 to Capel Curig: A4086 to Pen-y-Gwryd: A498 to Beddgelert: A4085 to Penrhyndeudraeth. 23 miles.—*5m.* **Capel Curig.**—*4m.* **Pen-y-Gwryd.**—*7m.* **Beddgelert.**—*7m.* **Penrhyndeudraeth.**
To Capel Curig up the wooded valley of the Llugwy. From Capel Curig to Pen-y-Gwryd across moor, then down beautiful Nant Gwynant, a valley of lush meadows and woods with high mountains on either side.

Betws-y-Coed, see p. 144.—*2m.* **Swallow Falls,** forming a broken cataract in surroundings of rock and woodland, is one of the most visited spots in Snowdonia. There is a hotel, with a huge car and coach park, and a fee is charged to visit the falls. A short way beyond there is a Forestry Commission picnic site and car park for the *Gwydir Forest Arboretum* (see p. 145). Beyond, where the road crosses the river, the stone building known as *Ty Hyll* (Ugly House) was once an overnight stop for Irish drovers bringing cattle from Holyhead to markets in England. They used the old road along the S. bank, rather less than 1 m. up which, between the road and the river, are the tree-covered earthworks of *Caer Llugwy* (no adm.), on some maps *Caer Bryn y Gefeiliau*, a Roman camp occupied apparently for only 50 years between 90 and 140. From Ty Hyll a small road climbs N. to Llyn Geirionnydd, with a branch to Gwydir Castle, on this latter being forest walks (see p. 145). A5 continues along the N. bank of the Llugwy, soon passing (l.) *Pont Cyfnyg* (Narrow Bridge), where the S. bank old road rejoins. Below the slender, single-arch bridge the stream forms a series of cascades.

Moel Siabod (see below), 2½ m. S.W., may be ascended by a track from here, or from Cobden's Hotel a little farther on.—From Pont Cyfnyg another track crosses the hills to *Dolwyddelan* (3½ m.).

Soon there appears to the left one of the finest and most famous views of Snowdon. The peaks, from l. to r., are Y Wyddfa (the summit), Crib Goch (lower and nearer), and Crib-y-Ddysgl, while soon Y Lliwedd appears farther left.

3 m. (from Swallow Falls) **Capel Curig** (pron. Kappel Kirrig). Encircled by mountains, the junction of the important mountain roads to Bangor, the Pass of Llanberis, and Beddgelert, and the home of the National Centre for Mountain Activities, the village is a small but important holiday centre, especially for climbers and walkers. The *National Centre for Mountain Activities* occupies Plas y Brenin (King's House), the former Royal Hotel, a short way down A4086. The Centre trains in all aspects of mountaineering, as well as in other outdoor activities, the facilities (also available for non-residential use) including an artificial ski slope and an outdoor heated pool for canoe rolling and paddling practice. The building dates from 1800, being called the Capel Curig Inn until 1871. The names of some distinguished visitors are scratched on a window pane, these including Queen Victoria and Sir Walter Scott.

Ascents and walks from Capel Curig. *Moel Siabod* (2860 ft), pron. Sha'bod, is a solitary peak 2½ m. southwest. Its geological feature is its rugged E. side, with a glacial amphitheatre in which lies small Llyn-y-Foel. The approach from Capel Curig crosses the clapper bridge just below the outlet of the Llynau Mymbyr, then heads upwards through afforestation, meeting at 1350 ft the track from Pont Cyfnyg, and reaching the summit by the N.E. ridge. The view embraces the finest escarpments of Snowdon (due W.), and the massive slopes of the Glyders and the Carneddau (N.W. to N.),with glimpses of the green valleys of the Llugwy, the Lledr, and Nant Gwynant. The descent may be to Pen-y-Gwryd.

Pen Llithrig-y-Wrach (2621 ft), 3 m. N., is worth ascending for its view of the lakes of Cowlyd, Eigiau, and Ogwen, as well as of the E. slopes of the Carneddau. The Bangor road is left ½ m. N. of Capel Curig by a track passing the farm of Tal-y-Waen. After an ascent of 1½ m. over open moor there is a view down to Llyn Cowlyd; here the track is left and the climb continued N. to the summit. The walk may be continued W. across the *Bwlch Trimarchog* (Pass of the Three Knights) to (1¼ m.) *Pen Helig* (2732 ft), and thence another 1½ m. along the narrow grassy ridge, precipitous on both sides and requiring care, to *Carnedd Llewelyn*. From Pen Helig an easy descent may be made along the shoulder of *Braich*, its S. spur, leaving on the right below the cliffs *Ffynnon Llugwy* reservoir (1786 ft). Thence viâ the farm of Tal-y-Braich A5 is reached 2 m. W. of Capel Curig. This route, reversed, is the most direct ascent of Carnedd Llewelyn from Capel Curig.

The long range of the *Glyders* may be reached direct from Capel Curig by a waymarked path following the ridge of Banc-y-Capel. The more interesting approach is from Ogwen Cottage.

From Capel Curig A4086 is taken along the N. shore of *Llynau Mymbyr* and up the moorland valley of Nant-y-Gwryd. To the S. Moel Siabod presents its dullest slope, and on the N. the Glyders are not here impressive, but ahead rises the fourfold peak of Snowdon.—*4 m.* **Pen-y-Gwryd Hotel** (850 ft), known to climbers as 'P.Y.G.', stands at the fork of the roads to Llanberis (Rte 9) and Beddgelert. Charles Kingsley introduced this lonely house into his 'Two Years Ago' (1857), and the landlord of those days (Harry Owen, d. 1891) was a noted climbers' guide. The hotel has mementoes of the Everest team of 1953, the first to conquer the peak, who trained in this area. Pen-y-Grwyd was the site of a Roman temporary fort or marching camp; traces of the square earthwork span both roads just below the fork.

Moel Siabod may be ascended from Pen-y-Gwryd in 2¼ hours by crossing the moor to (1½ m. S.E.) *Bwlch y Main*, and thence up the W. ridge of the mountain, leaving Llynau Dywaunedd below to the south. For the *Miners' Track* across the Glyders to Ogwen Cottage, see p. 157.

A498 descends ***Nant Gwynant**, a beautiful part wooded valley, with two lakes and mountains on either side. Traditionally this was the home of Madoc ap Owain Gwynedd (1150–80). (see also p. 111).

Just below Pen-y-Gwryd there is a car park high above *Cwm Dyli*. At the foot is the Snowdon power station, served by the pipes descending the mountain opposite, behind which rises the W. face of Snowdon.— *3 m. Llyn Gwynant* (217 ft) is nearly 1 m. in length. The road skirts the S.E. shore between the lake and *Hafod Lwyfog*, a property of 320 acres given to the National Trust in 1938 by Sir Clough Williams-Ellis; it includes the house (1638 reconstruction; no adm.) which was the birthplace of Sir John Williams, goldsmith to James I. Beyond the S. end of the lake is the hamlet of Glanaber (or Nant Gwynant), below which to the N. opens the great hollow of *Cwm-y-Llan*, with the peak of Snowdon at its head. Looking up this valley the S.W. slopes of Lliwedd are to the right, while Yr Aran, closer, is to the left. The Watkin Path up Snowdon starts at the bridge over the Glaslyn, as does also the Cwm-y-Llan Nature Trail (N.C., 2 m.), in part following the Watkin Path. Beyond, the road runs along the N. shore of Llyn-y-Ddinas (176 ft). *Dinas Emrys*, N. of the road a short way below the lake, is a hill on top of which are the remains of ramparts (12C). In legend it was here that

Vortigern tried to build his tower, and Merlin told of the red and white dragons (see Legend, p. 29, and also Nant Gwrtheyrn, p. 177). Some backing to legend is given by the discovery here of Iron Age relics.

4 m. (from Llyn Gwynant) **Beddgelért** (125 ft; pron, Beth-gélert) is a straggling village in a wooded and pastoral situation below rocky heights and at the confluence of two mountain streams, the Glaslyn and the Colwyn. It is also at the junction of three valleys (Nant Gwynant, described above; the road to Caernarvon, Rte 11; and Aberglaslyn, see below), all carrying main roads, the result being that in summer Beddgelert is crowded with visitors and, with its narrow bridge, is a traffic bottleneck.

History and Legend. A Celtic monastery was founded here in the 6C, this being, except for Bardsey, the foremost house in Wales. In the 12 or 13C it was succeeded by a small Augustinian priory, founded by Llewelyn the Great. Until the construction of the Porthmadog embankment in the early 19C the Glaslyn was navigable up to Pont Aberglaslyn, and in medieval times Beddgelert was a seaport.—The village owes its name (Grave of Gelert) to a legend first made familiar by the verses of William Spencer in 1800. Gelert was the hound of Prince Llewelyn, who, departing for the hunt, left one day in charge of his infant son. Returning to find the child missing, the cradle in disorder, and Gelert with bloodstained muzzle, Llewelyn slew the hound. Presently, however, the child was found safely sleeping, beside him being a dead wolf killed by the faithful Gelert. Variants of this tale are widespread; and a manuscript of 1592 mentions a Princess of Llewelyn ap Iowerth who brought with her from England a staghound, afterwards gored to death by a stag who perished at his side.

Of the Augustinian priory all that remains is the village *Church*, formerly the priory chapel. It retains triple lancet windows at the E. end, and a good arcade between the nave and its N. chapel, both 13C work. The reputed grave of Gelert, with stones erected by a visitor-conscious landlord of the Goat in the 18C, is in a meadow ¼ m. S. of the village, reached by a path from the bridge.

Ascents and Walks near Beddgelert. Local walks include the pleasant short ascent of *Moel-y-Dyniewyd* (1254 ft; 1½ hours), to the S.E., and also the track up the S. bank of the Glaslyn. Also local are *Beddgelert Forest Trail* (¾ m.; F.C.), starting from Beddgelert Forest Campsite 1 m. N. up A4085, and four waymarked *Beddgelert Forest Walks* (F.C.), starting from Pont Caer Gors (car park), 1 m. farther up the road. For *Cwm-y-Llan Nature Trail*, 3 m. N.E., see above. For walks from the area of *Pont Aberglaslyn* and *Nantmor*, see below.

Snowdon may be ascended by the Pitt's Head Route (p. 155) or the Watkin Path (p. 154). Of these the latter is incomparably the finer, and a good plan is to ascend by this route and descend by the other.

Moel Hebog (2566 ft), Bare Hill of Hawks, the nearest considerable mountain to Beddgelert, is 2 m. S.W. and may be ascended in rather over 2 hours. From the Caernarvon road, less than ½ m. N., the Colwyn is crossed and a tributary stream ascended to *Cwm Cloch* farm. Thence the way, marked by a line of cairns, lies up the steep righthand slope of a shallow cwm, avoiding a lower path which seems more inviting. The summit, at first hidden, is seen from a false top on the crest of the ridge, and is reached thence by a rather rough scramble. From the huge flat top the view to the N. is restricted by the mass of Snowdon, but towards the S.W. extends the Lleyn peninsula with Yr Eifl, while to the S. is Cardigan Bay, with Harlech and the mountain chain stretching from Cnicht to the Rhinogs. Cader Idris, beyond, forms a long ridge on the horizon. The vista N.E. looks up Nant Gwynant, a rich green valley in striking contrast to the nearer Nant Colwyn. A pleasant descent may be made by the easy S.W. slopes to (1 hour) the farm *Tal-y-Llyn*, near Llyn Cwm Ystradllyn. Another descent is N. via *Bwlch Meillionen* (1775 ft); in the hill face to the N. of this pass a cave is reputed to have been a refuge of Owen Glendower.

Yr Aran (2451 ft), the S. peak of the Snowdon group, rises rather over 2 m. N.E. of Beddgelert. A track is taken off A498, just N. of Dinas Emrys, to the farm of Hafod-y-Boeth, and thence another track for a short distance. The whole long hillside is now visible in front, and from here the summit can be gained in 1¾ hours. The view of the other Snowdon peaks is impressive, and much of the Gwynant, Glaslyn, and Gwyfrai valleys can be seen, along the last being a distant glimpse of Caernarvon and Anglesey. From Yr Aran Snowdon can be reached along the ridges of *Bwlch Cwm-y-Llan* and *Bwlch-y-Maen*; alternatively the return to Beddgelert can be made over *Craig Wen*, the rocky S.W. spur of Yr Aran.

For the walk to *Cnicht* and the two *Moelwyns*, all to the S.E., see below.

For Beddgelert to *Caernarvon*, and to *Porthmadog*, see Rte 11.

Below Beddgelert the road soon enters the **Pass of Aberglaslyn**, a picturesque narrow defile where the torrent of the Glaslyn and the road run side by side between steep fir-clad slopes. This is where the Glaslyn leaves the mountains, and, as noted above, until the beginning of the 19C the river was navigable as far as *Pont Aberglaslyn*, a beautiful spot but liable to be a traffic bottleneck in summer. Over 500 acres either side of the pass are owned by the National Trust. At the bridge A498 (Rte 11) continues S. to Porthmadog, while this Route crosses the bridge, about ¼ m. beyond which a small road (the old Ffestiniog road) branches east.

This small road in 1 m. reaches *Bwlch Gwernog*, where a turn N. leads along the pretty wooded *Nantmor Valley*. Cae Dafydd Forest Walk here is a 2 m. long circuit from the F.C. picnic site. Up the valley (c. 2½ m. from Bwlch Gwernog) a path crosses the road, leading W. to Dinas Emrys in Nant Gwynant and E. in 1 m. to the picturesque tarn of *Llyn Llagi* (1238 ft), with a view of Snowdon. The road continues N., in 1 m. joining the Nant Gwynant road between the two lakes.— *Cnicht* (2265 ft), pron. Kun-icht, and *Moelwyn Mawr* (2527 ft) may be reached on foot from Bwlch Gwernog. The old road, at this point a track (with hut circles to the S.), is followed E. for 1¼ m., rough moorland then being crossed, overlooking (S.) the glen of *Cwm Croesor* which separates the two mountains. The long shoulder of Cnicht, narrowing as it ascends, is at one point blocked by a crag. This is passed below on the right, the ascent being continued by a kind of rocky stairway (precipitous on one side) which soon reaches the summit. The view is extensive. To the N.W. is Snowdon, its central peak rising above Cwm-y-Llan; Moel Siabod is N.E.; due W. Moel Hebog stands out, and to the S.W. stretches Cardigan Bay.— To reach *Moelwyn Mawr* (another full hour's walk) a detour should be made around the head (1427 ft) of the deep Cwm Croesor. *Moelwyn Bach* (2334 ft) is ¾ m. S., *Stwlan Reservoir* (p. 146) lying in the col; the traverse of the twin mountains is a fairly difficult ridge walk.

From Pont Aberglaslyn the road skirts the reclaimed *Traeth Mawr* (see p. 162).—*7 m.* (from Beddgelert) **Penrhyndeudraeth** is a small town with a station of the Festiniog Railway and a National Park Information Centre.

For Penrhyndeudraeth to *Ffestiniog* and *Bala*, as also for *Portmeirion* and *Porthmadog*, see Rte 17.

9   PASS OF LLANBERIS. SNOWDON

The **Snowdon Sherpa Service** operates a regular bus service around Snowdon. This service not only allows the best of the scenery to be seen, but also gives walkers flexibility by freeing them from having to return to car parks. The service is also useful if the popular but small car park at Pen-y-Pass is full.

A   Pass of Llanberis
(Pen-y-Gwryd to Caernarvon)

A4086. 13 miles.—*1 m. Pen-y-Pass.—3 m. Nant Peris.—2 m. Llanberis.—7 m. Caernarvon.*

From Pen-y-Gwryd the Llanberis road (build c. 1850), cut into the hillside, ascends offering a splendid view down Nant Gwynant.—*1 m. Pen-y-Pass Youth Hostel* (1169 ft), at the crest of the pass, is the starting place for the Pyg Track and the Miners' Track to the summit of Snowdon. The road now starts its descent of the magnificent ***Pass of Llanberis,** the wildest valley in Wales, a narrow defile below black and towering walls of rock and almost blocked by boulders and debris. At *Pont-y-Gromlech,* just over a mile below the summit, the road crosses the Peris. Here there is parking space, below (E.) precipitous crags much used by rock climbers. Soon, to the W., the arms of Crib Goch open to give a fine view of the almost rectangular ***Cwm Glas,** approached by a footbridge ½ m. below Pont-y-Gromlech.

Cwm Glas, with its two little tarns (2200, 2700 ft) overhung by sheer precipices, is one of the finest and wildest cwms in Wales. The marks of glacial action are very distinct. On the W. side rises the rock bastion of *Cyrn Las* (Grey Horn), and on the E. side the N. ridge of Crib Goch ends in the spur of Dinas Mot (Hill Fortress). Beyond the first tarn is *Clogwyn-y-Person,* the Parson's Nose, a spur of Crib-y-Ddysgl noted among climbers.—The ascent from Cwm Glas to the summit of Snowdon leads viâ the ridge on the extreme right to strike the Llanberis ascent a little above Clogwyn Station.

3 m. (from Pen-y-Pass) *Nant Peris,* or Old Llanberis, has a rude cruciform church (mainly 14C), with a 15C timber roof, a screen with an old alms box, and a curious window in the W. wall. The Well of Peris, in a field across the road, was much visited for healing and wishing until comparatively recent times. As a wishing well it is said to indicate the granting of a wish by the appearance of a sacred fish, first mentioned by Pennant in 1781.—*Dolbadarn Castle*† is rather over a mile below Nant Peris. The castle's origins are lost, but its masonry suggests a building of the late 12 or early 13C. The main feature is the circular keep, probably built by Llewelyn the Great. Later, from 1255 for over 20 years, the castle was the prison of Owain Goch, elder brother of Llewelyn the Last.

2 m. **Llanberis** (350 ft) is a straggling community along the main road at the S. end of Llyn Padarn, here separated by a narrow isthmus from the smaller Llyn Peris. The natural beauty of the surroundings has long been marred by the scars of huge slate quarries which rise, tier upon tier, to a height approaching 1500 ft.

Quarrying finished in 1969 and the quarries are now in part becoming the site of the **Dinorwic Pumped-Storage Power Station,** which will be the largest such in Europe. The station is planned to be fully operational by 1982, but little will be seen from outside as almost everything will be inside mountain caverns. The upper reservoir is *Marchlyn Mawr* (2 m. N.E.), 1600 ft above *Llyn Peris,* the lower. The water will be carried from the upper reservoir to the generators by 3 km. of tunnels and a 412 metre vertical shaft. Visitors (after 1982) will be taken underground in electric buses; an environmental centre is planned to open in 1980.

Although best known for the starting station of the Snowdon Mountain Railway, Llanberis has three other things to attract the visitor. All are close to one another on the far side of the isthmus between the lakes. The *North Wales Quarrying Museum*†, a branch of the National Museum of Wales, occupies the workshops (1870) of the Dinorwic Quarry which functioned from 1809 to 1969. Foundry, smithies, pattern shop, woodworking shop, fitting shops, hospital, and messroom have all been preserved. There are film and slide shows. *Padarn Country Park* (1970) was the first in Wales. Extending along the shore of the lake, it includes a Nature Trail and Reserve, with one of the few remaining sessile oak woods; the Vivian Quarry, the first opened here, where something can be seen of the typical Llanberis gallery system of open quarrying in terraces between 60 and 70 ft high; and a choice of woodland walks.

The *Llanberis Lake Railway*† (now 1 ft 11½ inch gauge), originally the quarry railway (4 ft gauge) to Port Dinorwic between Bangor and Caernarvon, was in part saved by enthusiasts and now runs the length of the N. shore of Llyn Padarn. The total journey time is 40 minutes, but passengers may leave the train at the halfway station (picnic site) and catch a later train. Of the company's five steam locomotives, three (1889, 1904, 1922) belonged to the quarry.

Walks. A local walk is to the waterfall of *Ceunant Mawr* (½ m.), approached by the lane by the Victoria Hotel. The smaller *Ceunant Bach*, a little farther upstream, is also attractive.—The main longer distance walk is that up *Snowdon* (see below). There is also a track S. to *Llyn Cwellyn* (4 m.; 2 hours) and to Beddgelert (9 m.); the highest point reached is *Bwlch-y-Maes-Cwm* (1550 ft), below which the Snowdon Ranger Track is joined.

Beyond Llanberis the road skirts the S. shore of Llyn Padarn and soon emerges from the mountains. Just N. of *Waun* (1½ m. N. across the Seiont) *Ffynnon Cegin Arthur* is a chalybeate well with medicinal qualities ascribed to King Arthur.—*7 m.* **Caernarvon,** see p. 158.

B   Snowdon

*Snowdon, the highest mountain in England and Wales, is, despite its name, generally free from snow between April and October, though drifts may linger in the gullies until early summer. The massif forms a cluster of five peaks, linked by sharp ridges, and presents fine escarpments in all directions, especially towards the E. where the beautiful lakes of Glaslyn and Llyn Llydaw are overhung by sheer walls of rock. The principal heights, in their starfish formation, are *Y Wyddfa Fawr* (3560 ft), the central peak, now crowned by a cairn; *Crib-y-Ddysgl* (3493 ft), ½ m. N., skirted by the Llanberis Track; *Crib Goch* (3023 ft; Red Ridge), 1½ m. N.E., a splendid pile of rock, rich in pinnacles and buttresses; *Lliwedd* (2497 ft), the long craggy ridge running S.E., with a well-known rock wall; and *Yr Aran* (2451 ft), the outlying S. peak, forming a spur towards Beddgelert. Between these mountains are six cwms or hollows, of which *Cwm Dyli* and *Cwm Glas,* separated by Crib Goch, are the most impressive. Tracks cross all the ridges; exposed and liable to high winds, these are suitable only for the experienced.

Legend and History. To the ancient Welsh the mountain was Eryri, the High Land. Its English name of Snowdon it owes to the Saxons, who spoke of the distant Snow Dun, the Snow Hill or fortress. Its present Welsh name Y Wyddfa Fawr (Great Tomb) it owes to the legend that the summit was the tomb of the giant Rhita Fawr, slain by King Arthur. Arthur is supposed to have been mortally wounded on Bwlch-y-Saethau, and from this it is natural to accept Llyn Llydaw below as the lake into which Excalibur was thrown. Another legend is that of Vortigern and Merlin at Dinas Emrys in Nant Gwynant (see p. 148). That prehistoric man lived on the lower slopes is known from material found near Llyn Llydaw. In medieval times Dolbadarn became a castle of the Welsh princes, and the mountain is mentioned by Giraldus. Llewelyn the Last retreated into Snowdon before his final defeat and death; Edward I created a Royal Forest of Snowdon; and Owen Glendower is thought to have found refuge here. Thomas Johnson, a naturalist, is recorded as having ascended Snowdon in 1639, and Halley is said to have made astronomical experiments on the summit in 1697. It was in this century, too, that the first mining began. An ascent from Llanberis is fully described by Pennant

(1726-98), and Wordsworth writes of leaving 'Beddgelert's huts at couching time' to witness sunrise from the peak ('Prelude'). Victorian times were prosperous for guides and their ponies (George Borrow took his step-daughter up the mountain in 1854), but this era ended with the building of the railway in 1896.

ASCENT OF SNOWDON

The *View from the summit includes the whole mountain and hill system of north Wales, a large expanse of sea, and no fewer than 20 mountain lakes, while the ridges of the massif itself form an immediately striking feature, a wild fastness of rock towering frequently into swirling mist.—To the N.W. the whole of Anglesey projects flat into the Irish sea, with Holyhead Mountain rising on the island's farther side, while between is the thread of the Menai Strait with its bridges. Due N., some 5 m. distant, is the much quarried pyramid of Elidyr Fawr, overlooking Llyn Padarn. Over the Crib Goch ridge, in the foreground (N.E.), are the twin Glyders, with the peak of Tryfan just peeping over the saddle between them. Between Glyder Fawr and Y Garn (l.) are the Carneddau, 6-8 m. distant. To the right of Glyder Fach is Pen Llithrig-y-Wrach. Next, to the right of Crib Goch, in the foreground, comes the view down Cwm Dyli, sharply contrasted with the cliffs of Lliwedd (r.); beyond, over Llyn Llydaw, are the bare slopes drained by the Gwryd. The long Clwydian range forms an undulating horizon in this direction. Moel Siabod, dwarfed from this aspect, stands due E., masking the Conwy valley. The hollow of Cwm-y-Llan, to the right of Lliwedd (S.E.), gives a glimpse of green. Farther away are Cnicht and the twin Moelwyns, and, beyond, in the far distance, are seen (l. to r.) the Berwyns, the Arenigs, and the Arans. To the S., beyond the broad expanse of Traeth Mawr, is Harlech Castle (on the left, the Rhinogs), and farther off is the long ridge of Cader Idris. Closer, on the right of Yr Aran, rises Moel Hebog, while farther to the right are Y Garn and Mynydd Mawr, with Llyn Cwellyn at the foot of the latter and Llyn Nantlle Uchaf between them. Beyond Y Garn is the triple peak of Yr Eifl, with other hills of the Lleyn. Finally, to the N.W., the comparatively smooth slopes of Moel Cynghorion, Y Foel Goch, and Moel Eilio, spurs of the Snowdon range, complete the circle. The Irish (Wicklow) mountains are 80-90 m. to the W.; the Cumbrian hills are 90-100 m. N.N.E.; and the Isle of Man is 85 m. northwest.

Snowdon is ascended by the Snowdon Mountain Railway from Llanberis, or by any of the six signed traditional walkers' tracks, beginning at various points around the base of the mountain. Of these the finest and steepest are the *Watkin Path* from Nant Gwynant and the *Pyg Track* from Pen-y-Pass, to which the *Miners' Track*, also from Pen-y-Pass, is an interesting alternative skirting Llyn Llydaw and passing mine workings. The *Pitt's Head Track* and the *Snowdon Ranger Track*, both from the Beddgelert to Llyn Cwellyn main road, afford views of the lesser known W. escarpments. The *Llanberis Track* is the easiest but least interesting ascent.—The above ascents, all outlined below, are safe in clear weather, but it should be remembered that Snowdon is notorious for its sudden mists, and that parts of the group are dangerously precipitous and craggy. The inexperienced should not stray from the paths, especially on the N. and E. faces.

Expert cragsmen find first-class work on the great cliffs of *Lliwedd* (N. face), *Crib Goch* (ridge, pinnacles, and N. buttress), *Clogwyn-y-Person* and *Clogwyn-y-Ddysgl* (overlooking Cwm Glas), and *Clogwyn-du'r-Arddu* (very difficult).

Snowdon Mountain Railway†. From Llanberis to the summit (4½ m.) in one hour. This narrow-gauge rack-and-pinion line, the only one in Britain, with a maximum gradient of 1 in 5½, was opened in 1896 and is worked by steam, the engines being Swiss made. Refreshments are available at both Llanberis and the summit. Ample parking at Llanberis.—A sharp ascent begins soon after the station. A viaduct is crossed, with a good view of the Ceunant Mawr Falls, and, beyond, the Ceunant Bach Fall is also seen. After passing *Hebron* (1¼ m.; 930 ft) the line ascends the long N. spur of the mountain and crosses the Llanberis Track, Moel Eilio and Y Foel Goch being seen to the right. Beneath *Halfway* (2½ m.; 1600 ft), to the right is the deep valley of Cwm Brwynog (Cwm of Rushes), with its amphitheatre of cliff. The foot track is again crossed just beyond *Clogwyn* (3¾ m; 2550 ft) and there is a glimpse left into the precipitous gorge of Cwm Glas Bach with the Pass of Llanberis beyond. Curving to the right to ascend a slope above the cliffs of Clogwyn-du'r-Arddu (Black Precipice), with a tarn at their foot, the line affords a fine view extending as far as Anglesey. It then crosses the Snowdon Ranger Track (3200 ft) and reaches the saddle. *Snowdon Summit* station is just below the cairn of Y Wyddfa.

Llanberis Track. From Llanberis (Victoria Hotel). 5 m. in 3 hours. The track, originally a Victorian pony trail, never diverges far from the railway and generally affords the same views. A detour on the left beyond the second railway crossing leads to the cliff edge, with a splendid view of *Cwm Glas.* Near the summit *Bwlch Glas,* where the Pyg and Snowdon Ranger tracks join, is another viewpoint.

Pyg Track. From Pen-y-Pass. 2½ hours. This popular route was so named at the turn of the century by climbers from Pen-y-Gwryd Hotel (P.Y.G.), who wished to distinguish it from the Miners' Track. It is also often spelt Pig Track, some justification being that one translation of *Bwlch Moch,* reached at 1850 ft, could be Pigs' Pass. Llyn Llydaw and the sheer cliffs of Y Wyddfa and Lliwedd here come into view, and the track skirts the hillside under the crags of Crib Goch. Later a shoulder is crossed, looking down 400 ft into the cwm which contains Glaslyn, the Miners' Track being met above the W. end of the lake. The joint path bears right up zigzags to meet the Llanberis Track at *Bwlch Glas.*

Miners' Track. From Pen-y-Pass. 3 hours. The mine is Glaslyn, where copper was mined from the second half of the 18C until 1916. Its situation was so remote that the miners lived at the mine, returning on foot at weekends across the Glyders to their homes in Bethesda.—From Pen-y-Pass the track passes the small *Llyn Teyrn* (1238 ft) then crosses the N.E. end of *Llyn Llydaw* (1416 ft) by a causeway. The lake, more than 1 m. long, is dominated at its head by Lliwedd. The track skirts the N. shore for ½ m., then turns N.W., passing the abandoned copper workings near the smaller *Glaslyn* (1971 ft). From Glaslyn the path zigzags up to the Pyg Track, a route up which the miners carried their sacks to Bwlch Glas, whence the ore was dragged on sledges down to Llyn Cwellyn.

Watkin Path. From Nant Gwynant. 3 hours. Sir Edward Watkin was a Victorian railway entrepreneur whose dream was a train from Manchester to Paris, and who constructed nearly 2 m. of Channel

Tunnel before the government stopped the project. He retired to Nant Gwynant and soon built a path upwards from the South Snowdon Slate Quarries; it was opened by Gladstone in 1892. The path is perhaps the finest ascent, but it is steep and not for the inexperienced.—From the road, near the Glaslyn bridge, a cart-track is followed to a fork (5 min.). Here the branch to the left is taken, climbing above waterfalls to the right. At 850 ft the stream is crossed to a ruined house, a short way beyond which is *Gladstone Rock* (inscription), from which Gladstone, aged 83, opened the path, the theme of his speech being Justice to Wales. The cart-track ends at the old quarry, the point where the Watkin Path proper bears right and begins to ascend the long S.W. slope of Lliwedd. Approaching the ridge a short detour to the right affords a sudden and magnificent view from the edge of the precipice looking into Cwm Dyli. The narrow saddle which the track follows between Lliwedd and Y Wyddfa is *Bwlch-y-Saethau* (2690 ft), the Pass of the Arrows, traditionally a burial place of King Arthur. The ridge broadens, and another short detour gives a fine view of Glaslyn below.

Pitt's Head Track. From *Pitt's Head Rock* (2½ m. N. of Beddgelert on A4085) or from *Rhyd-Ddu*, 1 m. farther north. 3 hours. From the point where the two tracks meet (c. 1 m.) there is a gradual climb N.E. over open moor to the W. extremity of the *Llechog* ridge (2400 ft). Where the track is faint, there are small cairns. The precipitous N. face of Llechog is followed, with views down to the tarns in Cwm Clogwyn, the ridge narrowing into the rocky razor-edge of *Bwlch-y-Maen* (3056 ft), the Stone Pass. The Watkin Path is joined just below the summit.

Snowdon Ranger Track. From Snowdon Ranger hostel on Llyn Cwellyn. 2½ hours. After about ¾ m. the path to Llanberis is crossed. The slope of Moel Cynghorion is to the left, while to the right is the marshy ground of Cwm Clogwyn with its five tarns. From *Bwlch Cwm-Brwynog* (1600 ft), the steep ridge of *Clogwyn-du'r-Arddu* is ascended, and the Llanberis Track is met near Bwlch Glas.

An exhilarating high-level route is the *Snowdon Horseshoe, the traverse of the long precipitous ridges connecting Crib Goch and Lliwedd with Y Wyddfa. This route, which involves some scrambling, should only be attempted in fine weather and by experienced walkers. The normal start is Pen-y-Pass, and the round requires some 6 hours. The Pyg Track is taken as far as *Bwlch Moch* (1850 ft), from where a faint path leads to the foot of the Crib Goch arête. This, steep and narrow and in places rocky, is climbed to the summit of *Crib Goch* (3023 ft), with its pinnacles. Beyond is *Bwlch Goch* (2816 ft), the lowest point of the ridge, whence the ascent is made to the summit cairn of *Crib-y-Ddysgl* (or *Garnedd Ugain;* 3493 ft). There follows a descent to Bwlch Glas, where the Llanberis Track is followed to Y Wyddfa. From here the Watkin Path is taken to *Bwlch-y-Saethau,* this path being followed until it begins to drop off the ridge, at which point the Horseshoe runs S.E. up a steep and stony ridge to gain the summit of *Lliwedd* (2947 ft). From here the path E. along the ridge drops to Llyn Llydaw and the Miners' Track back to Pen-y-Pass.

10   CAPEL CURIG TO BANGOR

A5. 13 miles.—*5 m.* **Ogwen Cottage.—***4 m.* **Bethesda.—***3 m. Llandegai.—1 m.* **Bangor.**

As far as Ogwen Cottage, and down Nant Ffrancon, the road is through wild and grand mountain scenery.

Capel Curig, see p. 147.—The road ascends the N. bank of the Llugwy into country of increasing grandeur. The old road, now a grass-grown track, provides a pleasant alternative for walkers along the other bank. To the N. are the slopes of Pen Llithrig-y-Wrach and Pen Helig, with the Carneddau beyond in the distance, while to the S. Snowdon is soon hidden behind the long eastward extremity of the Glyders, the projection nearest the road being *Gallt-yr-Ogof* (Cliff of Caves). Soon the great rock-pyramid of *Tryfan* comes suddenly into view, with the mountains beyond Llyn Ogwen (Y Foel Goch, and, later, Y Garn) in the background. *Helyg Cottage*, below Gallt-yr-Ogof, is a hut of the Climbers' Club. The road crosses the Llugwy, which descends from its source of Ffynnon Llugwy to the N., while to the S. opens the great *Cwm Tryfan*, which may be ascended to Bwlch Tryfan. *Llyn Ogwen*, a lake 1 m. long and nowhere more than 10 ft deep, is grandly set in a deep hollow between the black and rock-strewn slopes of Tryfan and the Glyders to the S., and Pen-yr-Oleu-Wen, the precipitous S. spur of Carnedd Dafydd, to the north.—*5 m.* **Ogwen Cottage**, at *Pont Pen-y-Benglog* (993 ft), is a mountain school; adjacent Idwal Cottage is a youth hostel. This area is the southern end of the National Trust's huge *Carneddau Estate* of over 15,000 acres, which includes Llyn Idwal, the head of Nant Ffancon, and several mountains, amongst these being the N. slopes of the two Glyders, Tryfan, Carnedd Dafydd, and the N.W. slopes of Carnedd Llewelyn. For all of these, see below.

*Cwm Idwal Nature Reserve, ½ m. S., is reached by a path behind Ogwen Cottage. Established in 1954, the reserve is leased by the National Trust to Nature Conservancy, and is of such scientific importance that it is the subject of a special exhibition in the National Museum of Wales. The cwm was hollowed out by a huge glacier which, on its slow way downward, carved out Nant Ffrancon. It is this, and the associated Alpine flora, that give Cwm Idwal an importance which, even in the 19C., interested Charles Darwin who cited the cwm's hanging valleys, scored rocks, and Alpine flora in support of his glacial theory. *Llyn Idwal* (1223 ft), a sombre lake filling much of the cwm, is overhung by the main precipice of Glyder Fawr, to the right of which opens a fissure, with overhanging sides, known as *Twll Du* or the *Devil's Kitchen*. In legend Prince Idwal, son of Owain Gwynedd, was drowned here by his foster-father; his spirit haunts the lake, and that of his murderer the Devil's Kitchen. A Nature Trail c. 2 m. in length circles the lake anti-clockwise, passing 12 marked stations. Some of these are primarily viewpoints (Nos 1, 2, and 11); Nos 3 and 8 are beside N.C. enclosures used for studying the effects of grazing on mountain vegetation, while No 12 is beside an islet showing how differently vegetation can develop when inaccessible to sheep. Fossil fragments may be found near No. 4, No. 5 is on top of glacial moraine, and Nos 6 and 7 are, respectively, eroded peat and a scree slope. No. 9 is a particularly interesting station, with plants common in Britain at the end of the Ice Age but now restricted to certain mountain areas. The *Idwal Slabs* at No. 10 have been popular with climbers since 1895.

Walks and Ascents from Ogwen Cottage

This is one of the wildest parts of Wales, with precipices, boulders, and scree. Walks, parts of some of which involve rough scrambling, should only be undertaken in clear weather. Advice can be obtained at Ogwen Cottage.

The Glyders. The direct approach to *Glyder Fawr* (3279 ft; 1¾ hours), the highest peak in the range, is by the Nature Trail along the E. side of Llyn Idwal. To the left of Twll Du, a rock-strewn ledge, sloping steeply from right to left, is climbed to the saddle, marked by a cairn. Hence the ascent is S.E., the summit, a waste of shattered slate, being reached after a steep scramble over scree and boulders. The boulder-strewn summit of *Glyder Fach* (3262 ft) is reached by following the ridge E. for nearly a mile.—The path N.W. from Glyder Fawr crosses the dip between Twll Du and the small *Llyn-y-Cwm* (2350 ft), where Giraldus reported one-eyed fish. The path continues to *Y Garn* (3104 ft), whence the descent to Ogwen Cottage is between Y Garn and Y Foel Goch; alternatively the walk can be continued along the crest to *Carnedd-y-Filiast*, from here descending to Bethesda. An interesting geological feature, immediately S. below Carnedd-y-Filiast, is the way the cwm's smooth slab buttresses are slightly undulating, evidence of the ancient sea of the Upper Cambrian period. *Elidir Fawr* (3029 ft), 1½ m. W. of Y Foel Goch, drops steeply on its N. side to the large *Marchlyn Mawr Reservoir,* the upper lake of the Dinorwic Power Station at Llanberis.—Another approach (2¼ hours) to Glyder Fawr and Glyder Fach from Ogwen Cottage is viâ *Y Gribin,* separating Llyn Idwal from Llyn Bochlwyd. The path, with some scrambling towards the top, leads to the dip between the mountains; in mist it is better to keep to the right. A third approach is from *Bwlch Tryfan* on the Miners' Track (see below).—The view from the Glyders includes Snowdon, part of Anglesey, and Caernarvon Castle, seen between the twin lakes of Llanberis.

The **Miners' Track** is a route used in the 18 and early 19C by the copper miners of Glaslyn (see p. 154). Most of the miners would have walked from Bethesda to Glaslyn; the time from Ogwen Cottage to Pen-y-Gwryd is rather over 2 hours. Passing the foot of *Llyn Bochlwyd* (1806 ft), in a gloomy cwm, the track climbs to *Bwlch Tryfan* (c. 2350 ft), connecting Glyder Fach and Tryfan.—The route to the former ascends over scree (care required), at first to the right, under a rocky arête, but higher traversing to the left below some crags. *Tryfan* (3010 ft) has three precipitous faces, this N. approach from Bwlch Tryfan being the only one possible for walkers. From this col it is better to traverse to the left at first, avoiding the main ridge; thence a scramble over rocks leads to the summit, on which are two upright stones (natural, and not, as sometimes suggested, menhirs) locally known as Adam and Eve.—From Bwlch Tryfan the Miners' Track continues S.E., at first at the foot of the crags, then finding a break to reach the main ridge at c. 2500 ft. The descent is straightforward, and the track reaches A4086 a little E. of Pen-y-Gwryd.

Carnedd Dafydd (3426 ft) and **Carnedd Llewelyn** (3484 ft), both N.E. of Ogwen Cottage, the highest mountains in Wales after Snowdon, are named after the brother princes who opposed Edward I. The shortest and easiest ascent (3 hours) leads due N. from the farm of *Bodesi,* reached by a track off A5, ½ m. E. of Llyn Ogwen. The slope is climbed to the crest of *Cefn Ysgolion-Duon* (Ridge of the Black Ladders), which drops on its N. side in precipices to the great Cwm Llafar. Along the ridge Dafydd is ¾ m. W., and Llewelyn rather over a mile northeast. The view embraces most of the peaks of north Wales, and in clear conditions extends to the Cumberland fells. For the descent to *Aber,* see p. 121; to Bethesda, see below; to Capel Curig, see p. 148.

Immediately beyond Ogwen Cottage the road crosses the Ogwen, which here issues from the lake and, joined by the stream from Llyn Idwal, plunges down into the head of Nant Ffrancon in a series of cataracts known as the *Benglog Falls* (Falls of the Skull). The road, engineered by Telford in 1815-30, now enters *Nant Ffrancon, possibly named after Adam de Francton, traditionally the name of the man who killed Llewelyn the Last, but more probably deriving from Nant yr Afanc meaning Valley of the Beavers. This glaciated valley, fed by the great glacier of Cwm Idwal, is bounded on either side by rocky mountains, those on the W. side cut by cwms, each parent to its own glacier. Just beyond the hamlet of *Tyn-y-Maes* (3 m. from Ogwen Cottage) a bridge crossing the Ogwen gives walkers access by way of Cwm Ceunant to the area of *Carnedd-y-Filiast* and *Marchlyn Reservoir* (see above). The road up this W. side of Nant Ffrancon was built in the latter part of the 18C for the benefit of Irish M.P.s making for London.—The scenery now quickly changes, the rocks giving place to the woods of *Ogwen Bank* (E.), while to the W. are the Penrhyn Quarries.

4 m. (from Ogwen Cottage) **Bethesda** (4500 inhab.) owes its growth to the 19C development of slate quarrying. To the religious fervour of the same period it owes its present name, deriving from a Nonconformist chapel in the main street; previously the name was Glanogwen.

The **Penrhyn Slate Quarries**† were developed c. 1780 by Richard Pennant, the first Baron Penrhyn. The biggest opencast system in the world, the quarries form a vast amphitheatre, some 1000 ft deep, hewn in terraces out of the N. end of *Bron Llwyd*, the last shoulder of the Glyders. After being blasted out in huge slabs, the slate is cut by machinery into convenient sizes and shapes, then split, trimmed, and smoothed by hand. The slates are named, according to sizes, Queens, Duchesses, Marchionesses, Countesses, Ladies, Doubles, and Singles. The mules and carts of the early days were superseded in 1801 by the special railway to Port Penrhyn (see also Penrhyn Castle, Industrial Railway Museum). The quarry is noted for its red, blue, and green slates.

Bethesda is a good starting place for the ascent of the twin **Carneddau** (3¾ hours). From the farm of *Ty Slatters*, 1¼ m. S.E. by lane, a route is followed between the Llafar and Cenllysg streams to the shoulder of *Mynydd-Du*, which is then followed (rough scrambling; sharp drops on the left) to the summit of **Carnedd Dafydd**. A walk of 1¾ m. along the saddles of Cefn Ysgolion-Duon and Bwlch Cyfry-Drym reaches **Carnedd Llewelyn**.

3 m. **Llandegai**, see p. 121.—*1 m.* **Bangor**, see Rte 4.

11   BANGOR TO CAERNARVON AND PORTHMADOG

A487 to Caernarvon: A4085 to Beddgelert: A 498 to Porthmadog. 29 miles.—*5 m.* Port Dinorwic.—*4 m.* **Caernarvon.**—*5 m.* Betws Garmon.—*7 m.* **Beddgelert.**—*2 m.* Pont Aberglaslyn.—*5 m.* **Tremadog.**—*1 m.* **Porthmadog.**
Mountain and woodland on both sides between Betws Garmon and Pont Aberglaslyn; then mountains to the W. and reclaimed estuary to the east.

Bangor, see Rte 4, is left either by A5 as far as the Menai Bridge (1½ m.; heavy traffic in summer), then A487; or by A4087. The two roads meet roughly 3 m. outside Bangor.—*5 m.* (from Bangor) *Port Dinorwic*, now used by yachts, was the port at the end of the slate railway from Llanberis; all that now remains of this railway is the Llanberis Lake Railway. It seems probable that the crossing of the strait here to *Moel-y-Don* was used by Suetonius in 61 in his campaign against the Druids, and again in c. 78 by Agricola.

4 m. **CAERNARVON** (10,500 inhab.), near the S.W. end of the Menai Strait and on the right bank of the mouth of the Seiont, the busy and historic county town of Gwynedd, is visited for its great castle, its town walls, and the site of Roman Segontium.

Tourist Information. Quay, at S.E. end of the castle.
Parking. Quay, S. of the castle. Also N.E. off Castle Square (Pool Side, Bridge Street).
Main Shopping Area. Within the town walls. Castle Square (Sat. market).
Early Closing. Thursday.
Station. Nearest station is Bangor.
Coaches mostly operate from Castle Square.
Post Office. Castle Square.
Cruises. Menai strait cruises, Easter-Oct.

History. On Twt Hill evidence has been found of a Celtic settlement, and the Romans were at Segontium from c. 77 to c. 380. Otherwise the history of Caernarvon is that of its castle. In 1963 the Queen declared the town a Royal Borough.

Bangor Street leads into the town from the north. On its E. side, behind the Royal Hotel, *Twt Hill* (192 ft) affords a good general view; traces here of a ditch are evidence of a Celtic settlement. Bangor Street reaches Turf Square, once the site of the pillory and stocks. From here Eastgate Street leads W. through the walls, while Bridge Street continues S. into the large **Castle Square**, also known as *Y Maes*, site of a busy market on Saturdays. Statues here are of David Lloyd George (1863-1945), M.P. for the Caernarvon Boroughs from 1890 to 1945 (by W. Goscombe John), and of Sir Hugh Owen (1804-81), pioneer of Welsh university education. The castle, the quays along the mouth of the Seiont, and the walled town are all immediately W. and N.W. of Castle Square. The entrance to the castle is from Castle Street inside the walls, but it is worth going down to the quay, often busy with fishing boats and yachts, from where a far better impression of the great walls and their defensive strength is gained than is apparent from the town side.

The *Castle†, occupying an area of three acres within the angle of the Seiont and the Menai Strait, is, despite its low-lying site, a massive and imposing example of medieval fortification.

History. The first castle was a Norman motte-and-bailey of c. 1100, taken by the Welsh princes not long after its construction and remaining in Welsh hands until 1283, when Edward I set James of St George to building the castle that stands here today. The castle was completed in three main stages, the first being up till 1292, the second 1295 to 1308 when the master mason was Walter of Hereford, and the last 1309 to 1323. The associated English Borough was granted its charter in 1284. The use of polygonal towers has few English precedents, and that of banded masonry none. Both these are features of the walls of Constantinople, and, together with the use of the decorative eagle, suggest an intention to recall Segontium's tradition as the birthplace of Constantine the Great (what was believed to be the body of Constantine's father, Constantius I, killed at York in 305 while on an expedition against the Picts and Scots, was found in 1283 and reburied at Edward's behest). Edward II was born here in 1284, but not in the Eagle Tower as popularly supposed. The story of his presentation to the conquered Welsh as 'a Prince of Wales who could speak no English' is almost certainly apocryphal, and cannot in fact be traced earlier than 1584. In 1294 during Madog's rebellion the town was sacked by the Welsh, who breached the wall below Eagle Tower. In 1399 Richard II was here after his landing from Ireland, and in 1403 Caernarvon was unsuccessfully attacked by Owen Glendower. The Parliamentarian William Prynne was imprisoned here in 1637, and during the Civil War the castle changed hands three times, finally falling to Parliament. After 1660 it was dismantled. In 1911 the future Edward VIII was invested here as Prince of Wales, as was also Prince Charles in 1969.

Despite its externally complete appearance, the castle today is little more than a shell. It comprises two irregular wards, the upper or outer (E.) of which encloses the site of the Norman motte. There are two gates, the King's Gate (N.) at the join of the wards, and the Queen's Gate at the E. extremity. The many angles of the walls are marked by polygonal towers, crowned by picturesque turrets, Eagle Tower at the castle's W. end having three of these. The walls and towers along the S. side, between and including Eagle Tower and Northeast Tower, represent the earlier building phase (up to 1292), although the upper parts of Eagle Tower were completed later. An interesting defensive feature is the almost continuous system of mural passages, carried round the inner faces of the towers and pierced with loopholes. On the S. face of the castle these passages are doubled, this affording, in conjunction with the looped merlons of the rampart walk, positions for three tiers of archers.

The description below follows an anticlockwise circuit, starting with the lower ward. Visitors have a choice between using the mural passages or returning to the courtyard after each tower.

The ENTRANCE, on the N. side, is through the *King's Gate*, above which is a mutilated statue of Edward II. The gate was formerly approached by a drawbridge, traces of which and of its associated defences (portcullis, arrow slits) can still be seen. The entrance passage is flanked by strong octagonal towers, and the gatehouse would have incorporated quarters for the constable, with a hall, chapel, and living rooms. Beyond the entrance a range of buildings (now destroyed, except for *Prison Tower,* an inwards extension of the W. gatehouse tower) would have separated the two wards.—LOWER WARD. Along the wall between the W. gatehouse and the next tower (*Well Tower*) was the site of the kitchens. From the basement of Well Tower hooded fireplaces can be seen above. A postern here was perhaps for direct delivery of kitchen supplies. The westernmost tower is *Eagle Tower,* the largest of the castle, with walls 15 ft thick and an internal diameter at ground level of 34 ft. On the first floor there is an exhibition of armour. Here too is a small room, with a heraldic window, in which Edward II was once thought to have been born; in fact the tower would not by 1284 have reached this height. Stairs ascend to the roof with its three turrets. Stone eagles are among the weathered figures on the turret battlements, but only one (W.) is recognizable. In the basement of the tower is the castle watergate. Next comes *Queen's Tower,* housing the *Museum of the Royal Welch Fusiliers†,* telling the story of the regiment since its founding in 1689. Below the Queen's Tower the Hall (100 ft by 34 ft) filled the S.E. of the ward.—UPPER WARD. *Chamberlain Tower* contains a chapel (first floor, N.E.); *Black Tower* has small ten-sided rooms; and at *Cistern Tower* there is a stone tank. *Queen's Gate,* at the E. end of the castle, was originally approached by a drawbridge, evidence of which can be seen from a railed platform high above the quay. The next tower, the small *Watch Tower,* is entered through *Northeast Tower* beyond, which houses an Investiture Exhibition. The last tower is *Granary Tower,* between which and King's Gate the wall has arrow slits, so designed that two or three archers could shoot out of a single opening.

The **Town Walls,** nearly ½ m. in circumference and strengthened by towers, enclose a roughly rectangular area to the N. of the castle, to which, forming a single scheme of defence, they were joined at Northeast and Eagle towers. The town within, with several 16-19C houses, still retains the regular pattern standard to Edward I's English Boroughs. The walls are almost complete, and had E. and W. gates at either end of what is today's High Street. The tower at the W. gate (also known as *Porth-y-Aur,* or Golden Gate) is now the headquarters of the Royal Welsh Yacht Club (founded 1847). At the E. end the gate is also known as *Porth Mawr* or Great Gate. Below, in Greengate Street, the little window in the S.E. corner of the arch is that of the cell which until 1835 served as town lock-up. The most interesting building around the walls is the *Chantry of St Mary* (or Old Church), structurally incorporated within the walls at their N.W. angle where the adjoining tower serves as vestry and bell-tower. The church (restored) was built in the 14C by Henry de Elierton, later master mason of the castle.

The Roman fort of **Segontium†** is ½ m. S.E. of Castle Square on A4085 to Beddgelert. The site is owned by the National Trust, the museum is a branch of the National Museum of Wales, and the whole is under the guardianship of the Department of the Environment (A.M.). Probably founded in 78 by Agricola as a fort for auxiliary troops, the fort remained occupied until c. 380, one reason for its abandonment possibly being the withdrawal of troops from Britain by Magnus Maximus, who came to Britain as an official of Theodosius and was declared emperor by disaffected legions (he would later become Macsen Wledig of the 'Mabinogion'). There is a tradition that Constantine the

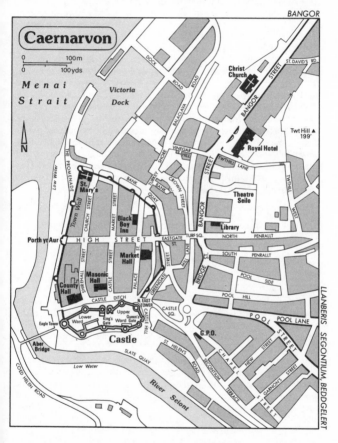

Great was born here, although in fact he was probably born c. 288 at Nis in Yugoslavia. Bar the ground plan outlined by foundations, little remains to be seen of the fort. Of more interest is the *Museum*, covering not only this site but the Romans generally. Among the subjects explained are the conquest and occupation of Wales; the military organization of the Roman army, with an accoutred model of an auxiliary infantryman; pottery making and Samian pottery, with some good examples of potters' name-stamps; the cult of Mithras; daily life at

Segontium.—*Llanbelig Church*, just E. of the site, is interesting for the continuity it provides from early pagan worship; it stands close to the Roman Mithraeum (located in 1959, but now covered; plaque on house), and the modern cemetery across the road stands on the Roman one. The church is dedicated to Peblig (Publicus), son of Magnus Maximus. The oldest part is the S. wall (probably 13C); the transepts and choir are mainly 14C; and the lower part of the tower is 15C. Once the tower was whitewashed as a navigation mark for ships.

A4085, leaving Caernarvon, passes Segontium and Llanbelig, crosses the Seiont, and ascends generally following the line of a Roman road. Ahead to the S.E. rises Moel Eilio (2300 ft) and to the S. Mynydd Mawr (2290 ft).—*5 m. Betws Garmon*, at the boundary of Snowdonia National Park, possibly derives its name from St Germanus. Hafoty House, just beyond, has pleasant walks in rock and water gardens beside the Nant Mill waterfall, a popular haunt of 19C artists. The road, beside the Gwyrfai and approaching wilder scenery, reaches *Llyn Cwellyn* (464 ft), on the farther side of which the bold crag of *Castell Cidwm* (Wolf's Castle) rises sheer from the water. About halfway along the lake is the *Snowdon Ranger Hostel*, starting point of one of the recognized routes up the mountain. The house was opened as an inn early in the 19C by a mountain guide, doubtless the pioneer of the track; later the place became a monastery, and it is now a youth hostel.—*4 m. Rhyd-Ddu* (600 ft) is a pleasantly situated hamlet from which a path joins the Snowdon Pitt's Head Track.

From Rhyd-Ddu B4418 passes in ½ m. (!.) a path leading to Beddgelert Forest, with many walks. In another ½ m. this road reaches *Llyn-y-Dywarch*, mentioned by Giraldus as possessing a floating island; it still occasionally happens that a piece of the peat shore breaks away and drifts about. This road continues W., to the S. in about 2 m., beyond *Mynydd Tal-y-Mignedd* (c. 2 m. away), being a remarkable circular cairn resembling a mill chimney. Local tradition ascribes the cairn to rivalry between the quarrymen of Rhyd-Ddu and Nantlle.

Pitt's Head Rock, 1 m. S. of Rhyd-Ddu, starting place of the similarly named Snowdon ascent, is so called because of its supposed resemblance to the statesman's profile. The watershed here is at 650 ft, and the road now descends Nant Colwyn, with *Beddgelert Forest* (F.C. walks) on the W., dropping over 500 ft in 2¾ m. to (*3 m.* from Rhyd-Ddu) *Beddgelert* and, *2 m.* farther, *Pont Aberglaslyn*. For these last three places. see pp. 149-50.

At Pont Aberglaslyn Rte 8 crosses the bridge to Penrhyndeudraeth, while this Route continues south. On the E. are the wide, marshy flats of *Traeth Mawr* (7000 acres). Until the early 19C a broad estuary navigable up to Pont Aberglaslyn, this became reclaimed land between 1807-11 when W. A. Madocks M.P. (1774-1828) built his great embankment (The Cob) across the mouth of the Glaslyn. Beyond the flats rise Cnicht and the Moelwyns, while to the W. of the road is Moel Ddu (1811 ft).—*3 m.* (from Pont Aberglaslyn) *Glaslyn Hotel,* beyond which the road skirts a range of steep, wooded cliffs. This is the *Coed Tremadog Nature Reserve* (permit from N.C.), a large area of oak, also botanically interesting because of the plants which have survived thanks to the absence of sheep. *Tan-yr-Allt*, S. of the road just before Tremadog, was the residence of W. A. Madocks.

Tan-yr-Allt was the scene of the 'Tremadog Incident', long a perplexity to Shelley's biographers. In Sept. 1812 the poet, attracted by Madocks's 'generous project', symbolizing a pre-eminence of mind over matter, came here with Harriet to offer his assistance. They occupied a house (now pulled down) at the W. end of the grounds, and here much of 'Queen Mab' was written. One night the following February, according to Shelley and Harriet, the house was forcibly entered, shots were fired, and Shelley's life was attempted. Thereupon the pair departed. The incident is now explained as a successful ruse to scare Shelley away, adopted by certain shepherds who objected to the poet's habit of putting sick or injured sheep out of pain when he came across them on his walks.

2m. **Tremadog** was built by W. A. Madocks between 1805-07, and, largely unaltered, remains a good example of early 19C town planning. T. E. Lawrence (Lawrence of Arabia, 1888-1935) was born here (plaque).—*1m.* **Porthmadog**, see p. 190.

12 ANGLESEY

The name Anglesey is generally accepted as meaning Island of the Angles, but some authorities derive it from the Norse 'öngull' meaning fiord. In Welsh it is Môn (the Mona of Tacitus), to which is sometimes added 'Mam Cymru' (Mother of Wales), a title arising from the island's extensive cornfields. Anglesey was occupied by man from very early times. Middle Stone Age remains of c. 7000 B.C. have been found, and the island is rich in later prehistoric sites. The island was the chief centre of the Druids, attacked by Suetonius Paulinus in 61 and almost exterminated by Agricola in 78, and later became a stronghold of the princes of Gwynedd. For some 200 years (850-1050) Anglesey was subjected to Norse raids.

Scenically Anglesey is for the most part undulating and somewhat monotonous, though there are some pleasant stretches of coast, this in 1967 being designated an Area of Outstanding Natural Beauty. Through the island run the main road and railway to Holyhead, an industrial town and increasingly important port, with the passenger and car ferry service to Dún Laoghaire in Ireland. Otherwise Anglesey is visited mainly for its prehistoric sites, for the mansion of Plas Newydd, for the great castle of Beaumaris, and for some unpretentious resorts.

The direct road from Menai Bridge to Holyhead (Rte 12A) is uninteresting. Visitors wishing to see the best of Anglesey should make the circuit of the island (Rte 12B).

A Menai Bridge to Holyhead

A5. 21 miles—*17 m. Valley.*—*4 m.* **Holyhead**

The **Menai Strait**, with for the most part green and pleasant banks, is a channel about 13 m. long and varying in width between a mile and 200 yards. The principal towns, both on the mainland, are Caernarvon (S.) and Bangor (N.). Near the latter the strait is crossed by road and rail bridges 1 m. apart. Before the construction of these bridges crossing was by ferry, and cattle herds for sale on the mainland had to swim across.— The building of the **Menai Suspension Bridge** by Thomas Telford in 1819-26 may be said to mark the zenith of stagecoach traffic, and the bridge remained the only link with Anglesey until the completion of Stephenson's railway bridge in 1850. The bridge was reconstructed in 1938-41, when the original light and graceful design was adhered to, except that the structure was strengthened, the roadway widened, and the number of chains supporting the roadway reduced from 16 to four.

The bridge measures 579 ft between the piers and 1000 ft overall. To allow for the passage of ships the roadway runs 100 ft above highwater mark. The strait is well seen from the bridge.—*Britannia Railway Bridge*, 1 m. W., carries the main line from London to Holyhead across the strait. The tubular bridge built by Robert Stephenson between 1846-50 was burnt out in early 1970, and the rail link was only restored with the completion of a new, conventional bridge in January 1972. Further reconstruction, including a road, is planned. A statue to Nelson, to the W. of the bridge, was erected in 1873 by Admiral Lord Clarence Paget as an aid to navigation.

Menai Bridge is a small town below the Anglesey end of the suspension bridge. *Tourist Information* on A5 past the first roundabout. The *Museum of Childhood*† specializes in aspects of childhood since the early 19C, exhibits including dolls, toys, magic lanterns, and suchlike. *Tegfryn Art Gallery*† shows works by north Wales artists. On *Church Island* (W. of A5), reached by a causeway, there is a little 14C church, originally founded in 630 by St Tysilio. This is thought to have been the landing place of Archbishop Baldwin in 1188.

A5 soon passes the *Anglesey Column* (90 ft), commemorating the 1st Marquess (1768-1854), who commanded the cavalry at Waterloo where he lost a leg. The column was erected in 1817, the statue by Noble being added in 1860. The top of the column affords an extensive and interesting view (115 steps. Fee). For more about the Marquess, see Plas Newydd, p. 167.

2m. **Llanfair P.G.** is the accepted abbreviation for *Llanfairpwllgwyngyllgogerychwyrndrobwllllantysiliogogogoch* (St Mary's Church in a hollow by the white hazel close to the rapid whirlpool by the red cave of St Tysilio), a name probably invented as a tourist lure, which it still is, at least to the extent that the longest platform ticket in the world is still the most popular local souvenir. The first Women's Institute in Britain was founded here in 1915.

For *Plas Newydd*, ½ m. S.W., see p. 167.—At *Penmynydd*, 2 m. N.W., the mansion (present building 1576; no adm.) was for centuries the home of the Tudors. Here was born Owen Tudor, believed to have married Catherine of Valois, widow of Henry V, their grandson being Henry VII. In the church (14C) is the alabaster tomb (c. 1385) of Gronw Tudor, uncle of Owen, and of his wife. The alabaster is chipped, due to a tradition that it could alleviate eye disease.

4m. **Pentre Berw,** beyond which the road crosses the *Malltraeth Marsh.* On the far side is the junction with A5114, 1 m. up which is *Llangefni* (3500 inhab.), the main market town of Anglesey. Tregarnedd (no adm.), a farm to the S.E. of the town, was the home of Ednyfed Fechan, counsellor to Llewelyn the Great.—*12m. Valley,* thought to have received its name from Telford when making a road-cutting through a small hill here, is now best known for its R.A.F. airfield, built in 1941 and in turn a fighter base, trans-Atlantic terminal, flying school, and missile practice camp. Iron Age bronze weapons and horse trappings, found at Llyn Cerrig Bach (2 m. S.E.), are now in the National Museum of Wales. Beyond Valley, A5 and the railway together cross a causeway 1200 yards long to **Holy Island** (see below), on which are the town of Holyhead with its important harbour, Holyhead Mountain at the N.W. with impressive cliff scenery, and several archaeological sites. *Penrhos Nature Reserve*†, at the W. end of the causeway, of interest for its variety of birds, is owned by *Anglesey*

Aluminium Ltd (W. of the road), a joint venture of the American Kaiser Aluminum and Chemical Corporation and the British Rio Tinto-Zinc Ltd. The plant produces some 100,000 tons a year. The company's jetty at Holyhead port has suction equipment for discharging alumina on to a conveyor belt to the plant about 1½ m. away.

3 m. **HOLYHEAD,** or *Caer Gybi* (10,500 inhab.), mainly a commercial and industrial town but also something of a resort, owes its

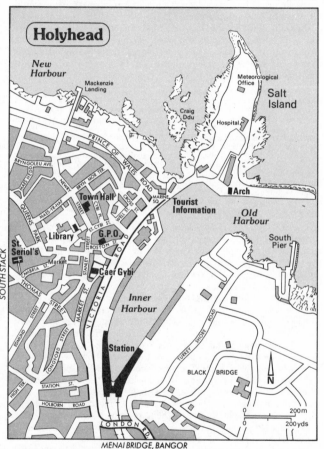

importance to its harbour. Francis Dodd (1874-1949), the painter and engraver, was a native of Holyhead. After curving across the railway, A5 reaches a fork, the left arm of which quickly reaches the main shopping streets (Market Street, extended by Stanley Street). Just E. of these streets is the small Roman fort of **Caer Gybi,** enclosing the churchyard of the church of the same name. The fort, dating from the 3-4C and probably built as a protection against pirates, forms a rectangle with round towers at the corners. Except on the E. the walls are largely intact. The N.E. and S.E. towers were largely rebuilt in the 18 and 19C respectively. In the 6C St Cybi used the walls as a protection for the church he founded here. Today's building is mainly 15-17C, though the choir is 13C (restored). In the Stanley Chapel the recumbent figure of the Hon. W. O. Stanley (d. 1884) is by Hamo Thornycroft (1897) and the windows are by Burne-Jones and William Morris. The smaller church to the S., known as Egylwys y Bedd (Church of the Grave) is said to contain the grave of a 5C pirate leader.

From the road fork the righthand road (Victoria Road) soon reaches Marine Square (*Tourist Information*). The port is beyond, while the road to the W., crossing open green slopes, skirts the *New Harbour* (Coast Guard, sailing clubs), opened in 1873 and protected by a breakwater 7860 ft long.

Port of Holyhead. Packet boats between Holyhead and Ireland are mentioned as early as 1573. Important later dates were 1801, when Holyhead was officially selected as the Irish packet station, at first to Howth but after 1834 to Dún Laoghaire; 1808, completion of the South Stack lighthouse; 1820, when steam began to replace sail; 1826, the opening of the Menai road bridge; 1850, the opening of the Menai railway bridge; 1873, completion of the New Harbour; 1880, when the Inner Harbour was opened; 1965, when the car ferry service was introduced; and 1970-71 when there was no rail traffic because of the destruction by fire of the Menai railway bridge. Recent developments have been the construction of a new terminal at Salt Island; the introduction of the 7836 ton multi-purpose 'St Columba'; and the growth of container traffic.—An arch (1821) at the entrance to Admiralty Pier, protecting the Inner Harbour, marks the end of A5 and commemorates the landing here by George IV. For the Anglesey Aluminium jetty, see p. 165.

The remainder of **Holy Island** is worth touring, both for its cliff scenery and its prehistoric remains, and the following round is suggested. From Holyhead, Cambria Street, passing the prominent, modern St Seriol's Church, leads towards South Stack, rounding *Holyhead Mountain,* or *Mynydd Twr* (710 ft), with many paths. The view includes Snowdonia, and sometimes the Isle of Man and the Mountains of Mourne in Ireland. The hillfort on the mountain has its best preserved rampart on the N. side. Approaching the coast the road turns right and climbs towards South Stack, about halfway up being a car park (l.). Across the road from here are the *Holyhead Mountain Hut Circles,* named and sometimes signposted as 'Irishmen's Huts' (Cytiau Gwyddelod) in obedience to a tradition, without any archaeological backing, that the huts were those of the Goidelic (Irish) Celts driven out by the Brythonic Celts in the 5C. The huts represent an extensive settlement of the 2-4C. Originally the settlement may have occupied something like 20 acres, but today only 20 huts remain, of which 14 are in the main group. The huts are circular or rectangular, some of the former having traces of central hearths and slabs indicating the positions of beds and seats.

The road (narrow, steep, and often very crowded) ends at a small parking area above *South Stack Lighthouse*†. Steps lead down to a small suspension bridge which crosses to the stack. The automated lighthouse (91 ft high and 197 ft above high water) was built in 1808 by David Alexander, who also built Dartmoor prison. The steps, with an associated nature trail, enable the seabird colonies to be well seen.

The road back passes the hut circles, just below which there is a T junction, the right arm of which is signed Treadour. In ½ m., a short way up a road to the left, are the *Penrhos Feilw Standing Stones,* two stones 10 ft high, traditionally at the centre of a circle though nothing of this is now visible. In another ¾ m. the coastal road reaches the head of the small bay of *Porth Dafarch* with a road junction at which there are traces of hut circles. Rather less than 2 m. farther E. the road meets B4545. Here, if B4545 is crossed, the road soon bears N. and in about 1 m. reaches *Trefignath Burial Chamber,* consisting of a long passage, once divided into several chambers. Today the E. chamber is the best preserved and is flanked by two upright stones. *Ty Mawr Standing Stone* is ½ m. farther up this road. If B4545 is taken S.E. for 1 m., a side road bears S. for *Rhoscolyn.* Here St Gwenfaen founded a church in the 6C, and her well on the W. slope of Rhoscolyn Head was long supposed to cure mental disorders.

B   Circuit of the Island

A4080 and A5 to Valley: A5025 to Pentraeth: B5109 to Beaumaris: minor roads to Penmon and back: A545 to Menai Bridge. 78 miles.—*2 m.* **Llanfair P.G.**—*9 m.* **Newborough.**—*6 m.*   *Aberffraw.*—*4 m.*   *Rhosneigr.*—*9 m.*   *Valley.*—*16 m.* **Amlwch.**—*5 m.* **Rhos Lligwy.**—*6 m.* *Pentraeth.*—*6 m.* **Beaumaris.**—*8 m.* **Penmon Priory** and back.—*7 m.* **Menai Bridge.**

Menai Bridge to **Llanfair P.G.** (*2 m.*), see p. 164.

A4080 bears S., in a little over 1 m. reaching ***Plas Newydd†**, a magnificent mainly 18C mansion beside Menai Strait, seat of the marquesses of Anglesey and since 1976 belonging to the National Trust. In addition to splendid rooms, furniture, and portraits, the house contains important works by Rex Whistler, including his largest wallpainting, and a museum devoted to the militarily renowned 1st Marquess who, as Lord Uxbridge, led the British cavalry at Waterloo.

History. The original house here was built in the early 16C by the Griffith family of Penrhyn, the estate later descending by marriage to the Bagenal, Bayly, and (1737) Paget families. An early Paget, a chief adviser of Henry VIII, had acquired the large estate of Beaudesert (demolished 1935) in Staffordshire and been created Baron Paget, the creation containing the unusual provision that the title should, if necessary, continue through the female line. This happened as the result of the marriage in 1737 between Caroline Paget and Sir Nicholas Bayly, their son becoming 9th Baron Paget in 1769 when the 8th Baron died childless. In 1784 he was created 1st Earl of Uxbridge, a title which in the first creation had already been held by the 7th and 8th barons Paget. From various sources this new 1st Earl of Uxbridge acquired immense wealth, and it was he who between 1783 and 1809 refashioned Plas Newydd from a medieval manor into an 18C mansion. The first phase was 1783-86 when, to match that at the S. end, another octagonal tower was built at the N. end of the E. front. In the second phase (1793-99) James Wyatt and Joseph Potter of Lichfield achieved a new entrance front on the W., created the Classical and Gothic interiors of the present main block, and built the stables. Potter added the N. wing between 1805-09. The grounds owe much to Humphry Repton, commissioned in 1798 to advise on the layout. In 1812 the estate passed to its most illustrious owner, the 2nd Lord Uxbridge, commander of the cavalry during the retreat to Corunna and at Waterloo and after the latter battle created 1st Marquess of Anglesey. Towards the end of the battle his leg was smashed, upon which he exclaimed to Wellington, riding beside him, 'By God, sir, I've lost my leg!', Wellington replying, momentarily glancing away from the retreating French, 'By God, sir, so you have!'. What must surely be a unique monument is the one in the town of Waterloo commemorating this leg. The Marquess eloped with Wellington's sister-in-law, fathered 18 children, and died aged 84. (See also Cavalry Museum below, and Anglesey Column p. 164). In the 1930s the 6th Marquess removed the battlements from the parapets, shortened the pinnacles on the E. front, giving them Tudor caps to match those on the entrance side, remodelled the N. wing, and created a long dining room, decorated by Rex Whistler, a close friend of the Pagets, between 1936-40. In 1976 the 7th Marquess gave the house and surrounding land to the National Trust.

The car park is beside the early 19C dairy, with a National Trust shop and information centre. From the front of the dairy can be seen the turreted and castellated stables (Potter, 1797). To the left of the stables are the large stones of a prehistoric burial chamber.

The *Gothick Hall* (1796-98) is a lofty rectangular room rising through two storeys and having a gallery. Pictures here include a contemporary portrait of the 1st Baron Paget; a portrait by Van Dyck; and two large works by Snyders. Another portrait is of Caroline Paget. The banners, both of the Royal Horse Guards, are of the Peninsular and Waterloo campaigns. The *Music Room,* also 1796-98 and the finest room in the house, occupies the site of the hall of the original building. The carved woodwork here, as elsewhere in the house, is that of Potter's craftsmen. Among the portraits are four by Hoppner (of the 1st Marquess, his sister and his second wife, and his younger brother Sir Arthur Paget), one by Lawrence of the 1st Marquess, and one by Romney of the Earl of Uxbridge. The *Hall and Staircase,* and the remaining rooms, are generally in the Neo-Classical style (note for instance the Doric columns) associated with Wyatt. In the hall there are two portraits of early Pagets, one attributed to Leandro Bassano and the other (1578), of the wife of the 2nd Lord Paget, by Marc Gheeraedts. The eight canvases of scenes of the Duke of Marlborough's campaigns are by Laguerre, and the full-length portrait of Wellington is by John Lucas. On the top landing there are Elizabethan portraits of the 1st Lord Paget (1549), of a young man (1585), and of Henry VIII and Queen Elizabeth. The *Landing and Gallery* and passages have more pictures, notably a group of the 1st Marquess's children, painted by Wilkin; early 19C watercolours of Beaudesert and Anglesey, the latter part of a set by John 'Warwick' Smith; and one, in the passage leading to Lady Anglesey's bedroom, of Florence Paget (the 'Pocket Venus') as a child (Henry Graves, 1850). She was the central figure of a Victorian scandal; courted by the Marquess of Hastings and by Henry Chaplin, both wealthy gamblers and rivals also of the turf, Florence accepted Chaplin but promptly eloped with and married Hastings, who however soon died of dissipation leaving Forence a widow at twenty-six. *Lady Anglesey's Bedroom,* occupying the octagonal S.E. tower, affords views along Menai Strait, including the family's private harbour (the 1st Marquess and his father always kept three yachts at Plas Newydd). The plaster frieze and chimneypiece date from the redecoration of 1793-99, but the present colour scheme was introduced in the 1930s by Lady Marjorie Manners, wife of the 6th Marquess, with the advice of Sibyl Colefax, a leading decorator of that period. *Lord Anglesey's Bedroom* also has a frieze and chimneypiece of the 1790s. The late 17 or early 18C state bed came from Beaudesert. The marine pictures are 19C English and Dutch.

The tour of the house returns down a spiral staircase of 1795 to the Gothick Hall, beyond which is the *Ante Room,* of Neo-Classical design signed and dated 1795 by Wyatt. The portrait of the 1st Earl of Uxbridge as a young man is attributed to Batoni, and the one opposite, of one of his sons, is by Lawrence. Among the furnishings are Louis XV chairs; a pair of Napoleonic Sèvres vases, with campaign scenes; gilt console tables in the style of Robert Gumley and James Moore, two leading craftsmen of the early 18C; and two gilt gesso pier glasses, bearing the Paget crest in medallions. The *Octagon Room* has an identical frieze to that in the Ante Room. Furnishings include early 19C Rococo games tables, one with a chessboard bearing the lions and eagles of the Paget arms; Louis XV chairs upholstered in a pattern of naval scenes; an 18C pier glass in the style of William Kent. The picture of the Menai Bridge was painted two years after its opening. The *Saloon* represents various periods. The bay window forms the base of a round tower added in 1751; the general form of the room may date to the alterations of 1783-86; the frieze, window mouldings, and double doors are Wyatt's of 1795. The elaborate marble chimneypiece was probably bought in 1796 from the elder Richard Westmacott. The room contains some interesting pictures, among these being four large pastoral scenes by B. P. Ommeganck; Queen Victoria and her suite riding at Windsor by R. B. Davis (1837); and the 1st Marquess, also by R. B. Davis (1830). The two busts, both by Reid Dick (1921 and 1925), are of Lady Caroline Paget and her mother, the 6th Marchioness. Outstanding among the furniture are the gilt pier tables and glasses (early 18C). In the *Breakfast Room* the frieze and pairs of double doors are all of c. 1795-98, and the chimneypiece is almost certainly by Westmacott. Most of the pictures are seascapes, including two watercolours showing Plas Newydd and Britannia Tubular Bridge (both Nicholas Pocock).

The *Rex Whistler Exhibition,* in the octagonal tower added in 1783-86, comprises a number of portraits of the family and also examples of Whistler's skills as book illustrator, stage designer, and decorative artist. Beyond, the long dining room created by the 6th Marquess is now the *Rex Whistler Room,* containing the artist's last and largest mural, in trompe l'oeil. The basic theme is an estuary with Renaissance cities, their buildings of every style and period, some genuine, others inventions. Throughout there are frequent references to the family, and Whistler includes himself as a young man sweeping leaves. In the small room beyond can be seen architectural drawings for the house, including Wyatt's and Potter's designs. The *Cavalry Museum* is in two parts. One room is devoted to the 1st Marquess. It includes a portrait by Winterhalter, and also an Anglesey Leg, an artificial limb used by the Marquess, invented and patented by James Potts of Chelsea. In the second room there is a vast picture of Waterloo (Denis Dighton), of particular interest for the accuracy of the uniforms.

2m. (from Llanfair P.G.) *Cefn Bach* is a hamlet at a crossroads. The road N. soon reaches the path to **Bryn Celli Ddu,** a well-preserved burial chamber of 2000-1500 B.C. The mound is modern protection and covers only a small part of the area of the prehistoric mound, which was 160 ft in diameter. The polygonal chamber, roofed by two stones and approached through an open outer passage (6 ft long) and an inner passage (20 ft long), was within but not in the centre of a circular area. It was surrounded by four concentric stone circles, three of which were within the cairn while the fourth marked the base. An incised stone found here, now in the National Museum of Wales, has been replaced by a replica (see also Barclodiad-y-Gawres, p. 171). The road S. from the crossroads in 1 m. reaches Menai Strait at *Moel-y-Don,* possibly the landing place of Suetonius and Agricola.—About 1½ m. farther along

A4080 another crossroads is reached, from which the lane S. soon reaches the little, disused church of *Llanidan,* known for its stoup which never dries up and reputedly had miraculous healing powers. There has been a church on this site since 616, when the first may have been founded by St Nidan, possibly a missionary from Scotland. The present building (13-15C) is part of an earlier church, the division between the aisles of which survives in the arcade outside. In the church there is an ancient stone reliquary, with a glass front, still showing bones, traditionally of St Nidan but in fact proven to be female.—*2m. Brynsiencyn* was once a Druid centre. Just beyond the village a road bears N., almost at once reaching *Caer Leb,* an Iron Age pentagonal enclosure defended by a double rampart. Excavation here in the 19C found remains of a rectangular building and a circular hut. From here a path leads S.W. to reach in ½ m. *Castell Bryn-Gwyn,* where a rampart and ditch enclosed a circular area of 180 ft diameter. The site appears to date from three periods, the first being New Stone Age; the second, of unknown date, when the width of the rampart was doubled at the expense of the ditch; and the third at about the time of the Roman conquest when a rampart was built over the earlier ditch. Little of this can now be recognized. Beyond Caer Leb the side road crosses another small road, ¼ m. beyond (r.) being *Bodowyr Burial Chamber,* with a capstone balanced on top of three uprights.

5 m. **Newborough,** formerly Rhosyr, is a small town which received its charter and English name from Edward I in 1303 when he transferred here people displaced by the construction of Beaumaris. From the 17C until the 1920s the weaving of marram grass ropes, baskets, and mats was a thriving local cottage industry. Around the town, except to the N.E., spreads the **Newborough Warren-Ynys Llanddwyn Nature Reserve** (F.C. and N.C.), the main interest of which is forest, marsh, and dunes. The reserve comprises five sections (see below) and can be seen by using a choice of recognized paths. The only motor road through the main reserve runs from Newborough for 2 m. through the forest to a car park and picnic site (fee in summer; information and leaflets) near the shore about halfway between Ynys Llanddwyn and Newborough Warren.

Malltraeth Pool, at the N. tip of the reserve, is beside A4080 2 m. N. of Newborough. It is protected by an embankment built by Telford as a sea defence, and is mainly a bird sanctuary.—South of here is *Cefni Saltmarsh,* reached by a path from near the F.C. office on A4080. An area of some 400 acres, the marsh is known for its sea plants and grasses.—To the E. and S. of the marsh stretches *Newborough Forest* of c. 2000 acres, planted in 1948 at which time sand often blocked roads and covered crops. Thanks to the trees (mostly Corsican pine) and other anti-erosion measures this drifting is a thing of the past. The path mentioned above and the motor road both cross the forest; also a path running from Newborough through the forest and out on to *Ynys Llanddwyn,* a promontory nearly 1 m. long, the Pre-Cambrian rocks of which are amongst the oldest in Britain (more than 600 million years). In the 5C this was the retreat of St Dwynwen, patron saint of lovers. The present ruined church is 16C. The lighthouse was built in 1873, before which the nearby tower (1800) marked the promontory.— *Newborough Warren,* the large S.E. section of the reserve, was, until the ravages of myxomatosis, the home of so many rabbits that as many as 80,000 were trapped annually. In the 13C this was agricultural land and Abermenai, at the S.E. tip and at the W. end of Menai Strait, was an important anchorage. Storms during the 14C caused sand to cover the fields and block the anchorage, and the warren has remained an area of dunes ever since. The decrease in the rabbit population has brought an increasing spread of vegetation, marram grass being the principal plant. A path from the car park skirts the warren's N.W. side as far as Llyn Rhos-Ddu, and another (from Pen-Lon, beyond the little lake) crosses the E. side.

Within the 2 m. beyond Newborough, A4080 crosses a finger of the forest, skirts Malltraeth Pool, and crosses the Cefni at the head of its estuary.—*4 m. Llangadwaladr* has a 13-14C church, interesting for a stone (nave wall, N.) commemorating Cadfan (Catamanus), a king or prince of Gwynedd who died c. 625. Translated, the latin inscription reads 'Cadfan the King, wisest and most renowned of all kings'. The village's name is that of Cadfan's grandson Cadwaladr, defeated by the Northumbrians near the Tyne in 634. About 2 m. N.N.E. of here, reached by side roads, is the burial chamber of *Din Dryfol*. In poor condition today, the chamber seems originally to have been some 50 ft in length.—*2 m. Aberffraw* was the capital of Gwynedd from about the 7-13C, but of this past there is now no trace other than perhaps a Norman arch reset in the church and traditionlly a part of the palace. On a small rocky island, 1½ m. S.W., reached by causeway at low tide, the little church of St Cwyfan (restored 1893) stands on 7C foundations.—*2 m. Barclodiad-y-Gawres Burial Chamber,* on the N. side of the small Trecastell Bay, is interesting for sharing with Bryn Celli Ddu the distinction of being a burial chamber with mural art, five of the stones here being incised with designs. The chamber, re-arranged to protect the stones, comprises a 20 ft long passage, a central chamber, and side chambers. The original mound, remains of which can be seen, would have been some 90 ft in diameter.—*2 m. Rhosneigr* is a small seaside resort, in the 18C notorious for the ship wreckers who hid in the Crigyll estuary to the north. Hanged in 1741 they are the subject of a ballad by Lewis Morris.—The loop of A4080 serving Rhosneigr is completed N. of the railway at *Llanfaelog*, ¾ m. N.E. of the church of which is *Ty Newydd Burial Chamber,* with a capstone resting on three uprights. A4080 continues N. to join A5; about halfway between Llanfaelog and A5 (r. beside the road, opposite a house called Maen Hir) there stands an inscribed stone.

4 m (from Rhosneigr). Junction with A5, where Rte 12A is followed for *5 m.* to *Valley.*

A5025 is now followed northwards.—*2 m. Llanynghenedl*, 2 m. E. of which, near the S. end of Llyn Llywenan, is *Presaddfed Burial Chamber,* in fact two chambers, one collapsed but the other with capstone and uprights.—*8 m.* **Tregele** is a hamlet at a crossroads. *Cemlyn Bay,* rather over 1 m. W., a small shingle beach, is part of a National Trust property which includes a bird sanctuary, chiefly for winter migrant wildfowl. A nature trail (2 m.) has been arranged by the local field study centre.

Carmel Head, 2 m. W. of Cemlyn Bay, is the N.W. extremity of Anglesey. *The Skerries,* a group of islets 2 m. farther N.W., have carried a lighthouse since the 18C, and until the 19C all passing ships had to pay a toll.

Llanfechell, 1 m. S.E. of Tregele, was the home of the 18C diarist William Bulkeley. At *Llanbabo,* 3 m. farther S., the church contains a 14C incised figure of St Pabo, thought to have been a local chief who found it necessary to seek asylum here. *Wylfa Nuclear Power Station*†, immediately N. of Tregele, has an observation tower and exhibition open to the public. A nature trail (1 m.) rounds the headland.—*1 m.* **Cemmaes,** on the bay of the same name, is a small resort with good bathing and cliff walks. The church of *Llanbadrig* (1 m. N.) is said to have been founded by St Patrick, on a journey to Ireland, possibly as thanks for being saved in a shipwreck on Middle Mouse rock. The church was restored in 1884 by Lord Stanley, the local landowner; a Muslim, he insisted on Islamic style in, for example, the tiles. Beyond, *Llanlleiana,* the northernmost point in Wales, is thought to be named after a female recluse who founded a chapel here in the 5 or 6C. The headland, which is Natural Trust property, includes the hillfort of Dinas Gynfor.

5m. **Amlwch** (3000 inhab.) is a port and resort whose fortunes have fluctuated with those of the copper mines of *Parys Mountain* to the south. Intermittently worked since Roman times, the mines were at their most prosperous in the late 18 and early 19C, at which time Amlwch was the most populated part of Anglesey. Abandoned in the later 19C, due to a combination of exhaustion, unstable prices, and American and African competition, the mountain today is a bleak, deserted place with many dangerous shafts. The small port, built for the mines in 1793, has however now regained importance with the construction of the *Shell Marine Terminal* which began in 1973. This comprises the single-buoy moorings 2 m. offshore, underwater pipelines to the shore station, and twin pipelines to a transit storage installation at Rhosgoch, 2 m. southwest. From here a pipeline runs 78 m. to the refinery at Stanlow in Cheshire.

The Parys Mountain mining company is also known for its penny and halfpenny tokens (1787-93). Minted when provincial tokens were introduced because of the shortage and poor quality of official copper currency, the Parys tokens became known both for their quality and for their design.

The church of St Eilian (¾ m. E.) is 15C, with a 12C tower. It contains a 15C rood screen and loft; 15C seats and book desks; wooden dog tongs; and an ancient painting of St Eilian (?), whose chapel adjoins the choir. In this chapel there is a curious semicircular piece of furniture, once believed to bring good luck to those who could turn round within it without touching the sides. St Eilian's Well, near the sea, was thought to have healing powers.

2m. Penysarn, 2 m. S.E. of which is *Traeth Dulas,* the now almost landlocked estuary of the small river Dulas. Beyond the estuary is the island of Ynys Dulas, with a 19C tower which served as a mark for ships. Dulas was the home of the Morris brothers (monument), together men of letters and patrons of the arts. The church at *Llandyfrydog* (2 m. S.W.) is mentioned by Giraldus as the scene of a sacrilege in 1098 when Hugh Lupus locked his dogs in the church overnight. The dogs went mad and the Earl was killed within the month.—*3 m. Rhos Lligwy.* Here a road (signed Moelfre) bears E., in ½ m. reaching a small crossroads (A.M. sign). The road ahead continues for 1 m. to the small resort of *Moelfre.* Off here in 1859 the 'Royal Charter', returning to Liverpool from Australia, was wrecked with the loss of 452 lives. Charles Dickens came here soon afterwards and used the tragedy as the basis of a story in 'The Uncommercial Traveller'. The righthand turn from the crossroads soon reaches a group of three archaeological sites. ***Din Lligwy** was a defended settlement, built (or rebuilt) by local people during the final stages of the Roman occupation. The site covers about half an acre and much can still be seen of the stonework of two circular and several rectangular buildings inside an irregular defence wall. *Capel Lligwy* is a now roofless chapel dating from the first half of the 12C, the upper walls of which were rebuilt in the 14C. A small S. chapel, with a crypt, was added in the 16C. Just S. of these sites, beside the road (r.), is *Lligwy Burial Chamber,* with a huge capstone (18 ft by 15 ft by 3 ft 6 in. and weighing 28 tons) supported by low uprights over a natural fissure, the greater part of the chamber thus being below ground. When excavated, bone fragments were found of thirty individuals.—The road reaches A5025, just E. up which the church of *Llanallgo* contains a memorial to the victims of the 'Royal Charter' (see above), buried in nine churchyards. *Traeth Bychan,* the bay to the S.E., was the scene of a submarine tragedy in 1939, when H.M.S. 'Thetis' failed to surface and 99 men lost their lives.

4m. (from Rhos Lligwy) **Benllech** is a family resort with some 2 m. of sand. The poet Goronwy Owen was born in the parish. *Red Wharf Bay* (Traeth Coch) to the S. has 3 m. of sand at low tide. Castell Mawr, on the N. headland, was a hillfort which, on the evidence of coins found here, may have been occupied by the Romans.—*2m. Pentraeth* was on the coast until stranded inland by land reclamation. Here B5109 is taken. In about 2½ m. a road bears S.W. to *Llansadwrn,* where the church contains a memorial of 520, unusual for being both to a holy man (Beatus Saturninus, i.e. Blessed Sadwen) and also to his saintly wife.

6m. **BEAUMARIS** (2000 inhab.) is a small resort and important yachting centre, pleasantly situated on Menai Strait with a view across Lavan Sands (see p. 121) to the mainland mountains. The town's earlier history is that of its great castle, today a major tourist attraction. The growth of tourism during the 19C brought the construction of a pier, the founding of the yacht club (Beaumaris is the home of the Royal Anglesey), and the building of Victoria Terraces, designed by Joseph Hansom of Hansom cab fame. Bathing is poor (shingle). In summer there is a passenger ferry to Bangor and Menai Bridge.

The *Castle†, now an extensive ruin, occupies an open site on level ground close to the shore. It is a concentric castle of almost perfect symmetry, encircled by a once tidal moat, and is particularly interesting for its sophisticated defences, which were, however, virtually never used. The outer curtain is superficially square, but since each of the four sides has a slight salient the form in practice is a flattened octagon, this allowing attack from any direction to be met. This outer wall is strengthened by towers. The more massive square inner defence is higher, permitting simultaneous firing from both outer and inner walls. The inner wall, also with towers, is noteworthy for its almost continuous internal passage. Another defensive trick is that the outer gateways are out of alignment with their gatehouses, this forcing an attacker to make an oblique approach.

History. Prince Madog had sacked Caernarvon in 1294, and it may have been this that prompted Edward I to start building Beaumaris, the last of his Welsh castles, the following year. At the same time the associated English Borough was granted its charter, taking the name Beau Marais (Beautiful Marsh) from an area soon to be drained by the castle moat system. The architect was James of St George and, although the castle was never completed, it was declared to be in a state of defence by 1298. Architecturally, the inner part of the S. gatehouse remained unfinished, the hall in the inner ward was scarcely started, and the towers were never properly roofed. In 1403 the castle was taken by Owen Glendower, but it was retaken in 1405. During the Civil War it was held (by a Bulkeley, the leading local family) for Charles I, but capitulated to General Mytton in 1646. At the Restoration Lord Bulkeley was reinstated as Constable, but the castle was abandoned in 1705. It nevertheless remained a Bulkeley possession until 1925 when it was made over to public ownership.

The moat, much wider than it is now, communicated with the sea by a short *Dock;* an iron ring to which boats were tied can still be seen. This dock was defended on its E. side by a projecting wing known as Gunner's

Walk, in a bastion of which was the castle mill, the sluice and spillway of which remain. A wooden bridge, replacing the former drawbridge, crosses the moat to the *Outer Ward*, which also had another gate at its N.E., a triple doorway which was never completed and is little more than a postern. Note the out-of-alignment arrangement, referred to above, of the gates and their gatehouses. The outer rampart walk, including twelve towers, affords fine views. The *Inner Ward* is entered by the S. gatehouse, guarded by a small rectangular barbican. The large gatehouses seem to have provided most of the living accommodation, that on the N. containing on its first floor what was intended to be the hall. The basement of the N.E. tower may have served as a prison. The tower on the E. face of the inner ward contains the beautiful Chapel, apsidal and vaulted and with a trefoiled arcade and doorway.

The *Bull's Head Hotel*, close to the castle, dates in part from 1472. During the Civil War it was commandeered by General Mytton, and later both Dr Johnson and Charles Dickens are said to have stayed here. The *Courthouse*, on the corner of Castle Street, was built in 1614. From farther along Castle Street, Steeple Lane leads to *Beaumaris Gaol†*, built in 1829 to designs by Hansom, and now a museum. Here can be seen the cells, including the punishment and condemned cells, a treadmill, and an exhibition of documents illustrating prison life in the 19C. The *Church of St Mary* (restored) dates from the early 14C, the nave having curious window-tracery and circular clerestory windows enclosing quatrefoils. The choir was rebuilt in 1500, but some original glass fragments have been set in the S. window. Among the monuments are the 16C altar-tomb of Sir Richard Bulkeley and his wife; a monumental stone to the father of Sir Philip Sidney; and, brought here from Llanfaes (see below), the carved stone coffin of Joan, wife of Llewelyn the Great and daughter of King John.

On rising ground N.W. of Beaumaris the *Bulkeley Monument* (1875) commemorates the family who were for generations Anglesey's leading landowners; their seat was *Baron's Hill*, between the monument and the town.

From Beaumaris this Route runs N. to Penmon Priory (c. 4 m. by side roads) before returning through Beaumaris to Menai Bridge.

Llanfaes, now a village, was until the 13C a commercial centre and port of some importance. In 1237 Llewelyn the Great founded a priory here over the tomb of his wife Joan; in 1295 Edward I removed all the inhabitants of Llanfaes to what is now Newborough and used the town's stonework as material for Beaumaris castle; and at the Dissolution the contents of the priory, including Joan's coffin, were removed to St Mary's in Beaumaris.—*Castell Llieniog* (E. of B5109, about 1 m. from Llanfaes) is a motte, perhaps erected by Hugh Lupus when he overran Anglesey in 1098, with fragments of a small square tower which withstood a Royalist siege in the Civil War. To the S. is the site of a battle of 819 in which the invading Saxons under Egbert gained a short-lived victory over the Welsh.

Penmon Priory was founded by St Seiriol in the 6C. The church was rebuilt between 1120-70, and in 1237 Llewelyn the Great granted the monastery and its property to the prior and canons of Priestholm (Puffin Island), who then apparently moved to Penmon, reorganizing the community as Austin Canons. The church and domestic buildings are now separate, the former serving as parish church and the latter being in the care of the Inspectorate of Ancient Monuments.

The *Church of St Seiriol*, as noted above, dates mainly from 1120-70, the nave being the oldest part (c. 1140) while the crossing and S. transept are of 1160-70. The choir is a rebuilding of c. 1220-40, coinciding with the arrival of the canons from Priestholm. There is a fine Norman pillar piscina in the nave; the base of a pre-Norman cross has been converted into a font; and another cross of the same period stands in the S. transept.—Immediately S. of the choir is the site of a small cloister, the W. side of which was the prior's house, now much altered and privately occupied. South of the cloister are the *Domestic Buildings*, a three-storey 13C wing containing the refectory, with a cellar below and dormitory above. Adjoining on the E. is an early 16C addition, which contained the warming room on the ground floor and the kitchen above.—Nearby is a square *Dovecot* of c. 1600, with a domed roof and open cupola, containing nearly 1000 nests. It was probably built by Sir Richard Bulkeley of Baron's Hill.—From near the church a path leads N. to *St Seiriol's Well*, possibly at the site of the 6C priory. The upper part of the small building covering the well seems to be 18C, but the much older lower part may incorporate something of the original chapel. The adjacent foundations of an oval hut may be those of the saint's cell. On the hill to the N.W. (¼ m.) stands a *Cross* of c. 1000, with intricate though mutilated carvings, including a Temptation of St. Anthony. The cross may have replaced an earlier one destroyed by the Norsemen.

The headland of *Trwyn Du*† is reached from by the dovecot. The lighthouse (1837) is automatic. Nearby is an old lifeboat station (1832-1915). To the S. are quarries, now disused, which provided stone for Beaumaris and, nearly six centuries later, for Telford and Stephenson for their Menai bridges.—*Puffin Island*, once known as Priestholm, is today also called Ynys Seiriol after the saint who established a settlement here in the 6C. The once large puffin population declined seriously when in the early 19C the pickled young birds were a popular delicacy. On the island are scanty remains of monastic settlement.

Small roads W. from Penmon lead in 3 m. to *Bwrdd Arthur* (500 ft), a bluff with a rampart enclosing traces of hut circles.

This Route returns from Penmon to (*4 m.*) Beaumaris, from where A545 skirts the wooded shore for *7 m. to* **Menai Bridge** (p. 164).

13   THE LLEYN

THE LLEYN (The Peninsula), some 25 miles long and 5-10 miles broad, thrusts S.W. into the Irish Sea. Scenically it is mainly mixed agricultural and wooded country, broken by groups of hills, those in the S.W. affording fine coastal views; in 1956 the coast was designated an Area of Outstanding Natural Beauty. The highest ground is to the N.E. where Yr Eifl rises to 1849 ft. Along the S. coast there are popular resorts such as Abersoch, Pwllheli, and Criccieth, but elsewhere, and particularly inland, the Lleyn is generally quiet and with something of a character of its own. It is a stronghold of the Welsh language. Places of specific interest are, along the N. coast, the church at Clynnog Fawr and the hillfort-village of Tre'r Ceiri; Bardsey Island, off the tip; and, along the S. coast, the 15C hall-house of Penarth Fawr, Llanystumdwy and its associations with Lloyd George, and the castle at Criccieth.

The Lleyn is described below as an anticlockwise circuit from Caernarvon.

A487 to Glanrhyd: A499 to Llanaelhaearn: B4417 and B4413 to Aberdaron: unclassified to Abersoch: A499 to Pwllheli: A497 to 1 m. W. of Porthmadog: A487 to Caernarvon. 78 miles.—*3 m.* *Glanrhyd.—7 m.* **Clynnog Fawr.—*4 m.* *Llanaelhaearn (Tre'r Ceiri).—6 m.* **Nefyn.—*13 m.* **Aberdaron.—*9 m.* **Abersoch.— *7 m.* **Pwllheli.—*7 m.* **Llanystumdwy.—*2 m.* **Criccieth.—*7 m.* *Dolbenmaen Church.—10 m.* *Glanrhyd.—3 m.* **Caernarvon.**

Caernarvon, see p. 158, is left by A487.—*3 m.* *Glanrhyd* is a road fork where this Route bears right on A499.—*2 m.* *Llandwrog* is just W. of the road.

From here a diversion (8 m. return) can be made N. to Belan. The road W. out of Llandwrog soon reaches the shore at *Dinas Dinlle,* a grass mound the summit of which is formed into a roughly oval fort by two ramparts and a ditch. It was probably used by both British and Romans, and it is also interesting as featuring, together with the islets of Arianrhod and Maen Dylan to the S., in one of the stories of the 'Mabinogion' ('Math, Son of Mathonwy'). The road now follows the shore through an area of shoddy building and across alluvial flats to *Fort Belan†* on the tip of the promontory which, with Abermenai to the N., forms the narrow entrance to Menai Strait. The fort was built by Thomas Wynne (of Glynllifon, S.E. of Llandwrog), 1st Baron Newborough, in 1775 as a garrison for the Royal Caernarvonshire Grenadiers, a force of 400 men raised and equipped at his own expense, a patriotic gesture which, by the time of his death in 1807, cost him a quarter of his fortune. Today's visitor can see the fort; the battery, with its cannons overlooking the Strait; and the 19C dock, with a small museum.

5 m. **Clynnog Fawr,** a typical Lleyn village, has a *Church* of outstanding interest. Founded by St Beuno c. 616 the church seems at first to have been monastic, but by 1291 it had become collegiate and it remained such until the Dissolution. The present building is of the early 16C. The N. porch has an exterior stair to an upper floor. Also noteworthy outside (S.W. angle of chapel) is a stone sundial of Anglo-Saxon type. The interior is an excellent example of late Perp., with fine windows. The choir has 14 contemporary stalls, and book-desks with linen-pattern panelling, and there is a rather plain rood screen (1531), with the base of its former loft curiously prolonged into the S. transept, where it is entered by a door communicating with a turret stair. Dog tongs (1815) are in the S. transept. The dugout chest beside the N.W. door is known as St Beuno's Chest. The church possesses a rare 15C mazer, shown only by prior arrangement. Under the tower arch is an

Elizabethan screen. From the tower, a passage (17C, and long used as the village lock-up) leads to *St Beuno's Chapel,* which contained the shrine or tomb of the saint, destroyed by fire in 1856 but until then regarded as miraculous. The chapel (restored 1913) is of a later date than the church, but the line of the foundations of an earlier building discovered during the restoration, perhaps Beuno's original church, is marked by dark floor-slabs. The stone with a cross is the original stone set up on the ground given to Beuno by Gwyddaint, Prince of Gwynedd. *St Beuno's Well,* beside the road (l.) just S. of the village, was a healing spring (Pennant writes of seeing a paralytic treated here). There are stone benches, steps down to the water, and niches probably intended for clothes.

Soon the road begins to leave the coast, ascending gradually, with the steep slopes of *Gurn Goch* (1607 ft) and *Gurn Ddu* (1712 ft) to the E. and a view of Holyhead to seaward.—*4 m. Llanaelhaearn,* a village at the foot of Yr Eifl, has a church entirely equipped with box-pews. An ancient stone in the N. transept is inscribed 'Aliortus Elmatiacos hic jacet'. From the village A499 continues S. to Pwllheli, but this Route follows B4417 along the S. flank of *Yr Eifl* (The Forks; 1849 ft), so called because of the triple peaks. The central peak, Yr Eifl proper, is flanked on the N.W. by a precipitous and much quarried summit (1458 ft) falling to the sea. To the S.W. below this, *Nant Gwrtheyrn,* is also known as Vortigern's Valley, one of a number (see also Dinas Emrys, p. 148) to which Vortigern is said to have fled. Here, according to one legend, he and his castle were destroyed by heavenly fire; according to another he was drowned by leaping into the sea. The quarrying village in the valley, deserted in 1954, has been acquired by an educational trust for use as a centre for Welsh language studies. On the peak to the E. of Yr Eifl is the hillfort-village of *Tre'r Ceiri (1591 ft), which can be reached by a path (¾ m.) which climbs from B4417 ¾ m. S. of Llanaelhaearn. Dating from the 2C, but perhaps earlier, this well-preserved site covers some five acres, enclosed by a rampart with an internal parapet. Inside there are remains of around 50 huts of varying shape and size. The enclosures outside the rampart were probably for cattle. The cairn above is Bronze Age in origin.

6 m. **Nefyn** (2000 inhab.), on the cliff, and *Morfa Nefyn* 1 m. W., with the adjacent twin sandy bays of *Porth Nefyn* and *Porth Dinllaen,* together form a quiet summer resort. Porth Dinllaen, a fine natural harbour, might have become the port for the packets to Ireland, but in 1838, as the result of a single vote in the House of Commons, Holyhead was chosen.—*5 m. Tudweiliog,* rather over 1 m. beyond which a road (signed Sarn) bears S.E., passing (r. after about 500 yards) a burial chamber.

8 m. **Aberdaron** is a picturesque holiday and fishing village, 2 m. short of the end of the Lleyn. A cafe and souvenir shop here was a 14C resting place for pilgrims on their way to Bardsey. The church, the graveyard wall of which is washed by the sea at high tide, consists of a 12C nave and choir, and a wide S. aisle added in the early 16C.; Gruffydd ap Rhys is said to have sought sanctuary here.

Aberdaron's best known native is Richard Roberts Jones (1780-1843), son of a local carpenter. Known as Dic Aberdaron, he was a strange vagabond and self-educated linguist, said to have spoken 35 languages and renowned for having compiled a dictionary in Welsh, Greek, and Hebrew. The dictionary can be seen at St Asaph, where its author is buried.

Roads run S.W. to within a short distance of *Braich-y-Pwll* and *Pen-y-Cil*, the two extremities of the Lleyn, both belonging to the National Trust. The former was the place from which pilgrims once embarked for Bardsey; there are a holy well and the foundations of a chapel. A road N.W. from Aberdaron leads in 2 m. to *Porthorion*, another National Trust property.

Bardsey Island†, 450 acres rising to 500 ft, is 2 m. off the tip of the Lleyn. The name is of Norse origin, and the Welsh name *Ynys Enlli* means Island of the Currents. Known also as the Island of 20,000 Saints, Bardsey was a major pilgrimage objective from the 5 or 6C onwards, three pilgrimages being reckoned as the equivalent of one to Rome. St Cadfan, from Britanny, is said to have founded the first monastery here in 429; in c. 545 St Dyfrig is thought to have died and been buried here (but see p. 321); and after the destruction in 607 of the great monastery of Bangor-is-Coed the surviving monks may have taken refuge here. In the N. part of the island are the 13C remains (little more than a bell-tower) of the Augustinian *St Mary's Abbey*, in the churchyard of which lie some of the 20,000 saints reputedly buried on the island. A nature reserve and now sparsely inhabited, Bardsey also has a lighthouse, an 18C cottage, and six 19C farmhouses, one of which is now the *Bird and Field Observatory*†. Opened in 1953, the Observatory's aims are to further interest in ornithology and other aspects of natural history (e.g. botany, entomology, marine biology etc.). In addition to the island's many birds, seals can normally be seen.

In 1977 the **Bardsey Island Trust Ltd** acquired an option (1977–80) to purchase the island. The Trust, springing from the Observatory, embraces many lovers of Bardsey and has received generous help from the World Wildlife Fund; a public appeal has been launched. The aims of the Trust are the purchase of the island; the protection of its beauty, its wildlife, its traditional farming system, and its interest as an ancient place of pilgrimage; and the guarantee of public access.

From Aberdaron an unclassified road is taken E., in *3 m.* reaching *Y Rhiw*, a hamlet on a miniature pass, commanding a wide view, including the sweep of Porth Neigwl or Hell's Mouth. The National Trust owns several properties around this coast. From here the road descends very steeply, at the foot of the hill being *Plas-yn-Rhiw*†, a small manor house, part medieval and part Tudor and Georgian.—*5 m. Llangian*, where in the churchyard (roughly in line with the S. centre window of the church) there is a particularly interesting 5C stone, inscribed Meli Medici/ Fili Martini/ Jacit (Here lies Melus the doctor, son of Martinus), the first mention of a doctor in Wales.

1 m. **Abersoch** is a small but growing resort at the end of the main coastal road from the north. Attractively situated with its harbour at the mouth of the Soch, with two large and sandy beaches, and recognized as an important yachting centre, the town can become very crowded. Boat trips can be taken to the *St Tudwal Islands*, the E. island having the remains of a small medieval priory. At *Llanengan*, 1½ m. S.W., there is a 15C church, tracing its origin to a foundation of the 6C. It consists of two naves, each crossed by a rood screen, one of which has an elaborately carved loft. Noteworthy also are the builder's 'credit' on the crossbeam of the vaulting of the S. nave; the tower, with bells from Bardsey; the old return-stalls, the 17C altar rails, and the dugout chest. South of Llanengan a road continues for 2 m. into the headland of *Mynydd Cilan* with good coastal scenery.

3 m. Llanbedrog, below the bold promontory of Mynydd Tir-y-Cwmwd (434 ft), is a sheltered resort. The path (3 m.) around the Mynydd offers views of St Tudwal's islands.

Just before Pwllheli, A497 bears northwest. *Bodvel Hall* (2 m.) was the birthplace of Dr Johnson's friend Mrs Thrale. At *Bodfuan,* 1 m. beyond, the church (1894) claims descent from a shrine founded in 595 by St Buan, to whom a cross has been erected.

4 m. **Pwllheli,** pron. Pool-thélli and meaning Salt Water Pool (4000 inhab. but much increased in summer), was created by the Welsh princes on the English Borough model, and received its first charter in 1355. Today it is both a crowded and popular resort and also the principal centre and market town for the Lleyn. The main town lies along A497, about ½ m. back from the long sand and shingle beach area with a promenade opened in 1890. At its E. end this seafront ends at a narrow hook of land forming one of the protecting arms of the almost landlocked harbour, with boatyards and providing shelter for many yachts.—*3 m. Penarth Fawr* (1 m. N. of the road. A.M. sign) is an interesting and attractive 15C hall-house, consisting essentially of one large room. A detailed explanation hangs on the wall.

The small road continues N. from Penarth Fawr across B4354 and through Llanarmon to (2 m.) *Llangybi.* Ffynnon Gybi (St Cybi's Well) here, 200 yards N.E. of the church, has a well-chamber with a paved walk, and niches in the wall. The beehive vaulting is thought to be unique in Wales, though found in Ireland.

After passing a huge holiday camp, A497 reaches (*4 m.*) **Llanystumdwy,** noted as the home of Earl Lloyd George of Dwyfor (1863-1945). Born in Manchester, he spent his early years at the cottage of his uncle (Highgate, on the main Criccieth road); he was educated at the church school at the W. end of the village; and he died at Ty Newydd, a house, above the Criccieth road, which he bought in 1939. His simple grave, designed by Clough Williams-Ellis, is beside the river. The *Lloyd George Memorial Museum†* contains many relics of the statesman. *Gwynfryn,* ¾ m. N.W., is the house to which Shelley moved in 1813 after the incident at Tremadog.

2 m. **Criccieth** (1700 inhab. but larger in summer) is a family resort. Near the corner of Cardigan Bay, here Tremadog Bay, the town enjoys fine views down the Lleyn, N.E. towards Snowdonia, and across the water to Harlech and the mountains behind. The *Castle†,* perched on a rocky green hill above the town, is a native Welsh stronghold built c. 1230 and strengthened by Edward I in 1283-84. It was taken in 1404 by Owen Glendower. The ruins consist mainly of a curtain enclosing the small rectangular inner ward (the oldest part of the castle) and the bold N. gatehouse flanked by towers. The larger outer ward, of which less remains, dates from c. 1260. The Leyburn Tower (W.) was probably the home of the constable. The Engine Tower (N.) was the launching site for missiles; the launcher would have been on the first floor, now disappeared.

3 m. Junction with A487, which this Route follows northwest. Effectively this is also the junction with Rte 11 (Caernarvon to Porthmadog) and Rte 17 (Bala and Ffestiniog to Porthmadog).—*1 m. Penmorfa Church* contains a memorial to the Civil War Royalist Sir John Owen.—*3 m. Dolbenmaen Church,* opposite which is a large motte, probably the 11C or earlier seat of the local rulers before they built Criccieth. From here a lane ascends N. 3 m. up the beautiful Pennant Valley.—*7 m.* *Pen-y-Groes* was until the beginning of the present century the centre for the slate and copper mines around Nantlle to the east.—*3 m.* *Glanrhyd,* where the circuit of the Lleyn is completed.—*3 m.* **Caernarvon.**

14   SHREWSBURY TO CHIRK AND LLANGOLLEN

A5. 27 miles.—*16 m.* Whittington.—*5 m.* **Chirk.**—*6 m.* **Llangollen.**

Shrewsbury, see Rte 21.—*4 m.* *Montford Bridge*, where the Severn is crossed.—*4 m.* *Nesscliff* is a village at the foot of a wooded hill, with a hillfort. Humphrey Kynaston's Cave here, approached by steps cut into the rock, was the refuge of a local highwayman. *Ruyton-XI-Towns*, 2 m. N., was formerly a borough made up of the 11 townships of the Manor of Ruyton (charter 1301).—*8 m.* *Whittington* is said to owe its name to the white flowers which were a feature of the surrounding swamps. The chief remains of the castle here, built by the Peverels and afterwards belonging to the FitzWarines, are the moat and the picturesque 13C gatehouse. One FitzWarine (Fulk) was an outlaw in hiding from King John. He is said to have married a lady on whom the King was forcing his attentions, the pair taking refuge in Sherwood Forest; hence a traditional identification of Fulk FitzWarine with Robin Hood. *Oswestry* is 2 m. southwest.

Approaching *(5 m.)* **Chirk,** just across the border, two adjacent viaducts, spanning the Ceiriog valley some 80 ft below, are seen W. of the road. One (1848) carries the railway, while the other, Telford's aqueduct of 1801, carries the Shropshire Union Canal. A pleasant small town, Chirk had its origins in a castle built here in the 11C, of which all that remains is a small motte near the church. The church has a 15C tower, a 15C roof to the N. nave, and monuments to the Myddeltons of the present Chirk Castle.

Chirk Castle†, 2 m. W. of the town, stands within a large park entered (from the E.) through ironwork gates of 1719 which are an outstanding example of the work of the Davies brothers. Originally these gates stood in front of the castle, a complete and still inhabited pile, begun possibly by James of St George c. 1290-95 and completed c. 1310 by Roger de Mortimer, on whom the land had been conferred by Edward I. Purchased in 1595 by Sir Thomas Myddelton, Lord Mayor of London and brother of Sir Hugh, the castle remains today in the ownership of the family. In general the castle has retained its original external appearance; that of a square, with a round bastion at each corner and a half-bastion at the centre of each face. The interiors have been frequently rebuilt, and today's visitor sees decorative styles ranging from the 16 to the early 19C. The park has a lake, N. of the castle, near which *Offa's Dyke* is clearly seen.

The generally wooded **Vale of Ceiriog** ascends W. into the Berwyns. At (6½ m.) *Glyn Ceiriog*, the Institute contains material illustrating the life and culture of the vale since the 18C, and commemorates its literary figures, John Ceiriog Hughes and Huw Morris, both poets who lived at *Llanarmon Dyffryn-Ceiriog* (4 m. farther). Just S. of Glyn Ceiriog a woodland walk (1 m.) can be taken along the course of the *Glyn Valley Tramway* (N.T.), the former 2 ft 4½ inch gauge quarry line.

A5 is the direct road to Llangollen. An alternative (3 m. farther) is via Ruabon and A539 up the N. side of the Dee (Vale of Llangollen). **Ruabon** (5700 inhab.) is an industrial centre for a district producing chemicals, ceramics, brick, and tiles. In the church, said to have been founded by St Mabon in the 6C, are a 14C (restored) wallpainting and monuments by Nollekens and Rysbrack to members of the Williams-Wynne family, whose seat was at *Wynnstay* (rebuilt after fire in 1858) immediately southeast. The house (no adm.) is now Lindisfarne College. Wat's Dyke runs through the park, and the estate was formerly called Wattstay. After *Acrefair*, 2 m. from Ruabon, there is a view of Telford's Pont-y-Cysylltau aqueduct (see below).

2m. Junction with A483 for Ruabon. A5 bears W. along the Vale of Llangollen.—*1m. Froncysyllte*, where a side road N. leads down to the river and Telford's **Pont-y-Cysylltau Aqueduct* (1795-1805) which carries the Shropshire Union Canal across the valley at a height of 121 ft. The viaduct is 1007 ft long and supported by 18 piers.

3m. **LLANGOLLEN** (3100 inhab.), crowded and often a traffic bottleneck in summer, lies mainly on the S. bank of the Dee, here flowing between wooded hills, on one of which to the N. is perched the conspicuous Castell Dinas Bran. Castle Street leads to *Llangollen Bridge*, parts of which date back to one built in 1345 by John Trevor, who later became Bishop of St Asaph. Rebuilt in Tudor times, the bridge has in turn been widened for coaches and strengthened for modern traffic. Llangollen and its environs offer several places of interest, most of these being on the N. side of the river. The town is the home of an annual (July) International Music Eisteddfod.

Tourist Information. Off W. side of Castle Street.
Parking. Off Market Street, which runs W. from Castle Street.
Eisteddfod. Office in Berwyn Street (A5). The International Music Eisteddfod was first held in 1947 and is now an annual July event attracting around 150,000 visitors. The competitions include events for choirs, soloists, folk singing, dancing etc. The general pattern is that competitions are held during the day, the evenings being reserved for concerts and other performances. The Eisteddfod ground is on the N. bank of the river.

Llangollen. South of the River

The **Church of St Collen**, in the town centre E. of Castle Street, owes its name to a 7C saint. Important in its own right during the 12C, it was made subordinate to Valle Crucis early the following century. The interior contains 15C hammer-beam roofs in the nave and N. aisle, and a 14C tomb-niche. In the churchyard is a monument, erected by the 'Ladies of Llangollen' (see below) to their faithful servant Mary Carryl (d. 1809), which afterwards served to mark their own burial place.

Plas Newydd†, S. of A5 about ¼ m. E. of its junction with Castle Street, is a picturesque, wood-carved black-and-white house, which was the residence from 1779 of Lady Eleanor Butler (d. 1829) and the Hon. Sarah Ponsonby (d. 1831). Inside, there is carved panelling and Spanish leatherwork, the latter given by the Duke of Wellington.

The two 'Ladies of Llangollen' were eccentric Irishwomen, who left their homes secretly in order to devote their lives 'to friendship, celibacy, and the knitting of blue stockings'. They became famous for their peculiarities of dress, their beneficence, and their collection of old oak and curios, to which it was recognized practice that their many visitors should contribute. Wellington, De Quincey (as a boy), Scott (who made the house a scene of 'The Betrothed'), and Wordsworth were among such visitors. Wordsworth's somewhat tactless sonnet, with its description of the house as a 'low browed cot' and its oblique reference to the ladies' age, is said to have given offence. The greater part of the collection was dispersed in 1832. The ladies' maidservant, Mary Carryl, bought the freehold of Plas Newydd with her savings, leaving it to the ladies at her death in 1809.

Llangollen. North of the River

Llangollen Station, immediately across the bridge, is now the home of the *Llangollen Railway Society*. Locomotives and carriages are being collected, and track organized, one aim being to run a steam service to Glyndyfrdwy (5 m.) by the 1980s.

The **Canal Exhibition Centre**† (Boat trips) is in an early 19C warehouse on the Shropshire Union Canal just above the railway station. Using working and static models, slides and films, pictures, and original material, the museum tells the story of the growth and use of canals. Among the themes covered are canal engineering; canals and coalmining; cargoes and how they were handled; and the life of canal people. A trip (¾ hour) may be taken by horse-drawn barge to Pentrefelis, 1 m. N.W.

The ruin of **Castell Dinas Bran** (1000 ft), conspicuous to the N. above Llangollen, is reached by a signed route from near the Canal Exhibition Centre. An Iron Age hillfort, and, later, a Welsh and for a brief period Norman wooden castle probably preceded the stone castle which seems to have been built c. 1236. Apparently little used, the place is known to have been a ruin by 1578. The climb is rewarded more by the view than by the ruin, which consists chiefly of the wall surrounding the hilltop. Much of the stone came from the ditch hacked out of the rock on the E. and south. The entrance passage, flanked by towers, is at the N.E. angle.

*Valle Crucis Abbey† is 1½ m. N.W. of Llangollen on A542. Where this road leaves the river, another road continues along the river for ½ m. to Telford's *Horseshoe Weir* and to *Llantysilio Church*, for both of which see p. 183.

The Cistercian Abbey was founded in 1201 by Madog ap Gruffydd, a prince of Powys who sided alternately with his own people and the English. A serious fire later in the same century led to major alterations, and the tower collapsed in 1400. The abbey was dissolved c. 1535. Today's quite extensive ruins comprise the church and some of the domestic buildings.

The *Church* adheres to the common early Cistercian plan of aisled nave, transepts with E. chapels, and short aisleless choir; the N. transept has been walled off from the crossing. In the walls of the N. aisle can be seen the original masonry, heightened by small flat stones added after the fire. The W. front is a beautiful composition (c. 1250–75), with three fine plate-tracery windows enclosed in a common frame, and with a delicate rose-window in the gable. The E. end (c. 1240) is notable for the manner in which its external pilaster buttresses split above the bottom row of lancets so as to embrace an upper pair. To be noted in the church are the remains of the pulpit (including the stairway) under the vanished W. arch of the crossing; the base of the altar; the curious recess, with remains of a shafted screen, on the N. side of the choir; the bases of altars in the two chapels on the E. side of the S. transept; and the arch (at the end of the S. transept) by which the dormitory was entered from the now vanished night-stairs. The piers of the crossing were heavily buttressed after the tower fell in 1400. In front of the choir there are six mutilated tombs, said to include those of Myfanwy Fechan, a beauty who inspired the bards and who lived at Castell Dinas Bran, and Iolo Goch, the bard of Owen Glendower.

The S. transept is adjoined by the Sacristy, to the S. of which is the vaulted *Chapter House* (rebuilt c. 1315-50), in three parallel aisles. In the central of these is the door from the *Cloister*, S. of which is the day-stair (blocked) to the dormitory, while to the N. is a curious little vaulted space, possibly for books. These mark the W. end of the two outer aisles of the chapter house and are contained within the thickness of the wall. The passage immediately S. of the chapter house led perhaps to the infirmary. To the S. of the *Dormitory*, which occupies the whole length of the upper floor, is the *Reredorter*. The N.E. corner of the dormitory was apparently the Abbot's Lodging. The S. and W. cloister ranges are no more than foundations.

Eliseg's Pillar, ¼ m. N. of the abbey, is a broken shaft, 8ft high, standing on what is supposed to be a burial mound. Its importance lies in its Latin inscription, originally of 31 lines but now so badly weathered that parts only of 15 remain. Luckily a scholar of 1696 made a record, so it is known that the cross was erected early in the 9C by Cyngen (or Concenn) who died c. 854 on a pilgrimage to Rome, in memory of his great-grandfather, Eliseg, who annexed Powys from the English. It may be that Eliseg lies under the mound, and it may also be that it is from this cross that the valley and abbey take their names.

To the E. of the valley stretches the line of *Eglwyseg Mountain*, forming the W. escarpment of the moorland plateau of Ruabon Mountain. The S. end is the great ridge of the *Eglwyseg Rocks*, a series of terraced limestone cliffs consisting of rounded promontories with gullies between. The ridge is well seen from the loop of *Horseshoe Pass* on A542 beyond the abbey; in 5 m. from the abbey this road reaches Rte 16. Another view of the rocks is from the small road from Llangollen which runs below the ridge to *World's End* (5 m.). Here there is a 1 m. long nature trail including a limestone gorge, moor, and afforestation (leaflet from Llangollen Tourist Information).

For Llangollen to *Corwen*, see Rte 15.

15   LLANGOLLEN TO CORWEN AND BETWS-Y-COED

A5. 31 miles.—*10 m.* **Corwen.**—*9 m.* **Cerrigydrudion.**—*5 m.* **Pentrefoelas.**—*7 m.* **Betws-y-Coed.**
Mainly undulating agricultural country and moor, with occasional distant views of mountains. The last 5 m. are down the narrow, wooded valley of the Conwy.

Llangollen, see p. 181.—*2 m.* *King's Bridge (Berwyn)*, which crosses a delightful stretch of the Dee. Below is *Chain Bridge*, the earlier crossing here, restored in 1929. Just across King's Bridge are Telford's *Horseshoe Weir* (1806), built to supply water to the Llangollen branch of the Shropshire Union Canal, and *Llantysilio Church* (Norman). Robert Browning worshipped here in 1886, a fact recorded by a brass on the S. wall placed here by Lady Martin (Helena Faucit, the actress; d. 1898), herself commemorated in a modern chapel N. of the choir. Sir Theodore (d. 1909) and Lady Martin lived at the adjacent mansion.—The road runs between two high areas of moorland, the Berwyns being to the S. and Llantysilio Mountain to the north.—*4 m.* *Glyndyfrdwy* was part of the possessions of Owen Glendower and the place from which he derived his name. A mound, 1½ m. W. between the road and the river, was almost certainly the site of his fortified manor. *Carrog*, just beyond across the river, is reached by a fine stone bridge of 1660.

4 m. **Corwen** (2200 inhab.), a small market town below a steep wooded hill, has its place in history as Owen Glendower's headquarters, where he gathered his forces before the battle of Shrewsbury. The *Church* (part 13C, restored) contains in the choir a curious raised monumental slab (14C) to a former vicar, and a Norman font. On the outer lintel of the priest's door (S. choir) is an incised dagger, known as Glendower's Sword and supposed to mark the point of impact of a weapon thrown by Glendower from the hill above in a moment of anger with the townsfolk. In fact it dates from the 7-9C. There is another dagger-mark on a 12C cross outside the S.W. corner of the church. Across the river, the hill of *Caer Drewyn* (½ m. walk from swimming pool), with a stone rampart ½ m. in circumference, probably dates to the immediate post-Roman period.

For Corwen to *Rhyl*, see Rte 6; to (N.) *Wrexham* and *Chester*, and (S.) *Bala*, *Dolgellau*, and *Barmouth*, see Rte 16.

Beyond Corwen, A5 crosses the Dee, and within the next 2 m. the junctions with the above Routes are passed. The valley of the Alwen is followed to *(4 m.)* *Maerdy*, where A5 enters that of the Ceirw. About 1 m. beyond Maerdy, on the S. (sign to Cwmain), a small road crosses a picturesquely set single-arch bridge 50 ft above the broken course of the river.—*5 m.* **Cerrigydrudion** is a village on a loop off the main road. The name, often wrongly written as 'druidion', means Place of the Brave and has no connection with Druids. Here B4501 leads N. for (4 m.) Llyn Brenig (see p. 136). *Caer Caradog*, 1 m. E. of Cerrigydrudion, is a hillfort where Caractacus (Caradog) is said to have been betrayed to the Romans by Cartismandua, Queen of the Brigantes, after his final defeat by Scapula in 51.—For the next 5 m. the road crosses rather dull moorland, relieved however by distant views of Snowdonia. Seen from *Cerrig* the panorama ranges (S. to N.) from Moel Siabod, past the two Glyders, Tryfan, the point of Y Foel Goch, and Pen-yr-Oleu-Wen to the two Carneddau; and a mile farther on Snowdon comes into view, with Crib Goch on its right and Lliwedd on its left. *Glasfryn* is just before the summit level (908 ft).—*5 m.* **Pentrefoelas**. The Levelinus Stone, now in the National Museum of Wales and replaced by a replica, stood just N. near the farm of Hen Voelas. It may have marked the grave of Llewelyn ap Sysyllt, slain in 1021. Several roads converge near the village.

Rte 5 (A543) from *Denbigh* joins here.

The road leading N.W. (B5113) reaches *Llanrwst* in 8 m., crossing a high point of 1056 ft, and commanding exceptional views.

One mile W. of Pentrefoelas, B4407 bears S., ascending the narrow valley of the upper Conwy and in 2 m. reaching the secluded village of *Yspytty Ifan*, which once belonged (yspytty=hospitium) to the Knights Hospitaller of St John. In the church (rebuilt 1858) there are recumbent effigies (15–16C) of the Rhys family, one of these being of Rhys ap Meredydd who carried Henry Tudor's Red Dragon standard at Bosworth. The road continues S.W., following the Conwy almost to its source in *Llyn Conwy*, about 4 m. beyond Yspytty Ifan and ½ m. N. of the road. Until the Dissolution this upper valley was officially sanctuary and, despite the presence of the Hospitallers, notorious for its lawlessness. Beyond, traversing open moor, the road joins Rte 17 at *Pont-ar-Afon Gam*.

At *Voelas Hall*†, immediately N. of A5 roughly opposite B4407, the Brachmael Stone of the 5 or 6C bears a Latin inscription recording the resting place of Brachmael and his wife. The stone was found in 1821 during the building of the road.—A5 soon crosses the river, following it down a deepening wooded glen. About 1 m. beyond the bridge a small road ascends N.W., in 1½ m. reaching *Capel Garmon Burial Chamber* (c. 1500 B.C.), the remains of a long barrow with three chambers, one of which still has its capstone in position. The stone base which surrounded the mound can be seen, with the 15 ft long entrance passage. An interesting feature of the site is what is thought to have been a false entrance, though it may have been a shrine.

In rather over another mile A5 reaches a road junction (B4406), above *Conwy* and *Machno Falls* (paths) by the confluence of these rivers in the steep, wooded valley below.

B4406, running S.W. above the narrow wooded valley of the Machno, soon passes *Penmachno Mills*. Here, in an attractive setting, a small road bridge crosses the river just above a packhorse bridge, the pleasant road descending through woods above the left banks of the Machno and Conwy (not visible from the road) to join the Betws-y-Coed to Ffestiniog road (Rte 7C). B4406 soon reaches *Penmachno*, formerly site of the Penmachno Stones†, one of the most interesting collections of Early Christian stones in Wales. One is inscribed with the sacred Chi-Rho (Christos) monogram; a second commemorates 'a citizen of Venedos' (ancient name for Gwynedd), cousin of Maglos the Magistrate; and a third states that it was erected during the time of the Roman consul Justinus. Inscribed in Latin and dating from the 5-6C, the stones suggest that some form of a Roman administration survived here even at this late date. Beyond Penmachno B4406 rounds the W. side of *Llyn Conwy* (½ m. E.; see above) and meets Rte 17 at *Pont-ar-Afon-Gam* (8 m. from A5).

7 m. (from Pentrefoelas) **Betws-y-Coed**, see p. 144.

16   CHESTER TO BALA, DOLGELLAU, AND BARMOUTH

A483 to Wrexham: A525 and A5104 to Corwen: B4401 to Bala: A494 to Dolgellau: A496 to Barmouth. 68 miles.—*9 m.* **Gresford.**—*3 m.* **Wrexham.**—*5 m.* **Bwlchgwyn.**—*5 m.* **Llandegla.**—*9 m.* **Corwen.**—*12 m.* **Bala.**—*5 m.* **Llanuwchllyn.**—*12 m.* **Dolgellau.**—*8 m.* **Barmouth.**

Pleasant if unexciting scenery to Bala, after which there is higher moor and mountain on both sides. From Dolgellau to Barmouth the road skirts the wooded Mawddach estuary. Views of Cader Idris (2927 ft).

Chester, see Rte 1, is left by Grosvenor Bridge.—*6 m.* **Pulford**, just beyond which the border is crossed into Wales.—*3 m.* **Gresford** has a 15C church with a fine tower and a noted peal of 12 bells, and an exterior frieze of small animals. Noteworthy features of the interior are the choir stalls and misericords; the glass, including the Te Deum E. window and, in the N. chapel, scenes from the life of the Virgin; the monument of John Trevor of Trevalyn (d. 1589), an interesting survival of a medieval semi-effigy; and a 15C font with sculptured panels. Gresford colliery, closed in 1973, was the scene of a tragedy in 1934 when 266 miners lost their lives as the result of an underground explosion. The town figures in 'The Angler' in Washington Irving's 'Sketch-Book'.—*3 m.* **Wrexham** (which may be bypassed), see p. 132.

5 m. **Bwlchgwyn**, with the *Geological Museum of North Wales*†, which provides a good geological background to the varied countryside of north Wales. There are indoor and outdoor geological displays; outdoor displays of industrial relics, including material from Gresford colliery, kilns etc.; an old silica quarry and geological trail; and a streamside walk in Nant-y-Ffrith, with footbridges across cascades.—*5 m.* **Llandegla** is a village with a holy well once known for curing epilepsy. A5104 is now taken, traversing what was the Hundred of Ial (Yale) and in 2½ m. reaching *Plas-yn-Yale,* former residence of the Yale family and birthplace of Elihu's father.—*4 m. Bryneglwys,* where the church has relics of the Yale chapel and family.—*5 m.* Junction with Rte 6 (A494) from Ruthin, and, just beyond, with Rte 15 (A5) from *Corwen,* which is ½ m. east.

Here there is a choice of roads to Bala, A494 being the main road (10 m.). B4401 from Corwen (12 m.), following the fertile valley called the *Vale of Edeyrnion* below the N.W. slopes of the Berwyns, is slower but more attractive.—*4 m.* Llandrillo is a starting point for walks into the high moor of the Berwyns, *Craig Berwyn* (over 2100 ft) being 4 m. southeast. The fine mass of Arenig Fawr comes into view ahead before the Dee is crossed to (*4 m.*) *Llandderfel* where the 15 C church has a contemporary rood screen and one parapet of its loft. In the N. porch, and visible through a window if the church is closed, there are two curious wooden relics, a headless animal and a piece of a pole. Known as St Derfel's Horse and St Derfel's Staff, these are said to be all that is left of an equestrian figure of the saint, the rest of which was taken to London to form part of the fire in which Friar Forest, Catherine of Aragon's confessor, was burnt in 1538.

4 m. **Bala** (1700 inhab.), at the N. end of Bala Lake, is a pleasant sailing and holiday centre, fortunate in having an attractive, tree-lined main street (High Street, A494) broad and straight enough to ease the flow of through traffic.

Tourist Information. (Wales Tourist Board and Snowdonia National Park). On E. side of High Street, soon after entering Bala from the north.

Parking. The Green, E. of A494 at N. entry to the town.

Early Closing. Wednesday.

History. The town's name derives from the Welsh 'bala', meaning 'outlet', because the Dee here flows out of Bala Lake. The motte in the town, as also the smaller one at the N.E. corner of the lake, is probably Norman, though some opinion suggests that it is Iron Age and that the Romans, who were certainly in this district (e.g. at Caergai), made use of it. The town was the centre of the more or less independent district of Penllyn within the Kingdom of Powys, and when the castle was taken in 1202 by Llewelyn the Great he annexed Penllyn to Gwynedd. Little else is known of Bala's history until the 18C when it became prosperous as a centre of the woollen industry, Pennant writing of a 'vast trade in woollen stockings' and of women and children 'in full employ, knitting along the roads'. This prosperity died in the early 19C with the Industrial Revolution. Bala's repute as a religious centre was more enduring, the town's best known figure being the Rev. Thomas Charles (Charles of Bala, 1755-1814), pioneer of the Methodist movement in north Wales, founder of the British and Foreign Bible Society (see also p. 226), and a leader of the Sunday School movement. Other local religious figures were Hywel Harris (1714-73), a Dissenter whose persecution here was marked by riots in 1741 (see also Trefecca, p. 256); Dr Lewis Edwards, who in 1837 started an academy for young preachers, later the Theological College for Calvinist Methodists and today a Christian Movement Centre; and the Rev. Michael Jones, who in 1865 fitted out a ship which took 153 people, most of them from Bala, to Patagonia where they could be free to practise their nonconformism. They founded the town of Trelew, with which Bala still keeps close touch. In 1967 the National Eisteddfod was held in Bala.

East of A494 on the N. edge of the town the large car park was once part of the Green, the town's market and the scene of large Methodist gatherings. Gorsedd stones nearby recall the National Eisteddfod in 1967. To the W., a short way up A4212, stands the former *Bala Theological College*. The motte, *Tomen-y-Bala,* with a path to the top, is just E. of the N. end of High Street. Farther on (r.) stands a bronze statue

(Goscombe John) of Thomas Ellis (1859-99), long M.P. for Merionethshire. Roughly opposite the White Lion Hotel is the house (tablet) where Thomas Charles lived. From here Tegid Street leads to the N. extremity of Bala Lake, on the way passing, in front of the Welsh Presbyterian Church, a statue of Thomas Charles.

For *Bala Lake*, see below. For Bala to *Ffestiniog* and *Porthmadog*, see Rte 17; to *Lake Vyrnwy*, see Rte 24B; to *Bwlch-y-Groes* and *Dinas Mawddwy*, see Rte 25B.

Bala Lake (530 ft) is known in Welsh as Llyn Tegid, a name deriving from Tegid Foel (Tegid the Bald), a shadowy figure who in the 5C was Lord of Penllyn, the ancient local district, and perhaps husband of Ceridwen, mother of the bard and seer Taliesin. The lake, lying pleasantly though undramatically below green hills backed by mountains, is several times mentioned in literature. Tegid Foel is a character in the 'Mabinogion'; Giraldus, who calls the lake Penmelesmere, possibly from the old English 'pemmel' meaning 'pebble', records that it 'rises by the violence of the winds'; it appears in Spenser's 'Faerie Queen'; and Tennyson in 'Geraint and Enid' refers to the sudden floods in the Dee valley caused by the S.W. wind 'that blowing Bala Lake fills all the sacred Dee'. This flooding has now been checked by the building of sluices below the river outlet, but in strong winds Bala can still be very rough. The lake (3¾ m. long by ½ m. broad) is the largest natural sheet of water in Wales, though it is nearly 40 acres smaller than the artificial Lake Vyrnwy. It is fed by several streams, one being the Dyfrdwy (Little Dee) at the S. end, and empties into the Dee which flows through Llangollen to its estuary N.W. of Chester. Bala is thought to be the only lake in which are found gwyniad, white fish of salmon species. The main road, skirting the W. bank, is described below. Along the E. bank run a narrow, rather enclosed road, and also the *Bala Lake Railway*†, which operates along a section of the former Great Western Railway's Ruabon to Barmouth line. In 1972 a local company laid 1 ft 11½ inch track, and today both steam and diesel trains run the length of the lake between Llanuwchllyn (the main station), and Bala (station at N.E. tip of the lake).

1 m. Llanycil, where the churchyard contains the graves of Thomas Charles, Lewis Edwards, and the Rev. John Parry (1812-74), compiler of a Welsh encyclopaedia. In another 2 m. the road crosses the Llafar, by the lake being *Glanllyn*, a main centre of the Welsh League of Youth (see below), then leaves the lake and passes below *Caergai* (no adm.), a 17C manor standing within the earthworks of a Roman camp occupied c. 98-117 and also traditionally site of the home of Sir Kay of Arthurian romance, Sir Rowland Vaughan (1590-1667), Royalist, hymnologist, and translator lived here. Beyond, the Lliw, Bala Lake's longest feeder, is crossed. For the lonely and beautiful road ascending this river and crossing high moor and afforestation to Bronaber on Rte 19, see p. 196 *Castel Carndochan*, S. of the river 1½ m. up the valley, is a Norman motte, still with something of its foundations. A 14C effigy in the church at (4 m.) **Llanuwchllyn** is probably that of one of the castle's owners. This church (rebuilt 1872) also contains a portable, wooden immersion baptistery of the 1850s; a brass communion plate, bearing a relief of the Temptation, said to have belonged to Cymmer Abbey; and a tablet to Rowland Vaughan of Caergai. The *Bala Lake Railway Station* is at the far end of the village. For the high scenic road to Bwlch-y-Groes and Dinas Mawddwy, see Rte 25B. At the main road entrance to Llanuwchllyn stand statues to Sir Owen M. Edwards (1858-1920), educationist and writer of books for children, and of his son Sir Ifan, founder of Urdd Gobaith Cymru (Welsh League of Youth).

Generally following the course of its Roman predecessor, the road now ascends the Dyfrdwy, through rather desolate country overshadowed by Aran Benllyn, to its highest point (770 ft). From here the descent is down the wooded Wnion valley, with Cader Idris ahead.

For *Aran Mawddwy* and *Aran Benllyn*, forming a high ridge to the E. of the road, see p. 224. From this side ascents can be made from Llanuwchllyn or Drws-y-Nant, 3 m. south.

9 m. Bont Newydd, where a road S. through Brithdir, avoiding often crowded Dolgellau, connects to the main roads to Dinas Mawddwy and Machynlleth.—*3 m.* **Dolgellau**, see Rte 18.

For the first 3 m. beyond Dolgellau there is a choice of roads, N. or S. of the Mawddach Estuary, the S. road being slightly shorter but crossing a tollbridge.

The northern road reaches in 1½ m. the bridge over the Mawddach, just before which are the modest remains of *Cymmer Abbey*, a Cistercian house founded in 1199 by monks from Cwmhir. The name, pronounced 'Kummer', was in full 'Kymer deu dyfyr' meaning 'meeting of the waters'. The ruins are principally those of the abbey's never completed 13C church. The N. nave arcade, three lancets at the E. end, battered sedilia, and a piscina in the S. wall survive. Of the cloister and domestic buildings little remains. The refectory is S. of the cloister, and something of the chapter house can be seen in the farm's yard. The farm is probably on the site of the guest house, important at a site where travellers were often delayed by river floods. For *Precipice Walk*, which can be reached from here, see p. 192. For the Mawddach valley northwards, see Rte 19.—In the churchyard at *Llanelltyd*, across the bridge, is buried Frances Power Cobbe (1822-1904), social writer and suffragist. The N. end of the tollbridge is reached in 1½ m.

New Precipice Walk, 1½ m. in length, is along the ridge above the main road between Llanelltyd and the tollbridge.

By the southern road from Dolgellau, *Penmaenpool* is at the S. end of the tollbridge. Here a signal box of the old railway (1865-1965, starting as the Aberystwyth and Welsh Coast Railway) has been arranged by the Royal Society for the Protection of Birds and the North Wales Naturalists' Trust as a *Nature Information Centre*† and bird observation post. Rte 26 from Machynlleth and Tywyn joins here from the south.

4 m. (from Dolgellau) *Bont-Ddu* lies below hills in which runs a gold reef. The mines, intermittently worked since Roman times, are now abandoned, though gold from here was used in the wedding rings of the Queen, Princess Margaret and Princess Anne.

The road N. from here, ending in 1½ m. and passing gold workings, was the old road to Harlech. From the end of the road walkers have a choice, the track to the left leading via Bwlch-Rhiwgyr to the coast at *Tal-y-Bont* or *Dyffryn Ardudwy* (c. 5 m.); that to the right via a packhorse bridge (Pont Scethin) to *Harlech* in c. 9 m.

The road leaves the shore, regaining it in 3 m. There is a fine view of the Cader Idris range across the estuary.—*4 m.* **Barmouth**, see Rte 20A.

17   BALA TO FFESTINIOG AND PORTHMADOG

A4212 and B4391 to Ffestiniog (Pont Tal-y-Bont): A487 to Porthmadog. 23 miles.—*3m. Frongoch.—7m. Pont-ar-Afon-Gam.—3m.* **Ffestiniog.**—*3m.* **Maentwrog (Tan-y-Bwlch).**—*4m.* **Penrhyndeudraeth.**—*3m.* **Porthmadog.**
Moor and mountain. After Pont-ar-Afon-Gam fine views down to the Vale of Ffestiniog and coast.

Leaving **Bala** (see p. 186), passing the former Theological College, A4212 ascends the pleasant open valley of the Tryweryn, in *3m.* reaching a road fork at *Frongoch*, where an upland road bears N. for Cerrigydrudion (8m.) on Rte 15. A memorial along this road commemorates Bob Tai'rfelin, singer of folk songs. Early in the century Frongoch boasted a whisky distillery; closed before the First World War, its buildings became a prison camp for Germans, and also for Irish interned after the 1916 Dublin rising.—*2m.* **Llyn Celyn**, in a beautiful moor and mountain setting, is a reservoir completed by Liverpool Corporation in 1965; it regulates the flow of the Dee and supplies water largely to Liverpool and the Wirral. The lake is 2½ m. long by up to 1 m. broad, and has at its E. end a dam 2200ft long carrying a road. Fish, which formerly swam up the river, are now collected in a trap and spawned artificially for stocking. The road skirts the N. shore, by the N.W. arm passing a modern chapel and memorial garden commemorating the chapel and burial ground drowned by the lake; some of the stone from the submerged chapel is incorporated in this new one.

About 1½ m. beyond the W. end of Llyn Celyn a road fork is reached. The road to the left (A4212) follows the track of the old railway past little Llyn Tryweryn to *Trawsfynydd*(8m.) on Rte 19. The old bridge near the fork is said to be Roman in origin.

Almost due S. rises **Arenig Fawr** (2800ft) which, isolated and barren, prompted Borrow to write that of all the hills he saw in Wales none made a greater impression. On the summit a tablet on an ancient cairn commemorates the crew of a Flying Fortress who lost their lives when their aircraft flew into the mountain in 1943. The mountain can be climbed by following A4212 for 1m., then a track left through afforestation and several gates to its end at the second deserted farm. From here the climb is on foot up the steep, grassy slope, becoming rough and rocky towards the top.

Now following B4391 across rather desolate moor, this Route reaches a watershed at 1507ft (2m. from the fork) and, in another *3m.*, *Pont-ar-Afon-Gam*, where the moorland road from Penmachno and Yspytty Ifan comes in from the north. A short distance beyond this junction there is a car park beside a *Viewpoint high above the deep slate cleft of *Rhaeadr Cwm* with its six cataracts.

Llyn Morwynion (Lake of the Maidens. 1292ft) is ¼ m. N. over the hill. The story goes that the men of Ardudwy, who had made a foray into Clwyd, were returning with their captive women when they were overtaken here by the pursuing men of Clwyd and slain. But so enamoured had the women become of their captors that, rather than return with their own men, they drowned themselves in the lake. Another story, from the 'Mabinogion', is that this is where the maidens of Blodeuwedd were drowned, after their mistress, who had murdered her husband in order to be with her lover, had been turned into an owl.

The descent to the Vale of Ffestiniog affords a superb view across Traeth Bach to Tremadog Bay and the long line of the Lleyn.—*3m.* **Ffestiniog** (600ft) is boldly situated on a bluff between the Vale of

Ffestiniog and the valley of the Cynfal. The knoll behind the church, reached by a path beside the S. wall of the churchyard, affords a view which, though now marred by the Trawsfynydd nuclear power station, still includes the full perspective of the valley and the sea and coast beyond. On the right rise the Moelwyns, with Moel Siabod in the distance farther right, and the Rhinogs are visible to the far left. A hill S.W. of the village, on which is the tomb of the 4th Baron Newborough, is another viewpoint. A local walk (sign by the church) is to the *Cynfal Falls*, just S. below the town. Above the falls a rock is known locally as Pulpud Huw Llwyd, a local mystic said to have preached from here. The walk can be continued up the valley via Bont Newydd to Rhaeadr Cwm.

For Ffestiniog to *Blaenau Ffestiniog* and *Betws-y-Coed*, see Rte 7C; to *Dolgellau*, see Rte 19; to *Harlech* and *Barmouth*, see Rte 20. For the *Festiniog Railway*, see below.

The Porthmadog road descends to the valley, at *Tal-y-Bont* merging with A496 from Blaenau Ffestiniog and in *3 m.* reaching **Maentwrog** (see p. 201), where Rte 20 from Barmouth and Harlech comes in from the south. A487 crosses the Dwyryd, on the farther side being **Tan-y-Bwlch** at the foot of the old road from Beddgelert.

Plas Tan-y-Bwlch is the Snowdonia National Park Residential Study Centre, and in summer there is also an Information Centre for passing visitors. The estate formerly belonged to the Oakley family, owners of the Blaenau Ffestiniog quarries. Bought in 1969 by the Countryside Commission and the National Park Committee, the study centre was opened in 1975. The visitor has a choice of two waymarked walks, both close to the Festiniog Railway, the first stone of which was laid by an Oakley in 1833.—The *Jubilee Trail* (c. 1 m.), starting from the car park, passes the house (1748, but much restored), then crosses the gardens, with 19C wrought-iron gates, and the wooded park to reach the mill pond and Llyn Mair, once used as water storage above channels down to the wheels at the saw and flour mills. From here a detour can be made to Llyn Mair Nature Trail, but Jubilee Trail now returns eastward, passing below Plas Halt on the railway and retracing itself to the garden. From here the walk continues, with views across the valley, to the nursery, once the fruit garden but now used for growing forest transplants.—*Llyn Mair Nature Trail* (¾ m.; parking off B4410 or at Tan-y-Bwlch station). The trail runs through a part of the reserve which preserves something of the original oakwoods that once covered much of Wales. Much of the woodland on the N. side of the valley was bought in 1965 by the National Trust, with help from the North Wales Naturalists' Trust, the woods then being leased to Nature Conservancy and declared a National Nature Reserve.

4 m. (from Maentwrog) **Penrhyndeudraeth**, where Rte 8 from Betws-y-Coed and Beddgelert comes in from the north.—*1 m.* **Minffordd**, 1 m. S. of which is **Portmeirion**†, a private village and tiny harbour in Italian style, the invention of the Welsh architect Sir Clough Williams-Ellis (1883-1978), who wished to create a seaside resort free from advertisements and careless building. Building has generally been in two periods, one before the war and the other from 1954 onwards. Apart from the hotel, the most conspicuous buildings are the *Campanile*, half Romanesque and half Baroque, and the *Bath House Colonnade* (18C), brought from Bristol in 1957 when the house itself was in danger of demolition. There is an audio-visual display in *Hercules Hall*. The village is surrounded by gardens (mainly rhododendrons), there is a long sandy beach, and, in addition to the hotel, there are cottages for renting and craft shops. Portmeirion pottery is well known, and can be bought at several places in N.W. Wales.

2 m. **Porthmadog** (3450 inhab.) is reached across *The Cob* (toll), the 1 m. long embankment carrying the road and Festiniog Railway across the mouth of the Glaslyn, built by W. A. Madocks, M.P. (1774–1828) in order to reclaim the 7000 acres of Traeth Mawr (see p. 162). Once the port for the Blaenau Ffestiniog quarries, Porthmadog today is primarily a holiday and sailing centre. The *Marine Museum*† at the harbour, includes a ketch of c. 1909 with material illustrating 19C harbour life, and a recreated slate quay. To the S. and S.W. are the beach areas of *Borth-y-Gest*, a small resort, and *Morfa Bychan*, with 3 m. of sand and several large caravan sites.

The **Festiniog Railway**† (12 m.), running above the estuary and the Vale of Ffestiniog, offers beautiful coastal and mountain views. Opened in 1836 as a horse-tram for the slate quarries of Blaenau Ffestiniog, and adapted for passengers in 1865, the line had a gauge of 1 ft 11½ inches, and was skilfully engineered with a continuous gradient of max. 1 in 70, this enabling laden trains to descend by gravity. The total rise is 700 ft. Closed in 1946, the line has been reopened in stages since 1954 with the help of the Festiniog Railway Society. There was a set-back when part of the course was drowned by the Tanygrisiau Reservoir, but a new alignment involving nearly 3 m. of earthworks was constructed, largely by volunteers. Trains are normally steam, but diesels are occasionally used. The stations between Porthmadog and Tanygrisiau are Boston Lodge, Minffordd, Penrhyndeudraeth, Tan-y-Bwlch, and Dduallt. The aim is to restore the railway to Blaenau Ffestiniog by about 1980.—The *Festiniog Railway Museum* is at Porthmadog station.

For Porthmadog to *Caernarvon* and *Bangor*, see Rte 11. For the *Lleyn*, see Rte 13.

18   DOLGELLAU AND CADER IDRIS

A   Dolgellau

Dolgellau (pron. 'Dol-geh-thly', meaning perhaps Meadow of the Hazels; 2300 inhab.), a compact little town distinctive for its grey-walled, slate-roofed houses, is the chief centre and market town for a large surrounding mountain district and thus very Welsh in both custom and language. Pleasantly situated on the S. bank of the Wnion at the foot of Cader Idris, within easy reach of beautiful and varied scenery, and at the junction of several main roads, the town is also a magnet for tourists and its attractive but narrow streets and bridge can become a traffic bottleneck in summer.

Tourist Information. (Wales Tourist Board and Snowdonia National Park). At S. end of bridge.
Parking. At S. end of bridge.
Early closing. Wednesday.
Market. Friday.
History. Owen Glendower held a Welsh parliament here in 1404, and later in the same year here signed an alliance with Charles VI of France, but otherwise Dolgellau figures little in history. The Vaughan (Fychan) family were for long the most important landowners, their seats being at Nannau (2 m. N.) and Hengwrt (1 m. N.W.). One of them was Robert Vaughan (1592–1667), the antiquary, who lived at Hengwrt and achieved renown through his priceless collection of manuscripts, now in the National Library of Wales; the remains of his house can be seen.

The seven-arch *Bridge* dates largely from 1638. The little town clusters mainly around Eldon Square and the smaller Queen's Square. The *Church of St Mary* was rebuilt, except for its tower, in 1776; inside there is a 14C recumbent effigy of Meurig ap Ynyr Fychan, a Vaughan ancestor.

There are a number of walks around Dolgellau, details and leaflets on which are obtainable from Tourist Information. The three best known are Precipice Walk, Torrent Walk, and New Precipice Walk.

Precipice Walk, c. 3 m. N., is a path some 3 m. in total length encircling the steep high ridge of Foel Cynwch, 1000 ft above the river Mawddach and with on its E. side the wooded small Llyn Cynwch. The walk affords superb views of Cader Idris and the length of the Mawddach estuary down to Barmouth. One approach is from Cymmer Abbey (see p. 188), but the shorter is from a parking space on the Dolgellau to Llanfachreth road near the entrance to Nannau Park, ancient seat of the Vaughans.

An older house on this site belonged to Howel Sele, whose Lancastrian sympathies brought him into conflict with his cousin Owen Glendower. It is said that Sele, out hunting, shot at Glendower but missed. Glendower then slew Sele, hiding the body in a hollow oak. This is 'the spirit's blasted tree' of Scott's 'Marmion', and the 'hollow oak of demonrie' of Lord Lytton's 'Arthur'. The oak was destroyed by lightning in 1813.

For the forest of *Coed-y-Brenin,* extending some 4 m. northwards from this area, see Rte 19.

Torrent Walk, 1½ m. E., is a 1 m. walk up the mossy fern-clad glen of the Clydewog, starting from where this stream runs into the Wnion and ending at the bridge at the junction of A470 with B4416 to Brithdir. The river descends over a series of small cascades.—For *New Precipice Walk* at Llanelltyd, see p. 188.

For Dolgellau to *Barmouth* (W.) and to *Bala* (N.E.), see Rte 16; to *Ffestiniog,* see Rte 19; to *Machynlleth,* see Rte 25A; to *Machynlleth* via the coast (*Tywyn*), see Rte 26; to *Dinas Mawddwy,* see Rte 25B.

B   Cader Idris

Cader Idris (2927 ft) means Chair of Idris, according to tradition and the bards a giant variously celebrated as warrior, poet, and astonomer. Tradition further insists that anyone sleeping the night in the chair, the exact position of which is obscure, wakes up as either a poet or a madman. More precisely it seems that Idris was a descendant of Cunedda, through Meirion (who gave his name to Merioneth), and that he was killed in about 630 fighting the Saxons.

Among the mountains of Wales Cader Idris, though excelled in height by many peaks, ranks next to Snowdon with visitors, thanks largely to its accessibility, its striking shape, the grandeur of its precipices, and the superb views afforded by the summit. The main core of the mass is a long ridge, some 8 m. in length and consisting of alternating bands of felspathic trap and slate. The summit is *Pen-y-Gader,* and the ridge, steep on all sides, presents almost perpendicular walls of rock towards the N. with an average height of 900 ft. To the S., for the most part, it descends in abrupt grassy slopes to the Dysynni valley, part of the crack in the earth's crust (the Bala Fault) which includes Bala Lake and Tal-y-Llyn. On this side there is also an impressive cwm, enclosed by Craig-y-Cau and Pen-y-Gader and containing the dark lake of *Llyn-y-Cau.*

Of the lesser heights of Cader Idris *Mynydd Moel* (2804 ft) is 1 m. E.N.E. of the summit, and *Tyrau Mawr* (2167 ft), a peak which commands a view at least equal to that from Pen-y-Gader, is 2¼ m. west. To the N.W. of Pen-y-Gader there is another deep cwm, in which lies *Llyn-y-Gader.* The narrow wall of rock, 1000 to 1300 ft high, separating the basin of this lake from that of Llyn-y-Cau, is the most striking feature of the mountain. *Llyn-y-Gafr* lies N.E. of Llyn-y-Gader and lower.

A national nature reserve since 1955, Cader Idris was bought in 1976 by the Nature Conservancy Council.—A hoard of Iron Age ornaments in the La Tène style, found under a boulder on the mountain in 1963, is now in the National Museum of Wales.

The *View, extensive because of the comparative isolation of the mountain and with a beauty enhanced by its nearness to the sea, is especially fine towards the north. Beyond the Mawddach estuary, stretching W. to Barmouth and its bridge, mountains extend N. behind the coast towards the loftier ranges of Snowdonia. Just to the right of Rhinog Fach (E. of Llanbedr) can be seen the peak of Snowdon itself, to the right of this being the Glyders and Moel Siabod, with the Carneddau farther in the rear. In the middle distance, still looking N., is the narrow Ganllwyd Valley (Dolgellau to Ffestiniog), and farther to the right, in succession, come the Arenigs, Rhobell Fawr, Moel Fammau (beyond Bala Lake), the Arans, and the wide moorlands of the Berwyns. To the E. and S. crowd indefinite hilltops, among which may be distinguished the huge lump of Plynlimon (S.S.E.). To the W. is the huge sweep of Cardigan Bay, from the mouth of the Dysynni at Tywyn to St David's Head. Across the bay to the N.W. is the line of the Lleyn.

Five recognized ascents are described below, three of these being from Dolgellau and two from the south from near Tal-y-Llyn lake, one of these latter, the Llyn-y-Cau Route, being the finest. A good short round from Dolgellau is to ascend by the Bridle Path and descend by the Fox's Path. Better, though longer, is an ascent by the Llyn-y-Cau Route, with a descent by the Bridle or Fox's Path. Lovers of long mountain walks can ascend by the Aran Route, traverse the whole ridge, and descend to Arthog (p. 227) or to Llanfihangel-y-Pennant (p. 226).

FROM DOLGELLAU BY THE BRIDLE PATH (5½ m. 2¾ hours, but 2½ m. may be by road.). This, the simplest and most used route, follows at first the old hill road from Dolgellau to Tywyn, which diverges left from A493 just W. of the town and ascends fairly steeply with the steep-faced Braich Ddu ahead. In 2 m. the road passes the reedy *Llyn Gwernan*, the high ground to the N. of which commands the most comprehensive view of the mountain's great escarpment. The Fox's Path (see below) starts here from opposite the hotel, but the Bridle Path leaves the road nearly ¾ m. farther on by the farm of *Dyffrydan*. The path (well marked) starts just short of the second of two little bridges and, keeping right of the farm, rises steadily over broken ground, heading S.S.W. towards the dip between Cyfrwy (l.) and Tyrau Mawr (r.), with the crags of Pen-y-Gader to the left. From the foot of the escarpment, steep but not precipitous at this point, the ridge (1838 ft) is gained by a series of zigzags. A little farther on, by a gate, the approaches from Arthog and Llanfihangel-y-Pennant (the continuation of the bridle path) are met. For Cader Idris a stile is crossed and the grassy ridge followed to the left. Higher up, a stony path keeps well to the right of the Saddle, though by skirting the edge of the cliffs fine views may be enjoyed. From the lip of the cwm above Llyn-y-Gader, a final rocky ascent reaches the summit cairn of *Pen-y-Gader*.

FROM DOLGELLAU BY THE FOX'S PATH (4½ m. 2½ hours, but nearly 2 m. may be by road). This is the shortest route and commands remarkable views of cliff scenery at close quarters; but the last 900 ft of the ascent, mainly over scree, are exceptionally steep and arduous, and hence this route may be considered better for the descent. From Dolgellau to the hotel on *Llyn Gwernan,* see above. Hence the path, not always easy to follow, ascends generally southwards. The Cader cliffs presently come into view, the Fox's Path being visible to the left of the summit. After crossing two small streams, the reedy *Llyn-y-Gafr* (1400 ft; 1¼ m. from Llyn Gwernan) is reached and the path skirts the lower end. Beyond, after a rough slope, is the foot of *Llyn-y-Gader* (1837 ft), celebrated as a mirror of cliff and sky. Directly above rises Pen-y-Gader, and the Fox's Path, inclining to the left, is now unmistakable among the scree. The scramble (c. 40 min.) begins almost immediately, the angle of ascent being about 35°. A small watercourse serves as a guide for most of the way, and the track emerges on a grass slope with two small cairns. Hence to the summit is a 5 min. rough walk to the right.

FROM DOLGELLAU BY THE ARAN ROUTE (5½ m. 3½ hours). This is a pleasant and easy ascent, but, since there is no regular path, one to be avoided in misty weather. Dolgellau is left by the Machynlleth road, a turn to the right being taken immediately beyond the Aran, which is followed upstream on its E. bank for 1½ m. skirting a wooded glen. Near the farm of *Maes Coch* a track bears left, in less than ½ m. gaining the low ridge (1250 ft). *Gau Craig,* the long E. buttress of Cader Idris, is now the objective; this is flanked on the Dolgellau side by swampy ground, which should be avoided by keeping first well to the left to reach the foot of the ridge, then turning to the right for the easier ascent along it. The tiny *Llyn Aran* is seen far below on the right at the foot of the cliffs, and beyond, 1 m. away towards Dolgellau, *Mynydd-y-Gader* stands out. The ridge, followed W., reaches the summit of *Mynydd Moel* (2804 ft), the fine view from which includes Dolgellau. Thence to the summit is an easy mile.

FROM MINFFORDD BY THE LLYN-Y-CAU ROUTE (3 m. 2½ hours). This is by far the finest ascent, though the path is steep and often stony. *Minffordd* is on A487, just N. of Tal-y-Llyn lake and 7 m. by road from Dolgellau. Walkers from Dolgellau can reach Minffordd in 5½ m. by following the Aran Route to the ridge above Maes Coch, descending thence S.E. to join A487 2 m. above Minffordd.

Much of the area around this route has been acquired by Nature Conservancy. While the path described below is not affected, access to the nature reserves is restricted. Visitors wishing to enter the reserves should apply to Nature Conservancy, Ffordd Penrhos, Bangor.

At Minffordd the route branches right from the main road, soon passing a private drive on the right to *Dol-y-Cau,* once the house of Dr Owen Pughe (d. 1835), the Welsh lexicographer. A little farther on there is a turn into a sometimes muddy drive leading to a footbridge. Beyond the stream a steep ascent begins through woods, mounting above the rushing torrent that issues from Llyn-y-Cau. Once above the tree level the gradient becomes easier, and the path swings W. towards the rock basin enclosing *Llyn-y-Cau* (1550 ft), the largest of the lakes on Cader Idris, overlooked by the sheer Craig-y-Cau (2617 ft) and the peak of Pen-y-Gader. The ascent away from the stream bears up left towards the foot of some outcrops, and, on reaching the rib of rock enclosing the lake, climbs steeply to the left (fair track). The lake at once comes into view below. (The alternative route skirting the S. shore of the lake, then climbing very steeply to the Bwlch-y-Cau, is not recommended). On gaining the ridge the route bears right along it, with a glimpse of Tal-y-Llyn to the left and Llyn-y-Cau far down to the right. The precipitous crags of Craig-y-Cau are traversed, followed by a descent to the grassy

Bwlch-y-Cau (2350 ft). The direct route from Tal-y-Llyn comes in on the left just before reaching the col. Thence to the summit is a plain walk of ½ hour by a good if stony track.

FROM TAL-Y-LLYN LAKE (3 m. 2 hours). The starting point is the N. shore of Tal-y-Llyn lake by the farm of *Rhiwogof.* This is rather over 1½ m. S.W. of Minffordd; it is also reached from Tywyn in 10 m. by B4405. This is a less strenuous but also less interesting ascent than Llyn-y-Cau. From where the track gives out beyond the farm, the route climbs the steep S. slope of the mountain, keeping well to the left of *Cwm Amarch* with its encircling crags. Passing left of a tarn, it traverses to the right over the top of the crags and, on gaining a ridge, bears down to the left of *Bwlch-y-Cau,* where Llyn-y-Cau comes into view below. Hence the summit is reached in ½ hour by a good if stony path.

19   DOLGELLAU TO FFESTINIOG OR MAENTWROG

A470. 17 miles.—*2m. Llanelltyd.—3m. Ganllwyd.—5m. Bronaber.—2m. Trawsfynydd.—3m. Junction of A470 and A487.—2m.* **Ffestiniog** or **Maentwrog.**
The first half of the road is up the beautiful Ganllwyd valley, beside the Mawddach and Eden and through the forest of Coed-y-Brenin. Afterwards comes open country with some views of mountains.

Dolgellau, see Rte 18. For Dolgellau to (*2m.*) *Llanelltyd,* see p. 188.

A470 (but see alternative road below) ascends the lovely *Ganllwyd Valley,* named for a hamlet and not for a river, following the W. bank first of the Mawddach and then of the Eden. The ridge above the opposite bank of the Mawddach is Foel Cynwch, with Precipice Walk high up on its slope. In 2 m., where the Wen and Las streams flow into the other side of the Mawddach, the road enters the wooded Ganllwyd Valley proper, in ¾ m., just beyond *Tyn-y-Groes Hotel,* passing above the bridge by which the alternative road joins this main road.

A pleasant and quiet alternative is offered by the little road which ascends the E. bank of the Mawddach. In 2½ m., where the Mawddach bears away N.E., the Las stream is crossed, just the other side being a road which leads W., in ½ m. reaching the Forestry Commission's *Glasdir Arboretum.* Trees include Japanese red cedar, Japanese larch, Norway spruce, balsam poplar, hemlocks, and Scots and Corsican pine. Returning, the Wen is crossed, beyond which the Mawddach is reached and crossed by the next bridge (c. 1½ m. from the Arboretum) to A470.

3 m. (from Llanelltyd) *Ganllwyd,* where the little Gamlan river flows in from the west. *Rhaeadr Ddu* (N.T.), a fine broken cascade on the Gamlan, is reached by a steep path (½ m.) up a rocky and wooded glen. National Trust land W. of the road here (Dolmelynllyn Estate, 1249 acres) includes a park, farms, and two hotels. Just beyond Ganllwyd, *Pont-ar-Eden* is a bridge across the Eden above its confluence with the Mawddach. The road now follows the W. bank of the Eden, in rather over 1 m. reaching *Pont Dolgefeiliau* (picnic site). The name means Meadow of the Smiths and recalls that in the early 19C this was where the drovers had their cattle shod before starting the long drive to London.

From Pont Dolgefeiliau a branch road leads in ½ m. to the **Coed-y-Brenin (F.C.) Visitor Centre†.** The forest of Coed-y-Brenin was mostly part of the ancient Nannau Estate, the first owner of which (1100) was Cadwgan, Prince of Powys, the property later passing to the Vaughans. After land had been bought from the Vaughans, the Forestry

Commission started planting in 1922. In 1935, to celebrate the Silver Jubilee of King George V, the name was changed from Vaughan Forest to Coed-y-Brenin (Forest of the King). The total area of forest, both sides of A470 and with a number of outlying sections, is some 21,700 acres, of which about 15,500 acres are planted, most of the remainder being agricultural land. The Visitor Centre provides an admirable introduction to all the main aspects of the forest, past and present, and includes also a display of gold mining machinery. The part of the forest most readily accessible is that to the E. of A470, reached (from the Visitor Centre) by walkers at Pont Dolgefeiliau, and by motorists at Pont-ar-Eden. The varied scenery includes forest proper, pasture, moorland, and the wooded glens through which tumble the Eden, Gain, Mawddach, and Wen. On the fringes the forest gives place to high, rolling moor. A map obtainable at the Visitor Centre clearly describes a network of many miles of paths, and also some motorable roads. The cascades of *Rhaeadr Mawddach* and *Pistyll Cain*, near gold mine workings (c. 2 m. on foot from the Visitor Centre, or a little less from the nearest car park), are particularly popular objectives. For an alternative approach from the N., see below.

A470 crosses the Eden at Pont Dolgefeiliau, gradually leaving the river's E. bank and in 1½ m. at *Bryn Eden* emerging from the forest on to open moor, with views of the Rhinogs to the west.—*5 m.* (from Ganllwyd) *Bronaber* is a scattered hamlet from which a choice of small roads traverse the lonely moorland to the east.

A road (signed Llanuwchllyn and Abergierw) ascends through a holiday village, on the hilltop above which a fork offers a choice. The righthand road, soon passing a chapel, leads across moor and through afforestation to (3 m.) a farm where the road ends. From here a path descends (25 min.) to the cascades of *Rhaeadr Mawddach* and *Pistyll Cain* (see above). The lefthand road soon reaches another fork. Here the righthand road (Abergierw) descends to the river Gain, before the bridge being two antiquities. *Llech Idris* to the right, is a 10 ft high standing stone. To the left is *Bedd Porius,* the grave of Porius, now just broken fragments. The 5-6C inscribed stone, which stood here until removed to the National Museum of Wales, records in Latin that Porius, a simple man (homo planus), lies here. The lefthand road at the fork wanders across remote high moor and afforestation to (12 m. from Bronaber) Llanuwchllyn at the S. end of Bala Lake. On the descent down the Lliw the road crosses the little tributary Erwent at the farm of *Buarthmeini;* here a short walk up the Lliw leads to a good cascade. For *Castell Carndochan,* S. of the road some 2 m. farther down the valley, see p. 187.

2 m. Trawsfynydd is a straggling village at the S.E. end of the lake of the same name, 2 m. long by 1 m. wide, created in 1930 as part of the Maentwrog hydro-electric scheme. In the village there is a statue to Hedd Wyn, a shepherd poet whose winning of the bardic chair at the 1917 Eisteddfod was declared after he had been killed in France. From here A4212 bears N.E., meeting Rte 17 in 8 m. just W. of Llyn Celyn.

The *Trawsfynydd Nuclear Power Station*† (Sir Basil Spence, 1959-64) was the first inland nuclear power station in Britain. It has a capacity of 500,000 k.w. and uses 35 million gallons of cooling water per hour from the lake. A nature trail (leaflet from power station) makes the 3 m. circuit of the lake.

Just over ½ m. beyond the power station, and just before the A470/A487 junction, a small road leads E. under a railway bridge, in 1 m., beyond a copse, reaching a tiny *Roman Amphitheatre,* with, a short way S.W., the mound of *Tomen-y-Mur* (no access). The name means Mound of the Wall, and the place is probably an early Norman motte raised inside the wall of the Roman auxiliary fort (1C) which stood here on Sarn Helen. The site figures in the 'Mabinogion' as a later seat of the princes of Ardudwy, and it was from here that the men of Ardudwy set out on the raid into Clwyd that ended in the drowning of the maidens in Llyn Morynion (see p. 189). The amphitheatre is the only example in Britain of one at an auxiliary fort.

3 m. Junction of A470 and A487. **Maentwrog** (see p. 201) is *2 m.* by A487. A470, crossing the Cynfal at Bont Newydd, in *2 m.* reaches **Ffestiniog**, see p. 189

20 BARMOUTH TO MAENTWROG

A Barmouth

Barmouth (2230 inhab.), in Welsh either *Y Bermo* or *Abermaw,* is a popular and overcrowded summer resort, largely a creation of the 19C. Situated at the N. extremity of the estuary of the Mawddach, on a narrow strip of level land between the sea and the hills, the town's chief attraction is its waterfront and beach with 2 m. of sands. This area is rather awkwardly separated from the rest of the town by the railway. Local walks are also an attraction.

Tourist Information (local, and Wales Tourist Board). Marine Parade, by the station.
  Parking. Marine Parade. Harbour.
  Railway and Bus stations. Marine Parade.
  Post Office. King Edward Street (inland of railway).
  Early Closing. Wednesday.
  Ferry. Passenger ferry to Fairbourne (miniature railway).

King Edward, High, and Church streets run parallel to the railway on its landward side, and on the steep slopes above, especially above Church Street and reached by a network of paths and alleys, cluster the houses of the old town. At the N. end is *St John's Church* (1890) with a large central tower. At the other end, above St David's Church, are *St George's Cottages,* belonging to the Guild of St George founded by Ruskin in 1871 (its purpose was to achieve model industry on co-operative lines). Above, *Dinas Oleu,* 4½ acres of cliffland, is the first property acquired by the National Trust (1895).

Along the waterfront the main promenade, a wide motor road and walk, extends 2 m. between Llanaber and the harbour (buses in summer). A house on the quay (*Ty Gwyn*), rebuilt but retaining an old door, is said to have been used by a Vaughan when plotting with Jasper Tudor to put Henry Tudor on the English throne. Also on the quay is the *R.N.L.I. Maritime Museum†,* with lifeboat and other ship models, lifeboat equipment, and interesting photographs dating from the mid 19C.

Three walks are popular. The *Railway Bridge* across the estuary also carries a footpath. The bridge is 800 yards long and has an iron swingbridge at its N. end where the navigable channel hugs the shore. The view is striking enough to have caused Wordsworth, who was here in 1824, to write of the 'sublime estuary'. On the right is the whole range of Cader Idris, from Tyrau Mawr, the nearest and most prominent peak, to Pen-y-Gader and Mynydd Moel. More distant, beyond the head of the estuary, appear Aran Mawddwy on the right, the highest peak in sight, and Aran Benllyn on the left. Again to the left are the lower and nearer summits of Moel Offrwm and Rhobell Fawr, the latter seen above the shoulder of Y Garn. To the N. the chain of the Llawllech hills is seen, with the rounded Diphwys, the highest peak, in the middle distance. Northwest across the bay extends the Lleyn.

Panorama Walk, reached by a lane off the main road 150 yards short of the railway bridge, undulates for some 3 m. along a steep slope 300-500 ft above the estuary.—The third walking area is the high ground above the town, reached either direct from the town or from Panorama Walk. The hillside, rising to 870 ft, is owned by the town and has been laid out with a network of paths.

B   Barmouth to Maentwrog

A496. 21 miles.—*5 m.* Llanddwywe.—*3 m.* **Llanbedr.**—*2 m.* Llanfair.—*2 m.* **Harlech Castle.**—*3 m.* Llanfihangel-y-Traethau.—*6 m.* **Maentwrog.**
At first the road traverses the district of Ardudwy, the narrow tract of country between the mountains and the sea which was the home of a people who, after the departure of the Romans, seem to have moved to Tomen-y-Mur. Scenically, beyond the flat coast with its many caravan sites, there is a seaward view across to the Lleyn, while ahead, after Llanfair, appear the mountains of Snowdonia. Inland there is moorland, comparatively dull as seen from the road, but, deeper in, with some wild scenery. With its many prehistoric remains, this is country popular with walkers. The best parts of the area are described below as diversions eastward from A496.

A496 runs above Barmouth sands.—*2 m.* **Llanaber Church,** standing between the road and the sea, is an ancient place (early 13C) with much of interest. Owing to the slope of the ground the floor is on different levels, five steps leading up from the nave to the choir and two more to the sanctuary. The interior work is unusually elaborate for what was, at the time of the church's construction, a remote corner of Wales, e.g. the choir and the S. doorway with its clustered shafts. The single E. lancet and the outer door to the porch are also rather unusual features. The alms chest, on the S. wall, incorporates old ironwork. In the N.W. corner there are two stones (before 10C); one of these, inscribed 'Caelexti Monedo Regi', though mentioned by early writers on Wales, is of unknown provenance. The roof timbers are 16C, and the cross on the interior W. wall is part of an ancient graveslab.—*1 m.* *Capel Egryn* lay-by.

From here two ancient sites can be reached on foot in rather over a mile. *Pen-y-Ddinas* is a hillfort on the N. of the valley, and, rather farther on the S. side, *Carneddau Hengwm* is the remains of a long cairn.

2 m. **Llanddwywe** is just beyond the Ysgethin, crossed at Tal-y-Bont. The church, on the W. side of the road, has a chapel begun by Gruffydd Vaughan of Cors-y-Gedol in 1615, with a monument to its founder; both are ascribed to Inigo Jones.

From the lodge opposite the church a drive, nearly 1 m. long, leads to *Cors-y-Gedol,* ancient seat of an extinct branch of the Vaughan family. The mansion (1593; no adm.) has been largely remodelled, but a gatehouse of 1630 is said to be to a design of Inigo Jones. A road round the S. of the house reaches a gate, 300 yards beyond which, beside the right side of the road, is *Cors-y-Gedol Burial Chamber* (on some maps called *Arthur's Quoit*), now little more than a large perched capstone. Not far beyond, this road reaches the Ysgethin. Walkers can ascend the stream, above the N. bank of which is the hillfort of *Craig-y-Ddinas* (1164 ft). *Pont Scethin* (2½ m. from the burial chamber) is on the old road from Dolgellau to Harlech, Bont-Ddu on the estuary of the Mawddach being 4 m. south. In wilder country above Pont Scethin are (¾ m.) *Llyn Bodlyn,* enlarged to form a reservoir for Barmouth, and, 1 m. farther, *Llyn Dulyn* at 1750 ft.

The straggling built-up area of **Dyffryn Ardudwy** begins immediately after Llanddwywe church. At the S. end, on the E. side of the road near a school, is *Dyffryn Cairn* (sign), one of the more important burial chambers in this part of Wales. Excavation in 1962-63 produced pottery and other finds, now in the National Museum of Wales. The cairn has been calculated to have been 100 ft long, narrowing in width from 54 ft at its W. end to 35 ft at the eastern. The remains visible today are some of the base stones of the cairn, and the two burial chambers. The W. chamber, with its own cairn, traces of which can be seen, is thought to have been built first and to have later been covered by the cairn of the larger E. chamber. Colonel Jones of Maes-y-Garnedd (see below) is buried at *Llanenddwyn,* ½ m. N.W. of Dyffryn Ardudwy; brother-in-law of Oliver Cromwell, he signed the death warrant of Charles I and was himself executed at the Restoration.—*3 m.* **Llanbedr,** with a 'craft village', is situated on the Artro. In the church there is a stone marked with a spiral design and considered to be Bronze Age. From here diversions can be made W. and E., the latter into some wild country.

The peninsula of *Mochras* or *Shell Island* (toll), 2¼ m. W., an island only at high tide, is noted for its variety of shells (some 200 varieties). From here, exposed at low tide, extends for several miles S.W. a broken line of rocks known as *Sarn Badrig,* St Patrick's Causeway, fabled to be a road which once led to the Lowland Hundred (see p. 225). The road from Llanbedr to Mochras passes standing stones.
A small road E. out of Llanbedr ascends the Artro. In 1 m., at Salem Chapel, starts the *Cefn Isaf Farm Trail,* a 2 m. walk explaining the working of a typical hill farm. The road up the Afon Cwmnantcol soon reaches *Cwm Nantcol Nature Trail,* a ½ m. riverside walk designed to show how nature has moulded the landscape. Beyond, the lane continues up Cwm Nantcol to *Maes-y-Garnedd* (4 m. from Llanbedr), birthplace of Colonel Jones (see above), and the point at which the walk described below ends.—The road up the Artro reaches *Pen-y-Bont* (2 m. from Llanbedr and, by a road which here bears N.W., 2½ m. from Harlech), a starting point for the easiest ascent of Rhinog Fawr (2362 ft; 2½ hours), to the E., a mountain remarkable for its chaos of enormous tumbled boulders. For cars the road proper ends at the farm of *Dolwreiddiog,* 2 m. beyond Pen-y-Bont.—Walkers may here make a loop of 6 m. to Maes-y-Garnedd. *Llyn Cwm Bychan* (505 ft) is a beautiful tarn, enclosed by steep heathery slopes and dominated on the S. by the cliffs of Craig-y-Saeth. The track ends at the farm of Cwm Bychan beyond the lake head, a path (an old packhorse trail) leading from here S. to the so-called *Roman Steps,* a strange staircase, or series of broken flights, formed of flat unhewn slabs of rock, edged with smaller uprights. The steps are variously attributed to British, Roman, and medieval builders, but their origin remains obscure. The steps climb through the craggy *Bwlch Tyddiad* (1450 ft), just E. being Llyn Morwynion, one of a number of lakes 'of the maidens' (see also p. 189). For 1 m. the walk now skirts the E. slopes of Rhinog Fawr, with an outlying section of Coed-y-Brenin immediately to the E. (paths E. to A470), rounding the mountain to bear S.W. along the narrow *Bwlch Drws Ardudwy* (1155 ft), the Pass of the Gate of Ardudwy, an impressive deep notch in the rugged mountain wall of the Rhinogs. The path crosses the marshy source of the Nantcol and reaches *Maes-y-Garnedd.*

2 m. **Llanfair,** site of former underground slate quarries. *Old Llanfair Quarry†,* on A496 between Llanfair and Harlech, enables visitors to see something of the workings excavated between 1875 and 1905. Ahead now is a view of the Snowdon group.

A small road, leading N.E. out of Llanfair, passing E. of Harlech and enabling A496 to be rejoined at a choice of points farther N., offers a scenic alternative to A496 as well as some ancient sites. *Muriau'r Gwyddelod* (¼ m. W. of the road, ¾ m. beyond Llanfair) are a group of hut circles. *Moel-y-Sensigl* (1019 ft), 1½ m. farther, with a nearby standing stone, is a good viewpoint. *Moel Goedog,* 1 m. farther, has cairn circles near its S.W. foot and a hillfort on top.

2m. ***Harlech Castle**† (Bold Rock), backed by its small town, rises foursquare on its rock platform some 200 ft above the marshes of Morfa Harlech, from which the sea has retreated, here for over ½ m. The castle is a notably complete and well-preserved example of Edward I's system of concentric fortification.—Access is from either above or below. The approach from below (car park) is through the old watergate and involves a long steep climb. B4573, from N. or S., is the easiest road to the town and the castle's upper entrance, the road from the station, immediately below the castle, being very steep and twisty. Parking close to the castle's upper entrance is limited, but there is a larger car park about ¼ m. south. The description below assumes use of the upper entrance.

History. Chosen by Edward I in 1283, this site was at that time immediately above the estuary which now runs out some 2½ m. to the north. The castle was started by James of St George in 1283 and completed by 1289, its builder staying on as constable until 1293. The town received its charter as an English Borough in 1285. With a garrison of only thirty-seven men the castle withstood a siege by Madog in 1294-95, but was not again besieged until 1404 when it was taken, but only after some treachery and bribery, by Owen Glendower. For four years, until retaken for the English in 1408, Harlech served as Glendower's capital. In 1460 Margaret of Anjou took refuge here after the battle of Northampton, and, although she soon moved on to Scotland, the castle remained in Lancastrian hands until taken by the Yorkists in 1468. It was the last stronghold in England and Wales to fall, and then only after enduring a siege of seven years. Among the survivors was a boy of 12, later to become Henry VII. The castle's stubborn resistance is said to have inspired the song 'The March of the Men of Harlech'. By the 16C Harlech had become a ruin, but during the Civil War, defended by Colonel William Owen, it held out for Charles I until, the last Welsh fortress to fall, it was taken by General Mytton in 1647. Never formally slighted, the castle was then allowed to lapse into ruin.

The **View** from the battlements includes the sweep of coast round Tremadog Bay and down the Lleyn, with to the N.W. Criccieth Castle. The mountain panorama starts with Mynydd Rhiw, near the tip of the Lleyn, then embraces, in succession and still on the Lleyn, Carn Fadryn, Yr Eifl, and the Bwlch Mawr group. Next come the mountains of Snowdonia with the Carnedd Goch group, Moel Hebog, the peaks of Snowdon itself, the Glyders, Cnicht, the two Moelwyns, and, at the head of the Vale of Ffestiniog, the bulky Manods.

The ENTRANCE is across the wide moat from the site of the barbican to a doorway flanked by two towers in the outer curtain. The outer defence here consists of a revetted terrace with a breastwork, rather than the full wall found at some other castles. Another surprising feature is that the gateways of the outer and inner defences are in line, there being no attempt, as for example at Denbigh and Beaumaris, to construct an oblique approach. The GATEHOUSE, three storeys high, is the principal feature of the castle. The residence of the constable, it had living rooms on the upper floors. It has two huge half-round towers facing outwards, and two large drum-towers, rising a further storey, at the inner corners. The rooms include an oratory, which was also a portcullis chamber, and a second oratory above that. This gatehouse, and the N.E. tower, were the only parts of the castle still roofed in the later 16C, the former then being used as judges' lodging and the tower as a prison.

A central passage admits to the INNER WARD, which is roughly oblong, enclosed by walls 40 ft high with a round tower at each corner. The rampart walk is corbelled out across the flattened inner faces of these towers, the outer two of which carry circular watch-towers. The S.E. and N.E. towers are similar, each having a dungeon entered originally by trapdoor from the room above. The rooms, not uniform in shape, are approached by wall stairs, at the top being privies. The outer towers represent the last part of the castle to be built and contain pentagonal rooms of one size. Various rooms can be traced around the interior of the ward. On the W. side are the *Kitchen* (S.) and *Great Hall* (N.). On the S. side are the *Granary* (E.) and, adjoining the kitchen, the site of a room known as the *Ystumgwern Hall,* so called because it was brought here complete from the residence of that name (4 m. away) of Llewelyn the Last. Opposite, against the N. wall, are the *Chapel* (W.) and *Bakehouse* (E.).

Between the chapel and bakehouse a passage with a postern leads to the OUTER WARD with, straight ahead, another postern, flanked by towers, that gave access to the precipitous CASTLE ROCK. On the N. and W. sides of the castle, following more or less the lower edge of the rock and connected by steep walls to the N.E. and S.W. corners of the outer ward, was a third line of defence, a wall added c.1295 after Madog's unsuccessful siege. The W. part of the rock is now reached by a gate behind the N.W. tower. Beyond can be seen the remains of a wall which ran from the tower to the precipice; also, to the S. of this wall and a little below the castle, platforms on which stood defensive engines. A path descends to the *Upper Gate,* once with a drawbridge, and thence, with a protecting wall, down to the *Watergate.*

There is a large heated swimming pool off A496 roughly opposite the station. At *Colleg Harlech*†, a residential college, there are periodic exhibitions by local artists, or arranged by the Welsh Arts Council.

For *Moel-y-Sensigl* (1019ft), 1 m. E., see p. 199.—For Harlech to *Pen-y-Bont* (2½ m. S.E.), for *Cwm Bychan, Roman Steps, Rhinog Fawr, Bwlch Drws Ardudwy,* and *Cwm Nantcol,* see p. 199.

3 m. Llanfihangel-y-Traethau is reached either by A496 across the flat Morfa Harlech, or, more pleasantly, by the higher B4573 which, just outside Harlech, skirts *Coed Llechwedd,* a woodland property given to the National Trust in 1937 in memory of the Irish writer A.P. Graves (1846-1931). At Llanfihangel-y-Traethau a narrow lane climbs to the small church above the village. When first built the church stood on a tidal island, and, although the sea receded in the later Middle Ages, there was still flooding until the building of a seawall in 1805. In the churchyard, close to the porch, stands a 12C stone. The Latin inscription records that it marks the grave of the mother of the builder of the church during the time of King Owain Gwynedd (1137-70). Portmeirion can be seen across the water.—A496 crosses the railway, passes the hamlet of *Talsarnau,* and reaches the head of the Traeth Bach estuary, where a road branches N. and W. to cross the Dwyryd by tollbridge and in 1 m. reach *Penrhyndeudraeth.* Here and beyond, the train of the Festiniog Railway may be seen high on the hill across the valley.—*5 m.* (from Llanfihangel-y-Traethau) *Maentwrog Power Station* is a small power station in woods, linked by pipe with Llyn Trawsfynydd.

A path here follows a glen to (1½ m.) *Rhaeadr Ddu,* the Black Cascade, a twisted water slide set among rocks and trees.

1 m. **Maentwrog,** a pleasant village below wooded hills, gets its name from its ancient stone, the 'maen' of Twrog, which stands in the churchyard and traditionally commemorates (there is no inscription) a 7C holy man known to have been a companion of St Beuno. The stone, though only 4 ft high, may be a prehistoric standing stone. Also in the churchyard is the grave of Archdeacon Prys (d. 1624), a former rector and author of the Welsh translation of the Psalter still in use.

For Maentwrog to (W.) *Porthmadog* and (E.) *Ffestiniog* and *Bala*, see Rte 17; to *Trawsfynydd* and *Dolgellau*, see Rte 19.

21   SHREWSBURY AND ENVIRONS

SHREWSBURY (83,600 inhab.), generally pronounced 'Shrowsbury', is the county town of Salop (Shropshire), its inhabitants being known as 'Salopians'. The town is encircled by a loop of the Severn, only a narrow gap being left to the north. Officially designated a Special Conservation area, Shrewsbury's wealth of black-and-white half-timbered houses, its picturesque and sometimes quaintly named streets, its museums, and the interest of its environs combine to attract many visitors.

Tourist Information. The Square (behind Old Market Hall).
Parking. Barker Street (by Rowley's House Museum). Abbey Foregate.
Main Post Office. Corner of Pride Hill and St Mary's Street.
Railway Station. N.E. quarter of the town, beyond the castle.
Bus Station. Barker Street.
Early Closing. Thursday.
Markets. *General:* Wed., Fri., Sat. *Cattle:* Tues.
Regimental Museums. Shrewsbury has six regimental museums. That of the *Queen's Dragoon Guards* is in the Clive House Museum. Those of the *Light Infantry* and of the *King's Shropshire Light Infantry* are in Sir John Moore Barracks, Copthorne, in the W. of the town. Those of the *Shropshire Yeomanry* and of the *Shropshire Battery, Royal Horse Artillery*, are at Sundorne Territorial Centre, beyond the N.E. of the town. The museum of the *4th Battalion (Territorial) King's Shropshire Light Infantry* is at the Territorial Centre, Coleham, in the southeast.
History. In the 5 and 6C local chieftains, including very probably that of Viroconium (see below), abandoned at about this time, recognized the strategic value of this bluff above the river, already used as a hillfort, and settled here. Later, with the name Pengwern, it became the seat of the princes of Powys. The place was taken by Offa of Mercia at the end of the 8C, then receiving alternative Saxon names; Scrobesbyrig (Fort in the Scrub) and Sloppesbury, from these evolving Shrewsbury and Salop. It is known that money was minted here in the 10C, and Shrewsbury was already a chartered town by the time of the Norman conquest, when it became part of a Marcher lordship, Roger de Montgomery (d. 1095) becoming Earl. In 1215 and 1232 the town was taken by Llewelyn the Great, and in 1234 by rebellious barons. Edward I made Shrewsbury the seat of his government during his subjugation of northern Wales, in 1283 here hanging Dafydd, brother of Llewelyn the Last. Richard II held a parliament here in 1288. At the Battle of Shrewsbury, fought three miles to the N. in 1403, Hotspur was defeated and killed. Under the Tudor era of stability Shrewsbury traded profitably in wool and flax with the Welsh, and it is from this time of prosperity that most of the half-timbered houses date. Shrewsbury School was founded by Edward VI in 1552. Charles I and Prince Rupert briefly made their headquarters here in 1642, Shrewsbury once again being used for the minting of coins. Rupert was again here in 1644, but the town fell to Cromwell's troops the following year. George Farquhar's play 'The Recruiting Officer', written in Shrewsbury in 1705, gives a picture of the town in Restoration times.
Among natives of Shrewsbury were Ordericus Vitalis (1075-1142), the chronicler; Thomas Churchyard (?1520-1604), the Elizabethan poet; Admiral Benbow (1653-1702); and Charles Darwin (1809-82). Here also lived John Weaver (1683-1760), an important figure in the history of dancing and associated with early forms of pantomime and the ballet.

The town centre is THE SQUARE, with the Old Market Hall. The main town is described below as two walks, both starting from here.

Northeast of The Square

In The Square stands a statue (by Marochetti; 1860) of Lord Clive (Clive of India), M.P. for Shrewsbury and mayor in 1762. Behind is the *Old Market Hall,* an Elizabethan building of 1595. For Clive House Museum, just behind, see below.

From The Square High Street descends between *Ireland's Mansion* (c. 1580) on the left and *Owen's Mansion* (c. 1592) on the other side, both splendid timber-framed houses. High Street joins Pride Hill, just opposite being a shop, (John Collier), the interior of which interestingly incorporates the remains of *Bennett's Hall,* which may have been the site of Charles I's mint in 1642. Pride Hill rises to the *High Cross* (Laurence Gotch) at the junction with St Mary's Street. The cross, presented by Shrewsbury School on its quatercentenary, stands on the site of the earlier cross where Dafydd was hanged in 1283 and the body of Hotspur hanged, drawn, and quartered in 1403.

Pride Hill becomes Castle Street, to the W. of which stood the Raven Hotel where George Farquhar wrote 'The Recruiting Officer' in 1705; this was the first play ever acted in Australia (at Sydney in 1789). On the right is the *Old Council House* (1625), occupied by Charles I in 1642 and by James II in 1687. Just beyond is the entrance to the *Castle†.* Standing on an Iron Age site, it was begun in 1067 and given to the Marcher lord Roger de Montgomery in 1071. All that remains of this early period are parts of the main wall and gateway. The castle was rebuilt by Edward I, modernized by Telford, restored in 1968, and now houses the local government council chamber. On the other side of the road stands the *Library,* occupying the old buildings (1630) of Shrewsbury School; in front is a bronze statue of Darwin. The road continues to the railway station.

From the High Cross St Mary's Street quickly reaches *St Mary's Church,* founded c. 970 as a collegiate church. The spire (222 ft) was the scene in 1739 of a dramatic and tragic event when one Cadman strung a rope from the top across the Severn and attempted to slide down it; the rope snapped and Cadman fell to his death (plaque on W. exterior wall). Inside, the sedile are Norman, the nave is E.E., and the N. aisle was rebuilt or restored during the Commonwealth. The church is known for its *Stained Glass,* collected from many sources. The windows are well labelled and explained. Outstanding are the large 14C Jesse window (from Old St Chad's) at the E. end; 16C glass from St Jacques, Liège, in the 15C Trinity Chapel (central two windows; the others are copies); and 19 panels (14 in the triple lancet on the N. side of the chancel, five in the middle window of the S. nave aisle) showing scenes from the life of St Bernard. These panels (1500) are by the Master of St Severin of Cologne and came from the abbey of Altenburg. Also noteworthy are, in the Trinity Chapel, an effigy of a 14C knight and 14C alabaster carvings; and, in the N. chapel, a tablet to Admiral Benbow (1653-1702), born at Coton Hill to the N. of the town.

Two very attractive half-timbered houses, *St Mary's Cottage* and *Draper's Hall,* stand immediately N. and S. of the church. Running S.W. from the church is Church Street, with *St Alkmund's Church,* founded in 911 by Ethelfleda, daughter of Alfred the Great, and rebuilt in 1795. The striking E. window (Francis Egington, 1795) is a copy from Guido Reni's Assumption. Adjacent to St Alkmund's, forming the corner of Church Street and Butcher Row (the latter with noteworthy 15 and 16C houses), is the mainly 15C *Prince Rupert Hotel,* a part of which, as Jones's Mansion, was where Prince Rupert lived in 1644.

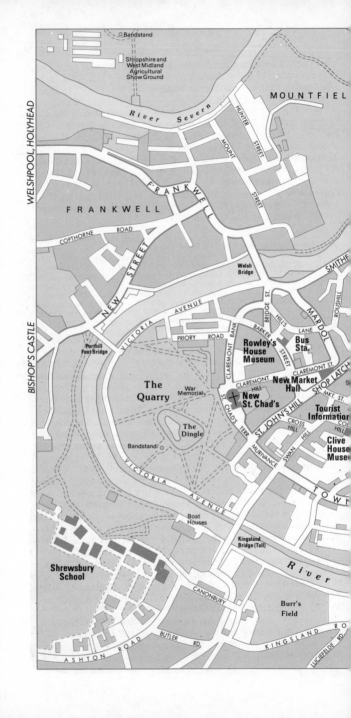

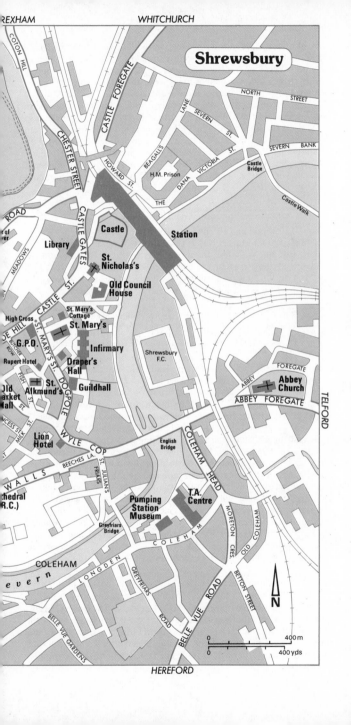

St Mary's Street continues as Dogpole, with on the left the *Guildhall* (1696) and the *Olde House,* once occupied by Mary Tudor. Dogpole runs into Wyle Cop opposite the *Lion Hotel,* in part Tudor but dating mainly from 1770, a coaching inn once with stabling for 100 horses. Among those who stayed here were the author Thomas de Quincey (1785-1859), who slept in the Assembly Room, all others being taken; William IV (as Prince William Frederick) in 1814; Charles Dickens in 1838, with his illustrator 'Phiz' (Hablot K. Browne); and Benjamin Disraeli in 1841. Madame Tussaud, of waxworks fame, presented an exhibition here in 1830, and Paganini held two concerts in 1831. Jenny Lind sang here in 1849 and 1856. Below the Lion Hotel is a half-timbered house in which Henry Tudor lodged in 1485 on his way to victory and the crown (as Henry VII) at Bosworth Field.

Southwest of The Square

For *The Square* and the *Old Market Hall,* see above.

Behind the Old Market Hall is **Clive House Museum.**† The building, mainly 18C but with 15C fragments, was until the Reformation the residence of the clergy of the nearby collegiate church of St Chad's (14-15C). In 1752 it was converted into three houses, and it was used by Lord Clive as residence when he was mayor of Shrewsbury in 1762.

GROUND FLOOR. Industrial archaeology (including, at Coleham Pumping Station, S.E. of the town across the river, two beam engines of 1900). Local ceramic (Coalport and Caughley). English glass. The Georgian Room, with church silver (17C) and a portrait by Zoffany.—FIRST FLOOR. *Regimental Museum of the Queen's Dragoon Guards.*—SECOND FLOOR. Costumes, including smocks. Local view pictures.

From behind the Old Market Hall, Market Street leads into Shoplatch, with the conspicuous *New Market Hall,* a modern building with a spacious, multi-level market through which it is possible to walk to Barker Street. Here, beyond the Bus Station, is ***Rowley's House Museum**†. The house (16C) was built as a warehouse by a wealthy cloth merchant who lived in the adjoining mansion (into which there are plans to extend the museum) and is worth visiting almost as much for itself, with its wealth of woodwork and huge beams, as for the museum. The museum is devoted almost entirely to the Roman town of Viroconium (p. 208), the outstanding exhibit being a large tablet (130), the largest Roman inscription ever found in Britain, which stood over the main entrance to the forum and is dedicated to the Emperor Caesar Trajanus Hadrianus Augustus. Other exhibits include a good model of the town; coins; military material, including an interesting time-expired soldier's discharge certificate; pottery; tradesmen's, household, and funerary material; mosaics and metalwork.

Welsh Bridge (1791) is just over 100 yards to the north.

Beyond the bridge is the district called Frankwell, the home of French settlers soon after the Norman conquest. Frankwell and The Mount lead to *Darwin House,* birthplace of Charles Darwin in 1809.

From Welsh Bridge Claremont Bank runs above **The Quarry,** a large public park within the loop of the Severn. Here Priory Road, beside the swimming baths, recalls a priory for Austin Canons, and in *The Dingle* stands the Shoemakers' Arbour, the only survivor of a number of such shelters put up by the various trade guilds. Claremont Bank continues past *New St Chad's,* a strangely planned circular church, built by Telford in 1792, with a Doric façade and tower. The road becomes Muirvance and then Town Walls, passing (S.) the town's only remaining tower and fragments of the 13C walls, and (N.) the *Roman Catholic Cathedral* (A. W. Pugin, 1856).

On the hill across the river is **Shrewsbury School,** founded in 1552 by Edward VI. The school originally occupied the site of the library, opposite the castle. The present main buildings, by Sir Arthur Blomfield, were opened in 1882; the Speech Hall was added in 1911. Among pupils have been Sir Philip Sidney, Fulke Greville, Judge Jeffreys, Dr Burney, Charles Darwin, Samuel Butler, Stanley Weyman and John Weaver. Dr Butler, later Bishop of Lichfield, was headmaster from 1798-1836.

East Shrewsbury

Wyle Cop drops to *English Bridge,* built by John Gwynn in 1769 and later widened, beyond which is Abbey Foregate where once stood the Monastery of SS Peter and Paul, founded by Roger de Montgomery in 1083 and now represented by **Abbey Church**† and, in an enclosure S. of the road, the elegant little 14C *Reader's Pulpit* of the refectory, the only relic of the domestic buildings.

The church has an imposing Dec. W. tower, the base of which, however, with the doorway, is Norman. The statue above the W. window is said to be of Edward III. The two W. bays of the nave were rebuilt at the same time as the tower; the other bays are plain Norman work. The transepts and chancel were built by J. L. Pearson in 1886-88. The monument of Speaker Onslow (d. 1571) in the N. aisle was brought from Old St Chad's, as was also the 13C effigy of a lawyer. Opposite the N. door are the fragmentary remains of a chantry, with figures of SS Winefride, John the Baptist, and Beuno, recovered in 1933 from a garden in the town. In the S. aisle is a tomb said to be that of Roger de Montgomery.

A little beyond Abbey Church, in Monkmoor Road (N. off Abbey Foregate), are *Shire Hall;* and *Whitehall,* a fine stone mansion of 1582, once belonging to Dr Butler. *Lord Hill's Column* (133 ft), just E., was erected in 1816 in honour of Viscount Hill (1772-1842), veteran of the Peninsular War.

Environs of Shrewsbury

There are a number of places of interest within 3-5 m. of Shrewsbury, all being to the N. or east.

Battlefield Church, 3 m. N. off A49, was built in 1408 to commemorate the Battle of Shrewsbury of 1403. The battle, fought in open country to the N. and W. of the church, marked the end of an attempt by the Earl of Northumberland and his son Henry Percy (Hotspur) to depose Henry IV, whom previously, on the death of Richard II, they had helped to put on the throne. The failure of Owen Glendower to meet Percy at Shrewsbury, as also a forced march by the King from Lichfield, led to the defeat and death of Percy. The battle features in Shakespeare's 'King Henry IV, Part One', in which Falstaff boasts that he killed Percy after a single combat lasting 'a long hour by Shrewsbury clock'. The church, neglected after the Reformation, was restored and made a parish church in 1862. It contains an early 15C Pietà, in oak, probably from the chapel of the nearby moated mansion of *Albright Hussey.*

Haughmond Abbey† is best reached from Battlefield Church by returning S. along A49 for 1½ m., then bearing E. on B5062 for 2 m. The abbey was founded by William Fitzalan in 1135 for Augustinian Canons. It was rebuilt towards the end of the century, at which time the church was much enlarged, and there was more rebuilding in the 14 and 15C. After the Dissolution a part was converted into a private mansion, which however burnt down, possibly during the Civil War. The ruins are mainly of the abbey's domestic buildings. The *Abbot's Lodging* (14-15C) has a graceful oriel window. Immediately W. of this is the large *Infirmary* (14C), once with nine doorways. The site of the *Kitchen*, still with its chimneys, extends N. from here, beyond being the sites of the *Refectory* and then the *Cloister*, of which virtually only the W. walls survive. The *Chapter House* (12C), on the E. side of the cloister, has a finely carved entrance and a 16C ceiling, the latter presumably a part of the conversion to mansion. What little is left of the *Church* (12C) is N. of the cloister. It had transepts, each with two chapels, and a nave, originally without aisles but later given one on the north. At the S.W. doorway of the church are figures of SS Peter and Paul. The site includes a small *Museum*, and, in the wood immediately E. of the site entrance, there is a *Monks' Well* (14 or 15C).

From the abbey minor roads S. in 4 m. reach *Atcham*, with a fine sandstone bridge across the Severn, built in 1771 by John Gwynn.

Attingham Park†, immediately N. of Atcham, comprising 3826 acres and a mansion, was acquired in 1953 by the National Trust under the will of the 8th Lord Berwick. The house, a pretentious aggrandisement in Palladian style around an older house, was designed in 1785 by George Steuart for the 1st Lord Berwick. The 2nd Lord Berwick put in hand the landscaping of the park (Humphry Repton, 1797) and also employed Nash to design the picture gallery. The pictures, largely portraits, include works by Angelica Kauffmann, Lawrence, Romney, Sickert, Ribera, Van Dyck (attrib.), and Kneller.

The part open to the public of the Romano-British town of *Viroconium*† (Wroxeter) is 1½ m. E. of Atcham.

History. There is evidence that Roman military activity in this area had started by 48, at the time when Scapula was fighting Caractacus, and a more permanent legionary fort seems to have been established a few years later. It was, however, shortlived, and with the transfer of the garrison to Chester in 88 Viroconium became civilian. What is interesting is that, whereas other abandoned forts in Britain became settlements for retired legionaries, Viroconium became a centre for the Cornovii, the local tribe. The town seems to have survived until around 500, when the unsettled times probably caused most of the inhabitants, by now possibly under the leadership of a mercenary chieftain, to move to a more easily defended site, such as perhaps Shrewsbury.

What the visitor sees is essentially the area of the Baths, at the centre of a town which, from here, extended some 700 yards N. and 400-500 yards in other directions. Although the town survived for perhaps another two centuries, the baths seem to have been abandoned as such by c. 300, the area afterwards serving various domestic purposes. From the site entrance (N.W. corner) the visitor passes (l.) the expanse of the huge *Exercise Hall*, stretching some 75 yards eastwards; the hall was demolished around the end of the 4C, its stones possibly being used for the town walls. A left turn is made into a passage, with (r.) the *Market Hall* and (l.) the long, narrow *Latrine*. Beyond are (l.) a *Caldarium* complex of a date later than the main baths, added perhaps to meet increasing demand, and (r.) the *Piscina*, a feature unusual in Britain.

Ahead now are three buildings. At the N. is the *Frigidarium,* the N. wall of which, the entrance from the exercise hall, is the most prominent feature of the whole site. On the S. side of the wall three tiled arches can be traced, and the original may be pictured as having niches with statues and spaces filled by mosaics. Either side of the Frigidarium were (N.) cold plunges and (S.) warming rooms. The central building was the *Tepidarium,* to the S. of this being the *Caldarium,* with its furnace on its S. side.—An admirable small *Museum* tells the story of Viroconium, and has good explanatory material on, for example, water supply, drainage, baths system etc. The *Forum* was immediately W. of the baths, and a length of its colonnade can be seen just across the road down the W. side of the site.—In the hamlet of *Wroxeter,* just S., the Saxon church (?9C) is evidence of continuing activity here after the abandonment of Viroconium proper.

For Shrewsbury to *Chirk* and *Llangollen,* see Rte 14; to *Welshpool, Newtown, Machynlleth,* and *Aberystwyth,* see Rte 22; to *Llandrindod Wells, Llandovery,* and *Swansea,* see Rte 29; to *Ludlow* and *Hereford,* see Rte 31.

22 SHREWSBURY TO MACHYNLLETH AND ABERYSTWYTH

A Viâ Welshpool and Newtown

A458 to Welshpool: A483 and A490 to Chirbury: B4386 to Montgomery: B4385 and A489 to Newtown: A492 to Caersws: A470 and A489 to Machynlleth. (OR, by Mountain Road, A470, B4518, and unclassified): A487 to Aberystwyth. 82 miles (or 85 miles by Mountain Road).—*12 m. Middletown.*—*6 m.* **Welshpool.**—*7 m. Chirbury.*—*3 m.* **Montgomery.**—*10 m. Kerry.*—*2 m.* **Newtown.**—*5 m.* **Caersws.** Then EITHER *5 m. Carno.*—*6 m. Llanbrynmair.*—*5 m. Cemmaes Road.*—*5 m.* **Machynlleth:** OR *7 m.* **Llanidloes.**—*17 m.* **Machynlleth.** Then *8 m. Tre'r Ddol.*—*8 m.* **Aberystwyth.**

After Welshpool the general course of the valley of the Severn is followed as far as Caersws. Then increasing moorland; higher, remoter, and more scenic if the Mountain Road is chosen. After Machynlleth, wood and moor inland and estuary flats to seaward.

Shrewsbury, see Rte 21, is left by Welsh Bridge and the suburb of Frankwell.—*6 m. Cardeston,* where the church preserves a barrel organ which plays hymn tunes. Just beyond, *Rowton Castle* is the Royal National College for the Blind.—*6 m. Middletown* is a hamlet just across the Welsh border.

The **Breidden Hills,** the isolated group of three peaks to the N., derive the second syllable of their name from the forts (duns) found on two of the hills, *Middletown Hill* (1050 ft) immediately N. of the village and *Breidden Hill* (1202 ft) beyond. The latter, supposed to have been the site of a battle between Welsh and English in 1292, has an obelisk commemorating Admiral Rodney's victory over the French off Domenica in 1782; the normal ascent is from Criggion on the north. *Moel-y-Golfa* (1234 ft), to the S.W., is the third and highest peak.

At *4 m. Buttington,* traditionally the site of a battle of 894 between the Saxons and the Danes, the church has a font made from a capital from the abbey of Strata Marcella. The Severn is crossed just beyond the village.

2 m. **Welshpool** (7000 inhab.), on the Shropshire Union Canal, is a generally red-brick, English-looking and English-speaking town, perhaps best known for its Monday agricultural and general market, known to have existed before 1263, in which year the town was granted a charter by the Prince of Powys. The town is entered by Salop Road and Church Street, the museum being on the right before the church, and *Tourist Information* and a cark park just below the church on the left. Below again, Church Street crosses Broad Street and Severn Street, this crossing being the town centre. The main theme of the *Powysland Museum†*, founded in 1874, is the social history of Powys. There is also archaeological material, this including local Roman finds and fragments from the nearby abbey of Strata Marcella, ransacked at the Reformation and of which nothing now remains. (The abbey was founded c. 1170 for Cistercians by Owain Cyfeiliog, Prince of Powys, who died as a monk here). A cottage just before the church is traditionally the birthplace of Grace Evans, who assisted Lady Nithsdale, daughter of the Marquess of Powis, in the rescue of her husband from the Tower of London in 1716 (see Powis Castle, below). The *Church*, restored by Street in 1871, contains work dating from the 13-19C, the earliest parts being the W. tower and the choir, the roof of which is decorated with armorial designs. Near the station are the remains of the early Norman motte-and-bailey castle, the bailey now being the bowling green.

For the *Welshpool and Llanfair Railway,* see p. 217.—For boat trips on the *Shropshire Union Canal,* operated by the Canal Society from Severn Street Lock, apply Tourist Information.

Guilsfield, 3 m. N., has a large 15C church. Of interest are the upper chamber over the S. porch; the late Dec. clustered pier shafts; the carved heads on the beams in the S. aisle, these coming from an earlier church; the 19C vaulting, each panel being different; and the Jacobean or earlier churchwarden's chest.

Long Mountain stretches some 4 m. along the Welsh side of the border to the S.E. of Welshpool. It is crossed by Offa's Dyke, and the highest point of the ridge is *Beacon Ring* (1338 ft), with a hillfort. At *Trelystan,* on the S.E. slope, a 15C wooden church was repaired and cased with brick in 1856.

For Welshpool to *Llanfair Caereinion* and *Mallwyd,* see Rte 22B; to *Oswestry,* see Rte 23.

Powis Castle†, 1 m. S.W. of Welshpool, inhabited for some 500 years, has since 1952 belonged to the National Trust. Although reconstructed in the 17C, the castle retains the general aspect of its 13-14C origin. Standing in beautiful grounds, which include terraced gardens, the castle contains late 16C plasterwork and panelling, a 17C staircase, early Georgian furniture, and a fair collection of portraits.

History. It seems probable that the remains of a motte-and-bailey in the park are those of the original castle here (c. 1100), destroyed by Llewelyn the Great in 1233 during his struggle with his rival, the local Gruffydd ap Gwenwynwyn, and again in 1275. Under the Treaty of Conwy Edward I granted the Gwenwynwyns the barony of De La Pole, but required that they renounce Welsh princely titles. The family then built the castle which is the nucleus of today's. The barony died out in 1551, and in 1587 the castle was bought by Sir Edward Herbert, a younger son of the Earl of Pembroke, and it was he who put in hand the conversion to Elizabethan standards. Sir Edward's son William, created Baron Powis in 1629, defended the castle for Charles I during the Civil War, but it fell to Parliament in 1644. The 3rd Baron (1667) undertook further rebuilding, but, as a supporter of James II, had to flee the country in 1688. It was his wife, a Lady of the Bedchamber, who smuggled out the future Old Pretender. In 1784, through marriage, the estate passed to Edward Clive (later Earl of Powis), son of Lord Clive of India. In 1807 the family took the name of Herbert. The 4th Earl was responsible for much remodelling of the interior (G. F. Bodley, 1891-1904), and it was he who gave the castle to the National Trust.

Ballroom. 18C decoration. Italian tapestry (1545), depicting the embassy of the Venetians to Cairo in 1502. French strongbox (17C).

Clive relics include the bed belonging to Tipoo Sahib, and Chinese and Indian bronzes (earliest 15C). Family portraits. Also portraits of Leopold II of Belgium (unknown artist); George III, copy of a Gainsborough in the Queen's collection; and the Nawab of the Carnatic and his son (? Thomas Hickey). *Billiard Room.* Pewter belonging to the 1st Baron Powis, which replaced silver sold during the Civil War. Portraits. *Staircase Hall.* Bust of Spencer Perceval, Prime Minister, by Nollekens (1814). *Dining Room.* This was formerly three rooms, and original plasterwork survives in the window recess and the doorway to the servants' staircase. Other decoration is Bodley's. Early 19C mahogany wine table. Among the portraits are two by George Romney and one by Joshua Reynolds; also others by N. Dance, J. M. Wright, M. Dahl, and R. Marientreu. *Library.* Ceiling painting by Lanscroon. Among the five daughters of the 3rd Baron (1st Marquess) depicted, the youngest, as Lady Nithsdale, rescued her husband in 1716 from the Tower of London; accompanied by her servant, she visited her husband, who, donning female's clothes brought by his wife, walked out with the servant. Portrait (unknown 17C artist) of 'Old Parr', who died in 1635 reputedly aged 152. Also a portrait of Lord Herbert of Cherbury, who surrendered Montgomery Castle to Parliament. *Oak Drawing Room.* Some original 16C plasterwork in W. window aperture. Other decoration and the inserted oriel window are by Bodley. William and Mary and early 18C furniture. Sèvres china, once belonging to Tipoo Sahib. Portraits include Charles II by Godfrey Kneller; 1st Earl of Powis as a boy, by Thomas Gainsborough; 1st Lord Clive, by N. Dance. *Gateway Room.* Mortlake tapestries of the life of Nebuchadnezzar (remainder of set is in Long Gallery). English 15C Book of Hours. Insignia of Lord Clive's Order of the Bath. Family and other portraits. *State Bedroom.* Decoration includes crowns and CR, presumably in honour of Charles I or II. Main decoration is mid 17C. Brussels tapestries (late 17C), illustrating the life of Sulieman the Magnificent. Mahogany bed (18C). Queen Anne chairs. Two toilet sets of c. 1700 in cloisonné enamel on brass.

Long Gallery, with 16C plasterwork. The painted wainscot is mid 17C. Furniture includes late 17C chairs; French walnut chest with carved portraits (1538); a 16C table, the top of which is inlaid with marble and semi-precious stones. Marble figures of the Elements (c. 1700). Greek vases of the 4C B.C. Mortlake tapestries, belonging to the set in the Gateway Room. Portraits (mainly family). The *Staircase* and landings were probably designed by William Winde (late 17C). The staircase murals are signed and dated by Lanscroon, 1705; on the right Vulcan forging the arms of love for Venus, and, on the left, Venus in Neptune's chariot, with Bacchus. On the landing the sword of the Lords of the Marches, said to date from c. 1500. *Blue Drawing Room.* Ceiling, by Lanscroon, with the daughters of the 2nd Marquess attended by allegories of Africa, Asia, and America. Early 18C panelling. Brussels tapestries, depicting Classical scenes (one signed Marcus de Vos, late 17C). Black lacquer commodes, attributed to Pierre Langlois, c. 1760. Enamel bowl and a large dish, both bearing the initials P. R. (Pierre Raymond of c. 1513-1584, first of a distinguished line of Limoges enamelists). Among the pictures are family portraits by M. Dahl, P.

Batoni, J. M. Quinkhard, Hugh Douglas Hamilton, and Anna Tonelli. Also Madonna and Child, attributed to Andrea del Brescianino.

Gardens. The main feature are the four *Terraces,* nearly 200 yards long, possibly the design of William Winde. Their limestone basis limits the species that can be grown here. The *Orangery,* at the centre of the terraces and once used as such, carries a balustrade with urns and four lead figures (? Van Nost, or Cheere) of shepherds and shepherdesses. Within the grounds, but outside the gardens, a Douglas Fir (185 ft) is the tallest tree recorded in the British Isles.

2m. (from Welshpool), Junction of A483 and A490. This Route follows the latter; more interesting, but taking 20 instead of 13 m. to reach Newtown.

The direct A483 reaches (5 m. from Welshpool) *Berriew,* a pleasant village on the Rhiew, traditionally associated with St Beuno who, on hearing an English voice across the Severn, wisely moved away, so great was the Welsh awe of the pagans to their east. Near *Garthmyl,* 1 m. farther, the Severn can be crossed. Beyond the bridge, a road N. parallel to the railway in 1 m. reaches (l.) the remains of a small Roman fort, probably a halt between Vircoconium and Caersws and apparently occupied until the 4C. In another 3 m. A483 crosses the Severn, on the steep narrow ridge N.W. of the bridge being the slight remains of *Dolforwyn Castle* (?13C).

A490 crosses the Severn.—*5m. Chirbury,* in England, where the church retains the 13C nave arcades of a small priory of Austin Canons founded c. 1180 (see also Montgomery church below). B4386 is now taken, leading S.W. (in 2 m. crossing a good section of Offa's Dyke, lined by trees) and returning to Wales.

3m. **Montgomery** (1000 inhab.), in Welsh *Trefaldwyn,* is a very small market town, attractively Georgian in character and standing on a hill below the ruins of its castle.

History. The site of the original castle, built by Roger de Montgomery c. 1072, is almost certainly the motte-and-bailey 1 m. N.W. known as Hen Domen (see below). The present castle was built by Henry III in 1223, and the town received its charter four years later. The 1st Lord Herbert of Cherbury (1583-1648; portrait at Powis Castle), philosopher and diplomat, spent his youth here and it was he who in 1644 surrendered the castle to Parliament. It was demolished in 1649 because the 2nd Lord Herbert was a Royalist. The 1st Lord Herbert's brother, George Herbert (1593-1633), the poet, was born either in the castle or in the town. What was left of the castle collapsed during the 19C.

The *Castle* site, a long, narrow, rocky ridge projecting boldly towards the N., is one of unusual strength, accessible virtually only from the south. This ridge is occupied by a series of four rectangular wards in a line, though it does not seem that the two outer (S.) sections were ever fully built. The *Church,* mainly 13C but with a tower rebuilt in 1816, has a good S. doorway. Inside is a double *Screen and rood loft, the original 15C part being the W. side of panels with traceried tops, five each side of the door. The panels at the foot are comparatively modern. The loft is thought to be made up of sections from the mother priory at Chirbury. From here also probably came the stalls and misericords (15C). Also in the church are the fine Renaissance tomb (1600) of Sir Richard Herbert, father of Lord Herbert and the poet; and two recumbent effigies, the smaller figure being probably Sir Edmund Mortimer (d. 1409), grandson of Owen Glendower, and the other Sir Richard Herbert (d. 1534), grandfather of the occupant of the Renaissance tomb. On the N. side of the churchyard is the *Robber's Grave,* on which the grass is said never to grow, because of the innocence of the wrongly convicted John Newton Davies (hanged in 1821) who lies beneath.

On the adjacent hill to the W. is the hillfort of *Fridd Faldwyn* (750 ft). *Town Hill*

(1050 ft), ¾ m. S. of this, crowned by the county war memorial, commands a view which includes (W.N.W.) Cader Idris.

B4385, leading W. out of Montgomery, in 1 m. reaches a small crossroads. In trees on the left side of the road N. (300 yards) is *Hen Domen,* the motte-and-bailey which is probably the site of Roger de Montgomery's castle of 1072.

B4385, S.E. out of Montgomery, in *3 m.* reaches A489, along which this Route bears west.—*7 m.* **Kerry,** which has given its name to a breed of sheep. Here, at the dedication of the church in 1176, a dispute as to episcopal jurisdiction led to a fight between the retainers of Giraldus and those of the Bishop of St Asaph. Of the original *Church* there remains the early Norman N. arcade and possibly part of the tower, with its buttresses of varying pattern and picturesque boarded top; most of the tower, though, was rebuilt in the 14C. In the interior are a chained Welsh Bible (1690); a 15C font, with the Instruments of the Passion; a 14C piscina (S. choir); a chest of 1759; and a pulpit which, though modern, bears 15C tracery.

The hill road leading S.E. (B4368) crosses Kerry Hill and Ceri Forest. On the descent towards *Anchor Inn,* 4 m. from Kerry and just in England, a distinctive earthwork called *Castell Bryn Amlwg* can be seen across the valley. It overlooks the junction of two streams, marking the meeting place of the former counties of Montgomery, Radnor, and Shropshire.

2 m. **Newtown** (5600 inhab.), on the Severn, is a bustling but pleasant market town with a number of places of interest to visitors. Despite its name, and despite also being designated a 'New Town' to have a population of 11,000, the town received a charter as long ago as the 13C. Formerly an important weaving and textile centre, Newtown was the birthplace of Robert Owen (1771-1858), factory reformer and founder of the co-operative movement. After many wanderings and experiments he returned here and is buried in the old churchyard of the now ruined St Mary's church.

Tourist Information. Shortbridge Street car park, opposite the *Post Office.*
Parking. Shortbridge Street.
Early Closing. Thursday.
Markets (High Street and Back Lane). Tues. and Sat.

Adjacent to the *Post Office* there is a small memorial park with a statue (Gilbert Bayes, 1953) of Robert Owen and a child. Shortbridge Street leads N.W. to the crossing of High, Broad, and Severn streets, the town centre. Here, in Broad Street, is the *Owen Memorial Museum†,* on the site of Owen's birthplace. The museum includes a reconstruction of the room in which he was born and display cases telling the story of his life. A visit is worth while to the nearby *W. H. Smith,* the booksellers. As a contribution to European Architectural Heritage Year the shop has been restored to its elegant style of 1927; there is also a museum of the history of the firm. To the S.W. is *Newtown Hall Park,* with the remains of a Norman motte-and-bailey. The *Davies Memorial Gallery,* in the park, commemorating the Davies sisters of Gregynog (see below), receives touring art exhibitions. By the river, to the E. off Broad Street, is the ruined 13C *St Mary's Church,* with Owen's grave in its churchyard. The church was abandoned in 1856, because it was too small and because also of repeated flooding, but the tower and other remnants were restored in 1939. At the end of Broad Street the river is crossed by Long Bridge, beyond in Commercial Street being the *Textile Museum†,* in a building which in the day of handloom weavers served as both home and workshop. The museum recalls the prosperity of c. 1790-1890, and the exhibits include handlooms, machines, costumes, documents, and pictures.

The village of **Tregynon,** 4 m. N. of Newtown, has a place in the story of the early use of concrete, two cottages and the school here being considered to be amongst the world's first concrete buildings. *Gregynog Hall*†, above the village in superb and extensive grounds (750 acres), has since 1960 been a residential educational centre of the University of Wales. The house was largely rebuilt in the mid 19C, following predecessors dating back to the 12C. In 1920 the estate was bought by the Misses Gwendoline and Margaret Davies (the latter gave it to the university) and developed as a music and conference centre, with also a press which produced fine limited editions and soon became a leader among private presses. The sisters were also art collectors, the bulk of their collection now being in the National Museum of Wales. At the hall may still be seen the press and sets of early special bindings; paintings by Richard Wilson, Romney, Lawrence, and Mathew Smith; two Rodin busts, of Victor Hugo and Mahler; and prints by, amongst others, Whistler and Augustus John.

Above Newtown the valley expands and the Severn receives the Carno and other tributaries.

5 m. Junction of A492 and A470 (*Caersws*). Here there is a choice of roads to Machynlleth; either the main A470 or the Mountain Road from Llanidloes. The latter is c. 3 m. longer and a good deal slower, but remote and scenically rewarding.

MAIN ROAD. **Caersws** is on the site of a 1C Roman station, known to have been garrisoned by troops from Spain. The main road crosses the N. part of the camp, traces of earthworks being visible on the town's W. outskirts. The town was for 20 years the home of the poet John Ceiriog Hughes, then manager of the local Van Railway (plaque on house just S. of the station). He is buried in the churchyard at *Llanwnog*, to the E. of A470 in 1½ m. The church here has a 15C rood loft, still with its stair, and some fragments of 15C glass in a window on the N. side. The scenery now starts to become moorland in character as the road follows the glen of the Carno.—*5 m. Carno.* It was here in 1081 that, both returning from exile, Gruffydd ap Cynan and Rhys ap Tewdwr joined forces, defeating their rivals and winning respectively the crowns of northern and southern Wales.—*3 m. Talerddig,* just before which the watershed (731 ft) between the Severn and the Dyfi basins is crossed. On the descent immediately beyond the village, in the right road bank, can be seen an anticlinal fold resembling a masonry arch.—*3 m. Llanbrynmair,* from where B4518 (S.) climbs across moor to join the Mountain Road in 6 m. *Llan,* 1½ m. along B4518, was the birthplace of Abraham Rees (1743-1825), the encyclopaedist; and the Rev. Samuel Roberts, social reformer and advocate of postal innovations, lived here from 1806-57. The early 15C church has a wooden tower enclosed inside the nave.— *5 m. Cemmaes Road,* from where to (*5 m.*) **Machynlleth,** see Rte 25B.

MOUNTAIN ROAD. From Caersws, A470 is followed south. An alternative (B4569) passes *Trefeglwys,* birthplace of Benjamin Piercy (1827-88), an engineer who built many of the railways in Wales and also those in Sardinia.—*2 m. Llandinam.* At the E. end of the bridge over the Severn is a bronze statue of David Davies (1818-90), a local boy who became a leading industrialist, developing the coal industry and founding the docks at Barry; the statue is by Sir Alfred Gilbert, sculptor of London's Piccadilly 'Eros'. The Severn, now little more than a stream, is here usually called by its Welsh name, *Hafren.*

5m. **Llanidloes** (2300 inhab.) is at the confluence of the Severn and its larger tributary the Clywedog. The town was a centre of Chartist riots in 1839. The *Old Market Hall,* a half-timbered building of c. 1600, is believed to be the only surviving free-standing market hall in Wales. The upper floor, originally used as court house, was in the 18 and 19C the meeting place of Quakers, Methodists, and Baptists, before they had their own chapels. It now houses a *Museum of Local History and Industry†,* the emphasis of which is textiles, lead mining, and the Chartist riots. Against the market hall exterior stands the *John Wesley Stone,* on which Wesley is said to have preached in 1748, 49, and 64. The *Church,* dedicated to St Idloes (7C), was restored and enlarged in 1881 but retains much of its earlier structure. The early 13C N. arcade, with heavily moulded arches and clustered piers, and the continuous hammer-beam roof (15C), may both have been brought here from Cwmhir Abbey. The 14C tower has an external batter, and, inside, the vaulted base has curious slate masonry.

Hafren Forest, on the E. slopes of Plynlimon and covering over 17 square miles, is some 6 m. W. of Llanidloes. From a F.C. car park there is a choice of several waymarked walks, ranging from 1 m. to 8 m. and leading through the forest, along the upper Severn, and on to Plynlimon. The most popular is the 1 m. long *Cascades Trail.*

The Mountain Road (B4518) bears N.W. out of Llanidloes. In 1 m. a road on the right makes a loop around Van Hill, and in another 1 m. there is a choice between skirting the N. or the S. bank of **Llyn Clywedog** reservoir, rather over 3 m. long. For the S. bank see below. B4518 runs some distance from the N. shore, on the right rising *Van Hill* (1580 ft). On the hill's slopes can be seen the chimneys of the now disused Van Lead Mine, and at the hill's S.E. foot the farm of Crowlym was where the first Sunday School in England and Wales was started by Jenkin Morgan in 1770. To the left, crowning a promontory into the lake, can be seen the hillfort of *Dinas* (1461 ft). The hamlet of *Staylittle,* at the N. end of the narrow finger that forms the head of the lake, owes its curious name to three blacksmiths who shoed horses so quickly that their smithy came to be called Stay-a-Little. The S. bank road (2 m. longer; picnic sites) soon passes the foot of the *Clywedog Dam* (1968; 214 ft high), regulating the flow of the Severn. From here a path leads to the now disused *Bryntail Lead Mine* (scheduled industrial monument). The *Llyn Clywedog Scenic Trail* is a walk of 2½ m. Immediately beyond the dam the road rounds the hillfort of *Pen-y-Gair* (1250 ft). Continuing round the lake the road enters *Hafren Forest* (see above) at a T junction and bears right, in another 2 m. rejoining B4518 just N. of Staylittle.—*7m.* (from Llanidloes by B4518) there is a road junction, the Mountain Road bearing W. while B4518 continues N. to (6 m.) Llanbrynmair on A470. The Mountain Road in 1 m. reaches a viewpoint above the *Ffrwd Fawr Falls,* with an impressive bare abyss. After crossing high open moor (road highest point 1671 ft), the road, with lovely views, descends along the N. edge of the Plynlimon plateau to reach (*10 m.*) **Machynlleth,** see p. 222.

Beyond Machynlleth the wooded valley of the Dyfi is descended (A487).—*6 m. Furnace,* where a diversion can be made up the beautiful *Cwm Einion,* or Artists' Valley. Here, 1 m. up the valley, a forest walk starts from the Forestry Commission office.—*2 m. Tre'r Ddol.* Here, in a disused chapel, *Hen Gapel†*, a museum founded by the late R. J. Thomas, a leading Welsh scholar, and now a branch of the Welsh Folk Museum, is devoted to 19C religious life. From Tre'r-Ddol, B4353 leads W. to sections of the Dyfi National Nature Reserve.

Dyfi National Nature Reserve (3973 acres) extends between the main road, the Dyfi estuary, and the coast. The reserve, established by the Nature Conservancy in 1969 and 1972, comprises the Estuary; Cors Fochno, or Borth Bog, inland; and (N.W.) Ynyslas Dunes. Other than as indicated below, access is restricted and application should be made to the Warden at the Nature Conservancy's Office, Plas Gogerddan, 3 m. N.E. of Aberystwyth. The *Estuary* (3525 acres), accepted as an important scientific site for many studies, is a haunt of wildfowl and migrant waders; a wildfowl refuge has been established in the E. part of the estuary, and to the S. of this a reserve (no adm.) is maintained by the Royal Society for the Protection of Birds. Access to the foreshore is limited to two footpaths; one from Tre'r-Ddol, following the river Clettwr, and the other (3 m. W. of Tre'r-Ddol) off B4353. Visitors are warned that the tides and mud can be very dangerous, and not to use these paths when the tide is coming in. *Cors Fochno* (access by permit only) is an area of raised bog to the S. of B4353. With layers of peat covering a period of some 7000 years, the bog is much used for botanical research. There is unrestricted foot access to *Ynyslas Dunes,* where there are a car park, an information centre, and a nature trail.

2m. **Talybont.** For the Scenic Route via *Nant-y-Moch* reservoir to *Ponterwyd,* see p. 231. From Talybont a lane leads N.E., climbing on to moor and in 2 m. reaching *Bedd Taliesin* (on right, just beyond a gate at which, by a farm, the lane turns into a track). Apparently the stones of a burial chamber, this is traditionally the grave of Taliesin, a (possibly mythical) bard and seer of the 6C.—*2m.* Junction with S. end of B4353.

Llandre is ½ m. up B4353. In woods above, *Castell Gwallter* is the motte of an early Norman castle founded by Walter de Bec and burnt by the Welsh in 1137. *Borth,* 2 m. farther N., a straggling village built along a storm beach, is a resort with fine sands, caravan sites, and a golf course. Millenia ago the storm beach was farther W., the present beach then being forest, and at low tide remnants of this can be seen between Borth and *Ynyslas* (1½ m. N.), beyond which is the dunes section of the Dyfi National Nature Reserve (see above). From Borth, Aberystwyth can be reached by B4572, crossing hills above cliffs; *Sarn Cynfelyn,* at Wallog, is a rock causeway said to be the remains of a road leading to the drowned Lowland Hundred (see p. 225).

4m. **Aberystwyth,** see Rte 27.

B   Viâ Welshpool, Llanfair Caereinion, and Mallwyd

A458 to Mallwyd: A470 to Cemmaes Road: A489 to Machynlleth: A487 to Aberystwyth. 70 miles.—*18 m.* **Welshpool.**—*9 m.* **Llanfair Caereinion.**—*16 m.* **Mallwyd.**—*11 m.* **Machynlleth.**—*8 m.* Tre'er Ddol.—*8 m.* Aberystwyth.
For the greater part agricultural scenery, but some moor between Llanfair Caereinion and Mallwyd. Green valley of the Dyfi to Machynlleth. After Machynlleth, wood and moor inland and estuary flats to seaward.

For **Shrewsbury** to (*18 m.*) **Welshpool,** see Rte 22A.—*3 m. Sylfaen Station* is, until the planned extension to Welshpool is achieved, the last station on the Welshpool and Llanfair Railway. The road descends into the valley of the *Einion,* which is crossed 2½ m. beyond Sylfaen. This river's name can be confusing since it is also called the *Banwy.* The Banwy proper rises at the watershed some 12 m. W. of Llanfair Caereinion, and the much smaller Einion feeds in near Neuadd, 1½ m. W. of Llanfair Caereinion, the single river then enjoying both names for some 7 m. until it flows into the Vyrnwy.—*4 m. Heniorth Station,* another station on the light railway.

Meifod, 4m. N.E., is reached by B4389 and then A495, the latter crossing the Vyrnwy just above where it is joined by the Einion or Banwy. The village, in a pastoral and wooded valley setting, is celebrated in Welsh poetry, because here or nearby was once a summer residence ('maifod') of the princes of Powys. The *Church,* consecrated in 1155, is of several periods (11, 16, and 19C), the oldest part being the 11C piers ahead and left of the entrance. In the S. aisle there is a 9-10C graveslab, with the Christian XP symbol and Norse features. The large churchyard has formerly contained at least one and possibly two other churches. The Roman Mediolanum has been variously located here; at Mathrafa (2½ m. S.W.), which succeeded Shrewsbury as a seat of the princes of Powys; at Old Oswestry; and at Caersws.

2m. **Llanfair Caereinion** is a small market town. The *Church,* rebuilt in 1868 as successor to a derelict 13C church which stood here, is entered through a surviving 13C doorway. Inside, all from the previous church, are the font, the oak vaulting of the choir, and the recumbent effigy (?14C) of a knight, unusual for being hollow and for having the inscription on the low-slung swordbelt rather than on the shield. Outside the porch the sundial of 1765 is the work of Samuel Roberts, a local clockmaker. *St Mary's Well,* a former healing well, is on the river bank below the church. The station of the *Welshpool and Llanfair Railway*† is in the N.E. of the town. With a gauge of 2 ft 6 inches, the line runs for 5½ m. through pleasant countryside to Sylfaen. The railway linked Welshpool and Llanfair Caereinion from 1903 to 1931 (passengers) and 1956 (goods). The present operators reopened the line in 1963 to Castell Caereinion, and in 1972 to Sylfaen, and there are plans to extend the run to Welshpool. Among the engines are two built for the line in 1903, one belonging to the German army, and one from a West Indian sugar plantation.

At *Llanllugan* (4m. S.W.) the 15C church, once that of a nunnery, contains an E. window with good contemporary glass.

2m. **Neuadd** may be reached by roads either side of the river, that on the N. crossing immediately below where the Einion joins the Banwy. A458 now leads N.W., in 2m. crossing the Einion.—*3m.* *Llanerfyl,* where the Banwy is again crossed. In the churchyard here, beneath a yew, there is a 5-6C gravestone. The road now ascends the N. bank of the Banwy, in *3m.* crossing the tributary Twrch and in another *4m.* the watershed (957 ft) between the Severn and the Dyfi. From here the pleasant valley of the Dugoed is descended, the road soon making a sharp curve where it crosses a glen. The name *Llidiart-y-Barwn* (Baron's Gate) here recalls that it was in these woods that Baron Owen (see p. 223) was murdered in 1555.

4m. **Mallwyd,** see p. 223. For Mallwyd to (N.) *Bala* and (S. *11m.*) **Machynlleth,** see Rte 25B.—For Machynlleth to **Aberystwyth,** see Rte 22A.

23 WHITCHURCH TO WELSHPOOL

A495 to Oswestry: A483 to Welshpool. 33 miles.—*2m. Redbrook.—9m. Ellesmere.—5m. Whittington.—2m.* **Oswestry.**—*3m. Llynclys.—2m. Llanymynech.—8m. Buttington.—2m.* **Welshpool.**

Whitchurch, see p. 131.—*2m.* **Redbrook** is just in Wales, in Maelor Saesneg, for which, as also for A525 which here branches N.W. for Wrexham, see Rte 5. A495 crosses Maelor Saesneg, with the peaty moorland of *Fenn's Moss* to the S., in 5m. leaving Wales and re-entering

Salop.—4m. **Ellesmere** (2700 inhab.), a pleasant small market town, stands on the bank of the small mere (Elli's Mere) from which it gets its name; Elli is said to have been founder of the first settlement here. To the S.E. of the town, within 2m., there are four more of the small but attractive meres characteristic of this district lying between the drainage systems of the Severn and the Dee. The *Motte* at the S.E. of the town is all that remains of the castle, originally that of the Earl of Shrewsbury and later given by King John to Llewelyn the Great. The *Church,* largely rebuilt by Sir Gilbert Scott, retains some Norman and Perp. work, with a 15C roof in the S. chapel. Inside are also the altar-tomb of Sir Francis Kynaston (d. 1590) and a diminutive sepulchral effigy of a notary with pen and inkhorn. The *Shropshire Union Canal,* which unites the Severn, Dee, and Mersey, passes a little to the S. of the town.—*5m. Whittington,* see p. 180 on Rte 14 which is crossed here.

2m. **Oswestry** (11,000 inhab.), a town with ancient roots, is today the busy market and general centre for a wide rural area, the site of an important cattle market, and the home of many people commuting to Wrexham, Merseyside, southern Salop, and even farther afield.

History. The great fort of Old Oswestry dates back to c. 300 B.C. and has also, with several other places, been suggested as the site of the Roman Mediolanum. In 642 Penda, pagan King of Mercia, defeated the Christian King Oswald of Northumbria at Oswestry (Battle of Maserfield), afterwards crucifying Oswald and thus giving the town its name deriving from 'Oswald's Tree'. The castle, possibly pre-Norman in origin, is mentioned in Domesday Book (1086) and was rebuilt in 1148 by Madog, Prince of Powys. In 1215 King John burnt the town, and in 1233 it suffered similar treatment at the hands of Llewelyn the Great. In 1398 Oswestry was granted its first Royal Charter by Richard II, and in 1536, under the Act of Union, the town, now prosperous as a wool trading centre, became officially English. During the Civil War Oswestry sided with Charles II but was taken by Parliament in 1644, the castle afterwards being slighted.—Sir H. Walford Davies (1869-1941), Master of the King's Musick, 1934-41, was born here.

The town centre is *The Cross,* at the corner of Cross Street being the *Llwyd Mansion* (1604), one of the town's best preserved half-timbered buildings. Now converted into shops, the house originally belonged to the Lloyds of Llanforda and still bears the crest granted to the family during the Crusades. From The Cross, Bailey Street leads N. up to Bailey Head, a square with the *Guildhall* and the new market (*Powis Hall*), opened in 1963 by the Earl of Powis on the site of an earlier market given by an ancestor in 1839. The name Bailey Head recalls the castle, the motte of which (all that now survives) rises as *Castle Bank* immediately behind the Guildhall; a short section of the demolished town wall has been erected here. Church Street, leading S. from The Cross, has some Georgian houses. The large *Parish Church* may have some 13C stonework in the tower, but has been frequently rebuilt. One rebuilding was made necessary by the damage caused during the Civil War when the Royalists removed the spire and there was skirmishing in the church; major work was carried out in 1874 by Street, and there was further restoration in the 1960s. From the church, Oswald's Well Lane leads W. to (c. 500 yards) *Maserfield,* the site of the battle of 642. *Oswald's Well* here traditionally gushed out when an eagle dropped a limb of the crucified Oswald on this spot. In the S.W. of the town the name Croeswylan Lane means 'Cross of Weeping' and recalls the market moved here during the plague of 1559. *Smithfield,* the new cattle market of 1968, is in the S.E. of the town on A4083 (markets Wed.).

*Old Oswestry (1 m. N.; sign off A483/495 in N.E. outskirts of the town) is a large and well-preserved earthwork. Occupied from c. 300 B.C. to A.D. 75, this great hillfort grew in stages by the addition of the several concentric ditches and banks, which, with N.E. and S.W. gates, are still much in evidence today. Old Oswestry is one of a number of places which have been suggested as the site of Roman Mediolanum.

From Oswestry to (N.) *Chirk* and *Llangollen* and (S.) *Shrewsbury,* see Rte 14; to *Lake Vyrnwy,* see Rte 24C.

3 m. **Llynclys,** a crossroads at which A495 (Rte 24C) bears W. for Lake Vyrnwy.—*2 m.* **Llanymynech** is just, though not entirely, in Wales. The name means either 'Enclosure of the Monks' or 'of the Miners', the latter being the more probable since there is no record of a monastery whereas silver, zinc, lead, and copper mining is known to have been a local activity on Llanymynech Hill to the S. in Roman times or earlier. In 1965 boys exploring a local cave found tools and silver denarii of Antoninus. The golf course on the hill straddles the border. Just S. of Llanymynech the road crosses the Vyrnwy.—*3 m.* Junction with B4392, enabling Welshpool to be reached via *Guilsfield* (see p. 210). The *Breidden Hills* rise to the E. beyond the very winding Severn which the road meets at (*3 m.*) *Pool Quay,* once a river port trading with Bristol in timber.—*2 m.* **Buttington,** see p. 209.—*2 m.* **Welshpool,** see p. 209.

24   LAKE VYRNWY AND ITS APPROACHES

A   Lake Vyrnwy

Lake Vyrnwy (pron. 'Verny'), at a height of 825 ft and beautifully situated below wooded hills, is a narrow strip 4 m. long and less than ½ m. wide. A road skirts the shore right round the lake, but in many places trees and undergrowth restrict the view, best enjoyed from the dam at the S. end. The lake, a reservoir for the water supply of Liverpool, was formed in 1880-90; tablets in the roadside rockface at the N. end of the dam record the various stages of the work and of the associated pipeline projects. Prior to the construction of the reservoir, the Vyrnwy, the chief Welsh tributary of the Severn, was here a small stream meandering across a marshy flat formed by the sands and gravels which had silted up a lake basin scooped out in glacial times. The present *Dam,* 390 yards long and 144 ft high, rests on the bar of glaciated rock that retained the early lake, and the reservoir can thus be regarded as the restoration of an ancient natural feature. The road is carried across the dam on a series of arches, through which surplus water escapes in cascades. The lake's surface area is 1121 acres, its storage capacity is 12,131 million gallons, and the catchment area covers some 36 square miles.

The hamlet of *Llanwddyn* was drowned by the lake, but a new village has grown up below the dam. On the N.E. shore, about 1 m. from the dam, a picturesque tower marks the entrance to the *Hirnant Tunnel* (2¼ m. long), which forms the first section of the aqueduct, 75 m. long, that carries the water to Liverpool. Farther on, at the mouth of the Cedig, is the site of the submerged village. The road from Bala viâ Cwm Hirnant reaches the lake at its N. tip, and that viâ Bwlch-y-Groes at *Pont Eunant,* 1 m. beyond on the W. shore, the site of the submerged Eunant Hall.

Approaches to Vyrnwy from Bala and Oswestry are described below, those from Bala being very scenic.

B   Approaches from Bala

Viâ LLANGYNOG. B4391 and B4396. 19 miles.—The road skirts the N. tip of Bala Lake, almost immediately afterwards passing the road to Cwm Hirnant (see below). Beyond, in another 3 m. at the junction with B4402/01, it climbs through woods, reaching open moor and (*8 m.* from Bala) **Milltir Gerig Pass** (1595 ft), a saddle in the long Berwyn range. The descent is above the precipitous valley of the Eirth.—*3 m.* **Llangynog** is a long village beautifully set below mountains at the meeting of the Eirth and Tanat glens. The lead mines and slate quarries are now closed, the former due to flooding.

The valley of the Tanat, a wooded and pastoral finger into the mountains, in 2½ m. reaches the little Norman church of *Pennant Melangell.* Inside are two 14C recumbent effigies, one said to be of a Welsh prince and the other of St Melangell; an 18C wooden candelabrum; and a rood screen of c. 1500. The loft of the screen, removed to the W. end of the church, has on its bottom beam mutilated carvings illustrating the 7C legend of St Melangell (or Monacella), according to which a hare, hunted by Brochwel Ysgythrog, Prince of Powys, took refuge under her robe. As a result Melangell became the patron saint of hares, thenceforward known as 'St Monacella's lambs' and treated as sacred in the district. Some carved fragments built into the S. outside wall of the church may have belonged to the saint's shrine, which is supposed to have stood in the small chamber behind the blank E. wall of the church. The valley ends in a rounded cwm, with the white thread of *Blaen-y-Cwm* waterfall.

The valley below Llangynog is that of the Tanat.—*2 m.* **Penybontfawr**, where the Tanat Valley and Llansilin approaches from Oswestry are met. For *Llanrhaeadr-ym-Mochnant* and *Pistyll Rhaeadr*, see below. From Penybontfawr B4396 ascends Cwm Hirnant (not to be confused with the other Cwm Hirnant described immediately below), in *6 m.* reaching **Lake Vyrnwy.**

Viâ CWM HIRNANT. Unclassified road. 9 miles. A beautiful drive through remote wood and moorland scenery.—B4391 is taken E. out of Bala, then, soon after leaving the lake, an unclassified road which climbs S. up the thickly wooded *Cwm Hirnant* (F.C. picnic site). Emerging from the woods, the road continues to climb across high moor (1641 ft) before, again in woods, descending beside the tumbling Nadroedd stream to reach the N. extremity of **Lake Vyrnwy.**

Viâ BWLCH-Y-GROES. A494 or B4403 to Llanuwchllyn, then unclassified roads. 14 miles.—*5 m.* **Llanuwchllyn** may be reached either by A494 (see p. 187) along the W. shore of Bala Lake, or by B4403 along the E. shore. From here an unclassified road (Rte 25B) ascends high up on the side of Cwm Cynllwyd to (*5 m.*) *Bwlch-y-Groes* (1790 ft; see p. 224), the highest road pass in Wales. Just beyond the summit a road branches E. away from the Dinas Mawddwy road to descend beside the Eunant stream, first across moor and then through woods, to (*4 m.*) **Lake Vyrnwy.**

C   Approaches from Oswestry

Viâ LLANSILIN. B4580 and B4396. 18 miles.—*3 m.* **Rhyd-y-Croesau,** where the Welsh border is crossed.—*2 m.* **Llansilin,** where Hugh Morris (1622-1709), the Royalist satirical poet, is buried.—*5 m.* **Llanrhaeadr-**

ym-Mochnant, of which Bishop Morgan (1545-1604), who in 1588 here made his translation of the Bible into Welsh, was vicar. In the church (S. aisle) there is a Celtic cross-slab (9-10C), of a type rare except in the Isle of Man and Scotland.

From the village a narrow, and in summer crow··:d, road leads in under 4 m. to **Pistyll Rhaeadr** (parking), said to be the highest falls in Wales and of which Borrow wrote 'I never saw water falling so gracefully, so much like thin beautiful threads as here'. The falls descend some 240 ft by a series of leaps, of which the first is an unbroken drop of more than 100 ft, falling into a cauldron from which the second cascade issues through a gap in the rock.—A track leads N. for 1½ m. to *Llyn Llyncaws* (2000 ft), a small tarn in a rock amphitheatre, and thence (½ m.) to *Moel Sych* (2713 ft), the highest point in the Berwyns.

2 m. Penybontfawr to (*6 m.*) **Lake Vyrnwy,** see above.

Viâ Tanat Valley. A483, A495, and B4396. 22 miles.—A483, S. out of Oswestry, in *4 m.* reaches *Llynclys,* from where A495 and B4396 are followed to (*2 m.*) *Llanyblodwel.* Soon the road reaches the N. side of the Tanat and crosses into Wales. At *Sycharth,* 1 m. N. and reached by the first road beyond the border, a motte is all that marks the site of the principal residence of Owen Glendower, described in a poem by the bard Iolo Goch as having nine halls, many guest rooms, and a church. It was destroyed in 1403 by the future Henry V.—*4 m. Llangedwyn,* where the church contains the recumbent effigy of a vested priest and a font, both from the previous church. At the E. exterior of the church there is a medieval stone cross. Llangedwyn Hall, N. of the road, was the residence of Sir W. Williams Wynn, the generous friend of the poet Southey, who, with Bishop Heber, visited him here. He gave the poet an allowance from 1797 until 1806, and in 1807 arranged a government pension.—*3 m.* Junction with B4580, up which (1 m.) is *Llanrhaeadr-ym-Mochnant* (see above).—*3 m. Penybontfawr* to (*6 m.*) **Lake Vyrnwy,** see above.

Viâ Llanfyllin. A483 to Llynclys: A495 to Llansantffraid-ym-Mechain: B4393 and A490 to Llanfyllin: B4393 to Lake Vyrnwy. 24 miles.—To just short of (*6 m.*) *Llanyblodwel,* see immediately above.— *3 m.* (by A495) *Llansantffraid-ym-Mecl.ain,* a short way into Wales and on the Vyrnwy, has a church with a Jacobean window (1619). Beyond the hamlet B4393 is taken for (*2 m.*) *Llanfechain,* where the church, dedicated to St Garmon (Germanus), contains an inscribed pulpit of 1636 and an iron chandelier of 1727.

4 m. **Llanfyllin** (1250 inhab.), a town which received its first charter in 1293, straggles along the upper Cain valley below steep wooded hills. In the early 18C red-brick *Church,* which has a noted peal of bells, are a chained copy of 'The Whole Duty of Man' (1687) and, on the altar frontal, a square of silk, embroidered I.H.S., found during the First World War by a soldier from here among the ruins of Ypres cathedral. Opposite the church a house (No. 27) has murals painted by French prisoners during the Napoleonic wars (apply to chemist, next door).— About ½ m. W. of Llanfyllin the road forks, the right branch in 4 m. reaching Penybontfawr. The left branch (B4393) leads S.W., ascending Nant Alan.—*5 m. Llanfihangel-yng-Ngwynfa,* just S. of the road, has a church containing old armorial pew backs (on the walls) and, in the vestry, graveslabs of c. 1400. In the churchyard there is a memorial to Ann Griffiths (1780-1805), well known as a writer of hymns in the Welsh language. Her home at *Dolwar Fach* (2m. S.) can be seen.—After an ascent to 1104 ft the road drops to (*4m.*) **Lake Vyrnwy.**

25   MACHYNLLETH TO BALA

A   Viâ Dolgellau

A487 and A470 to Dolgellau: A494 to Bala. 32 miles.—*5m. Corris.—3m. Minffordd.—4m. Cross Foxes Hotel.—3m.* **Dolgellau.—*17m.* Bala.**
The narrow wooded valley of the Dulas is followed by moor, a fine view of Cader Idris, and a craggy stretch along the mountain's E. foot.

Machynlleth (pron. 'Mahun'hleth'; 2000 inhab.), in the green valley of the Dyfi, is a market town, a shopping centre serving a wide surrounding district, and, being at the heart of much lovely scenery, a popular but not overcrowded holiday base. The town centre is the Clock Tower, from where Maengwyn Street, the broad main street, runs east.

Tourist Information. Owen Glendower Institute, Maengwyn Street (N. side, c. 300 yards beyond Clock Tower).
Parking. Off S. side of Maengwyn Street.
Post Office. Maengwyn Street (S. side, near Clock Tower).
Early Closing. Thursday.

The *Clock Tower* dates from 1872. On the left side of Penrallt Street, leading N., *Royal House* (no adm.) may have been a home of Owen Glendower. The *Owen Glendower Institute* (Tourist Information, Public Library) in Maengwyn Street is a 16C building said to occupy the site of a predecessor in which Owen Glendower held his first parliament in 1404. Opposite is the entrance to *Plas Machynlleth* (1671) which, with its fine grounds, was presented to the town by Lord Londonderry. The mansion now houses local government offices, and the grounds are a public park. Farther E., on the S. side of Maengwyn Street, the so-called *Mayor's House* (no adm.) is a half-timbered house of 1628. The *Dyfi Bridge*, N.W. of the town, first built in 1533, was rebuilt in c. 1800.

For Machynlleth to (S.) *Aberystwyth,* and (E.) *Newtown, Welshpool,* and *Shrewsbury,* and also by the Mountain Road to *Llanidloes,* see Rte 22; to *Dinas Mawddwy* and *Bala,* see Rte 25B below; to *Tywyn* and *Dolgellau,* see Rte 26.

A487 passes the station and crosses the Dyfi. Beyond the bridge, A493 (Rte 26) bears W., while this Route heads N., climbing the wooded, narrow and winding valley of the Dulas.—*3m.* The *Centre for Alternative Technology†,* in a now disused slate quarry, is an ecological exhibition of unusual interest, the theme of which is conservation and self-sufficiency. Sponsored by the Society for Environmental Improvement, the Centre demonstrates by practical example how the earth's limited resources can be exploited with a minimum of pollution and waste. Among the exhibits are solar collectors, with a solar heated hall; windmill and water driven generators; a conservation house, with wall insulation, heat pumps, and quadruple glazing; methods of organic gardening; fish culture; and the recycling of waste.

A short way farther up the road is *Tan-y-Coed Picnic Site* (F.C.), starting place for waymarked forest walks, which may be extended to the moorland ridge beyond (2187 ft) and down to the valley of the Dysynni.—*2m. Corris,* a village below the road at the junction of the Dulas and a small tributary. The *Corris Railway Museum†* preserves material relating to the slate quarries railway which ran between Aberllefenni and Machynlleth. Two of the railway's engines (1878, 1921) now operate on the Talyllyn line. Between Corris and Aberllefenni there is a F.C. picnic site (Foel Friog) with a 2 m. long trail passing the remains of buildings connected with the quarries. A487 now bears N.W., turning away from the Dulas and ascending past slate quarries to reach a height of 666 ft, with a splendid view of Cader Idris.—*3 m. Minffordd,* junction with B4405 which has ascended the Dysynni from near Tywyn. For this beautiful road (with the Talyllyn Railway, Castell-y-Bere, Llanfihangel-y-Pennant, and Tal-y-Llyn Lake, see Rte 26). Minffordd is immediately below Cader Idris, for the ascents of which from this side see p. 194. Beyond Minffordd the road climbs, with craggy heights on either side, to reach a pass at 938 ft; from here a moor and woodland path reaches Dolgellau in 3 m.—*4 m. Cross Foxes Hotel,* where A470 comes in from the E. from Dinas Mawddwy. In another 1½ m., at the head of *Torrent Walk* (see p. 192), B4416, diverging N.E. through *Brithdir,* offers a shortcut avoiding Dolgellau which can be a traffic bottleneck in summer.

3 m. **Dolgellau,** for which, with Cader Idris, see Rte 18. For Dolgellau to (*17 m.*) **Bala,** see Rte 16.

B Viâ Dinas Mawddwy and Bwlch-y-Groes

A489 to Cemmaes Road: A470 to Dinas Mawddwy: unclassified to Llanuwchllyn: A494 or B4403 to Bala. 30 miles.—*5 m. Cemmaes Road.* —*8 m.* **Dinas Mawddwy.**—*7 m.* **Bwlch-y-Groes.**—*5 m. Llanuwchllyn.* —*5 m.* **Bala.**

As far as Dinas Mawddwy the road follows the pastoral valley of the Dyfi, with high ground on either side. Beyond Dinas Mawddwy the narrow and steep direct road climbs through impressive, wild scenery across Bwlch-y-Groes (1790 ft), the highest road pass in Wales. Motorists preferring the main road can continue on A470 via Dolgellau.

Machynlleth, see Rte 22A above.—*2 m. Penegoes* was the birthplace of the painter Richard Wilson (1714-82).—*3 m. Cemmaes Road,* where A470 (Rte 22A) comes in from the east. At *Cemmaes,* 1½ m. farther, there is a memorial in the church to Dr Daniel Evans (d.1903), the first professor of Welsh at University College, Aberystwyth.—*6 m. Mallwyd,* where A458 (Rte 22B) joins from the east. In front of the church's wooden E. porch (1641) hangs a whale's rib dug up locally in the 19C. John Davies (1570-1644), the lexicographer and assistant to Bishop Parry in translating the Welsh Authorized Version of the Bible, is buried in the churchyard. The name 'Brigands' Inn' recalls that in the middle of the 16C this neighbourhood was terrorized by a gang known, from the colour of their hair, as the Red Robbers of Mawddwy. Eighty of the brigands were seized and executed in 1554, mainly through the activities of Baron Lewis Owen, who, the following year, was murdered by the gang's survivors at *Llidiart-y-Barwn,* about 2½ m. up A458. After this the gang was exterminated.

2 m. **Dinas Mawddwy** was long ago the centre of one of two local more or less independent districts within Powys, the other being Penllyn to the north (see p. 186). Mawddwy remained with Powys until the Edwardian conquest, when it became a part of the shire of Merioneth, although it retained the dignity of a mayor and corporation until 1668. Today a holiday and fishing centre, the village lies in a lovely amphitheatre below wooded hills and mountains at the junction of the Dyfi and the Cerist. Much of the hillsides is covered by rhododendrons, and in season the colour across the valley to the E. can be breathtaking. *Dinas Mawddwy Station,* by the Dyfi bridge, once the end station of the Cemmaes Road to Mawddwy railway (founded in 1868), is preserved and associated with a textile mill and craft shop. The fine wrought-iron gates have been reconstructed, and a short section of track is maintained (occasional rides in summer).

Motorists not wishing to take the direct Bala road across Bwlch-y-Groes can use the longer main road route via Dolgellau (10 m.). This road, for its first part very scenic, with steep cwms and waterfalls, ascends the valley of the Cerist, above the N. bank in 1 m. being National Trust property, given in 1947 by Squadron Leader J. D. K. Lloyd and his brother Dr W. E. B. Lloyd as a memorial to the men of Bomber Command who lost their lives during the war. Beyond, the road climbs steeply to the top of *Bwlch Oerddrws* (Cold Door Pass; 1178 ft), beyond which the country, though becoming open and bleak, is backed by a magnificent view of Cader Idris. At *Cross Foxes Hotel,* Rte 25A is joined.

1 m. At *Aber-Cywarch* a small road ascends the narrow valley of the Cywarch for 2 m. From the end of this road a path climbs N.E. up the steep slope of Hengwm valley for Dyrysgol and the range of the Arans.—Near *(3 m.) Llanymawddwy* there are some fine waterfalls, notably Pistyll Gwyn, 1¼ m. W. on the Pumryd. The scenery grows wilder, the Dyfi is crossed, and the valley ends in a cwm of precipitous mountain slopes, 800-1000 ft high, deeply scarred by watercourses. The Dyfi, from its source in the tarn of Craiglyn Dyfi (2½ m. N.W.), comes in through *Llaethnant* (Milk Valley) in a succession of cataracts, and the black, rocky peak of Aran Mawddwy stands out beyond the head of the glen. The road now climbs the steep side of the deep **Glen of the Rhiwlech,* passing the road to Lake Vyrnwy and, after a climb of over 1000 ft in c. 1¾ m., reaching the summit of *(3 m.)* **Bwlch-y-Groes** (1790 ft; parking), the highest point on any road in Wales. To the W. the dominant feature is the range of the Arans.

Aran Mawddwy (2970 ft) and **Aran Benllyn** (2901 ft) rise from a volcanic ridge running N. and S. between Bala Lake and Dinas Mawddwy. The names recall the semi-independent districts of Mawddwy (see above) and Penllyn (see p. 186). The range can be ascended from Dinas Mawddwy (Aber-Cywarch), from here, or from Llanuwchllyn, the easiest approach. Aran Mawddwy is curiously shaped, resembling a broken cone, while Aran Benllyn, with veins of white quartz, overlooks Bala. Between the two there is a fine ridge walk. The view from the range includes the Clwydian Hills and the Berwyns (N.E. and E.N.E.); Plynlimon a little W. of S.; and the Cader Idris range to the S.W., with the Mawddach estuary farther N. and a glimpse of the sea beyond. To the W. are the Llawllech range, the Rhinogs, and, nearer, Rhobell Fawr. The Snowdon group is seen to the N.W., and, slightly W. of N., Arenig Fawr with Bala Lake to its right. To the E. a narrow strip of Lake Vyrnwy may be visible, and Craiglyn Dyfi, source of the Dyfi, is 1000 ft below.

The descent is down the side of *Cwm Cynllwyd* to *(5 m.)* the lake level at *Llanuwchllyn* (see p. 187).—*5 m.* **Bala** (p. 186) is reached either by A494 (p. 187) along the N. shore of Bala Lake, or by B4403 skirting the S. shore with the little Bala Lake Railway.

26 MACHYNLLETH TO TYWYN AND DOLGELLAU

A493. 34 miles.—*4m. Pennal.—7m.* **Aberdovey.**—*4m.* **Tywyn.**—*2m.*
Bryncrug.—2m. Llanegryn.—7m. **Fairbourne.**—*2m. Arthog.—6m.* **Dolgellau.**
A pleasant coastal road with some good views. Interesting and scenic diversions
from Bryncrug up the valleys of the Dysynni or Fathew to the S. foot of Cader
Idris. Beyond Fairbourne the main road runs between the Mawddach Estuary and
the N.W. side of Cader Idris.

Machynlleth, see p. 222, is left by the bridge across the Dyfi, on the far
side of which A487 (Rte 25A) bears N., while this Route follows A493
southwest.—*4m. Pennal* is a village near the site of a Roman fort, traces
of which, with a motte, can be seen S. of the road.—At *(1m.) Cwrt* a
small inland road cuts across to Tywyn, and at *(2m.) Gogarth Station*
the main road reaches the estuary of the Dyfi. For the Dyfi National
Nature Reserve, see p. 216.—*4m.* **Aberdovey** (*Aberdyfi*) is a quiet
resort, with good sands, a well-known golf course, and sailing. The
Outward Bound Sailing Museum†, on the waterfront, contains general
material on sailing including model ships, early navigation instruments,
and early lifeboat equipment.

The song, 'The Bells of Aberdovey', was made famous through Charles Dibdin's
opera 'Liberty Hall' (1785). The legend is that of the *Lowland Hundred,* or
Cantref-y-Gwaelod, a low-lying land protected by dykes. One stormy night its
prince, one Seithenyn, was so drunk that he forgot to close the sluices and the
cantref was drowned. But its bells still peal below the water, and *Sarn Badrig* (p.
199) and *Sarn Cynfelin* (p. 216) are said to be ancient roads which once led to this
lost land. The earliest mention of this catastrophe is in a 13C manuscript, but the
story had a strong attraction for writers of the 17-19C who added their own
romantic embellishments. In fact the causeways are glacial deposits. See also
James Elroy Flecker's poem 'The Welsh Sea'.

4m. **Tywyn** ('yw' pron. 'ow' as in 'now') or *Towyn,* the name meaning
'Sand Dune', is an inland small town enlarged into a seaside resort, with
a sand and shingle beach extending 3m. S. as far as Aberdovey's golf
links, and many caravan parks and holiday camps to both the N. and
south. The station of the *Talyllyn Railway†* is at the S.W. end of the
town on the Aberdovey road. The line, opened for freight in 1866 and for
passengers the following year, was built to carry slate from the quarry
above Abergynolwyn (7m. N.E.) down to Tywyn, where it was
transferred to main line trains. The quarry closed in 1947, after which
(1950) the Talyllyn Railway Preservation Society was formed and as a
result a service, a world record, has operated every year since 1866. The
line has a gauge of 2 ft 3 inches and ascends (in c. 50 mins) the pleasant
valley of the Fathew to Abergynolwyn. There are seven stations and a
number of halts. Of the several steam engines, two date from the opening
of the line, two (1878, 1921) were used on the Corris Railway, and one
(1918) belonged to R.A.F. Calshot. The railway's *Museum†* at Wharf
Station contains material relating to narrow gauge railways in
general.—The *Church of St Cadfan,* founder of the monastery on the
island of Bardsey, is at the N. end of the town. It has an early Norman
nave (probably 11C), with massive short piers, curiously primitive
whitewashed arcades, and tiny splayed windows in the clerestory. There
is also some early work in the N. aisle, but the rest of the church is
rebuilding of 1884. St Cadfan's Stone (probably 7C), at the W. end of the
N. aisle, bears an inscription thought to be the oldest example of written
Welsh and certainly older than any extant manuscript. On the N. of the

choir are two recumbent effigies of the 14C, one of a knight, who seems to be in the act of drawing his sword; the other of a vested priest, with the amice drawn to form a hood. On the exterior of the church two curious old horizontal slabs have been incorporated into the 19C tower, one, on the S. side, bearing an inscribed cross.

Beyond Tywyn, while the railway and a minor road skirt the shore, crossing the mouth of *Broad Water,* a lagoon into which the Dysynni flows, the main road runs inland to *(2m.) Bryncrug,* burial place (chapel) of Mary Jones.

The roads up the Fathew and Dysynni valleys, both interesting and scenically worthwhile diversions, start from Bryncrug.—The **Fathew Valley** road is B4405, which in 3 m. at Dolgoch, with a waterfall, meets the Talyllyn Railway which it accompanies to *Abergynolwyn,* reached in another 2 m. Above was the Bryneglwys Slate Quarry (closed 1947), for which the line was built; a village Museum† illustrates the way of life of the mining community. Here the upper course of the Dysynni is met, and a road follows the river N.W. through a cut in the hills to its main valley just S. of Castell-y-Bere. B4405 continues N.E., ascending the upper Dysynni for 2½ m. to the river's source in *Tal-y-Llyn Lake,* 1 m. long and ¼ m. wide. The lake (at 270 ft) lies below the S. slopes of Cader Idris, for the ascents of which from this side see p. 194. The village, at the S. end of the lake, has a little church with a timbered roof (? 15C), curiously boarded and painted in the choir. A short way beyond the lake the road meets Rte 25A.

The unclassified road up the S. side of **Dysynni Valley** in 3 m. reaches *Craig-yr-Aderyn* (Bird Rock), a bold hill which, though well inland, is a breeding place for cormorants, an interesting natural continuation from the times when this valley was an arm of the sea. In rather over 1 m. farther the Dysynni valley, with its road to Abergynolwyn, turns S.E., the ancient Welsh fortress of *Castell-y-Bere* being a short way N. of the turning. Of unknown origin, but certainly Welsh rather than Norman, the castle, now only slight remains, occupies a high ridge. It was taken by the Earl of Pembroke in 1283 and rebuilt by Edward I, who however held it only until 1295 when it was retaken by the Welsh, by whom it was apparently finally destroyed. The plan of the place, conditioned by the site, is a long, narrow enclosure, at the S. end of which a postern protected by a tower can be traced. The borough established here in 1285 by Edward I seems not to have survived the retaking of the castle by the Welsh. The scattered hamlet of *Llanfihangel-y-Pennant* is a short way beyond Castell-y-Bere. The church has an old solid stone lychgate. Farther on, in a beautiful setting below mountains, the road crosses the Cader river by a modern bridge beside an old one, on the far side being the ruin of *Mary Jones's Cottage,* with a memorial. Daughter of a weaver, Mary Jones was born in 1784. When 10 years old she started to save for a Welsh bible, a task which took her six years. She then walked barefoot across the mountains to Bala where, so she had been told, she would be able to buy a bible from Thomas Charles, only to find that none was available. Thomas Charles, however, gave Mary his own bible, and, as a result of this incident, founded the British and Foreign Bible Society. Mary Jones lived to the age of 88 and is buried at Bryncrug. Her bible is preserved in the Society's headquarters in London. The cottage is at the end of the road, but a path continues N., ascending to the saddle of Cader Idris, where there is a choice between climbing to the summit or descending W. to Arthog or straight ahead to Llyn Gwernan and Dolgellau.

After Bryncrug A493 crosses the Dysynni, just beyond the bridge (S). being a motte, an early seat of the princes of Gwynedd, in use before the construction of Castell-y-Bere. *2m.* (from Bryncrug) *Llanegryn,* where the little church, on a hill to the N.W., has a font that is possibly Norman and a magnificent *Rood Screen and loft, by one tradition brought here by the monks of Cymmer Abbey at the Reformation but more probably an example of local craftsmanship. Opinion on the age of the screen varies between early 14C to mid 16C. On the S. exterior wall of the choir, to the left of the window, an incised cross, possibly a consecration cross from an earlier church, can be made out. The road reaches the coast shortly before *(2m.) Llangelynin Church,* a very primitive mainly 12C

structure above the shore, dedicated in the 7C to St Celynnin, a local saint. Inside are a unique double horse-bier; murals of unknown date, discovered during restoration in 1917; old pews with painted names; and a stoup, once reputed to be miraculously kept supplied with water.—
2m. **Llwyngwril** is a seaside village, with extensive caravan sites and holiday camps. Beyond, Barmouth and the estuary of the Mawddach come into view.—*3m.* **Fairbourne** is a growing holiday resort, with 2m. of sand stretching N. to the point that marks the S. side of the narrow entrance of the Mawddach Estuary. Barmouth, on the other side, can be reached either by passenger ferry or by the path across the railway bridge (see Rte 20A), access to this being by a road 1m. east. The *Fairbourne Railway*†, with a gauge of only 15 inches the smallest of Wales's little railways, started as a horse-drawn railway carrying materials for the construction of the village. Using steam and diesel engines, the railway runs for 2m. between the village and the ferry.

2m. **Arthog**, E. above which, surrounding twin lakes, is the National Trust property of Cregennan (705 acres), given in 1959 by Major C. L. Wynne-Jones in memory of his two sons killed in the war.

Cader Idris can be climbed from Arthog by following a track up the left bank of the stream to the farm of *Pant-y-Llan*, just short of a road and at the S.W. corner of the National Trust estate. The road is followed N.E. for ¼m. to a house called *Hafod-y-Fach* (790 ft), opposite which a steep climb eventually joins the Bridle Path from Dolgellau.

3m. **Abergwynant Valley**, a narrow, wooded glen which ascends south. The lane up the valley in 6m. reaches *Llyn Gwernan*, near two paths climbing Cader Idris.—Passing *Penmaenpool* (p. 188), with its tollbridge and Nature Information Centre, **Dolgellau** (Rte. 18A) is reached in *3m.*

27 ABERYSTWYTH

ABERYSTWYTH (12,000 inhab.) combines several features, being the main town on Cardigan Bay and thus a general centre serving a wide area; a popular and lively seaside resort; the base of the Vale of Rheidol Railway; with its castle a place of some historical interest; and the home of the National Library of Wales and of the University College of Wales.

Tourist Information. 6 Park Avenue. Promenade (summer only).
Parking. Park Avenue. Promenade (limited).
Railway and Bus Station. Alexandra Road.
Main Shopping Area. Great Darkgate Street and Terrace Road. Northgate.
Main Post Office. Great Darkgate Street.
Early Closing. Wednesday.
History. (Town and Castle). The present suburb of Llanbadarn Fawr is on the site of a 6-8C bishopric and settlement, which can be regarded as the parent village of Aberystwyth, known as Llanbadarn until the 15C. In 1110 Gilbert FitzRichard of Clare built a primitive castle, the earthworks of which can still be seen, on a site 1½ m. S. of the present castle and at that date near the mouth of the Ystwyth. For over a hundred years this castle suffered a violent history, being burnt down no less than five times, usually in wars between Welsh princes. The last recorded incident was the taking of the castle by Llewelyn the Great in 1221. The present castle, dating with its associated borough from 1277, was started by Edmund of Lancaster, brother of Edward I. Progress, in any case slow, was halted in 1282 when the Welsh took and briefly held the castle, but by 1284 the place was fit enough to receive a visit by Edward I. In the revolt of 1294 a Welsh siege was unsuccessful. During Owen Glendower's revolt the Welsh destroyed the town in 1401 but failed to take the castle until 1404, after which it remained a Glendower

headquarters for four years. Coins of Welsh silver were minted here between 1637-42, and during the Civil War Aberystwyth was held for the King. The castle was surrendered in 1646 and blown up in 1649. At the close of the 18C the discovery of a chalybeate spring led to a shortlived attempt to turn Aberystwyth into a fashionable spa.

The general pattern of the town is a seafront, running N.-S. and broken by the castle headland, backed by an area of pleasant and mostly small streets, with to the E. the station and to the S. the harbour. The district of *Penglais* (National Library, and new University College) is on rising ground to the northeast.

From the seafront there is a view of the whole of Cardigan Bay, from Snowdon and the Lleyn to Strumble Head and the Presely Hills. Beyond the N. end of the town rises *Constitution Hill* (400 ft), reached by footpath or by the *Aberystwyth Cliff Railway*†, opened in 1896 and between then and 1922, when it was electrified, operated by water balance tanks. The bandstand, and King's Hall used for a variety of entertainment, are on Marine Terrace, farther S. being the *Pier,* opposite which is the *Theological College of the Presbyterian Church of Wales* (formerly of the Calvinistic Methodists; removed from Trefecca in 1906). Just S. again, the most conspicuous feature on the seafront, is the old building of the *University College of Wales* (see below). Originally intended for a hotel, the building was rebuilt after a fire of 1885; it now houses arts departments, the General Library, and the Registry. In front are statues of Thomas Charles Edwards (1837-1900), the first Principal, and the Duke of Windsor (Chancellor of the University while Prince of Wales), both in their robes of office.

The **Castle** ruins occupy the low hill of a promontory immediately S. of the college. For the castle's history, see above. The site is an unusual diamond shape, with a large inner ward above and surrounded by a narrow outer ward. Of the outer ward there survive most of the length of the curtain (much restored), and remains of the E. and N.W. gates and of the angle-towers. The inner ward, its line marked by a bank, has virtually disappeared except for its E. and N.W. gates and fragments of angle-towers. East of the E. angle of the outer ward, there was a barbican, now marked by a mound; and it is thought that the War Memorial at the tip of the promontory may stand on the site of an outlying defended area.

The **Harbour**, S.E. of the castle, with the mouths of the Rheidol and Ystwyth, is used by fishing boats and yachts.

In the town there are two museums. *Aberystwyth Yesterday*†, in old St Paul's, Upper Darkgate Street, is an exhibition explained by its name. Among the exhibits are 300 hats from the stock of a shop closed in 1923, and, in a nearby building, there is a replica of a Victorian shop. The *Ceredigion Museum*†, at 14 Vulcan Street, is devoted to the story of Ceredigion (Cardigan). Themes include lead mining, weights and measures, seafaring, butter making, lighting, and the 17C Aberystwyth mint. One room has been converted to a replica of a cottage interior of 1850.

The **University College of Wales**†, founded in 1872, mainly by the efforts of Sir Hugh Owen (1804-81), has since 1893 ranked as the senior constituent college of the University of Wales. For the original buildings on the seafront, see above. Other buildings lie to the E. of the station, but the main recent development has been the *New*

Campus, on Penglais Hill in the N.E. outskirts of the town. Among the buildings here are the Institute of Rural Science (pre-war); Biology (1959); Physical Sciences (1962); Llandinam (1965), for geography,

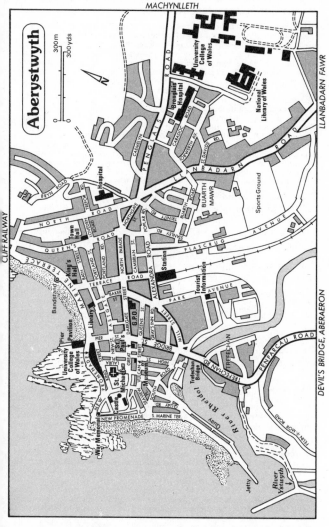

geology, and social studies. The Great Hall and Theatre together form part of the *Arts Centre*†, with touring exhibitions.

The ***National Library of Wales** occupies a commanding site on Penglais Hill, the land of which was presented by Lord Rendel. Begun in

1911, the *Readers' Room*†, *Manuscripts Block,* and the *Exhibition Gallery* were finished in 1916. The *Administration Block* and the surrounding terraces were completed in 1937, and the *Central Block* in 1955. Loan exhibitions and exhibitions from the library's own collections are held in both the *Gregynog Gallery*† and *Central Hall*†.

The movement for a national library dates from 1873, and a Royal Charter was granted in 1907. Under this the task of the library is to collect, preserve, and make available all books, manuscripts etc. in Welsh and other Celtic languages, or which deal with the Welsh and other Celtic people; also to hold works on all subjects and in all languages which help to achieve the purposes for which the University of Wales and other Welsh educational institutions were founded. In 1912, under the Copyright Act, the library became one of the six libraries entitled to claim a copy of all books, pamphlets, maps etc. published within the British Isles.

Among the library's chief treasures are the 'Black Book of Carmarthen' (12C), the oldest manuscript in Welsh; the 'Book of Taliesin' (13C); the 'White Book of Roderick' (13-14C), containing the oldest known versions of the Mabinogion tales; Latin and Welsh manuscripts of the Laws of Hywel Dda; early manuscript of Geoffrey of Monmouth's 'Chronicle'; the Henwrt manuscript of Bede's 'Ecclesiastical History of Britain' (12C) and Chaucer's 'Canterbury Tales' (c. 1400); the so-called 'Bangor Missal', really a Sarum missal of the late 14 or early 15C, finely decorated; one of the only two vellum copies of 'The Great Bible' of 1539; a 15C 'Passionale' probably made for Henry VII; and several illuminated Books of Hours and versions of 'Le Roman de la Rose'; early editions of Euclid.

The **Vale of Rheidol Railway**† (gauge 1 ft 11½ inches), British Rail's last steam line, ascends the lovely Vale of Rheidol for 11¾ m. from Aberystwyth to Devil's Bridge. It is the best way of seeing the Vale, as the main roads (Rte 28) run well above and clear of the valley. For the minor road along part of the N. side, see p. 231. There are five stations in all, and the single journey takes one hour. After *Llanbadarn* (see below) the railway keeps to the S. bank of the Rheidol. Beyond *Capel Bangor* the average gradient is 100 ft per mile, and, thanks to the narrowing and winding valley, there are constantly changing views, including, after *Aberffrwd* where the gradient becomes 1 in 50, the Rheidol Falls. For *Devil's Bridge,* see p. 234.—The line was opened by a private company in 1902, partly to carry lead from the Rheidol valley mines, but also largely to satisfy tourist demand; today only passengers are carried. In 1962 it was in danger of closure, but was saved by local effort and advertising which has been rewarded by ever increasing passenger figures.

The suburb of **Llanbadarn Fawr,** 1 m. S.E., the ancient parent village of Aberystwyth, was in the 6-8C the seat of a bishopric founded by St Paternus, Bishop of Vannes. In the 8C the see was merged into that of St David's. The aisleless cruciform *Church,* 140 ft long and 90 ft across the transepts, and with a central tower of 40 ft square, is one of the largest in Wales. Except for the sanctuary, which may be a 15C extension, the church is a plain building of the early 13C, its austerity relieved by a beautiful S. doorway. An unusual feature is the arrangement of the three lancets at the W. end, and the three on the S. of the S. transept. In this transept there are two Celtic crosses. The smaller one, much mutilated, is the older; traditionally it was once a standing stone, and it may have stood on a shaft. The larger may date to the early 8C. The legend associated with the crosses tells how St Samson, brother of Padarn, was threshing corn two miles away, using the stones as a flail, when the head flew off and landed at Llanbadarn; piqued, Samson threw the handle after it. The 14C poet Dafydd ap Gwilym, who eloped with an Anglesey princess, may have been a native of this parish, although his birthplace was more probably Broginin, 6 m. northeast.

For Aberystwyth to *Machynlleth* and beyond, see Rte 22; to *Devil's Bridge, Ponterwyd, Llanidloes, Rhayader, Builth Wells,* and *Brecon,* see Rte 28; to Carmarthen, see Rte 44.

28 ABERYSTWYTH TO RHAYADER AND BUILTH WELLS

Between Aberystwyth and Rhayader there is a choice of roads, both of them scenic with moor and forest. These are either viâ Ponterwyd (with a silver-lead mine museum) and Llangurig, with if wished a diversion to Llanidloes (31 m. to Rhayader); or a more southerly route viâ Devil's Bridge, and then a wild and remote mountain road (29 m. to Rhayader). The two routes, here only 2½ m. apart, are linked by a road between Ponterwyd and Devil's Bridge.

A Viâ Ponterwyd, Llangurig, and Rhayader

A44 to Llangurig: A470 to Builth Wells. 44 miles.—*4 m.* **Capel Bangor.**—*6 m.* **Ponterwyd.**—*5 m. Eisteddfa Gurig.*—*7 m.* **Llangurig.**—*9 m.* **Rhayader.**—*7 m. Newbridge-on-Wye.*—*6 m.* **Builth Wells.**

Aberystwyth, see Rte 27.—*1 m. Llanbadarn Fawr,* see p. 230—*3 m. Capel Bangor.* Here a minor road ascends the Vale of Rheidol beside the N. bank of the river, in 4 m. reaching *Rheidol Power Station*† (with a nature trail along the river), just short of Rheidol Falls.—*4 m.* At *Nant-yr-Arian,* just N. of the road, there is a F.C. Visitor Centre, from which starts a 2 m. long walk (moor, woodland, and a small lake).—*1 m. Llywernog Silver-Lead Mine*†. Prospecting began here in the 1740s, the mine reaching its greatest activity during the following century although it was abandoned in the 1880s. Restoration (started 1973) as a museum now offers the visitor an audio-visual programme; an indoor exhibition, with material covering Welsh mining generally; a large area with relics of machinery etc; and underground workings, which include a pit sunk in 1795.—*1 m.* **Ponterwyd** is a hamlet where the upper Rheidol is crossed, and where roads N. and S. enable worthwhile diversions to be made. The Borrow Arms recalls that it was here that Borrow dried out after floundering through peat bog, much of which is now covered by the reservoirs of Nant-y-Moch (see below).

A4120, leading S., in 2½ m. reaches *Devil's Bridge* on Rte 28B, on the way passing the church of *Ysbytty Cynfyn,* set within the remains of a stone circle (five stones surviving) and thus providing a continuity of ritual building, pagan and Christian, from prehistoric to present day times. Cynfyn was a hospice (Ysbytty) of the abbey of Strata Florida. A path from the church leads in 10 min. to the *Parson's Bridge,* below which the Rheidol rushes through a narrow passage.

A 'Scenic Route' northward from Ponterwyd, through bare mountain scenery below the W. flank of Plynlimon, passes above the small *Dinas Reservoir* and in 4 m. reaches *Nant-y-Moch Reservoir,* an irregular narrow sheet of water some 3 m. long forming part of the Rheidol hydro-electric scheme. The reservoir (named after a chapel drowned here), with its dam, 170 ft high and 1150 ft long, was inaugurated in 1965. The dam is crossed and the road skirts the S. and W. shores of the reservoir, the scenery here being broken and softened by plantations, Leaving the reservoir the road bears W., crossing a watershed at 1300 ft, then dropping down the fine Cwm Ceulan to *Talybont* (p. 216), 9 m. beyond the dam.

A44 rises steadily along the S. slopes of Plynlimon, crossing rather desolate moor broken by afforestation. *Dyffryn Castell* and (*5 m.*) *Eisteddfa Gurig* (1359 ft), the top of the pass, are the usual starting points for the ascent of the mountain.

Plynlimon (2468 ft), notorious for its bogs and with several abandoned mines on its slopes, is a large moorland dome, on which are the sources of five rivers; Severn, Wye, Dulas, Llyfnant, and Rheidol. Featureless, and notorious also for its mists, the mountain is no place for the inexperienced and ill-equipped; map and compass are essential. *Plynlimon Fawr* (2 m. from Eisteddfa Gurig; 2468 ft), the first summit reached, is just S. of *Llyn Llygad Rheidol,* a tarn which supplies water to Aberystwyth. The secondary summit of *Arwystli* (2427 ft) is 1¾ m. E.N.E., the source of the Wye being between the two. The Severn rises on the hillside of *Blaen Hafren,* 1½ m. N. of Arwystli. Another approach to the mountain is through Hafren Forest (see p. 215).

The view is extensive, and because of the mountain's central situation includes most of the hill ranges of Wales. To the W. is the sweep of Cardigan Bay, with the estuary of the Dyfi; and to the N.W. the line of the Lleyn may be seen. Cader Idris is N.N.W., with, slightly right of its highest point, something of Snowdonia, but distant and with Snowdon itself masked by Cader Idris. Arenig Fawr is almost due N., with Aran Mawddwy to the right of it and nearer. To the N.E. are the Berwyns, and to the E. the Kerry Hills. Radnor Forest lies E.S.E., and S.E. and S. are the Black Mountains and the Brecon Beacons. To the S.W. the Presely Hills stand out.

The road descends beside the Tarenig, with afforestation to the S., just in these woods, 2 m. below Eisteddfa Gurig, being traces of a small Roman outpost fort. In another mile the Wye coming in from the N. is crossed and then followed, in gentler scenery, to (*7 m.*) the village of **Llangurig.** The church, dedicated to St Curig (d. 550), a rebuilding of 1879 by George Gilbert Scott, retains some older parts. The tower is 14C, and from the 15C survive the arcade between the nave and the N. aisle, the choir arch, and the tracery of the E. window. For *Llanidloes* (4 m. N.E.), see p. 215.

A470 continues to descend the now narrowing and increasingly beautiful Wye Valley, keeping to the E. bank.—*9 m.* **Rhayader** (1200 inhab.) is in Welsh *Rhaeadr Gwy,* the 'waterfall of the Wye', a name which recalls falls here that virtually disappeared when the river bridge was built in 1780. The castle built here by Rhys ap Gruffydd in the 12C has long disappeared, and Rhayader today is a country centre much used by holiday visitors, among the attractions being pony trekking, fishing, walking, and the beautifully situated reservoirs a short distance to the west.

The diarist Francis Kilvert was in 1876-77 vicar of *St Harmon,* 3 m. north. The church contains a Norman font.—For *Cwmhir Abbey,* 6½ m. N.E., see p. 237. For Rhayader to *New Radnor* and *Leominster,* see Rte 30.

The ***Elan Valley and Claerwen Reservoirs,** completed respectively in 1892-96 and 1952 and supplying water to the Birmingham district by means of an aqueduct some 73 m. long, are reached in 3½ m. by B4518 S.W. out of Rhayader. In a setting of mixed woodland and rocky bare hills, the Elan reservoirs comprise a chain of four narrow lakes, each with its dam, extending 9 m. from N. to south. The flooding of the valley provided the theme for the novel 'The House Under the Water' by Francis Brett Young. Claerwen reservoir, aligned roughly E.-W. and nearly 4 m. long, lies to the west. The dams are particularly attractive when cascading. Roads skirt the entire length of the reservoirs, and there are a number of parking places. The road from Rhayader in 3 m. passes Birmingham Corporation's *Elan Village* on the S. bank of the Elan, then reaches the dam on the E. side of *Caben Coch,* 1 m. beyond which is the *Garreg Ddu Viaduct,* where there is a choice of roads. The road beyond the viaduct skirts the W. side of Caben Coch, towards the S. of which, if the water is low, can be seen the garden wall of Nant Gwyllt where Shelley and Harriet lived in April-June 1812. At the lake's end the road bears W., in 2 m. reaching *Claerwen,* the dam of which is 1166 ft long. A road continues the length of the N. shore.—The other road from Garreg Ddu Viaduct heads N. beside this narrowing reservoir, below which lies Cwm Elan, the house where, after his expulsion from Oxford in 1811 because of his pamphlet 'The Necessity of Atheism', Shelley visited his cousin Thomas Grove and wrote that 'all was gloomy and desolate'. Next the *Pen-y-Garreg* reservoir dam (528 ft long, 123 ft high) is reached, with a car park from which a very attractive short walk leads to the foot of the dam. The roads along either side of the reservoir meet at the dam (513 ft long, 120 ft high) at the foot of *Craig Goch* reservoir, clear of woodland and in open moor. From here the road N. runs above and a short way back from the reservoir, at its head (*Pont-ar-Elan*) meeting Rte 28B.

South from Rhayader A470 descends the glen of the Wye, which in 2 m. is joined from the W. by the Elan.—*3 m. Llanwrthwl,* a village with a standing stone in its churchyard. *Doldowlod House,* between the road and the river 1½ m. farther S., was once the home of James Watt (1736-1819), the engineer. The valley opens out before (*4 m.*) the straggling village of *Newbridge-on-Wye,* just S. of which the Wye enters upon one of its most broken and beautiful reaches.—*5 m. Llanelwedd,* site of the Royal Welsh Agricultural Society showground (July). Rte 29 comes in from the E., and the road crosses the Wye by a bridge of six arches (1779; widened in 1925).

1 m. **Builth Wells** (1500 inhab.) lies on the S. bank of a pastoral stretch of the Wye. There is a convenient car park (with *Tourist Information* in summer) beside the river.

History. The town probably originated as a settlement below the early Norman motte-and-bailey castle, thought to have been built by Bernard of Newmarch in 1091. The castle was partially destroyed by Llewelyn the Last in 1260, and in 1282 the refusal of the garrison, in Welsh history the 'traitors of Bu-Allt', to give Llewelyn protection led to his death at nearby Cilmeri. At about this time Edward I built a stone castle here (see picture in Llandrindod Wells museum); it is known to have been in good repair in the time of Henry VIII, but was probably destroyed under Elizabeth I. Later Builth became an important centre on the cattle route to England (it still has a weekly market), and for a period the town was known for mineral springs.

The *Castle Mound,* just beyond the S. end of the bridge, is reached by a path to the right of the Lion Hotel. Of Edward I's stone castle virtually nothing remains, what is seen today being the large early Norman motte-and-bailey. The earthworks are notable for the unusual width of their ditches, and for the way in which the bailey is divided by another ditch. The *Church,* W. of the car park, was rebuilt after 1875 except for the restored 12C tower. In the porch there is an effigy of John Lloid (d. 1585), one of Elizabeth I's body-squires.

For Builth Wells N.E. to *Llandrindod Wells, Knighton,* and *Shrewsbury,* and S.W. to *Llandovery* and *Swansea,* see Rte 29; to *Abergavenny,* see Rte 32.

B   Viâ Devil's Bridge and Rhayader

A4120 to Devil's Bridge: B4574 to Rhayader: A470 to Builth Wells. 42 miles.—
11 m. **Devil's Bridge.**—*2 m.* **The Arch.**—*11 m.* **Pont-ar-Elan.**—*5 m.* **Rhayader.**—
13 m. **Builth Wells.**
For the *Vale of Rheidol Railway* from Aberystwyth to Devil's Bridge, see p. 230.

Aberystwyth, see Rte 27. The Rheidol is crossed, the road then
skirting the E. side of a hill (415 ft) with a hillfort and an unsightly
monument to the Duke of Wellington.—*1 m.* **Penparcau,** a suburban
village and crossroads from which A487 (Rte 44) bears south.

From the crossroads, B4340 in 2 m. reaches **Nanteos†**, a Georgian mansion the
principal part of which was built in 1739 for Thomas Powell, who had made a
fortune from property and lead mines. *Entrance Hall:* An 18C side table.
Cantonese porcelain (18C). *Morning Room:* Victorian decoration. Dresden,
Newhall, Coalport, and Swansea porcelain. Italian bureau-bookcase (18C). Self-
portrait by D. G. Rossetti. *Library:* Books (mainly 18C). Letter written by Lord
Byron. Regency furniture. Family portraits. *Dining Room:* Italian 19C souvenir
miniatures, showing Rubens and Van Dyck. Family portraits. Spode chinaware.
Copies of pictures by Reni and Greuze. *Inner Hall:* Chinese blue and white, and
Japanese Amari porcelain. French chandelier (1810). Portrait of Elizabeth Owen,
who haunts the Pink Bedroom. *Gallery:* Note the false doors, inserted for
symmetry. Chinese blue and white porcelain. *Music Room:* Portrait of Richard
Wagner, reputed to have composed part of 'Parsifal' while at Nanteos. Marble
fireplace (18 or 19C), with inlay of Aesop's fox and stork fable. *Main Bedroom:*
Victorian furnishing. Fireplace replica of Iron Bridge. Swansea porcelain. *Pink
Bedroom:* Haunted by Elizabeth Owen, who for ever searches for the jewels she hid
to prevent their passing to a hated sister-in-law and then forgot where she had put
them. *Kitchen, Scullery, and Cellars:* Collection of early domestic material.

The road gradually ascends along the S. side of the Rheidol valley,
with occasional views down to the river and, at the highest point (989 ft),
2 m. beyond Henffordd Arms Inn, across to the steep N. side. During the
descent hills mask the valley.

10 m. **Devil's Bridge,** a popular beauty spot with a hotel, a huge car
park, and the terminus of the Vale of Rheidol Railway, is in a landscape
of wooded glen, rocks, and torrent. Here the Rheidol suddenly changes
direction from S. to W., at the bend being joined from the E. by the
Mynach, which falls 300 ft through a rocky chasm in a series of cataracts
which in spate become an almost continuous fall. An iron bridge (1901)
spans the stream at the lip of the falls. Just below this is the stone bridge
of 1753, and, lower still, the original *Pont-y-gwr-Drwg* (Bridge of the
Evil One), traditionally ascribed to the Devil. It may have been built by
the monks of Strata Florida, and Giraldus writes of crossing a bridge
here in 1188. The *Mynach Falls* (fee for non-residents) are in the grounds
of the Hafod Arms Hotel. Paths offer views of the basin above the falls,
of the three bridges, and of the distant Gyfarllwyd Falls up the Rheidol,
Farther down, the whole series of the Mynach Falls is seen from a
platform, from where steps descend steeply to a footbridge across the
river at the foot of the falls.

For Devil's Bridge to *Ysbytty Cynfyn* and (2½ m.) *Ponterwyd* on Rte 28A, see p.
231.
B4343, leading S. from Devil's Bridge and crossing the valley of the Ystwyth, in
8 m. reaches the abbey of *Strata Florida* (see p. 348).

Devil's Bridge is left by B4574 which ascends into woodland to (*2 m.*)
The Arch, with a Forestry Commission picnic site in a scenic setting and
a choice of three forest trails. There is a viewpoint 300 yards N. of the

picnic area. The stone arch was put up in 1810, to honour the Golden Jubilee of George III, by Thomas Johnes (1748–1816) of Hafod Uchtryd (demolished 1958), 2 m. south. When in 1783 Johnes inherited the estate, then apparently neglected and impoverished, he resolved to transform the place through sound farming and afforestation, in the latter context becoming a pioneer and between 1796 and 1813 planting over four million trees, mostly larch. He can thus be said to have anticipated the present Forestry Commission estate. Johnes was also a scholar and issued his own translations of Froissart's and Monstrelet's 'Chronicles' from a private press. (See also Croft Castle, p. 245, where can be seen aquatints of Hafod.)

After The Arch the road leaves the forest for open moor, ascending the Ystwyth, passing large disused lead mines, and traversing remote and desolate country to cross the watershed at 1320 ft. The descent is then down the Elan to (*11 m.*) *Pont-ar-Elan,* a road junction above the head of Craig Goch Reservoir into which the Elan flows. The small road leading S. offers an alternative route to Rhayader viâ the beautiful Elan Valley Reservoirs (see Rte 28A).—*5 m.* **Rhayader,** for which and for Rhayader to (*13 m.*) **Builth Wells,** see Rte 28A.

29   SHREWSBURY TO LLANDRINDOD WELLS, LLANDOVERY, AND SWANSEA

A488 to Penybont: A44 to Cross Gates: A483 to Llandovery: A40 to Llandeilo: A476 or A483 and A48 to Swansea. 114 miles.—*9 m. Minsterley.*—*12 m.* **Bishop's Castle.**—*5 m.* **Clun.**—*6 m.* **Knighton.**—*5 m. Monaughty.*—*2 m. Bleddfa.*—*9 m.* **Cross Gates.**—*3 m.* **Llandrindod Wells.**—*7 m.* **Builth Wells.**—*6 m.* **Garth.**—*6 m.* **Llanwrtyd Wells.**—*10 m.* **Llandovery.**—*6 m. Llangadog.*—*6 m.* **Llandeilo.** *14 m.* **Pontardulais.**—*8 m.* **Swansea.**

From Shrewsbury to Knighton generally undulating agricultural country. After Knighton, and more so after Builth Wells, increasingly moorland and afforestation, with the road running below the Cambrian Mountains to the N. and Mynydd Epynt and Black Mountain to the south.

Shrewsbury, see Rte 21, is left viâ Welsh Bridge.—*9 m. Minsterley* has a 17C church in which hang Virgin Crants or Maiden's Garlands, paper crowns with decorative flowers. Those in this church are mid 18C, but the tradition may reach back as far as the 5C. In Shakespeare's 'Hamlet' the priest at Ophelia's funeral protests that, although 'her death was doubtful . . . Yet here she is allow'd her virgin crants.' Beyond Minsterley the road ascends the Hope Valley, reaching a height of over 1000 ft, with to the E. the rocky *Stiperstones* ridge, rising to over 1700 ft. From the watershed the descent is for 3 m. along the Welsh border, with volcanic *Corndon Hill* (1684 ft) to the west.—*12 m.* **Bishop's Castle** is a small town with some picturesque houses but no castle, though there is a tower of a border keep of the bishops of Hereford 2 m. E. at *Lea.*

A488 continues S., rising again to 883 ft before dropping down into (*5 m.*) **Clun,** where the river of the same name is crossed by an old bridge. The little town was created a borough by Edward II, but lost this status in 1886. The ruined *Castle,* probably dating from the 12C, was blown up by Parliament after the Civil War; like Painscastle it is sometimes identified with the 'Garde Douloureuse' of Scott's 'The Betrothed'. The

Church has a squat Norman tower and 11-12C arcades, restored in 1876. The porch and lychgate are early 18C.

CLUN TO NEWTOWN. B4368 and A489. 15 miles. This hillroad runs N.W. across moorland, in 3 m. reaching *Newcastle*, just beyond a good section of Offa's Dyke. Above the village there is a large hillfort. In another 6 m. the road reaches the border at *Anchor Inn* and the earthwork of *Castell Bryn Amlwg* (see p. 213). *Newtown* is reached via *Kerry* (see p. 213).

Beyond Clun A488 again climbs, this time to 1154 ft, crossing a rather monotonous upland. *Caer Caradoc,* 1 m. E., is the traditional scene of the defeat of Caractacus in 51 by Ostorius Scapula (see also p. 58). The road then descends a wooded glen into the valley of the Teme and enters Wales.

6 m. **Knighton** (2200 inhab.) is a border market town on the steep Welsh bank of the Teme. There are two mottes; one, first mentioned in 1181, at the top of the town, and the other (Bryn-y-Castell), possibly an outlying defence of the first, in the valley just E. of the station. *Offa's Dyke* crosses the S.W. edge of the town, giving it its Welsh name of *Tref-y-Clawdd* (Cantref of the Dyke). A good section of the dyke can be reached by a path beside *Tourist Information* near the top of the hill.

KNIGHTON TO NEWTOWN. B4355 and unclassified. 18 miles. This hillroad ascends the Welsh bank of the Teme, in 3 m. reaching *Knucklas,* with a hillfort ¼ m. north. *Beguildy,* reached in another 5 m., has a church with a rood screen and the base of its loft. From here small roads lead generally N. for 1 m. to the remote church of *Betws-y-Crwyn* (1300 ft), with a fine rood loft and panelled roof. Hence by minor roads in 3 m. to *Anchor Inn* on the border and the earthwork of *Castell Bryn Amlwg* (see p. 213). *Newtown* is reached via *Kerry* (see p. 213).

5 m. Monaughty (W. of the road) is a stone Tudor farm which was once a monastery grange. It is said that a tunnel once ran between the grange and *Pilleth* (1 m. E.), this being used as an escape route by the monks when attacked. In 1402 Pilleth was the scene of an important battle in which Owen Glendower defeated and captured Sir Edmund Mortimer, fighting for Henry IV, and established his claim to be the Welsh national leader. Mortimer, advancing from the E. along the flank of the hill, seems to have been ambushed by Glendower who was hidden on the reverse slope above. After the battle Mortimer sided with Glendower. The news of Mortimer's capture provides part of the opening scene of Shakespeare's 'Henry IV. Part 1.' *Castell Foel-Allt,* beside the river below Pilleth church, is a motte-and-bailey dating from the late 11C, whose primitive castle is known to have stood for barely a century.

At *Cascob* (1½ m. S. of Monaughty, but, other than on foot, reached in 5½ m. viâ Pilleth and Whitton) the church has a mound at its W. end which may be the remains of a tower burnt by Glendower. The present tower is of unusual ground plan, being twice as long from N. to S. as from E. to west. Inside the church are a triangular aumbry and square piscina (both 13C), a 14C font, and a restored rather plain 16C rood screen.

2 m. Bleddfa, where the church had a mound at its W. end. Excavation (1962) revealed a small doorway and the base of a tower, probably that of the earlier church destroyed by Owen Glendower at about the time of the battle of Pilleth. The road now climbs along the N. flank of *Radnor Forest,* a plateau (2166 ft) some 5 m. square, well afforested on this side. Walkers can cross by a nature trail of 8 m. which starts about 1 m. W. of Bleddfa (at sign F.R.P.7) and ends near *Water-break-its-neck* (see p. 243) on A44. After reaching a height of 1201 ft the road descends to

(*4 m.*) *Llanfihangel Rhydithon* (with a track to Water-break-its-neck), 2 m. beyond which a road (sign) leads S. for 1 m. to *The Pales*, an early 18C Friends' Meeting House.—*3 m. Penybont*, a village in which there is a still functioning 19C forge. Rte 30 is met here and followed for *2 m.* to **Cross Gates.**

Cwmhir Abbey, 5 m. N. of Cross Gates, is in a beautiful pastoral setting in the winding valley of the Clywedog ('cwm hir' means 'long valley'). The abbey was founded in 1143 for Cistercian monks from Whitland, and a second foundation followed in 1176. It was also twice destroyed, first by Henry III in 1231, and in 1401 by Owen Glendower who is said to have suspected that the monks were Englishmen in disguise. At the Dissolution there were only three monks. Although after Henry III's destruction an ambitious rebuilding was planned, in fact the choir was never built, the transepts were left unfinished, and the nave (242 ft long) was destroyed by Glendower. Today's remains comprise little more than the foundations of the nave and some battered lower courses of its wall. Traditionally the body of Llewelyn the Last was brought from Cilmeri and buried below the altar, the position today being marked by a blackthorn.
A483, a hillroad leading N. from Cross Gates up the valley of the Ithon for (22 m.) Newtown, in its first 10 m. passes four churches of interest. That at *Llanddewi Ystradenny*, although a rebuilding, retains a late 12C doorway. At *Llanbister*, a foundation of the 6C, the 12 or 13C church adapts to a sloping site by interior flights of steps. The tower, unusual for being at the E. end, is entered by a door N. of the altar. Also to be noted are a stoup and piscina, both 13C; what is left of the carved 16C rood screen; the 17 or 18C W. gallery; and the modern baptistry for immersion. *Llananno* contains an early 16C *Rood Screen and loft, with later work (1933) distinguishable by its darker tone. Twenty-three figures face into the nave. There is also a churchwarden's pew of 1681. If the church is closed, something of the screen can be seen through the N. windows. At *Llanbadarnfynydd* the rebuilt church retains an early E. window and some relics of its rood screen.

This Route now turns S. on A483, almost at once passing the church of *Llanbadarnfawr*, with a 12C S. doorway and fine carved *Tympanum of c. 1140. The lefthand supporting capital bears two naked figures, possibly Adam and Eve, with the Devil below. A Roman stone, inscribed with the name of Valerius Flavinius, is inserted in the left wall of the porch. Almost certainly coming from Castell Collen, the stone was found embedded in the wall of the old church during rebuilding in 1878 and suggests that the original church may have used Castell Collen as a quarry.

3 m. **Llandrindod Wells** (3500 inhab.), the county town of Powys, though no longer a spa is still a not unfashionable holiday centre·which with its wide streets and large hotels retains much of its spacious Edwardian character. The town is divided into two by the railway, the station being to the N.W., and the main street (Temple Street) with the Town Hall (*Tourist Information*) to the east.

History. Although today's Llandrindod Wells dates only from the late 19C the town has ancient roots. The Romans were nearby at Castell Collen and probably knew the springs (saline, sulphur, magnesian, and chalybeate), and the parish church of the Trinity, which gives the town its name, traces its origins to the 12C. The saline spring is recorded in 1696, the sulphur spring in 1736, and in 1748 the springs were the subject of verses in the 'Gentleman's Magazine'. At this time the place was no more than a scattered hamlet. A hotel was built in 1749 and, until closed in 1787, gave Llandrindod a few years notoriety as a haunt of gamblers and rakes. It was the arrival of the railway in 1867 that changed everything, and by the end of the century the spa had developed, receiving as many as 80,000 visitors a year, a prosperity which was to last until the Second World War.

The *Llandrindod Wells Museum*†, in War Memorial Gardens, Temple Street, is largely, though not exclusively, devoted to finds from the Roman fort of Castell Collen. Other exhibits include an interesting series of photographs and descriptions of local churches; a dugout canoe found in the Ithon, of unestablished date but perhaps contemporary with the later occupation of Castell Collen; and a collection of dolls from many parts of the world. At the *Automobile Palace* (Temple Street) can be seen the Tom Norton Collection of bicycles and tricycles, covering the period from 1869-1938. In *Rock Park,* in the S.W. of the town, the waters can still be taken at the now privately owned pumproom, and to the S.E. is *Llandrindod Lake* (boating, fishing), above being the parish church (see above) and the golf course at a height of 1100 ft.

The Roman fort of **Castell Collen,** 1¼ m. N.W. of the town, is reached from A4081 (take the lane N. immediately W. of the Ithon bridge and ask for permission to park at the second farm). The fort seems to have known four phases, namely an original turf and timber site of 75-78, the work of Julius Frontinus during his campaign against the Silures; stone construction of the mid 2C; a reduction in size in the early 3C; and a strengthening in the late 3 or early 4C. The rectangular earthworks of a fort of between three and four acres are clearly visible, and to the W. can be traced something of the area abandoned in the 3C.

Cefnllys, 1 m. E. of Llandrindod Wells, has a 13C church. In 1893 the rector removed the roof because he wanted his parishioners to attend the church in Llandrindod, now at its height as a spa, but so indignant were the parishioners that they reroofed the church two years later. On the motte-and-bailey above the church stood a castle built in 1242

Between Llandrindod Wells and Howey, to the W. of A483 beyond the railway, aerial photographs have shown traces of a Roman road and practice camps. At *Disserth,* just W. of the main road, the church has a three-level pulpit and a box-pew, both 17C. The *Carneddau Hills* (1430 ft), to the E. of the road, provide good walking, and are of geological interest for the way in which the Llandovery and Lower Silurian flags here have been disrupted by intruding volcanic rocks, while ice markings, perched blocks, and moraines are evidence of later glacial action.—For *6 m. Llanelwedd* and *1 m.* **Builth Wells,** in the Wye valley, see p. 233.

Beyond Builth Wells A483 runs between the long ridge of Mynydd Epynt (1650 ft; a Ministry of Defence range) to the S.E. and the southern end of the Cambrian Mountains to the northwest. Both areas include high moor and forest and are crossed by a number of unclassified roads, those through the Cambrian Mountains being through some of the remotest country in Wales.—*2 m. Cilmeri* is where Llewelyn the Last, denied help by the garrison at Builth, was killed in 1282 during a skirmish with the English. A roadside monument (1956, replacing one of the 19C) stands at the place where he is supposed to have fallen. One tradition holds that he is also buried near here, but Cwmhir Abbey seems a more probable site. Glan Irfon, ¼ m. S. of the road, was a home of the eccentric Lady Hester Stanhope (1776-1839).— *4 m. Garth.* Here there is a choice of roads for the next 5 or 6 m. The main road loops N. through *Beulah,* a village which has given its name to a breed of sheep; from here an unclassified road N.W. in 5 m. joins the drover road (see below) at Abergwesyn. The valley road, 1 m. shorter, passes through **Llangammarch Wells,** in parkland scenery at the confluence of the Irfon and Cammarch. The village gained its former reputation as a spa because its water contained barium chloride, not found elsewhere in Britain and recommended for heart disease and rheumatism. The now disused pumphouse and the well are in the grounds of the Lake Hotel. Llangammarch was the birthplace in 1559 of John Penry, the Puritan writer and publisher, hanged in London in 1593 for sedition. The Royalist Bishop Howell (1588-1646) was also born here, and Theophilus Evans (1694-1767), author of a popular book on Welsh antiquities said to have run through 30 editions, was vicar. The book was translated into English under the title 'View of the Primitive Ages'; it was highly imaginative and asserted that Arthur was as real as Alexander the Great.

6m. **Llanwrtyd Wells,** once. a spa known for its sulphur and chalybeate springs, is now a modest country holiday and pony trekking centre. The small modern town is on the main road, the old village being about a mile northwest. The *Cambrian Welsh Tweed Factory* (visitors welcome), a mill established in 1918 and considerably extended in 1944 and 1970, is run for the disabled by the Royal British Legion. Yarn made wholly from Welsh wool (something of a rarity) can be bought here. The artificial *Abernant Lake* (50 acres; boating and fishing) is under a mile southeast.

From Llanwrtyd Wells, a former drover hillroad can be followed N. and W. through forest and across remote moorland to (18 m.) Tregaron on Rte 44B. Along the road there are a number of Forestry Commission picnic sites. The narrow rocky glen of the Irfon is ascended through *Abergwesyn,* beyond which the road bears W. through a corner of *Towy Forest.* From here a path follows the E. side of the Towy for 2 m. to the N. tip of Llyn Brianne. After crossing the Towy the road runs across moor for 4 m., passing a road S. to *Llyn Brianne* and reaching over 1500 ft before skirting another section of forest in which is the little *Llyn Berwyn.* From here the Berwyn and the road drop down to **Tregaron** in the valley of the Teifi.

Beyond Llanwrtyd Wells the road ascends through remote country to cross the *Sugar Loaf Pass* (949 ft).—At (*6m.*) *Llanfair-ar-y-Bryn* the 13-15C church is built within the walls of a Roman station, possibly the Luentium of Ptolemy, and fragments of Roman brick may be seen below the E. window and in the N. wall. The Rev. William Williams (see below) is buried in the churchyard.

4m. **Llandovery** (2000 inhab.), a leading market town, owes its Welsh name of *Llanymddyfri* (Church amidst the Waters) to its position at the confluence of the Gwydderig and the Bran, and about 1½ m. above that of the Bran and the Towy, this last, with a course of 68 m., being the longest river entirely in Wales. Of the Norman *Castle* a few remains (oval motte, a roughly square bailey, and some later masonry) stand on a knoll beside a large parking area in the S. of the town. It was partly burnt by Gruffydd ap Rhys in 1116, and does not seem to have been long held by the English. *Llandovery College,* near the railway, was founded in 1848. Rhys Pritchard (1579-1644), known as the 'Vicar of Llandovery', celebrated for his preaching and as the author of 'The Welshman's Candle', a paraphrase of the Gospels in Welsh quatrains, was born at Llandovery and in 1602 became vicar of the parish church (Llandingat). William Williams ('Williams Pantycelyn', 1717-91), the revivalist and hymn writer, was born at *Cefncoed,* 4 m. northeast.

The most attractive excursion from Llandovery is that up the upper **Vale of Towy** to Llyn Brianne, a distance of 11 m. to the S. end of the lake. Roads follow either side of the river, and at *Craig Bron-y-Rwrt* (8 m. from Llandovery) a small road bears off N.W. and then S.W. for Pumpsaint on Rte 34. Just beyond, another road bears N. across the river for the R.S.P.B.'s *Dinas Reserve* (information room; walk). Near the farm of *Ystradffin,* 1½ m. farther N., is *Twm Shon Catti's Cave,* the retreat, remarkable only for its narrow entrance, of 'Tom John, son of Catherine' (1530-1620), a poet whose youthful freebooting escapades gained him the title of the 'Robin Hood of Wales'. Later he married the heiress of Ystradffin and became a magistrate. *Llyn Brianne,* with a dam at its S. end, boosts the water supply of Swansea. The irregularly shaped lake is over 3 m. long from the dam to the N. tip of its long, narrow E. finger. A minor road, with a Forestry Commission picnic site, skirts the E. shore, beyond the lake continuing for 4 m. to join the drover road between Llanwrtyd Wells and Tregaron (see above).

For Llandovery to (E.) *Brecon,* and (W.) *Lampeter* and *Aberaeron,* see Rte 34.

From Llandovery there is a choice of roads either side of the Towy to (*6 m.*) *Llangadog.* A40, N. of the river, should be taken for Rte 34 to Lampeter, which bears away W. at *Llanwrda,* 4 m. from Llandovery. From Llanwrda a road also leads across (5 m.) to *Talley Abbey* (see below). Llangadog is a small market town lying between the Sawdde and the Bran, two tributaries of the Towy. *Mandinam,* 2 m. E., was the home of Joanna Bridges, Jeremy Taylor's second wife (1656), rumoured to have been a natural daughter of Charles I. *Carn Goch,* 3 m. S. of Llangadog, is a large hillfort with a stone rampart and earthworks covering some 15 acres.

After Llangadog there is again a choice of roads. The more direct road to Swansea is A4069, which ascends the valley of the Sawdde and crosses the long moorland stretch known as Black Mountain before descending to the iron-smelting centre of Brynamman. But this Route follows the more interesting road through (*6 m.*) **Llandeilo,** centre for a number of worthwhile diversions. The town (1800 inhab.), occupying the slope of a hill above the Towy, takes its name from St Teilo, who is said to have died in a monastery here in 560. The *Church,* the N. aisle of which serves as parish hall, is in origin 13C but was almost entirely rebuilt in 1840. It preserves the heads of two stone crosses of the 9 and 10C. A path leading W. from the bridge (1848) along the N. bank of the river soon reaches the little church of *Llandyfeisant,* said to be on the site of a Roman temple. To the W. of the town is *Dynevor Park* (no adm.), in the S. part of which, on a hill overlooking the Towy, stand the ruins of the *Old Castle,* well seen from B4300 to the south; the ruins comprise a circular keep, a drum-tower, and some fragments of curtain wall.

According to tradition, the first castle was built in 876 by Rhodri Mawr, as a palace for his son Cadell, to whom he gave the sovereignty of South Wales. Later the castle became the seat of the House of Rhys. It was taken in 1203 by the usurper Maelgwn ap Rhys, who was ousted by the sons of his brother Gruffydd. An English siege of 1257 was raised by Llewelyn the Last. Dynevor was granted to Sir Rhys ap Thomas FitzUrien by Henry VII, but confiscated by Henry VIII, who beheaded the owner on a trumpery charge of treason. The present Lord Dynevor is a descendant of Urien, Prince of Reged. Spenser places Merlin's cave 'amongst the woody hills of Dynevowre'.

Diversions from Llandeilo

The remains of **Talley Abbey**†, 7 m. N., are reached by B4302 up the pleasant valley of the Dulais. Talley was founded by Rhys ap Gruffydd (d. 1197), Prince of South Wales, for Premonstratensian Canons and was the only monastery of this Order in Wales. The canons were ejected in c. 1200 by the powerful Cistercians of Whitland, but by 1208 had been reinstated as the result of an appeal to the Archbishop of Canterbury.

The name is a shortened form of Tal-y-Llychau (Head of the Lakes) and refers to the situation of the abbey on the more southerly of two small lakes. The remains of the church, of very plain architecture, consist chiefly of the transepts with their chapels, part of the choir, and fragments of the nave and tower. To the S. of the nave are the lower courses of cloisters. Talley claims to be the burial place of Dafydd ap Gwilym (c. 1320-80), described by Borrow as 'the greatest of his country's songsters'.—From *Llansawel,* 2 m. N. of Talley, B4310 leads S.W. to *Abergorlech* and *Brechfa* on the S.E. flank of Brechfa Forest, with a forest trail from the former place.

WEST OF LLANDEILO. A pleasant and interesting round of 12 m. can be made either side of the Towy to the W. of Llandeilo, starting along B4300, to the N. of which the ruin of *Dynevor Old Castle* (see above) can be seen on the hill above the valley. Soon afterwards the mansion of *Golden Grove* stands above the road on the S. side. Now a college of technology and agriculture, the present building (by Wyatville, c. 1824; best seen from Cilsan Bridge just N.) is successor, on a different site, of a mansion burnt down in 1769, in which Jeremy Taylor found a refuge with Richard Vaughan, 2nd Earl of Carbery, the mansion's owner, during the ten disturbed years of 1645-55. While here Taylor wrote many of his best works, including his 'Holy Living', 'Holy Dying', and 'Golden Grove', and at the same time kept a school in the neighbouring Newton Hall. B4300 continues W., with a view ahead of *Nelson's Tower* (or *Paxton's Tower*), a folly built in 1811 by Sir William Paxton as a memorial to Lord Nelson and now owned by the National Trust. Before reaching Nelson's Tower, B4297 is taken N., just across the river being the ruin of *Dryslwyn Castle,* an early Welsh stronghold known at one time to have been held by Rhys ap Gruffydd. The ruins are interesting for being to some extent the result of deliberate undermining by besiegers in the late 13C, an operation which apparently cost many of the sappers their lives. The return to Llandeilo may be made along A40, with, on the S. side before the turn to Llangathen, *Grongar Hill* (410 ft) with a hillfort. The charms of the hill, as also of Dryslwyn, were sung by the poet John Dyer (1700-58), who was born at nearby Aberglasney. In the church of *Llangathen* there is a monument to Bishop Rudd of St David's (d. 1615), who also lived at Aberglasney.

*Carreg Cennen Castle†, 4m. S.E. of Llandeilo, is strikingly placed on a precipitous limestone rock, rising 300 ft above the ravine of the Cennen. From the ruins, which are some distance above the car park, there is a view over much of the W. part of the Brecon Beacons National Park.

History. There was a fortress of some kind on this site in very early times, tradition ascribing one castle to Urien, a knight of the Round Table. The present castle, the name of its builder unknown, dates from the late 13 or early 14C. It was taken by the Lancastrians during the Wars of the Roses, but in 1462 was destroyed by William Herbert of Raglan because it had become a haunt of brigands.

The castle, without a keep, was quadrangular with inner and outer wards. The ruins are entered on the N. by a gatehouse with a portcullis at each end. The solid tower at the S.W. angle of the quadrangle is scarcely more than a buttress, and the S.E. corner, above the cliff, is unprotected. Strangely, the hall is placed on the N. and weakest sector of the curtain. The most remarkable feature of the ruins is the long dark passage (torch recommended) cut through the solid rock and lighted by loopholes, that leads from the S.E. corner to the so-called well, a cavity in the floor that may have served as a cistern but contains no spring.—About 1½ m. S.E. of the castle, the Loughor issues from a limestone cave, known as the *Llygad Llwchwr* (Eye of the Loughor).

From Llandeilo Swansea can be reached in 22 m. by a choice of roads which meet at Pontardulais.

Viâ Cross Hands. A476 and A48. There is an ascent over bleak moorland to (*8 m.*) **Cross Hands.** Two huge slagheaps here were levelled in the early 1970s to provide an area of playing fields and grazing land. *Cwmgwili Colliery,* 1 m. N.E., is a drift mine established in 1960 and *Cynheidre Colliery,* 3 m. S.W., is a complex dating from 1939 and now one of the area's major anthracite producers. A476 continues S. to Llanelli, but this Route bears S.E. on A48, descending the Gwili valley.—*6 m.* **Pontardulais,** where the Loughor is crossed just above the head of its winding estuary, is an industrial town just N. of the M4 motorway. In the 1840s Pontardulais was a centre of the Rebecca Riots. A road S. through Gorseinon and Gowerton offers an approach to the Gower Peninsula avoiding Swansea.—*8 m.* **Swansea,** see Rte 42.

Viâ Ammanford. A483 and A48. The valley of the Cennen is followed, then, before (*5 m.*) *Llandybie,* that of the Loughor.—*2 m.* **Ammanford** (6300 inhab.) is a busy valley town in the South Wales coalfield. *Betws Drift Colliery,* ¾ m. E., was started in 1974. Underground workers ride direct from the pithead to the coal face, and mined coal travels by conveyor direct into rail wagons.—*7 m.* **Pontardulais,** see above.—*8 m.* **Swansea,** see Rte 42.

30   RHAYADER TO NEW RADNOR AND LEOMINSTER

As far as Walton, 22 m. from Rhayader, Rtes 30A and 30B, across mixed moor, pasture, and woodland, are the same. At Walton there is a choice, both roads however running through a district noted for its attractive half-timbered houses. Pembridge and Eardisland on Rte 30A, the main road, are particularly picturesque. Rte 30B, following minor roads an average of 3 m. farther N., includes the site of the Battle of Mortimer's Cross and the N.T. property, Croft Castle.

A   Viâ Walton and Pembridge

A44. 38 miles.—*7 m.* **Cross Gates.**—*2 m. Penybont.*—*2 m. Llandegley.*—*4 m. Junction with A481.*—*4 m.* **New Radnor.**—*3 m. Walton* (**Old Radnor**).—*3 m.* **Kington.**—*6 m.* **Pembridge.**—*2 m.* **Eardisland.**—*5 m.* **Leominster.**

Rhayader, see p. 232. A44 ascends E., rounding the flank of *Gwastedyn Hill* (1566 ft).—*4 m.* From *Nantmel* a lane runs S.W. to (1½ m.) the pretty small *Llyn Gwyn.*—*3 m.* **Cross Gates** (see p. 237). where Rte 29 is met and followed for *2 m.* to *Penybont* (see p. 237).—*2 m. Llandegley,* where the church has a 15C rood screen, and a blocked priest's doorway with a curious seven-foiled head. The early 18C Friends' Meeting House (*The Pales*) is ½ m. north. For the next 8 m. the road loops around the S. of the moor and forest upland of Radnor Forest (for access see below).—*4m*. Junction with A481 to Builth Wells. To the N. at the junction *Tomen Cas* is a conspicuous tumulus.

To BUILTH WELLS. A481. 11 miles. The road almost immediately reaches its highest point (1243ft) above the little tarn of *Llyn Hili*, after this descending through open scenery into the upper valley of the Edw. This is crossed at *Hundred House Inn*, ½m. beyond being *Maud's Castle*, a motte and bailey, now a farm, mentioned in the first half of the 12C. The undulating road passes below (N.) *Caer Einon*, a hillfort on an 1100ft spur, and reaches the valley of the Wye. For *Aberedw*, 3m. S. on the E. bank of the Wye, see p. 255. At *Llanelwedd* Rte 28 is joined.

1m. Llanfihangel-nant-Melan, about 1m. beyond which (steep rise by a road bend) a motorable lane (N.W.), keeping right at a fork, leads in 1m. into woods in which a cascade, attractively named *Water-break-its-neck*, tumbles down a narrow ravine. A pleasant walk can be made around the top of the ravine, and a track and path cross Radnor Forest to respectively Llanfihangel Rhydithon and Bleddfa (8m.) on A488 (see p. 236).—*3m*. New Radnor, once the county town of Radnorshire, is now a large village, the most interesting feature of which is the large *Motte-and-Bailey* behind the church, all that is left of an 11C castle, destroyed by King John, rebuilt by Henry III, and finally destroyed by Owen Glendower in 1401. This was the starting point in 1188 of Archbishop Baldwin's tour through Wales with Giraldus to preach the Third Crusade. In the 13C the town was laid out in square blocks, but of this street plan virtually nothing now survives, although just outside the S.W. of the town something can be seen of the protective boundary earthwork.

New Radnor is the best starting point for walks across **Radnor Forest** to the north. A number of tracks and paths lead to *Llanfihangel Rhydithon* and *Bleddfa* (p. 236), and also to *Cascob* (p. 236). The highest point of the plateau (2166 ft), an almost level expanse of peat, offers a wide view, especially E. into England and S. to the Black Mountains.

3m. Walton, with the hamlet of **Old Radnor** (850ft) ½m. S. on the side of a hill. This was once a base of Harold Godwinson, notorious for being defeated and killed by William the Conqueror at Hastings in 1066. The small motte in a field some 300 yards S.E. of the church was the site of his castle, and must also have been the 'Cruker Castle' mentioned by Giraldus. The **Church*, though wholly English in style, is one of the finest parish churches in Wales. With its imposing W. tower, the church is a good example of late 14C work, though showing in the N. aisle and S. chapel traces of an earlier style. Inside there are several things of interest, these including the parclose screens N. and S. of the choir; the rood screen, still with the base of its loft; the ancient stalls and book-desks, one of the latter still with chain and clasp; the organ case of c. 1500, with linen-fold and Tudor roses; and the huge, rudely circular **Font*, among the largest in Britain, made from a glacial boulder which may have served as a prehistoric pagan ritual stone. The floor slab with a floreated cross at the entrance to the choir is 13C. In the N. chapel are, at the E. end, a late 15C St Catherine window, an Easter sepulchre built into the N. wall, and a huge medieval vestments chest.

At Walton Rte 30B (B4362) branches northeast. A 44 in 1m. passes below (N.) *Stanner Rocks* and enters England.—*3m*. **Kington** is a small market town on the Arrow, with some good Georgian houses. Mrs

Siddons, then aged about 17, made her debut in a barn here in 1772 or 73. The *Church* has an E.E. chancel and a Dec. nave and S. chapel, this last containing a fine 15 C alabaster tomb of the Vaughans of Hergest. Margaret Vaughan, who in 1632 founded the Grammar School (enlarged in 1860 and 1907), was widow of Sir John Hawkins, the Elizabethan adventurer. The collection (50 acres) of rhododendrons, azaleas, and other trees and shrubs at *Hergest Court Gardens*†, 1 m. W., is one of the best in Britain. *Bradnor Hill*, ½ m. N.W., owned by the National Trust, is common land with a golf course. The golf course, occupying the summit (1284 ft), is the highest in Britain.—*2 m.* **Lyonshall** has a motte with some castle ruin, and a church with a Norman tower.

4 m. **Pembridge** is a town noted for its many old half-timbered houses, and its rustic Tudor Market Hall, originally with an upper storey. The *Church* was built between 1320-60, this rather long period being due to the ravages of the Black Death. It is successor to a 12C church, sections of the arches of which can be seen in the N. and S. walls of the choir. Worth noting are the N. door with its sanctuary knocker; the medieval glass in the window at the W. end of the S. aisle; the Jacobean altar rails, pulpit, and lectern; and the brass candelabra (1722) above the crossing. On the 14C detached **Belfry* the carving on the stone entrance jambs may be from the earlier church, and the holes in the door are said to be shot holes, perhaps from the time of the Civil War. Inside are magnificent beams, and a clock of 1889, the works of which can be clearly seen.

Weobley, 5 m. S., is a notable half-timbered village. The church contains a memorial to Colonel John Birch, Cromwell's commander who besieged Hereford and was later a signatory of the King's death warrant.

2 m. **Eardisland**, on the Arrow, is a village with several half-timbered houses, an outstanding example being the 14C *Staick House*. The *Church* (restored 1864) is basically 14C, though part of the nave is 12C. Note the 14C glass (E. window); the unusual stepped sedilia (13C); and, on the external S. wall of the choir, a curious recess which may have been an anchorite's cell. There is a small motte or tumulus immediately N. of the church. *Burton Court*†, 1 m. S., has a 14C hall, but otherwise is late 18C. The front of the house was redesigned in 1912 by Clough Williams-Ellis. The house contains an exhibition of European and Oriental costumes.—*5 m.* **Leominster**, see p. 254.

B   Viâ Walton, Presteigne, and Croft Castle

A44 to Walton: B4362 to beyond Croft Castle: B4361 to Leominster. 44 miles.—*22 m. Walton.—6 m.* **Presteigne.**—*6 m. Shobdon.—2 m.* **Mortimer's Cross.**—*2 m.* **Croft Castle.**—*6 m.* **Leominster.**

To (*22 m.*) *Walton*, see Rte 30A. B4362 runs N.E., passing below (N.) the hillfort of *Burfa,* briefly entering England, and in *6 m.* reaching **Presteigne** (1300 inhab.), an attractive old town with half-timbered houses. The Lugg, which skirts the N. edge of the town, is here the border. John Bradshaw (1602-59), the regicide, was born here and is said to have lived in the Radnorshire Arms, a half-timbered house of 1616. The Lugg bridge dates from the 17C. The *Church* is 14-16C, but has earlier fragments; a jamb and segment of choir arch (E. end of N. aisle) are pre-Norman, and there are two early Norman window fragments in the N. wall. Also noteworthy are a mosaic of old glass (S. chapel); a late 13C sepulchral slab (N. aisle); and an early 16C Flemish tapestry representing the Entry into Jerusalem. The low hill W. of the town, known as *The Warden*, now a public park, is the site of the Norman castle destroyed by Llewelyn the Last in 1261. At *Norton*, 2 m. N., the church has a bell-turret supported on timber framing, and a tree stump by the churchyard entrance stills bears manacles suggesting its use as a whipping post.

B4362 runs E. through a short tongue of Wales, in 2 m. entering England below (S.) isolated *Wapley Hill* (1000 ft), on which is an oval hillfort with at one point five lines of defence works.—*6 m.* (from Presteigne) *Shobdon*. Opposite the Bateman Arms a driveway leads in ½ m. to a Gothick church of 1755; the choir arch and other remains of the predecessor church, with some excellent Norman sculpture, have been erected on the hill to the north. To the S. of Shobdon is an airfield (gliding and parachuting).

2 m. **Mortimer's Cross**, site of the battle fought on 2 Feb. 1461, in which Edward, Duke of York, defeated the Lancastrian Earl of Pembroke, soon afterwards deposing Henry VI and becoming Edward IV. This was the first battle of the Wars of the Roses to be followed by the massacre of the common people and the beheading of the captured gentlemen; amongst the latter was Owen Tudor, grandfather of Henry VII, who was taken to Hereford and there executed. Of the actual battle little is known, other than that some meteorological quirk caused a triple sun to appear and that, after the victory, Edward incorporated the sun in his banner.

At *Aymestrey*, 1 m. N., the church has a 16C rood screen. *Wigmore*, 3 m. farther N., once boasted a castle and an abbey. What little is left of the castle, Edward's base before Mortimer's Cross, a Mortimer stronghold and later owned by Robert Harley, Earl of Oxford, is just north. The abbey remains are now part of farm buildings near *Adforton*, another mile north. The ruined castle at *Brampton Bryan*, 3 m. N.W. of Adforton, was from the 13C the property of the Harleys (see also Berrington Hall, p. 252). The church at *Aston,* 4 m. E. of Adforton, has a good Norman door. *Leintwardine*, 2 m. N. of Adforton, is the site of the Roman Bravonium, a station on Watling Street, In the church are 15C stalls, and the tomb of General Tarleton (1754-1833), who served in the American War of Independence.—A4110, S. from Mortimer's Cross, in part coincides with Watling Street.

1 m. **Lucton School** is a Queen Anne building of 1708.

1 m. ***Croft Castle**† (N.T.), ancient seat of the Croft family and still lived in by them, is basically of the 14-15C (outer walls and towers), modified in the 16 and 17C and given a new internal structure in the mid 18C. The grounds are noted for their magnificent trees, and the castle interior for its generally Georgian decoration.

History. There was a fortification here as long ago as the 4C B.C., the earliest date ascribed to Croft Ambrey, the hillfort on the ridge 1 m. N.W. of the present castle. The first recorded Croft was Bernard de Croft, mentioned in Domesday Book, and the present stone castle, possibly successor to an earlier structure, was built in the 14-15C. Sir James (d. 1590) was Comptroller of the Household to Elizabeth I; it may have been he who planted some of the avenues and who rebuilt the N. face of the castle. The Crofts supported the King during the Civil War, Sir William being killed at Stokesay in 1645. Another well-known Croft was Hubert, Bishop of Hereford, who in a bold sermon so upbraided Cromwell's soldiers that they came close to shooting him (see p. 275). In 1746, because of debts, the castle was sold to an ironmaster, Richard Knight, whose daughter Elizabeth married Thomas

Johnes, father of the builder of Hafod Uchtryd (see p. 235). It was the elder Thomas Johnes who put in hand the rebuilding in 1765, much of the work being by Thomas Pritchard (1723-77), this being known from the discovery in 1964 at the American Institute of Architects, Washington, of Pritchard's record book containing drawings for Croft Castle. The younger Thomas Johnes, heavily committed to his schemes at Hafod, in 1785 sold Croft to Somerset Davies of nearby Wigmore, from which family the Crofts re-purchased the property in 1923. The National Trust took over the freehold in 1957, but members of the family continue to live in the castle, most of the contents of which remain Croft property.

EXTERIOR. The approach is by oak and beech avenues ending at a late 18C wall. The castle is roughly square in shape, the walls and towers, though in part rebuilt, generally representing original structure. The N. front is the least altered. The towers, all except the N.W. with rebuilt tops, have 16C windows. The central part of the E. front is 18C, except for the battlemented porch which is an addition of 1913.

INTERIOR. The *Hall*, a courtyard until the mid 18C, has 17C panelling, presumably taken from elsewhere in the castle. Among the subjects of the portraits are Elizabeth I; Sir James Croft, Comptroller of the Queen's Household; and the Earl of Leicester. The furniture is largely 17C. The *Gallery*, also mid 18C, contains portraits, including Bishop Croft (by P. Gent) and the Man of Ross (see p. 290) by Josef van Aken. Also a portrait by Lemuel Abbott of the 5th Baronet (Herbert Croft, 1751-1816), known as the 'Dictionary Maker', a literary figure who produced a revised edition (which never got beyond manuscript stage) of Doctor Johnson's 'Dictionary', and in 1780 published a work with the intriguing title 'Love and Madness, a Story too true, in a series of letters between Parties whose names could perhaps be mentioned were they less known or less lamented'; in this Croft included material from hitherto unpublished letters of the poet Chatterton. In the *Courtyard* there is an early 19C fire engine. The *Gothick Staircase* is noted for its plasterwork (restored 1974), ascribed to Thomas Pritchard. In the *Dining Room* the 'Georgian' decoration of 1913 incorporates some mid 18C work. The Venetian window is ascribed to Pritchard. Among the portraits are the Children of Sir Richard Croft, attributed to Sir W. Beechey; Sir Richard Croft by J. J. Halls; and the 1st Lord Croft and Lady Croft by Phillip de Lazlo. In the *Oak Room*, S. of the Gothick staircase, the panelling was painted white at the same time that Pritchard made his ceiling. The *Blue Room* is so called because the Jacobean panelling was probably originally painted blue; note the trompe l'oeil effect of the gilded rosettes. The ceiling is mid 18C. The Rococo chimneypiece and overmantel, originally in the Oak Room, frames a portrait (1760s) by Gainsborough of Elizabeth Cowper (d. 1805), wife of the 3rd Baronet. There is also a portrait of the actress Peg Woffington by H. R. Morland. The furniture is William and Mary (walnut), Queen Anne (knee-hole side table), and early Georgian (five chairs). In the *Drawing Room* the painted panelling is early Georgian and the ceiling 18C. Among the painting are an Italian landscape by J. F. van Bloemen (1662-?1740); Leda and the Swan, and Cupid and Psyche, by Jacopo Amigoni (1675-1752); and Judgement of Midas, and the Triumph of Galatea, both attributed to G. Chiari. The *Library* includes a copy of Dr Johnson's 'Dictionary', annotated by Herbert Croft; books and tracts published by Bishop Croft; and books written by the younger Thomas Johnes and printed at Hafod. A possibly unique piece of furniture is the combined writing table and filing cabinet designed for Herbert Croft. In the *Ante-Room* the Rococo chimney-frame, originally in the N.W. tower, is the work, to Pritchard's design, of Nelson and Van Hagen of Shrewsbury; according to Pritchard's record book the former worked on the frame for four weeks and three days and the latter for eight days and nine hours. Also in this room are portraits by Thomas Lawrence of Herman Wolff (drawing) and Mrs Wolff, and a miniature self-portrait; and three pictures of Elizabeth Croft (a close friend of Lawrence), one as a girl in the 1780s, a later portrait with her cousin by J. Slater, and one of her as an old lady by William Beetham. On the *East Staircase* are aquatints of Hafod by J. 'Warwick' Smith (1792). In the *Gothick Bay Room* hang pictures of Herefordshire, and of Croft Castle in 1792 and 1840. Also shown here are some finds from Croft Ambrey hillfort.

THE GROUNDS represent a late 18C preference for the natural, as opposed to the more formal style of 'Capability' Brown; the steep Fish Pool Valley (N. of the entrance drive) is typical of the new thinking. The Oak Avenue, with some trees of great girth, and the Beech Avenue have already been mentioned. The Spanish Chestnut Avenue, a ½ m. long row running W. from the castle, may date back to the early 17C. The nearby Lime Avenue is a 1970s replacement of an avenue which was referred to in 1792.—*St Michael's Church*, immediately E. of the castle, is of the 14-15C, enlarged in 1515. It contains the elaborate altar-tomb of Sir Richard Croft (d. 1509) and his wife (d. 1520); the latter was governess to the sons of Edward IV at Ludlow. The tomb was probably originally in a chapel (demolished early 18C) on the N. of the castle. Also worth noting are some early stained glass, and a boarded vault (17-18C), with clouds and stars.—A path (1 m.) leads N.W. across park and through woods to the hillfort of *Croft Ambrey* at 1000 ft. Occupied from the 4C B.C. until the arrival of the Romans, the fort covers some 38 acres and comprises a main enclosure (the original fort) with a later outer enclosure on its south. The N. side is above a steep drop, but the other sides are protected by banks and ditches.

Beyond Croft Castle B4362 in *2 m.* joins B4361, which leads S. to (*4 m.*) **Leominster**, see p. 254.

31   SHREWSBURY TO HEREFORD

A49. 54 miles—*4 m.* Condover.—*4 m.* **Acton Burnell.**—*7 m.* Church Stretton.—*3 m.* Acton Scott Farm Museum.—*5 m.* Craven Arms.—*8 m.* Ludlow.—*8 m.* **Berrington Hall.**—*3 m.* **Leominster.**—*4 m.* Hope-under-Dinmore.—*8 m.* Hereford.

Shrewsbury, see Rte 21, is left by English Bridge, immediately across which A49 bears south.—*2 m. Bayston Hill*, ½ m. S.E. of which is *Bomere Pool*, the 'Sarn Mere' of Mary Webb's 'Precious Bane'. Beyond Bayston Hill, for 10 m. as far as Church Stretton, there are more places of interest a short way to the E. than actually along A49. The first is (*2 m.*) *Condover*, where the church has a late Norman N. transept and a 17C nave formed by combining the early nave and N. aisle into one after the fall of the central tower in 1660. *Condover Hall†*, an imposing mansion of 1598, is a school for handicapped children. The interior has a fine contemporary fireplace and panelling. Approaching *Pitchford* (2½ m. S.E.) the road rounds Pitchford Hall (no adm., but visible), a beautiful half-timbered house of 1473. In the village church there is a wooden effigy of a knight (c. 1250).

4 m. **Acton Burnell.** In the beautiful E.E. *Church* (early 13C, restored by Robert Burnell, see below) there are three monuments of interest, all in the N. transept. The *Brass of Sir Nicholas Burnell (1382) is considered to be one of the finest in England. The other two monuments are of Sir Richard Lee (d. 1591) and Sir Humphrey Lee (d. 1632), ancestors of Richard Henry Lee, a signatory of the American Declaration of Independence, and of General Robert E. Lee the Confederate commander. The monuments (that of Sir Humphrey by Nicholas Stone, master mason to Charles I) are intriguing for the small figures of all the children, Sir Humphrey having five daughters and one son, and Sir Richard three sons and a formidable row of nine daughters. The small hole in the N. wall of the choir may have been the inner window of an anchorite's cell, the possible remains of which can be seen against the external wall.

Acton Burnell Castle, adjacent to the church, is a ruined late 13C fortified manor house.

History. Acton appears in Domesday Book as a manor belonging to Roger FitzCorbet, and in another record of a century later as belonging to William Burnell. In 1249 another William Burnell was outlawed for murder and the estate reverted to the Corbets. By about 1266, however, the estate was owned by Robert Burnell, powerful favourite of Edward I who in 1274 became Chancellor of England and Bishop of Bath and Wells. In 1283 he here entertained Edward I in a timber house which, the following year, was superseded by his new stone mansion; it was on this occasion that Edward enacted a statute safeguarding the rights of merchants. Burnell was created a baron, but the direct line died out in 1420, after which his mansion seems no longer to have been used as a residence. Much later, probably in the 18C, the place became part of a large barn.

The ruins are interesting for being almost entirely of their original date and free of significant alteration so long as the house was occupied. The place was clearly too small for the large staff that would have surrounded a man of Burnell's lay and Church importance, and it can be presumed that there were extensive outbuildings. The site comprises a rectangular main block, a narrow W. extension, and four rectangular corner towers. In the main block the ground floor seems to have had four rooms, that on the S.E., entered through the S.E. tower, probably being for Burnell's lay officers. The important rooms were on the upper floor, these being the *Hall,* which occupied the three E. bays, and the *Great Chamber* within the W. bay. From this latter a stair in the S.W. tower led to the *Private Apartments,* these including a living room above the great chamber, a bedroom in the W. block, and a garderobe in the N.W. tower. The small octagonal room on the groud floor of the S.W. tower was probably a strongroom. The N.E. tower, originally about twice its present size, housed the chapel.

Langley Chapel†, 1½ m. of S. of Acton Burnell, was built by Robert Burnell and restored in 1601.

From Acton Burnell the line of the Roman Watling Street is followed S.W., meeting A49 and in *7m.* (from Acton Burnell) reaching **Church Stretton** (3300 inhab.), at 650 ft and lying below higher ground on both sides. *Long Mynd* to the W. is a moorland ridge stretching some 7 m. from N. to S., the greater part of which (4530 acres) was acquired by the National Trust in 1965 with money raised by public subscription. The highest point is 1700 ft, and within the area there are some 15 prehistoric barrows, many of these being either side of the Port Way, running the length of the ridge, an ancient road used by prehistoric axe traders, later a section of the drovers' road from Montgomery to Shrewsbury, and today still is use and serving as parish boundary. *Caer Caradoc,* 1½ m.

N.E. of Church Stretton, is one of the many Welsh and borders hillforts traditionally associated with Caractacus, whose name has been given to a local cave.

3 m. The *Acton Scott Working Farm Museum*† is to the E. of A49. Covering some 22 acres, the museum demonstrates life on a Shropshire upland farm as it was in the days before the internal combustion engine. Local craft material and local produce can be bought, and there is a programme of demonstrations of traditional occupations, these including spinning, leather work, wood turning, lace making, corn dollies, beekeeping, and textile design. There is also sometimes Morris dancing.—*5 m.* **Craven Arms,** a village named after a coaching inn, is now a railway junction for the lines to central Wales and Swansea.

*Stokesay Castle†, just S. of Craven Arms, is the oldest and probably the finest example in England of a moated fortified manor house (13-14C).

History. The original name of this place was simply Stoke (Dairy Farm), this becoming Stokesay in the early 12C when the first owners, the Lacy family, passed the property to the Say family which had originally come from Sai in Normandy. The Says built the lower storeys of the N. tower (c. 1240), only a few years before selling the estate to a wool merchant, Lawrence of Ludlow, who c. 1281 set about building the rest of the mansion which was completed by 1305, nine years after his death. In the Civil War, Stokesay, now owned by the Royalist Lord Craven, surrendered to Parliament in 1645. From 1648 on, the castle was leased and sub-leased until by the mid 19C it was in derelict condition. In 1869 the castle was bought by Mr J. D. Allcroft, who undertook much restoration work and whose descendants are still the owners, although the castle itself is not inhabited.

Across the moat, dry since the 18C, the entrance is through a beautiful, half-timbered **Gatehouse,* probably early 17C and successor to a stone building. The wood carving is noteworthy. The *Courtyard,* now a clear space, would formerly have been cluttered with buildings, one of which, the kitchen, was in the N.W. corner. The well is in the courtyard, and beyond, at the S.E. of the S. tower, can be seen a piece of the original late 13C curtain wall. Apart from the earlier lower storeys of the N. tower, the whole range of buildings along the W. side of the courtyard was put up between 1285 and 1305. The *North Tower* carries attractive projecting timber work, most of which is contemporary with the main structure. In the basement, probably a store, can be seen the now blocked door which led to the kitchens. In a room on the first floor are medieval tiles from the church, and in the second floor room there is a fine original fireplace. The *Hall* has a particularly pleasing timber ceiling. Although opinion differs as to its age, many of the timbers are probably original. The hearth is 13C, as are also the windows with their seats. The *Solar* is on the first floor, above an undercroft and cellar, parts of the walls of which may be the oldest structure of the castle (perhaps 1200). The stone stairway up to the solar is successor to a timber one. Noteworthy are the peepholes into the hall; the ancient stone fireplace; and the carved Flemish overmantel and the panelling, both of the 17C. The so-called *Passage Block* is in fact two rooms; that on the ground floor, reached from the undercroft, is original, but the upper room is a 17C addition. The original entrance to the *South Tower* would have been by drawbridge from the solar entrance to the door on the first floor. Within the walls are garderobes, and a stair which leads to the roof, a flat lead 19C replacement of an earlier tiled arrangement.

Stokesay Church was founded in the 12C as chapel to the castle, but of this early church only parts survive in the doorway, tower, and choir. The church suffered badly in the Civil War, when Royalists took refuge in it, and was largely rebuilt in 1654. Inside are some primitive pews (below the gallery), with rests to keep feet clear of the rubble floor; and 17C box-pews, pulpit (a despoiled three-decker), and murals.

At *(5 m.) Bromfield* there are some remains of a priory, including the 12C gatehouse, with a wooden upper storey, and the nave of the church, now incorporated in the parish church. The choir ceiling, with heraldic painting, is 17C.

3 m. **Ludlow** (7500 inhab.), on a hill above the junction of the Teme and the Corve, is an interesting and attractive old town with a castle, several half-timbered houses, and some narrow alleys.

Tourist Information. 12 Brand Lane (between Broad Street and Old Street).
Parking. Castle Square. Broad Street. Mill Street.
Post Office. Corve Street.
Early Closing. Thursday.
History. Prehistoric and Roman routes traversed the site of the town, this line still being followed by today's Corve and Old streets, and there may well have been an ancient settlement here, possibly near today's Dinham bridge. At the Conquest William I gave this district to Walter de Lacy (hence Stanton Lacy 3 m. N.), and it was his son Roger who in 1086 began to build the castle, around which in c. 1130 the town was founded, built to a squared pattern still apparent today. By the 14C Ludlow was a prosperous wool centre, complete with walls and seven gates. The De Lacy line died out in 1307, and Ludlow passed in turn to the Mortimers and the Plantagenets. During the Wars of the Roses Ludlow was staunchly Yorkist and, though sacked in 1459, was rewarded on Edward IV's accession two years later with a charter. Ludlow Castle now belonged to the Crown and was much used by Royalty. The 'Princes in the Tower' lived here; Arthur, elder son of Henry VII, was here briefly with his bride Catherine of Aragon, dying within months of his arrival; and Mary Tudor lived here. Perhaps 1475 was Ludlow's most important date, the year in which it was chosen as the seat of the Council of the Marches, a position which ensured the continuance of prosperity, despite the now declining wool trade. One President of the Council was Sir Henry Sidney (from 1559-86), and his better known son Sir Philip spent his youth here. But prosperity did not long survive the Civil War (in which Ludlow was the last Royalist town in Shropshire to fall) and the abolition of the Council of the Marches in 1689. Abandoned, the castle became a ruin. There was a revival between the mid 18 and mid 19C when Ludlow became a commercial centre for glove making and a social centre for the surrounding nobility and gentry, many of whom built town houses for the season. With the arrival of the railway in 1851, however, society moved farther afield, and Ludlow declined until the 20C brought light industry and tourism.

Entering the town from the N. by Corve Street, the *Feathers Hotel* stands at the top on the left. It is a magnificent half-timbered hotel (built as such in 1521) and contains early Jacobean carving of 1606. The *Butter Cross* (1746) is at the town centre; the upper room was once used as a Blue Coat Charity School. At the rear of the building, in Church Street, is the *Museum†*, covering local history, geology, and zoology. The museum includes (in Old Street) the County Natural Science reference collections, the collection of over 30,000 fossils being especially noteworthy.

To the N. is the large *Church of St Lawrence,* with a tower 130 ft high. Of many periods, the church is mainly early 15C, though on the S. side some fragments may date back to 1199. There was a major restoration in 1952-59. The ashes of A. E. Housman (1859-1936), the poet and scholar, best known for 'A Shropshire Lad', lie in the churchyard (plaque on church exterior N. wall). The church is entered through an early 14C hexagonal porch, unique except for one at St Mary Redcliffe, Bristol. Noteworthy in the interior are the E. window, with 15C glass (re-arranged 19C) depicting the story of the martyred St Lawrence; the organ of 1764 by John Snetzler; in the chancel, the reredos, screens, and misericords, much of the carving being 14 and 15C; the monuments to Marcher officials and lords; and the tomb of Ambrosia (d. 1574, aged 19), sister of Sir Philip Sidney. The Lady Chapel contains a 14C Jesse window; interesting 17 and 18C benefaction boards; and, a reminder that in the 17C it served as fire station, the pegs on which hung the leather buckets and the niche through which the engine emerged. In the N.W. corner of the church there are two tombs, one of which, with a Tudor Rose, is traditionally where the heart of Prince Arthur was buried.

Opposite the E. end of the church stands the picturesque *Reader's House,* (open in summer, apply at church), a half-timbered Tudor building with a Jacobean porch, incorporating some fragments of a much older stone 'church house', acquired in the 14 or 15C by the ancient Palmers' Guild. In the 18C it was the residence of the reader, an assistant to the parish rector.

From Butter Cross High Street leads W., passing the market erected to commemorate Queen Victoria's Diamond Jubilee, to Castle Square, in which is the Tudor *Castle Lodge,* a 14C stone house, with 16C timberwork, once the official residence of the honorary 'Porter' of the castle. The *Town Hall,* occupying the centre of the square, dates from 1887.

The ruined **Ludlow Castle**† was begun by Roger de Lacy in 1086 and received additions down to 1581. The general plan is a large outer ward to the E., with a smaller inner ward at the N.W. corner. For the history of the castle, see that of the town.—The entrance is through the late 12C *Gatehouse,* over which were the rooms in which Samuel Butler, then steward to the Earl of Carbery, wrote a great part of 'Hudibras' (1661-62). On the left are battlemented ruins (Tudor period), once serving as stables and barracks. On the far W. side of the outer ward is the late 13C tower known as *Mortimer's Tower* and traditionally the site of the prison (1189) of Hugh de Mortimer, an opponent of Henry II; to obtain his release, he not only had to pay a large sum, but also hand over all his plate, horses, and hawks. In fact this tower was a postern giving access to Dinham bridge. To the right of the tower the *Inner Moat,* which was always dry and which was the source for much of the stone for the earlier castle, was crossed by a drawbridge. It is now crossed by a stone bridge.

The INNER WARD is entered by a *Gateway* (1581), built by Sir Henry Sidney and bearing his arms and those of Elizabeth I. On the right are the *Judges' Lodgings,* also built by Sir Henry. On the left is the Norman *Keep* (late 12C), the oldest part of the castle, with a stairway leading to the top (110 ft). Originally the keep was larger, but its N. part was demolished in the 15C. In the ward stands the exquisite late Norman (c. 1120, but much altered) **Round Chapel,* one of the first such built in Britain under the influence of the Knights Templar; the decoration of the W. door, chancel arch, and wall arcade should be noted. On the chapel's E. side the foundations of the chancel and apse have been exposed. To the N. of the chapel is a range of 13-14C buildings, of some historical interest, built by the Mortimers as a fortified palace. *Pendower Tower,* at the E. end, was where the little Prince Edward and his brother were held for nearly ten years until 1483 when Edward became Edward V and the pair were removed to London and murdered. Immediately W. are the *Armoury;* a state apartment of unknown purpose; and then (running E.-W.) the *Great Hall*. Today's visitor stands in the cellars, above which would have been the main floor; here Milton's masque of 'Comus' was presented in 1634 before the Earl of Bridgewater, President of the Council of the Marches, the Earl's youngest three children playing some of the roles. The W. rooms (*Prince Arthur's Apartments*) were those occupied by Prince Arthur with Catherine of Aragon (1501-02); they were married in Oct. 1501, when Arthur was 14 and Catherine 16, and Arthur died in Spring 1502. Between Prince Arthur's Apartments and the keep lie the site of the Tudor *Bakery*, with, at its W. corner, a square Norman tower and the well; and, at the S.W. corner of the inner curtain, another square Norman tower, the lower storey of which has been converted into a large oven.

From Butter Cross, Broad Street, with some of the most attractive old houses in Ludlow, descends S. through *Broad Gate*, the only survivor (much restored) of the original seven gates. At the foot of Lower Broad Street, a furniture factory occupies the site of the town's old fulling mill, while, opposite, a garage occupies that of the Hospital of St. John. *Ludford Bridge* dates from the 15C.—Mill Street, to the W. parallel to Broad Street, has several Georgian houses. The *Guildhall*, on the W., is in origin 15C but was rebuilt with a new frontage in 1768. The *Grammar School*, on the opposite side of the road farther down, includes a 14C house which has been used as the school hall since 1527. From Lower Mill Street can be seen a stretch of the town wall.

Across the river a pleasant road W. ascends to (½ m.) *Whitcliffe*, a bluff which commands a splendid view of the town and castle, with the Clee Hills beyond. The small *Mortimer Forest Museum*† here illustrates aspects of forest activity and includes a Deer Room, with skins and antlers. There is a 1 m. long Nature Trail.

A49 crosses Ludford Bridge and continues S., in 1½ m. reaching a junction with B4361 offering an alternative approach to Leominster (1 m. longer). Along this latter road *Richard's Castle*, reached in 2½ m., has (1 m. N.W.) a possibly pre-Conquest but Norman-style motte-and-bailey, and a Norman and 14C church with a detached tower. Farther S. (2½ m.) B4362 leads W. for *Croft Castle* and *Mortimer's Cross* (see p. 245).

8 m. (from Ludlow) **Berrington Hall**† is a mansion of 1778-81, built by the younger Henry Holland (also responsible for Claremont, near Esher, Brook's Club, Carlton House, parts of Sloane Street and other development in London). The grounds, which include an artificial lake and island, were landscaped by 'Capability' Brown, whose daughter was married to Holland. The mansion is notable for its fine marble and plasterwork.

History. The earliest recorded owners of the estate were the Cornewall family, who later moved to Moccas, their manor probably being on a site (where there are traces of foundations) about 1000 yards N.E. of the present mansion. In about 1775 the estate was bought by Robert Harley, whose family had held the castle at Brampton Bryan since the 13C. On Harley's death in 1804 the estate passed through his daughter Anne to the lords Rodney (Anne married the son and heir of Admiral Lord Rodney), in whose hands it remained until sold in 1900 to Mr Frederick (later Lord) Crawley. In 1957 the Treasury, to whom the mansion and park had been surrendered in payment of estate duty resulting from the death of the 2nd Lord Crawley, transferred the property to the National Trust. The greater part of the pictures and furnishings remain the property of the family.

In the *Marble Hall* the floor is of mixed marble, and the ceiling is typical of Holland's simplified design. The wool tapestry panels (Aubusson-Felletin, c.1901) are part of a series in the house adapted from the paintings of Nicholas Lancret (1690-1743). The *Drawing Room* contains the best and most elaborate of the house's ceilings. Its central medallion is a composite scene taken from the ceiling of the Villa Farnesina in Rome and is believed, with the minor roundels, to be the work of Biagio Rebecca (1735-1806), a decorative artist who is known to have designed panels for Holland's alterations to the Brighton Pavilion. The chimneypiece, with caryatids, is of Carrara marble and encloses a contemporary steel grate, notable for the row along the front of Wedgwood cameos of Roman emperors. The small rectangular *Boudoir* has a barrel ceiling of simple pattern. The columns are of scagliola (plaster composition). The *Business Room* has undergone alteration, both soon after completion and again more recently, and has lost a door which was on the right of the fireplace. Redecoration in 1975 repeated after much careful study the original colour scheme. The ceiling female figures representing the seasons are the work of Biagio Rebecca. The house contains four pictures (three by Thomas Luny, 1759-1837), showing the exploits of Admiral Rodney, the picture in this room (by Luny) being of the 'Formidable' at the battle off Dominica in April 1782, when Rodney defeated the Comte de Grasse (it was Rodney's last battle, and the one which earned him his barony). The *Back Hall,* with a portrait of Thomas Harley, leads to the *Staircase Hall,* lit by a beautiful glass dome. Here are two more wool tapestry panels (see Marble Hall). The pillars are of scagliola. The *Dining Room* contains a fine chimneypiece, which once had a central plaque made, very unusually, of silver; it was sold by the last Lord Rodney to live here. In this room are the remaining three naval battle pictures. Two, by Thomas Luny, depict the destruction of the Spanish flagship off Cape St Vincent (Jan., 1780), and Rodney's flagship 'Sandwich' being attacked by the French off Martinique (April, 1780). The third picture shows the surrender of the French flagship (a present to Louis XVI by the city of Paris) at the Dominica battle of April 1782 (see Business Room). The decoration in the *Library* is particularly delicate. At the corners the grisaille panel paintings of the Muses are attributed to Biagio Rebecca, as are also the rectangular panels in the frieze and the panel over the white marble chimneypiece. The ceiling medallions, also attributed to Rebecca, are of English men of letters (clockwise from the fireplace—Prior, Milton, Pope, Shakespeare, Chaucer, Newton, Bacon, Addison). The Axminster carpet (early 19C) was probably woven specially for this room.—Around the *Courtyard* are the 19C Laundry, the Dairy, Servants' Hall, and Stables.

Eye Manor†, 1 m. W. of Berrington Hall, was built in 1680 for Ferdinando Gorges, a West Indian trader in slaves and sugar. The house has notable late 17C plaster ceilings, and also exhibitions of period costumes, dolls, needlework, and books produced by the private Golden Cockerell press. In the adjacent church, with a 13C porch, there are two 16C alabaster monuments to the Cornewall family, once owners of Berrington and Moccas.

Approaching Leominster on A49, *Eaton Hall* (no adm.) is to the S. about 1 m. short of the town. A moated house (14C), now a farm, this was long the home of the Hakluyt family. A Hakelute was M.P. for the local borough as long ago as 1304, and Richard Hakluyt (c. 1553-1616), the geographer, although not born here was a member of the family.

3m. (from Berrington Hall) **Leominster** (pron. 'Lemster'; 7250 inhab.), on the Lugg, is a market town and centre for light industry. There are a number of attractive Georgian and older houses, and a large and interesting church.

Town Centre. Corn Square and High Street.
Parking. Corn Square.
Post Office. Corn Square.
Market. Friday. First Monday in month.
Early Closing. Thursday.
History. The town originated in a priory founded in 660 by Merewald, King of Mercia, a Northumbrian missionary, Ealfred being the first abbot. One tradition tells that, when at court, Ealfred offered bread to a ravening lion which, however, accepted the bread meekly. This was taken to mean that the fierce pagans would in the same way accept Christianity, and hence the founding of the priory and the town's name, Leonis Monasterium. However Leofric of Mercia later endowed a nunnery here, and it is as Leofminstre that the place is recorded in Domesday Book. In the 12C the original priory was succeeded by a Benedictine priory, sister to that at Reading, and it was from about this period that the town started to grow. In 1207 both town and priory were plundered by William de Braose, a Marcher baron, and Leominster suffered again in 1402 when taken by Owen Glendower, who here imprisoned Mortimer whom he had taken at Pilleth. As early as the 13C Leominster had been known for the quality of its wool (known as Lemster Ore), and this trade was at its most prosperous between the 17-early 19C.

The *Priory Church,* of SS Peter and Paul, illustrates every style from Norman to Perpendicular. The original Norman structure was extended and rebuilt in the 13 and 14C. When the priory was suppressed in 1539 the whole E. end and the central tower were demolished, but the local people built a wall across the naves and preserved the remainder as parish church. Almost totally destroyed by fire in 1699, the church was partially rebuilt by 1705 and completed in the late 19C by Sir Gilbert Scott. There was further restoration in 1921-23 and 1948-50.—The Norman parts of the church are the nave on the N., with unusual arcading to its N. aisle, and the fine W. doorway, which should be seen from outside. Also, the wall at the W. end of the main nave is the original wall of the S. aisle of the Norman church; on the floor, immediately below this wall, are some 14C tiles. The main nave, added in 1239 as parish church, has a beautiful Perp. window, 45 ft high. The S. aisle was built c. 1340 and has ballflower ornamentation, a style which also appears on the exterior of the church. The tower is of three periods, 12 and 15C, when the Perp. arches were inserted, but the battlements and pinnacles are 19C. In the chapel at the E. end of the S. aisle are a beautifully displayed pre-Reformation silver chalice, an old Leominster seal, and a piscina of c. 1239 surrounded by three expressive heads. A curiosity housed by the church is the long ducking stool, used for the last time in 1809, for the disciplining of scolds, tradesmen giving short measure etc. *Priory House,* now part of an old people's home, was part of the domestic buildings, and the *Forbury Chapel* (13C) was also part of the priory.

Of the town's several old houses the best is the lovely half-timbered *Grange Court,* now in a public park just S. of the church. It was built in 1633, by John Abel the 'King's Carpenter', at the junction of High Street and Broad Street, where it served as civic centre until 1853 when a new town hall was put up. Sold by auction, it was demolished and lay in pieces in a builder's yard until bought a few years later by a Mr. Arkwright who re-erected it on its present site. It served as a private house until 1939 when it became municipal offices. The *Leominster Museum†* in Etnam Street just S. of Corn Square, is a folk museum with material of both general and local interest.

For Leominster to *Eardisland, Pembridge, Croft Castle, Mortimer's Cross, Presteigne, Walton (Old Radnor), New Radnor,* and *Rhayader,* see Rtes 30A and 30B.

4m. **Hope-under-Dinmore,** a short way E. of which is *Hampton Court* (no adm.), a castellated mansion built by Sir Rowland Lenthall with the ransom of prisoners taken at Agincourt in 1415.—*2m. Dinmore Manor†* is to the W. of the road beyond wooded Dinmore Hill. Visitors are admitted to the 12-14C Chapel of the Knights Hospitaller, the Cloisters, Music Room, and Gardens.—*5m. Holmer,* where the church has a detached half-timbered belfry.—*1m.* **Hereford,** see Rte 36.

32 BUILTH WELLS TO ABERGAVENNY

The alternative Routes described run roughly parallel and up to 8 m. apart, meeting at Tretower, with its medieval manor and ruined Norman castle, 7 m. N. of Abergavenny. Rte 32A is for its first 13 miles scenically the more attractive, descending a particulary lovely stretch of the Wye. Rte 32B, on the other hand, includes the interesting cathedral town of Brecon, with access to some beautiful country to its south. The best of both Routes will be achieved by choosing Rte 32A as far as Talgarth, with some nearby places of interest, then cutting across to Brecon (following part of Rte 37) and reaching Tretower and Abergavenny by Rte 32B.

A Viâ Talgarth and Tretower. Wye Valley

A470 to Llyswen: A479 to just beyond Tretower: A40 to Abergavenny. 33 miles.—*7m. Erwood Bridge.—1m.* **Erwood.—***4m.* **Llyswen.—***3m.* **Bronllys.—** *1m.* **Talgarth.—***10m.* **Tretower.—***7m.* **Abergavenny.**
Between Builth Wells and Llyswen the road descends the wooded and pastoral valley of the Wye, this being followed, between Talgarth and Tretower, by the upland W. slopes of the Black Mountains. Beyond Tretower the pleasant valley of the Usk is descended.

Builth Wells, see p. 233. The main road (A470) follows the W. bank of the Wye. An alternative—quieter, scenically equally attractive, and passing Aberedw (see below)—is down the E. bank from Llanelwedd, just N.E. of Builth Wells. The first bridge (Erwood) is 7 m. S. by the main road, and 3 m. S. of Aberedw.

By the main road, soon after *(4m.)* *Alltmawr,* the *Aberedw Rocks,* an outcrop of the Silurian formation rising in terraces of slabs to a height of nearly 600 ft, can be well seen across the river.—*3m. Erwood Bridge.*

From across the bridge B4567 leads N. below Aberedw Rocks, in 3 m. reaching the village of **Aberedw,** at the wooded mouth of the glen of the Edw. There are fragments of a small castle, but the church, a good example of the primitive Welsh mountain type, is more interesting. A small building, probably late 13C, it was restored in Tudor times. The large N. porch was once used as parish hall, being closed by doors the hinges of which can still be seen. The church has a hammer-beam roof and a late 14C rood screen surmounted by curious 17C balustrading. *Llewelyn's Cave,* in woods across the Edw, a traditional hiding place of Llewelyn the Last, was perhaps the retreat of Cewydd, a local saint. At *Llanbadarn Garreg,* 2½ m. up the Edw valley, the church is 15C and virtually untouched.

1m. **Erwood** (pron. 'Errod'). The name is a corruption of the Welsh *Y Rhyd* (The Ford), which was much used by cattle drovers. It was here in 1841 that Henry Mayhew, a frequent visitor, and others decided upon the foundation of 'Punch', of which Mayhew became a first joint-editor. Below Erwood the valley opens. *Llangoed Castle* (no adm.), attractively situated between the road and the river, was rebuilt in 1911 by Clough Williams-Ellis but retains the gabled porch of the earlier mansion (1632).—*4m.* **Llyswen.**

From here A470 may be taken across to (11m.) Brecon, in 2m. passing *Llandefalle* with a mainly 15C church and a churchyard containing several ancient yews. A4153, crossing the bridge at Llyswen, leads to *Maesronen* and *Llowes* on Rte 37A.

This Route continues S.E. as A479, crossing Rte 37A at (*3m.*) **Bronllys**, just S.E. of which is *Bronllys Castle*, a single circular tower of c. 1200, but with later alterations, with a vaulted basement. The tower stands on an earlier motte.

1m. **Talgarth** (1900 inhab.) is a little market town, perhaps best known for its association with Hywel Harris of Trefecca (see below). The *Church* has a 14C tower of strongly defensive type and contains, in the S. aisle, an elaborate 14C sepulchral slab. Hywel Harris is buried here. The *Tower Shop.* near the bridge in the town centre, is a fortified tower (11-13C) which once served as the jail.

Trefecca House†, 1¼ m. S.W. on B4560, was founded in 1752 by Hywel Harris (1714-73), a Methodist revivalist, as an institution ('The Connexion') organized on communal religious-industrial lines. The museum here includes rare books published by the institution press, field pulpits, and other material associated with the community. **Llangorse Lake**, 3m. farther S., is 4m. in circumference and, after Bala Lake, the largest natural lake in Wales. Shallow and reedy, the lake was excavated by glacial action. Today it is a leading centre for water sports of many kinds. An island towards the N. side is the only place in Wales where definite traces of prehistoric lake-dwellings have been found (see model in Brecon museum), and it may be this early occupation which gave rise to the local tradition of a submerged town. The best general view of the lake is from B4560 above the lake's S.E. end., the road from here continuing to Bwlch on Rte 32B. In the village of *Llangorse*, beyond the lake's N. end, the church is 14-15C. The churches at *Llanfihangel Tal-y-Llyn* and *Llan-y-Wern*, a short way N.W. of Llangorse, both contain 17C survivals of the floreated cross motif (see p. 260). The oval shape of the churchyard at Llan-y-Wern suggests that this was a very early foundation.
In the hamlet of *Llanelieu*, at 800 ft 2m. E. of Talgarth, the church (restored) retains its medieval S. door and ironwork. Inside there is a double rood screen, with part of the skeleton floor of its loft. At the back is the original boarded and painted tympanum, rising above the tie-beam of the roof. Cut on the front of the tie-beam is the socket for the rood. The tympanum is pierced by a number of small openings, presumably serving as squints for the occupants of the gallery. The church gets its name from St Ellwy, a granddaughter of King Brychan of Brecknock, said to have had a castle near here.

A479, leading S., now crosses the W. slopes of the Black Mountains, the E. extremity of Brecon Beacons National Park.—*3m. Pen-y-Genffordd*, above which is *Castell Dinas*, once a motte-and-bailey castle, complementing Tretower Castle at the foot of the glen. From here a track ascending the S. bank of the Rhiangoll stream leads towards (3m.) *Waun Fach* (2660 ft), the highest summit of the Black Mountains, with a flat, heather-covered top. *Ty Isaf Burial Chamber* is ¼ m. E. of the road, ¾ m. S. of Pen-y-Genffordd. The chamber is on private land, but the mound and stones can be seen from the lane.—The road descends beside the Rhiangoll to (*5m.*) *Cwm-Du*, where the church has a late 14C tower, a sanctuary arch (though none to the choir), a curious small porch towards the S., and an early inscribed stone (S. exterior).

2m. **Tretower.** *Tretower Court†, entered through a gatehouse of c. 1480, was the mansion of the Vaughans and is an unusually complete and picturesque example of a medieval manor house. The oldest part, the stonework on the N., is 14C; the woodwork is possibly 15C. Sir Roger Vaughan made extensive alterations in the 15C but retained the house's earlier character. The wall-walk, originally a defensive structure, was given its roof and windows in the 17C. The outstanding features of the house are its beautiful oak woodwork, well seen in the large empty rooms, and the generous number of garderobes. *Tretower Castle*† was built by the Normans early in the 12C. With Castell Dinas at the head of the glen, it was intended to guard this pass against the incursions of the unconquered Welsh. It was successfully besieged by Llewelyn the Last, and was partly destroyed by Owen Glendower in 1403, after which it seems to have been abandoned and allowed to fall into ruin. The castle design of a circular tower (c. 1235) within the enclosure of an earlier (mid 12C) square keep, which had been partly demolished, is thought to be unique. The large ward, on the E., now encloses a farmyard.

1m. Junction with Rte 32B, the road now becoming A40. In about 1 m., beside the road near the entrance to *Gwernvale Manor Hotel*, can be seen cist stones formerly covered by a long barrow. Gwernvale was the birthplace of Sir George Everest (1790-1866), Surveyor General of India, after whom Mount Everest was named.

1m. **Crickhowell** (1400 inhab.) owes its name to the hillfort (crug) of Hywel on the hill (Table Mountain) 1 m. north. On the W. of the road at the N. entrance to the town stands the picturesque 15C gateway of a now vanished mansion of the Herberts. The *Church* (14C), with a shingle spire unusual in Wales, contains in its choir five tomb-niches with two recumbent effigies. Of the Norman *Castle* all that remains are its motte and two broken towers. The river Usk is spanned by a medieval bridge of 13 arches, beyond which the church of *Llangatwg* has a 15C tower.

Beyond Llangatwg the Beaufort road in 1½ m. (first cattle grid) reaches *Craig-y-Cilau Nature Reserve* (N.C.). Access is by a track from the cattle grid, a path then running the length of the reserve (1¼ m.) below the 400 ft high escarpment. The reserve (157 acres) is one of the best botanical sites in the Brecon Beacons National Park with over 250 recorded species, and is also known to be the breeding place of 49 kinds of bird. The reserve also includes entrances to a cave system of about 12 m., but access is only for members of approved clubs.

On A40, 1 m. S. of Crickhowell, there is a fine standing stone to the E. of the road. Approaching Abergavenny, a steep and narrow road (N.T. sign) climbs up on to the *Sugar Loaf* (1955 ft), a National Trust property of 2130 acres presented in 1936 by Viscountess Rhondda. From a car park there is an easy upland walk of about 1½ m. to the highest point.—*5m.* **Abergavenny,** see Rte 35.

B Viâ Brecon and Tretower

B4520 to Brecon: A40 to Abergavenny. 33 miles.—*5m. Mynydd Epynt watershed.—10m.* **Brecon.**—*3m. Llanhamlach.—3m. Llansantffraid.—2m. Bwlch.—3m.* **Tretower.**—*7m.* **Abergavenny.**
Across the open moorland of Mynydd Epynt before descending the part wooded valley of the Honddu to Brecon. After Brecon, a gradual descent of the valley of the Usk with, to the W., the high ground of Brecon Beacons.

Builth Wells, see p. 233. The road climbs across the open upland of *Mynydd Epynt*, with Ministry of Defence ranges to the west.—*5m.* At the watershed (1560 ft), with a road across to Garth on Rte 29, the E. edge of the ranges is skirted before the descent into the valley of the Honddu.—*8 m. Llandefaelog Fach*, where the church has a Celtic cross slab (10C) under the tower arch, bearing the name and figure of Briamail.—*2 m.* **Brecon**, see Rte 33.

3 m. Llanhamlach, where the rebuilt church contains an unusually well-preserved effigy of a lady, and a 10-11C slab with sculpture representing the Crucifixion. In the N. porch there are several graveslabs with the floreated cross motif (see p. 260). Ty *Illtud* (¼ m. E. of the junction with the minor road to Pennorth) is a prehistoric long cairn with a well-preserved mound containing a small chamber and capstone. The carved crosses on the capstone supports are medieval.—*3 m.* *Llansantffraid*. In the churchyard here, near the E. wall, is the tombstone of Henry Vaughan, the 'Silurist' (1622-95), born at Scethog, 1½ m. farther on. The tomb bears the Vaughan crest of three heads, said to recall the birth in c. 1100 of triplets who survived despite being strangled by the umbilical cord. Vaughan was himself a twin. For *Talybont Reservoir*, 2 m. S.W., and beyond, see p. 264.—*2 m. Bwlch*, ½ m. N. of which is *Castell Blaenllynfi*, the scanty remains of a Norman castle of the De Braose family. For *Llangorse Lake*, 2 m. farther N., see p. 256. *Llangynidr Bridge*, 1 m. S. below Bwlch, is a particularly attractive four-arch bridge on a lovely stretch of the Usk.

The road now descends, rounding the wooded hill of *Myarth*, passing (*3 m.*) **Tretower** (see Rte 32A above), plainly seen just E., and just beyond reaching the junction with A479. For Tretower to (*7 m.*) **Abergavenny**, see Rte 32A.

33   BRECON. BRECON BEACONS, TALYBONT, AND TAF FECHAN

A   Brecon

BRECON (*Aberhonddu;* 6300 inhab.), occupying high ground N. of the Usk at its junction with the Honddu and the Tarell, is a town of ancient origin visited largely for its interesting 13-14C cathedral. At the crossing of several important roads, with some narrow streets, and also within easy reach of the mountain scenery of the Brecon Beacons and of the larger National Park of the same name, the town can become a traffic bottleneck in summer.

Tourist Information. E. end of Glamorgan Street (local, Wales Tourist Board, Brecon Beacons National Park).

Parking. Northeast of St Mary's Church, which is town centre; approach from Lion Street (one-way W. to E.) and Lion Yard. Also by the Usk, either side of the bridge.

Post Office. St Mary Street.

Early Closing. Wednesday.

History. The Romans were near here (at Y Gaer, 3 m. W.) in about 75, and in the 5C, after the Roman departure, the Brecon area was under the chieftain Brychan, from whom it derived its name. During the reign of William II at the close of the 11C the Norman Bernard of Newmarch built his castle on a virgin site here, and it was around this that the town began to grow, gaining its first charter in 1246. Brecon was besieged by Llewelyn the Last in 1282, and later the neighbourhood suffered raids by Owen Glendower. By the 15C the town had developed a considerable cloth trade. During the Civil War the citizens, anxious to demonstrate and secure their neutrality, demolished the town walls and much of the castle.—Among natives of Brecon were Sir David Gam (d. at Agincourt, 1415), who is supposed to be the original of Shakespeare's Fluellen; Dr Hugh Price (1495-1574), founder of Jesus College, Oxford; Dr Thomas Coke (1747-1814), founder of the American Methodist Episcopalian Church; Mrs Sarah Siddons (1755-1831), the actress, and her brother, the actor Charles Kemble (1775-1854). Henry Vaughan, the 'Silurist', worked here for some years as a physician.

St Mary's Church, at the town centre, has a bold 16C tower and a nave arcade which retains one fluted Norman capital on the N. side. The nearby *Sarah Siddons Inn* was the birthplace of the actress in 1755, and the actor Owen Nares died here in 1943. In Glamorgan Street, S. of St Mary's, is the *Roman Catholic Church,* where Adelina Patti was married in 1898.

Bulwark, with a bronze statue (1852) of Wellington by J. E. Thomas, a local sculptor, leads S.E. from St Mary's, at its end being joined by Glamorgan Street. In the latter, near its junction with Bulwark, is the *Brecon Beacons National Park Information Centre.* Just E., within the angle of Glamorgan Street and Captain's Walk, the classical *Shire Hall* (1842) contains the **Brecknock Museum**†.

The museum, concerned principally with the former county of Breconshire, until about 1939 generally known by its earlier name of Brecknockshire, is of its kind outstanding both as to its material and the way in which it is shown. There are four sections. *Work in Brecknock:* Reconstruction of an early 19C kitchen. Agricultural implements and machinery up to the end of the 19C. Laundering and other domestic devices. *Man in Brecknock:* Cases exhibiting Palaeolithic to Norman material, with good accompanying descriptions, pictures, and models. A beautifully displayed copy of the town charter granted by Queen Mary (and her husband Philip II of Spain), with explanatory notes on town charters generally. Roman and Early Christian stones. A dugout canoe of c. 800. A reconstructed Assize Court. The town stocks, last used in 1826. *Arts, Crafts, and Social Life:* Furniture. A collection of love-spoons, the traditional Welsh courting gift up to about the 17C. Sewing machines. Victorian toys. Costumes, with contemporary photographs. *Natural History:* Rocks, soils, climate, and wildlife.

Captain's Walk, descending towards the Usk and passing some remains of the old town wall, is said to have been a favourite promenade for French officers interned at Brecon during the Napoleonic wars. The *South Wales Borderers Regimental Museum*†, displaying as many as 15 Victoria Crosses, is in the barracks on A40 rather over ¼ m. southeast.

The *Cathedral, or Priory Church of St John the Evangelist, stands on high ground above the Honddu in the northern part of the town.

History. The priory was founded, very probably on the site of an earlier church, by Bernard of Newmarch at the close of the 11C as a cell of the Benedictine monastery of Battle in Sussex, a connection recalled by the village of Battle 3 m. northwest. Giraldus was archdeacon of Brecon in c. 1172, but of the early church nothing remains except parts of the nave walls immediately W. of the crossing. The choir and transepts were entirely rebuilt in the first half of the 13C, when the tower was added; and during the 14C the nave, with the N. and S. aisles, was newly built, and the E. chapels of the transepts were reconstructed on a larger scale. The church was restored in 1862-65 by Sir Gilbert Scott. In 1923 the church was made cathedral of the diocese of Swansea and Brecon, and in 1927 such parts of the priory domestic buildings as had survived the Reformation were restored by W. D. Caröe and rededicated for cathedral chapter use.

The NAVE is entered by the N.W. porch, above which is an upper chamber. The present beautiful vista up the whole length of the church was before the Reformation broken by a rood screen, reached by the still remaining staircases W. of the crossing. The screen divided the church into two, the E. part being for the monks and the W. serving as parish church; above the screen was suspended a great rood, the Crog (Cross) Aberhonddu, of miraculous virtue, which gave the church its second title, Church of the Holy Rood, and which is celebrated by the Welsh bards of the 15C. At the W. end of the nave are a Norman font; a remarkable stone cresset with 30 cups, unique in Wales and the largest found in Britain; a stone thought to have been used by archers for sharpening their arrows; and several sepulchral slabs, notable for their retention as late as the 17C of the medieval floreated cross, a practice common in this neighbourhood though rare elsewhere. Similar slabs will be found in other parts of the cathedral. The *North Aisle,* the former Chapel of the Corvisors (shoemakers) and Tailors, has a beautiful 14C tomb-niche and recumbent effigy; an old parclose screen; a dormer window portraying three early Welsh saints, Cynog, Brychan, and Alud; and a case of old religious books, including a rare breeches-bible. In the *South Aisle,* the former Chapel of the Weavers and Tuckers, are the tombs of Sir David Williams (d. 1613) and his wife Elizabeth Vaughan; the wooden effigy of a lady (c. 1555), the only surviving figure from a tomb made up of three tiers of oak beds; and, at the W. end, a medieval cope chest. The *North Transept* was known formerly as the Chapel of the Men of Battle, and the *South Transept* as that of the Red Haired Men (the Normans).

The *CHOIR, the vaulting of which was first completed by Gilbert Scott, contains the most beautiful work in the cathedral. The E. window, of five large lancets, completely fills the wall space, while at the sides are graduated triplets of unusual character. The full effect of those on the N., however, is impaired by the later (14C) blocking of their lower parts. Also worth noting are the exquisite 13C sedilia; the rare triple piscina; the trefoiled niches (concealed by the reredos), N. and S. of the altar, that seem once to have opened on the outer air but perhaps afterwards served as aumbries; and the supulchral slab on the N. wall of the sanctuary, with a curious carving of the Crucifixion. The reredos (W. D. Caröe, 1937) has figures of saints and others in relief. Rich archways at the W. end of the choir open into the transept chapels on either side. In the *Havard Chapel* (N.), with a 14C doorway to the sanctuary combined with a squint, is the tomb of Walter Awbrey (? 1312), with an inscription in old Saxon and Norman French characters. Here also are four old houselling benches (two now cut down for footstools) that formerly took the place of fixed altar rails at the celebration of Holy Communion. This is now the regimental chapel (1961) of the South Wales Borderers. The *Chapel of St Lawrence* (S.), after lying in ruins for 300 years, was rebuilt by Caröe in 1930; it contains a small 13C piscina.

The domestic buildings of the priory (entered from the S.W. door), after serving as stables etc. for three centuries, have been skilfully fitted up by Caröe as the canonry, deanery, and chapter house.—On the steep bank of the Honddu above the church are the pleasant *Groves,* a public park, once a retreat of Henry Vaughan.

The **Castle** (no adm.), between the cathedral and the Usk bridge, is in two parts. The main ruin, in the grounds of the Castle Hotel, dates from a reconstruction during the reign of Edward I and consists of one side of the Great Hall and of the *Ely Tower.* It was in this tower that in 1483 the

Duke of Buckingham, a lord of Brecknock, held Morton, Bishop of Ely, prisoner. Morton had been arrested on the accession of Richard III; he succeeded in persuading his gaoler into rebellion, but the venture failed and Buckingham was executed though Morton escaped. On the rise opposite the hotel are the motte and part of the bailey of Bernard of Newmarch's original 11C castle, still with fragments of keep and gatehouse.

The suburb of **Llanfaes** is S.W. of the town across the attractive old seven-arch Usk bridge. Here *Christ College*†, originally a Dominican friary, was refounded by Henry VIII in 1541 as a collegiate church and school. The buildings are largely modern but incorporate the 13C monastic church, the nave of which is in ruins, while the choir is now the school chapel. The former refectory is the school dining hall, and another ancient room is now the library.

The remains of the Roman fort of **Y Gaer,** 3 m. W. of Brecon, can be reached on foot by the track of the Roman road S. of the disused railway. By car, the Cradoc road is taken W. out of the town; at Cradoc the left fork (signed Aberyscir) reaches a small crossroads in rather over ½ m., the left turning leading to a farm where permission to park and visit the site should be asked. Probably known to the Romans as Cicutium, the fort occupies a site guarded on the S. by the Usk, on the W. by the Yscir, and on the other sides by a ditch. It was founded c. 75, at the time of the final Roman conquest of Wales, rebuilt c. 105 and again c. 140, and finally abandoned c. 290. Among the garrisons seem to have been the Vettonian Spanish cavalry and the 2nd Legion. Later much of the masonry was removed by Bernard of Newmarch as material for his castle at Brecon. The site was excavated by Sir Mortimer Wheeler in 1924-25. Most of what was found was later covered, but the outer face of the N. wall, in good condition and up to 10 ft high, can be seen; and the other walls, with the usual rounded angles, and something of the N., E., and especially W. gates can be traced.—The village of *Battle,* 1 m. N. of the fort, recalls that Brecon priory was originally a cell of Battle Abbey in Sussex. Dr Thomas Coke is buried here. Between Y Gaer and Battle, visible from the minor road near the disused railway bridge, there is a 13 ft high standing stone.

Pen-y-Crug (1088 ft), 1 m. N.W. of Brecon, is a hill with a fort, reached by a bridleway and footpath.—At **Llanfrynach,** 2½ m. S.E. of Brecon, there is a *Salmon Hatchery*†.

For Brecon to (N.) *Builth Wells* and (S.) *Abergavenny,* see Rte 32; to *Aberaeron,* see Rte 34; to (E.) *Hay-on-Wye* and *Hereford,* and (W.) *Swansea,* see Rte 37. To *Merthyr Tydfil,* see Rte 33B below.

B   Brecon Beacons, Talybont, and Taf Fechan

Together the Brecon Beacons with Talybont and Taf Fechan forests make up a mixed mountain, moor, forest, and lake area of great beauty and variety, bounded on the W. by A470 (Brecon to Merthyr Tydfil, see below), on the S. by A465 (Merthyr Tydfil to Abergavenny, see Rte 37B), and on the E. by A40 (Brecon to Abergavenny, see Rte 32B). There is a network of walks, and a motor circuit (see below) can be made which takes in much of the best of the scenery.

Brecon Beacons, which are only one part of Brecon Beacons National Park (see p. 24), fill the N.W. section of this area. The Beacons themselves, with over 8000 acres surrounding them, were given to the National Trust in 1965 by Sir Brian Mountain. The principal summits, barely ½ m. apart, are *Pen-y-Fan* (N., 2906 ft) and *Corn Ddu* (S., 2863 ft), a distinctive pair of sandstone peaks facing sharply N. and on this side broken by cwms. Southwards the slopes are generally gentle, while a ridge extending E. in nearly 1 m. reaches the lesser peak of *Y Gribin* (2608 ft). Continuing E. from Y Gribin the ridge is broken by *The Gap*, a col between the N.-S. ridges of Bryn Teg and Cefn Cyff across which runs the track which was once a Roman road and later (until the 19C) became the main link between Brecon and Merthyr Tydfil.

The **View** from the Beacons includes, on the N., glimpses of the green Usk valley, with its background of moorland, far beyond which (60 m. N.N.W.) Cader Idris may sometimes be distinguished. To the N.E. and E. is the massif of The Black Mountains, with Llangorse Lake and the Sugar Loaf, and behind them, though rarely seen, the Malvern Hills. The view to the S., relieved in the foreground by reservoirs, extends across moorland to the industrial Valleys; and the Bristol Channel, with the distant outline of Exmoor and the Quantocks, can often be made out. To the W. the Carmarthen Van masks the Vale of Towy and a great part of the Pembrokeshire peninsula.

BRECON BEACONS WALKS. The Beacons are very popular with walkers and are crossed by several recognized routes which, because of the relative compactness of the area, can be combined as wished. These routes are outlined below, foot starting points being indicated by Ordnance Survey references, and distances being from the starting point to the summit of Pen-y-Fan. Although cars can be driven to starting points, the approaches are generally by narrow lanes with, unless otherwise stated, very limited parking space.

One of the most popular routes is that via **The Gap**, 3½ m. A road (Bailehelig) heads due S. from Llanfaes, leaving the hospital on the right. In 2½ m. a T junction is reached, from where the righthand lane crosses a stream and ends at a stony track. From here (O.S. 036235) the track follows the E. slope of Bryn Teg to The Gap, where walkers can either turn W. for the summits or descend S. to the Neuadd reservoirs and the road through Taf Fechan and Talybont forests.—An alternative (2½ m.) from the same starting point is along the spur of *Bryn Teg*, with a steep scramble to the summit of Y Gribin.—The Gap can be reached by two other routes with starting points farther east. One of these, **Bryn** (6½ m.), starts from near the farm of Blaen-Nant (O.S. 080244) and ascends W. of the summit of Bryn to bear W. above the head of the valley of Menascin. The other, **Cefn Cyff** (5 m.), starts from near Rhiwiau (O.S. 057240), the ascent being by the spur of Cefn Cyff.

There are two other approaches from the north. The **Cwm Gwdi** path (2½ m.) is reached by taking Ffrwdgrech Road S.W. out of Llanfaes (left fork after St David's Church), in ¾ m. reaching a choice of three roads, the lefthand of which is taken to a small car park beyond the second cattle grid (O.S. 024247). From here the ascent is by a bridleway over Allt Ddu and then along the spur of Cefn Cwm-Llwch. Particular care must be taken to keep E. of the Ministry of Defence rifle range S. of the starting point. The other approach, **Cwm Llwch** (3¼ m.), is reached by the same road out of Llanfaes but the central road is taken at the triple road choice. This passes the miniature Ffrwdgrech falls, then follows the stream through woods to a small crossroads where the lane deteriorates into a motorable track. After ¾ m. this track ends at a beautifully sited green parking and picnic area (O.S. 006244). From here the foot route ascends to Llyn Cwm Llwych, a tarn in a glaciated cwm, then zigzags up the steep slope to the W. of the lake, past the Tommy Jones Obelisk, erected to the memory of a boy of five who climbed to this point alone and died here (1909). Thence via Corn Ddu to Pen-y-Fan.

From the W., off A470, there are three approaches, the northernmost (3¾ m.) climbing **Pen Milan** to the W. of Cwm Llwch. The starting point (O.S. 001249) can be reached either by the small road leading S.E. from the bridge at Libanus, or by branching off the Cwm Llwch approach. After ascending Pen Milan this route reaches the Tommy Jones Obelisk.—Farther S. two ascents start from near Storey Arms (O.S. 982203), a Youth Adventure Centre. There is parking at a lay-by. The **Y Gyrn** ascent (3 m.) strikes N. to the top of Y Gyrn, then curves E. round the head of a stream to reach the Tommy Jones Obelisk. The **Storey Arms** ascent (2 m.), the most direct of all, can be wet and muddy. The path starts just S. of the plantation, and white posts lead viâ Bwlch Duwynt to Corn Ddu.

Talybont and Taf Fechan forests, with their long narrow reservoirs of the same names and, on the lower S.E. slopes of the Beacons, the two beautifully situated *Neuadd Reservoirs,* angle as valleys across the middle of the area. The valleys, which are water catchment zones, were first planted by the Forestry Commission in 1937; large scale planting of conifers started in 1945, but the earlier oak, ash, and other trees have been preserved. A number of car parks and picnic sites have been provided.

To the S.E. are the moorland heights of *Mynydd Llawgatwg* (1734 ft) and *Mynydd Llangynidr* (1805 ft), forming the N. rim of the South Wales coalfield, crossed by various tracks and also by B4560 which runs N.-S. (Llangynidr to Beaufort) between the two heights.

MOTOR CIRCUIT FROM BRECON. 37 miles round trip.—*6 m.* Brecon Beacons National Park **Mountain Centre**† (1000 ft) is on the upland **Mynydd Illtyd Common** in the angle between A40 and A470. It is reached by a minor road (sign) off A40 just beyond the roundabout on the W. outskirts of Brecon. (An alternative approach, more suitable for larger vehicles, is from Libanus on A470). Ascending on to the common the minor road passes (½ m. N. from a road fork) the earthworks of the hillfort *Twyn-y-Gaer* with, to its E. and S., mounds which are probably Bronze Age burial cairns. In another mile, after passing a pond, there is a small standing stone on the left, probably a route marker since a line projected S.W. from here hits two similar stones at the edge of the common. About 200 yards farther, by another little pond, is *Bedd Illtyd,* now no more than two stones in a hollow but by local tradition the grave of St Illtyd (b. 425), founder of the monastery at Llantwit Major. Beyond, a left turn passes *Illtyd Church,* built in 1858 on a site the circular shape of which suggests a very early foundation, possibly by Illtyd. The *Mountain Centre* (1966; additional facilities 1969), ¼ m. farther, with a fine view, offers National Park information, buffet, picnic facilities etc. Across the W. section of the common can be traced a length of the Roman Sarn Helen; and, by contrast, the underground oil pipeline from Milford Haven to the Midlands (1972) crosses the common.

A road from the Mountain Centre drops down (rather over *1 m.)* to *Libanus* on A470.—Ascending the valley of the Tarell to round the W. flank of the Beacons, the road in *3 m.* reaches **Craig Cerrig-Gleisiad Nature Reserve** (N.C. Picnic site nearby), a 698 acre glaciated area of crags, gullies, and mountain streams, rising from 1200 to 2000 ft. More than 300 species of plants and 60 of birds have been recorded. A footpath skirts much of the reserve's boundary, but otherwise access is by N.C. permit only.—*1 m.* The watershed is at 1440 ft, and just beyond is the former inn and now Youth Adventure Centre *Storey Arms,* a popular starting point for two routes (Y Gyrn and Storey Arms) up to the Beacons' summits.

A470 now descends the valley of the Taff, passing plantations of *Coed Taf Fawr,* and, in succession, *Beacons, Cantref,* and *Llwyn-On* reservoirs, all providing water for Cardiff. Near the N. end of this last reservoir is *Garwnant Forest Centre*†, providing information on all three forests S. of Brecon Beacons (Coed Taf Fawr, Taf Fechan, and Talybont), and setting the forestry scene within the context of water catchment, farming, and the National Park. There is a short forest trail.

8 m. (from the watershed) there is a major crossroads with A465. Here a small road is taken N.E. to (rather over *1 m.)* *Pwll Glas,* a hamlet and road junction lying below a limestone crag on top of which are the very scanty remains of *Morlaix Castle* (late 13C). The ruins include traces of two round towers, a vaulted basement, and a deep pit (unfenced and dangerous); the easiest approach is to follow the Merthyr Tydfil road for c. ½ m. and then walk along the W. side of the golf links.

Continuing N.E. from Pwll Glas through increasingly wooded scenery, the road skirts the W. length of *Taf Fechan Reservoir,* at the N. end (*4 m.*) bearing right at a fork. (But a diversion should be made to the left for 1½ m. to the *Neuadd Reservoirs,* lying in wood and moorland below the Beacons. Above the E. side of the reservoirs runs the old Roman road, until the 19C also the Brecon to Merthyr Tydfil road; this, rising to *The Gap,* is one of the most popular walkers' routes across the Beacons).

At *Pont Blaen-y-Glyn,* less than *2 m.* beyond the road fork, there are Forestry Commission picnic sites marking the starting points of four short waymarked walks. The Waterfall Walk, though the most strenuous, is perhaps the most rewarding and includes five waterfalls.— The road continues N., skirting the W. side of *Talybont Reservoir,* 2 m. long and with a dam at its N. end. *Danywelt* (just N. of the dam), a National Park study centre with residential courses, occupies a farmhouse and barn restored (1977) from a derelict condition; the plans were partly drawn up by architectural students from Kingston Polytechnic, and the local labour was employed under a government job creation scheme.

5 m. *Talybont village.* From here Brecon can be reached in *6 m.* by B4558. Alternatively A40 can be joined at *Llansantffraid,* ¼ m. northeast.

34   BRECON TO ABERAERON

A40 to Llandovery: A483 to Llanwrda: A482 to Aberaeron. 51 miles.—*2 m.* **Llanspyddid.**—*4 m.* **Trallong.**—*3 m.* **Sennybridge.**—*3 m.* **Trecastell.**—*1 m.* **Llywel.**—*8 m.* **Llandovery.**—*4 m.* **Llanwrda.**—*7 m.* **Pumpsaint.**—*7 m.* **Lampeter.**—*12 m.* **Aberaeron.**

Brecon, see Rte 33A. Just W. of the town a minor road ascends W. to the *Mountain Centre,* see Rte 33B.—*2 m.* **Llanspyddid,** where the 14C church has a contemporary barge board on the N. porch, and a curious pulpit canopy. In the churchyard is the reputed gravestone of Brychan, or of Aulach his father.—*3 m.* **Penpont.** Oaks from the estate provided beams to support London's Big Ben.—*1 m.* The church at *Trallong* contains an Ogham stone of the 5-6C, though the ringed cross may be two centuries later.—*3 m.* **Sennybridge** is a town dating mainly from the arrival of the railway in 1872. Rte 37A bears S. here for Swansea. *Castell Ddu,* just W. of the town, now only slight remains, dates from the 14C and is believed to have earlier been the home of Sir Reginald Aubrey, friend of Bernard of Newmarch.—*3 m.* **Trecastell** is an old coaching village with a small motte-and-bailey.

The nearly 2 m. long wooded *Usk Reservoir* is 3 m. west. One of the most massive standing stones in Brecon Beacons National Park, weighing perhaps 20 tons, can be seen from the road ¼ m. S.E. of the reservoir's E. end. The road running S. of the reservoir crosses the Usk, 2 m. below its source. Near the E. bank, about half-way to the source, there is a prehistoric monument made up of a circle and an ellipse. Of the circle seven stones are standing, with seven fallen; and of the ellipse twelve are standing and three have fallen.

1 m. **Llywel,** where the Llywel Stone (a cast of the original now in the British Museum), inside the church, is particularly interesting for bearing carving of three early periods. The Ogham probably dates from at least the 5C; the Latin commemorates one Maccutrenus Salicidunus, believed to have been a local man of c. 500; and a small cross, carved between the above names, is probably of the 7C. The intricate work on the other side of the stone merits attention. Also in this church are another Ogham stone and a portion of the 16C rood screen. A part of the rood loft, removed in 1869, now forms the entrance to the vestry, in which are an ancient font and the stocks (1798).—About 3 m. short of Llandovery, beside the S. side of the road, the *Mail Coach Pillar* stands as a dramatic warning against driving and drinking.—*8 m.* (from Llywel) **Llandovery,** see p. 239.—*4 m.* by A40, **Llanwrda,** where A482 is taken N. while A40 continues S.W. as Rte 29. A482 ascends the valley of the Dulais to (*4 m.*) the watershed at *Bwlch Cefn-Sarth* (759 ft).

3 m. **Pumpsaint** (Five Saints) is a village on the site of a Roman settlement concerned with the exploitation and protection of the nearby gold mines. Of the settlement nothing visible survives, though a bath house just S. of the village was excavated and covered, and Sarn Helen runs N. from A482 1 m. beyond Pumpsaint. The **Ogofau Roman Gold Mines,** ½ m. S.E. of Pumpsaint, are at the S. end of the National Trust's *Dolaucothi* estate of 2577 acres, given in 1941-44 by Mr H. T. C. Lloyd-Johnes as a memorial to his family, owners since the time of Henry VII. At the car park are a N.T. information hut; the ancient Five Saints Stone, of unknown story; and a mound that was probably a motte, though it may have been an ancient mining tip. There is evidence that the mines were exploited in prehistoric times, but it was the Romans who, starting in c. 75, really developed the site. Of medieval mining there is no sure evidence, but the site has been twice worked in recent times, the first being between 1888-1910 (Mitchell Mine) and the second between 1933-38 (Roman Deep Holdings). On neither occasion did the return justify continuing operations, and the mining carried out did not significantly affect the pattern of the Roman workings. The site is a complex one and visitors should first study the explanatory material at the N.T. hut. The two main features are the aqueducts, with their reservoirs, tanks, and sluices, visible today as hillside ledges; and the opencasts, with associated shafts. Visitors are warned that shafts can be dangerous, and should use the waymarked walks which lead past the most interesting features.—The small road passing the mines continues up the remote valley of the Cothi, descending to that of the Teifi, and in 11 m. reaching *Llyn Brianne.*

Beyond Pumpsaint the watershed between the Cothi and the Teifi is crossed at 1025 ft, the road then descending to (*7 m.*) **Lampeter,** see p. 347, where Rte 44B is crossed. A482 ascends for 4 m., then drops into the rich *Vale of Aeron.*—*12 m.* (from Lampeter) **Aberaeron,** see p. 346.

35   ABERGAVENNY

**(Including Abergavenny to Ross-on-Wye,
to Monmouth, and to Newport)**

A   Abergavenny

ABERGAVENNY (10,000 inhab.) is a busy market town at the confluence of the Usk and the Gavenny.

Tourist Information. Monk Street (Local, Wales Tourist Board, Brecon Beacons National Park).
Parking. Tourist Information. Bus Station, Cross Street.
Market. Tuesday.
Early Closing. Thursday.
History. Abergavenny was known to the Romans as Gobannium. Later it became a stronghold of the Lords Marcher, the first Norman lord being Hameline de Balun (1085-1135) who built the castle. This later passed into the hands of William de Braose who in 1175, in revenge for the killing of his uncle by the Welsh, here murdered many of the Welsh lords of Gwent whom he had invited to be his guests. The town was sacked by Owen Glendower in 1404, and again by Parliament in 1646. A Jacobite riot at the accession of William III resulted in the suspension of the town's charter. Smollet, in his 'Humphry Clinker', places the home of Squire Bramble near Abergavenny.

At Tourist Information in Monk Street there is an excellent *Brecon Beacons National Park Exhibition†*. The large **Church of St Mary**, a short way down the road, was formerly the chapel of a small Benedictine priory, founded by Hameline de Balun as a cell of the abbey of St Vincent at Le Mans in France. Of this nothing remains, today's church, apart from the mainly modern nave, being mostly of the 14C. The Choir lost its clerestory and received the present lath-and-plaster groining in a restoration of c. 1828. The **Monuments* (13-17C), although in more than one case patched with figures from an alabaster reredos, form an outstanding series. In the S., or *Herbert Chapel* are the recumbent effigies of the Herbert, Cantelupe, and Hastings families, and also what is thought to be a 14C Herbert graveslab found buried in the churchyard in 1961 In the centre are Sir William ap Thomas (d. 1446), father of the 1st Earl of Pembroke of the Herbert line, and of his wife. In the nave there is a fine wooden figure of George de Cantelupe, Baron Bergavenny (d. 1273). In the N. or *Lewis Chapel* are effigies of Eva de Braose (d. 1246) and of Eva de Cantelupe (d. 1257). The latter, sometimes attributed to Christina Herbert (d. c. 1307), is a rare example of a figure of a woman with a shield. The monument of Dr David Lewis (d. 1584), the first principal of Jesus College, Oxford, was erected by himself during his lifetime. The large 15C wooden recumbent figure evidently formed the root of a Tree of Jesse, probably once part of the reredos of the high altar. In the *Choir* the old stalls, with latticed backs, and the seats for the prior and sub-prior beneath tall tabernacled canopies, date probably from the late 14C. On the N. floor of the choir a small brass to the Stephens (father and son) bears on intriguing rhyming epitaph. The font has a good circular Norman bowl and 'rope' carving.

The slight remains of *Abergavenny Castle* are a short distance southwest. Of De Balun's early castle only the motte and the roughly pentagonal bailey remain, and of the later stone defences, which were incorporated with the town walls, all that is left is part of the N.W. curtain, with the ruins of the entrance gate and two mural towers. The

Abergavenny and District Museum† in the castle includes a late-Victorian Borders Kitchen and a Saddlery, the latter based on an actual saddlery in use until 1920.

Blorenge (2½ m. S.W.; 1834 ft), forming the N.E. bastion of the South Wales coalfield, is capped by mountain limestone and is noted for its sink, or swallow, holes. A road leads to close to the summit, where there are car parks, one of which, *Foxhunter*, was presented by Colonel Llewellyn in memory of his famous horse (d. 1959), buried near here; Foxhunter represented Britain 35 times and had 78 international wins.

For **Sugar Loaf**, 2½ m. N., see p. 257.

For Abergavenny to (E.) *Hereford* and (W.) *Merthyr Tydfil, Neath,* and *Swansea,* see Rte 37B.

B   Abergavenny to Ross-on-Wye

B4521 and A49. 21 miles.—*5m.* **White Castle.**—*6m.* **Skenfrith.**—*7m. Old Pike.*—*3m.* **Ross-on-Wye.**

The road crosses the S. slopes of the isolated hill of *Skerrid Fawr* (1596 ft), 205 acres of the summit of which are National Trust property given by Major Jack Herbert in 1939. The notch at the N. end of the ridge is locally attributed to an earthquake at the time of the Crucifixion, and the hill is sometimes referred to as Holy Mountain, either on account of this or, more likely, because of St Michael's Chapel which stood on the summit until the 17C and was a place of pilgrimage. A waymarked path leads from the road to the summit.

5m. (beyond *Llanvetherine*), a small road leads S. to ruined **White Castle**†, interesting for being of two distinct periods (12 and 13C). The general plan of the castle is a large outer ward to the N., an inner ward protected by stone curtain and moat, and to the S. a defensive hornwork, also protected by a moat.

History. The 12C name was Llantilio Castle, the name of the local manor. In the 13C, however, the castle became White Castle, from the white plaster coating which the place then wore and of which traces can still be found. The earthworks are evidence of an early Norman fortification, but the present stone remains are of the 12 and 13C. In 1201 King John granted White, together with Skenfrith and Grosmont, to Hubert de Burgh, the three forming what came to be known as the 'Three Castles' or the 'Welsh Trilateral'. Except for 1205 to 1219, during which period the castles fell into the hands of William de Braose and his son, they were held by Hubert de Burgh until his fall from favour in 1232. Soon afterwards the castles reverted to the Crown. It was in c. 1263, at the time of the threat by Llewelyn the Last, that White was refortified, a major process involving the transfer of the main entrance from S. to north. After the subjugation of Wales by Edward I, White Castle became no more than an administrative centre and already by the 16C it was roofless and abandoned.

The visitor enters the castle through the *Outer Gatehouse* on the E. side of the outer ward, an addition of the 13C refortification. The structure was essentially a broad, rectangular passage with gates at both ends. The portcullis groove can be seen by the outer gate, and the modern bridge crosses the pit formerly covered by the drawbridge. The large *Outer Ward* formed part of the original defences, these surviving as a bank beyond the ditch (never a real moat and probably always dry) on the N. and west. The wall and towers all date from the 13C., one of the latter (N.W.) being rectangular and serving as offices, possibly of the quartermaster. A recess in the W. of the wall was a garderobe. The moat is crossed to the *Inner Ward*, the oldest part of the castle with walls of the late 12C. The gatehouse and towers, however, represent the 13C refortification. The Gatehouse is of standard pattern, with towers of four storeys flanking the passage; the portcullis groove can be seen. Inside the ward only the outlines of the rooms survive. The Hall (with its kitchen on the opposite side of the ward) was against the N.E. wall, the outer foundations representing the original 12C hall (a tall building which probably rose higher than the wall), and the inner the hall known to have been built in 1244. South of the hall are the well and the E. tower, with, beyond, the Constable's Solar and, S. again, the latrine pit. The Chapel occupies the S.E. corner of the ward, the choir being provided by the S.E. tower, while the nave projected into the ward. The base course of the S. of the ward, the oldest masonry of the castle (early 12C), is all that is left of the original small keep. Only the inner part survives, the remainder being cut by a section of 13C wall linking the S.E. and S.W. towers. This was the site of the castle's main entrance prior to the refortification, the entrance being protected by the moat and the *Hornwork* beyond. Although a length of 13C wall crosses to the hornwork, it does not seem that this latter was ever given any stonework defences.

The village of **Llantilio Crosseny**, 1½ m. S., has an ancient and interesting origin. In 556 this was the land of a chief called Ynyr who, when threatened by pagan Saxons, appealed for help to St Teilo. Teilo responded with prayer, Ynyr set up a large wooden cross, and the Saxons were defeated. In gratitude Ynyr gave land to Teilo for the founding of a church, and hence the village's name meaning Holy Enclosure of Teilo at the Cross of Ynyr. The *Church*, successor to several since 556, is mainly of the 12 and 13C. Originally cruciform, the church's N. transept was absorbed by a 14C chapel (Cil Llwch), and a clerestory was added in the 15C. The Nave was originally considerably lower, as indicated by the low arches at the crossing, and the present Perp. structure is of the 15C. In the N. aisle the main windows are modern restoration, but the small window of two lights at the E. end, discovered during this restoration, is 16C. It now carries the arms of two men thought to have been local lords of the manor; a Herbert beheaded after the Battle of Banbury in 1469 (see also Raglan below), and Sir David Gam (d. at Agincourt), said to have been the original of Shakespeare's Fluellen ('Davey Gam Esquire'). Steps in the wall of the tower, facing the nave, led to the now vanished rood loft. On the W. pier of the central crossing arch is a 'Green Man', with foliage coming from his nostrils, an interesting example of the way in which Christianity adapted what had been a pagan fertility symbol into one of new life and Resurrection. In the Choir the sepulchral *Floor Slabs in low relief are especially noteworthy, a particularly attractive one being that of a father, mother, and three sons. There is also (N. wall) a marble relief by Flaxman to Mary Ann Bosanquet (d. 1819). The Cil Llwch Chapel, the former N. transept, derives its name from an ancient manor house, now Great Hillough Farm, 1 m. southwest. Points of interest are the squints, suggesting that the chapel may have been private to the manorial family; and, either side of the altar, stone brackets in the shape of youth's heads, representing according to one local tradition the Princes in the Tower.—At *Llanvapley*, 2 m. W. of Llantilio Crosseny, the *Rural Crafts Museum*† exhibits farm wagons, agricultural implements, craft tools etc.

6 m. **Skenfrith Castle** (N.T.) is an unusually small ruined castle, consisting of a circular keep near the centre of an irregular foursided enclosure.

History. There was almost certainly a primitive early Norman fortress here. Today's Skenfrith, with White and Grosmont one of the 'Three Castles' (see White Castle, above), was largely built by Hubert de Burgh, probably between 1229 and his fall from favour in 1232. Soon after this the castle reverted to the Crown and the finishing touches were put to the place. The W. tower seems to have been added c. 1263, at the time when Llewelyn the Last was threatening. By the 16C it seems probable that Skenfrith was roofless and derelict, and the last Governor of the 'Three Castles' (John Morgan, d. 1557) lies in the local church.

The entrance is through what little remains of the *Gatehouse* in the N.

wall. The mound on which the *Round Tower* (completed c. 1244) stands is not a survival of an early Norman motte but a mound built from spoil from the moat and designed to give the tower sufficient height to enable defenders to fire beyond the curtain wall. The tower is of three storeys. There is no communication between ground and first floor, both having individual entrances, but the second floor and the roof were reached by a stair, partly in the W. wall and partly in a turret. The *West Range* of buildings was revealed by excavation in 1954. The central room, reached by shallow steps, is divided from the N. room by a wall, but it seems probable that the two were originally one. In the central room are a blocked fireplace, blocked probably when it was found that flooding made these rooms unusable, and at the S. end a recess which may represent the site of a stair to a floor above. Of the *East Range* virtually nothing was built, though the kitchens were probably between the Round Tower and the E. curtain.

Skenfrith Church. Although there was almost certainly an earlier church, the present one is mainly of the early 13C, but with aisles which may be up to 200 years later. It is dedicated to St Bridget, and the ancient carving of the head of a nun over the porch is reputed to represent her. The tower is semi-defended, with thick walls, this and the upper storeroom suggesting its role as a refuge. In the N. aisle hangs the Skenfrith Cope, an example of English 15C embroidery. Here also is the *Altar-tomb* of John Morgan (d. 1557), last Governor of the 'Three Castles', and of his wife (d. 1564), his four sons, and his four daughters; the tomb is remarkable for the way in which it shows the detail of the dress of the period. Nearby is the Morgan family pew. The church's stone altar is its original one, dating from 1207. Thrown down at the Reformation, it formed part of the floor for several years until, comparatively recently, replaced as altar on new pillars. The slab bears some small incised consecration crosses (e.g. front 1. corner). The front of the reading desk in the choir includes a part of the early rood screen.

At **Garway**, 2 m. N. in England, the *Church* is known for its Knights Templars' Chapel in which the Templars were initiated. Note the incised crosses and other signs both inside the chapel (e.g. above the door) and outside. The corbels of the exterior E. window of the chapel bear a head of a Grand Master and a mask, and the Lamb and Flag sign is above the W. end exterior window. In the church the nave is 14C, while the choir of c. 1170 has a carved arch bearing (1.) a Green Man (see Llantilio Crosseny above). The detached tower of c. 1200 contains an old long-chest. The nearby dovecot (1326) was built by the Hospitallers, who succeeded the Templars.

Just beyond Skenfrith, B4521 enters England.—*7 m.* Old Pike, where Rte 38 (A49) is joined.—*3 m.* **Ross-on-Wye,** see p. 290.

C   Abergavenny to Monmouth viâ Raglan

A40. 16 miles.—*4 m.* *Llanfihangel-y-Gobion.*—*5 m.* **Raglan Castle.**—*7 m.* **Monmouth**.

The direct road to Monmouth is B4233. For *Llanvapley, Llantilio Crosseny*, and *White Castle*, along or close to this road, see Rte 35B.

The road descends the valley of the Usk, with Blorenge to the west.— *4 m.* *Llanfihangel-y-Gobion*, where Rte 35D diverges S. on A47 for Usk. Leaving the river A40 crosses the *Clytha* estate, with to the N. a Classical early 19C mansion and to the S. on a hill a late 18C mock castle.

5 m. **Raglan Castle†**, a striking ruin on a knoll, interestingly combines medieval defensive requirements with those of manorial elegance and comfort. Built mainly in the 15 and 16C the castle represents the last, though not the least impressive, example of medieval fortification in Britain.

History. The original motte, on which the Great Tower now stands, was raised by William FitzOsbern after the Norman conquest of Gwent in 1067-71. The present castle was started by Sir William ap Thomas, who had been knighted by Henry VI and made Steward of Usk and Caerleon. He built the Great Tower (c. 1430-45), and probably also the S. gate. His son was William Herbert, Earl of Pembroke, a leading Yorkist who helped to put Edward IV on the throne but was later (1496) defeated in battle and beheaded. It was he who completed the greater part of the present buildings. Later the property passed to the earls of Worcester, the 3rd Earl (William Somerset) between 1548-89 rebuilding the hall and enlarging the Pitched Stone Court to a mainly domestic pattern. In the Civil War Raglan, a principal Royalist centre, was defended for eleven weeks in 1646 against Fairfax by the 5th Earl, aged 84. The castle's fall in August marked the end of the first phase of the Civil War, Raglan later being slighted. At the Restoration the ruins were returned to the 6th Earl. Field Marshal Lord Raglan (d. 1855), who commanded the British army in the Crimea, was a later member of the family.

Approaching the *Gatehouse* the gargoyles above and the heraldic stonework to the left are worth notice. Although this gatehouse was protected by a drawbridge and two portcullises, everything beyond, except for the Great Tower, is residential building in which the fine doorway arches and windows are pleasing features. Beyond the gatehouse the *Pitched Stone Court* is crossed to the *Kitchen* (N. corner of castle) containing two large double fireplaces. To the left of the kitchen is the *Pantry*, and the rooms lining the W. side of the court are the *Buttery* and the *Great Hall*, the latter with a fine oriel window. From the hall stairs descend to the huge cellars. On the W. of the hall are the slight remains of the *Chapel*. The hall and chapel divide the Pitched Stone Court from the *Fountain Court*, occupying the site of the early Norman bailey. In the N.W. corner the *Grand Staircase* ascended to living apartments. At the S.W. corner of the court a gateway leads to the *Bowling Green*, from where steps descend to the *Moat Walk*, with niches (late 16C) which once held statues of Roman emperors. The *Great Tower*, reached from Fountain Court, is a hexagonal detached keep, surrounded by a moat and designed as a self-contained last point of defence. One side was blown up by Fairfax, but the stairway to the top remains.

7m. **Monmouth**, see p. 291.

D   Abergavenny to Newport viâ Usk and Caerleon

A40 to Llanfihangel-y-Gobion: A471 to Usk: unclassified to Caerleon: B4236 to Newport. 20 miles.—*4m. Llanfihangel-y-Gobion.*—*7m.* **Usk.**—*7m.* **Caerleon.**—*2m.* **Newport**.

As far as (*4m.*) *Llanfihangel-y-Gobion* this Route is the same as Rte 35C.—In rather under *3m.* A471 for the second time crosses the Usk. At *Betws Newydd*, 1m. N.E. of the bridge, the church has a small but good 15C rood loft, retaining its boarded tympanum. Just N. of Betws Newydd the height of *Coed-y-Bwynydd* is a National Trust property of 25 acres with good views of the Usk valley.

4m. **Usk** (1900 inhab.), on the E. bank of the river and probably occupying the site of the Roman Burrium, is a market town much of which dates from the 18C. The small *Castle*† (12C), belonging to the De

Clares and the earls of March, was taken by Simon de Montfort in 1265. The ruins include the keep (1169-76), altered in the 15C, a round tower on the 13C curtain, and a gatehouse. The parish *Church* was once that of a Benedictine nunnery, refounded by Richard de Clare, son of 'Strongbow', in 1236. The nunnery gatehouse survives by the churchyard gate. In the church the nave is early 13C, but the arches of the crossing, the choir, and the tower are of the first half of the 12C. The aisle was added in the 13C, but in the 15C was rebuilt on a wider scale, its two elaborate porches (N. and W.) being added at the same time. Worth noting are the large circular stair turret that projects into the aisle; the unusually tall 15C rood screen; and a fine brass inscription of c. 1400 in an early Welsh dialect.

The Caerleon road leads due S. from Usk, descending the W. side of the valley.

An alternative is to use the main A449 down the E. side of the valley. This skirts (c. 6m. from Usk) *Wentwood Forest,* see p. 299.

7m. **Caerleon** (7000 inhab.), now to a great extent a dormitory town for Newport, is visited for its Roman remains and associated museum.

History. The Roman fortress, founded c. 75, was called Isca, the modern name being a corruption of Castra Legionis (Fort of the Legion). The legion was the 2nd, which came here permanently after its subjugation of the Silures and remained until late in the 4C; its normal strength was 5-6000 men. There was also a civil settlement or town, and it is known that a bishop of Caerleon was present at the Synod of Arles (314), the first general council of western Christianity. The bishopric is said to have been transferred in the 6C to St David's by St David himself, as foretold by Merlin. During this post-Roman period Arthur is said to have been both crowned and to have had his capital here, a tradition supported however only by the local name for the amphitheatre of King Arthur's Round Table. Be this as it may Tennyson came to Caerleon in search of local colour for his 'Idylls of the King'. In 1188 Giraldus passed through Caerleon and enthusiastically described the Roman remains.

The Roman fort and town occupied the area between today's town and the Usk, access now being by a road opposite the museum. On the left of this road are the amphitheatre and, to its left, a length of town wall (originally a rectangle of c. 540 by 450 yards), virtually all that can be seen of the town. To the right of the approach road is the site of the *Barracks*, of which only earthworks and the plan of foundations survive.

The **Amphitheatre†*, dating from 80-100, comprises an oval area, 184 ft long by 136 ft wide, hollowed out of the ground, surrounded by an earth bank rising to 28 ft in height, and supported by stone walls. Inscribed stones (not easy to find) record progress in the arena's construction. There are eight entrances, all originally vaulted so that seats could be carried over them. Two of these were for performers, and six for spectators. Those for performers were the more elaborate ones on the N.E. and S.W., both with traces of a small waiting room and stone benches, and the latter with two inscribed stones nearby. At the N.W. entrance can be seen the drain which ran the length of the amphitheatre.

The *Legionary Museum†*, a branch of the National Museum of Wales, occupies a building of 1850 built in the style of a classical temple. Stonework includes carved heads (of local stone) wearing Phrygian caps, and a large tablet celebrating the opening of an important fortress building. Also exhibited are coins, pottery, domestic implements, weapons, glass, and a figure of a legionary, showing his clothing and accoutrements. In the basement (admission normally only by prior application) is more stonework and also a tessellated floor.

It was at the *Hanbury Arms*, a Tudor inn overlooking the river, that Tennyson stayed while gathering material for his 'Idylls of the King' (1859). Roughly opposite, in private property surrounded by a high wall, can be glimpsed the motte of an early Norman castle.

2m. **Newport,** see p. 299.

E   Abergavenny to Newport viâ Pontypool

A4042 (4051 through Cwmbran). 17 miles.—*10m.* **Pontypool.**—*3m.* **Cwmbran.**—*4m.* **Newport**.
The road skirts the E. edge of the South Wales mountains and main industrial area. It also runs just E. of the *Brecknock and Monmouthshire Canal.* Dating from 1797-1812, the canal was closed to commercial traffic in 1932, but is now used for recreational purposes.

The road heads S:, with Blorenge to the west.—*2m.* The Usk is crossed.—*8m.* **Pontypool** (39,000 inhab.), today a diversified industrial town, is the home of the Welsh iron industry. The first forge here was established at Pontymoel, in the S.E. part of the modern town, in 1425, and the first ironworks followed in 1577. It is said that the first forge in America (1652) was built by Pontypool emigrants. In 1682 the first rolling mill is thought to have been started here by Thomas Cooke, and in the early 18C Thomas Allgood (d. 1716) developed 'Pontypool Japan', a novel and attractive treatment of iron plates by a brilliant and heat-resistant lacquer. In 1829 the town was a centre of the Chartist riots, the Pontypool leader, William Jones, marching to Newport to help in the assault on the Westgate Hotel; for this he was transported. The town's main attraction is the large *Pontypool Park*, lying N. of the river; the fine iron gates at the park's Pontymoel entrance were presented by Sarah, Duchess of Marlborough. *Llandegfedd Reservoir*, 2m. E., a water supply for Cardiff, serves also as a recreational area (sailing, fishing). From two picnic areas to the S. of the lake start a choice of waymarked walks varying in length between 1 and 5m.

Blaenavon (8000 inhab.) is 6m. up the largely built-up valley of the Lwyd. Ironworks were established here in 1757, and coalmining started in earnest in c. 1782 when it was realized that coal could meet the demands of the ironworks better than wood, supplies of which were everywhere fast running out. To a great extent industrial estates have taken over from the mining and heavy industry of the past, one such for example, the Gilchrist Thomas Industrial Estate, recalling the man who solved the problem of separating phosphorus from iron in the Bessemer converter, his theory being successfully tested in 1876 at the Blaenavon Ironworks. Derelict industrial areas, particularly to the N.W., are steadily being treated and converted to industrial estates and recreation sites.

3m. **Cwmbran** (22,000 inhab.), county town of Gwent, is a 'new town'. The *Llantarnam Grange Arts Centre* is home to both touring and local exhibitions. At *Llantarnam*, at the S. of the town, the modern abbey occupies the site of a 12C Cistercian abbey, a gateway of which survives.—*4m.* **Newport,** see p. 299.

36   HEREFORD

HEREFORD (47,000 inhab.), on the N. bank of the Wye, is a city of ancient origin, the seat of a bishop since 672 when its see was detached from Lichfield. Today it is both an important market centre serving a wide rural area and also the home of diversified industries which include cider, nickel alloy, canning, poultry, and lighting. The city is visited mainly for its beautiful and very interesting cathedral, but it also offers some lengths of its old walls, some attractive old houses, a number of museums, and, with its extensive and central pedestrians' streets, convenient shopping.

Tourist Information. N. side of Commercial Street.

Parking. Several car parks around and close to the ring road. Those just S. of Blueschool Street are convenient for Tourist Information and the city centre. For the cathedral the most convenient is between Bridge Street and Greyfriars Bridge viaduct.

City Centre. High Town (pedestrians).

Main Post Offices. St Peter's Street, off High Town. Broad Street, near the cathedral.

Railway and Bus Stations. Commerical Road (N.E. city).

Market. Wednesday.

Early Closing. Thursday.

History. The city's name is Saxon, meaning Army Ford, a clear indication that Hereford was from early times a military post along the approaches to southern Wales. The bishopric dates from 672, when it was detached from Lichfield, and at about the same time the town was laid out by Millfrith of Mercia. In c. 760 either Ethelbald or Offa of Mercia built the first earthwork defences, these protecting the area between the Wye and the present East and West streets, once together Behind-the-Wall Street. In the 10C King Athelstan summoned the Welsh chieftains to Hereford, the meeting fixing the Wye as the border. A century later Edward the Confessor granted Hereford to his Norman nephew Ralph, who built one of the first Norman castles in England on the site now known as Castle Green. But in 1055 Ralph was routed by the Welsh and the town was sacked and burnt. Under the Normans Hereford became an important border garrison and trading centre, receiving a Royal Charter in 1154. It suffered badly during the troubled years of Stephen's reign; and again during the struggle between Henry III and Simon de Montfort, when the latter for a while held both Henry III and the future Edward I prisoner in Hereford (1264). By the end of the 13C stone city walls and towers had been completed. In 1326 Hugh Despenser, after capture at Neath, was hanged here, and Owen Tudor was executed at High Town in 1461 after the battle of Mortimer's Cross. During the Civil War Hereford, twice taken by Parliament, was in 1645 unsuccessfully besieged for a month by a Scottish army. After this the city stagnated, perhaps the main event of the 18C being the widespread demolition (1774) of the ancient walls and gates and other older buildings in an attempt to modernize what was still an essentially medieval and notoriously unhealthy city. But it was only in the mid 19C, thanks to proper sewage and water supply and the arrival of the railway, that modern Hereford started to develop.—David Garrick (1717-79) is the town's most famous native. Thomas Traherne (1636-74), the poet, was the son of a Hereford shoemaker.

The main city is enclosed by the Wye to the S. and a succession of ring roads following the line of the old walls (see below). Within this crescent (about ½ m. from N. to S. and E. to W.) the city centre (High Town) and principal shopping streets are to the N., while the cathedral is to the south.

City Centre

HIGH TOWN is a broad pedestrian precinct. At its S.E. end is the ***Old House**†, a beautiful half-timbered building of 1621, designed by John Abel, the 'King's carpenter', originally one of a group known as

Butchers' Row, demolished in the early 19C. The house is now a museum devoted mainly to Jacobean furnishing and other material of the same period, and containing also some interesting pictures of the Kemble, Siddons, and Garrick theatrical families, all with Hereford connections. *St Peter's Church,* to the E., contains good 15C canopied stalls. Thought to have been founded c. 1074, the present much rebuilt church retains some work of c. 1300 (N. aisle and arcade) and an early 13C tower. Opposite one another at the N. end of St Owen's Street are (N.) the Classical *Shire Hall* (Smirke, 1819) and (S.) the *Town Hall* (1904), where the city plate, insignia, charters and other records can be seen on prior application.

Widemarsh Street, out of the N.W. corner of High Town, soon passes the end of Maylord Street, a plaque on a house on the corner here commemorating the birthplace of David Garrick (1717).

From High Town, High Street runs W., very soon turning S. as Broad Street. The westerly continuation of High Street is Eign Gate, a pedestrian street. **All Saints Church,** at the junction of the three streets, is mainly late 13-early 14C, but the remains of an earlier 13C church can be seen in the walls of the choir. The spire (14C) has a kink, this being due to the fact that the N. wall of the tower, built on the site of a ditch, subsided when the spire was added; when the spire was restored in the 19C the top section was built vertical. Noteworthy in the interior are the 14C canopied stalls and misericords; timber roofing of the 15C; a 14C chest; the 16C font at which David Garrick was christened; and a collection of some 300 chained books.

On the W. side of Broad Street, roughly opposite the cathedral, are the **City Museum and Art Gallery†**. The former is concerned mainly with local archaeology, natural history, and domestic life. Exhibits include Roman material, costumes, toys, farm implements, bygones, and military equipment. The Art Gallery (exhibitions changed roughly monthly) contains paintings, applied art, silver, glass, and pottery.

Cathedral and Castle Green

The ****Cathedral,** of St Mary the Virgin and St Ethelbert the King, is a beautiful and interesting building of many architectural styles.

History. The see of Hereford dates from 672 when it was detached from that of Lichfield, the first bishop to be recorded being Putta (676). In 794 Ethelbert of East Anglia, coming to marry the daughter of Offa of Mercia, was murdered by the latter near Hereford, and tradition has it that his ghost demanded burial at Hereford. Miracles then occurred at the tomb and Ethelbert became a saint. In 825 what was probably the first stone church on this site was built over Ethelbert's tomb, this being followed by another built by Athelstan and probably destroyed when the Welsh burnt the town in 1055. The first Norman bishop, Robert de Losinga, began to rebuild in 1079, but if, as tradition asserts, his church was circular, it must have been largely obliterated by Bishop Reynelm (1107-15) who is styled on his tomb 'founder of the church'. Yet the 11C character of parts of the E. end suggests that Reynelm's claim is excessive. During Stephen's reign supporters of Matilda captured the cathedral and used the tower for launching missiles at the castle, forcing Stephen's followers to surrender. Robert de Bethune (1131-48) completed the nave and restored the choir, and William de Vere (1186-99) radically altered the E. end and probably began the Lady Chapel (completed c. 1220), beneath which was constructed a spacious crypt. Bishop Peter of Aquablanca (also known as Peter of Savoy, d. 1268) built the N. transept c. 1260. A favourite of Henry III, he was so unpopular that the local citizens sided with Simon de

Montfort and in 1263 drove Peter out of the cathedral. The inner N. porch was added by Bishop Swinfield (1283-1316). The central tower (165 ft), erected on Norman piers and arches, and the chapter house are due to Bishop Adam of Orleton (1312-27), and Bishop Booth (1516-35) added the outer N. porch. In 1646 Dean Croft, preaching here, berated Cromwell's soldiers for their destructiveness and was only saved from being shot on the spot by the intervention of an officer. The fall of the W. tower in 1786 gave Wyatt the opportunity to pull down the W.

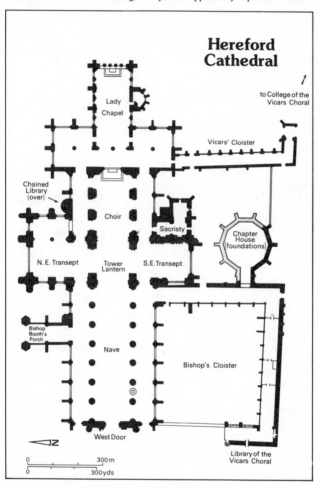

Hereford Cathedral

to College of the Vicars Choral

Lady Chapel

Vicars' Cloister

Chained Library (over)

Choir

Sacristy

Chapter House (foundations)

N. E. Transept

Tower Lantern

S.E. Transept

Bishop Booth's Porch

Nave

Bishop's Cloister

N

0   300 m
0   300 yds

West Door

Library of the Vicars Choral

bay, destroying much Norman work in the nave, and to erect a new W. front after his own idea of Gothic. The latter has since been replaced by a new 14C style façade (J. Oldrid Scott, 1908). The E. end and crossing were restored in 1843, and the whole building in 1856-63.

EXTERIOR. The best view is that from the N.E., this embracing the E.E. Lady Chapel (1220), the clerestory of the choir (1240), Peter of

Aquablanca's N. transept of 1260, and the Dec. Gothic N. choir aisle and N.E. transept of 1290. On the W. front the N. medallion depicts Dean Croft being menaced by Cromwell's soldiers.

Visitors usually enter the cathedral by *Bishop Booth's Porch* on the N. side, where the varied and intriguing small figures around the arch are worth studying. The NAVE (12C), one of the richest Norman designs in England, is notable for its massive piers, its main arches with their rich carvings and mouldings, and the arches that support the tower. The triforium and clerestory are the work of James Wyatt (1788), who refaced the former and completely rebuilt the latter. The sculptured font is 12C, but rests on a 14C pedestal. The pulpit (early 16C) is the one from which Croft berated the soldiers. The *Aisles* are late Dec. on Norman lower courses. In the N. aisle there is a monument to Bishop Booth (d. 1535), complete with its original grille, and in the S. aisle one to Sir Richard Pembridge (d. 1375), who fought at Poitiers. A curious feature is that his effigy has a new right leg; the wooden leg, which for a while served as substitute, and which incorrectly wore the Garter, is in the Library.

The NORTH TRANSEPT was built c. 1260 by Peter of Aquablanca, probably to house his own exquisitely designed tomb. Here too is the shrine of Bishop Thomas Cantelupe (d. 1282), whose remains worked miracles and attracted pilgrims. He was the last Englishman to be canonized (1320) before the Reformation. The pedestal is notable for its naturalistic foliage and the figures of Templars. Broken up at the Reformation, the shrine was discovered in the 19C and rebuilt on or close to its original position. Under the great window, one of the largest examples of geometrical tracery in England, is the canopied tomb of Bishop Thomas Charlton (d. 1344). The SOUTH TRANSEPT retains its Norman character, much of it probably being Robert de Losinga's work (1079) and thus the oldest part of the cathedral. On the wall is a triptych of the South German School (c. 1530). Bishop Trevenant (d. 1404), who made the Perp. alterations in this transept, lies under the S. window. On the W. side there is a fireplace of probably Norman origin but with 18C alterations, beside it being a few 14C stalls with their original canopies. Note also in this transept the coloured effigies of Alexander Denton (d. 1577), and of his first wife and child.—The *Tower Lantern*, with its many shafts and curious gratings, was hidden by a 15C roof until 1843.

In the CHOIR, dedicated in 1110, the rich Norman triforium is below a graceful E.E. clerestory, which, like the vaulting, dates from the 13C. The main arches are supported by massive piers, and the capitals of the semi-detached shafts are elaborately carved. At the E. end there is a grand Norman arch, surmounted by a blind arcade, which originally gave access to the central of three apses, all over a long period (c. 1190-1371) replaced by transepts. In the axis of this arch now rises a pier of the processional aisle which was an important part of Bishop de Vere's alterations of 1186-99. The stalls (note the carved animals) and the Bishop's throne are of the 14C. A marble slab opposite the throne marks the supposed site of St Ethelbert's shrine, and a 14C statue of the saint is in the S. side of the Sanctuary. The late 12C chair to the left of the altar is said to have been used by King Stephen, and the brass of Bishop Trilleck (1360) in the floor (l.) is a good one. The organ (1893) includes a few pipes from the organ of 1676.

In the NORTH CHOIR AISLE hangs the **Mappa Mundi,* executed on vellum c. 1313 by Richard of Haldingham, a prebendary of the cathedral. This is a typical medieval map, with Jerusalem at the centre

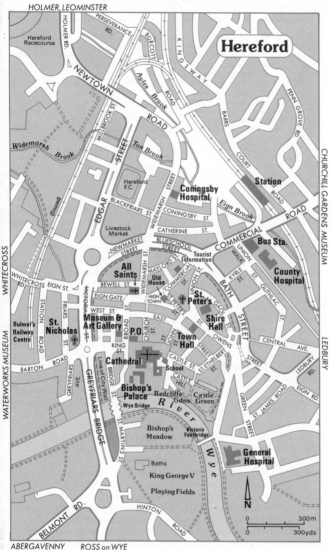

and, at the top beyond the circular sea, the Day of Judgement. Within the map, representing of course a flat world, Asia is at the top, Africa to the right, and Europe to the left. Many Biblical events are depicted, and it is likely that the map, based on the authority of the Bible amongst many other sources, was used for teaching purposes. Opening from the North Choir Aisle is the *Chantry of Bishop Stanbury* (1480-96), with rich fan-vaulting and heraldry and an original oak door.—In the S. Choir Aisle there are several 14C effigies of early bishops.

The *CHAINED LIBRARY†, reached by a stairway (? 14C) opposite the Mappa Mundi, occupies a room which was built for muniments by Bishop Aquablanca. The room is said to have formerly been reached by a bridge across the N. window of the N. transept, and a door at the N.W. corner of the room opposite a similar one by the window seems to support this tradition.

The first recorded library was in the W. cloister, but in 1595 this was moved to the Lady Chapel, where it remained until 1842. For 13 years the books were kept in the College of the Vicars Choral, before, in 1855, being brought to the present room.—With some 1450 chained books the collection is the world's largest. Among the manuscripts the oldest is two pages of the Gospel according to St Matthew (7C). There are 227 manuscript volumes dating from the 8C onwards. These include the Four Gospels (8C); the Hereford Breviary (1265-70), with music, lost between the Reformation and the early 19C when it was found in a London shop; the 'Cider Bible' (15C), in which the words 'wyn ne sidir' have been substituted for 'strong drink'; and also many early texts, books on canon law, commentaries etc. Except for two using paper, the manuscripts are all on parchment. Of the printed books over 50 are prior to 1500, two of these being Caxton's.

The EAST TRANSEPTS replaced the Norman apsidal chapels, the work occupying c. 1190-1371. The main work dates from 1290, but that on the S.E. transept, on cheaper lines, was not carried out until 1364-71. This transept contains a bust by Roubiliac, probably of James Thomas (d. 1757), and several brasses on the walls.

The *LADY CHAPEL (1220) is a beautiful example of E.E. work, especially the clustered window shafts and the E. end with its five lancets (restored). On the S. side is the 15C tomb of Precentor Swinfield, with his 'swine', and some of the windows contain 14C glass from St Peter's church. On the N. side are the monument of Joanna de Bohun (d. 1327); and the fine tomb of Sir Peter de Grandisson (d. 1358), unusual for the dog which, instead of lying passive, is actively watching its master.—The *Audley Chantry* (1500) is behind a screen of painted stone. Having built the chantry for himself, Bishop Audley was transferred to Salisbury where he built another before his death in 1524. The main features are the original oak door and the lierne vaulting (short ribs joining bosses) of the upper chamber.—The *Crypt* is believed to be the only example of an E.E. crypt.

A covered walk with a carved oak roof, known as the *Vicars' Cloister,* leads from the S.E. transept to the *College of Vicars Choral,* built around a quadrangle (1472). At the end of the walk there is a collection of carved stonework dating from the 11C. A second cloister, of two walks (Perp.), known as the *Bishop's Cloister,* is entered from the S. side of the nave; dating from the 15C this cloister was to give access to the Bishop's Palace and the *Chapter House,* the foundations of which can be seen E. of the E. cloister walk. Unusual for being ten-sided the chapter house, built in the early 14C, was stripped of its lead roof during the Civil War (the lead being made into bullets) and used as a quarry in the 18C. The square tower at the S.E. corner of the Bishop's Cloister is called *Ladye Arbour,* from, it is thought, Our Lady's Herbarium. The S. walk is blocked, and the W. walk was demolished in 1760. At the S.W. corner is the *Library* of the Vicars Choral.

The *Bishop's Palace* (no adm.), with a Norman hall, stands between the cathedral and the river. In Gwynne St, on the wall of the bishop's garden, is a tablet marking the alleged birthplace of Nell Gwynne (or Gwyn, 1650-87).
The *Cathedral School,* immediately E. of the cathedral, dates back to 1381 and includes the cathedral choristers among its pupils. The Three Choirs Festival dates from c. 1720 when the choirs of Hereford, Worcester, and Gloucester cathedrals met 'to make musick' together. Now much expanded this annual festival, held at each place in rotation, includes not only the cathedral choirs but also other singers, both amateur and professional.

Redcliffe Gardens, just S.E. of the cathedral and reached by Quay Street, occupy the site of the Norman castle. *St Ethelbert's Well,* at the junction of Quay Street and Castle Hill, though now only a wall fountain, recalls an ancient healing well. *Castle Green,* E. of Redcliffe Gardens, was the castle's bailey, and *Castle Pool* to the N. is all that is left of the moat. The grounds contain a mortar, used in 1646 by Parliament's Colonel Birch against Goodrich Castle; and a column (60 ft; 1809), celebrating Nelson's victories.

At the S.E. corner of Castle Green the *Victoria Suspension Bridge* (1898, rebuilt 1967), a footbridge, crosses the Wye to the extensive *Bishop's Meadow* and *King George V Playing Fields,* together filling the S. bank westward to Wye Bridge.

The Ring Roads and Beyond

The ring roads, an arc of about 1½ m., follow the course of the medieval **City Walls,** at one time with 15 bastions and five gates. What survived the demolition of the 18C was revealed by the roadworks of 1967, and several stretches can now be seen, one being below Greyfriars Bridge viaduct. This includes a bastion at St Nicholas Street. There is another length, with another bastion, farther N. along Victoria Street. Beyond this, a grass bank (1968) extending to West Street marks the line of Saxon earthwork defences. Further sections of wall can be identified round most of the remainder of the ring.
Greyfriars Bridge (1966) is at the S.W. corner of the ring. To its E. is *Wye Bridge,* originally built in 1490 and widened in 1826. The bridge has six arches, the third of which from the city side was destroyed during the siege of 1645. The southernmost arch is in part an 18C rebuilding. This bridge is successor to two others, a wooden one of about 1120 and a stone replacement of the 14C.
The W. ring roads are Greyfriars Bridge and Victoria Street. The **Waterworks Museum**† is ¾ m. W. by Barton Road and Broomy Hill. Occupying Hereford's first waterworks (1856), the museum is operated by a trust formed in 1974. It contains a boiler of 1895, the oldest triple-expansion pumping engine in Britain, a unique two-cylinder engine, and a boiler feed pump, all of these being demonstrated. There are also other pumps, engines, gauges, etc., and the long-term aim of the trust is to preserve the Victorian waterworks in its entirety.—Eign Street, leading W. off the N. end of Victoria Street, soon becomes Whitecross Road in which is **Bulmer's Railway Centre**†, home of the steam locomotive King George V (1927) and five pullman coaches, one of which is an unaltered former Royal coach. Others house a cinema and museum. The train runs a short distance on public open days. Farther along Whitecross Road (1 m. from Victoria Street) is the *White Cross,* erected by Bishop Lewis Charlton in 1361 in thanksgiving for the departure of the Black Death,

during which markets were held on this site. The cross was much restored in the 19C and only the stepped base is wholly original.—It was from *Widemarsh Common*, ½m. N. of the end of Victoria Street, that in 1265 the future Edward I escaped from Simon de Montfort's guards, soon afterwards defeating and killing De Montfort at Evesham.

The N. ring roads are Newmarket and Blueschool streets. From the junction of these Widemarsh Street soon reaches **Coningsby Hospital**†, an almshouse erected in 1614 by Sir Thomas Coningsby for old soldiers, sailors, and servants, on the site of a commandery of the Knights Hospitaller. The chapel (in origin c. 1200, but much restored) is now a museum of the Order, and there is also an exhibition illustrating the life of the Coningsby pensioners. Adjacent are a Preaching Cross (c. 1350), and the ruins (refectory walls and parts of the cloister) of the *Black Friars Monastery* (c. 1322).

Bath Street forms the E. side of the ring road. From its N. end Commercial Road, passing the bus and railway stations, becomes Aylestone Hill, off which, in Venn's Lane, is **Churchill Gardens Museum**† (¾ m. from ring road), with pictures, furniture, glass, porcelain, and a large collection of costumes.—The *Regimental Museum of the 1st Bn Herefordshire Light Infantry*† is in Harold Street, rather over ¼ m. S.E. of the S. end of Bath Streeet.

For Hereford to *Shrewsbury*, see Rte 31; to *Swansea* (viâ *Brecon* or *Abergavenny*), see Rte 37; to *Ross, Monmouth,* and *Chepstow,* see Rte 38.

37   HEREFORD TO SWANSEA

A   Viâ Brecon and Sennybridge

A438 and B4350 (or A465, B4349, and B4352) to Hay-on-Wye: B4351 to Clyro: A438 to Bronllys: A470 to Brecon: A40 to Sennybridge: A4067 to Swansea. 72 miles.—*20m.* **Hay-on-Wye.**—*1m.* **Clyro.**—*5m.* **Three Cocks.**—*2m.* **Bronllys.**—*8m.* **Brecon.**—*8m.* **Sennybridge.**—*7m.* **Bwlch Bryn-Rhudd.**—*3m.* **Dan-yr-Ogof.**—*11m.* **Pontardawe.**—*7m.* **Swansea.**

Mixed scenery which includes the pastoral Wye valley, narrowing between higher ground near Hay; high, open moorland after Sennybridge; and the largely industrial valley of the Tawe S. of Dan-yr-Ogof.

To Hay-on-Wye there is a choice of roads, N. or S. of the river. There are bridges, linking the two roads, at Bridge Sollers, Bredwardine, and Whitney.

To HAY NORTH OF THE WYE. **Hereford** (see Rte 36) is left by White Cross (p. 279).—*3m.* Junction with A480. At *Credenhill,* 1m. along A480, the church contains a tablet to Thomas Traherne (1636-74), the poet, who was rector here from c. 1657-66. At *Brinsop,* 1m. farther, the small church has a Norman tympanum of c. 1150, with St George and the Dragon, and memorial windows to Wordsworth and his sister, who stayed at the half-timbered Brinsop Court, ¾ m. north.—*2m.* The road crosses a National Trust property, which includes *The Weir* (gardens open), a house of 1784. *Kentchester,* ½ m. N., is the site of a large Roman station of Castra Magna, on the road from Viroconium to Caerleon, the line of which crosses A438. All that survives is some earthwork and traces of wall in the N.E. part.—*1m. Bridge Sollers,* just S., has a bridge across the Wye.—*2m. Portway* is a hamlet at a crossroads.

Monnington-on-Wye, ½ m. S., is traditionally the place where Owen Glendower died and was buried in 1415. One of his daughters married the owner of Monnington Court.

A pleasant and interesting diversion of c. 10 m. can be made to the N., rejoining A438 at Willersley. The minor road N. from Portway, soon joining A480, in 4 m. reaches *Sarnesfield* crossroads. The church, a short way N.E. on A4112, has a nave first built in the late 12C, the interior window under the tower arch being of the same period. The remainder of the church is mostly 14C. In the churchyard there is a memorial (W. of and near the porch, but illegible) to John Abel (d. 1674), the 'King's Carpenter', builder of, amongst other places, the Old House in Hereford and Grange Court at Leominster. He executed his own monument here at Sarnesfield when over the age of ninety. *Weobley* (see p. 244) is 2 m. northeast. At *Almeley Wooton,* 3 m. N.W. of Sarnesfield, can be seen the oldest Quaker meeting house in Britain (1672). *Eardisley,* 2 m. S. of Almeley Wooton, is a village with several half-timbered houses. The church contains a well-preserved and elaborately carved *Font of c. 1150; note also the angle taken by the S. piers of the nave. The main road is rejoined at Willersley, 1 m. south.

5 m. **Willersley.**—*3 m.* **Whitney,** a short distance beyond which B4350 is taken across the Wye (toll).—At *(2 m.)* *Clifford* are the small remains of a castle, first built by William FitzOsbern, Earl of Hereford. The remains include FitzOsbern's early Norman motte-and-bailey, with a curious small subsidiary bailey S.W. of the mound, and the ruins of the hall and a mural tower of a later Edwardian stone castle. 'Fair Rosamond' (d. c. 1176), daughter of Walter de Clifford and romantic mistress of Henry II, may have been born here. In the church (at *Llanfair,* just S.E.) is the finely carved wooden figure of a vested priest (1280), probably a member of the local priory.—*2 m.* **Hay-on-Wye,** see below.

To HAY SOUTH OF THE WYE. **Hereford** (see Rte 36) is left by Greyfriars Bridge, beyond which A465 forks right.—*2 m.* *Belmont Abbey* (Benedictine) is a school. The abbey church is open daily and there is a complete round of services, with, primarily, Gregorian plainchant. Beyond the abbey B4349 bears right for *Gorsty Common* where another right fork is taken on to B4352.—*4 m.* (from Belmont) **Madley,** said to be the birthplace of St Dyfrig (Dubritius). The large *Church* is mainly 13 and 14C but has an early 12C N. porch which was a transept of an earlier church. There is a double S. aisle, the outer one (Chilstone Chapel) being added c. 1330; here the roof timbering is original, and the carved woodwork (installed 1953) behind the altar is thought to be of medieval Spanish origin. The crypt, something of a rarity in parish churches, is beautifully vaulted from a single central pillar. The glass in the central of the E. windows is 13 or 14C, and the local sandstone cross in the churchyard is probably contemporary with the church.—*2 m.* *Tyberton* has a church of 1720 (incorporating the Norman door of its predecessor), designed by John Wood who built Bath's Royal Crescent. The interior is a Restoration period-piece, including box-pews and elaborate oak carving.

3 m. **Moccas Park,** with huge and ancient oaks, was designed by 'Capability' Brown. In the park the *Church* is an almost perfect example of a Norman village church, and *Moccas Court†,* designed by Robert Adam, is a fine Georgian mansion of 1775.—*1 m.* *Bredwardine* is an attractive village near the Wye, here crossed by a graceful bridge. To the S.E. are the remains of a 13C motte-and-bailey castle of the Baskervilles. Francis Kilvert (1890-79), the diarist, was vicar here from 1877 until his death and is buried in the churchyard. A large burial chamber known as

Arthur's Stone stands on high ground near Llan Farm, 1½ m. southwest; the entrance passage, chamber, and capstone can be seen. At *Dorstone,* 2 m. S.W. of Bredwardine, there is a motte-and-bailey of unusual shape, the motte being oval and the bailey kidney. Beyond Bredwardine the road curves S.W., rounding Merbach Hill (1045 ft) and in *5 m.* at *Hardwick* joining B4348. About 1 m. beyond the join, a motte known as *Mouse Castle* can be seen to the south.

2 m. **Hay-on-Wye** (1400 inhab.), on the S. bank of the Wye and just in Wales, is a small but important market town and general centre serving the needs of the surrounding rural community. The large market grounds are the scene of important cattle, sheep, and horse sales, Clun and Kerry sheep being a principal feature. Hay is also much concerned with the book trade and boasts the largest secondhand bookshop in the world, the various sections being scattered around the town. The town derives its name from the Norman-French 'haie' (hedge or enclosure). The 11C *Castle* (no adm.), in the centre of the town, was burnt by King John in 1216 and again by Owen Glendower. Despite much rebuilding while in Lancastrian hands during the late 14C, little now remains beyond a ruined gatehouse (blown up in the Civil War) and parts of the walls. In Elizabethan times a manor house was grafted on to the castle. An early Norman motte-and-bailey castle, first mentioned during the reign of Henry I, is in the S.W. of the town. *St Mary's Church* (restored 1834) incorporates parts of the tower and porch of a church of c. 1200. The ancestors of W. D. Howells (1837-1920), the American author, were natives of Hay and his father emigrated from here.

The Black Mountains

The **Black Mountains,** a large area of high moorland included within Brecon Beacons National Park, extend some 16 m. southwards from Hay to end in the Sugar Loaf above Abergavenny. On the W. the mountains are bounded by the Talgarth to Tretower road (Rte 32A), while to the E. the massif (in England) eases gently down to the lower ground across which lies Hereford. From the S. (A465 forming the boundary) the mountains are cut by several valleys, some of these being mentioned under Rte 37B below.—A small road S. out of Hay-on-Wye crosses the mountains from N. to S., leaving the highest ground to the W. (*Waun Fach,* 2660 ft), descending to *Llanthony Priory,* and reaching A465 at *Llanfihangel Crucorney.* Above Hay this small road reaches *New Forest,* a road fork.

The road to the left in 3 m. reaches *Craswall* in England, 1 m. N. of which by a footpath are some remains of a Benedictine priory founded by Roger de Lacy in 1222. Beyond Craswall the road descends the Monnow to *Longtown* (see Rte 37B below).

Above New Forest the road emerges on to open moor and soon crosses *Offa's Dyke,* clearly seen on the E. side with *Hay Bluff* (2219 ft) beyond. *Lord Hereford's Knob* (2263 ft) later stands close on the W. side, the road then descending to *Capel-y-Ffin* with a little whitewashed chapel. A monastery was founded here in 1870 by the Rev. Joseph Leycester, an Anglican clergyman who took the name Father Ignatius. The monastery did not long survive his death in 1908, but has now become a retreat for a R.C. community. The summit of Waun Fach is

2½ m. S.W. of here. For *Llanthony Priory,* 3 m. farther S., see Rte 37B below.

A network of walks cross the Black Mountains, the above small road providing a useful starting base. *Hay Bluff* is a popular objective, the view embracing the Wye valley, the Brecon Beacons (S.W.), Radnor Forest (N.), the Malvern Hills (E.), and even sometimes the Cotswolds (S.E.). From here walkers can bear S.E., crossing the border and following the shoulder to the left, to *Black Hill* (2102 ft). Beyond, the shoulder tapers rapidly to a narrow ridge, from which a descent of rather over 1 m. reaches a lane which leads to *Llanveynoe,* then *Longtown* and *Clodock* (for the two latter places, see Rte 37B below). An alternative from Hay Bluff is to take a path along the S.W. flank of Black Hill to the lane at *Blaen Olchon,* here bearing left for Llanveynoe. Yet another choice, for those wishing to return to Hay, is viâ *Craswall Priory.*—*Waun Fach* can be reached from Castell Dinas (p. 256) or from Capel-y-Ffin viâ the small Grwyne Fawr reservoir.

After Hay-on-Wye this Route for about 5 m. follows the more interesting N. side of the Wye, crossing the river to (*1 m.*) **Clyro,** where there are remains of a motte-and-bailey castle. Francis Kilvert was curate here from 1865-72, living in the 18C house opposite the Baskerville Arms and here writing much of his famous diary which describes the surrounding countryside. He is commemorated by a tablet in the church.—*2 m.* **Llowes,** where the church contains a Celtic stone with two faces, the simpler cross dating from the 7C and the wheel from the 11C. Known as the Great Cross of St Meilig, the stone is thought first to have stood on a nearby height, until brought to the churchyard in perhaps the 12C; it was moved into the church in 1956.

Painscastle, 3 m. N., has an early Norman motte, ascribed to Payn FitzJohn (1130). The castle, rebuilt in stone by Henry III, is sometimes identified as the 'Garde Douloureuse' of Scott's 'The Betrothed', the siege described in the novel being that of Gwenwynwyn of Powys, which took place here in the late 12C when Gwenwynwyn was fighting Llewelyn the Great.

About 1 m. beyond Llowes a road to the N. in ½ m. reaches *Maesyronen,* a curious Nonconformist chapel of 1696 complete with its contemporary fittings.—*2 m. Glasbury,* where the river is crossed.—*1 m. Three Cocks* is named after a locally famous coaching inn. Near Felindre, 1½ m. S.E., is *Gwernyfed Old Hall* (accommodation), a beautiful Tudor mansion visited by Charles I after his defeat at Naseby. The outer face of the S. porch incorporates a late 12C doorway, while the inner has a nail-studded door with a wicket. Inside are a minstrels' gallery; a staircase newel made from the mast of a Spanish galleon; and two portraits by Kneller.—*2 m.* **Bronllys** (p. 256), where Rte 32A is crossed.—*2 m.* At *Llanfilo,* S. of the road, the restored little church has a good 15C rood screen and loft, still with its original plaster tympanum, box-pews of 1600, and a simple font that may be pre-Norman.—*5 m.* Approaching Brecon the village of **Llanddew,** just N. of the A470, has some slight remains of a former palace of the bishops of St David's. Of the house of the archdeacons of Brecon, though, mentioned and occupied by Giraldus, there remains no trace. The church (12 or 13C) exhibits the external batter (probably copied from military architecture) typical of many churches in this neighbourhood. The transepts are entered by unusually small arches and have very narrow squints.

1 m. **Brecon,** see Rte 33A. Rte 32B is crossed here.—For Brecon to (*8 m.*) **Sennybridge,** see Rte 34.

This Route now turns S. on A4067, in ¾ m. reaching *Defynnog,* with a mainly 15C church founded in c. 450. A curious external feature is the 5-6C stone, bearing a Latin inscription and traces of other decorative work, which has been built into the S.W. angle of the tower. Inside the church the font bears a Runic (ancient Anglo-Saxon) inscription, believed to be the only specimen of Runic in Wales. The road now climbs to upland moor, passing *Cray Reservoir* and reaching *Bwlch Bryn-Rhudd* (1212 ft), *7 m.* from Sennybridge, with to the N.W. Cefn Cul (1844 ft) and to the S.E. Fan Gihirych (2381 ft).

In a little less than 2 m. below Bwlch Bryn-Rhudd a minor road ascends N. up the valley of the Tawe. *Cerrig Duon* (1270 ft), 2 m. up the valley and just W. of the road and river, is a prehistoric stone oval, a rather rare shape of which there are only about ten examples in Britain. The stones are small, and other curious features are the large standing stone just N. of the oval, and the rows of small stones starting from near the E. side. There is another standing stone ½ m. N. on the E. of the road.

The road now descends the Tawe all the way to Swansea.—*3 m.* **Dan-yr-Ogof**†. The caves here are the main feature of a tourist complex which includes a tourist information desk; a small museum; a geological trail; a dinosaur park; a motel, and a caravan site. Discovered in 1912 and opened in 1938 the caves, with about 1½ m. accessible to visitors, claim to be the longest and largest public caves system in Britain.—At **Craig-y-Nos,** just S. of the caves and in a lovely setting beside the Tawe, the grounds of the mansion have been converted into a country park with over 40 acres of wood, water, and open meadow. The summer programme includes demonstrations of the use of sheep and gun dogs, drystone walling, horse shoeing, sheep shearing, and other country activities. The mansion, known as *Craig-y-Nos Castle* and now a hospital, was built in 1842. In 1878 it was bought by the singer Adelina Patti, who built a small private theatre and lived here until her death in 1919.

Saeth Maen, 1 m. W. at 1280 ft and accessible only on foot, is a prehistoric alignment of seven stones (five still standing), pointing in the direction of Cerrig Duon.

Henrhyd Falls (N.T.), within the wooded ravine of the Llech, are reached by a road leading S.E. off A4067 1 m. S. of Craig-y-Nos.

The road now starts to enter the coal and industrial area, though there are many signs of reclamation.—*11 m.* **Pontardawe** is near collieries. *Abernant* (2 m. N.W.), completed in 1958 and virtually entirely mechanized, produces some 300,000 tons annually and will be considerably expanded. *Treforgan* (2 m. E.), a drift mine (1963-66), also almost entirely mechanized, produces about 227,000 tons yearly.—*4 m.* A4067 crosses the M4 motorway.—*3 m.* **Swansea,** see Rte 42.

B   Viâ Abergavenny, Merthyr Tydfil, and Neath

A465 to Neath: A483 to Swansea. 68 miles.—*7 m.* St Devereux (for **Kilpeck**).—*4 m.·* **Pontrilas** (for **Golden Valley**).—*6 m.* Pandy.—*2 m.* Llanfihangel Crucorney.—*5 m.* **Abergavenny.**—*16 m.* **Merthyr Tydfil.**—*6 m.* Hirwaun.—*4 m.* Glyn Neath.—*9 m.* **Neath.**—*9 m.* **Swansea.**

Between Hereford and Abergavenny the road skirts the gentle S.E. slopes of the Black Mountains, penetrated by several pleasant valleys. Rather bleak, part industrialized moorland between Abergavenny and Glyn Neath is followed by the part wooded and part industrialized Vale of Neath.

Hereford, see Rte 36.—*2m. Belmont Abbey,* see p. 281.—*5m. St Devereux* derives its name from St Dyfrig. At **Kilpeck,** just S., the 12C *******Church,* well restored in 1848, embodies some of the richest and most imaginative Norman carving in Britain, what is seen here being the most complete surviving example of the local-style of the mid 12C. Especially noteworthy are, on the exterior, the superb S. doorway and the W. window, with more carving on the belfry above; and, inside the church, the carving on the arch to the choir and within the apse. The church, once that of a now vanished priory, stands on the site of a 6 or 7C predecessor, a fragment of which can be seen at the lower exterior N.E. corner of the nave. The adjacent *Castle* is now no more than earthworks, a moat, and some ruined pieces of keep walls. The moat, immediately W. of the church, separates the old and new churchyards.

4m. **Pontrilas,** just short of the Welsh border and near the S.E. corner of the Black Mountains, is a hamlet where several roads meet. Various diversions can be made from here.

GOLDEN VALLEY, following the river Dore, slices N. for some 12m. through the lower E. slopes of the Black Mountains. The name is incorrectly derived from the river's name (Welsh, 'Dwr')), which has nothing to do with gold but means 'water'. At (1 m.) *Ewyas Harold* there is a motte-and-bailey which probably dates from the time of the Norman adventurers invited by Edward the Confessor. The church contains a 14C tomb of Lady Clarissa Tregoz, with her heart-cup in her hands.— ***Abbey Dore,** 1 m. farther N., is the church of a Cistercian abbey founded in 1147 by Robert of Ewyas, grandson of Ralph, Earl of Hereford. Of Robert's church nothing survives, and the present church, consisting of choir and transepts only, dates from 1180 to c. 1280, being architecturally mainly E.E. Allowed to fall into disrepair after the Dissolution, the church was restored in its present form by Lord Scudamore in 1633, and there was again a major restoration in 1902. In the Transepts, each with a single chapel, the murals are of the 17C. The screen, by John Abel, bears the arms of Charles I in the centre, flanked by those of Scudamore (N.) and Archbishop Laud (S.). Beyond, the Choir, with its clustered columns, represents E.E. architecture at its simplest and best. On the floor, either side of the altar, there are 13C tiles collected together after the restoration of 1902, and under an arch (S.) there is a mutilated 12C effigy of the monastery's founder. Except for the lectern, all the furniture here is the work of John Abel. The E. end of the church comprises an Ambulatory with five chapels, the foundations of the dividing walls of which can be seen. On the floor of the chapels there are 13C bosses, possibly from the former nave.—At *Bacton,* 1½m. N., the church, with a good cradle roof, contains the effigy of Blanche Parry, maid of honour to Elizabeth I.—At *Vowchurch,* 3m. farther N., the church, with a half-timbered belfry-spire, is unusual in that the main weight of the roof is carried on internal timber piers. From here a road leads W. across to the Escley and Monnow valleys (see below).

At **Rowlstone,** 1 m. W. of Pontrilas, the 12C church contains two unique 14C brackets, one bearing cocks and the other swans. On the choir arch there are two inverted figures, one being St Peter and the other an angel. The S. door has good ironwork (note the serpent entwined around the ring of the door handle), and a mid 12C tympanum with a Majesty.

Kentchurch Court†, 1½m. S.E. of Pontrilas, once a 14C fortified manor house, was largely rebuilt by Nash between 1795 and 1807. An older gateway survives, and the lower part of the N.W. tower is original. The court has long been the home of the Scudamores. One of Owen Glendower's daughters married Sir John Scudamore, who, with his three sons, was executed after Mortimer's Cross. For John Kent (John of Kentchurch) see Grosmont Church below.

The road crosses into Wales at (*1 m.*) *Monnow Cap.* **Grosmont Castle,** 1 m. S.E., was, with White and Skenfrith, one of the 'Three Castles' granted to Hubert de Burgh in 1201 but which he lost on his fall from power in 1232. It was besieged by Llewelyn the Great in 1233, but saved by the timely approach of Henry III; and again by Owen Glendower in 1405, this time being saved by the future Henry V. Mostly of the early

13C, but with some 14C additions on the N., Grosmont differs from the other two in the greater development of its residential character, but nevertheless, like White Castle, is remarkable for the strength of its earthworks. To the right on entering are the ruins of the unusually large Hall (c. 1210), curiously on the outer side of the later curtain (1220-40). Little else remains other than the ruins of curtain towers. In *Grosmont Church* (mostly 13C) only the choir and transepts are in use. Noteworthy are the late Norman arches of the nave, the Norman font, the E.E. arcading in the choir, and the Dec. piscina. John Kent (fl. 1400), also known as John of Kentchurch, is said to be buried here. A bard, his patrons the Scudamores sent him to Oxford and he later became priest at Kentchurch. Many stories surround him: that he was a magician, that he lived to 120, and that (presumably because of the Scudamore marriage link) he was Owen Glendower in hiding. The large figure in the S.E. of the nave, once thought to represent him, seems more likely to be of a knight. In the churchyard there is a preaching cross.

From Monnow Cap the road runs just within the border as far as (*5 m.*) *Pandy.*

From Pandy a diversion can be made N. up the valley of the Monnow. The border is crossed back into England in 2 m., *Clodock,* bearing the name of a grandson of the chieftain Brychan, being 1 m. farther. Here the church, with a Norman nave, has outstanding 17 and 18C woodwork, from the later period being the three-decker pulpit and the gallery. At *Longtown* (½ m. N.), with a ruined Norman keep on its motte, there is a choice of valleys, all, by small roads or on foot, ascending into the moorland of the N. part of the Black Mountains described on p. 283 above. In the church at *Michaelchurch Escley,* 4 m. N. up the valley of the Escley, there hangs a painted Christ of the Trades (in poor condition), a theme common in Cornwall but unusual in this part of the country.

2 m. Llanfihangel Crucorney is at the S. end of the road crossing the Black Mountains from Hay (see p. 282 above). *Llanfihangel Court*† is a Tudor and Stuart manor house, remodelled on a medieval predecessor. The plaster ceilings date from 1559 and the fine yew staircase from 1600.

The ruins of **Llanthony Priory** are 5 m. N. along the road to Hay.

History. In 1100 William de Lacy founded a religious community here on the site of a chapel dedicated to St David. Three years later he was joined by one Erniseus, a former court chaplain, the two men and their followers then building a church and the community becoming Austin Canons. The monks, however, having 'no mind to sing to the wolves' migrated first to Hereford and then to Gloucester. In 1175 however the community returned to Llanthony, building a new church, the ruins of which are those seen today. The priory was dissolved in 1538 and fell into neglect. In 1807 the estate was bought by the poet Walter Savage Landor. But his ambitious plans (involving a school, 10,000 cedars of Lebanon, and merino sheep) soon put him at loggerheads with his tenants, his neighbours, and the local authority, until, bankrupt, he assigned the estate to trustees in 1815.

Of the church (212 ft long) the W. front, with its twin towers, and portions of the nave, transepts, central tower, and choir remain. The style is a plain and severe early Transitional combined with E.E. There was no triforium; doorways rather than arches lead from the aisles to the transepts; and there is generally a sparing use of capitals and correspondingly frequent use of continuous mouldings. The Abbey Hotel cellars in part incorporate the remains of the prior's house, and a farm stands on the site of the domestic buildings. The old gatehouse forms part of a barn beside the road a short way north.—The adjacent *Parish Church* dates from the 13C and was probably the priory infirmary.

From Llanfihangel Crucorney another small road, W. of the one to Hay, ascends *Grwyne Fawr* to (9 m.) the small reservoir of the same name in the heart of the Black Mountains. This is a starting point for walks, including to Waun Fach (2660 ft) which is under 1 m. southwest. —At *Pont-y-Spig,* just under 3 m. along this road, lanes bear W. and then N. for the secluded little *Partrishow Church (or Patricio). The story goes that a holy man named Issui had a cell near here, probably at the holy well just below the church, the approach to which is marked by a stone cut with a Maltese cross. In the early 11C a church was built, tradition says with money left by a pilgrim who had been cured of leprosy, and it has been suggested that the chapel built on to the W. wall of today's church may mark the site of this. Giraldus came here in 1188 and is said to have preached from the cross (in part original) which stands in the churchyard. The church (restored in 1908 when in danger of collapse) is of various periods, the earliest part being the N. wall of the chapel and the windows in its W. wall, both 13C or earlier. The S. wall of the chapel and its roof, and the nave porch date from the 14C, while the remainder of the church seems to be of the 15 and 16C. Features of interest inside the church are the small but beautiful rood screen and loft (late 15C and probably local work); two very early stone altars in front of the screen, and a third in the chapel; the 15C cradle roof; a Welsh bible of 1620; and a decorated font which may be dated from the inscription round the rim saying in Latin that it was made 'in the time of Genillin', who has been identified as an 11C prince of Powys.

The road runs between the *Sugar Loaf* (N; p. 257) and *Skerrid Fawr* (S; p. 267).—*5 m.* (from Llanfihangel Crucorney) **Abergavenny,** for which (and the roads to Ross, Monmouth, and Newport) see Rte 35.

Between Abergavenny and Methyr Tydfil, and on to Hirwaun, A465 crosses rather bleak moorland between the S. part of Brecon Beacons National Park (Rte 33) and the South Wales industrial valleys (Rte 41).—*5 m. Clydach* was the birthplace of Sir Bartle Frere (1815-84), the maker of Sind and the first High Commissioner of South Africa (1877).—*2 m. Brynmawr* (7000 inhab.) developed with the growth of the iron smelting industry in the 19C. Although economically a part of the industrial valleys, the town lies on high ground. In turn the heads of the Ebbw Fach, Ebbw, Sirhowy, and Rhymney valleys are passed.

9 m. **Merthyr Tydfil** (61,000 inhab.), though once dependent upon coal, iron, and steel, is now a modern town which has largely cleared the scars of the past and today lives from diversified industries operating from the several industrial estates which surround the town and lie close to many modern housing estates.

History. The Romans were here, with a fort on the site of today's Penydarren Park, but the town derives its name from St Tydfil, a pious daughter of Brychan, who was murdered here in the 5C. A settlement grew around her shrine, this developing into a village dependent on Morlaix Castle (1 m. N.), built in 1275. In the 17C Merthyr Tydfil, by now a scattered hill village, became a centre for Dissenters. Industry came with the 18C, and by 1783 there were four ironworks in the area. The opening in 1795 of the Glamorganshire Canal between Merthyr and Cardiff (substituting water transport for slow and costly packhorses) gave a major boost to the town's prosperity. In 1804 the earliest steam locomotive, constructed by Richard Trevithick (1771-1833), was tried on the horse-tramway between Merthyr and Abercynon (8 m. S.), and in 1841 Brunel's railway to Cardiff was opened. By now, with around 22,000 inhabitants, Merthyr was the largest town in Wales, with numerous ugly iron and coal workings and their associated tips and slag-heaps. But decline came in the earlier part of this century when the import of cheaper ore from abroad not only killed ironstone mining but also led to the transference of the steel mills (1928-30) to the coast with its fast developing ports.—Joseph Parry (1841-1903), the composer, was born here. From 1900 the town's M.P. was James Keir Hardie (1856-1915), founder of the Independent Labour Party and the first Labour member.

The redeveloped town centre includes a shopping area (pedestrians only) of over 50 acres, close to the bus and railway stations, to the High

Street, also with many shops, and to a large car park by the river Taff. *St Tydfil's Church* (1809), successor to possibly several others, is said to stand on the site of the saint's murder; it contains two inscribed stones of the 6-9C. *Cyfarthfa Castle*†, in a large park about 1 m. N.W. of the town centre, was built in 1825 by the ironmaster William Crawshay and is now the town museum and art gallery. The museum tells the town's story from Roman to modern times, with particular reference to the industrial period, and the art gallery includes a collection of 19C paintings and watercolours of early Merthyr.

For Merthyr Tydfil to *Brecon* (Brecon Beacons, Talybont, and Taf Fechan), see Rte 33B.

6 m. Hirwaun is a colliery town at the head of the Cynon valley. About 1 m. W., by a colliery, A4061 climbs S. in a large loop over Hirwaun Common to descend into the Rhondda valley (Rte 41A).—*4 m. Glyn Neath*, at the head of the Vale of Neath.

From Glyn Neath a moorland road (picnic sites) leads N. across Fforest Fawr, the section of Brecon Beacons National Park to the W. of the Beacons. As far as (5 m.) the mountain village of *Ystradfellte* the road is wooded, with a number of waterfalls along the Mellte and Hepste rivers about 1 m. east. Beyond Ystradfelite the road ascends the valley of the Llia, the Roman Sarn Helen, here a track, coming in from the S.W. about 2 m. N. of the village. *Maen Madog*, ½ m. down the track, is a 9 ft high standing stone bearing a Latin inscription that this is the stone of Dervacus, son of Justus, who lies here. The stone was probably put up in prehistoric times, and the inscription is thought to date from some time between the 5 and the 9C. *Maen Llia*, near the road 2 m. farther N., is a 12 ft high standing stone.

A465 now runs S.W. down the **Vale of Neath,** a narrow but almost level valley, part wooded and part industrialized.—*4 m.* Above *Resolven,* on the other side of the valley, is the *Melincourt Waterfall.*— *4 m. Aberdulais.* Near Cilfrew, 1 m. N., is *Penseynor Wildlife Park*†, specializing in exotic birds.

1 m. **Neath** (29,000 inhab.) is a busy industrial town mostly on the E. bank of the river, though the abbey and the small Roman remains, the only things likely to interest the visitor, are on the W. side. Once noted as a centre of the copper industry, the first smelting house in South Wales was built here in 1584 by copper miners from Cornwall. The *Castle,* N.E. of the station, was founded by Richard de Granville in c. 1130, as successor to a motte-and-bailey on the more vulnerable W. bank, but was nevertheless burnt by Llewelyn the Great in 1231. All that now survives is the outer face of the gateway with two drum-towers linked by a flying arch.

The somewhat smoke-begrimed 13C ruins of **Neath Abbey**† are by the W. bank of the river a short way S. of the bridge.

History. The abbey was founded by Richard de Granville, on land taken from the Welsh, at the same time that he built his castle (1130), originally for Savigniac monks although in 1147 it became Cistercian. Becoming prosperous, mainly by trading in wool and hides, the monks built the present church between 1280 and 1330 and the abbey remained prosperous until dissolved in 1539. Later in the 16C part of the abbey was converted into a mansion by Sir John Herbert. With the rapid industrial development of the 18C the abbey was used as a forge while the Herbert mansion housed the workmen.

Beyond the entrance the Lay Brothers' quarters form the W. range of the site, the chimneys on the E. side of the quarters being relics of the period of industrial use. Moving N.E., the site of the main refectory (with at the N. end the washing bays) is crossed to the cloister, beyond the N. side of which is the *Church,* of which little remains except the outer walls of the nave and part of the W. front. It comprised a nave of seven bays and two aisles, and a presbytery of three bays. The transepts were each of two bays with two chapels. In the S. transept can be seen two altars, a piscina, and, on the W. side, the night-stairs. To the S., beyond the sacristy, is what little remains of the chapter house, beyond this being the *Herbert Mansion,* standing on the medieval foundations of the abbot's house. The *Dormitory Undercroft,* with good medieval vaulting, houses various abbey stones.

The remains of the *Roman Fort* of Nidum, established in 75-80 on the road from Caerleon to Carmarthen, were discovered in 1949 during the construction of a housing estate. What little there is to be seen (the lower courses of two gateways) can be found by taking the road signed 'Pontardawe' from the roundabout at the W. end of the river bridge; the remains are then on the right in about ¼ m. behind two sets of railings.

9 m. **Swansea,** see Rte 42.

38   HEREFORD TO CHEPSTOW

The Lower Wye Valley

A49 to Ross-on-Wye: A40 to Goodrich: B4432 to Lower Berry Hill: A4136 to Monmouth: A466 to Chepstow. 42 miles.—*8 m.* **Llandinabo.**—*6 m.* **Ross-on-Wye.**—*5 m.* **Goodrich Castle.**—*3 m.* **Symond's Yat Rock.**—*3 m. Lower Berry Hill.*—*1 m. Staunton.*—*3 m.* **Monmouth.**—*5 m. Bigsweir Bridge.*—*4 m.* **Tintern Abbey.**—*2 m. Wyndcliff.*—*2 m.* **Chepstow.**

The **Wye** (Welsh *Gwy*) rises on the slopes of Plynlimon, only 2 m. from the source of the Severn, flowing to the S.E. and E. past Rhayader, Builth Wells, and Hay to Hereford, and then S. to join the Severn just below Chepstow after a course of 135 miles. For a few miles N. of Hay, and again over its lower course below Monmouth, the river forms the border between Wales and England. The river is scenically lovely over virtually its entire length, but particularly so between Rhayader and Hay and between Ross and Chepstow.

This latter stretch, the **Lower Wye Valley**, with places such as Symond's Yat and Tintern Abbey, is the most popular, visitors having come here in increasing numbers since the valley first became fashionable with the tourists of the mid 18C.—From the 13C until as recently as 1901 the valley was industrially important, being the principal iron producing place in Britain and known for its wire mills. During these centuries, and particularly during the 18 and 19C, the river was a vital waterway, many places building ships. Ships of up to 90 tons ascended to Brockweir, from where goods continued upstream by barge. There was no valley road until the end of the 19C, the road from Monmouth to Chepstow running across the higher ground to the west. The Monmouth to Chepstow railway, opened in 1876, closed in 1959. The forest of the valley was ruthlessly exploited from medieval times until the 1920s when the Forestry Commission took over with the dual aim of improving productivity while at the same time preserving the scenery and developing recreational facilities. In 1938 the Wye woodlands became a part of the *Dean and Wye Valley Forest Park.*— For walkers there is the waymarked *Lower Wye Valley Walk,* provided

by the Gwent County Council with the cooperation of the Forestry
Commission and local landowners. This extends from Monmouth to
Wyndcliff, a distance of 14 miles. Details of this and other walks can be
obtained from County Hall, Cwmbran, Gwent. The *Offa's Dyke
Footpath* runs along the E. bank.

Hereford, see Rte 36, is left by Greyfriars Bridge. To the E. *Dinedor
Hill* has a hillfort, as does also farther S. *Aconbury Hill*, higher and
nearer the road.—*8 m.* At *Llandinabo* the church contains a particularly
fine Tudor rood screen carved with a marine theme of dolphins and
mermaids.—*2 m. Pengethley Park* is a National Trust property
(footpath access).

4 m. **Ross-on-Wye** (6000 inhab.) is a market town on a hill above the
E. bank of the Wye. The town centre is the Market House, with *Tourist
Information* just below at 20 Broad Street and car parking a short way
N.E. off Henry Street. Ross owes much to John Kyrle (1637-1724), born
in the nearby village of Dymock. A barrister, he was a noted local
benefactor who, amongst other things, did much for the poor, preserved
the church, and gave the town its water supply. He became known as the
'Man of Ross' and was eulogized by Pope ('Moral Essay', 1732); his
portrait hangs at Croft Castle.—The *Market House*, in local red
sandstone, was designed by John Abel and built between 1660-74. On
the E. wall is a medallion of Charles II, also commemorated, on the S.E.
corner, by a monogram, F.C. intertwined with a heart, thought to imply
'Faithful to Charles in heart' and to have been put up by Kyrle. Kyrle's
house, bearing his bust, is adjacent, and the garden with its summer
house can be seen on application to the shop now here. *St Mary's
Church*, just S.W. of the Market House, a large Dec. and Perp. building,
was founded in the 13C but underwent much rebuilding in 1743 and
again in 1862. The 14C spire was rebuilt (pinnacles being added) in 1721,
much of the cost being born by Kyrle whose grave is in the church. Also
noteworthy in the church are the monuments to the Rudhall family, in
particular those to John (d. 1636) and his wife, and to Colonel William
(d. 1651) in Roman armour. The Plague Cross in the churchyard
commemorates the 315 people who lost their lives in 1637. The adjacent
Prospect offers a good view of the Wye's horseshoe bend. It was in the
nearby *Royal Hotel* (1837), on the site of a manor of the bishops of
Hereford, that in 1867 Charles Dickens first met his biographer John
Forster. Old Gloucester Road, just S.E. of the Market House, was once
the town's main through road. It is said that George IV, after being held
up here by traffic (plaque 'King George's Rest' at junction of Old
Gloucester Road and Copse Cross Street) ordered the new road
(Gloucester Road) to be built.

Leaving Ross this Route crosses *Wilton Bridge*, built in 1597 and
widened during the Second World War. To its N. ruined *Wilton Castle*
(no adm.), built in the 13C to defend the river ford, was destroyed by the
Royalists during the Civil War.

A40 in *5 m* reaches the road to **Goodrich Castle**†, superbly sited on
bedrock above the river.

History. The castle takes its name from Godric, who built the first fortress here,
of which however nothing survives. Today's ruins are of the 12C (keep) and 13C
(remainder of the castle). The castle was held by the earls of Pembroke throughout
most of the 13C, passing in c.1326 to the Talbots, created earls of Shrewsbury in
the 15C, whose principal residence it became. During the Civil War Goodrich was

held first by Parliament and then by the Royalists who, under Sir Henry Lingen, defended it against an attack in which the stables were burnt. Later it was slighted. It was here that Wordsworth met the little girl who inspired 'We are Seven' (1793).

The entrance is at the N.E. at the Barbican, beyond which the moat is crossed to the Gatehouse with, on its S., the Chapel. Turret stairs climb to the rooms above, from where a wall-walk leads to the S.E. tower. Below this, in the inner ward, are the entrance to the dungeon and the mid 12C *Keep*. The Hall lines the W. side of the ward, to its N., beyond a small room, being the Solar. Note here the slender pillar from the room below, splitting into two arches at the W. end of the solar. From here a postern gives acess to the outer ward.

All that remains of *Flanesford Priory*, an Augustinian house founded in 1346, is the refectory, now incorporated in a farm just E. of Goodrich village. The river is crossed by *Kerne Bridge* (1828), from the other side of which the village of *English Bicknor* is c. 4m. south. The 12-15C church here was built within the perimeter of the Norman motte-and-bailey. It contains 12C N. and S. arcades and, at the E. end of the nave but thought to have originally been the S. door, an archway carved with chevrons. *Symond's Yat Rock* is c. 3m. farther.

From Goodrich the direct road to *Symond's Yat Rock* (*3m.*) is due S., crossing the river by Huntsham bridge (B4432). The rock, a famous beauty spot (473 ft), rising between two reaches of the river which at their nearest point are only 500 yards apart, commands a glorious view in which the river below loops through pastoral and wooded scenery. To the E. are the steep Caldwell Rocks, where the Wye makes a wide bend to the N., while to the S.W. the river sweeps round the Great Doward (661 ft). A log cabin at the car park provides leaflets describing forest and geological trails and the Forest of Dean (see 'Blue Guide to England').—The small ferry to the village of *Symond's Yat*, on the W. bank, is below the W. side of the rock (½ hr on foot).

A40 southwards from Goodrich in 2m. reaches *Whitchurch*, from where B4164 leads in 1m. to the popular village of **Symond's Yat** below the rocks which here wall the Wye. Beyond Whitchurch the hill of Great Doward rises on the S. of the road, on its S. slope being *King Arthur's Cave* (accessible by road and path), in which fossil remains of mammoth, rhinoceros, and hyena and also Neolithic flint implements have been found. Between the cave and Ganarew on A40 is *Little Doward Camp*, a large hillfort in which, according to tradition, Caractacus held out against Scapula.

From Symond's Yat Rock this Route continues S. on B4432 to (*3m.*) *Lower Berry Hill* where A4136 is taken west.—*1m.* In the church at *Staunton*, built between 1100 and 1325, there is a curious pulpit which incorporates an entrance to the now vanished rood loft. The road, now crossing into Wales, descends through woods, on the right being the *Robinson Oak* (sign), planted in 1790. Reaching the valley the road turns S.W. and soon passes (1.) a road which climbs *Kymin Hill* (850 ft), a National Trust property bought in 1902 with local subscriptions. On the hill there is a 'Naval Temple' erected in 1800 by a dining club in honour of 16 of Nelson's admirals. Nelson breakfasted here in 1802, while on a visit to Monmouth with Lady Hamilton. The road crosses the Wye and then A40 at *Monmouth School*, founded in 1614, though most of the present buildings are mid and late 19C.

3m. (from Staunton) **Monmouth** (6700 inhab.) is a pleasant market town on the W. bank of the Wye just N. of where it is joined by the Monnow. Its best known feature is its unique 13C fortified bridge. For the most part the town's street plan has been unchanged since c. 1450.

Tourist Information. Market Hall, just N.W. of Agincourt Square, the town centre.

Parking. Just N. of Agincourt Square.

Early Closing. Thursday.

History. Monmouth was probably the site of the Roman Blestium. Later, in succession came Saxon and early Norman (1068) fortresses, followed by a 12C stone castle. The town grew around this castle, and around a Benedictine priory founded at about the same time. Geoffrey of Monmouth was born in the town in c. 1100 and, though there is no certainty about this, the future Henry V (Harry of Monmouth) in the castle in 1387. When in 1535 Henry VIII created the county of Monmouth, hitherto under the jurisdiction of the Lords Marcher, the town became its capital, a position it has now lost with the creation of the county of Gwent. 'Monmouth caps', woollen headgear worn by medieval soldiers, are mentioned in Shakespeare's 'Henry V' as having been worn at Agincourt ('Welshmen did good service . . . wearing leeks in their Monmouth caps').

Agincourt Square, the old market, is the town centre. *Shire Hall* (1724) carries a statue of Henry V, placed here in 1792 when the Wye valley was becoming so popular with tourists. It was in this hall that John Frost and other Chartists were tried in 1839. In front of the hall stands a statue (Goscombe John) to the Hon. C. S. Rolls, born at nearby Hendre, one of the founders of Rolls Royce, killed in a flying accident in 1910. In the bar of *The King's Head* there is a fine plaster likeness of Charles I, dating from the Restoration. Of the *Castle*, approached by Castle Hill roughly opposite Shire Hall, little survives beyond the early 12C keep (or Great Tower), traditionally birthplace of Henry V. The adjacent *Great Castle House*, now army property, was built in 1673 by the 3rd Marquess of Worcester because, it is said, he wanted the birthplace of his grandson to be as near as possible to that of Henry V.

Priory Road, leading N. out of Agincourt Square and constructed in 1837, represents the only significant addition to the town's medieval street plan. Here the *Market Hall*, a 1969 rebuilding of a Victorian hall burnt down in 1963, houses the post office and also the *Local History Centre†* and the *Nelson Collection†*, consisting largely of material collected by the mother of C. S. Rolls, an admirer of the admiral. Included in the collection are portraits of Nelson and Lady Hamilton, letters, and a model of the Battle of Trafalgar. *St Mary's Church*, a short way N.E. of the Market Hall, on the site of the church of the priory, is mainly a rebuilding of 1881 by G. E. Street, though the tower and spire are older. In the baptistry there are some 15C tiles and a cresset stone from the earlier church (c. 1102). In the nearby *Roman Catholic Church* there are relics of John Kemble, a priest executed in Hereford in 1679.

From Agincourt Square Monnow Street leads S. to **Monnow Bridge* (13C), a unique example in Britain of a fortified gateway on a bridge. Just across the bridge is the *Church of St Thomas Becket* which, though much restored, retains its Norman choir arch and a N. door (c. 1180). The mock-Norman porch is of the 19C. To the S.W. of Monnow Bridge is the *Clawdd Du*, with a small medieval bridge, an early earthwork constructed to defend this outlying part of the town.

For Monmouth to *Abergavenny*, see Rte 35C.

There are a number of places of interest in the area S. of Monmouth lying between the Wye and the A449 from Raglan to Newport. B4293 out of Monmouth, the main road to Chepstow before c. 1820, in 5m. reaches **Trellech**. Here the *Church* (early 14C) is successor to an earlier church founded in the 7 or 8C, to which period the base of the Preaching Cross in the churchyard and the Saxon font may belong. The *Harold Stones*, 250 yards S. of the church, have nothing to do with King Harold but are prehistoric standing stones. The *Tump*, S.W. of the church, is a Norman motte, and the *Virtuous Well* (S.E. on the road to Tintern), with some medieval stonework, probably owes its reputed healing qualities to the iron content of the water. Rather less than 4 m. farther S., a road bearing S.W. in 2 m. reaches *Wolves Newton Folk Museum*†, with domestic and agricultural bygones housed in old barns. At *Llangwm Uchaf*, 2 m. W. of Wolves Newton, the church of St Jerome (at the road's end) has a 15C locally carved rood screen and loft, still with tympanum. At the base of the choir arch are three 'green men', two on the N. and one on the south. With oak leaves in their mouths they link pagan with Christian tradition. The road from Llangwm to Chepstow (B4235) in 3 m. reaches a junction of six roads, just N. of which, behind a hedge on the N. side of the road, is *Gaer Llwyd Burial Chamber*, now little more than collapsed stones. For *Wentwood Forest,* S.W. of here, see p. 299.

From Monmouth A466 is followed down the E. bank of the Wye.—*2 m. Redbrook* was during the 17 and 18C a copper smelting centre, and tinplate works started at Lower Redbrook in 1771 were closed in 1961.—*3 m. Bigsweir Bridge* where the road crosses to the W. bank.—*3 m. Brockweir Bridge*. When the Wye was an important commercial waterway, this was the point at which goods were transferred from ships into barges.

1 m. *Tintern Abbey† is pleasantly situated beside the Wye below wooded hills.

History. The Cistercian abbey was founded here in 1131, but of this abbey little remains, most of today's ruins dating from rebuilding in the 13 and 14C. Occupied mainly with agriculture, the abbey was at its most prosperous during the early 14C. Edward II visited here in 1326, prior to trying to escape from Chepstow. After the Dissolution the abbey was neglected until made popular by the romantically minded travellers of the 18C.

Before entering the site the W. exterior face should be noted, particularly the fine tracery of the great window of seven lights and of the moulded arch enclosing the two trefoil-headed openings of the W. doorway.—From the entrance a passage to the right leads into the W. end of the *Nave* (mostly late 13C), which retains its clerestory on the S. side. The W. window and doorway have already been noted. The four large and beautiful arches of the crossing formerly supported a tower, and beyond is the huge and beautifully proportioned *East Window, covering almost the whole of the wall. The nave may be left by the Processional Doorway beside the N. transept, beyond being the E. walk of the *Cloister*. On the right are the *Library* and the *Vestry*, now, because of the disappearance of the wall between them, one room. From the vestry there is a door into the *North Transept*, which incorporates remains of the original 12C church and retains the night-stairs and a six-light window with much of its tracery. Continuing along the E. walk of the cloister the *Chapter House* and *Parlour* are passed, a walk along the N. side of the latter reaching the *Infirmary Cloister*, across which (E.) is the *Infirmary*, with to its N. its *Kitchens*. Note here the great drain. To the N. of the Kitchens are the *Abbot's Quarters*, with his lodging and adjacent chapel on the E. and his hall to the west.

To the W. of the Abbot's Hall is the admirable *Exhibition*, telling the story of Tintern and its abbey. Among the themes illustrated are the geology of the district; early man; and the various stages of the abbey (including information on the Cistercians and monastic life generally) from its founding to today's rescue and conservation.

From the Exhibition a walk leads S. back to the Infirmary Cloister, passing on the right the *Reredorter* and its drain. Beyond, the *Novices' Lodging* is on the right. If this is left by its S. door, a right turn passes the

Tintern Abbey

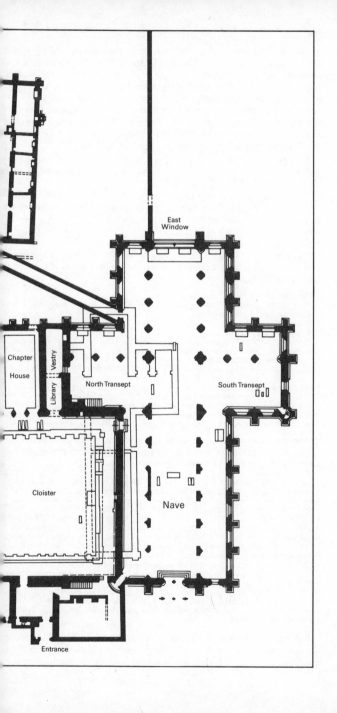

East
Window

Chapter
House

Vestry

Library

North Transept

South Transept

Cloister

Nave

Entrance

Day-Stairs and arrives at the N. walk of the main cloister. Along this walk are in turn the *Warming House*, the *Monks' Refectory*, the *Kitchen* (note the serving hatch), and the *Lay Brothers' Refectory*. This last is larger than that of the monks since, with the Cistercian emphasis on agriculture, the lay brothers normally outnumbered the monks.

The abbey made much use of the river as a waterway, and the adjacent Anchor Hotel is on the site of the *Watergate*; a 13C arch leading to a slipway can be seen.—Just W. of the abbey, beside the car park, the *Guest House* and other buildings have been excavated.

Chapel Hill Walk (1½ m.) and *Barbadoes Walk* (2 m.) are two waymarked walks in Tintern Forest, both starting from the Forestry Commission car park ¼ m. up the Llanishen road from the Royal George Hotel.

2 m. Wyndcliff is a well-known viewpoint, the view being dominated by the Severn Bridge. The viewpoint can be reached either by steps from a car park on the main road, or by a path from another car park a short way up the road signed 'Wyndcliff' (Forestry Commission plan of local walks).—*Chepstow Racecourse* was developed in 1926.

2 m. **Chepstow** (8000 inhab.) stands on the W. bank of the Wye, 2 m. above its junction with the Severn, and is most visited for its impressive and finely sited castle.

Tourist Information. High Street.
Parking. Off Beaufort Square in town centre. Castle (also for museum).
Caravan Site. Racecourse.
Post Office. Station Road.
Early Closing. Wednesday
History. The town's name is Saxon, meaning Market Town. To the Romans it was known as Castell Gwent and to the Normans as Striguil. Of the Romans there is little evidence except the remains of a ford a short way upstream of the castle, and the excavation of coins and, in 1973, cremation sites near St Mary's Church. From Norman times until the Civil War the town's story was largely that of the castle, within the shelter of which, and of a priory of about the same period, it developed. The town was granted a charter in 1524. Chepstow also developed as a port and shipbuilding centre, an activity which was at its most prosperous in the late 18 and early 19C. Today ships are still seen, but shipbuilding (during the last war mainly landing craft) has now been superseded by general engineering.

The *Castle†*, covering a considerable area and comprising three wards, a keep, and a barbican, occupies a striking situation strung along a steep platform of rock washed by a broad reach of the Wye.

History. Erected by William FitzOsbern, Earl of Hereford, soon after the Conquest, the castle is unusual for having been built from the outset in stone. This original Norman keep (or Great Tower) survives, making Chepstow one of the oldest stone castles in Europe. As the result of a rebellion FitzOsbern's son lost both castle and title in 1075. In 1189 the castle passed by marriage to William Marshal, who, with his five sons, each of whom succeeded in turn, much increased the place's strength. In the 13C Chepstow was held by the Bigods, earls of Norfolk, and in the 15C it passed to William Herbert, Earl of Pembroke, remaining in this family until the present century. In 1326 Edward II, pursued by his relentless wife Isabella, sailed from Chepstow, but was soon blown back into Cardiff. During the Civil War the castle was twice taken by Parliament; in 1645 it surrendered after only brief resistance, but later was again held for the King, on this second occasion the defender being Sir Nicholas Kemeys who, though deserted by his men, fought on alone until killed.—Henry Marten, the regicide, was imprisoned here in what is now called Marten's Tower from 1660 until his death in 1680, and Jeremy Taylor for six months in 1655.

Entrance is through a Gatehouse (1225–45), flanked by towers, beyond being the Inner Ward. To the N. are the remains of domestic quarters, including the Hall and Kitchens and, below the former, a

Crypt. This part of the castle, overhanging the cliff, offers a good view down to the river, and upwards to the Great Tower. On the S.E. of this ward stands Marten's Tower. The Middle Ward is crossed to the Great Tower, the original castle (1067-72). The E. door and the S. and W. wall arcades are the oldest features. Beyond are the Upper Ward and the Barbican.

The *Chepstow Museum*†, across Bridge Street from the castle car park, is concerned with local history, including that of the Wye and the Forest of Dean. Near here two bridges cross the Wye; the road bridge dates from 1816, and the railway bridge, although modernized, was originally built by Brunel. *St Mary's Church* was once that of a Benedictine priory, traces of which were excavated on the S. side of the church in 1973. Of the early church the Norman nave and aisle and W. door arch remain, although this last was originally the N. porch, removed to this position during rebuilding of 1841. Inside the church are the tomb of Henry Marten; the canopied tomb of the 2nd Earl of Worcester (d. 1549) and his wife; and an elaborate monument to Margaret Clayton (d. 1620), with effigies of her two husbands and 12 children. In Beaufort Square a German gun serves as memorial to Able Seaman Williams of Chepstow, who won the Victoria Cross at Gallipoli. The 13C *Port Wall*, which enclosed the medieval town on the S. and W., can be traced throughout much of its course, one good place being the main car park. The W. gate, though probably more or less true to the original design, is a rebuilding of 1524.

The S. end of *Offa's Dyke* is across the Wye from Chepstow.

For the *Severn Bridge*, and the S. coast to *Newport, Cardiff, Swansea,* and *Carmarthen,* see Rte 39.

39 SEVERN BRIDGE TO CARMARTHEN

A48 and A4161 to Cardiff: A4160 and A4055 to Barry: B4265 to St Bride's Major: B4524 to Bridgend: A48 to Penllergaer: A484 to Carmarthen. 105 miles.—
5 m. **Caerwent.**—*3 m.* **Penhow Castle (for Wentwood Forest).**—*6 m.* **Newport.**—
11 m. **Cardiff.**—*3 m.* **Penarth.**—*4 m.* **Barry.**—*3 m.* *Rhoose Airport.*—*7 m.* **Llantwit Major.**—*6 m.* *St. Bride's Major.*—*4 m.* *Ogmore Castle.*—*2 m.* **Ewenny Priory.**—
2 m. **Bridgend.**—*8 m.* **Margam Park.**—*5 m.* **Port Talbot (for Cwm Afan).**—*3 m.* *Briton Ferry* (for **Swansea**).—*8 m.* **Penllergaer.**—*3 m.* **Loughor.**—*3 m.* **Llanelli.**—
9 m. **Kidwelly.**—*10 m.* **Carmarthen.**

For most of its length this Route crosses industrial South Wales. Nevertheless industry tends to occur in pockets and there are several stretches which are clear of it, while diversions either side of the road quickly lead either to a pleasant coast or to often scenic valleys ascending to moorland. The M4 motorway is never far from the roads described.

The **Severn Bridge** (toll), which also crosses the mouth of the Wye, was opened in 1966 as part of the London-South Wales M4 motorway. It has an overall length of 5240 ft, and a central span between the 400 ft suspension towers of 3240 ft, while the suspended structure has the shape of an aerofoil to reduce both weight and wind resistance. There is a footpath. The view is exposed and, especially at low water, somewhat bleak. *Beachley,* the peninsula separating the Wye and the Severn, the tip of which is crossed by the bridge, was where in 603 the Celtic bishops crossed in order to meet St Augustine and attempt, though without success, to reconcile the differences between the Celtic and Catholic Churches. *Offa's Dyke* starts at Sedbury Cliffs, c. 1 m. N. of the bridge.

The **Severn Tunnel**, through which runs the London to South Wales railway, is 3 m. downstream of the road bridge. The longest tunnel in Britain (4 m., 638 yards), it was constructed in 1873-86 by Charles Richardson, a pupil of Brunel. At places the tunnel is 100 ft below the bed of the river.

Chepstow (see p. 296) is reached by a spur off the motorway.—*5 m.* (from Chepstow) ***Caerwent** is the site of an extensive and interesting Romano-Welsh town, and, according to some scholars, also the birthplace of St. Patrick.

History. The capital of the native Silures was the hillfort of *Llanmelin,* 1 m. north. On occupying new territory it was the Roman custom to transfer the inhabitants of capital hillforts to new towns, built of course to a Roman pattern, this happening to the Silures in c. 75. Their new town of Caerwent, or Venta Silurum, was easily controlled by the Romans whose main E.-W. road, considerably wider than the present road, ran through its centre. The town would have been at its most prosperous during the 2C, at which time or a little later the original earthwork boundary was strengthened by a stone wall. Insecurity came with the 3C, and in c. 340 the town's defences were improved by the addition of bastions. With the departure of the Romans (c. 400) Caerwent, though partially reoccupied from time to time, began to fall into ruin. Later came the Normans, building their motte-and-bailey castle in c. 1070.—Finds from Caerwent are displayed in the museum at Newport.

The town is a rectangle covering some 44 acres, divided by streets into 20 regular blocks. The *Church* (13C, but probably successor to an earlier one), roughly halfway along the E.-W. road, makes a good starting point. In the porch there are two exceptionally interesting inscribed stones. One records the erection of a statue by the tribal senate of the Silures to Paulinus, successively commander of the 2nd Legion and governor of the Gaul provinces of Narbonensis and Lugdunensis. The other, dedicated to Ocelus Mars, indicates how native and Roman gods became merged into one. Across the road from the church the village war memorial stands on a Roman platform. A few yards W. from here, Pound Lane leads N. to the remains of a combined shop and house and, just beyond, a house. Farther W. along the Roman road the *West Gate* is reached, a stone stile here giving access to the town walls which can be followed round to the E. gate. The most interesting section is the *South Wall,* with the remains of bastions (the addition of 340) attached to the outer face. From the *South Gate,* contemporary with the 2-3C wall, there is a choice between continuing round the wall, passing (S.E. corner) the *Norman Motte;* or a lane may be taken due N. to its junction with the E.-W. road, opposite being the site of the *Temple.* The *North Gate* can also be visited.

Caldicot Castle†, 2 m. S.E. of Caerwent, has a round 12-14C keep and a large gatehouse. Now owned by the District Council, the castle is used for medieval jousting and banquets and also contains a museum with a collection of 18C costume, antique furniture etc. The figurehead of Nelson's flagship 'Foudroyant' and some cannon are in the grounds.—At *Portskewett*, 1 m. E. of Caldicot Castle, there is a long barrow ¾ m. N.E. of the church beside a road; it has traces of two chambers. On the shore *Sudbrook Camp,* dating from the early 1C, contains the ruin of a Norman chapel.

3 m. **Penhow Castle†,** a small fortified manor dating from the 12-16C, was first held by the St Maur family, a name which soon corrupted to Seymour. Later the castle changed hands frequently, at one time becoming a farm, until bought in 1973 by Mr Stephen Weeks whᴏ put major restoration in hand. The oldest part is the 12C keep. The curtain wall probably dates from the 13C, the two halls (originally one) from the 14 and 15C, and a Tudor wing was added in the 16C. The adjacent church (reconstructed in 1914 on its 13C plan) was within the outer ward and thus served as a defence point (note the arrow slits in the tower).

Wentwood Forest, lying 1½ m. N. of Penhow, originally belonged to the Marcher lordship of Striguil (Chepstow) but at the end of the 15C passed to the 1st Earl of Worcester. By this time tenants' rights were clearly defined, the law being applied twice yearly at a court held at *Foresters' Oaks,* now a road junction just N. of Wentwood Reservoir. During the 17 and 18C the demand for timber for shipbuilding and for oak bark for tanning led to the enclosure of much of the forest, and exploitation continued well into the present century. The forest now comprises some 3000 acres, over half of which is managed by the Forestry Commission. There are several picnic sites, from which start waymarked walks, the most popular being *Wentwood Reservoir,* with two walks (2 and 4 m.) and also a Countryside Trail (2 m.) ascending *Gray Hill,* on the slope of which there is a stone circle. The hillfort of *Llanmelin,* ancient capital of the Silures, is 1 m. E. of *Llanvair Discoed* (S.E. of Wentwood) where there are fragments of a 13C castle. *Cas Troggy,* the slight remains of another 13C castle, is on the N. edge of the forest, in or near which are a number of other earthworks and similar remains.

A48 crosses M4 and runs through the E. suburbs of Newport. At a fork reached in 2½ m. A48 bears left, crossing the Usk by George Street Bridge. The righthand fork soon reaches Newport Bridge, just across which are the castle and the city centre.

6 m. **NEWPORT** (137,000 inhab.), on the tidal Usk, is a busy industrial and commercial centre and port which has also been an episcopal see (Diocese of Monmouth) since 1921. Among places of interest are the cathedral, the museum, the murals in the civic centre, and the transporter bridge.

The compact **City Centre** (High Street, Commercial Street, and John Frost Square pedestrian precinct) is a short way beyond the W. end of Newport Bridge. The *Bus Station* and a *Car Park* are alongside John Frost Square; the *Post Office* is in High Street; and the *Railway Station,* with another car park, is just west.

History. The castle was first built in 1171, and by early medieval times the town had developed into a trading centre, called 'Novus Burgus' or 'Castell Newydd' in distinction to the 'old port' at Caerleon. The town was seized by Simon de Montfort, and in 1402 was sacked by Owen Glendower. Major change came with the industrialization of South Wales from 1750 onwards, this particularly affecting the docks, hitherto little more than river wharfs, and with the opening of the valleys' canals in the 1790s Newport became the principal coal port of South Wales. In 1839 Newport was the scene of Chartist riots under the local leader John Frost. The Transporter Bridge was built in 1906, and the George Street Bridge (A48) in 1964.

The **Castle,** at the busy road intersection W. of Newport Bridge, was first built in 1171, rebuilt in the 14C, considerably modified in the 15C, slighted after the Civil War, and what was left was restored in 1930. Virtually nothing remains other than the E. side of a former courtyard rising directly from the mud banks of the Usk, the ruins consisting chiefly of a square central tower (at the top the chapel, and in the bottom the watergate) between two octagonal towers with rectangular bases.

The old *Westgate Hotel,* at the N.W. end of Commercial Street, was held by the mayor during the Chartist riots, and the bullet-marked pillars of its porch are preserved in the present hotel. The good **Museum and Art Gallery**† is in John Frost Square, a pedestrian precinct off Commercial Street and beside the bus station. The Roman material from Caerwent and Caerleon includes casts of the two interesting inscribed stones at Caerwent church. Other themes in the museum are the Chartist riots; natural history; and local activities and industries, including sections on iron and the docks. In the Art Gallery are early English watercolours, including 18 and 19C local scenes; Pontypool and Usk japan ware; and sculpture which includes works by Epstein, Rodin, and Goscombe John. The **Civic Centre,** a handsome group of buildings in Clytha Park ½ m. W. of the city centre beyond the railway, is known for its murals (Hans Feibusch, 1961-64) telling the story of Monmouthshire. The subjects are Celtic settlement; Roman Caerleon; the coming of Christianity; the building of Tintern Abbey; the burning of Newport Castle by Owen Glendower; the Battle of Agincourt (Henry V having been born at Monmouth); the surrender of Raglan Castle during the Civil War; the Chartist riot; steelworks; the arrival of American troops during the last war; the building of George Street Bridge (1964).

St Woolos Cathedral, until 1921 the parish church, is at the top of Stow Hill, ¾ m. S. of the centre.

History. The name is a corruption of Gwynllwy, a local 6C lord who was converted to Christianity and then built the first church on this hill. A Norman church followed; in the 15C, after Owen Glendower's destruction, the N. and S. aisles were rebuilt and the tower was added. With the creation of the Diocese of Monmouth the church became pro-cathedral in 1921 and cathedral in 1949. The E. end was extended in the 1960s.

On the W. exterior the headless statue is supposed to be that of Jasper Tudor (d. 1495), uncle of Henry VII and reputed builder of part of the tower. The *Lady Chapel,* immediately E. of the tower, is thought to occupy the site of the first church and to be the oldest part of the present one. Its E. wall is 12C; the other walls are 13C, and it has been suggested that they may include pre-Norman material. The *Nave* (12C, with 15C aisles) is entered through a remarkably fine Norman arch, the columns of which are thought to be of Roman origin from Caerleon. The nave itself is typically Norman, with a clerestory of narrow round-headed windows.

The interesting **Transporter Bridge** is reached by Commercial Street and its extension Commercial Road. Built in 1906, there are only three others similar, one being at Middlesbrough and the other two in France. A movable platform carries cars and pedestrians, up to a load of 120 tons. A staircase (fee) climbs to the top span, from where there is a fine view. Once very busy, the bridge has now been largely replaced by the George Street Bridge.

The L-shaped **Docks** lie S. of the Transporter Bridge. Entered by a lock, they comprise a N. and S. dock with a combined water area of 125 acres. The docks handle general cargo, iron and steel, and cars, and there are specialized facilities for timber. An oil tank farm enables coastal tankers to discharge.

Llanwern Steelworks, to the E. of Newport S. of the railway, started production in 1962 and can claim to be the first in the world to be reliant entirely on basic oxygen steelmaking; the first to install automatic charging of blast furnaces; the first to incorporate full computer control from furnaces to coilers; and the first works to be built in Britain after the 1956 Clean Air Act.

Tredegar House Country Park, 2½ m. S.W. of the city centre, is 90 acres of park acquired by the local authority in 1974 as a recreation area (walled gardens; picnics; boating and fishing; children's farm etc.). The 16 and 17C mansion (visits) is undergoing a 20 year programme of restoration.

For Newport to *Caerleon, Usk,* and *Abergavenny,* see Rte 35D; to *Pontypool* and *Abergavenny,* see Rte 35E; to the *Ebbw* and *Sirhowy* valleys, see Rte 41E.

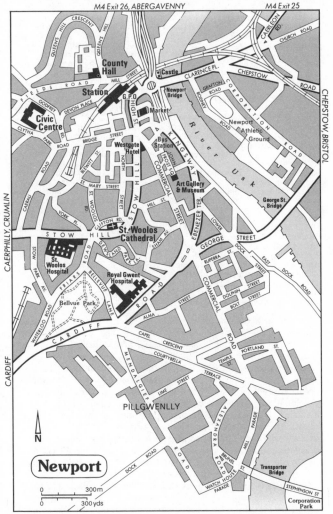

Beyond Newport A48 skirts the marshes of the *Wentloog Level,* bordering the Bristol Channel.—*7 m. St Mellons,* where the E. suburbs of **Cardiff** (see Rte 40) are reached, the road in *4 m.* arriving at the city centre.

In addition to the M4, there is a choice of three roads between Cardiff and Bridgend. This Route follows the most interesting through Barry and Llantwit Major. The other choices, the main A48 through Cowbridge and a northerly road† viâ Llantrisant, are described immediately below.

CARDIFF TO BRIDGEND VIÂ COWBRIDGE. (20 m). With the castle on the right, Cardiff is left by Cowbridge Road which in 7 m. reaches *St Nicholas,* ½ m. S. of which is *Tinkinswood Long Cairn.* Excavated in 1914 this large and quite well-preserved burial chamber has, from the grave goods discovered, been dated to about the middle of the third millenium B.C. The weight of the capstone has been estimated as c. 40 tons. The bones of around 50 people, flint implements, and pottery were found here. *Dyffryn House*†, just beyond, a residential educational centre, is known for its garden. About 1 m. farther a left turn almost immediately reaches *St Lythan Long Cairn,* smaller and in less good condition than Tinkinswood.—**Cowbridge** (1500 inhab.) is 6 m. beyond St Nicholas. A turning S. off the long main street leads to the 14C walls and gatehouse, with, adjacent, the Grammar School, endowed in 1685. A short way beyond the walls, a right turn at a T junction soon reaches the small ruin of *St Quentin's Castle,* with a 14C gateway. At *St Hilary,* 1½ m. S.E. of Cowbridge, there is a Norman church, and ruined *Beaupré Castle,* 1 m. S. of St Hilary, is a late Elizabethan mansion with Renaissance doorways.—**Bridgend** (see below) is reached in 7 m.

CARDIFF TO BRIDGEND VIÂ LLANTRISANT (19 m.). Cardiff is left by Cathedral Road and Llandaff, **Llantrisant** being reached in 10 m. The town, picturesquely sited in a saddle between two steep hills, takes its name ('Three Saints') from SS Illtyd, Gwyno, and Dyfod, to whom its church is dedicated. There are some scanty remains of the 13C castle, where in 1326 Edward II and Hugh Despenser fell into Isabella's hands after being betrayed by a monk of Neath Abbey. The *Royal Mint,* transferred from Tower Hill, London, is on a trading estate N.W. below the town (Rhondda road).—Near *Llanharan,* 3 m. W., there is opencast coalmining.—The 13C church at *Coychurch,* 4 m. farther W., has several architectural peculiarities, these including a blank bay before the crossing; lobed quatrefoil windows in diamond frames at the W. of each aisle; a cinquefoiled clerestory (S. only) in the nave; and unusual buttresses to the choir and N. transept. The tower (since rebuilt) fell in 1877, destroying the S. transept and shattering one of the two Celtic crosses of interlaced pattern which then stood in the churchyard. Fragments of the damaged cross, bearing the name Ebisar, and the undamaged cross are now in the church.—**Bridgend** (see below) is reached in 2 m.

3 m. **Penarth** (24,000 inhab.) stretches back from Penarth Head, opposite Cardiff docks across Penarth Flats. The town is a summer resort, among the attractions being the Esplanade, the Pier (Marina Pavilion, excursion steamers), the Italian Gardens, and Alexandra Park. The docks, opened in 1865 and now disused, are being filled in. *Turner House Art Gallery*†, in Plymouth Road c. ¼ m. W. of the pier, was built in 1888 by James Pyke Thompson for the public exhibition of a selection of his private collection. Now a branch gallery of the National Museum of Wales, it is used for changing exhibitions from the museum's collections. A cliff walk (2¼ m.) leads to *Lavernock Point,* off which are various rocks and uninhabited islands. Marconi's early experiments in transmitting radio waves across water were made between Lavernock and the island of *Flat Holme,* 3 m. southeast.—*1 m. Dinas Powis* where, ¼ m. N.W., there are the small remains of a medieval castle.

3 m. **Barry** (42,000 inhab.), named after the 7C St Baruch, owes its modérn development (the population was only 85 in 1881) to its *Docks,* founded by David Davies, a coal owner, between 1884-99. With a water area of 114 acres, the docks handle general cargoes, including in particular bananas (Geest Line), processed sugar, and timber. There is an expanding import of oil and chemicals, and Seaspeed Ferries Ltd operate a roll-on/roll-off freight service to Dublin. A good view of the docks can be obtained from the N. end of *Barry Island,* a peninsula resort, largely given over to a large holiday camp. *Barry Castle,* in the W. part of the town, dates from the 12-13C. Thought to have been held by the De Barri family in the 12 and 14C, it is known to have already been a ruin by the 16C. All that can be seen today is the ruined S. gate and some wall of a fortified manor (restored 1964). Immediately W. of the castle a road descends through *Porthkerry Country Park,* a green and wooded valley running down to the sea.—*3 m.* (from Barry) *Rhoose* is Cardiff Airport.

At *Penmarc,* 1½ m. N., the ruined castle (behind the church, overgrown and neglected) belonged to the Umfravilles; in 1664 it was acquired by the Parliamentarian Philip Jones. At *Llancarfan,* 1 m. farther N., the farm of Llanvithyn to the N. is said to stand on the site of a school founded by St Cadoc in the 6C and destroyed by the Danes in 987; reputedly the school rivalled that of St Illtyd at Llantwit Major, its most famous pupil being St Malo, the Breton bishop. *Fonmon Castle* (no adm.), 1 m. S.W. of Penmarc, is a small late Norman keep with a 17C mansion built on its N. side; like Penmarc, it was acquired in 1664 by Philip Jones. John Wesley often stayed here.

The road skirts the S. side of the airport, passing *Font-y-Gary,* another place where John Wesley stayed. *Aberthaw* has a large cement works, and *St Athan* is known for its R.A.F. Technical School.

7 m. (from Rhoose Airport) **Llantwit Major** (6500 inhab.), with a picturesque 15C town hall and an unusually interesting dual church, is a place of historic importance in the early story of Christianity in Wales.

It was here in c. 500 that St Illtyd (see also p. 263), a teacher and craftsman (he invented an improved plough) from Brittany, founded his monastery and school of divinity. An early 7C 'Life of St Samson' of Dol in Brittany records that Samson was brought by his parents to the school of Illtyd 'the most learned of all the Britons in knowledge of the Scriptures'. Other pupils included St Gildas, the historian, St Paul Aurelian, the bard and seer Taliesin, and even perhaps St David. The pupils were divided into 24 groups, each responsible for an hour of worship, a system ('laus perennis' or 'continual praise') traditionally also associated with Glastonbury and Old Sarum. The school did not survive the Normans, but the monastery continued until the Dissolution, though only as a cell to Tewkesbury Abbey.

The interesting and curious *Church* is in two parts, and it seems that the Old (or West) Church, in origin c. 1100 and probably occupying the site of St Illtyd's early church, was the parish church, while the New (or East) Church of the late 13C was the monastery church. Of the original Old Church there remain only the lower courses of the crossing (below the tower of c. 1200) and the arched S. doorway. The transepts disappeared about the middle of the 13C; aisles were added to the original chancel, which then became the nave of the New Church, and to this a new chancel was added on the E., while a chapel was built on the W. of the original nave. In the 15C the Old Church was rebuilt on the original foundations, this becoming at least the third to occupy this site.—The *Old Church* contains a collection of Celtic stones. A shaft (c. 800), once surmounted by a wheel-cross, is known as the Cross of St Illtyd and bears his name (Iltut) on the back. In front the Latin inscription records that Samson placed this cross here. The adjacent 6 ft high wheel-cross has interlaced carving on both sides and was erected by Howel (Houelt) for the soul of Res his father. Alongside, a cross shaft, without inscription, includes four crosses in its elaborate interlacing. On the N. side stands the Samson stone, erected by Abbot Samson for his own soul and for those of Ithael (Iuthahelo) and Arthmael (Artmali), recorded 9C chieftains. Also here are the ancient curfew bell, recumbent effigies of medieval priests, and the effigies of a lady and her child in Elizabethan costume. The principal features of the *New Church* are the murals (14-15C, restored 1950), and the Jesse niche (13C) at the E. end of the S. aisle.

At the mouth of the *Colhugh Brook,* on which Llantwit stands, is a small estuary said once to have been used as a harbour. On the cliffs to its E. *Castle Ditches* are Iron Age earthworks, while to the W. *Tressilian Caves* were used by smugglers. *St Donat's Castle,* 2 m. W. near the coast, a restored 15-16C baronial mansion, was owned by Randolph Hearst the American publisher in the 1930s and is now Atlantic College, an international school.

6 m. The church at *St Bride's Major* contains (immediately N. of the altar) an elaborate 13C sepulchral slab; alongside is an early 16C altar-tomb. B4524 follows the exposed coast past the little resorts of *Southerndown* and *Ogmore-by-Sea,* then ascends the E. side of the estuary of the Ogmore.—*4 m.* Ogmore Castle was the centre of the lordship of Ogmore, established in early Norman times by William de Londres. The ruins comprise two rectangular wards, each surrounded by a moat. In the larger inner ward, enclosed by an early 13C curtain wall, are an early 12C rectangular keep (probably built by William's son Maurice), a 13C hall (N.E.), and a late 12C building (E.) of unknown origin. Ancient stepping stones cross the river here.—*2 m.* **Ewenny Priory,** though on private land, for the most part lies along the road and can be well seen. It was founded by Maurice de Londres in 1141 as a cell to the Benedictine abbey of Gloucester; the church, which became the priory church, had already been built by William de Londres. The priory is a good example of early Norman part ecclesiastical and part defensive building, the military character appearing in the crenellation (at this period not mere ornament) in the remains of the strong precinct wall (12-13C) and in the gateways (c. 1300), in both of which are loopholes, that on the N.W. also having a portcullis. The *Church* is in two parts; the nave, which is the parish church and was probably always parochial, and the chancel, now disused, which was monastic. The two parts are separated by a 13C stone rood screen. The Nave exhibits good Norman work in its arcade, in the arches of the crossing, and in the open wall arcade (late 12C) on the W. of the S. and only surviving transept. The nave was heightened and the central tower was built in the late 12C, and the N. aisle, built at the same time, was rebuilt in the 16C and again (partly) in 1895. The font has a basin of c. 1200, and under the E. arch of the crossing there is a wooden screen of the 14-16C. In the surviving transept are the tomb of the founder, and various monuments and stonework fragments. Traces of the chapel (mid 12C) to the E. of the now vanished N. transept can be seen outside.

A pleasant and interesting short diversion can be made to **Merthyr Mawr** (1½ m. W. of Ewenny), an attractive village with whitewashed and thatched cottages. Beyond the village the road continues for 1 m. to a car park and picnic site beside an area of dunes where evidence of early Iron Age (500-50 B.C.) occupation has been found (brooches, pins, fragments of smelting crucibles). *Candleston Castle,* at the car park, is the neglected ruin of a fortified 15C manor house. To the N. of Merthyr Mawr the winding Ogmore is crossed by two narrow road bridges. The southern of the two is dated 1827, while the northern bridge (on the road signed Laleston) is known as the Dipping Bridge because of the parapets arranged for sheep washing.

Above this bridge stands *Merthyr Mawr House†*, with, in the grounds, the remains of a 15C chapel in which are two 11C inscribed stones.

2 m. (from Ewenny Priory) **Bridgend** (14,700 inhab.) is a fast expanding industrial town on the Ogmore, site (to the S.E.) of the Ford engine works, the construction of which was agreed between the government and the Ford Motor Company in 1977. During the last war the German prisoner-of-war camp here (Island Farm) was in the news when in March 1945 67 officers tunnelled to shortlived freedom. In Newcastle, the N.W. section of the town, high on the hill are the remains of the 12C *Castle†*, of obscure history. The main feature of interest is the Norman gateway bearing elaborate decoration.

The extensive ruins of **Coity Castle†** are 1½ m. N.E. of Bridgend.

History. Coity was probably first built by Sir Gilbert de Turbeville around the end of the 12C, remaining in the family until the line died in the 14C. The castle was then owned in turn by Sir Roger Berkerolles and Sir William Gamage, the latter being besieged here by Owen Glendower. When the Gamage line became extinct towards the end of the 16C, the estate passed by marriage to the 2nd Earl of Leicester and the castle was deserted.

The plan is a large, irregular outer ward (14C), on the E. of which is a circular inner ward. This latter is entered by the badly ruined Middle Gate, to the left being the keep and to the right against the curtain wall the domestic buildings. The walls of the keep date from the late 12C, but most of what is inside it is 14C. In Tudor times a four-storey addition was built on the N. side. Most of the curtain wall is contemporary with the keep, but the buildings inside are mainly 14C. In these buildings the principal rooms, reached by a staircase between the chapel and the hall, were on the first floor above small, vaulted ground floor rooms; the chapel is opposite the Middle Gate, with the hall to its W., and then the kitchens. The large rectangular building which occupied much of the N. part of the inner ward is of unknown date and purpose.—*Coity Church* (14C, with a 15C tower) contains two small De Turbeville effigies, and a wooden chest with carvings of the Instruments of the Passion, possibly a rare example of a portable Easter Sepulchre (c. 1500).

3 m. Junction with A4106.

At **Newton**, 2 m. down A4106, the parish *Church* (13-15C), E. of the road, has some interesting features. High on the E. side of the tower is a doorway, intended to give access to a wooden parapet that could be erected on the corbel immediately below thus providing defence. The S. porch is another curiosity, the Norman pillars supporting the outer arch here being upside down, this presumably happening after they had been brought from somewhere else. Noteworthy inside the church are the 13C floreated cross on the ledge N. of the chancel arch; the E. window by Burne-Jones; and, in the chancel, the stone altar, with original base and table, a rare survivor from the time when Edward VI ordered the destruction of all stone altars.—**Porthcawl**, just beyond Newton, is a popular seaside resort, with numerous amusements, a Grand Pavilion, a miniature railway leading to Coney Beach pleasure park, a golf course, and one of the largest caravan parks in Europe (3000 vans). To the N.W. of Porthcawl, a region of sand dunes, planted with stabilizing grass, stretches almost to the Margam steelworks on the outskirts of Port Talbot. The dunes are split into two by the river Kenfig, the S. part being *Kenfig Burrows*. Here, between the river and the freshwater Kenfig Pool, are the last remnants of the town and castle of Kenfig, overwhelmed by sand in c. 1400. The Elizabethan *Sker House,* near the shore, is described in Blackmore's 'Maid of Sker'.

5 m. **Margam Park†**, to the N. of the road, the beautiful park of the Tudor-Gothic *Margam Castle* of 1840 (damaged by fire in 1977), is now a large recreational area. The castle is successor to a mansion built in 1537 by Sir Rice Mansel who acquired the estate when Margam Abbey (see below) was dissolved. Cars must be parked at the entrance, visitors then either walking or using the park's bus service (free). The park includes a *Park Centre,* picnic sites, gardens, a herd of over 300 fallow deer, and a heronry (no adm.). The *Orangery* (Anthony Keck, 1790) has been restored by West Glamorgan County Council and is in part used for receptions and exhibitions. Also within the park (and accessible only from the park) is the ruin of the 13C *Chapter House* of Margam Abbey with a beautiful vaulted vestibule. Unlike most Cistercian chapter houses, which were rectangular, this one is twelve-sided outside but circular within. It was originally vaulted from a central shafted pillar, the foliated capitals of which remain. For the *Coed Morgannwg Way* long distance footpath, one end of which is at Margam Park, see below.

1 m. **Margam Parish (Abbey) Church.** The abbey was a Cistercian house founded by Robert, Earl of Gloucester, in 1147 near the site of a long vanished Celtic monastery. The greater part of the nave (115 ft) of the original abbey church survives in what is today the parish church. The lower part of the W. front, the plain and massive arcades, and perhaps the groining of the aisles, date from the 12C. The twin Italianate campaniles were added in 1808. The windows at the W. end contain glass by William Morris, and in the S. aisle there is a group of alabaster tombs of the Mansel family, who bought the abbey estate at the Dissolution.— The adjacent **Margam Abbey Museum**†, in a building which was one of the earliest church schools in Wales, contains an important collection of inscribed and sculptured stones, mostly from this neighbourhood. These include a Roman milestone (309–13) from Port Talbot, with the original Latin inscription on one face, and an early Christian one on the other; two pillar stones commemorating Bodvoc and Pumpeius Carantorius, both of whom lived in the 6C, the latter stone carrying Ogham writing and the former found on the summit of Mount Margam; several pre-Norman crosses, including that of Einion (late 9C), the Wheel-Cross of Cynfelyn (c. 900), richly decorated and bearing representations of the Virgin and St John, and others from Margam (9–11C); tombstones of abbots (13–14C); a damaged military effigy of the 14C; and several post-Reformation gravestones.—*Capel Mair,* a ruined 15C chapel on a spur above the church, may have been either a private oratory or a place for lay worship. For the *Chapter House,* see Margam Park above.

4 m. **Port Talbot** (with Aberavon, 50,000 inhab.) boasts the largest steel strip mill in Europe and the newest and largest deep-water harbour in Britain. There is a controversial redeveloped town centre (1976). *Aberavon,* the N. part of the town, is popular for its sandy beach and amusements.

The British Steel Corporation's *Margam Works* were opened in 1923, but began their real expansion in 1951 after four large steel and tinplate firms amalgamated to form the Steel Company of Wales, which, on nationalization in 1967, was absorbed by British Steel Corporation. The complex extends over 4½ m. and includes five blast furnaces, 300 coke ovens, strip mills, and rolling mills.

The *Harbour* has grown out of the early riverside wharves. With the Industrial Revolution and the build-up of activity around the mouth of the Afan, it became necessary to provide a dock, so a new cut was made for the river and its former course was converted in 1837 into what is now called the Old Dock. No significant expansion took place until the recent (1960s) construction by the British Transport Docks Board in conjunction with the British Steel Corporation of the modern deep-water harbour, with a breakwater a mile long and a water area of 464 acres. Opened by the Queen in 1970, the harbour enables virtually the entire throughput of bulk iron ore for the steel industry, including Llanwern at Newport, to be concentrated here. There are ambitious expansion plans.

Cwm Afan Scenic Route (A4107) leads N.E. from Port Talbot. From the 18C until recent times the valley was largely given over to coal mining and industry. The South Wales Mineral Railway came in 1859, linking Briton Ferry with Glyncorrwg, and passengers rail services in 1885. A4107 was built in 1930-32 as a measure to relieve the depression. Today the railway and the pits have gone, and A4107 has been designated a Scenic Route (with picnic sites and other facilities being organized by West Glamorgan Council and the Forestry Commission), an increasingly afforested valley linking the industrial coast with the high moorland above Rhondda. The focal point of the Scenic Route is *Afan Argoed Countryside Centre*† (opened 1976), 6 m. above Port Talbot. Among the facilities are the information centre, picnic sites, guided walks, film shows and lectures, and, for schools, a Field Studies Centre. Here too is the interesting *Welsh Miners Museum*, telling both the technical and the social story of mining in Wales.—From Afan Argoed there are several waymarked walks. It is also roughly the halfway point along the *Coed Morgannwg Way* (opened 1977), a 23-25 m. long waymarked route linking Craig-y-Llyn (1969 ft; off A4061 3 m. S.W. of Hirwaun) with Margam Park. The walk, traversing high moor and the forests of Cymer and Margam, generally follows waymarked tracks but is steep in places.

3 m. (from Port Talbot) *Briton Ferry,* where A48 crosses the dock and the mouth of the river Neath by viaducts. For **Swansea,** 5 m. W., and **Gower** beyond, see Rte 42. A48 heads N., soon passing *Llandarcy,* with an oil refinery linked by pipelines to Swansea's Queen's Dock, and then rounding the northern and in part industrial outskirts of Swansea to *(8 m.)* **Penllergaer.** Here A48 bears N. offering an inland approach to Carmarthen, while this Route continues W. on A484 for *Gorseinon* and *(3 m.)* **Loughor,** at the head of Burry Inlet where it is entered by the river Loughor. This was the Roman Leucarum, and later, in c. 1110, the Norman Henry de Newburgh built his castle at the S.E. corner of the Roman fort. All that is left, the ruin of a 13C square tower, stands on its motte beside the road before it drops down to the river, crossed by a long bridge.

3 m. **Llanelli** (28,000 inhab.) is an industrial centre with various steel (tinplate), chemical, and engineering works. British Steel Corporation's large *Trostre Works* are to the S. of the road entering the town. In the town centre there are a large shopping centre and covered market, with direct access from a multi-storey car park, and nearby (Vaughan Street) the *Public Library Exhibition Gallery*† exhibits paintings by modern local artists and receives touring exhibitions. In the N. part of the town (Felinfoel Road) is the *Parc Howard Art Gallery and Museum*†, with material of local interest; a good collection of Welsh porcelain, paintings by Welsh artists; and an interesting case explaining the manufacture of tinplate. The writers George Meredith (1829-1909) and Richard Savage (d. 1743) both lived for a time in Llanelli.—The road skirts the N. side of *Burry Inlet,* here some 3 m. wide. In June 1928 Amelia Earhart, the first woman to fly across the Atlantic, reached Burry Inlet from Trepassy Bay in Newfoundland in 20 hours 40 minutes.

9m. **Kidwelly** (3000 inhab.), at the head of the estuary of the Gwendraeth, grew up around the castle and priory established here in the early 12C. The town's name is pronounced as in English. The main town is S. of the river, here being the *Priory Church of St Mary,* once the church of the Benedictine priory founded c. 1130 by Roger, Bishop of Salisbury, as a cell to Sherborne Abbey. The present building dates mainly from c. 1320, but was restored in 1884 after the spire, which had already crashed twice, had been struck by lightning. Features of the interior are the unusually broad nave, which was originally longer and extended west; the squint, discovered in the sanctuary wall in 1973; and the mural staircase in the vestry leading up to an anchorite's cell, with a loophole to enable him to hear services.

The river is crossed by a 14C bridge, beyond being the site of the original town which lay within the defences of **Kidwelly Castle**†. Built by Roger, Bishop of Salisbury, at about the same time as his priory, the castle, sometimes Welsh and sometimes English, several times changed hands until passing to the Crown under Henry IV. The extensive ruins above the river comprise a rectangular inner ward, surrounded by a semicircle of outer ward ending at either end at the river. The wall walk around the outer curtain affords a good general impression. The inner ward dates from c. 1275, its domestic buildings (hall, solar, and chapel) being late 13 or early 14C. The outer curtain and gatehouse are of the 14C, as are also the upper parts of the inner ward's towers, all this being the work of Henry of Lancaster, nephew of Edward I. The *Gatehouse* (S. end of the castle) is unusual for being sited on the outer rather than the inner curtain, and also for being a part of the defences of the original town; it contains dungeons and (N.E. corner) an oubliette. In the *Outer Ward* a later period hall of c. 1500 lies outside the inner ward between its S.W. and N.W. towers, this hall's kitchen being beyond against the outer curtain. At the N.E. corner of the outer ward, beyond the N. gate, are the Stables. The *Inner Ward,* the oldest part of the castle, is entered at its N.E. corner. Along the E. side are the Solar and the Hall, beyond being the Chapel, the most interesting place in the castle, occupying the third storey of a tower which projects boldly towards the river. The large kitchen occupies the S.W. corner of the ward. To both the N. and the S. of the castle there are subsidiary earthworks.

Tregoning Hill, 4m. W. on the shore, is a National Trust cliff property of 20 acres (public access) offering good views of Carmarthen Bay.

10m. **Carmarthen,** see Rte 43.

40   CARDIFF

(Including Llandaff Cathedral and St Fagans, Welsh Folk Museum)

A   Cardiff

CARDIFF (285,000 inhab.), in 1955 officially confirmed as the capital of Wales, is a fine city which successfully combines such varied roles as national and county capital; home of a historic castle and cathedral (at Llandaff), and of a more modern but not less notable university college; shopping, commercial, and industrial centre; and major port. The spacious central part of the city is both interesting and attractive with its striking castle, its riverside park, its pleasant pedestrian precincts and shopping arcades, and, in Cathays Park, one of the most pleasing and distinguished groups of public buildings in Europe.

City Centre. Castle, Duke, and Queen streets, with the streets running S. off these.

Tourist Information. 3 Castle Street (opposite entrance to castle).

Parking. Multi-storey off Westgate Street; adjacent to Bus Station; Greyfriars Road, just N. of Queen Street.

Caravan Site. Pontcanna municipal site (off Cathedral Road, 5 min. drive from centre).

Railway and Bus Stations. Adjacent off Wood Street (¾ m. S. of castle). Also *Queen Street,* only for trains to the Valleys.

Main Post Office. Westgate Street (½ m. S. of castle).

Airport. Rhoose (12 m. S.W.).

Theatres. *New Theatre* (general productions, and Welsh National Opera Company seasons). *Sherman Theatre* (university and other productions).

Summer Events. *Llandaff Festival* (first half of June). *International Show Jumping* in the castle. *South Wales Miners' Gala and Eisteddfod* (second Sat. in June).

History. The Romans are known to have settled here in c. 60-90 after their defeat of the Silures, a small civil settlement developing to the S. of their fort. Of the period between the Roman withdrawal and the arrival of the Normans virtually nothing is known, through by one tradition Lancelot is said to have fled by sea from here, and there must also have been some association with the chieftain Morgan Mwynfawr (d. c. 975), from whose name the modern Glamorgan derives. In 1093 Robert FitzHamon arrived, building his primitive fortress on the site of its Roman predecessor, and in 1158 the later castle was successfully stormed by Ifor Bach, ruler of Senghenydd, the district to the N. of Cardiff. It was not long before a town began to grow within the castle's protection. By the late 13C there were 2000 inhabitants, already enjoying a charter, confirmed by others in 1340, 1421, 1581, 1600, and 1608, this last continuing until the Municipal Corporations Act of 1835 which brought to an end municipal dependence on the lord of the castle.

Cardiff was overrun by Owen Glendower in 1404, and in 1490 both castle and town came into the hands of Jasper Tudor, uncle of Henry VII. In 1551 Cardiff was presented by Edward VI to Sir William Herbert. During the Civil War the place, with Royalist sympathies, was held alternately for the King and Parliament, but afterwards remained in the possession of the Herberts and their descendants, the marquesses of Bute.

Modern Cardiff was born of the Industrial Revolution, its population increasing from 1000 in 1801 to 30,000 by the middle of the century and over 180,000 in 1911. Important steps were the construction of the Glamorganshire Canal (Merthyr Tydfil to Cardiff) in 1794; the digging of the first dock, on the initiative and at the personal expense of the 2nd Marquess of Bute, in 1839; the arrival of the railways between about 1848-64; and the opening of another dock in 1860. By the latter part of the 19C Cardiff, largely through being the leading port handling iron and coal, was at the height of its prosperity. At the turn of the century Cathays Park was acquired, the first building, the City Hall, being opened in 1905, the year in which the official status of City was granted. In 1922 the city's boundary was extended to include Llandaff with its cathedral.

After the First World War there was a serious drop in the trade through the docks, and in the last war the city, the docks, and the cathedral all suffered severe damage from air raids. The coal trade declined and disappeared and the docks shrank, but new prosperity has come with the replanning of the docks for oil, timber, and general cargoes, and with the development of new industries.

*Cardiff Castle†, conveyed to the city in 1948 by the 5th Marquess of Bute, is enclosed within 19C walls, generally following the line of the Roman enclosure, and architecturally spans from Roman to modern times. The castle's history is essentially that of the town. The principal stages of its construction are c. 1093 when Robert FitzHamon threw up the motte, this being followed by the first stone building, probably erected by Robert of Gloucester ('The Consul'), a natural son of Henry I; the building on the motte of the keep in the late 12C; the building by Gilbert de Clare in the later 13C of the Black Tower (today's entrance), the wall linking it to the keep, and the keep gateway, this work dividing the castle into two wards; during the 14 and 15C the move from the keep to more roomy and purely residential apartments along the W. wall, this range being extended in Tudor and Stuart times; the removal in the late 18C of the outer buildings of the keep and of the wall dividing the wards; and finally the reconstruction in 1867-75, by William Burges for the 3rd Marquess, of the entire S.W. part of the castle, this including the addition of a spire to the Octagonal Tower and the erection of the 150 ft high Clock Tower in the place of a small turret. At the same time the internal decoration was redesigned throughout in fantastic and colourful style.

The castle is entered by the *Black Tower* where, to the right, a fine length of Roman wall, probably of the 3C, can be visited. From the tower the line of Gilbert de Clare's wall runs across to the *Motte* and *Keep,* this last offering a good view.—The S.W. buildings can only be visited by conducted tour (45 min.). In the *Clock Tower* the rooms are the Winter Smoking Room (first floor); the Bachelors' Bedroom with, in the adjoining dressing room, a marble bath of Roman (but not local Roman) origin; and, at the top, the Summer Smoking Room, designed on the theme of the firmament. The *Herbert Tower* (16C) is the southernmost of the projecting towers along the W. wall. Here is the Arab Room (1881), with a decorated ceiling in gold leaf and a chimneypiece of white marble and lapis lazuli. Much of the work here is that of imported Arab craftsmen. Beyond is the *Banqueting Hall* of c. 1428, with murals depicting the life of Robert of Gloucester. The windows represent the various lords of Cardiff. Next comes the *Octagonal Tower* (early 15C), forming part of the medieval defences. Here the Chaucer Room (decoration 1889) contains windows illustrating the 'Canterbury Tales'; the floor is tiled as a maze and there are alphabet tiles in the hearth. A richly decorated staircase leads down to the frescoed *Chapel* (1848), formerly a dressing room but converted after the death of the 2nd Marquess. In the *Bute Tower* the Dining Room has a fine ceiling in gold leaf in Moorish style. At the top of the tower is the Roof Garden (1876), open only May-Sept. The *Library* (early 15C) contains windows inserted by Jasper Tudor, but the room's decorations are 19C. The carved and inlaid bookcases are noteworthy. The *Entrance Hall* has stained glass windows depicting English monarchs who have owned the castle.—The castle also houses the *Museum of the Welch Regiment†.*

Castle Street skirts the S. side of the castle. To the W. it crosses the Taff with, to the N., parks and gardens on both sides of the river. On the W. bank are, from S. to N., *Sophia Gardens,* with a concert pavilion; the *National Sports Centre* (1972); *Glamorgan County Cricket Ground;* and *Pontcanna,* with sports grounds and the municipal caravan site. Cathedral Road, running along the W. of these open spaces, leads to Llandaff and St Fagans. *Bute Park,* on the E. side of the river, stretches almost 2½ m. to Llandaff. Here, between the castle and the river, have been marked out the foundations of a medieval priory.—Beyond the Taff, Castle Street becomes Cowbridge Road East, off which, in Market Road (¾ m. beyond the river bridge) are the *Chapter Workshops and Centre for the Arts*†, where visitors can see artists of many kinds at work in their studios and workshops. The Art Gallery not only has its own exhibitions but also receives Welsh Arts Council and other touring exhibitions.

Westgate Street, leading S.E. off Castle Street, passes *Cardiff Arms Park* (named after a former pub), home of Welsh rugby. Beyond are the General Post Office (1896), and, close to one another, the bus and central railway stations and the *Empire Swimming Pool,* built in 1958 for the British Empire and Commonwealth Games.

Eastwards Castle Street is prolonged by Duke Street, while High Street, becoming St Mary Street, both shopping streets, leads south. To the E. of High Street is the attractive Victorian *Market* (1886-91), surrounded by pedestrian precinct. Farther on, the elegant *Morgan Arcade* of 1896 leads E. off St Mary Street.—Queen Street, the eastward extension of Duke Street, is a spacious pedestrian precinct. *St John's Church,* S. of Duke and Queen streets, is the parish church. Restored in 1890-99, the church dates mainly from 1453 and is unusual for having a clerestory in the chancel but not in the nave. The tower (1473) was built by Ann Nevill, wife of the future Richard III. The oldest part of the church, a survival from a predecessor, is the 13C S. chancel aisle. Noteworthy inside the church are the altarpiece in the S. aisle by Goscombe John; and the N. (or Herbert) chapel, with a monument to two Herbert brothers (Sir William, d. 1609, Keeper of Cardiff Castle; and Sir John, d. 1617, secretary to Queen Elizabeth and James I). The *Oriel*†, at 33 Charles Street, leading S. off the E. end of Queen Street, is the gallery and bookshop of the Welsh Arts Council. Art exhibitions change roughly every two weeks, and there are also poetry readings, folk music events etc.

Cathays Park, to the N. of Queen Street, is Cardiff's Civic Centre, an area of distinguished white stone buildings, most dating from the early years of this century, set along broad avenues broken by gardens. The following are some of the more noteworthy buildings. The *City Hall* is the central of the three along the S.E. side, built in 1905 by Lanchester and Rickards in Renaissance style with a dome surmounted by a Welsh dragon and with an imposing clock tower, 194 ft high. The fountains and the pool in front were completed in 1969 to commemorate the investiture of Prince Charles as Prince of Wales. Inside, in the Marble Hall on the first floor, which has pillars of Siena marble, is a series of 11 statues presented by Lord Rhondda (d. 1918) illustrating Welsh history. These include St David (Goscombe John), Owen Glendower, Henry Tudor, and Sir Thomas Picton, one of Wellington's leading commanders. The Council Chamber contains a collection of city treasures; the Assembly Hall has a rich segmented ceiling; and in the Lord Mayor's Parlour there is a mosaic of 86,000 marble pieces. The *Law Courts* (1906, Lanchester and Rickards) stand to the left of City Hall, while to the right is the National Museum of Wales (see below). To the S. of the museum are the Gorsedd Gardens, with a stone circle commemorating the National Eisteddfod of 1899. The statues here include David Lloyd George (Rizzello, 1960), and three others by Goscombe John. The *Welsh National War Memorial* (J. Ninian Comper, 1928), behind City Hall in Alexandra Gardens, bears a plaque commemorating also those who fell in the last war. Museum Avenue runs along the N.E. side of Cathays Park, with, beyond the National Museum, various buildings of the *University College of South Wales.* The W. wing (W. D. Caröe) dates from 1903-09. The N. wing (1930s and 1950s) and the S. wing (1960s) are additions in the same style. Founded in 1883, the college in 1893 became one of the constituent colleges of the University of Wales, the others being Bangor, Aberystwyth, Swansea, and Lampeter. The college's *Sherman Theatre Gallery*† receives monthly touring art exhibitions. To the N. of Alexandra Gardens is the *Welsh Office* (P. K. Hanton, 1938). The University of Wales *Institute of Science and Technology* stands at the N.W. corner of the park. From here King Edward VII Avenue leads S.E., with, from N. to S., the *Temple of Peace* (Percy Thomas, 1938), built as a headquarters for Welsh people fighting war and disease and now housing a variety of organizations concerned with international affairs and health; another building (Ivor Jones and Percy Thomas, 1916) of the *Institute of Science and Technology; Mid Glamorgan County Hall* (Vincent Harris and T. A. Moodie, 1908-10), with a S. extension of the 1930s by Ivor Jones and Percy Thomas; and the *University Registry* (Wills and Anderson, 1901-3), extended in 1933 by Alwyn Lloyd. The modern *Cardiff College of Music and Drama* is off the S.W. side of the park.

The long Bute Street leads S. into much redeveloped **Butetown,** the dockside district, in which stands the *Exchange* building, chosen as the meeting place of the Welsh Assembly. The fine **Welsh Industrial and Maritime Museum**†, a branch of the National Museum of Wales opened in 1977 to exhibit large and heavy machines, is at the S. end of Bute Street.

Natural power is represented by a waterwheel of 1907. Steam and other engines include a single cylinder beam engine of 1851-1921, used by Cardiff waterworks; a single cylinder colliery haulage engine (1870); a single cylinder engine used at Barry refuse yard (1900); a two cylinder compound engine (1910), coupled to an alternator; a colliery four cylinder ventilation fan engine (1911); a single cylinder suction gas engine of 1914 used at Llandrindod Wells pumping station; a four cylinder diesel compressor (1951); a turbo-alternator (1925); a single cylinder table engine of the early 19C, used successively in a brewery and a saw mill; a single cylinder engine of 1865, rebuilt in 1895, and used until 1974; There are also several pumping engines, while power for transport is illustrated by a Pratt and Whitney Wasp Major aero engine, and a Rolls Royce Conway bypass jet. Out of doors there are railway engines, and, in an adjacent dock, boats, including a pilot cutter of 1911 and a canal boat of 1934.

Cardiff Docks. Although ships had used the Taff estuary from at least medieval times, it was only with the Industrial Revolution that there became a need for enclosed docks. West and East docks were opened in 1839 and 1860, these being followed by Roath Dock in 1887 and Queen Alexandra Dock in 1907, this last completing the system. The peak of a prosperity which was dangerously founded almost entirely on coal was 1913 when 10 million tons were handled. Two wars and the depression, and above all the gradual change from coal to oil, made clear the need for new thinking, and, with the creation of the British Transport Docks

Board in 1963, a policy of diversification and modernization was put in hand. Among the many measures since taken have been the closure of the obsolete West and East docks; the redevelopment of large land areas formerly required for the coal railways system; the construction of new deep-water berths; the development of specialized timber handling; the development of oil terminals; and the provision of terminal facilities for cargoes as diverse as fruit, mineral ores, grain, feeding stuffs, and refrigerated produce. The water area of the docks is now 144 acres, with 26,260 ft of quays.

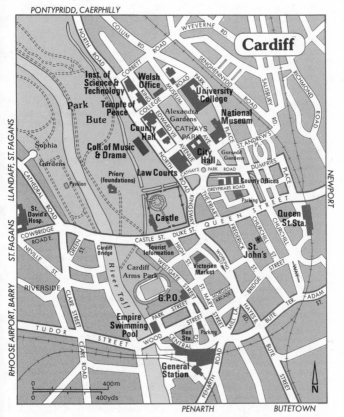

Parks and Open Spaces. Cardiff boasts some 2700 acres of parks and open spaces, many of these having planned walks and trails, leaflets about which can be obtained from the Parks Department at City Hall. *Bute Park, Sophia Gardens,* and *Pontcanna* have already been mentioned. *Roath Park* (100 acres), 1½ m. N.E. of the city centre, has a lake (boating and fishing), a children's playground, and a rose garden and conservatory. A miniature lighthouse commemorates Captain Scott's departure from Cardiff in 1909 on his Antarctic expedition. *Glamorgan Canal Wharf* is a nature reserve with bird and waterplant life along a short surviving stretch of the Glamorgan Canal (opened 1794, closed by 1900). Access is off Velindre Road, W. of Whitchurch Hospital, 4 m. N.W. of the city centre. Other parks are mentioned below under Llandaff and St Fagans. For *Cefn-Onn* and *The Wenallt,* see p. 331.

For Cardiff to (E.) *Severn Bridge* and (W.) *Carmarthen,* see Rte 39; to *The Valleys,* see Rte 41.

B   *National Museum of Wales†

The **NATIONAL MUSEUM OF WALES,** one of the largest museums in the United Kingdom and largely supported by government funds, contains important archaeological, art, botanical, geological, industrial, and zoological collections. Although the emphasis is on the story of Wales, there is much of broader scope and interest, notably the outstanding collection of modern European art. A feature of the museum are the New Galleries, using the most modern display techniques.

The proposal for a national museum was aired in parliament in 1903, and a Charter of Incorporation was granted by Edward VII in 1907. In 1910 the design by the architects Smith and Brewer was chosen out of 130 entrants in an open competition. The foundation stone was laid by George V in 1912, but work was held up by the war and it was not until 1922 that the western part of the main hall and the galleries from it were opened to the public. George V formally opened the museum in 1927. The E. wing was opened in 1962 and the W. wing in 1960. Future plans, already in hand, include the extension of the former to match the length of the west, and the completion of the quadrangle by a N. gallery.

Museum facilities and activities include regular temporary exhibitions; a large specialized library; a bookshop, selling a wide range of books published by the museum as well as a selection of other titles; a schools service; lecture programme; and restaurant and snack bar.

Branch Museums. The museum has several branch museums, each concerned with a specialized theme. *Welsh Industrial and Maritime Museum,* Butetown, Cardiff (p. 312). *Welsh Folk Museum,* St Fagans, Cardiff (p. 322) *Turner House,* the art gallery at Penarth, South Glamorgan (p. 302). *Legionary Museum,* Caerleon, Gwent (p. 271). *Graham Sutherland Gallery,* near Haverfordwest. Dyfed (p. 360). *Museum of the Woollen Industry,* Dre-Fach, Felindre, Dyfed (p. 350). *Segontium Roman Fort Museum,* Caernarvon, Gwynedd (p. 160). *North Wales Quarrying Museum,* Llanberis, Gwynedd (p. 151). *Hen Gapel Museum* (19C religious life), Tre'r-ddol, Dyfed (p. 216).

The MAIN HALL, with the bookshop, contains the permanent Collection of Sculpture, which includes the following. *W. Goscombe John:* St John the Baptist. David Lloyd George. Boy at play. Lady Goscombe John. Morpheus. The Drummer Boy. *Peter Lambda:* Aneurin Bevan. *John Gibson:* Narcissus. Meleager, or the Hunter. Wounded Amazon. Aurora. *John Evan Thomas:* Death of Tewdric, King of Gwent. George Price Watkins. *Auguste Rodin:* St John the Baptist. The Kiss. The Earth and Moon, and Eve (both on the E. stair). *Henry Moore:* Upright Motive No.8 (E. stair).

NEW SCIENCE GALLERIES (WEST). **Discover the Countryside of Wales** presents, with the help of scenic paintings, simulated environments, sound effects, and other means, a dramatic and informative picture of the Welsh countryside. Themes include Cwm Idwal (p. 156); open moorland; bog, with Tregaron (p. 348) as the example; woodland and forest, grassland; lakes and marshes, Llangorse (p. 256) being the example; dunes, cliffs, and the shore.—The **Animal Kingdom** is a largely specialist exhibition, dealing with modern thinking on animal classification. Cases bear colour-codings, explained by a panel at the entrance.

NEW SCIENCE GALLERIES (EAST). **Botany in Wales** includes themes such as an introduction to the identification of flowering plants, illustrated by life-like wax models; the history of plant hunting in Wales; forestry, pollution and reclamation. Recreational facilities such as Nature Trails, Country Parks, Picnic Sites, National Parks etc., are also featured.—The **Unity of Science** gallery aims to demonstrate the inter-relationship between physics, chemistry, and astronomy. Among the themes illustrated are electromagnetic and gravitational forces acting against each other; the tracks of sub-atomic particles, shown by a continuously working 'cloud-chamber'; the growth of crystals; division of cells (film); and the outer universe (slides).

ZOOLOGY. **Ground Floor.** Whales and dolphins. Reptiles. Birds, with dioramas illustrating the bird life in various environments, e.g. shore,

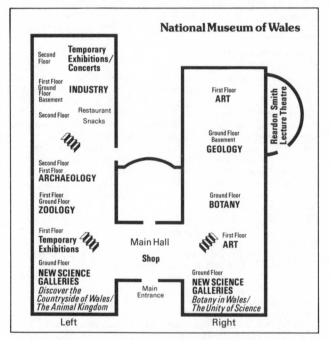

hill and moor, streams, woodland. Life-history of Kittiwake gull. British mammals. An observation beehive. The **First Floor** material illustrates concepts interesting modern scientists. On the left, the evolution of animal life, including the role played by inheritance (the cell; natural selection; evolution of the skull; origins of birds, horses, and other mammals; ancestry of man). On the right, the relationship between man and animals (protection of birds; nature conservation, and population growth; introduction of animal life by man; destruction of life by man). Special exhibits of the Great Auk, and a giant egg of the extinct bird Aepyomis.

INDUSTRY. An **Introductory Gallery** (first floor) illustrates the variety of Welsh industries from early to modern times. Industries covered include copper mining (18C); lead and coal mining, and the making of iron and steel (19C); oil refining and cement making (20C). The **Coal Mining Gallery** (basement) comprises two roadways, together showing the complete range of roof supports. There are also niches in which techniques such as hand drilling, shot firing, the pneumatic pick etc. are illustrated. The **Iron and Steel Gallery** (ground floor, beyond the Introductory Gallery) traces the story of iron, steel, and tinplate manufacture from the 16C to today. The **Modern Industries Gallery** (first floor) includes such industries as synthetics, gas, power generation, telecommunications, vehicle and aviation engines, electronics, nickel refining, wire drawing, and nail manufacture. The **Shipping Gallery** (first floor) contains models of ships and lighthouses, figureheads, and the optic (c. 1870) taken from the South Bishop lighthouse.—Larger industrial material will be found at the Welsh Industrial and Maritime Museum (p. 312).

ARCHAEOLOGY. The archaeological story of Wales is told more or less chronologically, starting at the N. end of the second floor.—**Prehistory.** *Old Stone Age* material includes an axe of local quartzite from Cardiff (perhaps 200,000 years old), and stone implements and ivory ornaments from Paviland (p. 342) and other sites. From the *New Stone Age* are a model of Bryn Celli Ddu (p. 169), finds from the Mynydd Rhiw axe 'factory', and simple grave goods from communal tombs. The *Bronze Age* is represented by a cist from Brymbo (near Wrexham), with bones; grave goods from other cists and from round cairns, including early metalwork, flint arrowheads, and faïence beads, possibly imported from the Mediterranean c. 1400 B.C. The increasing wealth and skill of the Bronze Age are illustrated by the gold ornaments, outstanding being neck-rings, bracelets, and the *Caergwrle Bowl, with elaborate gold decoration and representing a boat on the waves. From the later Bronze Age or early *Iron Age* are a sheet-bronze bucket from Arthog (Gwynedd) and two cauldrons from Llyn Fawr (Mid Glam.). By about this time (say 300 B.C. and later) the first Celts were arriving in Wales, bringing with them metalwork in the La Tène tradition. (La Tène: a site in Switzerland at which were first discovered ornaments and other objects produced by a culture spanning roughly the last 600 years B.C.). Especially noteworthy are shields; a wrought-iron *Firedog from Capel Garmon (p. 185); and ornaments from Tal-y-llyn (Gwynedd) and Llyn Cerrig-Bach (Anglesey). Much other Iron Age material comes from the many hillforts of Wales.—**Roman Period** military equipment is mainly in the museums of Caerleon and Segontium, though here there is a model of a typical auxiliary fort. Other material includes a mosaic pavement (4C) from Caerwent; pottery and tiles from Holt, where the 20th Legion had its kilns; and evidence of Roman mining activities.— The **Early Christian Period** is principally represented by the *Gallery of Stone Monuments,* a collection of 23 stones and 14 casts ranging from the earliest inscribed stones of the 5C., through the sculptured high crosses introduced in the 9C., to the locally developed styles which probably survived into the 12C. The stones are arranged in a stepped circular setting, with clusters representing different chronological groups. Each stone is numbered, and information boards are provided.—**Medieval Period** material includes rood figures (14-15C); one leaf from a fine ivory *Diptych (14C, French work) from Llandaff; a comparative display of decorated floor tiles (13-16C); and finds from castles, mostly pottery and metalwork reflecting Anglo-Norman influence.—The **Coin Room** displays include specimens from the early medieval mints at Cardiff, Pembroke, and Rhuddlan, and a series from the Aberystwyth mint of Charles I, where Welsh silver was coined. Also from Wales are the tradesmen's tokens of the 17-19C. From elsewhere there are panels containing British, Gaulish, Greek, Roman, Byzantine, and medieval European and English coinages.

BOTANY. A large collection of Welsh plant portraits, and possibly the finest collection of wax models of plants in the world. Cases illustrate the economic importance of plants, their preservation, pollination, breeding, and dispersal mechanisms. Working experiments show how plants function. Other cases cover plant diseases, moulds and man, fungi and lichens, mosses and liverworts, the utilization of seaweeds, marine and fresh-water algae, ferns and other spore-bearing plants. Representative plants are shown under the classifications of coast, woodland, mountain, moor, heath, grassland, marsh, and water; also carnivorous and parasitic plants. There is a large section devoted to Welsh timber trees and their products. Dioramas illustrate reafforestation (Lake Vyrnwy, p. 219). Related subjects include pine cones and Dutch elm disease. Temporary topical exhibits, usually with selections of colour slides, are changed at intervals.

GEOLOGY. Geological maps and photographs, including a large relief model illustrating the geology of Wales and the Marches. Fossils, arranged stratigraphically. Minerals, arranged according to chemical composition. Welsh gold specimens. A rock collection, containing specimens from most of the geological formations in Wales and including representative sets of the rocks of economic importance.

FINE ART. The fine arts are arranged more or less chronologically in a series of rooms from S. to N., except for the collection of Impressionists which is in the Pyke Thompson Gallery (first floor, S.E. corner of museum).

The most notable collection is that of the sisters Gwendoline and Margaret Davies of Gregynog Hall (p. 214), bequeathed to the museum in 1952 and 1963. The collection includes Old Masters, works by the Barbizon School, British paintings and drawings, and, above all, French art of the late 19C with particular emphasis on the Impressionists.

Northern Art (c. 1500-1650). *Marc Gheeraedts:* Queen Elizabeth. *Anon:* 2nd Earl of Pembroke. *Lucas Cranach:* Portrait of a man. *Anon:* Sir Roger Mostyn. *Anon* (Antwerp): Katheryn Tudor of Berain. *I. Laudin:* Mater Dolorosa (Limoges enamel).

Italian Religious Art (1450-1580). *Giovanni Cima (da Conegliano):* Madonna and Child (c. 1505). *Alessandro Allori:* Virgin and Child, with Saints Francis and Lucy (altarpiece). *Studio of Botticelli:* Virgin and St John adoring the Child. *After El Greco:* Christ led to Calvary.— Also the *Nynehead Tabernacle (c. 1460, Florence) in marble. Originally made for the small church of Santa Maria alla Campora, outside Florence, the tabernacle was brought to England in the 19C and given to the church at Nynehead, Somerset. The door is not the original, but is part of an altarpiece of 1520 by *Francesco Granacci.*

Seventeenth Century. *Jusepe de Ribera:* St Jerome in the desert. *Frans Hals* and *S. de Bray:* Family group in a landscape. *Nicolas*

Berchem: Figures by a well. *Anthony van Dyck:* Portrait of a man. *Aelbert Cuyp:* River landscape with horsemen and peasants. *Benjamin Cuyp:* The blind leading the blind. *Jacob van Ruisdael:* Waterfall. *Jan van Goyen:* River scene. Dunes scene. *Meindert Hobbema:* River scene. *Rembrandt:* Catrina Hooghsaet. *Karel Dujardin:* Travelling musicians. *Andrea Sacchi:* Hagar and Ishmael. *P. P. Rubens* and *Frans Snyders:* The fig. *Gaspard Poussin:* Hilly landscape with classical figures. *Nicholas Poussin:* The body of Phocion carried out of Athens. *Louis* and *Mathieu Le Nain* (?): A tavern quarrel.

Eighteenth Century. The emphasis is on the Welsh landscape artist *Richard Wilson,* many of his works showing the influence of Claude Lorrain of a century earlier. Wilson was more concerned with the emotion aroused by a landscape than with detail. Paintings to be seen include Pistyll Cain; Landscape with banditti round a tent; Penn Ponds, Richmond Park; A Maid of Honour; Rome and the Ponte Molle; Landscape with banditti, the murder; Pembroke town and castle; Caernarvon Castle; Dolbadarn Castle; and View of Dover.—Also in this gallery are Roman ruins, by *Giovanni Panini;* Viscountess Bulkeley as Hebe, by *George Romney;* and Llanthony Abbey, by *William Hodges,* a pupil of Richard Wilson. Also porcelain and furniture of the period, and a silver-gilt Rococo toilet service made by *Thomas Heming,* goldsmith to George III, for the marriage of Sir Watkin Williams-Wynn who appears on the left in the portrait group by *Pompeo Batoni.*

Nineteenth Century. *J. M. W. Turner:* Tobias and the Angel. Thames backwater, with Windsor Castle. Fishing boat in a mist. *John Constable:* Landscape near Dedham. *E. Landseer:* Encampment on Loch Avon. The ratcatchers. Landscape with waterfall. *David Cox:* Moorland landscape. *D. G. Rossetti:* Fair Rosamund. *Ford Maddox Brown:* King René's honeymoon. *J-F. Millet:* The Good Samaritan. Faggot gatherers. The shooting stars. The little goose girl. The storm. The peasant's family. *Honoré Daumier:* Head of a man. Workmen in a street. Lunch in the country. A famous case. By the Seine. Don Quixote reading.—The ***Collection of Impressionists,** with some others, is in the Pyke Thompson Gallery. *Van Gogh:* Rain at Auvers. *Henry Moret:* Village in Clohars. *Pierre Bonnard:* Sunlight at Vernon. *C-F. Daubigny:* Morning on the Oise. *Eugène Boudin:* The port of Fécamp. River at Bordeaux. Village fair. Venice, jetty at the mouth of the Grand Canal. Beach at Trouville. *J. B. C. Corot:* Fisherman moored to the bank. Distant view of Corbeil, morning. Castel Gandolfo. The pond. *Pierre August Renoir:* Head of a girl. Peasants resting. La Parisienne. *H. Fantin Latour:* Immortality. Larkspurs. *Camille Pissaro:* Pont Neuf, Paris. Sunset at Rouen. *Alfred Sisley:* View in the village of Moret. *Edgar Degas:* Woman putting on a glove. Ballet dancer, aged fourteen (sculpture). Dancer looking at the sole of her foot (sculpture). *Edouard Manet:* Argenteuil, 1874. The rabbit. The church of Petit-Montrouge, Paris. *Auguste Rodin:* The fallen Caryatid (sculpture). *Claude Monet:* Water lilies (1905, 1908. 1906). Rouen Cathedral, sunset. Twilight, Venice. Charing Cross Bridge, London. Palazzo Dario, Venice. San Giorgio Maggiore, Venice. *Paul Cézanne:* Edge of a wood in Provence. Still Life with a teapot. Mountains seen from L'Estaque.

Twentieth Century works are in the northernmost gallery and the adjacent circular gallery. Welsh artists are well represented, these including the following. *Augustus John:* Study of a woman's head. A peasant family. Study of a boy. Grace. Aran Islands. La désespérance d'amour. Old Ryan. Dylan Thomas. Madame Suggia. Romany folk. Portrait of Dorelia. *Gwen John:* Dorelia John (drawing). Girl in blue. Girl in profile. Study for 'The brown teapot'. Study of a seated nude. *J. D. Innes:* Pembroke coast. Canigou in snow. *Frank Brangwyn:* Venice, St Mark's. *David Jones:* Annunciation in a Welsh hill setting.—The major European movements also find a place here. Pure Cubism is represented by a small bronze of 1912 by *Archipenko,* and its influence can perhaps be traced in the bronze head Henriette III, by *Matisse* (1929), and the painting Loom + Woman, by *Natalia Goncharova* (1913). German Expressionism is represented by Lake near Moritzburg, by *Erich Heckel* (1909), and Coast scene with red hill, by *Alexei Jawlensky* (1911). Surrealism is seen in The empty mask, by *René Magritte,* and something of abstract art in Three figures with black, by *Willi Baumeister* (1920).—Sculptures in the circular gallery and the small gallery adjoining it include Head of Augustus John by *Jacob Epstein* (1916) and Madame Chia Pi by the same artist (1942).

APPLIED ART is shown in the China Room (off the Fine Art galleries) and on the first floor balconies around the main hall. The **China Room** contains Welsh china, much of it Swansea and Nantgarw of the Nance Collection (E. Morton Nance, d. 1953; author of 'The Pottery and Porcelain of Swansea and Nantgarw').—The **East Balcony** contains British and European glass. Also the Jackson Collection of Spoons, including a unique Anglo-Saxon spoon, one bearing perhaps the earliest extant example of the London hallmark, and a complete set of 13 Apostle spoons (Sir Charles Jackson, d. 1922; author of 'History of English Plate', and of 'English Goldsmiths and their Marks'). The **North and South Balconies** display ceramics, japanned wares, ivory etc., and also the Investiture Regalia of the Prince of Wales. The **West Balcony** provides the setting for an exhibition (changed monthly) showing the work of modern artist-craftsmen.

C Llandaff Cathedral

*LLANDAFF CATHEDRAL (12-13C), in the suburb of the same name rather over 2 m. N.W. of the city centre, is reached by Cathedral Road or, by walkers, through the parks either side of the Taff.

History. That this was once a pagan site is known from the evidence of pre-Christian probably Romano-British burials discovered under the W. part of the cathedral. Tradition connects the founding of the church with St Teilo (d. c. 580), appointed Bishop of South Wales by St Dyfrig (d. c. 546), and it is known that a pre-Norman church stood here or near here. Another saint, associated with Teilo and Dyfrig, was Euddogwy, the trio being the reason for the three mitres on the present coat-of-arms of the see. The existing church was begun c. 1120 by Urban who, though probably a Welshman, would have been appointed by the Normans. Of this early church the chief remains are the Norman arch dividing the presbytery from the Lady Chapel and some traces of blocked windows in the S. wall of the presbytery. It seems that the completion of the nave was delayed by some 50 years, for the N. and S. doorways (perhaps no longer in situ) date from c. 1170. Two events of the 12C may be mentioned, one being the death of Geoffrey of Monmouth at Llandaff in 1154, and the other the visit in 1188 by Archbishop Baldwin, accompanied by Giraldus, preaching the Third Crusade (the next visit by an Archbishop of Canterbury would not be until 1972). The present nave and chancel arcades, as well as the W. front, which was flanked by E.E. towers, date from the earlier 13C, and the chapter house was completed in 1250. In 1266 the cathedral was the scene of a great dedication service, this coinciding with the enthronement of Bishop William de Braose, during whose time the Lady Chapel was added in Geometrical style. During the 14C the nave walls and aisles, which on the N. had apparently begun to lean outwards, were rebuilt, and large windows with pointed heads were inserted. The presbytery was also remodelled by the cutting of arches through Urban's outer walls and windows, and the medieval history of the fabric closed with the rebuilding of the N.W. tower by Jasper Tudor.

There followed nearly 300 years of neglect. The building was already in dangerous decay by 1575; Cromwell's soldiers used the nave as a tavern and post office, and the font as a pig trough, and burnt the cathedral's books at a formal ceremony at Cardiff Castle; after storms in 1703 and 1723 the S.W. tower collapsed and the nave roof fell in; and in the 18C 'restoration' took the strange form of an Italian Temple, built within the walls by John Wood, better known for his work at Bath.

Real restoration began in 1835 when Precentor Douglas devoted two years of his stipend to this purpose. Later years saw the removal of Wood's temple (all that remains are two urns outside the N.W. of the cathedral); the restoration of the Lady Chapel, presbytery, choir, and part of the nave; and the reopening of all these parts for divine service in 1857. Much of the later restoration was under the care of John Prichard, son of a priest of the cathedral and a pupil of Pugin, who rebuilt the S.W. tower, gave the chapter house its distinctive roof, added the row of sovereigns' heads (S. wall; modern heads N. wall), and carved four Evangelists on the E. face of the tower. It was Prichard's partner, J. B. Seddon, who brought in the Pre-Raphaelite work in glass, carving, and painting. In 1880 Dean Vaughan refounded the Cathedral School (perhaps founded in the 9C), abandoned in the 17C. In Jan. 1941 a German landmine destroyed virtually the whole of the previous century's work, Llandaff being, next to Coventry, the worst damaged of Britain's cathedrals. Restoration, completed in 1960, was largely by George Pace, who added the parabolic concrete arch, the Welch Regiment Memorial Chapel (David Chapel), and the Processional Way.

EXTERIOR. Llandaff is unique among British cathedrals in having no transepts, and the absence of a triforium is also remarkable in so early a building. Externally the most notable feature is the gracefully irregular W. front with its 13C centre. The curious pendent tympanum of the doorway (there never was a central shaft) has an original statue (St Dyfrig or St Teilo), and in the apex of the gable there is a Majesty. The S. doorway of the nave (c. 1170) is a rich example of Norman Trans. work. Jasper Tudor's N.W. tower is of Somerset design, but the elaborately panelled battlement and pinnacles are modern. The S.W. tower and spire, rebuilt from Prichard's designs of 1869 and bearing figures of saints and clerics, resemble those found in southern Normandy. Prichard and his father are buried in the churchyard near the S.E. door.

The INTERIOR is at once striking, the dominant feature being Pace's concrete arch, surmounted by a cylindrical organ case (with gilded Pre-Raphaelite figures, formerly in the niches and canopies of the pre-war choir stalls) bearing Jacob Epstein's huge Christus in unpolished aluminium. The effect is to separate nave and choir while not interfering with the lower level vista. The long arcades of the Nave and Choir, with foliated capitals, are 13C; the flat-panelled ceiling is modern, the hardwood being from Central Africa and Malaya. At the N.W. corner of the nave is the Illtyd Chapel, dedicated to the fallen of the 53rd (Welsh) Infantry Division. The Rossetti Triptych (1846-64) here, forming the reredos of the high altar until 1939, illustrates the Seed of David; Swinburne, Burne-Jones, and William Morris and his wife were the models. The font, at the S.W. corner of the nave, is by Alan Durst (1952) and depicts Man's fall, Christ's Redemption, and scenes from the lives of SS Dyfrig and Teilo. Most of the windows in the S. aisle are Pre-

Raphaelite, but the small panels in the second window are English 17C glass. Above the S. door hangs a Madonna and Child, attributed to Murillo. In the *South Presbytery Aisle* a 10C Celtic Cross is the only relic of the pre-Norman church; hidden at the time of the Commonwealth, it was found in 1870 in the garden of the Bishop's Palace. The *Teilo Chapel,* at the E. end of the S. aisle, contains an alabaster figure of Lady Audley (?early 15C).

The *Lady Chapel* (c. 1287), finely proportioned and with lovely vaulting, contains in its N.E. corner the tomb of the builder, Bishop William de Braose. The E. window tracery is 19C, and the glass is modern. In the niches of the 15C reredos are bronze panels, each with a wild flower named in Welsh in honour of Our Lady. The richly carved *Urban Arch* dividing the Lady Chapel from the *Presbytery* is a remnant of Bishop Urban's church of c. 1120. On the S. side of the presbytery, on the site of St Teilo's shrine, is a 13C effigy of the saint. The silver-gilt shrine, a centre of pilgrimage, stood here until the Reformation when the canons dismantled it rather than have it destroyed, the various pieces soon disappearing. Note the remains of the old Norman window on the S. wall. On either side of the altar are heavy Florentine candlesticks (17C), and the windows above the Urban Arch contain stained glass by John Piper and Patrick Reyntiens (who together also did a huge window in Coventry cathedral). In the *Choir* the Bishop's Throne and the stalls are 19C work (restored 1960).

The *Dyfrig Chapel,* the E. end of the N. aisle, is so called because Urban is said to have buried the saint's bones here in an attempt to boost his cathedral's repute. It contains the badly broken 14C reredos (originally 3-tiered), removed from its place behind the high altar during the 19C restoration, and, to its S., the tombs of Sir David Mathew, standard bearer to Edward IV at Towton in 1461, and of Sir Christopher Mathew (d. 1500). The family had the right of burial in this N. aisle until the 18C when they failed to continue to maintain the roof. Six porcelain panels on the W. Organ Case were designed by Burne-Jones and are from the Della Robbia pottery at Birkenhead; the model was Elizabeth Siddal, wife of Rossetti and inspiration to the Pre-Raphaelites. West of the organ case is the *Euddogwy Chapel,* commemorating the third saint traditionally associated with the founding of the cathedral and now the memorial chapel of the R.A.F. Auxiliary Squadron. Here, opposite a painting of the Assumption (15C, on board), is the marble monument of Dean Vaughan (d. 1897) by Goscombe John. Farther W., on the S. side of the N. aisle, a modern pulpit commemorates Archbishop John Morgan (d. 1957), below it being another Mathew tomb (Sir William and his wife, 1526).

The Norman *Teilo Doorway* leads into Pace's *David Chapel* (1956), the memorial chapel of the Welch Regiment, with furnishings that are gifts from Commonwealth regiments. In the *Processional Way* (also 1956) there hang four medieval gargoyles, rescued from the damage caused by the 1941 landmine.

CATHEDRAL CLOSE. On the green, immediately S. of the cathedral, are a restored *Cross* and the remains of a 13C *Bell-Tower,* a ruin since the early 15C; traditionally Exeter cathedral's bell known as 'Great Peter' came from here. Beside the green are the modern Deanery and Canon's Residence, while to the E. a pleasant garden (1972) is surrounded by fragments of the former *Bishop's Palace.*

In the village, near the main crossroads, is *St Michael's Theological College* (1907), with a chapel by George Pace. *Llandaff Court,* ¼ m. S.W. of the crossroads, is a library and community centre in eight acres of park and gardens. *Fairwater Park* (31 acres), ½ m. farther W., contains an artificial ski slope.— Francis Lewis, a signatory of the Declaration of Independence, was born at Llandaff in 1713.

D   *St Fagans, Welsh Folk Museum†

The **WELSH FOLK MUSEUM,** the largest branch museum of the National Museum of Wales, is at St Fagans, some 4 m. W. of central Cardiff. The museum is in three adjacent parts—the Galleries (New Buildings, containing also the bookshop, restaurant, and offices, and with the car park and picnic area close by); the Re-erected Buildings (Outdoor Museum); and St Fagans Castle. A folk museum was made possible in 1946 when the Earl of Plymouth offered St Fagans Castle to the National Museum of Wales and arranged for the transfer of 80 acres of park on generous terms.

GALLERIES. The **Agricultural Gallery** tells the story of farming in Wales, illustrating this with a fine collection of implements and machines. The various sections include Ditching and Hedging; Drainage; Ploughing and Harvesting, with machines ranging from the 18C to present times; Threshing, winnowing, chaff cutting, and corn grinding; Livestock. Below the gallery, off the courtyard, there is a collection of carts, sleds, etc.—The **Costume Gallery** is particularly attractive with its admirably displayed groups in period costume. The displays are changed at regular intervals.—The **Gallery of Material Culture,** comprising several small sections, illustrates aspects of the domestic, social, and cultural life of Wales. *The House* includes two 16C oak screens, and furniture characteristic of Wales, with fine cupboards and dressers; also chairs, selected to show their development. *Cooking* is illustrated by a collection of utensils, including spits and jacks, and *Dairying* by several butter churns (one operated by a dog), dairy hand-tools etc. In the *Laundering* section can be seen a box mangle, a selection of early washing machines, and a sequence showing the development of the iron. A panel is devoted to *Welsh Heraldry.* The *Lighting* section covers from the rushlights and tallow candles widely in use in Wales even in the late 19C, to tinder boxes, matches, and oil lamps. The *Arms* display ranges from crossbows to muskets, and from rapiers to pistols, with a special case devoted to these last. Also shown are shotguns, a blunderbuss of c. 1800, and a seven-barrelled rifle of c. 1820. In the section devoted to *Fire Fighting and Law and Order* can be seen insurance fire-marks; a fire engine of 1786; stocks, a scold's bridle, mantraps, and a daunting Schedule of Sentences (1831). The *Folklore* section contains objects associated with festivals, family occasions, and suchlike. Also collections of Welsh Valentines, and of love-spoons. The *Friendly Societies,* developing between about 1790 and 1850, were both a social focus and a means of social insurance. Something of their story is told here. The *Sports and Games* section contains material relating to rugby from 1881 to 1927. Also equipment used in bando (a rough 19C game), quoits, tennis, and chess. Under *Medical* can be seen instruments and 'cures' of the past, including tooth extractors, leech jars, an electric

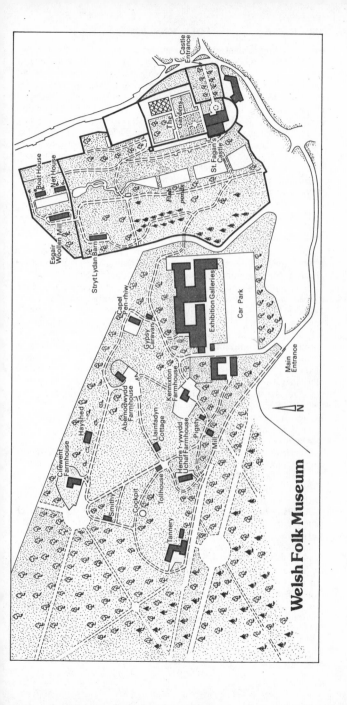

Welsh Folk Museum

treatment for rheumatism, and examples of the inventions of the 19C orthopaedic surgeon Owen Griffith. The *Education* section contains some of the museum's outstanding collection of 19C samplers and embroideries; school exercise books; and an unpleasant 19C device called the Welsh Not, a piece of wood hung around the neck of any pupil caught speaking Welsh. *Ecclesiastical* material includes communion cups and plates (17-18C), a preaching desk used by John Wesley, dog tongs, and Sunday School material. The *Eisteddfod* section shows material relating to the 18C societies which fostered the institution, and also to the Gorsedd of the Bards. The *Music* section is devoted to both instrumental and choral music. Among the instruments are triple harps, a hornpipe, a 'cwrth' (1742), and pianos. Church music is represented by precentors' pitch pipes and by a number of organs.

Outside the Gallery of Material Culture a wall-display outlines the work of the museum's *Department of Oral Tradition and Dialects.* The subjects receiving particular attention are the pattern of agriculture, the crafts, and domestic life; folklore and song; and dialect speech.

The RE-ERECTED BUILDINGS are mostly spread around the park N.W. of the Galleries, and there are other buildings to the E. in the castle grounds. Further buildings will be added as opportunity offers.

Immediately behind the Galleries there is a *Gypsy Caravan,* whence the following is a convenient round.—**Capel Pen-rhiw** (from Dre-Fach, Felindre, Dyfed-Carmarthen) is a Unitarian chapel, in origin possibly a barn adapted in 1777. At this time there was a loft, but a gallery was substituted in the early 19C, the aim being to increase the accommodation without adding to the building. The pews, probably a family responsibility, show individual variations, and the arcaded one next to the three-decker pulpit may have been for the elders. The floor is of beaten earth, except for the boarded communion place. The stone seats outside were used for overflow congregations during preaching festivals. Schools were once housed in the chapel, a Welsh Not (see Education, above) being among the quill pens and other articles found when it was dismantled.

Abernodwydd Farmhouse (from Llangadfan, Powys-Montgomery) was built in the 16C and renovated in the 17C, when the present loft, chimney, and windows (unglazed, with sliding shutters) were inserted. The furnishing is 17C. To be noted are, in the kitchen, the chest; in the dairy, the cheese press and churn; in the chamber, a box bedstead; and, in the room beyond the kitchen, a 17C chest.

The **Hayshed** (from Maentwrog, Gwynedd-Merioneth), with large slate pillars, dates from the 19C. It is passed on the way to the **Cilewent Farmhouse** (from Dyffryn Claerwen, Powys-Radnor), a typical moorland longhouse occupied by both the family and its cattle. The family lived in the N. end, with two rooms on the ground floor and two above, this part being separated from the cowhouse and stable by a passage from which the cattle were fed. The entrance, for both men and beasts, is wide enough for longhorn cattle. The cowhouse has stalls and a pen for calves; the stable, with its own entrance, is beyond, and above there is a loft for hay. Note the arrangement for draining the liquid manure, and also the opening in the W. wall of the cowhouse through which manure was thrown out. The peathouse is in the yard, and N.W. of the house are the sheep pens. Built in 1579 or earlier of local shaly stone and river stone, the house was much altered c. 1734.

The **Smithy** (from Lawr-y-glyn, Powys-Montgomery) is late 18C but altered. Beyond is the **Tannery** (from Rhayader, Powys-Radnor). Dating mainly from the 18C, this tannery was the last oak-bark tannery in Wales and mainly produced heavy leathers for boots and harness, a process which required at least 18 months. On the S. side of the yard can be seen the clean-water pit for the initial washing of the hides, and three lime pits in which the raw hides lay for several days before unhairing and fleshing, these tasks being carried out in the Beam House immediately behind the pits. At the back of the Beam House are three pits used for the further softening of soft hides (the recipe was a mixture of water, pigeon droppings, and dog excreta). The end pit in front of the Beam House was for fleshings that went to glue works. On the N. side of the yard are a room where hides were cut prior to tanning, and a cellar in which horse hides were stored under damp conditions to produce the white leather which was so popular for footwear in the 19C. The tanyard comprises a series of pits, some open, others covered by the main building. Eight of the oak-lined pits in the centre were for the mixing of the oak-bark (stored and ground in the large building at the back of the tannery) with water in order to produce the tanning liquor; the others were for the actual tanning by immersion. Further processes were scrubbing and washing (stone table in the centre of the yard); drying on the racks on the first floor; dressing by the currier, if required for harness or shoe uppers.

The **Cockpit** comes from the yard of the Hawk and Buckle Inn, Denbigh. The walls and roof are original (early 18C), but the remainder is reconstruction. The **Tollhouse** (from Aberystwyth) was originally built in 1771, but the roof is later. Note the fascinating list of charges and exemptions. **Llainfadyn Cottage** (from Rhostryfan, Gwynedd-Caernarvon), dating from 1762, is an excellent example of the use of boulders, some of the larger of which extend right through the walling. The single room has been divided by placing two cupboard beds at the sleeping end. Boards resting on the bed testers form a loft.

Hendre'r-ywydd Uchaf Farmhouse (from Llangynhafal, Clwyd-Denbigh) dates from the late 15C. The wood-mullioned windows are part of the timber framing. The roof is of wheat straw, with an underthatch of oak rods woven on riven oak stakes. The building comprises dwelling and cowhouse, the division being a wattled and daubed cruck truss. The dwelling had an open hearth with no chimney, the smoke escaping through windows and doors; the furnishing, as sparse as it would have been at the time, is mainly early 16C.

The **Melin Bompren Watermill** (from Cross Inn, Dyfed-Cardigan) was built in 1853 and is typical of a country mill of the period. The conical **Pigsty** is of a type found only in the S. of Wales. Although this particular sty is 18C, the technique of corbelling is an ancient one. **Kennixton Farmhouse** (from Llangennydd, Gower), illustrates development over a period of about a hundred years. The E. part of the building is the oldest (c. 1630); note the scissors-tie in the room to the right at the top of the stairs. The kitchen was added later in the same century, and the whole house was renovated in the early 18C when the back-kitchen and all the windows were added. Of constructional interest are the mortar floors, characteristic of Glamorgan; in the kitchen, the ceiling recess which here serves as a place for hanging bacon and, above, forms a child's bed; and the woven straw mats which form the underthatch of the roof. The furniture includes, in the kitchen, a Glamorgan dresser, an interesting bacon-cupboard chair, and a box bed; in the parlour, a small dower chest, a Bible box (1716), and a chair with a drawer below the seat, all from Gower; in the back-kitchen, articles associated with dairying, including a cheese press and a butter-working table.

The path past the Gypsy Caravan leads E. through a tunnel to the castle grounds (see below), in the N. part of which are more buildings.

The **Stryt Lydan Barn** (from Penley, Clwyd-Flint) consists of two sections joined by a drifthouse, into which the loaded wagons entered. The S. part is the older (c. 1550). Constructed on crucks, this part of the barn divided into three bays. The corn, unloaded from the drifthouse into the N. bay, was threshed with flails in the central bay (note the central doors which provided a draught for winnowing), and the straw was stacked in the S. bay. The N. part of the barn (c. 1600) is of post and truss construction.

Esgair Woollen Mill (from near Llanwrtyd, Powys-Brecknock) was built c. 1760, though the interior was altered during the 19C. The mill is worked by water, pumped from the swimming pool to the top of a bank whence it runs to the wheel by gravity. The mill is still producing, and its products can be bought.

The **Boat House and Net House** is a replica of a building that stood on the river bank at Chepstow until the 1940s. Material relating to fishing in Wales is exhibited, this including nets, traps, and gaffs used in salmon fishing, and equipment used in inshore fishing for lobsters, cockles, and mussels. There is a unique collection of coracles.

The **Castle Grounds** are either side of a steep valley, along the foot of which are the fishponds, which are kept stocked. The *Gardens,* on the E. side to the N. of the castle, include a formal garden with topiary, a fountain garden, and herb, rose, and knot gardens. There are also a vinery and flower house, grapes and flowers sometimes being for sale, and two bronzes by W. Goscombe John (Joyance and the Elf). The large lead cistern in front of the house (E. side) dates from 1620.

ST FAGANS CASTLE is an attractive Elizabethan mansion, built between 1560 and 1590 on the site of a 12C stronghold whose 13C curtain wall still surrounds it. The house has been whitened to restore it to its probable early appearance.

History. The early castle was built by Sir Peter le Surs, on whom the lordship of St Fagans had been bestowed by Robert Fitzhamon, the Norman conqueror of Glamorgan. By the early 16C the castle was a ruin, but in 1560 a part of the estate came into the possession of Dr John Gibbon, who built the present house, incorporating something of the old N. wall. In 1616 Sir Edward Lewis of Caerphilly bought St Fagans. In 1648 the parish was the scene of a battle in which the Parliamentarians, under Horton and Jones, decisively defeated the Royalists under Poyer and Laugharne. In 1730 the estate passed by marriage to Other Windsor, 3rd Earl of Plymouth. By the early 19C. the place was in disrepair, but in the 1860s considerable renovation was carried out, the main staircase was probably inserted, and the tower and servants' hall were built.

The *Back Hall* contains an 18C Sedan chair.—The *Kitchen* has two 16C fireplaces and 16-18C utensils. Note the spits (especially the dog-driven one), and the bacon rack and bread crate suspended from the ceiling.—The *Hall* was used by both family and servants. The 16-17C furnishing includes a baluster-turned 'justice's chair' (c. 1550), two buffets (c. 1590 and 1630), and a two-piece cupboard (early 17C.). The overmantel bears the Windsor arms. The Welsh Bible is the edition of 1620.—The *Drawing Room* has 17 and early 18C furnishing. The Flemish tapestry (Brussels, early 18C) has scenes copied from David Teniers the Younger. The musical instruments are an 18C triple harp, once belonging to the harpists of Powis Castle, and a virginal of 1654. The arms on the overmantel are those of the Lewis family.

On the first floor the *Long Gallery* has Mortlake tapestries (17C) illustrating the legend of Diane and Calisto from Ovid's 'Metamorphoses'. Portraits are of Elizabeth Lewis (d. 1733) and her husband Other Windsor (the marriage which brought St Fagans to the Windsors, earls of Plymouth), and of William Williams, a blind harpist. The 17-18C furniture includes a pier glass in black lacquer frame (18C), a long-case clock of c. 1775 by David Parry of Carmarthen, and an early piano.—The *Dining Room* represents that of Glantorvaen House, Pontypool, for which all the furniture was made in the 1860s by Trapnell of Bristol and Newport. Note the six-light gas chandelier.—The *17C Bedroom* has a frieze of c. 1620 and an overmantel of 1635. The intricately carved bed has been much restored.—The *Library* generally represents that at Coed-coch (Abergele, Clwyd-Denbigh), most of the furniture having been made for John Lloyd Wynne, whose portrait hangs here with that of his wife (both 1811). Not from Abergele are the clock, by John Thackwell of Cardiff (1740-1830), and the books, most of which are from the National Library of Wales.—The *Parlour,* furnished in 17C style, has a carved frieze inscribed EBL/1624, for Sir Edward Lewis and his wife Blanche; Sir Edward's initials also appear, together with the Lewis arms, on the iron fireback (1620). Of the two tapestries, with scenes from paintings by David Teniers the Younger, one was probably woven in Soho under the supervision of John Vanderbank (d. 1727), and the other at Lille in the 17C.—The frieze in the *18C Bedroom* is of 1620, and the stone mantel, brought from a house in Whitchurch (Glam.), of 1583. The tapestries, part of the Diane and Calisto series, are, like those in the Long Gallery, 17C Mortlake. The bed is early 18C.

The *Exhibition* shows domestic appliances of the late 19 and early 20C. Most are intriguing, particularly so being the bathroom appliances.

In the *Castle Yard* there are a number of coaches. A *Wood Turner* and a *Cooper* work nearby. They, and other craftsmen, may eventually be housed in re-erected workshops.

41   THE VALLEYS

The **Valleys** covered by this Route are Rhondda, Cynon, Taff, Rhymney, and Ebbw. The first four are described as from Cardiff, and Ebbw, which includes Sirhowy, as from Newport.

Until the second half of the 18C these valleys, a fan of steep-sided narrow clefts extending some 20 miles into the South Wales mountains, were virtually untouched wild countryside. The change came with the Industrial Revolution which exploded in this part of Wales through the combination of high grade coal in the valleys, the plentiful iron ore along their heads, and the several ports that could be developed at their feet. Communications were at first by packhorse or mule along atrocious roads. This was soon followed by the digging of canals, the Glamorgan Canal between Merthyr Tydfil (and later Aberdare) and Cardiff being opened in 1794, closely followed by the Monmouth Canal in 1796 and the Swansea Canal in 1798. A measure of the speed of industrial development can be judged from the fact that the 50,000 tons carried on the Glamorgan Canal in 1820 had increased to 350,000 tons by 1839. The usefulness of the canals lasted some 50 years, until the railways took their place. The Taff Valley railway was authorized in 1836, and the Rhymney Valley dates from 1854-64. By the middle of the 19C the valleys, though untouched on their heights, had below been transformed into disfigured strips into which crowded towns, mines, iron and associated works, and railways.

The first step in the long decline came with the invention of improved processes for the large-scale manufacture of steel. These processes demanded better quality iron ore, this in turn meaning either the closure of ironworks or their transfer from the heads of the valleys to the coast with its fast developing ports, where foreign ore could be imported and treated. The depression, two wars, the replacement of coal by oil, and the need for steelworks to be near the ore ports combined to bring about an accelerating decline, and after the last war it became clear that two related steps needed urgent attention. The first was the substitution of diversified industry for the mining and heavy industry of the past, an aim which has largely been achieved, with modern industrial estates now proliferating. The second requirement was reclamation, the removal or softening of the scars. This task began to be tackled seriously in the 1960s, although progress was slow and by 1966 only some 99 acres had been treated. The Aberfan tragedy of 1966, when a sliding tip killed 144 people, including 116 children, shocked public opinion, and subsequent progress has been notable to the extent that by the mid 1970s the officially treated areas totalled over 7000 acres. The responsibility is now that of the Welsh Development Agency (established 1976), whose ambitious plans are directed towards more than another 30,000 acres, awaiting conversion to industrial estates, recreation areas, country parks etc.

The view, still often held, that these valleys are a 'black country' is now far wide of the mark. While there are still collieries, seemingly endless built-up areas, and some ugly industrial patches, far commoner features today are the long low terraces of houses, built in local stone, brightly painted, and following the contours; the clean industrial estates; and the smooth, green, landscaped hills that were once hideous tips. Contrasts are as frequent as they are unexpected, and from most places there is quick access, on foot or by car, to the generally untouched moorland above. Today the roads ascending the valleys provide convenient, not uninteresting, and often scenic links between the coast and Brecon Beacons National Park.

A Rhondda Valley (Cardiff to Hirwaun)

A470 to Pontypridd: A4058 to Treorchy: A4061 to Hirwaun. 29 miles.—*5m.* **Castell Coch.**—*6m.* **Pontypridd.**—*3m.* **Porth.**—*2m.* **Tonypandy.**—*3m.* **Ton-Pentre.**—*3m.* *Treherbert.*—*4m. Hirwaun Common Pass.*—*3m. Hirwaun.*

Comprising the two valleys of Rhondda Fawr and Rhondda Fach, and with a chain of towns, **Rhondda** is a borough of some 88,500 people. The borough stretches from Pontypridd to Hirwaun Common, is an average of 4m. wide, and is typical of the general description of The Valleys given above. Three collieries continue to operate.

With Cathays Park on the E., Cardiff is left by North Road, a left fork being taken just after crossing Inner Bypass. The valley of the Taff is then ascended.—*5 m.* **Castell Coch**† (Red Castle), to the E. of the main road and beautifully situated on a steep wooded slope guarding a glen, is a folly built in 1865-85 by William Burges for the 3rd Marquess of Bute. It stands on the foundations of a 13C castle, recorded as having already been in ruins centuries ago, fragments of which survive in the base of the tower nearest to the car park and in its dungeon. The name derives from the previous castle's red sandstone. The building, fantastic both in construction and interior decoration, is triangular with at each angle a round tower crowned by a conical roof of Rhineland character. Drawbridge and portcullis are working copies of the originals, and the castle's rooms are decorated with romantic murals, with scenes from Aesop's fables and Greek mythology, birds, animals etc. There is an interesting exhibition explaining the castle's design and construction.— *1 m.* Taff's Well was at one time noted for its tepid medicinal springs. At *Nantgarw,* just beyond, good porcelain, now greatly valued by collectors, was produced for a short period in the early 19C. Important collieries have been developed here in an area which is the biggest reserve of coking coal in Britain, and a coke-oven and by-products plant is associated with *Nantgarw-Windsor Colliery.* Beyond Nantgarw the road passes *Treforest Trading Estate,* founded in 1936 and the first in Wales.

5 m. **Pontypridd** (34,000 inhab.) is an industrial town at the confluence of the Taff and the Rhondda. It owes its name (Bridge near the Earthen Hut) to a graceful bridge (disused) over the Taff, built in 1756 by William Edwards, a local stonemason, after two unsuccessful attempts. The bridge, 35 ft above the river, has a single span 140 ft across, forming a segment of a circle 170 ft in diameter; a special feature of the design is the lightening of the haunches by three cylindrical tunnels on each side, thus lessening the inward and upward thrust of the masonry and reducing wind resistance. In *Ynysangharad Park* statues by Goscombe John commemorate Evan and James James, father and son and author and composer of the Welsh National Anthem; they were local cloth makers. *Ty Mawr/Lewis Merthyr Colliery,* 1 m. N.W. of Pontypridd, was sunk in 1875 and given major reconstruction in 1962.

Rtes 41B and 41C lead N., while this Route continues N.W., now ascending the valley of the Rhondda.—*3 m.* **Porth** ('Gateway') is at the junction of the Rhondda Fawr and Rhondda Fach valleys. At *Cymmer,* just S., is the oldest Nonconformist chapel in the valley (1748).

B4277 ascends **Rhondda Fach**. Penrhys, to the W. of the valley after 2½ m., may owe its name to a tradition that Rhys ap Tewdwr was beheaded here in 1093. St Mary's Well (restored) was a popular place of pilgrimage until the Reformation. At *Ferndale,* 1½ m. farther up the valley, factories provide employment for several disabled people, mainly from the mining industry. *Darran Lake* is used for boating and fishing, and the land up to the crags above is a nature reserve.—*Maerdy,* 1½ m. farther N. at the head of the valley, was the first Rhondda colliery town to feel the depression, three of its four pits closing between 1932-40. However between 1948-52 there was a major modernization by which a new colliery was constructed on the site of the closed pits. The road continues over the mountain to (3 m.) *Aberdare* in the Cynon Valley.

It was at *Dinas,* S. of the river 1 m. W. of Porth, that the first Rhondda commercial mine was opened in 1809. The greater part of this area has now been redeveloped, and at *Penygraig,* just W., two large tips have been cleared and levelled to provide some 100 acres for a school and playing fields.

Gilfach Goch, c. 4½ m. S.W. of Dinas by A4119, A4093, and B4564, is in a small valley which was entirely given over to mining from 1860-1960 but which is today a model of what can be achieved by imaginative reclamation and landscaping. At the same time the industrial past is recalled by the *Industrial Trail,* 2 m. long (short cuts possible), starting at the site of the former Six Bells Hotel towards the N. end of W. loop of B4564. Nine interpretive panels tell the story of six collieries, the Six Bells, the Prince of Wales Plantation, and the former railway station. The valley was the subject of Richard Llewellyn's novel 'How Green was my Valley'.

2m. **Tonypandy** was the scene of mining riots in 1910. In *Nantgwyddon Woods,* to the N., the Pentref Bowmen, Rhondda's archery club, have established a large Field Archery Centre, now of international repute.—*3m.* **Ton-Pentre** is Rhondda's administrative centre, and in Gelligaled Park there is the valley's large Sports Centre (1975).—*1m.* **Treorchy**. The establishment here in 1939 of a large clothing factory was the first main step towards diversification in Rhondda. The Royal Male Voice Choir, the oldest in Wales, was granted its title by Queen Victoria after a Command Performance at Windsor in 1885.—*2m.* **Treherbert** is the terminus of the railway. *Blaenrhondda,* on a side road, 1 m. N., has been designated a conservation area because of its late 19C houses. *Fernhill Colliery,* beyond, is one of the only three collieries remaining in Rhondda.

After Treherbert the road, built in 1930-32 by unemployed miners, climbs the N.E. flank of the head of the valley, crossing Forestry Commission land with several waymarked paths.—*4m.* **Hirwaun** *Common Pass* (1600 ft), with a parking place offering a fine view N. to the Brecon Beacons across the partly industrialized valley far below. Late Bronze and early Iron Age finds at *Llyn Fawr* (below, N.W.) are in the National Museum of Wales. A sign indicates the start of the *Coed Morgannwg Way* walk (see p. 307) to Afan Argoed (13 m.) and Margam Park (23 m.). Descending in a large loop the road in *3m.* reaches *Hirwaun* on Rte 37B.

B   Cynon Valley (Cardiff to Hirwaun)

A470 to Abercynon: A4059 to Hirwaun. 25 miles.—*11m.* **Pontypridd.**—*3m.* **Abercynon.**—*4m.* **Mountain Ash.**—*4m.* **Aberdare.**—*3m.* **Hirwaun.**

To (*11m.*) **Pontypridd,** see Rte 41A.—*3m.* **Abercynon** can be reached either by A470 or B4273 along the E. or W. sides of the Taff respectively. The town is the birthplace (1933) of Dai Dower, the flywright boxing champion. A470 (Rte 41C) continues N., while this Route bears N.W. up the valley of the Cynon. *Lady Windsor/Abercynon Colliery,* neighbouring collieries sunk in 1886 and 1896, were linked underground in 1975 to form a single unit.—*4m.* **Mountain Ash**, just S. of which is *Penrikyber Colliery,* sunk between 1872-78 and modernized in 1963-64. *Deep Duffryn Colliery,* to the N. on the N.E. side of the valley, was sunk in 1850.

4m. **Aberdare** (40,000 inhab.) is the chief town of the valley. *St John's Church* dates from c. 1189 and has, outside the W. door, curious iron gates made at the nearby Abernant Ironworks (founded 1802) and consisting of a series of the figure 3. In Victoria Square there is a statue to Caradog, leader of the South Wales Choral Union Choir which won the Crystal Palace Cup in 1872 and 1873. *Dare Valley Country Park* (1972), to the W. of the town, has been created on land that was until recently collieries and tips; today there are over 25 attractively landscaped acres with over 20,000 mixed trees, and four waymarked trails (1 to 5 m.; leaflet from site warden) illustrating natural history and some local industrial archaeology. At *Trecynon,* the N. suburb of Aberdare, there is an iron bridge of 1811 which once carried the tramway linking the ironworks with the Glamorgan Canal.—*3 m. Hirwaun* on Rte 37B.

C   Taff Valley (Cardiff to Merthyr Tydfil)

A470. 23 miles.—*14 m.* **Abercynon.**—*2 m.* **Treharris.**—*2 m.* *Aberfan.*—*5 m.* **Merthyr Tydfil.**

To (*14 m.*) **Abercynon,** see Rte 41 A and B.—It was along the horse-tramway between Merthyr Tydfil and Abercynon (the route of today's road) that in 1804 Richard Trevithick tried out the earliest steam tram-locomotive, covering the distance in four hours and five minutes and carrying 10 tons of iron and 70 men.—*2 m. Quaker's Yard,* at the foot of the Bargoed valley, takes its name from an old burial ground. It is a part of **Treharris,** near which are two collieries. *Deep Navigation Colliery* was sunk in 1894 and wholly reorganized in the 1960s; its original name was Harris's Navigation Pits, Harris being the principal shareholder who also gave his name to the town. *Taff Merthyr Colliery,* recently improved for future development, was sunk in 1924.—*2 m.* A road leads W. to *Aberfan,* where in 1966 Pontglas School and a row of houses were engulfed by a sliding coal tip. Of the 144 dead, 116 were children and a Memorial Garden now occupies the site of the school.

The valley becomes more upland in character and at (*2 m.*) *Troedyrhiw* it widens considerably.—*3 m.* **Merthyr Tydfil,** see p. 287.

D   Rhymney Valley (Cardiff to Rhymney)

A469. 19 miles.—*5 m.* **Thornhill.**—*2 m.* **Caerphilly.**—*4 m. Ystrad Mynach.*— *3 m. Bargoed.*—*5 m.* **Rhymney.**

With Cathays Park on the E., Cardiff is left by North Road, which, beyond the intersection with Inner Bypass, becomes Caerphilly Road, passing through the suburb of *Llanishen* with (E. of the main road) a huge complex of government tower-offices.—*5 m. Thornhill.* To the E. (1 m.) is *Parc Cefn-Onn,* some 200 acres of open country and wooded hillside, noted for its rhododendrons and azaleas and offering good views. The park, with a station on the Cardiff to Caerphilly railway, was acquired by the city of Cardiff in 1944. To the W. (1 m.) of Thornhill is *The Wenallt* (750 ft; 140 acres), another open space belonging to Cardiff. The park is a rolling area of woodland and heath with a view across Cardiff and the Bristol Channel.—From the watershed (888 ft), ½ m. N. of Thornhill, there is a good panorama down to Caerphilly and the valleys beyond.

2 m. **Caerphilly** (36,000 inhab.), an industrial and market town which started as a Roman station, is known for its fine white cheese and for ****Caerphilly Castle†**, after Windsor the largest in England and Wales (30 acres, including the earthworks) and architecturally important as being the model for the concentric plan adopted by Edward I for his great fortresses. The castle's defences are remarkable for their elaboration and novelty.

History. The earliest fortification here was the Roman fort of c. 75, the site of which is now occupied by the Civil War earthwork (the Redoubt) to the N.W. of the castle. In 1268 Gilbert de Clare, fearful of the threat to Cardiff from Llewelyn the Last, began to build a castle here, but this was destroyed in 1270 by Llewelyn when he invaded the surrounding district of Senghenydd. The following year Gilbert de Clare started again, continuing to build despite a siege by Llewelyn, whom he eventually forced to withdraw. From the Clares Caerphilly passed in 1317 to the Despensers, Edward II finding brief refuge here from Isabella. After this the castle lost its military value and before the middle of the 16C had already fallen into decay. During the Civil War a redoubt for artillery was built beyond the N.W. of the castle, but later Cromwell drained the lakes and blew up the towers, his attempt on one of which (S.E.) clearly being only partially successful. Later Caerphilly passed viâ the earls of Pembroke to the Butes, the 4th Marquess in 1935–37 making careful and extensive restoration before handing the castle over to the Crown.

The castle is a magnificent example of the concentric plan, borrowed, largely through the experience of the Crusades, from Europe and the Near East. It comprises four separate groups of fortification, these being the castle proper, a complex of two concentric wards completely surrounded by a lake; a large barbican system to the E. of this, defended by an outer moat; a large hornwork on the W.; and, to the N.W., the outlying Civil War redoubt. The lake (c. 15 acres), created by damming the small Nant-y-Gledr, washed the outer defences on the S. and W. and was separated only by a narrow bank from the moat (itself filled from the lake) which on the N. side flanked the outer ward.

The visitor's approach is across the EAST BARBICAN, a line of embattled curtain wall, in places 60 ft high, stretching N. and S. over some 340 yards. This wall, sheltering a raised earthen platform and strengthened by several bastions, also formed a dam for the lake. Approximately in the middle there is a large *Gatehouse,* which was approached by two drawbridges resting at their ends on the hexagonal stone pier that still survives in the outer moat. The two halves of this barbican could be defended independently, as they were divided by a transverse wall, 20 ft high, across the platform. The doorway that connected them was sealed by a portcullis and by a drawbridge over the adjoining overflow channel, which controlled the amount of water in the lake. At the N. end of the N. platform there is a postern. On the S. platform are the remains of a mill, worked by water from the lake, and beyond, at the S. end, a large gateway, facing W. to prevent the barbican being outflanked and commanding the brook at the point where it was dammed.

The *Inner Moat,* formerly with a drawbridge, is crossed to the castle proper, the OUTER WARD being reached through the ruins of its E. gate. This ward, which surrounds the inner with a terrace 48–60 ft wide, was defended by the moat on every side except the south. Its outer boundary was little more than a breastwork above the revetted scarp of the moat, but it was reinforced by wide semicircular bastions at the corners. Just S. of the outer ward entrance there are the ruins of what may have been a granary, and, against the wall of the building next to the leaning tower, are the remains of an oven.

The INNER WARD, roughly rectangular (200 by 160 ft), has massive gatehouses on the E. and W., both with half-drum-towers to the field. The *East Gatehouse* (usually closed) is the more impressive and contains on its second floor a hall and (S.) an oratory. Of the drum-towers at the angles of the ward, blown up by Cromwell, that on the N.E. has largely disappeared, while that on the S.E. survives as a 50 ft high segment overhanging its base by 11 ft 6 inches. The other towers have been restored. The *Great Hall* (70 by 35 ft and c. 30ft high) is along the S. side of the ward. It was probably rebuilt c. 1317 by Hugh le Despenser. Note the ball-flower ornament inside. Now restored, the hall is sometimes used for official and charity functions. To the E. of the hall are the buttery and a small chapel, together now used as modern kitchen and boiler house; and to the W. is a range of state apartments. The *Kitchen,* very unusually placed, projects S. into the outer ward, which, with the adjoining watergate, it effectively blocks on this side. Communication

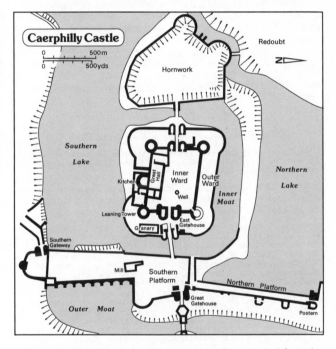

with the fortifications here was by a covered gallery, reached from the ground at the S.W. corner of the inner ward.

Opposite the W. gatehouse of the outer ward, perhaps originally the castle's principal entrance, is the large revetted HORNWORK of c. 3 acres, once defended by yet another moat and drawbridge. Beyond, to the N.W., is the REDOUBT, the site of the Roman fort, possibly also the site of Gilbert de Clare's first castle, and in the Civil War used for artillery.

B4263 ascends the Nant-y-Aber N.W. from Caerphilly to (4 m.) the former mining village of *Senghenydd.* The worst colliery disaster in Britain occurred here in 1913 when 439 miners were killed as the result of an explosion.

Rudry Forest, stretching E. from Caerphilly, has four waymarked walks (1 to 2 m.). Three of these start from Llwyncelyn car park and picnic site on the minor road skirting the S.E. side of the woods, and a fourth starts from the N. side ½ m. E. of Rudry.

Bedwas Colliery, 2 m. N.W. of Caerphilly, sunk in 1908, was reconstructed in 1958-60.

4 m. Ystrad Mynach, where A472 is crossed, leading W. to the Taff and Cynon valleys and E. to the Sirhowy and Ebbw valleys. *Hengoed Viaduct,* just N., dates from 1867. *Penallta Colliery,* to the N. of Hengoed, was sunk in 1905 and considerably extended in 1960.—*2 m.* Junction with B4254. At *Gelligaer,* on high ground 1 m. W., the 13C church contains the village stocks (14C) and the St Gwladys Stone (9-10C), formerly on Gelligaer Common (1 m. N.W.) and probably standing near the site of Capel Gwladys, founded by this saint in the 6C. Behind the church can be clearly seen the earthwork outlines of a small Roman fort built early in the 2C on the road from Cardiff to Brecon, the course of which runs along the mountain ridge N.W. across the common.

1 m. Bargoed, with a colliery dating from 1897.—*5 m.* **Rhymney** was an important iron working town, the first works being started here in 1800. St David's Church (1843) was endowed by the Rhymney Ironworks Company for the benefit of their workers. A465 (Rte 37B) is 1 m. north.

E   Ebbw and Sirhowy Valleys (Newport to Ebbw Vale)

A467 to Aberbeeg; A4046 to Ebbw Vale or A467 to Brynmawr. 17 or 18 miles.— *6 m.* **Sirhowy Valley.**—*1 m.* **Cwmcarn Scenic Forest Drive.**—*2 m.* **Newbridge.**— *3 m. Aberbeeg.*—*5 m.* **Ebbw Vale** or *6 m.* **Brynmawr.**

A467 runs W. from St Woolos Cathedral.—*2 m. Rogerstone* has large aluminium works. The road continues through industrial *Risca* to (*4 m.*) the junction with A4048, which ascends Sirhowy Valley.

SIRHOWY VALLEY. In 5 m. A4048 crosses A472, linking (W.) Rhymney Valley and (E.) Ebbw Valley. The industrial town of **Blackwood** (6500 inhab.), spreading 1 m. westwards, is the main place up Sirhowy Valley and has two nearby collieries. *Britannia Colliery,* N.W. at Pengam, was sunk in 1912, and *Oakdale Colliery,* 1 m. N.E., sunk in 1908, has recently been much modernized. At **Markham,** 3 m. N. of Blackwood, the colliery dates from 1913. The valley ends at **Tredegar** (17,500 inhab.), a former iron working town, 5 m. farther N., beyond which A4048 meets A465 (Rte 37B). There are three disused collieries near Tredegar. *Yard Level* (1802-73) was one of the first levels to supply the Tredegar Ironworks; *Ty-Trist* (1834-1959); and *Pochin* (1876-1964), where although, due to rock, five years elapsed between first sinking and the first coal production, the colliery soon afterwards became the most extensive in this district. Aneurin Bevan (1897-1960) the Labour politician was born at Tredegar.

1 m. Cwmcarn is to the E. of A467. This is the starting point for the Forestry Commission's **Cwmcarn Scenic Forest Drive†,** seven miles of mountain forest with superb views both N. towards the Brecon Beacons and S. to the Bristol Channel. The woodland here, mostly dating from the 1920s, is successor to the medieval Forest of Machen, destroyed over the centuries by the demands of sheep, tanning, iron smelting, and mining. There are several car parks and picnic sites, two of these (Nos 3 and 7 in the S.E. part of the drive) being just below the hillfort of *Twmbarlwm* (1374 ft).

1 m. **Abercarn** is another industrial town. At *Craig Wen,* 1 m. E. in Nant Gwyddon, there is a Forestry Commission office, beyond which a car park marks the start of Cwm Gwyddon Forest Walk (2 m.). A short way N. of Abercarn there are two collieries, *Celynen South* and *Celynen*

North, sunk respectively in 1873 and 1913 and the latter much modernized in 1963.—*1m.* **Newbridge** has a fine Roman Catholic church by P. D. Hepworth (1939). A472, linking Abercynon to Pontypool, is crossed at *Crumlin,* a N. extension of Newbridge. The large fan-ventilation engine of Crumlin's Navigation Colliery (1907-68) is now in the Welsh Industrial and Maritime Museum, Cardiff. Penyfan Pond, once a colliery feeder lake, is now a country park (information centre).

3m. Aberbeeg, where there is a choice of valleys, the W. fork being Ebbw Fawr and the E. Ebbw Fach.

EBBW FAWR. *Marine Colliery,* just S. of (*2m.*) *Cwm,* opened in 1891, is the only colliery still operating in Ebbw Fawr.—*3m.* **Ebbw Vale** (29,000 inhab.), a crowded industrial town, was from 1929 the constituency of Aneurin Bevan. Over dependent upon steel, the town has been seriously affected by British Steel Corporation's problems of the 1970s and steel making ended in 1978.

EBBW FACH. Approaching (*1m.*) **Abertillery** (40,000 inhab.) *Six Bells Colliery,* opened in the 1890s, has been modernized. In 1960 45 miners lost their lives in an explosion here. In Abertillery the small *Museum†,* in the Library, covers local industrial history. *Abertillery New Mine,* developed between 1956-59, is a drift mine which integrates two former collieries here.—*5m.* **Brynmawr,** see p. 287.

42   SWANSEA AND GOWER

A   Swansea

SWANSEA (*Abertawe.* 172,500 inhab.), an industrial city, port, and the main shopping centre of southwest Wales, lies on the N.W. shore of Swansea Bay, mostly on the W. bank of the mouth of the river Tawe. The docks stretch away from the E. bank of the river's mouth, and, with industry confined to the outer edge, the city centre, mostly reconstruction after the air raid damage of the last war, is spacious and modern. Development has also allowed for extensive parks and gardens. Although without a cathedral, Swansea was granted city status following the investiture of the Prince of Wales.

City Centre. The Circus, just N. of the castle.
Tourist Information. *Guildhall,* over 1½ m. W. of the centre.
Centre Parking. Multi-storey off Orchard Street and Kingsway. Near *Leisure Centre,* for Royal Institution of South Wales, and Maritime and Industrial museums.
Market. Between Oxford and Orange streets. Open Mon.-Sat.
Railway Station. High Street, to N. of the castle.
Bus Station. Singleton Street.
Main Post Office. Castlewind Street.
Airport. Fairwood Common (5 m. W.).
Entertainment. *Grand Theatre* (repertory). *Brangwyn Hall* (concerts; music festival in Oct.).
Boats. Car ferry to Cork. Summer excursions to Ilfracombe.
History. The name probably derives from 'Sweyn's ey', suggesting that Swansea originated as a Viking settlement, possibly founded by Sweyne Forkbeard who is known to have been active in the Bristol Channel. The castle was first built by Henry de Newburgh, or Beaumont, who in 1099 led an expedition into Gower, and the town which grew around it received a charter from William de Braose in 1210. Later, the castle was destroyed by Owen Glendower. Shipbuilding and coalmining began in the Swansea district in the 14C, if not earlier, and trade was early

established with Ireland, France, and the Channel Islands. Swansea furnished ships for coast defence for Elizabeth I. In the Civil War the town was Royalist until 1645, when Colonel Philip Jones, a native Parliamentarian, was made governor; the town later received a charter from Cromwell. By 1700 Swansea was the largest port in Wales. Smelters were attracted to the district (many from Cornwall) by the rich coal, and in the 18C numerous copper works were developed (mostly a little inland; the first at Landore), Nelson's ships being sheathed with Swansea copper. In the 19C not only copper, but silver, lead, tin, nickel, zinc, cobalt, and iron ores were imported for smelting and refining on a large scale. For a short time too, in the early 19C, Swansea porcelain was a noted local manufacture. The Swansea Canal, opened in 1798, had a rapid effect on the trade of the port, which increased from 90,000 tons in 1799 to 500,000 tons by 1839, and the first of the enclosed docks (North Dock) was opened in 1852, South Dock following in 1859. Both these docks were on the W. bank of the Tawe. As steelmaking developed in the area, and as tinplate and coal became the principal exports, pressure grew for more docks and two were built on the E. bank between 1879 (Prince of Wales) and 1909 (New King's). The copper smelting industry began to decline from c. 1880, and later, with the rest of South Wales, Swansea suffered from two wars, the depression, and the ousting of coal by oil. This last, however, was turned to good account when in 1918 the first oil refinery in Britain was opened near Swansea, the associated Queen's Dock for tankers following in 1920. During the Second World War (1941), the town centre was so badly damaged by bombing that rebuilding afterwards was to a new plan.

Among eminent natives are Bishop Gower (d. 1347), who founded and endowed the original Swansea Hospital; Philip Jones (1618-74), the Parliamentarian; Beau Nash (1674-1762); Count Albert de Bellerocle (1864-1944), the painter, and friend of Manet, Degas, and Lautrec; and Dylan Thomas (1914-53), the poet. Richard Savage, the poet, lived here in 1739-40, on a pension of £50 to which Pope contributed £20.

The focal point of the rebuilt city centre is the CIRCUS, from which five ways radiate; three of these are post-war creations, while Orchard Street, leading N., retains its old alignment. College Street (pedestrians only) links the Circus to what was Swansea's original main street, High Street leading N. to the *Railway Station* and Castlewind leading S. past the remains of the *Castle*. These are the ruins not of Henry de Newburgh's castle, but of a fortified manor erected on its site in 1330-32 by Bishop Gower. Features are a circular turret, and a tower with the open arcading characteristic of Gower's work. Below the castle is the site of the North Dock of 1852, now filled in, the river here flowing through the associated New Cut.

The **Glyn Vivian Art Gallery**†, in Alexandra Road a short way N. of the Circus, has a permanent collection and also temporary exhibitions. The sculpture, in the entrance hall, includes Angel Torso by *Jacob Epstein*, Silent Five by *Austin Wright*, Curved Form by *Barbara Hepworth*, and Janet by *W. Goscombe John*. Among the paintings are works by *Stanley Spencer* (Marriage at Cana. Garden at Whitehouse); *Augustus John* (Irish Coast. The Tutor); *Richard Wilson*, *J. D. Innes*, *Christopher Williams*, *John 'Warwick' Smith*, *Nicholas Pocock*, *Edward Lear*, *Lucien Pissaro* (Cefn Bryn), and *Muirhead Bone* (The Bridge, Sheringham). The gallery also has an outstanding display of Swansea and Nantgarw pottery and porcelain; a collection of 17 and 18C glass; and collections of English and Continental paperweights and miniatures.

Princess Street leads S. from the Circus, to its W. being the covered *Market*, the largest in Wales. *St Mary's Church*, rebuilt in 1897 by Blomfield, was gutted by bombing in 1941 and built again after the war. Beyond the S. end of Princess Street is the huge *Leisure Centre* (1977), catering for all manner of sports.

The **Royal Institution of South Wales Museum**† (Victoria Road, just

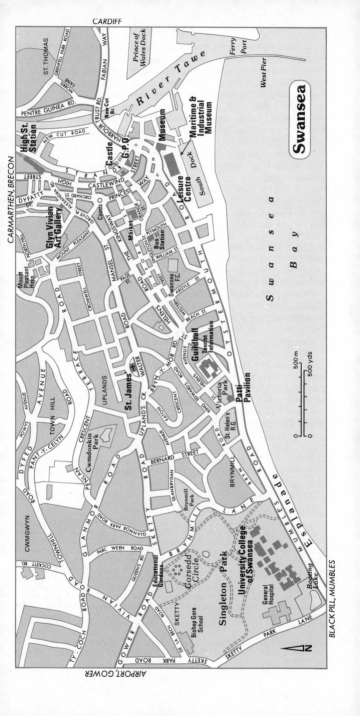

Swansea

CARDIFF

CARMARTHEN, BRECON

AIRPORT, GOWER

BLACK PILL, MUMBLES

River Tawe

Prince of Wales Dock

West Pier

Ferry Port

ST. THOMAS

GRENFELL PARK ROAD

MORRIS LANE

FABIAN WAY

NEW CUT ROAD

HARBOUR TRUST RD.

PENTRE GUINEA RD.

New Cut Br.

High St. Station

STRAND

Castle

G.P.O.

Museum

Maritime & Industrial Museum

South Dock

HIGH STREET

NEW CUT ROAD

ORCHARD ST.

PRINCESS WAY

CASTLEWIND

Leisure Centre

DYFATTY ST.

ALEXANDRA ROAD

GROVE PL.

Glyn Vivian Art Gallery

NORTH HILL

Mount Pleasant Hosp.

MOUNT PLEASANT

Clocks

PRINCESS

The Market

KINGS WAY

MANSEL ST.

CROMWELL STREET

PAGE ST.

ORANGE ST.

PLYMOUTH ST.

MONTPELIER

NELSON ST.

Bus Station

WILLIAM ST.

Swansea F.C.

ST. HELENS

PICTON TERRACE

TOWN HILL

POWYS AVENUE

DYFED AVENUE

PANT-Y-CELYN ROAD

GLANMOR ROAD

Cwmdonkin Park

CRESCENT

UPLANDS

St. James'

WALTER

BRYN-Y-MOR RD.

BRYNYMOR ROAD

EATON CRESCENT

AGNES

MANSEL

WESTERN ST.

BEACH ST.

ARGYLE ST.

Swansea Bay

Guildhall

Tourist Information

Victoria Park

Patti Pavilion

OYSTERMOUTH ROAD

UPLANDS CR.

ST. HELEN'S ROAD

EDWARDS

BRYNMILL

St. Helen's R.G.

BERNARD STREET

GLANBRYDAN

Brynmill Park

CWMGWYN

TOWNHILL ROAD

COCKETT RD.

TY COCH ROAD

VIVIAN ROAD

GOWER ROAD

GLANMOR PARK ROAD

PARC WERN ROAD

PENFILIA

SKETTY ROAD

QUEEN'S RD.

STA. VR. BECH RD.

Educational Gardens

Bishop Gore School

BRYNMILL LANE

Gorsedd Circle

Singleton Park

University College of Swansea

General Hospital

Boating Lake

ESPLANADE

SKETTY PARK ROAD

PARK LANE

SKETTY LANE

BRYN ROAD

500 m

500 yds

N

E. of the Leisure Centre) was founded in 1835. At the *Entrance* are a Roman milestone from the military road between Nidum (Neath) and Bovium (Boverton), and the Gnoll Stone, the shaft of a Celtic cross of c. 1100. On the *Ground Floor* are a model of Singleton Abbey (see below), Welsh porcelain, and a natural history section with an aquarium. The *First Floor* houses three sections. Egyptology. Archaeology, including (on the staircase) a Roman altar with traces of Ogham inscriptions; a well displayed and explained series of cases running from the Ice Age to medieval times; the Gwindy and Penard Roman coin hoards; and a case devoted to finds in the Paviland caves. The Welsh History section includes a reproduction of an early 19C Gower kitchen, souvenirs of the Mumbles Tramway, and relics of Petty Officer Evans, born in Gower, who died accompanying Scott to the Antarctic (1912).

The **Maritime and Industrial Museum**†, opened in 1977, includes a part of the otherwise now disused South Dock (opened in 1859) with ½ m. of railway track. The museum covers the history of the port of Swansea and of the industry of the city and its environs, together with material on transport and agriculture. Among the exhibits are a 200 ton tug; a lightship; and the Abbey Woollen Mill, brought here from Neath and maintained in full production.

Oystermouth Road runs W. close to the shore, in 1 m. reaching the **Guildhall** (Sir Percy Thomas, 1934), set back but recognized by its 160 ft tower. Inside is the *Tourist Information* office. *Brangwyn Hall*†, on the S., contains the British Empire Panels by Sir Frank Brangwyn, originally painted as a war memorial for the House of Lords. The corridors are hung with sketches by Brangwyn, watercolours of Welsh scenes etc. The **University College of Swansea,** in a fine park ¾ m. farther W., occupies Singleton Abbey, formerly the residence of Lord Swansea, and modern adjacent buildings. One of the five constituent colleges of the University of Wales, the college was founded in 1920 and has over 3000 students and some 400 teaching staff. The New Buildings house the faculties of Science, Engineering, Social Studies, and Arts; also a Music, Arts, and Drama complex. The *Exhibition Gallery*† (South Arts Library Hall) receives regular visiting art exhibitions. The *Wellcome Collection*†, presented to the university in 1971, comprises a large part of the antiquities collected by Sir Henry Wellcome (d. 1936), the manufacturing chemist. The collection, formerly housed in the Wellcome Medical Museum, London, contains over 2000 items, deriving mostly from Ancient Egypt.

The Port. For the growth of the port see History above. Entered from seaward by *King's Lock* (875 ft by 90 ft), with a helicopter pad on its N. side, or by road off A483, the docks comprise *Prince of Wales Dock* at the N., *King's Dock* in the centre, and *Queen's Dock* to the south. The total deep water area is 206 acres, and the length of quays 33,266 ft. In addition to steel and tinplate products and general cargo, the port is still active in the export of coal, with rail yards and special facilities on King's Dock. Milford Haven has taken over the import of crude oil, but in place of this Swansea's export of refined spirits has increased, Queen's Dock having five tanker jetties, all with pipelines to the B.P. refinery at Llandarcy 3 m. northeast. In addition to the enclosed docks there are facilities along the E. shore of the river mouth, the most important being the *Roll on/Roll off Terminal* (1969) for passengers and accompanied cars (service to Cork) and all types of wheeled freight traffic.

Parks. Swansea has 48 parks, totalling 700 acres. *Victoria Park,* by the shore W. of the Guildhall, includes Patti Pavilion (dancing, concerts, variety). *Singleton*

Park, farther W., in part of which is the University College of Swansea, contains a boating lake and, at its N. end, the *Educational Garden,* with conservatories and rare and subtropical plants. *Brynmill Park,* just N.E. of Singleton, has a bowling green, a lake, and a children's zoo. *Cwmdonkin Park,* ¾ m. N.E. of Brynmill, was a favourite of Dylan Thomas and contains a memorial to him. Between Swansea and Oystermouth are *Clyne Valley,* noted for its flowering shrubs, and, by the shore, *Blackpill Lido,* with children's amusements.

B   Gower

TOURIST INFORMATION. **Swansea Guildhall,** at the start of the circuit described below. **Fairwood Common** (Easter-Sept.), on A4118 1 m. N. of the airport; quickly reached in 2½ m. from the junction of A4118 and B4436 near Pennard. Before touring the peninsula, visitors are advised to get local information and leaflets on:—

Caves. Access is sometimes dangerous, and it is also important to know low tide times both for caves and for the promontories of Worms Head and Burry Holms.

Nature Reserves. Oxwich, Gower Coast, and Whitford Burrows.

Walks. Leaflets for Oxwich Sand Trail, Port Eynon Point Walk, Gower Farm Trails, and Gower Coast Nature Trail.

The **GOWER PENINSULA,** a mass of carboniferous limestone, 15 m. long by 4-8 m. broad, projecting W.S.W. from Swansea into the Bristol Channel, is best known for its S. coast bays, beaches, and rocky cliff scenery. In 1956 it was designated an Area of Outstanding Natural Beauty. The bays, often with limited and expensive parking, can be very crowded in summer. Along the centre are, from E. to W., Fairwood Common, with the airport, Cefn Bryn, and Rhossili Down, these last two being old red sandstone uplands (over 600 ft) offering magnificent vistas. On the W. are Rhossili Bay and Whitford Sands, both with estuary conditions and unsafe for swimming, while the N. shore is largely salt marsh. Much of the scenic land, whether cliff, common, or marsh, has been acquired by the National Trust, and there is nearly always footpath access. Walking is the best way to see many parts of Gower, perhaps the most popular stretches being those between Port Eynon Point and Rhossili, and from Rhossili N. along Rhossili Down to Llangenydd and Llanmadoc.

The inhabitants are the descendants of Flemish colonists planted here and in Pembroke by Henry I.

The *Caves* of Gower are famous, but archaeologically rather than scenically, for in many have been discovered the bones of animals either long extinct or no longer found in Britain or even in Europe. Such animals include lion, elephant, rhinoceros, hippopotamus, mammoth, bison, bear, wolf, and hyena. The fact that access to these caves is now often difficult is evidence of major change in sea level, or, in some cases, that the remains of larger animals would have been dragged into the caves by, for example, wolves or hyenas. In some caves, notably Paviland, Palaeolithic human remains have been found. Finds from the caves are in the National Museum of Wales (Cardiff) and in the Royal Institution Museum in Swansea. Visitors are warned that access is in some cases not only difficult but also dependent on tides.

Also of interest on Gower are burial chambers, hillforts, ruined castles, nature reserves, and churches (usually basically 13C), notable for their small chancels and battlemented towers, the latter recalling the time when churches rather than castles were the ordinary person's places of refuge.

The description that follows starts at Swansea's **Guildhall,** with

University College beyond (for both see above), and makes a meandering clockwise circuit of, including diversions, some 45-50 miles.

The electric tramway which ran along the bay to Mumbles until closed in 1960 was opened as a horse-tramway in 1807. For *Blackpill* and *Clyne Valley*, see above.—*3 m.* **Oystermouth** has been included in Swansea since 1920. The *Castle*† is strikingly placed on a green hill above the N. end of the town.

History. There appear to have been a series of Norman wooden structures here, the first perhaps put up by Henry de Newburgh in c. 1099. The first mention of a castle is 1215 when, the lordship having been given to the De Braose family by King John, a castle was burnt by the Welsh. Rebuilt, it was again destroyed by the Welsh in 1256-57 when Llewelyn the Last was in Gower. The keep, the nucleus of today's ruin, probably dates from c. 1280 as it is known that Edward I visited here in 1284; the gatehouse and the ward walls are of a few years later. Afterwards the lands passed to the Mowbrays, who during the 14C converted the castle to residential use (the wings to the E. and W. of the keep dating from this period), and eventually to the Beauforts who presented the castle to Swansea in 1927.

The Gatehouse, originally flanked by two towers, of which traces remain, gives access to a single ward. Immediately on the left is the guardroom, beside which steps lead up to one of the governor's apartments, popularly though for no good reason known as the White Lady's Chamber. The ruins of the barracks are on the right of the ward, and those of kitchens on the left. At the top of the ward is the Keep, the oldest part of the castle, to its left being a three-storey building with a cellar, state rooms, and, on the middle floor, the banqueting hall. To the right is another three-storey building, comprising a basement kitchen (note the roasting-jack holes by the fire), what may have been either a priest's or retainers' room, and, at the top, the chapel, with Dec. windows (restored 1845), an aumbrey, and a piscina. Oystermouth *Church,* reputedly built on the site of a Roman villa, has a battlemented 13C tower and an E.E. east window. In the churchyard is the tomb of Dr Thomas Bowdler (1754-1825), who by expurgating Shakespeare added his own name to the English language.

Mumbles, from the French 'mamelles' meaning 'breasts', strictly refers only to the two islets (accessible at low water) off the small promontory beyond Oystermouth. Today the name is generally applied to the whole promontory, a popular resort area with a pier from which in summer there are steamer trips to Ilfracombe. On the outer islet are a lighthouse (1793) and a fort (1861). To the W. of Mumbles are popular *Langland* and *Caswell* bays.

From (*3 m.*) *Bishopston* the National Trust's narrow and wooded Bishopston Valley (footpath) winds for nearly 2 m. down to *Pwlldu Bay. Pennard Church* (15C), just W., incorporates parts of an earlier church buried by the dunes 1 m. W. near Pennard Castle (see below). Possibly from this earlier church are two lancets in the chancel, a window with moulding (nave, S. wall), the font, and the beam supporting the gallery.

Pennard Cliffs are a fine stretch of National Trust land extending nearly 2 m. from Pwlldu Head to Southgate. Below the cliffs are two caves, *Bacon Hole* and *Minchin Hole,* in both of which ancient animal bones have been found (c. 1850). There is evidence that the latter was used as a hiding place during Roman and Dark Age times. The scanty remains of *Pennard Castle* (13 or 14C) lie N.W. of Southgate. The main feature is the gate towers.

Just N. of Pennard B4436 joins A4118, **Fairwood Common Tourist**

Information being 2½ m. N. beyond the airfield. This Route bears W. to **Parkmill**, *3 m.* from Bishopston. At the W. end of the village a lane leads N. round the front of a wood, in ½ m. reaching a clearing at which meet a number of other lanes. In a meadow, c. 200 yards N., is *Parc Le Breos Burial Chamber*, also known as *Giant's Grave*, a long unroofed passage with four chambers (restored). When excavated in 1869, the remains of four or more people were dicovered. In *Cathole*, a cave about 300 yards N. of the burial chamber, flint tools excavated in 1968 suggest that this cave was used in about 12,000 B.C.—*1 m*. *Penmaen*, to the S. of which are *Penmaen Burrows* with a Norman earthwork, a burial chamber, and the slight remains of an ancient church. *2 m. Penrice Park*. Application should be made at the lodge to visit *Penrice Castle*, a ruin of the middle and late 13C consisting of an irregular single ward with a gatehouse to the N. and a round keep on the W., the oldest part of the castle (c. 1250). Adjoining the E. curtain there is an early 16C dovecot. The castle was built by the Mansel family (Norman origin from Le Mans) and stands above a late 18C mansion with a 19C E. wing.

From Penrice Park entrance a road leads S. to (*1 m.*) **Oxwich** by the shore. The *Burrows Nature Reserve* (N.C.), an area of salt marsh and dunes through which a freshwater stream flows, is of both botanical and ornithological interest. Parking is only allowed in the official car park, where there is an Information Centre. There is no restriction on access to the beach or to the dunes near the car park, but for elsewhere a permit is necessary. The Sand Trail explains the effects of sand and its movements. The *Church*, a little S. above the shore, dates from the 13C and has a tiny chancel which may be a Celtic cell (tradition holds that the ancient font was brought here by St Illtyd). The so-called *Castle* remains are those of a Mansel manor house built c. 1541.

From Oxwich A4118 can be rejoined by following the minor road along the W. side of Penrice Park through (*1 m.*) the village of *Penrice*, with an early Norman motte and, on the green, the base of a medieval cross. At A4118 a left turn, followed by a right turn, leads in under *2 m.* to **Reynoldston**. Here a road running E. climbs in ½ m. on to **Cefn Bryn**, a ridge (610 ft) of open common offering a fine vista. Parking is easy. To the N., visible from the road, is *Arthur's Stone*, a large burial chamber capstone formed of an erratic block of millstone grit, 14 ft by 7 ft and weighing 25 tons.

1 m. (from Reynoldston) **Knelston** where there is a ruined 12C church. *Llanddewi*, just W., has a church in which the nave and chancel are curiously out of line, presumably due to different building periods. The village is also the start of three Farm Trails (2 m.-6 m.; leaflet from warden at Llanddewi Farm).

From Knelston this Route now describes S. to Port Eynon Point and W. to Rhossili and Worms Head. To continue the motor circuit of the peninsula it is necessary to return from Rhossili to Llanddewi-Knelston. The diversion to Port Eynon, Rhossili, and back to Llanddewi-Knelston amounts to c. 12 m.

1 m. Scurlage is at the junction with B4247.—*2 m.* **Port Eynon Point** is beyond the village of the same name at the finish of A4118. This limestone headland, with magnificent coastal views, is a National Trust property (footpaths). There are two caves near here, one at the point's S. tip being an animal bone cave, and *Culver Hole*, on the W. of the point, being largely man-made in the 15C as a dovecot. Some of the best cliff walking in Gower, much of it across National Trust land, is between Port Eynon Point and Worms Head.

Returning to (*2 m.*) *Scurlage*, B4247 is taken west.—*1 m. Pilton Green* from where there is a footpath to *Paviland Caves* (access difficult, and only possible at low water), famous for having been occupied by man at the end of the Ice Age. In one of the caves (Goat's Hole) Dr Buckland, excavating in 1823, found part of the skeleton of a young man, since radio-carbon dated to the 17th millenium B.C. (The bones, stained with ochre, were at first incorrectly identified, their owner becoming known as the Red Lady of Paviland). This man would have been one of the hunters who moved along this coast as the ice receded. Flints and ornaments discovered here are evidence that man continued to use these caves over millenia. Cliffs near Paviland, and commons at Pilton Green and (*1 m.*) *Pitton Cross*, are National Trust property.

Thurba Head, ½ m. S. of Pitton, is a 200 ft headland (with a hillfort) marking the S. end of *Mewslade Bay*, perhaps the most scenic and rocky inlet along this coast. *Red Chamber*, a cave ¼ m. E. of Thurba Head, is so called from the ochre colouring of its walls.

1 m. **Rhossili**, a village at the W. end of B4247, lies above the S. end of the 5 m. long sandy crescent of remote and windswept *Rhossili Bay* which marks the W. extremity of Gower. The church, with a 12C doorway, contains a memorial to Petty Officer Evans, born here, who died with Scott in the Antarctic in 1912.

Gower Coast Nature Reserve (N.T. and N.C.) lies below Rhossili village and includes Worms Head. The *Limestone Trail* (c. 3 m.) starts from the National Trust collecting box W. of Rhossili car park and makes an anticlockwise circuit passing seven points of interest. These include (1) the wreck of the 'Helvetia' (1887); (2) Old Castle, earthwork traces of an Iron Age defended village; (3) Rhossili Vile, an open field system of narrow strips dating from Saxon times; (4) Kitchen Corner, where limestone was quarried in the 18 and 19C and loaded into boats at the foot of the cliff; (5) Coastguard Lookout; (6) Tears Point, with bared limestone which is the top of deposits several thousand feet thick; (7) Fall's Bay, with a raised beach of conglomerate shells.—*Worms Head*, deriving its name from the Norse for serpent, consists of two rocky islets connected with the mainland by a natural causeway for c. 2½ hours each side of low tide and with each other by a narrrow neck of rock always above water. The outer head rises abruptly to a height of 200 ft and in rough weather the breaking seas are a magnificent sight; ancient animal bones have been found in the cave at the foot, which must in those distant times have been a lot more accessible. The water thrown up by the nearby blowhole can be seen from Rhossili.
Rhossili Down (N.T.) popular for hang-gliding, stretches for nearly 2 m. N. from the village. The *Beacon* (633 ft), near the S. end, is the highest point in Gower. Farther N., on the E. slope, there are two burial chambers known as *Sweyne's Houses*. The name 'houses' derives from the Saxon for 'mound', and one tradition is that this is the burial place of Sweyne Forkbeard, said to have given his name to Swansea.

Walkers can descend from Rhossili Down to Llangennydd. Motorists must return a little over *4 m.* to Llanddewi, from where a narrow road in *2 m.* reaches *Burrygreen*.—*2 m.* **Llangenydd**, where the church, the largest in Gower, is an early 12C rebuilding of the church of a small priory founded in the 6C by St Cenydd and destroyed by Norse raiders in 986. The tower, curiously placed N. of the nave, has a saddle-back roof and is an outstanding example of the Gower fortified type. An ancient graveslab inside the church may be that of St Cenydd.

Burry Holms, 1½ m. N.W., an islet marking the N. end of Rhossili Bay, is accessible for c. 2½ hours each side of low water. On the islet are traces of Iron Age earthworks, the ruins of a medieval monastic settlement, and a lighthouse. At low water the remains can be seen of the 'City of Bristol' which ran ashore in Rhossili Bay in 1840. In this area, too, have been found doubloons and other coins from a Spanish galleon wrecked in the 17C. *Culver Hole Cave (Burry)*, ¼ m. N.E. and accessible only for a short time at low water, produced the bones of thirty or more human beings, fragments of Bronze Age urns, and also Iron Age artifacts. *Spritsail Tor Cave*, near Prissen's Tor 1½ m. N.E., produced human and animal bones and Roman pottery fragments.

2 m. **Cheriton,** where the 13C church is one of the most beautiful in Gower. Notable features are the S. doorway, the good E.E. arches, and the tower with its saddle-back roof. The church at *Llanmadoc*, ½ m. W. of Cheriton, is said to have been founded by St Madog, a follower of St Cenydd; rebuilding of 1865 left little of the earlier 13C church.

The *Bulwark* (N.T.) is a large hillfort S. of the Cheriton to Llanmadoc road. **Whitford Burrows** (N.T.), the peninsula reaching N. into Burry Inlet, is a Nature Reserve (N.C.) of dunes and saltmarsh. Cars must be parked at Llanmadoc, and visitors are asked to keep to the paths, one of which (4 m. return) leads to Whitford Point. The warden's house is at the start of the path. Visitors are warned that swimming is dangerous (currents and undertow) and that unexploded shells may be found away from the paths.

1 m. (from Cheriton) *Landimore* has fragments of a castle.—*1 m.* **Weobley Castle**† is the ruin of a large 13-14C fortified manor. Owned by the De la Bere family until the 15C and damaged during Owen Glendower's uprising, the property later passed to the Herberts and the Mansels. Beyond the gatehouse (14C) there is a single ward with the keep (mid 13C), the oldest part, to the right. The remaining ruins, mostly later 13C, include the chapel, completing the S. side, and the kitchens and hall on respectively the E. and north. There is a standing stone in a field S. of the road behind Windmill Farm, roughly opposite the castle approach.—At (*1 m.*) *Llanrhidian* a stone on the green, possibly the remains of the village cross, seems later to have been used as a pillory. In the church porch there is a carved stone bearing human and animal figures and thought to date from the 9C. Note also, on the exterior S. wall, the intriguing rhymed epitaph of Robert Hary (d. 1646).

Below the village the road skirts *Llanrhidian Marsh* (N.T.).—*4 m.* *Penclawdd* is known for its cockles industry, and also for 'laverbread', minced and boiled seaweed tasting not unlike strong spinach. The seaweed is brought from Pembroke as the local variety is too sandy. From here there is a choice of roads to (c. *7 m.*) Swansea's **Guildhall.**

43   CARMARTHEN

CARMARTHEN (12,900 inhab.), the county town of Dyfed, is on the W. bank of the Towy some 8 m. above the river's mouth. Coracles, of the local oval type, may sometimes be seen on the river (see also p. 350).

Town Centre. Guildhall.
Tourist Information. Darkgate, just N.W. of Guildhall.
Parking. Off John Street, N. of Guildhall. Behind library, N.W. of St Peter's Church.
Post Office. King Street.
Market Day. Wednesday and Saturday. **Early Closing.** Thursday.
History. Carmarthen is the site of the Roman Caer Maridunum; the ruined walls were still standing in the time of Giraldus and something of the amphitheatre survives today. Later, in popular mythology, Merlin was born here, son of a king's

daughter and of a spirit (see p. 29). In c. 1096 the Normans established a castle and walled borough here, the former being restored by Edward I c. 1313, in which year the town was granted its first charter, soon becoming an important port and centre of the wool trade, exporting to Flanders and elsewhere and in 1353 being declared the staple (monopoly) wool centre of Wales. Prosperity was interrupted in the early 15C, when the town was taken by Owen Glendower in 1403 and 1405, but by 1450 the first festival officially using the name 'eisteddfod' could be held here; metrical rules codified for this occasion are still applied to the Chair Poem of the National Eisteddfod. In 1555 Robert Ferrar, Bishop of St David's, was burnt at the stake in what is now Nott Square as soon as the heresy laws were reintroduced by Mary I. During the Civil War the castle was held for the King, but soon capitulated (1646) to General Laugharne and was later slighted. Carmarthen continued to prosper as both port and administrative and trading centre; iron smelting and tinplate works were established in the 18C and trade was boosted by the arrival of the railway in 1856. Change and some decline followed the port developments farther E. along the coast (the tinplate works closed in 1900), Carmarthen gradually becoming of administrative rather than industrial importance.

Sir William Nott (1782-1845), victor of the First Afghan War; Brindley Richards (1819-65), composer of 'God Bless the Prince of Wales'; Sir Lewis Morris (1833-1907), the poet, and E. W. Tristam (1882-1952), best known for his work in preserving medieval wallpaintings, were natives of the town. Sir Richard Steele, the Irish man of letters, died of a stroke in King Street in 1729.

The *Guildhall,* rebuilt in 1767, is successor to one of 1583. The large covered *Market* is N.W. beyond Red Street. In Nott Square, a short way E. of the Guildhall, a monument commemorates the martyrdom here of Bishop Ferrar. To the S.E., on a bluff above the river, the County Offices occupy the site of the *Castle,* the only surviving features of which are the motte, a length of curtain wall, and the 14C gatehouse. *St Peter's Church* (12-14C), with a tower of the fortified type, stands at the N. end of King Street. In the S. chapel are an altar-tomb with effigies of Sir Rhys ap Thomas (d. 1525), who fought for Henry Tudor at Bosworth, and of his wife, and memorials to Bishop Ferrar, Sir Richard Steele, and General Nott. A Roman altar stands in the W. porch.

Priory Street, leading N.E. from St Peter's Church, recalls the Augustinian priory which stood between here and the river. Founded c. 1130 and burnt in 1435, the priory is important as the place where the 'Black Book of Carmarthen', the oldest manuscript extant in Welsh (now in the National Library of Wales), was written in the late 12C. At the junction of Priory Street and Oak Lane stands the *Old Oak,* now a withered stump, for centuries associated with Merlin's prophecy that should the oak fall so also would the town. The remains of the *Roman Amphitheatre* are beside the main road about ¼ m. farther east.

In the W. of the town, to the E. of Morfa Lane, the *Bulwarks* are a survival of Royalist earthwork defences of the Civil War.

The **Carmarthen County Museum**† occupies a former palace of the bishop of St David's at *Abergwili,* on A40 2 m. E. of Carmarthen. The finest exhibit is a Roman gold chain and pendant found at Dolaucothi. It was at Abergwili that Bishop Davies and William Salesbury worked together to produce their Welsh Book of Common Prayer and New Testament (1567).

A house called Tygwyn (now a farm) at *Llangunnor,* on the E. bank of the Towy opposite Carmarthen, was the property of Mary Scurlock, Sir Richard Steele's second wife and the 'Dearest Prue' of his letters. Steele lived here from 1724 until his death in 1729, and is commemorated by a monument in the church.

Llanstephan, 7 m. S. of Carmarthen on the W. bank of the Towy near its mouth, has a ruined *Castle* overlooking the estuary. Built during the late 13C the castle, successor to early defensive earthworks on the same site, comprises an outer and an inner ward, with, on the curtain of the former, a large gatehouse (1280), which seems to have been converted to a keep and main living quarters shortly after completion. In the *Church* the chalice, in use since 1756, is a rare example of

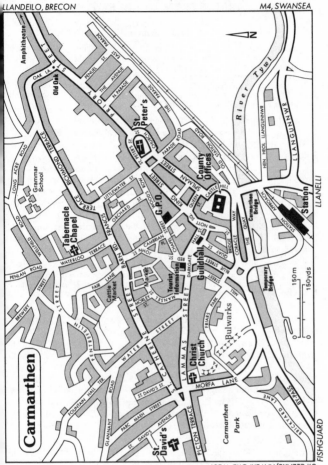

hallmarked (1569) 'coconut' cup. *St Anthony's Well,* ¼ m. S.W. of the castle, a wishing well said to have medicinal properties, has a niche in which the figure of a saint probably once stood.

For Carmarthen to *Aberystwyth* viâ *Aberaeron,* see Rte 44A and viâ *Lampeter* and *Strata Florida,* see Rte 44B; to *Cardigan, Fishguard,* and *St David's,* see Rte 45; to *Haverfordwest* and *St David's* or *Fishguard,* see Rte 46; to *Tenby, Pembroke,* and *Milford Haven,* see Rte 47.

44 CARMARTHEN TO ABERYSTWYTH

A Viâ Aberaeron

A484 and A486 to Synod Inn: A487 to Aberystwyth. 48 miles.—*7 m. Cynwyl Elfed.*—*6 m.* Road fork (Rte 45) for *Museum of the Woollen Industry.*—*3 m.* **Llandyssul.**—*5 m. Ffostrasol* (for *West Wales Farm Park*).—*5 m. Synod Inn.*— *6 m.* **Aberaeron.**—*13 m.* **Llanfarian.**—*3 m.* **Aberystwyth.**
The first part is scenically pleasant, ascending narrow, winding, and wooded valleys and passing several wool mills. Later the Route crosses duller country. For the first 13 miles Rte 45 coincides with this one.

Carmarthen, see Rte 43.—A484 ascends the twisting wooded valley of the Gwili to a short way before (*7 m.*) *Cynwyl Elfed,* where B4333 bears N.W. providing an upland shortcut to Newcastle Emlyn while this Route continues N., now ascending the Duad.—*2 m. Cwmduad,* where the valley divides into three, A484 taking the central one.—*4 m.* Road fork, Rte 45 bearing left and this Route right. For the *Museum of the Woollen Industry* at Dre-Fach, Felindre (2 m. N.W.), see p. 350.—The Teifi is crossed before (*3 m.*) **Llandyssul,** a wool centre with several mills. The church has a Norman tower into which a 6C inscribed stone has been built. Christmas Evans (1766-1838), the Baptist preacher, was born here.—*5 m. Ffostrasol.* For *West Wales Farm Park* (3 m. N.W.) see p. 379.—*5 m. Synod Inn* on A487.

The small seaside resort of New Quay (1000 inhab., but many more in summer) is 4 m. N. by A486. The town is built on a steep, rocky slope above a curving sandy bay, popular with caravanners and campers. From *New Quay Head* (300 ft) there is a view across Cardigan Bay to the Lleyn, Snowdonia, Cader Idris, and Plynlimon.

6 m. **Aberaeron** (1300 inhab.), developed during the 19C, contains several Georgian-style houses, notably in Alban Square to the E. of the main road. There are a pleasant small harbour and a shingle beach. The *Aquarium,* at the harbour, specializes in the marine life of Cardigan Bay. For Aberaeron to *Brecon,* see Rte 34.—*1 m.* In the porch of the church at *Llanddewi Aberarth* there are two incised stones, one a 9C cross and the other a hog-backed stone.—*6 m. Llanrhystyd.* The church at *Llangwyryfon* (3½ m. E.) is the only one in Europe, except for that at Cologne, dedicated to St Ursula and the 11,000 Virgins.—*6 m.* **Llanfarian,** where Rte 44B comes in from the S.E. and the Ystwyth is crossed.

A minor road along the W. side of the river leads to *Bryn-Eithyn Hall Folk Museum†,* in a house which was once the home of Sir Ifan Edwards, founder of the Welsh League of Youth (see also p. 188). The exhibits include early Welsh oak furniture, model sailing ships, and arms and armour. A motte-and-bailey, ½ m. N., is probably the site of Gilbert FitzRichard of Clare's first Aberystwyth castle, built in 1110 near what was then the mouth of the Ystwyth.

About 1½ m. beyond the river a crossroads is reached. Rte 28B leads E. along A4120. This Route turns N.W. passing on the left *Pen Dinas* (415 ft), with a hillfort and a monument to the Duke of Wellington.— *3 m.* (from Llanfarian) **Aberystwyth,** see Rte 27.

B   Viâ Lampeter and Strata Florida Abbey

A485 to Lampeter: B4343 to Pontrhydfendigaid: B4340 and B4575 to Lanfarian: A487 to Aberystwyth. 52 miles.—*5 m. Pont-ar-Sais.—11 m. Llanybydder.—5 m.* **Lampeter.—***4 m. Llanfair .Clydogau.—4 m.* **Llanddewi Brefi.—***3 m.* **Tregaron.—***6 m. Pontrhydfendigaid* (for **Strata Florida Abbey**).—*1 m. Llanfarian.—3 m.* **Aberystwyth.**

Carmarthen, see Rte 43.—A485 heads N., on the outskirts of Carmarthen leaving *Abergwili,* with the Carmarthen County Museum (see p. 344) 1 m. to the E. on A40.—*5 m. Pont-ar-Sais,* 1½ m. W. of which is *Llanpumpsaint,* the 'Church of the Five Saints' (SS Ceitho, Celynen, Gwyn, Gwyno, and Grynnaro). The medieval altar-slab in the church bears nine consecration crosses. The road now runs across hilly wooded country, leaving on the W. several roads to Llandyssul on Rte 44A, and on the E. hill roads across to the Cothi valley.—*11 m. Llanybydder,* a weaving centre on the E. bank of the Teifi, with a number of mills open to visitors, is also known for its horse fairs (last Thurs. of the month).—At (*1 m.*) *Pencarreg* the church contains a curious ancient font bearing human heads.

4 m. **Lampeter** (2300 inhab.), also called *Llanbedr Pont Steffan,* lying below wooded hills on the W. side of the Teifi, is the chief centre and market town of the upper valley of the Teifi. *St David's College,* the oldest Welsh degree-granting institution, was founded in 1822 by Bishop Burgess of St David's for Church of England students, becoming a constituent college of the University of Wales in 1971. The original buildings, by C. B. Cockerell (1827), are grouped around a quadrangle and lie within pleasant grounds containing a motte and modern extension buildings. The sculpture group, by P. W. Nicholas, was winner of a Welsh Arts Council competition. The library of some 80,000 volumes contains a good collection of theological and historical works, as well as several early manuscripts and printed books, including a Lübeck missal that is unique in Britain. For Lampeter to (W.) *Aberaeron* and (E.) *Brecon,* see Rte 34.

A485 follows the W. side of the Teifi, but this Route takes the more interesting B4343 along the E. side.—*4 m. Llanfair Clydogau,* the site of Roman silver mines, was on the Roman Sarn Helen. South from here (now modern minor roads) this reached the Ogofau goldmines; northwards the road crossed the river and in c. 4 m. reached a fort (*Bremia,* ¼ m. S.E. of the junction of A485 and B4578, the continuation N. of Sarn Helen).—*4 m.* **Llanddewi Brefi,** where St David attended a synod in 519, possibly for the purpose of confuting the Pelagian heresy, but more probably for the enactment of local rules of discipline. The present *Church of St David* (Dewi) stands on a mound which, tradition holds, rose under the saint as he preached here. The church, from which the transepts have now disappeared, was probably rebuilt c. 1287 in connection with a college established here by Bishop Beck of St David's for a precentor and 12 prebendaries. Of the three Celtic crosses in the churchyard, the middle one is called St David's Staff. Built into the N.W. exterior angle of the church are two small fragments of the gravestone of Bishop Idnert, the last bishop of Llanbadarn Fawr, who was murdered in c. 720.

3 m. **Tregaron** (4000 inhab.), a little market town and centre for the surrounding hill sheep farms, owes its name to Caron, a chieftain and self-declared bishop of the 2-3C. Twm Shon Catti (p. 240) was born here (1530), as was also Henry Richard (1812-88), advocate of international arbitration and founder of the Peace Union, to whom there is a memorial. *Yr Oriel†* displays outstanding Welsh craftwork. At *Llangeitho,* 4 m. W., a centre of Methodism, there is a statue to the Rev. Daniel Rowlands (1713-90), the revivalist, who was born there. For the drover hillroad across to (18 m.) *Llanwrtyd Wells,* see p. 239.

Cors Tregaron Nature Reserve† lies immediately W. of B4343 for a distance of 4 m. N. from Tregaron. The reserve, an area of some three square miles either side of the meandering Teifi, includes three raised peat bogs, the largest being on the W. side and the other two on the east. The bogs are 'raised', in that they appear as domes with the centre up to 20 ft higher than the edge. This feature has developed over millenia through several stages: briefly, the dropping of glacial moraine forming a dam; the growth of a lake; the silting of the lake, the arrival of vegetation, and the formation of a fen; the vegetation rots, becoming waterlogged, sinking, and under pressure turning to peat; and the shaping of a dome because the peat has formed more easily above the waterlogged centre than above the edges from where the rainfall can seep away. The natural state of the bogs has been damaged by peat cutting (which however ended in 1960), the W. bog being the least affected but the other two having only the centres of their domes undisturbed. These two E. bogs touch the road at *Ty Coed* (Warden's house) just over 1 m. N. of Tregaron, and again 1 m. farther, just before the point where the disused railway track bears away. The reserve is of particular interest to botanists and ornithologists, and is the subject of a special feature at the National Museum of Wales.

6 m. (from Tregaron) *Pontrhydfendigaid* means 'Bridge near the ford of the Blessed Virgin'.

*Strata Florida Abbey† (1 m. S.E.) was once one of the most celebrated abbeys in Wales.

History. The name is a Latinized form of 'Ystrad Fflur' meaning 'Plain of Flowers'. Although this abbey, a Cistercian house, is known to have been founded in 1164, tradition suggests that there may have been a predecessor, perhaps Cluniac, near Old Abbey Farm, 1½ m. S. of Pontrhydfendigaid, where in the 19C the foundations were excavated and removed. The founder of 1164 was probably Robert FitzStephan, a vassal of the Clares. Two years later his lands were overrun by Rhys ap Gruffydd. Grandson of the founder of the earlier house, and perhaps finding Cistercian ideals of simplicity and poverty akin to local monastic tradition, Rhys refounded the abbey in 1184 and began the existing church, although he died before its dedication in 1201. The greater part of the ruins date from this time, or a few years later (the E. extension of the presbytery). The chapter house and the monks' choir are of the 14C, while the cloister is 15 or early 16C. The abbey, wholly Welsh in character, was the political, religious, and educational centre of the country in the 12 and 13C, in 1238 witnessing an assembly of Welsh princes summoned by Llewelyn the Great to swear allegiance to his son Dafydd. Economically the abbey flourished largely from wool, provided by the sheep which grazed on its lands which extended as far as Rhayader. During the Owen Glendower troubles the abbey was abandoned as such, being used as military stables. The building of the stone cloister dates from some time after the return of the monks. After the Dissolution the estates passed through various hands, the Crown assuming responsibility for the ruins in 1931.

Apart from remains of the cloister and the chapter house, the ruins seen today are those of the church. At the entrance there is a small *Exhibition* telling something of the story of the Cistercians and of the abbey. Here too are fragments of sculptured work of a delicacy and richness strangely at variance with the orthodox Cistercian severity of this period.

The CHURCH, in Trans. Norman style, is on the usual Cistercian plan, having an aisled nave of seven bays, transepts (each with three chapels), and an aisleless presbytery. At the W. end of the *Nave* the doorway (not quite in its original medieval form) is richly ornamented, with a framing cluster of rolls, continuous from the ground, tied together at intervals by bands ending in crosier-like ornaments. Inside, the arcades were of unique local character, the clustered piers being raised on plain screen walls c. 5 ft high, an arrangement not known elsewhere in England or Wales, though occasionally found in Ireland. The *Crossing* was filled by a monks' choir, with screen walls largely blocking all directions except east. On the E. of the choir narrow openings gave access to the *Transepts,* each with three E. side chapels, originally vaulted. Remains of altars can be seen, and many of the medieval tiles have been relaid (not in situ). The designs on the tiles merit study. In the N. transept there is a memorial (1951) to Dafydd ap Gwilym (c. 1320-80), described by Borrow as 'the greatest of his country's songsters'. Born near Aberystwyth, he may be buried either here at Strata Florida or at Talley. The *Presbytery* belongs to two periods, the two W. bays being the earlier part and the E. bay an addition of c. 1250. Later came two more alterations. In the 14C the floor was raised, two steps being placed under the E. arch of the crossing; and in the 15C the altar was raised and moved W., leaving space behind for two chapels. Some of the tiles laid during the 15C alteration have been reset. Beyond the S. end of the S. transept is the *Sacristy,* with doors from both the cloister and the transept.

The CHAPTER HOUSE, immediately S. of the sacristy, is in two parts and of two periods (13 and 14C), the oldest masonry being the S.E. and E. wall remains. It seems that the older E. part of the building was abandoned, becoming part of the cemetery (note the two graves through the walls). Rhys ap Gruffydd belonged to the princely house of Dynevor, many members of which were buried here. It is thought that the line of tombs outside the angle of the S. transept and presbytery represents earlier burials (two of the headstones bear pre-Norman ornamentation). Later burials were in the chapter house, where one slab has been exposed. The CLOISTER, with two doors to the S. aisle, had five bays on its N. side, each with a window, some of the sills of which survive. The alcove at the centre of the N. side was for a lectern. After the Dissolution the W. walk was divided into rooms which, with the now ruined W. building, formed part of a house.

Teifi Pools, a cluster of small lakes in wild country 2½ m. N.E. of the abbey and accessible by a lane and paths, are the source of the Teifi.
B4343, leading N. from Pontrhydfendigaid, in 8 m. reaches *Devil's Bridge.*

B4340 is now followed N.W. through *Ystrad Meurig,* where there are traces of a castle of the Clares. Beyond, reaching Ystwyth Forest, the Ystwyth is crossed; there is a F.C. picnic site ¼ m. E. of the bridge beside the road on the S. bank.—*6 m.* (from Pontrhydfendigaid) *Black Covert, Trawscoed,* near the junction of B4340 and B4575, is another F.C. picnic site and the start of a forest walk which includes a hillfort and a butterfly reserve.—*5 m.* (by B4574) *Llanfarian,* where Rte 44A is joined. For Llanfarian (with *Bryn-Eithyn Hall Folk Museum*) to (*3 m.*) **Aberystwyth,** see Rte 44A.

45   CARMARTHEN TO CARDIGAN AND ST DAVID'S

A484 to Cardigan: A487 and B4582 to Nevern: A487 to St David's. 61 miles.—
16 m. Henllan.—3 m. **Newcastle Emlyn.—***3 m. Cenarth.—4 m. Llechryd.—3 m.*
Cardigan.—*7 m.* **Nevern.—***2 m.* **Newport.—***3 m. Dinas.—4 m.* **Fishguard.—***7 m.*
Mathry.—9 m. **St David's.**
Diversions should be made down side roads in order to see the coastal scenery.

Carmarthen, see Rte 43.—For Carmarthen to (*13 m.*) road junction
A484/A486, see Rte 44A.—*3 m. Henllan,* a village on the Teifi, has a
picturesque bridge, and some earthworks thought to be pre-Norman.
The **Museum of the Woollen Industry**†, at Dre-Fach, Felindre 1 m. S., is
a branch of the National Museum of Wales and administered by the
Welsh Folk Museum. Opened in 1976, and occupying part of a working
mill, the museum tells the story of the industry from medieval times to
the present day. The collection of textile machinery dates from the
18C.—The road now descends the Teifi, as known today for its salmon
as it was in the 12C when Giraldus praised it for abounding with finer
salmon than any other river in Wales. Giraldus also reported beavers
here.—*3 m.* **Newcastle Emlyn** (700 inhab.) is a small centre serving the
surrounding farming community. Of the original Norman castle,
thought to have been on the N. bank, there is no trace. The 'new' castle
was a 16C rebuilding of an earlier one by Sir Rhys ap Thomas. Although
designed as a fortified manor, it was held for the King during the Civil
War and afterwards slighted. Little remains above ground other than
the gateway to the inner ward. It was in *Adpar,* across the river, that the
first printing press in Wales was set up in 1719.—*3 m. Cenarth.*

Coracles. It is along the stretch of the Teifi between Cenarth and Cilgerran
(c.7 m. downstream) that the art of using the coracle is most preserved, not only out
of sentiment but also practically for netting salmon and sea trout. The boats are
made of intertwined laths of willow and hazel to a design which has been little
changed since the Iron Age. Unlike the oval Towy coracle, used in calm water, that
of the Teifi narrows at the waist, lies deeper in the water, and can cope with the
local eddies. Coracle races are held, and there is an annual regatta (July) in which
junior events are a feature.

4 m. Llechryd. At *Manordeifi,* across the river from here, the old
church is known as the 'Coracle Church'. For *Cilgerran Castle,* 1½ m.
W., see p. 378.

3 m. **Cardigan** (3900 inhab.) is a pleasant small market town on the
Teifi, some 3 m. above the river's mouth (hence the Welsh name
Aberteifi).

History. A port and the site of a primitive fortification in pre-Norman times, the
first castle here was built in the late 11 or early 12C by Gruffydd ap Rhys. Later
(c. 1170) this became a residence of Rhys ap Gruffydd, who strengthened the
fortifications and in 1176 organized here the first recorded eisteddfod (although
this word is not used in contemporary chronicles). Town and castle passd to the
Earl of Pembroke, who in 1240 rebuilt the latter. Town privileges were granted by
Edward I and confirmed by a charter of 1542. In 1645 the castle fell to Parliament,
Jeremy Taylor being among the captured garrison. The town's prosperity declined
during the 19C with the silting up of the estuary.

The *Castle* remains (no adm.), no more than portions of the keep and
two ruined towers, embedded in later work, are those of the Earl of
Pembroke's rebuilding. The *Church,* to the E., has been rebuilt with the
exception of the chancel, in the E. window of which there is some ancient
glass. The *Priory* (near the church), on the site of a Benedictine house,

was the home of Mrs Katharine Philips (1631-64), the 'matchless Orinda' who inspired Jeremy Taylor's 'Discourse of Friendship' (1657). The old bridge (rebuilt 1726) is one of the town's attractive features.

Gwbert-on-Sea, 3 m. N. of Cardigan on the E. side of the estuary, is a small resort with a golf course and cliff scenery. Beyond, just offshore at the estuary mouth, is the cliffbound *Cardigan Island,* home of seals, birds, and half-wild Soay sheep (no landing; round-the-island boats from Gwbert or St Dogmaels). *Mwnt,* 1½ m. E. of Cardigan Island, is a coastal National Trust property of nearly 100 acres.

For Cardigan to (N.) *Aberaeron* and (S.) *Tenby,* see Rte 49.

St Dogmaels, on the S. bank of the Teifi 1 m. below Cardigan, has the remains of an *Abbey,* founded in 1115 by Robert Martyn, Lord of Cemaes, for monks of the reformed Benedictine Order brought over from Tiron in France; it was successor to an early Welsh house, sacked by the Vikings. The small ruins comprise part of the church (14-15C) and fragments of the refectory. Of the church the N. and W. walls of the nave survive, the most notable feature being the ball-flower ornament on the moulding of the N. door. In the S.E. corner of the site there are inscribed stones, effigies etc. In the *Parish Church* (1850), within the abbey precinct, the Sagranus Stone, inscribed in Latin and Ogham, in 1848 provided the key for the interpretation of the Ogham alphabet.

7 m. (by B4582) **Nevern**. On a hill to the N.W. are the remains of the *Castle,* originally a fortress of the local chieftains of Cemaes and c. 1100 built as a motte-and-bailey by the Norman Robert Martyn, who became Marcher Lord of Cemaes. His grandson, William, moved to Newport before the end of the century, Nevern being taken over by Rhys ap Gruffydd (his father-in-law), who built a stone castle on the E. angle of the ward. The ruins are overgrown, but the motte can be seen and also some fragments of the stone castle. The *Church of St Brynach* (15-16C, with a Norman tower) is of interest for its many carved stones. The two inside the church, now forming window sills in the S. transept, were found in 1906 embedded in the wall of the passage to the chamber over the chapel. The Maglocunus Stone (?5C) bears both Latin and Ogham inscriptions commemorating Maglocunus (Welsh Maelgwn), son of Clutor. It is of interest that the chieftain who granted land to St Brynach for his church was called Clether or Clutor and was related to Brynach's wife, but there is no evidence that this Clutor and the one on the stone are the same. The other sill, the Cross Stone (10C), bears a cross of entwined Viking pattern. There are two more stones in the churchyard. The Vitalianus Stone, immediately E. of the porch, is inscribed in both Latin and Ogham. The *Great Cross, farther E., is one of the most perfect Celtic crosses in Wales. Dating from the 10C the cross is 13 ft high and bears elaborate patterning. Note, on the E. and W. sides, the examples of the abbreviated writing of the period, that on the W. standing for 'dominus', and that on the E. possibly for 'Halleluiah!'. There are several other items of interest around the churchyard. To the E. of the Great Cross the tombstone epitaph to the infant children of the Rev. D. Griffiths is as amusing as it is touching. Just beyond, a memorial stands to the Rev. John Jones (vicar here 1842-52), who helped Lady Charlotte Guest in translating the 'Mabinogion' into English. A faintly inscribed stone will be found on the N. wall of the church (W. corner of the sill of the second chancel window); this has been cut to fit its present position and is thought to bear part of a vertical Latin inscription of

c. 400. On the N.E. corner of the N. transept, there is an ancient consecration cross, and by the churchyard entrance there is a mounting block. A short way W. of the church, beyond a stile, the Pilgrim's Cross, cut into the rock, was probably a shrine along the road from Holywell to St David's.

*Pentre Ifan Burial Chamber (restored), close to a side road c. 3 m. S.E. of Nevern, shows rather more of interest than many. A communal burial place dating from before 2000 B.C., the main structure consists of a 16 ft long capstone supported by massive uprights 7 to 8 ft high. Immediately S. of the chamber there is a 'portal' (three stones in H setting) with, on either side, two more stones, the whole forming an arc. To the N.E. of the chamber is a large stone, thought originally to have been upright and to have served a ritual purpose associated with the fire-pit immediately to its south. There were two more fire-pits to the north.— There are two other burial chambers to the S. of the coastal road between Newport and Moylgrove. *Trelyffant*, 2 m. N. of Nevern, is a rectangular tomb, the capstone of which is cut with cup-marks. *Llech-y-Drybedd*, just over 1 m. E. of Trelyffant, is a polygonal chamber.

2 m. **Newport** (1000 inhab.), once capital of the Marcher Lordship of Cemaes, the only one not abolished by Henry VIII, and said to have had a brisk wool trade through its port until, in Tudor times, the plague diverted the market to Fishguard, is now mainly a holiday centre. The *Castle* (no adm.), dating from the 13C and successor to Nevern, is now incorporated into a modern mansion. For the *Presely Hills* to the S. of Newport, see p. 377.

About 1½ m. W. of Newport, beside the main road (N.), there is a group of five burial chambers (*Cerrig y Gof*) forming a circle, an arrangement unique in Wales.—*3 m.* (from Newport) *Dinas* is a village at the base of *Dinas Island*, a 400 acre promontory culminating in Dinas Head (463 ft). A walk (3 m.) leads round the promontory, below which seals may be seen; limited parking at either end. At *Cwm-yr-Eglwys* only the belfry and a wall survive of a church (said to have been founded in the 6C), destroyed by a storm in 1839.

4 m. **Fishguard** (with *Goodwick*, 5000 inhab.) is a pleasant little town, perched high above the *Old Harbour*, an inlet at the head of which, at the mouth of the Gwaun, is the picturesque Lower Town. This was the setting for Dylan Thomas's 'Under Milk Wood', filmed here in 1971. Fishguard is associated with the last invasion of Britain, when on 22 Feb. 1797 three French frigates arrived off Carreg Wastad Point (2 m. N.W.) and landed 1400 convicts under the command of the Irish-American, General Tate. Local people and militia gathered under the Earl of Cawdor, and on 24 Feb. Tate, appreciating that his position was hopeless (according to tradition he mistook red-cloaked Welshwomen for British soldiers), signed unconditional surrender at the Royal Oak, where relics of the occasion are preserved.

The narrow **Valley of the Gwaun** ascends S.E. from Fishguard. In c. 3½ m., in the parish of Llanllawer, *Parc-y-Meirw* (O.S. 998359; rather hidden in a hedge) is one of the longest prehistoric stone alignments in Wales. Some 130 ft in length, it is made up of eight stones, some of which have fallen.

The main road descends to the *Parrog*, a ½ m. long beach between Fishguard and *Goodwick*, once a fishing village but now the expanding base for **Fishguard Harbour**, known for its sea services with Rosslare in Ireland. The harbour (as also that at Rosslare) was built between 1894-1906 by the specially formed Fishguard and Rosslare Railways and Harbours Company, and it was on 30 Aug. 1906 that services, previously running from Neyland (Milford Haven) to Waterford, were transferred to Fishguard and Rosslare. In 1972 Roll on/Roll off facilities were inaugurated, this opening the route to large commercial as well as private vehicles. The crossing takes 3½ hours, and during the summer there is a motorail service from London.

A diversion can be made into **Pen Caer** (lanes and paths), the promontory to the W. of Goodwick. The principal hamlet is *Llanwnda,* best approached by motorists from the W. end of Goodwick. Reaching the high ground this road turns right, then left for Llanwnda; at this second turn there is a small incised stone set in the road bank. (Walkers can ascend the lane which starts c. ¼ m. W. of the lifeboat station; this passes (r.) the remains of three burial chambers and joins the motorists' road at the small incised stone). Giraldus was for a while rector at Llanwnda. Note the stone cross cut into the E. end of the exterior nave wall of the church. Just S. of the church there is a burial chamber, interesting for the labour-saving way in which one end of the capstone rests on the ground and the other on a stone standing in a pit. *Carreg Wastad,* ¾ m. N.W., was the landing place of the invaders of 1797, their leader Tate making *Tre-Howel Farm* (1 m. W. of Llanwnda) his base. *Strumble Head,* at the N.W. of Pen Caer, has a lighthouse and commands fine views of most of Cardigan Bay. *Carn Fawr* (600 ft), beside the road c. 3 m. W. of Llanwnda, is crowned by a hillfort. At *St Nicholas,* 2 m. S. of Carn Fawr, the church has an inscribed stone built into its wall, and two Ogham stones in the choir. There is a burial chamber (*Carn Llys*) ½ m. S. of the village, and a standing stone ¾ m. east.

The direct road (A487) between Fishguard and St David's is of little interest, but there are several side roads down to the coast, with its cliff scenery, these all being linked by minor roads running close to the coast. For *St Nicholas,* see above. From *Mathry* (*7 m.* from Fishguard) a road leads N.W. to *Abercastle,* ¼ m. W. of which there is a burial chamber (*Longhouse Farm*), with a nearly 16 ft long capstone resting on three of its original seven supports.

9 m. **ST DAVID'S** is a straggling village on an almost treeless windswept plateau above the small river Alun ¾ m. from the sea. Since the 6C a bishopric, it is the smallest cathedral city in Britain. The *Pembrokeshire Coast National Park Information Centre* is at City Hall, High Street. The partly ruined *Tower Gate* is the main entrance to the cathedral close, a large enclosure, c. ¾ m. in circumference, still mostly surrounded by a wall (c. 1300, though often restored). The gatehouse is the last survivor of four, and it and the precinct wall are in the main attributed to Bishop Gower (1328-47); but it has been suggested that the octagonal flanking tower on the N., which is 50 years older than the rest, was originally a detached bell-tower.

St David's is mainly visited for its Cathedral and ruined Bishop's Palace, both of which are in the deep Alun valley, also known as *Glyn Rhosyn* (Valley of the small bog). The village can be very crowded in summer and visitors with cars may find parking easier in the valley. The foot approach to the cathedral is by a flight of 39 steps, known as the 'Thirty-nine Articles'.

**St David's Cathedral, the largest, finest, and perhaps most interesting church in Wales, is in core a late 12C building, but alterations have given its exterior a style largely of the 14C.

History. The see was traditionally founded by St David, the patron saint of Wales, c. 550, when he transferred his monastery from Whitesand Bay (N.W.) to Glyn Rhosyn, but both the church and monastery he is supposed to have built here have long disappeared. William the Conqueror is known to have paid homage at the shrine of St David, but in 1088 the town was sacked by the Norsemen and the cathedral burnt. Despite this, St David's flourished, kings continuing to make it a place of pilgrimage, two pilgrimages here being equated with one to Rome.

The present building was begun in 1180 during the episcopate of *Peter de Leia* (1176-98), the third Norman bishop (the first was Bernard, who succeeded the Welshman Wilfred). His nave still stands. Giraldus gives a gossiping account of the see in 1188; he was himself afterwards nominated to the bishopric, but failed to secure it (in spite of three appeals to Rome), partly because of his connection with the Welsh royal line, and partly, no doubt, because he argued for the independence of the Church in Wales. In 1220 the central tower fell, demolishing the choir and transepts; but these, with the lower stage of the tower, were rebuilt practically in the original style by 1250. The successive addition of the chapel of St Thomas, the ambulatory, and the Lady Chapel (by *Bishop Martyn*, 1296-1328) completed in broad outline the ground plan of the church. *Bishop Gower* (1328-47) raised the height of the nave and chancel, inserting the Dec. windows, and added the middle stage of the central tower. *Bishop Houghton* (1361-88), Lord Chancellor to Edward III, achieved fame by being excommunicated and then himself excommunicating the Pope from the cathedral steps; *Bishop Vaughan* (1508-22) completed the top stage of the tower, and also vaulted the Lady Chapel. Other bishops during the 16C were *Bishop Ferrar* (1548-55), the Marian martyr, burnt at Carmarthen, and *Bishop Davies* (1561-68), who procured the first Welsh translation of the Bible.

Archbishop Laud (1621-26) was appointed bishop on relinquishing the presidentship of St John's College, Oxford, but he never came to St David's. During the Civil War much of the lead was stripped from the roofs, and the E. parts of the cathedral became dilapidated. *Bishop Bull* (1705-10) was known for his strong anti-Catholic preaching during the reign of James II, and *Bishop Thirlwall* (1840-74) as a classical historian and for his addresses relating the attitude of the Church to contemporary political issues.

The W. front was rebuilt by Nash at the end of the 18C. The modern work of restoration, begun in 1846, was afterwards carried on (1862-78) by Sir Gilbert Scott who rebuilt the W. front to what is thought to be its original design.

The see now embraces all the modern county of Dyfed.

The **Exterior** is plain but dignified. Points to note are the lack of high-pitched roofs to the nave and choir; the 125 ft high tower; and the huge buttresses on the N. side of the nave. The 13-14C building (Chapel of St Thomas, and library) in the angle between the N. transept and the presbytery was originally of three storeys. The S. porch is the work of Bishop Gower, except that the parvise was added in c. 1515.

The **Interior** has a total length of 298 ft; a width across the nave and aisles of 68 ft; and a width across the transepts of 131 ft. General features are the softly tinted purple slate and the lavish late-Norman ornament.

The NAVE is of six bays, clerestory, and triforium, with a varied wealth of chevron and other ornament. The flat *Roof of Irish oak, probably erected during the treasurership of Owen Pole (1472-1509), is unique in having a number of arches of fret-like delicacy that apparently carry the ceiling but are in fact pendants of it. The slope of the floor, due to its original construction on ill-drained and ill-prepared ground, is very noticeable; there is a rise of 14 ft between the W. door and the high altar. Under the second arch from the E. of the S. arcade is the monument of Bishop John Morgan (1496-1504), with his recumbent effigy and sculptures round the base, including, at the foot, a vigorous panel representing the Resurrection. On the adjacent (W.) pier there are traces of murals. At the E. end of the S. aisle there is a beautiful 13C tomb-niche of a vested priest with a curiously shaped canopy. The elaborate and beautiful *Rood Screen, one of the chief glories of the cathedral, is the work of Bishop Gower, whose tomb, with effigy, occupies the S. compartment. To the N. of the central opening, which is notable for its unusual skeleton vaulting, is a striking stone reredos.

The TRANSEPTS, entered from the nave aisles by Norman doorways

St. David's Cathedral

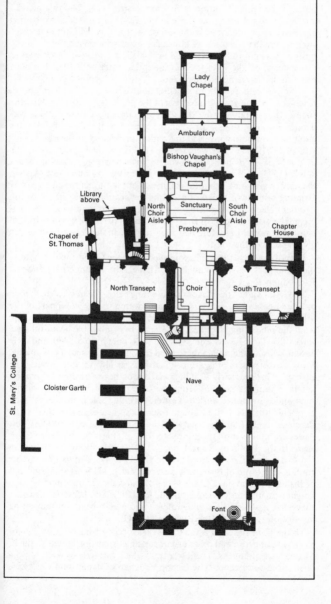

instead of by the usual arches, were largely rebuilt after the fall of the tower in 1220; but here, and in the presbytery, the builders, though adopting the pointed arch, assimilated their new work to the Norman character of the nave. In the *North Transept*, at the back of the choir stalls, is the reputed Shrine of St Caradoc (d. 1124). The two pierced quatrefoils in the base (like those in the shrine of St David, see below) may have been intended for the insertion of a diseased limb in hope of cure, or for the reception of alms. The great window on the N. of the transept was put in by Butterfield in 1846. The *Chapel of St Thomas of Canterbury*, off the E. of the N. transept, a vestry until 1952, has been restored as a memorial to Bishop Prosser (Archbishop of Wales; d. 1949); it contains a beautiful 13C double piscina. The room above, reached by a stair from the N. aisle of the presbytery, was originally the chapter house but is now the *Chapter Library*†. Originally this was divided into two floors, of which the upper was the Treasury, but this latter has now been converted into a gallery in memory of Bishop Havard (1956). The library cases were restored in 1955 by the Pilgrim Trust. The oldest book is Bishop Lyndewode's 'Provinciale sue Constitutiones Angli' (1505), still today quoted as an authority on Church law. Also in the library are some beautiful fragments of the former organ case (? by Grinling Gibbons), broken up during restoration work. In the *South Transept* there are fragments of two Celtic slabs, one of which commemorates the two sons of Bishop Abraham (1076-78), who was bishop before the present building had been started. In the W. wall a doorway gives access to the tower.

East of the nave there follow in succession the Choir, the Presbytery, the Sanctuary, Bishop Vaughan's Chapel, the Ambulatory, and the Lady Chapel.

The CHOIR takes the place of the crossing below the tower, which rests on four fine arches. The circular-headed arch on the W. is part of the original wall of Peter de Leia, while the other three are pointed and date from the rebuilding after 1220. The *Lantern* exhibits the beautiful Dec. work of Bishop Gower. The 28 Choir Stalls date from c. 1470, and their design, without the usual tabernacled canopies, is unusual if not unique. Most of the misericords are original and, as always, interesting. The Bishop's Throne, nearly 30 ft high and one of the few medieval examples left in Britain, is perhaps from the time of Bishop Morgan, though surrounded by earlier work by Gower. On either side there is a seat for a chaplain. Another rarity (though found in some parish churches) is the Parclose Screen (late Dec.) between the choir and presbytery. The Choir Aisles are either side of the presbytery and sanctuary. In the *North Choir Aisle* is the tomb of Rhys Gryg (d. 1233), fourth son of Rhys ap Gruffydd; the effigy is, however, of the 14C. The *South Choir Aisle* contains the tomb of Bishop Gervase (Iorwerth; 1215-29) alongside that of Bishop Anselm de la Grace (1231-47), and the recumbent effigy of a knight who may be Rhys ap Gruffydd (d. 1197). Another effigy has been suggested as being that of Giraldus, and a slab bears an interesting inscription to Silvester the Physician (?13C).

To the E. of the choir is the PRESBYTERY, comprising three and a half bays, with chevron and other ornament, and originally lighted on the E. by two tiers of lancets. The lower row, which formerly looked into the open space now occupied by Bishop Vaughan's Chapel, is now blocked, and enriched with glass mosaics by Salviati. The jambs and arches are decorated with imitation ornament that is richer than any other in the cathedral. The upper tier was reconstructed by Gilbert Scott, from surviving fragments, in place of a poor but genuine window of the 15C. The roof, of 1461, was likewise restored by Scott. On the N. of the presbytery is the late 13C *Shrine of St David,* once a magnet for crowds of pilgrims. In the middle is the large altar-tomb (with a handsome modern brass) of Edmund Tudor (d. 1456), father of Henry VII, brought here at the Dissolution from the church of the Grey Friars at Carmarthen. On the S. is the beautiful recumbent effigy of Bishop Anselm de la Grace (1231-47), alongside that of Bishop Gervase (1215-29).—On the S. side of the SANCTUARY is a rare series of wooden sedilia (1460-81), and here the floor is paved with encaustic tiles, many of which are old.

BISHOP VAUGHAN'S CHAPEL, entered from the aisles, is a fine example of late Perp. work, with a fan-tracery *Roof (1508-22). Originally this was an open space, bounded by the presbytery and by the three walks of the ambulatory; it was also apparently neglected and dirty, being described as 'vilissimus sive sordidissimus locus in tota ecclesia' and the sum of fourpence paid for its cleaning in 1492. The arrangement, unique among British cathedrals, may have been due to the 13C builders' reluctance to block up the three lower lancet windows on the E. of the presbytery. An unexplained feature is the recess on the W. side, with an opening at the back that looks into the presbytery. This is 12C work of De Leia's time; but of the four crosses (brought from elsewhere) immured around the opening, the one below it, hidden by a coffer, may possibly be a relic of a pre-Norman church. This recess, found walled up by Gilbert Scott, concealed a quantity of bones—possibly those of St David or St Justinian, or both—embedded in mortar and probably hidden here at the Reformation; they are now in the coffer just referred to. On the E. side of the chapel stands the Altar of the Holy Trinity, made up of old fragments, with a niche and window on either side, an unusual and curious arrangement.

The AMBULATORY contains several 13-14C recumbent effigies. Its E. walk is vaulted, while the side walks show evidence of a like but unfulfilled intention at three different periods.—The LADY CHAPEL was the last part of the cathedral to be restored, with a replacement for Bishop Gower's vault which fell in 1775. In addition to fine sedilia, the chapel contains two tomb-niches, probably the work of Gower. The one on the S. (restored; no effigy) is thought to be that of Bishop Martyn (1296-1328), the original builder of the chapel. The other (N.), perhaps the tomb of Bishop Bek (1280-96; builder of the Bishop's Palace), has been restored as a tomb for Bishop Owen (1897-1926).

On the N. side of the nave, and once connected with it by a cloister, are the ruins of ST MARY'S COLLEGE (restored since 1933), founded for secular priests in 1377 by Bishop Houghton and John of Gaunt, fourth son of Edward III. The chief feature is the *Chapel,* above a barrel vault, with a plain tower attached to its S.W. corner. This originally formed the S. range of the quadrangle. During work on the conversion of the buildings into a cathedral hall (1965), a tomb, believed to be that of Bishop Houghton, was discovered.

The remains of the *Bishop's Palace† are on the farther side of the Alun rivulet. Started by Bishop Bek and continued by Gower, the palace was mostly built between 1280-1350 and may have had the additional purpose of serving as reception centre for pilgrims to the shrine of St David. The decay of the palace dates from the time of Bishop Barlow (1536-48), who stripped the lead from the great hall, though perhaps not, as local tradition asserts, to portion his five daughters, all of whom he married off to bishops.

The palace consists of a single large quadrangle. The open arcade and parapet that run round the top of the whole building on the outer side are typical of Gower's work. The entrance to the quadrangle is by a disproportionately plain gateway at the E. end of the N. face. Immediately to the left of this is what is supposed to have been the *Private Chapel* (c. 1350), raised, like the rest of the palace, on a series of vaults, which provided basement rooms and storage. The *Bishop's Hall* (late 13C; c. 60 ft by 24 ft), on the E. side of the quadrangle, has a later entrance porch with a curious doorway, exhibiting the semi-octagonal head characteristic of Gower's work. To the S. of this hall is the *Kitchen;* to the N., the *Solar.* The *Great Hall* (1327-47; c. 120 ft by 31 ft), on the S. side, is noticeably larger than the Bishop's Hall and was doubtless used for public purposes. It is approached by a fine porch at its N.E. corner, with a striking ogee doorway enriched by canopied niches with now mutilated figures, and has a beautiful rose window at the E. end. At its N.W. corner is the *Chapel,* with a piscina and a W. bell-turret. The W. side of the quadrangle seems to have been occupied by domestic buildings, stables etc.

Environs of St David's

The promontory, in the S. part of which St David's lies, is a sparsely inhabited windswept district, known for its cliff scenery, its sandy bays, and its associations with David and other saints. It was described by Giraldus as a remote and infertile corner, but, though the latter term still applies, the remoteness today can be crowded in summer. Much of the coastal land is owned (15½ m.) or protected (8½ m.) by the National Trust, largely as the result of an appeal in 1939 and substantial help from the Pilgrim Trust. Small roads or lanes fan out from St David's to many of the bays, and the National Park Coastal Path follows the coast.

For St David's to *Haverfordwest,* see Rte 46.

Caerfai Bay, ¾ m. S., is the nearest bathing place. In *St Non's Bay,* the next bay W., are the ruins of the Chapel of St Non (or Nonnita), the mother of St David; and here, according to tradition, David was born, probably early in the 6C. Another legend relates that she fled to Brittany before the birth. The chapel lies N. and S., and this, together with the primitive masonry of the still fairly perfect S.W. angle, suggests a possible rare survival of early British church building. A little inland, St Non's holy well is said to rise and fall with the tide.

Porthstinan is 2 m. W. of St David's. The remains of a chapel here are those of a pilgrimage chapel of St Justinian, the confessor of St David; the building, with primitive internal wall arcades, is said to be the work of Bishop Vaughan (1508-22). In summer, a number of boats do trips to and around *Ramsey Island* (1 m. W., boat round 1½ hours). The island, privately owned, is a R.S.P.B. nature reserve, and the beaches are a breeding place of grey seals. Traditions associated with the island are that St Devynog founded a monastery here as early as the 2C; that St

Justinian was murdered here; and that St David and St Patrick met at the monastery. Ancient stone coffins have been found on the supposed monastery site. The rocks to the W. of Ramsey Island are known as the *Bishops and Clerks.* There is a lighthouse on South Bishop.

Whitesand Bay, 1½ m. N.W. of St David's and reached by a good road, is a popular sandy beach. In prehistoric times it was from here that traders sailed to Wicklow in Ireland for copper and gold. The *Burrows,* skirting the bay, has a golf course and is traditionally the site of the probably legendary Roman settlement of Menevia, and of St David's first monastery.

St David's Head (no road), a bold promontory with cliffs 100 ft high, juts out as the N. protection of Whitesand Bay. The head is the Octopitarum Promantarium mentioned by Ptolemy. *Clawdd-y-Milwyr,* or Warriors' Dyke, a double rampart of stones across the base of the promontory, is of unknown origin, and, approaching the tip, there are the remains of a chamber tomb. *Carn Llidi* (595 ft) is a distinctive height 1 m. E. of the tip of the head; on the N. slope of the height's W. extremity, are the remains of two more chamber tombs.

46 CARMARTHEN TO HAVERFORDWEST AND ST DAVID'S OR FISHGUARD

A40 to Haverfordwest: Either A487 to St David's or A40 to Fishguard. 44 miles.—*9 m.* **St Clears.**—*5 m.* **Whitland.**—*7 m. Robeston Wathen* (for **Llawhaden Castle**).—*1 m. Canaston Bridge.*—*3 m. Slebech Church* (for **Picton Castle**).—*4 m.* **Haverfordwest.**—*15 m.* **St David's** or **Fishguard.**

Carmarthen, see Rte 43. The road skirts the N. side of the alluvial plain at the mouth of the Taf.—*9 m.* **St Clears** is a small agricultural centre straggling N. and S. of the main road. In 1406 Owen Glendower was defeated here by the men of Pembroke, and in 1843-44 the village was a focus of the Rebecca Riots. The *Church,* on A4066 to the S., with a tower that batters to the top, retains the carved Norman chancel arch of a small Cluniac priory which was attached in 1291 to St Martin-des-Champs in Paris. Rtes 47A and B bear S.W. and S. from St Clears.—*5 m.* **Whitland,** a small market town on the Taf, is historically important as the meeting place of the assembly convened by Hywel Dda in 930 to codify Welsh tribal customs into a single legal system; so successful was the assembly that the code lasted until the time of Edward I. The *Abbey,* today an insignificant ruin 1¾ m. N.E., was once a great Cistercian house, the 'Alba Domos' of Giraldus, founded by Bernard, the first Norman bishop of St David's, in 1143; the abbey colonized Cwmhir in the same year, and Strata Florida in 1164.

Beyond the Taf, A40 ascends out of the valley, in *5 m.* crossing A478 (Rte 49). *Narberth* is 1 m. south.—*2 m. Robeston Wathen,* 1 m. N. of which is ruined **Llawhaden Castle** (mainly 14C), once an important residence of the bishops of St David's.

History. The land around Llawhaden was a rich possession of the see of St David's, and in 1115 Bernard, the first Norman bishop, built a circular motte fortification here. In 1192 Rhys ap Gruffydd assaulted and razed this castle, of which all that remains today is the moat, and in the early 13C, when the bishops had recovered the place, a stone castle was built. Later, in the early 14C and probably under the direction of Bishop Martyn, Llawhaden was rebuilt and extended as a large fortified mansion. Bishop Barlow (see p. 358) is generally supposed to have stripped the roof of its lead and to have left the castle to decay.

Within its circular moat, the castle comprises a single irregular ward round which lie the domestic buildings. The *Gatehouse,* at the S.W. corner, is largely a late 14C addition. To its W. are the *Garrison's Quarters,* today a ruined two-storey building which would probably have been a hall above an undercroft, with, at an angle, the kitchen beyond. Adjoining and immediately N.W. of the garrison's hall are the foundations of a circular tower (internal diameter 12 ft), a survival of the early 13C stone castle's curtain wall, which can be traced along the exterior of the garrison's hall. In the *North Range* of buildings, too, the main rooms were on the first floor above vaulted storerooms, but of this upper floor little remains. In the centre the hall extended N.W. to S.E., with on its left the Bakehouse (W.) and Kitchen (E.), and to its right the Bishop's Private Chamber. The *South Range,* to the E. of the gatehouse, comprised two storeys of rooms above undervaults, with beyond, at the castle's S.E. corner, the Chapel, originally joined to the bishop's chamber. The S.E. tower contained the chaplain's living quarters.— *Llawhaden Church* dates mainly from the 14C, but has a N. tower which is somewhat older.

1 m. (from Robeston Wathen) *Canaston Bridge,* 1½ m. S.W. of which, on the minor road to Minwear, there is a Forestry Commission viewpoint and picnic site above the narrow estuary of the Eastern Cleddau; *Slebech Forest Trail* makes a 1 m. long round from here. In the 12C Slebech became a Commandery of the Knights Hospitaller. In Slebech Park, 2 m. W. on the N. side of the river, there is a ruined church of a preceptory of the Knights Templar. *Blackpool Mill†* (1813) is a restored tidal mill.

Just beyond (*3 m.*) *Slebech Church,* a minor road leads S. off A40, in 1½ m. reaching **Picton Castle†**, with gardens and the Graham Sutherland Gallery. Originally a Norman motte guarding the confluence of the Eastern and Western Cleddau, the stone castle dates from c. 1302 when it was built by Sir John Wogan, who was Justiciary of Ireland from 1295-1313. The castle was taken by Owen Glendower in 1405, by the Royalists in 1643, and by Parliament in 1645. In 1800 a four-storey block was added, and since 1954, when the estate passed to the Hon. Hanning Philipps, a descendant of the medieval owners, Picton has been converted to a modern residence. The *Gardens,* in neglected condition in 1954, have now been cleared and nurtured, and include plants and shrubs from Scotland's famous Lochinch Gardens, the home of Lady Philipps's family. The *Graham Sutherland Gallery* (1976), a branch of the National Museum of Wales, includes oil paintings, watercolours, aquatints, lithographs, etc., presented by the artist and his wife as a token of the inspiration he drew from Pembrokeshire over many years; some of the works were made especially for the gallery.

Wiston, 2 m. N. of A40, takes its name from Wizo the Fleming. The motte and bean-shaped ward of his castle of c. 1120 survive. It was destroyed in 1220 by Llewelyn the Great, and the keep on the motte is probably later 13C rebuilding.

4 m. **Haverfordwest,** (9000 inhab.) is a solid and busy market town on the Western Cleddau, which is navigable up to here for small craft. With some steep streets and several good Georgian houses, the town was designated a conservation area in 1976.

Tourist Information. *Wales Tourist Board:* Riverside car park. *Pembroke Coast National Park:* 40 High Street.

Parking. *Riverside* (E. of river). *Castle Lake* (N. above High Street; convenient for castle and St Mary's Church).

Post Office. Quay Street (W. of river).

Early Closing. Thursday.

History. Although the name is a legacy of Viking raids, the town grew around the Norman castle built here in c. 1120 by Gilbert de Clare. Flemish settlers arrived during the reign of Henry I. Gruffydd ap Rhys took town and castle in 1135, but it was back in Norman hands by 1153 when Henry II visited here. Other kings who came here were John (1210), Edward I (1284), Richard II (1394), and Henry Tudor (before Bosworth, 1485). In 1220 Llewelyn the Great burnt the town, and in 1407 Owen Glendower's French mercenaries did so again, though they failed to take the castle. During the Civil War the town changed hands several times. In 1642 it was held for Parliament; in 1643 for the King; in 1644 it was occupied by Parliament's General Laugharne, and in 1645 by the Royalist Sir Charles Gerard; later in 1645 Laugharne returned, and finally the castle was slighted. The town became a prosperous port during the 18 and 19C, trading regularly with Bristol and Ireland; and recent years have seen conservation measures such as an extensive listing of scheduled buildings and the diversion of heavy traffic away from the centre.

The main town is on the W. bank of the river. The principal bridge is *New Bridge,* W. of which Victoria Place leads into Castle Square. From here High Street, with many Georgian façades, climbs up to St Mary's Church (see below).

The remains of the *Castle,* to the N.W. above Castle Square, are the shell of the mainly 13C inner ward. By the mid 15C the place was already a ruin, but in 1779 a county gaol was built in the ward against the S. wall; used only until 1820, it was not demolished until 1964. The castle now houses the town *Museum and Art Gallery†.* The museum is concerned mainly with the story of the town and surrounding district, and the gallery receives regular touring exhibitions. *St Martin's Church,* to the W. of the castle, is mainly of the 14C. The *Regional Library†,* in Dew Street, regularly receives touring art exhibitions, some sponsored by the Welsh Arts Council.

St Mary's Church, at the top of High Street, dates originally from c. 1250-70, but the N. aisle was rebuilt and the clerestories added in the 15C. The entrance is by the N. door. From the S. door 13 steps descend to the nave, the W. end of which is raised by several steps. The nave has three E.E. lancet windows, somewhat unusually placed at its W. end (the glass forms a war memorial), and, like the N. aisle, a good 15C roof. At the W. end is also the mutilated effigy of a pilgrim with scallops on his satchel, perhaps indicating a visit to the shrine of St James of Compostella in Spain. At the E. end there is an elaborate 15C bench-end (the end of the adjacent pews of the sheriff and mayor) showing St Michael and the dragon. The **Arches* of the chancel and those of the N. arcade are exceptionally good 13C work, retaining uninjured their capitals of stiff foliage enlivened with masks and small animals. The windows in the chancel, especially the great E. window, are splendid examples of plate-tracery.

Quay Street, leading S. out of Castle Square, becomes Old Quay, where a small open space above the old slipway provides a setting for 18C warehouses, one of which may have been the port's original custom house. Farther S. (¼ m. from Castle Square), beside the river, are some remains of a *Priory Church,* founded for Augustinian Canons by Robert de Hurlford (Haverford) in 1207.

For the peninsula (*Marloes* and *Dale*) to the S.W. of Haverfordwest, see p. 367. B4329 leads N.E. for (25 m.) Cardigan. After 7 m. *Llys-y-Fran Reservoir Country Park* lies under 1 m. to the E. of the road. The Reservoir (dam opened by

Princess Margaret in 1972) supplies water for the whole area of what was the county of Pembroke; and the Country Park provides picnic sites, sailing, fishing etc, and a nature trail which starts at the car parks at either end of the dam and skirts the reservoir, a total distance of 7½ m. In another c. 3 m. B4329 starts to climb across the *Presely Hills* (see p. 377).

To St David's. A487. *6m. Roch Castle* (no adm.), to the N. of the road, takes its name from the outcrop of rock on which it stands, a site said to have been chosen by Adam de la Roche because of his fear of snakes (as so often in such cases, he was killed by a snake, brought in unobserved in some fire wood). What is seen today is one surviving 13C D-shaped tower with projecting chambers; a block of flats has now been added. In the roof of the S. porch of the nearby small church, stone has been interestingly used in the same way as wood. The stream just beyond Roch marks the N. boundary of English-speaking southern Pembroke i.e. the district colonized by the Flemings.—*2m.* the coast is briefly reached at *Newgale,* a scattered holiday village with a 2½ m. long beach. Here, at exceptionally low tide, can be seen the stumps of a submerged forest, known to Giraldus and described by him as a grove of ebony. From here on, much of the coast is either owned or protected by the National Trust. The road turns inland.—*3 m. Solva* is a secluded fishing village at the head of its narrow winding creek; up to the mid 19C this was quite an important port.—*4 m.* **St David's,** see p. 353.

To Fishguard. A40. *3m. Poyston,* 1m. E. of the road, was the birthplace of Sir Thomas Picton (1758-1815), Governor of Trinidad and distinguished commander during the Peninsular War, who was killed at Waterloo.—In about *2m.* (near *Treffgarne*) A40 crosses the Western Cleddau and runs, with the river and the railway, through the narrow, wooded *Treffgarne Gorge,* with hillfort earthworks lining the heights on both sides. Brunel brought his railway as far as here in 1845, but was defeated by the old, hard rocks, and it was not for another 60 years that the line was completed. Here *Nant-y-Coy Mill Museum*† contains Victoriana, all of local provenance. The mill, dating back to 1332 or earlier, was rebuilt in 1844; there is a 1½-m. long nature walk through a wildlife conservation area. Owen Glendower is said to have been born at Little Treffgarne, on the E. side of the river. The *Triffleton Waterfowl Collection*†, 1m. E. on the Puncheston road, includes over 50 varieties of geese and duck.—*2m. Wolf's Castle,* where there is a motte. *Sealyham,* 1m. N.E., gives its name to a breed of terrier. To the E. now rise the *Presely Hills.*—*8m.* **Fishguard,** see p. 352.

47   CARMARTHEN TO PEMBROKE AND MILFORD HAVEN

Two routes are described; the direct, inland main road, or generally minor roads along the coast. The two come within a little over a mile of one another at Kilgetty and Saundersfoot, and meet at Pembroke. The coastal route, longer by ten miles, is by far the more scenic and interesting.

A   Direct

A40 to St Clears: A477 to Pembroke: A4139, A477, and B4325 to Milford Haven. 39 miles.—*9m.* **St Clears.**—*12m.* **Kilgetty.**—*6m. Carew Cheriton* (for **Carew Castle**).—*4m.* **Pembroke.**—*8m.* **Milford Haven.**

Carmarthen, see Rte 43. For Carmarthen to (*9m.*) **St Clears**, see Rte 46.—*2m. Llanddowror.* Griffith Jones (1684-1761), the pioneer of Welsh education and organizer of travelling schools, was vicar here.—*8m. Killanow*, a hamlet on a minor crossroads. *Amroth*, on Rte 47B, is less than 1 m. south.

2m. **Kilgetty**, where there is an important *Information Centre* (Wales Tourist Board, A.A., R.A.C., National Park; bookings for Walks and Talks). The centre includes an exhibition illustrating the story of local anthracite and iron ore mining, the main activity here until the first half of this century. Alongside the centre, glassmaking and blowing can be seen at *Avondale Glass†.* A *Coalfield Trail* starts from the centre (leaflet obtainable). The trail (2½ m.; can be wet in places) starts along the embankment of the tramroad which was built in 1829 and ran to Saundersfoot harbour, and passes various remains of former mining activity. A few yards beyond the centre A478 (Rte 49) is crossed, *Tenby* being 4 m. south.

6m. Carew Cheriton has a large 14-15C church (with a mounting block at the entrance) containing tombs of the Carew family, one of these being that of Sir Nicolas (d. 1311), who built the earliest part of Carew Castle. On the N. of the chancel is the effigy of a vested priest (c. 1325), and on the S. a very small recumbent female figure (c. 1300; either a child or perhaps a 'heart burial'). The tiles (c. 1500) on the chancel floor may have come from Carew Castle. The detached 14C chantry or mortuary chapel, used in 1846 as a school, is a rare survival of an, in any case, uncommon feature.

The imposing ruins of **Carew Castle†**, to the N. of A477, stand on a ridge above a tidal creek.

History. The earliest castle, of which nothing survives, is said to have been built by Gerald de Windsor, an Anglo-Norman chieftain, at the close of the 11C. Another tradition is that the estates came to him as the dowry of his wife Nest, daughter of Rhys ap Tewdwr, sister of Gruffydd ap Rhys, and mistress of Henry I. Their son assumed the name of Carew, and their daughter was the mother of Giraldus. The earliest authentic stone structure was the fortified mansion of the Carews, built c. 1270-1320. In 1480 Carew was sold to Sir Rhys ap Thomas, who remodelled the place and added the Great Hall. Sir Rhys entertained Henry Tudor after his landing on Milford Haven in 1485, and in 1507 here held a great tournament to celebrate the Garter bestowed on him by Henry, now Henry VII. In 1558 the castle was granted to Sir John Perrot, who rebuilt the whole of the N. side in a purely domestic Tudor style. In the Civil War Carew was held for the King in two sieges (1644 and 45), but the damage was apparently such that it was not lived in after 1686. The castle is still owned by Carew family descendants.

Architecturally Carew spans the period between the military structures of the 13C (W.) to the fortified manors of Tudor times (N.). The plan is roughly rectangular with a three-quarter drum-tower at each corner, the two on the W. being strengthened externally by curious semi-pyramidal spurs. The entrance on the E., the weakest side, was specially protected, the whole front being covered by an outer ward and the actual gateway by a narrow barbican which compelled approach at right angles; it was also flanked on the S. by the drum at the S.E. angle, and on the N. by a special tower protruding from the curtain. The original *Carew Manor House* was built inside this E. curtain and included a chapel in the special tower just referred to; it is representative of the period when defence was moving outwards to a curtain and away from a keep. The late 15C *Great Hall* built by Sir Rhys ap Thomas, with its fine entrance tower, is on the W. of the ward (upper storey), while on the N. is *Sir John Perrot's Manor* with its large windows and oriels.—Beside the road near the castle entrance stands **Carew Cross*, a magnificent early Christian monument, nearly 14 ft high, erected c. 1035 to commemorate Maredudd (killed in battle that year), co-ruler with his brother of Deheubarth. The cross was made in two parts, the wheel-cross at the top fitted into position by a tenon. The elaborate geometric and intertwined patterns show both Celtic and Scandinavian influence. *French Mill*†, just W. of the castle, a tidal mill, is known to have existed in Elizabethan times; the present building is early 19C and the mill ground corn until c. 1918.

Upton Castle, 2m. N.W. of Carew Cheriton, is a mansion which incorporates parts (13C) of a castle which was the seat for some 250 years of the Malefant family. There is no admission to the castle, but the *Grounds*†, with over 250 specimens of trees and shrubs and since 1976 maintained by the National Trust, are open to visitors. There is a wooded picnic site by the car park, and a path leads through woodland and past formal terraces. A chapel, close to the castle, contains three Malefant effigies (13 and 14C). The parts of the 13C castle incorporated into the mansion are at the rear and cannot be seen.

4m. (from Carew Cheriton) **PEMBROKE** (14,600 inhab.) is an ancient town with a single main street which runs for over ½ m. along a narrow ridge above Pembroke River. In October this street is the scene of a centuries old fair. Lengths of the 13C town walls survive, particularly on the S., these originally being integral with the castle and having three gates, West and East gates being at either end of the main street and North Gate guarding what is now the bridge across the river. *Tourist Information* is at the Drill Hall in Main Street, and there is convenient parking on the S. below the town wall.

The large and imposing ruins of ***Pembroke Castle**†, occupying the W. end of the ridge, sprawl over a promontory above the river and Monkton Pill.

History. Roman coins have been found on this site, and it may later have been a Viking stronghold, but the first castle here was built c. 1095 by Arnulf de Montgomery. Described as a 'slender fortress of stakes and turf', it was left in the hands of Arnulf's steward, Gerald de Windsor (probably builder of Carew), who withstood a siege by the Welsh in the following year and in 1102, when Montgomery fell from favour, was granted the castle by Henry I. Three years later Gerald rebuilt the place. The earldom of Pembroke was created in 1138, (the first earl was Gilbert de Clare), the title later passing to the Marshals, who were largely responsible for the castle the remains of which are seen today. The oldest part is the keep, thought to have been built by William Marshal in c. 1210, and the whole castle seems to have been completed, initially by his five sons in succession, by the end of the century. In 1452 Henry VI granted Pembroke to Jasper Tudor, and in 1457 his nephew Henry Tudor was born here. Throughout the Civil War the castle was held for Parliament, but in 1648 the town's military governor John Poyer surprisingly declared for the King. Cromwell then besieged Pembroke for 48 days, subjecting it to continual artillery battering until, after capturing the water supply, he was able to compel surrender. The castle was then slighted, and Poyer was shot in London early the following year. Neglected and used as a quarry for over 200 years, the castle was restored in 1880, 1928, and later.

The ground plan is an outer ward to the E., and beyond, above the curve of the promontory, the smaller and rather older inner ward. The entrance to the OUTER WARD is across the ditch, now filled in, which separated the castle from the town, and then by the *Gatehouse*, noteworthy for its external barbican (restored 1880-85), compelling oblique approach, and for its internal semicircular angle-towers connected by a flying arch, possibly intended to carry a wooden platform manned by defenders. Within the gatehouse (with a small local museum, open in summer only) there is a maze of rooms and passages. The walls of the ward are strengthened by five circular drum-towers, connected by passages. On the S. and W. sides the first tower is the *Henry VII Tower,* confidently stated by Leland (official antiquary to Henry VIII) to be Henry's birthplace. Note the very individual privy in the adjacent wall. *Westgate Tower* (destroyed 1648, restored 1931) stands at the point where the southern town wall, with the West Gate, joined the castle. The *Monkton Tower* is different from the others in having separate entrances to its floors. It stands to the S. of the *Inner Gatehouse,* surviving only as foundations, on the inner curtain. This, approached from below by a twisting path, was the original and only entrance to the castle during the period when it consisted of the inner ward only; when, not long afterwards, the outer ward was built, the path was built over and a new and higher *Water Gate* opened beside Monkton Tower. On the E. side of the ward *Northgate Tower* marks the point where the N. town wall joined the castle curtain. Much of the tower's outer wall, destroyed in 1648, is a rebuilding of 1934. To the N. the *Mill Gate* marked the exit to the tidal mill below, the dam of which, with a drawbridge, was the entrance to the town through the North Gate. Mill Gate and the mill were protected by the rectangular *St Ann's Bastion* (restored 1929).

Just within the INNER WARD stands the circular *Great Keep,* 75 ft high and 24 ft in diameter internally at the bottom, with walls 19 ft thick at the base. It was possibly built by Gilbert de Clare, but more probably by William Marshal in c. 1210. Originally four storeys, it is now open from ground level to the domed stone roof. The chief entrance was on the first floor, up wide steps, the foundations of which were discovered in 1932; the basement entrance was apparently added at an early date. The staircase is a restoration of 1928. At the top, square holes in the outer parapet were probably for the attachment of an archers' platform. The domestic apartments, largely crowded into cramped space N.E. of the keep, are not on the scale of the rest of the castle. From S. to N., beside the inner curtain are the *Dungeon Tower*; the *Oriel*, probably a Tudor adaptation of an earlier antechamber; the *Norman Hall*, the hall being above a basement, and access through either the Oriel or the *Northern Hall*, again a main floor above a basement. A stairway (dark and often slippery) leads from the Northern Hall down to the *Wogan*, a large natural cavern, roughly 80 ft long and 60 ft broad, probably used as a store; the cavern can also be reached by the path around the base of the castle. The *Chancery*, to the W. of the Norman Hall, seems to have been a Tudor addition. In the S.W. of the inner ward are the scanty remains of the *Chapel*, alongside the gloomy *Western Hall*.

For *Castlemartin Peninsula*, see Rte 48.

Monkton Priory, ½ m. W. of the castle across Monkton Pill, here dammed to form a mill lake, was founded by Arnulf de Montgomery in 1098 for Benedictine monks; a cell of Sées in Normandy, the priory was given to St Albans in 1473. The church has a long, narrow, barrel-vaulted nave, and the monastic chancel, though part of the original structure, was recast in the 14C. The church lay in ruins for many years until a restoration of 1878-87. The detached chapel to the N. is apparently contemporary. Under the tower is the altar-tomb of Sir

Francis Meyrick (d. 1603), the upper part in a style suggesting Italian Renaissance influence. On the exterior, the tower is of the local fortified type; in the gable above the E. window there is a decorated niche with a headless figure; and, from traces of two small half-blocked windows on the N. exterior of the nave, it has been suggested that the masonry incorporates the S. wall of a pre-Norman church.

A4139 crosses Pembroke River. **Pembroke Dock**, 1 m. W., is a town which developed after 1814 when the Admiralty Dockyard moved here from Milford Haven; the first ships, 'Valorous' and 'Ariadne', were launched in 1816. Greatly expanded during the First World War, the government dockyard was in 1930 handed over to the R.A.F., and Pembroke Dock became well known as a flying boat base which played an important part in the Atlantic patrols of the Second World War. Its role ended with the demise of the flying boat. The town was planned on a generous squared pattern with wide streets, and some solid Victorian architecture survives. In summer there are boat excursions (from Hobbs Point on the N. of the town) in Milford Haven, to see giant oil tankers and the shore terminals, and up Daucleddau, the joint estuary of the Western and Eastern Cleddau rivers. The *Pembrokeshire Motor Museum*† traces the history of road transport since the mid 19C. Exhibits include vintage cars; a horsedrawn fire engine of 1896; a replica of a country garage of the 1920s; an amphibious car; and a hovercraft.

A477 crosses upper Milford Haven by a toll bridge, opened in 1975, which has superseded the ferry (just W.) between Hobbs Point and *Neyland*. The latter was the main trading port to southern Ireland until superseded by Fishguard in 1906. About 1 m. beyond the bridge, B4325 is followed W. past oil refineries.

8 m. (from Pembroke) **Milford Haven** is the name both of the huge natural harbour and of the town (see below) on its N. shore. The magnificent natural harbour, described by Nelson as the best in the world and with sheltered roadsteads for the largest ships, is some 10 m. long by ½ to 2 m. broad, and at its head breaks into several tidal inlets reaching far inland, the longest being the estuaries of the Western and the Eastern Cleddau. Until c. 1800, however, the haven served only as temporary refuge. The Norsemen came here (in King Alfred's time one expedition wintered with 23 ships), and both Henry II and John, each with 4-500 ships, set sail from here to conquer Ireland. In 1407 12,000 French mercenaries landed here to fight for Owen Glendower against Henry IV, and in 1485 Henry Tudor, Earl of Richmond, came ashore at Mill Bay with a small retinue from Brittany to begin the campaign that would end with victory at Bosworth Field and his crowning as Henry VII. In the late 18C Sir William Hamilton (best known as husband of Nelson's Lady Emma) inherited from his first wife the local manors of Pill and Hubberston. He appreciated the potential of the haven but, far away as Envoy Extraordinary to the Court of Naples (a post he held from 1764-1800), there was nothing he could personally do, so he appointed his nephew, the Hon. R. F. Greville, as his agent. In 1790 an Act of Parliament sanctioned the establishment of a town, and Greville imported a group of Quaker whalers who had been unsettled by the American War of Independence. It was they who laid out Milford Haven town in the squared pattern to which they were accustomed. At about the same time a naval dockyard was opened, which, however, in

1814 moved to Pembroke Dock. The railway came in 1863 but, although there was some optimistic investment (Milford Haven docks were completed by 1888), large ships failed to use the place. However the Neyland trawler fleet moved to Milford Haven, which by the opening years of the 20C had become one of Britain's largest fishing ports. During both wars the haven was busy with Atlantic convoys, but after the Second World War there was a general decline and trawling has now virtually disappeared.

New life came with the 1960s as the haven began to develop into a major oil port, and today it is used by the leading oil companies whose activities have brought huge tankers, and a growing spread of oil terminals and refineries, from which there are pipelines to the Midlands. The haven is under the operational control of the *Milford Haven Conservancy Board* (1958), whose jurisdiction extends over all tidal waters, which means from the sea to as far inland as Haverfordwest, Canaston Bridge, and Carew. In 1964 the Board's permanent headquarters and signal station at Hubberston Point (W. of Milford Haven) were opened by Princess Marina, Duchess of Kent.—In summer the best way to see the tankers, terminals, and general port activities, is by the ship which operates out of Pembroke Dock (Hobbs Point).

In **Milford Haven** town (14,000 inhab.) *Tourist Information* (National Park) is in the Town Hall. *St Katharine's Church*, built by Greville in 1801-08, was extended in 1907 by the addition of two bays to the E. nave and a new chancel and Lady Chapel. A case contains a bible and prayer book presented by Nelson. In the porch are an Egyptian porphyry bowl and a replica of the truck of the French battleship 'L'Orient' which blew up at the Battle of the Nile (1798). The urn had been acquired by Greville, the genuine truck had been presented to the church by Lady Hamilton in memory of Nelson, and Greville proposed to combine these into a font. However the bishop objected on the grounds that the bowl was pagan and that the truck had been 'polluted . . . by blood and carnage'. The bowl remained in the church but the truck is now in the National Maritime Museum at Greenwich. Sir William Hamilton (1730-1803) is buried in the churchyard; he lived at *Castle Hall*, E. of the town. The small remains of *Pill Priory*, built in 1200 by Adam de la Roche, are to the N.W., and to the N.E., beyond the head of the Pill Inlet, there are very slight remains of the medieval *Castle*. *Gellyswick Bay*, to the W. of the town, is popular for bathing and sailing.

MARLOES AND DALE PENINSULA

An indented peninsula, ending as two promontories, extends some 10 m. westward from Milford Haven. The main road into the peninsula is B4327 from Haverfordwest, the two principal villages towards the W. end being Marloes to the N. and Dale to the south. To the W. there are several islands. The National Park footpath, crossing some National Trust land, follows the coast with its cliff scenery, and sandy bays. The National Park's *Countryside Unit* is at **Broad Haven**, a small resort on the coast at the N. end of the base of the peninsula.

Marloes is an inland village, with *Marloes Sands* around the bay ¼ m. southwest. Marloes Nature Trail (2 m.) explores the cliffs and the area immediately inland of the sands. The W. extremity of the bay is marked by *Gateholm Island* (Norse, Goat Island), which is an island only at high tide. On the island there are traces of a large number of rectangular huts, survivals of a Dark Ages (possibly monastic) settlement. *Albion Sands*, immediately W. of Gateholm, recall the 'Albion', a paddle-steamer wrecked here in 1840; iron shafts can be seen at low tide. From *Martin's Haven*, at the road's end 2 m. W. of Marloes, there are boat trips to Skomer (see below).

St Ishmael's, a village in the S. central part of the peninsula, is named after a 6C colleague of St Teilo. On the N. outskirts of the village there is a motte, and the Long Stone (½ m. N.W.) is the tallest standing stone in the National Park. A story attaches to *Mullock Bridge*, on B4327 roughly halfway between St Ishmael's and Marloes. Sir Rhys ap Thomas of Carew Castle is said to have given his word to Richard III that if Henry Tudor entered Wales it would only be by riding over his body. When Henry landed at Mill Bay Sir Rhys both satisfied his conscience and ensured his own future by lying under the bridge while Henry rode across; he then hurried to Carew where he received Henry.

Dale, to the S., is a small holiday village and sailing centre (boat excursions to Skomer). *Dale Castle* (no adm.), a modern residence, stands on or near the site of a medieval manor first mentioned in 1293 as belonging to Robertus de Vale. Around the promontory to the S. are Iron Age earthworks across the base of Dale Point; *Dale Fort*, a Victorian fort now the home of a Field Studies Centre (no adm.), with courses in biology, geology, geography etc.; *West Blockhouse Point*, site of coastal defences first erected c. 1580, rebuilt 1852-57, and in occupation until 1950; and *Mill Bay*, where Henry Tudor landed on 7 Aug. 1485. On the night of 9 Nov 1866 six ships were wrecked here, and on 14 March 1964 a ship being towed to Swansea for scrapping broke away and was driven ashore (wreck still visible). At *St Ann's Head*, accessible by road, there are a coastguard station and lighthouse.

Skomer Island† (722 acres), a National Nature Reserve administered by the West Wales Naturalists' Trust, is known for its seabirds, seals, and spring and early summer wild flowers.—Between Skomer and the mainland is *Midland Isle* or *Middleholm* (21 acres).—**Skokholm Island**† (242 acres), also a bird sanctuary administered by the West Wales Naturalists' Trust, has the first Bird Observatory to be established in Britain (1933; accommodation and courses).—**Grassholm Island**† (23 acres), 7 m. W. of Skomer, was purchased in 1948 by the Royal Society for the Protection of Birds and is famous for its gannets.

B   Viâ the Coast and Tenby

A40 to St Clears: A4066 to Pendine: unclassified to Saundersfoot: A478 to Tenby: A4139 to Pembroke: A4139, A477, and B4325 to Milford Haven. 49 miles.—*9 m.* **St Clears**.—*4 m.* **Laugharne**.—*5 m.* **Pendine**.—*8 m.* **Saundersfoot**.—*3 m.* **Tenby**.—*2 m.* **Penally**.—*4 m.* **Manorbier Castle**.—*4 m.* **Lamphey Bishop's Palace**.—*2 m.* **Pembroke**.—*8 m.* **Milford Haven**.

Carmarthen, see Rte 43. For Carmarthen to (*9 m.*) **St Clears**, see Rte 46.

4 m. **Laugharne** (pron. 'Larn') is a quiet rural town, with Georgian houses, on the W. bank of the estuary of the Taf, here over ½ m. wide and about to broaden farther as it meets that of the Towy.

History. For long the history of the town was that of the castle. Founded during the 12C and for a while held by Rhys ap Gruffydd, it was destroyed by Llewelyn the

Great in 1215, then rebuilt by the De Brians.It was Sir Guy de Brian who in 1307 granted a charter, by which the town was administered by a portreeve (chief officer) elected every six months by the citizens, a system which in main respects still obtains today. In Tudor times the castle came to Sir John Perrot, who, as he did at Carew, converted the place into a mansion. In the Civil War Laugharne was the home of the general of the same name, who held the castle for Parliament in 1647 but later sided with the King. In the 18C Mrs Bridget Bevan (d. 1779), associate of Griffith Jones of Llanddowror, lived here, and in recent years Laugharne was the home of the poet Dylan Thomas (d. 1953), who is buried in the churchyard.

The *Castle* (adm. by appointment only), of which little survives, comprises two 12-13C towers and traces of Perrot's mansion. King Street commemorates a visit by Henry II, and the tower of the *Town Hall* contains a curious small prison furnished with a wooden bench with a pillow end. In *St Martin's Church* (14C, modernized 19C) are the remains of a Bronze Age man (in a chest on the 1. side of the entrance to the vestry), found during the construction of a local housing estate; a 10C Celtic Cross (restored); and a wood carving of St Martin of Tours, brought from Oberammergau in 1866, executed by a member of the Lang family, long associated with the Passion Play. Dylan Thomas did much of his writing in a small boat house above the water to the N.E. of the town (reached by Victoria Street, off King Street, then at the end of narrow Cliff Road; if not open, the interior can be seen through a window).

Llandawke, 1½ m. W. by narrow but motorable lanes, has a very primitive 13C church (unused), in which are a 5-6C stone bearing writing in Ogham and Latin, and an effigy, by some considered to be that of St Margaret of Marlos, daughter of Sir Guido de Brian, to whom the church is dedicated. The effigy, of c. 1400, was originally in the churchyard.

5 m. **Pendine** is a small resort whose sands, stretching away to the E., have an honoured place in motoring and aviation history. Between 1924-27 the world's land speed record was five times attempted here, three times by Malcolm Campbell (1885-1948) and twice by J. G. Parry-Thomas, the latter being killed here in 1927; his car was buried near the beach until dug up in 1969 for restoration. The final speed achieved by Campbell was 174.88 mph in 1927, though by 1935 (at Bonneville, Utah) he raised this to over 300. In 1933 Jim and Amy Mollison (Johnson) took off from the sands for a non-stop flight to New York via Canada; lack of fuel forced them down only 60 m. short of New York. For a fee, modern motorists can drive, but not speed, along the beach. The *Burrows*, stretching E. to the Taf estuary, are a Ministry of Defence area (danger zone).—The road climbs inland to (*2 m.*) *Marros* (450 ft), with a quaint 'neolithic' war memorial, before dropping to (*3 m.*) *Amroth*, a seaside and inland village where the stumps of a submerged forest can be seen at low tide. This is the S.E. extremity of the Pembroke Coast National Park.—*3 m.* **Saundersfoot**, today a holiday resort with good bathing and a harbour crowded by small sailing craft, dates from 1829 when the harbour was built to export the anthracite mined a short way inland and brought here by tramroad. For the important *Kilgetty National Park Information Centre* and the *Coalfield Trail*, 1½ m. inland, see p. 363 *Wiseman's Bridge*, to the N. of the town, was the scene of a D Day rehearsal, watched by Winston Churchill.

3 m. **TENBY** (5000 inhab. but many more in summer), an ancient and picturesque walled town, today a lively resort, sprawls along a steep promontory, narrowing to only a few yards at its E. end, which separates North Sands and the harbour from South Beach and Castle Sands.

Town Centre. Tudor Square.
Tourist Information (Local and National Park). Civic Centre, The Norton (at N. entry to town).
Parking. At Tourist Information. Limited parking by the harbour.
Early Closing. Wednesday.
History. From the evidence of coins found on St Catherine's Rock during the construction of the fort there in the 19C, Tenby may have existed in some form in Roman times, but the first mention of the place is in a poem of c. 875 which names the fortress on the promontory as Dynbych-y-Pysgod (Fortlet of the Fishes), the modern word Tenby being a development of Dynbych. This poem praises the court here of the prince, Bleiddudd ap Erbin, a patron of bards. Around 1111 the town, growing to the W. of the castle, was settled by Flemish clothworkers, but soon afterwards suffered the usual violence of the times. The castle was taken in 1153 by Rhys ap Gruffydd, in 1187 his son sacked the town, and in 1260 it was taken by Llewelyn the Last. During a part of this time (1172-75) Giraldus was rector here. Although by 1386 the castle was close to ruins, the town, granted a charter by Henry IV, became a flourishing port (importing wines and salt and exporting coal and cloth), a status which lasted until well into the 16C. In 1457 the town walls were strengthened by Jasper Tudor, and in 1471, after the Battle of Tewkesbury, Henry Tudor found refuge here before escaping to Brittany. The defences were again strengthened under the threat of the Armada. Although garrisoned for the King during the Civil War, Tenby surrended in 1644 after a siege of only three days. After decline during the 17 and 18C, the town was rescued in the 19C by Sir William Paxton and others who, helped by the opening of the railway, were able to develop the resort to which Tenby largely owes its present day character.—Robert Recorde, author of 'Ground of Artes', the earliest important mathematical treatise, and inventor of the = sign, was born here in 1510. Augustus John, the artist, was born in 1878 at Belgrave House, now the Belgrave Hotel.

South Parade starts 220 yards S. of Tourist Information, along it running the surviving section of the **Town Wall**. This, ¼ m. in length and ending at South Cliff, lies across the base of the promontory and, with a short return section on the N., now destroyed, was the town's inland defence. The wall, first built perhaps in the 13C, was, as noted above, strengthened by Jasper Tudor in 1457, and again in 1588; it is some 20 ft high and is strengthened externally by bastions, of which all except one are cylindrical. About halfway down the length of the wall is the *South Gate*, protected externally by a semicircular barbican (*Five Arches*), which retains its sole original entrance on the N. side, with (a favourite medieval trap for attackers) a rightangled turn. From Five Arches, St George Street leads E., passing on the left below the church an old archway, once giving access to the churchyard and prison.

St Mary's Church is of many and mixed periods, the oldest being a 13C rebuilding of an earlier church. Much of today's structure dates from the 15C, with extensive modification during the 19C, these two periods reflecting the town's peaks of prosperity. Features of the Exterior are the large *South Porch* (c. 1500) with, above the inner door (refashioned 18C), a small window of a 13C chapel; the late 13C *Tower*, unusual for being to one side of the chancel, with a 15C spire; the 15C *West Door*, inserted into an older wall and ornamented with moulding and a double-ogee head, all that survives of a large W. porch built in 1496 and demolished in 1831; and, to the W., the slight ruins of a building erected in conjunction with this porch, probably as a chantry and school.

The *Nave*, basically 13C, was extensively altered in the 15C when the N. arcade and a row of arches on the S. side were added. The roof was restored in 1966, as was also the pulpit of 1634, with ample ladies around the top. The N. aisle is an early 15C addition. The S. aisle results from a throwing together in the late 15C of a number of chapels. The fine roof dates from the same time. The *Chancel* (13C) was enlarged c. 1470 by the addition on the E. of steps and a raised Sanctuary, with a crypt below. The panelled ceiling (restored 1962) has elaborately carved bosses, 75 of which are original. The *Chapel of St Nicholas* (N.) is an addition of 1480; the monuments include the tomb of Bishop Tully of St David's (1460-82). *St Thomas's Chapel* (S.) is also a 15C addition; among the monuments are two with effigies of Thomas White (d. 1482) and of his son John (d. 1490), both mayors, the former at the time of Henry Tudor's escape in 1471.

Below the main street, roughly E. of St Mary's, is the late 15C **Tudor Merchant's House**†. Beautifully furnished, the house contains a fine Flemish chimney, remains of early murals showing Flemish patterns, and a National Trust Information Centre; restored in 1938, this is one of the few surviving old town houses in South Wales. From the *Harbour* there are boat trips to Caldy Island, around Caldy and St Margaret's islands, to Lydstep etc.; boats for shark and other fishing; and diving cruises. South of the harbour, beyond the narrow neck of the promontory, is *St Catherine's Rock*, a detached spur not accessible at high tide, with a dismantled fort (built 1868-75) and a small zoo. Castle Hill, the small green extension promontory E. of the harbour, is laid out as a promenade, with a marble statue of Prince Albert (J. E. Thomas). Of the *Castle* all that survives are a gatehouse, a double tower, and traces of domestic buildings. **Tenby Museum**† here contains archaeological and historical material relating to Pembrokeshire, and to Tenby in particular; finds from Hoyle's Mouth (see below), including human teeth and the bones of now extinct animals; and a collection of shells.

Scenic walks can be taken N. or S. along the cliffs, that northwards to *Saundersfoot* (4½ m.) viâ *Monkstone Point* being particularly popular. Southwards the National Park coastal path leads to *Penally* and *Lydstep*, for both of which see below. See below also for *Hoyle's Mouth* (1 m. S.W.), another popular objective.

At *Gumfreston*, 1½ m. W. on B4318, there is a small and primitive 12C church (14C tower), with a unique semicircular recess (perhaps a baptistry) on the N. of the nave; some ancient murals; and a bronze Sanctus bell. In the churchyard there are three medicinal springs, the central one being chalybeate.—For *St Florence*, 3 m. W. of Tenby, see below.

For Tenby to *Cardigan* and *Aberaeron*, see Rte 49.

CALDY ISLAND

Caldy Island†, 2¼ m. S. of Tenby and owned by Cistercians, is 1½ m. long (E. to W.) and ¾ m. across at its widest point; but it is so broken by bays and inlets that the coast is some 9 m. in length. Features of the island are the abbey (the monks of which farm the island), the flowers, the souvenir shop, and the seabirds, these being especially numerous on the S. side.

History. Excavations have revealed evidence of early occupation in the form of Neolithic human remains, flint implements, and Roman pottery of the 1 C.A.D. The first monastery on Caldy (late 5C) was probably established by a colony from St Illtyd's foundation of Llantwit Major (though some authorities maintain that Caldy was the older foundation). Its most famous abbot was St Samson of Dol, the patron saint of Caldy, some of whose relics are still preserved. How long this Celtic monastery lasted is unknown, but it was presumably in existence when the Caldy Ogham stone was put up. This is a slab of sandstone, with a cross and a double inscription, one in Ogham (5-6C), and the other in Latin added in the early 9C; the inscription bids those who pass to pray for the soul of Catuoconus (Cadogan). Nothing more is heard of the island, except that it became a nest of pirates and fell prey to Norse raids, until 1127, when it was given by the mother of Henry FitzMartyn to the Benedictines of St Dogmaels. The monks held peaceful possession of Caldy for over 400 years, leaving evidence of their occupation in the three fishponds, the medieval buildings etc. In 1534 the monastery was dissolved and the island given by Henry VIII to secular owners. It passed through various hands, until in 1906 it was purchased by Aelred Carlyle and became the home of the Anglican community which he had founded and which, in 1913, was received into the Church of Rome as Benedictine. In 1928 the Benedictines moved to Prinknash Park, in Gloucestershire, their place being taken by Cistercian monks from Chimay in Belgium. The monastery was raised to the status of abbey in 1958.

On the cliffs, facing Tenby, there is a round Norman tower, now converted to a chapel. The principal building on the island is the *Abbey* (1907-11; conducted tours for male visitors only); the church, seriously damaged by fire in 1940, was restored in 1950-51. The peal of bells is one of the largest in Wales. Near the abbey is *St David's Church*, in plan closely resembling the Irish churches of the 8 and 9C and most probably in origin as old if not older. It has a Norman W. door.

Beyond, the *Old Priory* dates from the 13-14C, with 15C additions, and is of interestingly defensive character. Visitors may enter the restored *Church of St Illtyd*, with a leaning tower and, at the E. end of the nave, the Caldy Ogham Stone. Beyond the Old Priory the track continues to the lighthouse (1828).

St Margaret's Island, off the N.W. tip of Caldy, is a nature reserve and bird sanctuary under the care of the West Wales Naturalists' Trust. No access without permit.

Tenby is left by A4139. Just outside the town there is a road to the right signed Penally, off which almost immediately there is a small road, again to the right, which in a few yards reaches a path up to *Hoyle's Mouth* (torch required), a cavern over 50 ft deep and containing several chambers. Excavations during the 19C produced Palaeolithic flint implements, a human jaw and teeth, and bones of extinct animals such as a cave bear and reindeer. Some of these finds are in the museum at Tenby. Hoyle's Mouth has been popularly identified with the Cave of Belarius in Shakespeare's 'Cymbeline' (Act III, Scene VI).

2m. The village of *Penally* is by one tradition both the birth and burial place of St Teilo. The 13C church contains a fragment of a cross shaft with Northumbrian motifs (9C, and unusual in Wales) and a wheel-cross of the 10C; also the sepulchral slab of William and Isemay de Raynoore (1260-90), in dark slate, with the alabaster faces of the deceased let into it in low relief. Both inscription and style are French.—*2m.* **Lydstep Head** is a promontory of precipitous limestone cliffs; the headland of 54 acres was given by the Pilgrim Trust to the National Trust in 1936. Steps lead down to the *Lydstep Caverns*, all, except for Smuggler's Cave, accessible only at low tide. A nature trail (1½ m.), organized by the West Wales Naturalists' Trust, starts at the car park.

2m. **Manorbier Castle**†, in a commanding position above the attractive red sandstone bay of the same name, is famous as the birthplace of Giraldus. A mainly 13-14C structure, the castle has been 'peopled' by model figures, these including Giraldus, prisoners in a dungeon etc.

History. The name derives from Maenor Pyr (Mansion of Pyr), the first abbot of Caldy. The castle was probably built by Odo de Barri in the early 12C, Giraldus being born soon afterwards in c. 1147. The De Barri line died out in 1359, and Manorbier was held by the earls of Huntingdon until 1461 when it was seized by the Crown. Later, Elizabeth I sold the estate to Thomas Bowen of Trefloyne and it passed by marriage to the Philipps of Picton, to a member of which family it still belongs.

Of Odo de Barri's original building virtually nothing remains, except perhaps the inner side of the gateway. The buildings seen today are of the 13-14C and comprise an outer and an inner ward. The latter is roughly oblong, with (N.E.) a *Gatehouse*. The small tower immediately N.W. of the gate is probably late 12C and the oldest part of the castle. The residential part (S.W. end) is of two dates. The *Hall* and the original two-storeyed chamber to the N.W. of it are contemporary with most of the early castle; the *Chapel* and another two-storeyed chamber were built c. 1260. Both chapel and hall are raised on pointed barrel vaults, each being approached from the court by an external staircase; the chapel contains a sedile niche and a fireplace. Tradition has it that Giraldus was born in the N.W. tower, which, though, is almost certainly of a later date.—*Manorbier Church*, on the opposite side of the valley, has a curiously irregular appearance, this resulting from successive additions to the original Norman structure. Features of interest are the 13C tower of local type; the pointed barrel vaults; the primitive arches cut in the walls of the earlier (12C) nave; the base of the rood loft in the N. aisle and the gallery by which it is reached; and the 13C recumbent effigy of a De Barri. *King's Quoit*, above the E. arm of Manorbier Bay, is a sub-megalithic burial chamber, the capstone of which at one end rests on two short pillars and at the other on the ground.

St Florence, 2 m. N.E., was in medieval times a harbour (today's Ritec stream was a sea inlet) and a centre of Flemish influence, and the round, external chimneys on some of the cottages are still locally known as 'Flemish chimneys'. The rude 13C church of local type has a curious little dark S. transept chapel. *Manor House Leisure Park†*, comprising 12 acres of wooded grounds, has exotic birds and animals; a model railway exhibition; a children's adventure playground; wild and formal gardens, and a tropical planthouse.

Climbing N.W. out of Manorbier Bay the minor road passes a good clifftop parking areas.—*3 m. Hodgeston* (pron. 'Hodson') where the church chancel contains a double piscina and mutilated triple sedilia.

1 m. The ruins of **Lamphey Bishop's Palace†**, dating from the early 13 to the late 16C, lie just N.E. of Lamphey village. This was one of the several manors of the medieval bishops of St David's. Despite the troubled early medieval period, and in contrast to the palace at St David's itself, Lamphey has virtually no defensive features and survived as a country retreat of some elegance and comfort.

History. It is known that Wilfred, the last Welsh bishop before the appointment of the Norman Bernard, was here in 1096. The earliest surviving stonework (early 13C) is parts of the walls of the old hall, to the W. end of which the camera (private apartments) was added later in the century. Bishop Gower (1328-47) much extended the palace, adding a new hall (Great Hall), angled away from the S.E. corner of the earlier one, a battlemented wall enclosing the courtyard, and (N.W.) the gatehouse. In the 15-16C, largely under the influence of Bishop Vaughan (1509-22), the camera was remodelled and a chapel was added beyond the N. side of the old hall. Finally, with the Reformation, Lamphey passed to the Crown, being granted in 1546 to the Devereux, earls of Essex; Robert, the favourite of Elizabeth I, lived here as a boy.

Approaching the palace by road a stream is reached, the marshy hollows on either side of which mark the site of the fishponds; these are first mentioned in a survey of 1326. At the palace the most notable architectural features are Bishop Gower's typical high battlemented parapets carried on arcades which rise above the roofs, and the circular chimneys above the camera and great hall marking the period of Devereux ownership.

The main range of the palace extends roughly W. to E. to the S. of the *Gatehouse* with its arcades. The *Camera* (c.1250, and 15-16C), at the W. end, was a two-storeyed building, the attendants occupying the ground floor and the bishop having his private apartments above, these comprising a main room and, projecting to the S., bedroom and garderobe. Access for the bishop was by either of two stairs at the N.E. and S.E. corners. The bedroom and garderobe area was extended in the 15C. Of the fireplace in the centre of the N. wall, the lower part is original, but the circular chimney above, as also that at the N.W. angle of the building, are Devereux insertions. The *Old Hall* (early 13C), extending E. from the camera, is a much ruined two-storeyed building in which the actual hall occupied the upper floor. A garderobe juts out to the S.W., and it has been suggested that this and the bishop's garderobe were drained by a channel from the stream, though no trace of this has been found. The *Chapel* (early 16C), on the N. side of this hall, must have replaced a chapel elsewhere. Also on the upper floor, it has a fine traceried window of five lights in its E. wall, and two other windows, each of three lights, in the N. wall. The small projection to the N.E. was the Sacristy. Bishop Gower's *Great Hall* (1328-47, and 16C), forming the E. end of the palace range, is a two-storeyed building with a huge, long vaulted ground floor lighted by slits. The hall above was over 70 ft long, and from the camera the bishop reached it by crossing the old hall and then using a short passage. The fireplace in the N.E. corner and the southward projecting garderobe are the main Devereux features. The Gower arcaded parapet is best seen from the N. side.

For (*2 m.*) **Pembroke** and Pembroke to (*8 m.*) **Milford Haven**, see Rte 47A.

48   CASTLEMARTIN PENINSULA

The **CASTLEMARTIN PENINSULA**, some 9 m. from E. to W. and 8 m. from N. to S., extends W. and S.W. from Pembroke between Milford Haven and the outer Bristol Channel. The peninsula is best known for its sandy bays and rugged cliff scenery along the S. and W. coasts between roughly St Govan's Head and Angle. The National Park footpath follows much of the coast, but is forced inland between St Govan's Head and Freshwater West by Ministry of Defence ranges, which, when in use, can prevent access to interesting St Govan's Chapel and some of the best of the coast (red flags and roadside warning notices). The northern part of the peninsula, along Milford Haven, is spoilt by oil refineries and a large power station. The peninsula is the winter home of the mountain sheep of the Presely Hills.

The clockwise round described below covers, without diversions, some 29 m., made up of 6 m. from Pembroke to St Govan's Chapel; 6 m.

from St Govan's Chapel to Castlemartin; 7 m. from Castlemartin to Angle; and 10 m. from Angle back to Pembroke.

Pembroke is left by B4319. After about 2 m. a minor road leads E. for 1 m. to the church of *Stackpole Elidor* (or Cheriton Elidor) with a Norman tower and several effigies, these including Richard de Stackpole and his wife (14C) and the painted kneeling figure of Roger Lort, with his wife and 12 children (17C). On the coast to the E. is a National Trust property (1976) of some 2000 acres, with 8 m. of cliffs, two beaches, and a hillfort on *Greenala Point.*—After rather over another mile along B4319, another minor road bears S. for **Bosherston,** with a church (1250-70) of local type, interesting for a passage-hagioscope which projects externally in the angle between the S. transeptal chapel and the chancel. The Preaching Cross in the churchyard (c. 14C) may have been adapted from an older Crucifixion, the evidence being the face in the centre. Probably dismantled at the Reformation, the original shaft seems to have been lost and replaced by the present stumpy one. The *Lily Ponds* (or Fish Ponds), to the N.E., are formed by the damming of an inlet by blowing sands. The lilies are at their best in June, and the ponds are popular with fishermen. A standing stone, c. ½ m. N. of the ponds, carries two cup marks.

The Ministry of Defence tank ranges stretch W. from Bosherston, and a notice board beside the road states whether or not the road is open to ***St Govan's Chapel** (1 m. S.), fascinating for its primitiveness, its age (at least 11C and possibly as early as 6C), its legends, and for its extraordinary position blocking a narrow cleft halfway down the cliff.

St Govan, a 6C Irishman of Wexford, was a follower of St Ailbe (d. 527), a native of Solva near St David's, who founded the monastery at Dairinis, Wexford. After a visit to Rome, St Govan entered Dairinis, of which he eventually became abbot. It was as an ageing man that he came to Pembroke, possibly because of the connection with St Ailbe. Tradition now takes over, maintaining that the cleft opened to save St Govan who was being attacked by pirates, closed around him, then opened again when the pirates had left. St Govan then built his cell here, remaining until his death in 586, when, tradition continues, he was buried beneath the chapel altar. March 26 is St Govan's Day.

The Chapel, easily reached by steps, measures 17 ft 6 inches by 12 ft 6 inches. At the E. end is the stone altar, to the side of which steps lead to a small cell cut in the rock; here there is a fissure, said once to have sheltered St Govan, and which today grants the wishes of anyone able to turn round within it. On the S. wall of the chapel are a piscina, an aperture, and a window. In the upper plastering of the W. wall there is a circle containing an inscription of unknown age or meaning. There was apparently once a well in the floor near the main door, known for its ability to cure eye and skin complaints. The *Well* outside the chapel, now dry, was effective for both wishing and healing. The boulder outside the chapel, known as *Bell Rock,* contains a silver bell, once in the little bell-tower, stolen by pirates, brought back by angels, and secured within the rock.

When the range is clear, walkers can follow the fine coast W., with precipitous, tortured cliffs 100 to 160 ft high, soon reaching *Huntsman's Leap,* a narrow fissure over which a horseman is said to have leapt, dying thereafter of fright. Beyond there are remains of cliff fortifications. At *Bullslaughter Bay* there are large caves, and beyond is the *Devil's Punch Bowl,* (or the *Cauldron*), a hollow enclosed by steep cliffs 130 ft high and connected with the sea through a natural arch. The two isolated *Elegug Stacks* (roughly 3 m. from St Govan's Chapel) are massive limestone pillars, covered by breeding birds between April and early August ('elegug' is Welsh for guillemot). From Elegug Stacks a small road leads N., in 1½ m. joining B4319.

The road is retraced from St Govan's Chapel, through Bosherston, to B4319, which is now followed west. After 2 m. along B4319 a small crossroads is reached. The road S. leads in 1½ m. to *Elegug Stacks* and a fine stretch of cliff scenery (see above; road can only be used if the range is clear). To the N. is the village of *Warren*, with a tall church spire. The church (restored 1855) has some c. 13C barrel vaulting. **Castlemartin** is associated with the Castlemartin Yeomanry, who repulsed the French landing near Fishguard in 1797 and thus earned the distinction of having the only Battle Honour awarded for action on British soil. Castlemartin Black Cattle were one of the two breeds which early in this century were interbred to produce today's Welsh Black. In the Church there is an organ of 1842, once owned by Mendelssohn.

B4319, continuing N.W., now returns to the coast above *Freshwater West*, with a magnificent beach which, however, with Atlantic rollers, is dangerous for bathing. Near where the road joins B4320 is the *Devil's Quoit*, a burial chamber with a 12 ft capstone resting on a single pillar; other collapsed pillars lie around. The fishing village of **Angle**, at the end of B4320, stands on the W. of Angle Bay which opens into Milford Haven. On *Thorn Island*, 1½ m. W. of Angle, the fort was built in 1852-59.

B4320 is now followed east. *Rhoscrowther* and *Pwllcrochan*, to the N. of the road, are close to oil refineries. At the former the Norman church includes a curious little chapel on the S. of the nave and what may be an Easter sepulchre. The *Pembroke Power Station* (2000 MW), to the W. of Pwllcrochan and completed in 1974, is the largest oil-fired station in Europe. Built on reclaimed land in the deep Pennar Gut, the station is virtually out of sight. It uses locally refined oil (up to 11,000 tons a day), some of which is obtained by pipeline from Wear Point on the N. side of Milford Haven. To the S. of B4320 is *Orielton*, an 18C house on a site occupied since the 12C; it is now a Field Studies Centre. B4320 reaches Pembroke through *Hundleton* and *Monkton* (see p. 365).

49   TENBY TO CARDIGAN AND ABERAERON

A478 to Cardigan: A487 to Aberaeron. 56 miles.—*5 m.* **Begelly.**—*3 m.* Templeton.—*2 m.* **Narberth.**—*5 m. Llandissilio.*—*9 m.* **Crymych (Presely Hills).**—*7 m.* **Cilgerran Castle.**—*2 m.* **Cardigan.**—*5 m. Blaenannerch.*—*5 m. Sarnau.*—*4 m. Plwmp* (for **West Wales Farm Park**).—*3 m.* **Synod Inn.**—*6 m.* **Aberaeron.**
The first half crosses the Presely Hills, with many prehistoric archaeological sites, and a choice of walks and minor roads. Between Cardigan and Aberaeron diversions can be made to the coast with its fine cliff scenery.

Tenby, see p. 369.—*5 m.* **Begelly**, where A477 (Rte 47A) is crossed. For *Kilgetty Information Centre* and the *Coalfield Trail*, see p. 363.— *3 m. Templeton* once belonged to the Knights Templar of Slebech, who may have had a hospice here. Traditionally it was near here that a battle was fought in 1081 which established Gruffydd ap Cynan and Rhys ap Tewdwr as princes of North and South Wales.

Sentence Castle, a motte to the W. of Templeton, is, with nearby *Narberth Castle*, traditionally the site of the 'Mabinogion's legendary court of Pwyll, Prince of Dyfed. Perhaps Narberth was the site of the court, and perhaps Sentence was the nearby mound of Gorsedd Arberth to which Pwyll liked to withdraw. The mound had the magical property that, if anyone high-born sat there, he could only leave after either receiving a wound or seeing a wonder. Pwyll was lucky, and met the beautiful if sometimes sarcastic Rhiannon.

2m. **Narberth** (1000 inhab.), originally Castell yn Arberth and, as noted above, traditionally associated with the 'Mabinogion', is a market town sprawled over a steep hill. It was burnt by the Norsemen in 994. The *Castle* (no adm.), in the S. part of the town, is now no more than fragments of the castle built c. 1246 by Sir Andrew Perrot, given by Henry VIII to Sir Rhys ap Thomas, and dismantled after the Civil War; it is successor to an early Norman castle, destroyed by the Welsh in 1115, of which nothing remains. The *Church,* in origin 13C, was rebuilt in 1879.

A40 (Rte 46) is crossed 1 m. N. of Narberth. Beyond *(5 m.) Llandissilio* the road climbs the ridge that separates the E. Cleddau valley (W.) from that of the Taf.

The **Presely Hills** (sometimes Prescelly or Prescelli) stretch away westwards almost to Fishguard Bay, a rolling moorland rising to 1760 ft, with patches of afforestation and, because of the water held by the boulder-clay, extensive areas of bog that can bring difficulties for the ill-prepared walker. Walkers are also reminded that sudden mists are a feature of the hills, and that good maps and suitable clothing are essential. Flocks of Welsh mountain sheep graze their home areas, from which they rarely stray, and an increasing number of mountain ponies is to be found. The main interest of the hills lies in their prehistoric archaeology. Not only are they dotted with cairns, burial chambers, standing stones, stone circles etc., but the hills also provided (1500-2000 B.C.) the 'blue stones' for Stonehenge, these (weighing up to four tons) being dragged some 140 miles, part of the way along the old trade route from Ireland; a route which, incidentally, explains Geoffrey of Monmouth's belief that the stones in fact came from Ireland. The hills are crossed by A478 (this Route), by B4313 running S.E. from Fishguard, and by B4329 running S.W. from Cardigan; the latter two cross at *Greenway.* Many minor roads and lanes link these, but not across the main mass of the hills which lies between A478 and B4329, between *Crymych* on the former and Greenway. Most of this part of the hills is accessible only to walkers, who can follow the Bronze Age Track (c. 8 m.) which links Crymych with *Bwlch Gwynt* on B4329 (1½ m. N. of Greenway) and passes close to several prehistoric sites.

The **Bronze Age Track,** dating from c. 1500 B.C., grew out of the movement between the main centre of the Beaker people on Salisbury Plain and Whitesand Bay (N.W. of St David's), and thence by boat to Ireland's Wicklow Hills with their copper and gold. From the E. the starting point is *Croesfihangel Tumulus,* 1 m. S.W. of Crymych and reached by road. The much eroded tumulus burial mound (Middle Bronze Age) produced urns and cremated remains dated to c. 1000 B.C. To the S., on the other side of the road, there is a Neolithic burial chamber of c. 2500 B.C., with a capstone 16 ft long and 10 ft broad (permission to visit should be requested at Mountain Farm). On *Foeldrygarn* (1200 ft), ½ m. N.W., there is an Iron Age stone-walled hillfort; ramparts defend the E. gate, but the S. and W. gates rely on the steep slopes. Hut sites here were excavated in 1899, finds, now in the museum in Tenby, including beads, pottery, and a stone lamp. The cairns on the top may be Bronze Age burials. Foeldrygarn provided five volcanic dolerite stones for Stonehenge. *Carn Ferched,* beside the track ¾ m. after Croesfihangel, is a small Bronze Age burial mound. To the S. of the track, after another ¾ m., is *Carnmenyn*

(Cairn of the Boulders), the main source of Stonehenge's dolerite stones. *Carnalw,*
1 m. N. of Carnmenyn, provided four blue rhyolite stones. In another ½ m. the
track reaches *Bedd Arthur* (Arthur's Grave), an oval of 12 stones, probably Bronze
Age and erected perhaps 2000 years before Arthur's time. Next, in ½ m., a branch
track S. in 1½ m. reaches *Cerrig Meibion Arthur* (see below). The main track
continues W., in 2 m. beyond Bedd Arthur reaching a point ½ m. N. of *Foel
Cwmcerwyn* or *Presely Top* (1760 ft), the highest point of the hills, with four
Middle Bronze Age burial cairns. The view from here can extend from Dunkery
Beacon on Exmoor (76 m. S.E.) to Snowdon (85 m. N.N.W.) and include also the
Irish coast. In legend ('Mabinogion, Culhwch and Olwen') it was on Foel
Cwmcerwyn that Arthur and his men had one of their running fights with the great
boar Twrch Trwyth. Two of Arthur's sons were among the many warriors killed by
the boar, and are commemorated by the name borne by the two Neolithic Cerrig
Meibion Arthur (see below), the Stones of the Sons of Arthur. In another 1½ m.
the track reaches B4329 at *Bwlch Gwynt* (Windy Pass). Note, where the track
continues across the road, the way in which it is stepped along the slope, this
resulting from users choosing new lines as stretches became waterlogged. Also W.
of the road, N. of the track, can be seen *Foel Eryr* (Eagle Mountain; 1535 ft), with a
Bronze Age cairn.

On B4329, the name *Tafarn-y-Bwlch* (Tavern of the Pass), 1 m. N. of Bwlch
Gwynt, now a farm, recalls that this was once a coaching inn. The track due S. from
here, which crosses the Bronze Age Track in under 1 m., was a drovers' road.
Brynberian is another 1½ m. farther N. on B4329; *Bedd-yr-Afanc* (Monster's
Grave), ½ m. S.E. to the E. of the streams, seems to be a Neolithic long cairn, or
gallery grave, of perhaps 2500 B.C. This type of site is unique in Wales, but known
in Ireland.

Sites S. of the Bronze Age Track. There are a number of sites within the area
between the Bronze Age Track and the roads linking Greenway viâ Maenclochog
and Llangolman to A478. At *Rosebush,* 1 m. S.E. of Greenway, a disused railway
track is crossed. The line (Fishguard to Rosebush and, 8 m. farther S.,
Clunderwen) operated from 1899 to 1937 (passengers) and 1949 (goods). A short way
beyond, small roads to the W. reach in 1½ m. *Dyffryn Circle* (O.S. 059285), an
Early Bronze Age (1500 B.C.) burial mound surrounded by stones. To the E. stands
the single *Budloy Stone.* Roughly opposite the road to Dyffryn, a small road leads
N.E. off the Greenway-Maenclochog road, in 2½ m. reaching (W.) *Maen-y-Parc*
(O.S. 111303), a probably Early Bronze Age standing stone which may have been
deliberately shaped. *Cerrig Meibion Arthur* (O.S. 118310; Stones of the Sons of
Arthur), N. of the road in about another ½ m., are two Neolithic stones, one large
and square at the top, the other thinner and pointed (see also Foel Cwmcerwyn
above). From here small roads can be followed generally S.E. for 1½ m. to *Gors-
Fawr Stone Circle* (O.S. 135294) of the Early Bronze Age with 16 stones and two
outliers. It may be of some ritual significance that the line of sight between these
outliers aims directly at Carnmenyn. From *Glan Rhyd* (O.S. 153319), 2 m. N.E. of
here, can be seen (½ m. S.E.) the *Waun-Lwyd Stones* (O.S. 158312; no adm.),
similar to Cerrig Meibion Arthur.

9 m. (from Llandissilio) **Crymych** is the starting point for the Bronze
Age Track walk described above.

7 m. **Cilgerran Castle**† ruins are 1 m. E. of the main road. Though
small, the ruins are strikingly and romantically sited on a steep
promontory above the tidal limit of the Teifi and have inspired a number
of artists, notably Richard Wilson and J. M. W. Turner. In the 18 and
19C the boat excursion from Cardigan to Cilgerran was a principal
tourist attraction, and the trip can still occasionally be made today (from
Gwbert).

History. An early castle may have been built by Roger de Montgomery c. 1093,
but it is known that this site was developed by Gerald de Windsor, to whom it was
granted by Henry I. It was taken and at least partly destroyed by Rhys ap Gruffydd
in 1164; taken by William Marshal, Earl of Pembroke, in 1204; recovered by
Llewelyn the Great in 1213; and finally retaken by William Marshal's son, William,
in 1233. This last rebuilt the castle, and it is to this period that most of the surviving
structure belongs. But Cilgerran was soon neglected, and is recorded as being in
ruins by 1326. There were frequent changes of ownership during the Wars of the
Roses, and, with the abolition of the Marcher Lordships in 1536, Cilgerran passed

to the Vaughans who seem to have lived here until the early 17C. Thereafter the place became no more than romantic ruins. Cilgerran was acquired by the National Trust in 1938, and has since been placed under the guardianship of the Crown.

Occupying a steep promontory above the Teifi and a tributary stream, the castle required little defence on the W. and N., but was vulnerable from other directions. The main castle is the inner ward, protected on the E. and S. by two large round towers and a gatehouse, joined by curtain wall. This inner ward is separated by a ditch from a much larger outer ward to the S., itself defended by a wall and ditch.

The modern entrance is at the S.W. corner of the OUTER WARD, which represents the bailey of the early Norman motte-and-bailey castle. On the W. little defence was necessary. On the S. there was a ditch and wall, but though the fomer can be made out, very little survives of the wall. On the E. there was a wall, but this collapsed during slate quarrying in the 19C, and, apart from a short section at the N.E. corner, the wall seen today is 19C replacement. The most interesting feature of the outer ward is the rock-cut ditch which separates it from the inner ward.—The INNER WARD is entered at its S.W. corner by the *Gatehouse* (early 13C), which stood beyond a drawbridge over the ditch and was defended by two portcullises. The two round towers and associated curtain wall all date from the early 13C. The *East Tower,* probably the first to be built, was of four storeys and projects outwardly well clear of the curtain wall, this enabling the wall to be covered by fire from the tower. The ground floor is entered directly from the ward. The room on the top floor had a fireplace, and the tower's only outward-facing window. The *West Tower* is generally similar, though one difference was that the entrance was at the first floor, probably by wooden steps, the ground floor being reached by a trap-door from the first (the present doorway into the ground floor is a 14C modification). Other 14C work included the wall dividing the ground floor into two, and the stair on the E. side of the new ground floor entrance. The very ruined *Northwest Tower* was a rectangular 14C addition. Of the buildings that would have filled the ward only traces survive. The *Kitchens* would have been against the curtain to the S. of the Northwest Tower, and in the S.W. corner of the ward something of a 13 or 14C limekiln can be seen. The oldest parts of the castle (12C) are two short sections of wall; one between the kiln and the gatehouse, and the other some remains on the edge of the cliff halfway along the ward's N. side.

2 m. **Cardigan,** see p. 350, where Rte 45 is crossed.—A487 runs at some distance from the sea, but diversions can be made to the coast with its cliff scenery. Near (*5 m.*) *Blaenannerch* there is a Ministry of Defence rocket-testing station. *Aberporth,* on the coast 2m. away, is an attractive fishing and holiday village.—*5 m. Sarnau,* from where a road leads to *Penbryn* on the coast, a hamlet with a beach. Llanborth Farm, immediately N. of the hamlet, was acquired by the National Trust in 1967. *Llangranog,* 1½ m. farther N. up the coast, is a hamlet in a narrow ravine between high headlands. *Lochtyn Farm,* N. of the hamlet, was acquired by the National Trust in 1965; the property of 213 acres includes 1½ m. of cliffs, an island, two beaches, and a hilltop (public access, except to island).—*4 m.* **Plwmp.** From here a small road S. in 2 m. reaches **West Wales Farm Park**† (60 acres; opened 1977). The park, an approved station of the Rare Breeds Survival Trust, has as its aim the preservation and exhibition of rare breeds of farm animals and poultry. Signs lead to Cattle, Sheep, Pigs, Horses, Goats, and Poultry, and among the many breeds to be seen are shire horses and Shetland ponies; 'wild' white cattle, Britain's oldest breed, used for sacrificial purposes by the Druids and Romans; shaggy Highland cattle; two-horned Soay, two to six-horned St Kilda, and two to four-horned Jacob sheep; Iron Age pigs; golden Guernsey goats, the only pure British breed and very rare. For children there is a Pets Corner.

3m. Synod Inn, where Rte 44A is joined. For *Newquay,* 4 m. N., see p. 346. For (*6m.*) **Aberaeron,** see p. 346.

INDEX

Topographical names are in bold print; names of persons in italics; other entries in Roman print. Where there are several references, the more important are in appropriate cases printed bold.

Notes

Notes

Key page to Map numbers

0	5	10	15 km
0	5		10 miles

Reference

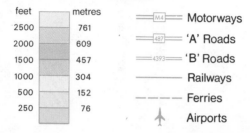

feet		metres
2500		761
2000		609
1500		457
1000		304
500		152
250		76

═══ M4 ═══	Motorways
═══ 487 ═══	'A' Roads
═══ 4393 ═══	'B' Roads
────────	Railways
─ ─ ─ ─	Ferries
✈	Airports

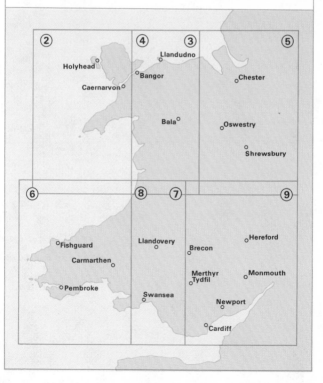

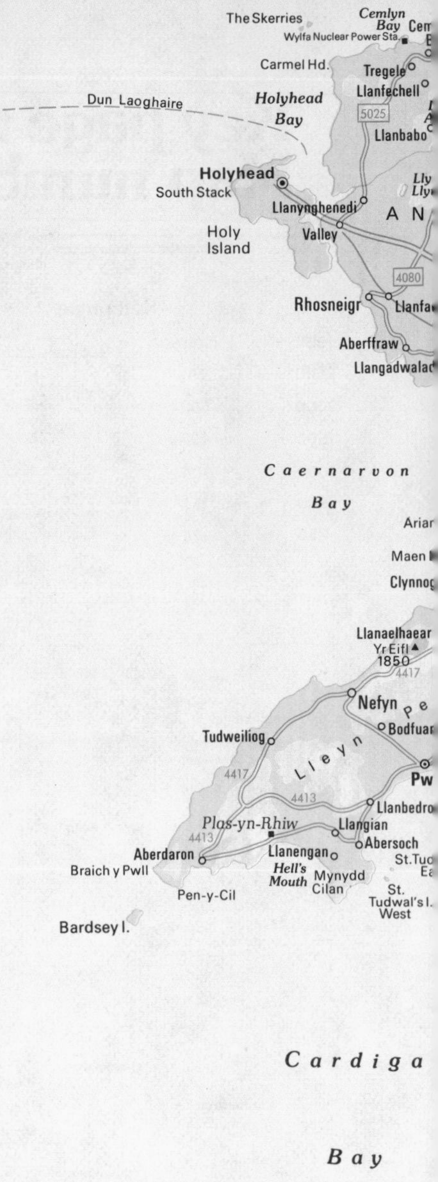

The Skerries
Cemlyn Bay Cem
Wylfa Nuclear Power Sta. E
Carmel Hd.
Tregele
Llanfechell
Holyhead Bay
5025
Dun Laoghaire
Llanbabo

Holyhead
South Stack
Llanynghenedl
Lly
Lly
A N
Holy Island
Valley
4080
Rhosneigr
Llanfa
Aberffraw
Llangadwalad

C a e r n a r v o n

B a y

Ariar

Maen

Clynnog

Llanaelhaear
Yr Eifl
1850
4417
Nefyn
P e
Bodfuar
Tudweiliog
L l e y n
4417
4413
Pw
Llanbedro
Plas-yn-Rhiw
4413
Llangian
Abersoch
Aberdaron
Llanengan
St.Tuc
Braich y Pwll
Hell's Mouth Mynydd
Ea
Pen-y-Cil
Cilan
St.
Tudwal's I.
West

Bardsey I.

C a r d i g a

B a y

Puffin I.
Gt. Ormes Head
Little Ormes Head
Pt. of Ayr

Penmon
Llandudno
Penrhyn Bay
Prestatyn
Rhyl
Trelawnyd
Whitford
Mosty

Llanfaes
Conwy Bay
Deganwy
Colwyn Bay
Rhuddlan
Dyserth
Gorsedd
Gree

Beaumaris
Conwy
Llandudno Junction
Llanddulas
Abergele
St. Asaph
Holywell
Basi

Penmaenmawr
Dolwen
Bodelwyddan
Caerwys
He

Llanfairfechan
Bodnant
Llanfair Talhaiarn
Nann

Penrhyn Castle
Tal-y-Fan 2000
Ro-wen
Tal-y-Cafn
Henllan
Rhyd-y-Mw

Bethesda
Llyn Anafon
Foel Fras 3092
Tal-y-Bont
Llansannan
Denbigh
Cilcain

Carnwedd Llewelyn 3484
Llyn Eigiau
Bychau
Llanrhaeadr
Llandyrnog
Moel

Pen Llithrig-y-Wrach 2622
Llyn Cowlyd
Llanrwst
Pentre
Moel Fammau 1820
Llan

Nant-Peris
Capel Curig
Pont Cyfnyg
Gyffylliog
Ruthin

Pen-y-Pass
Llanberis Pass
Moel Siabod 2860
Betws-y-Coed
Mynydd Hiraethog
Brenig Res.
Efenechdyd
Llanfair-Dy-Clwyd

Pen-y-Gwryd
Conwy Falls
Clocaenog Forest
Llana

Snowdon 3560
Nant Gwynant
Pont-y-Pant
Alwen Res.
Clocaenog
Llandegla

Dolwyddelan
Pentrefoelas
Derwen
Bryneglwys

Blaenau-Ffestiniog
Llyn Conwy
Ysbytty Ifan
Cerrigydrudion
Carrog
Valle Cruc Abbe

Cnicht 2265
Tanygrisiau
Gwyddelwern

Tal-y-Bont
Pont-ar-Afon-Gam
Llyn Celyn
Maerdy
Corwen
Llangoll

Maentwrog
Ffestiniog
Frongoch

Penrhyndeudraeth
Tomen-y-Mur
Arenig Fawr 2259
Llanderfel
Llandrillo
Glyn Ceiric

Talsarnau
Trawsfynydd
Bala
Lake Bala
Berwyns

Bronaber
Llanuwchllyn
Llanarmon Dyffryn Ceiriog
Llansi

Rhinog Fawr 2362
Coed-y-Brenin
Bryn Eden
Pennant-Melangell
Llanrhaeadr ym Mochnant

Nantcol
Pont Dolgefeiliau
Aran Benllyn 2901
Bwlch-y-Groes
Lake Vyrnwy
Llangynog
Penybontfawr
Llangedwy
Llansantff-ym-Mech

Llyn Bodlyn
Ganllwyd
Llanfachreth
Aran Mawddwy 2970
Llanymawddwy
Llanfyllin

Bont Newydd
Brithir
Llanwddyn

Llanelltyd
Bont-Ddu
Dolgellau
Dinas Mawddwy
Nant-y-dugoed
Meifod

Penmaenpool
Llyn Gwernan
Cader Idris 2804
Minffordd
Mallwyd
Llanerfyl
Guilsfi

Arthog
Tal-y-Llyn
Neuadd
Welshp

Fairbourne
Corris
Llanfair Caereinion
Pow Cas

Llanfihangel-y-Pennant
Cemmaes Road
Llanbrynmair
Llanllugan

Abergynolwyn
Dovey
Llan
Talerddig
Tregynon

Dysynni
Pennal
Machynlleth
Llanwnog
Montgor

Bryncrug
Cwrt

Furnace
Llanidloes
Llandinam

Ynyslas
Tre'r-Ddol
Staylittle
Van Hill 1580
Caerwys
Newtown
Kerry

Cors Fochno
Borth
Talybont
Llyn Clywedog
Hafren Forest
Plynlimon
Eisteddfa Gurig
Llandinam

Llandre
Nant-y-Moch Res.
Severn
Anc

Llanidloes

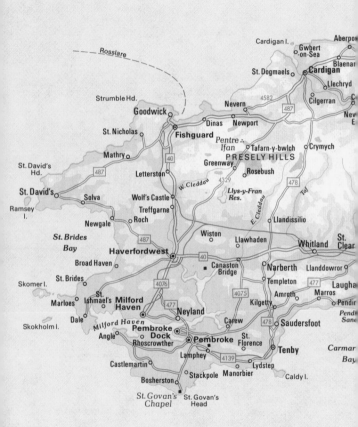

Rosslare

Cardigan I.
Aberpo
Gwbert
on-Sea
Blaenar
St. Dogmaels
Cardigan
Llechryd
Strumble Hd.
Nevern
4582
Cilgerran
Ce
Goodwick
487
Nev
Dinas
Newport
E
St. Nicholas
Fishguard
Pentre
Ifan
Tafarn-y-bwlch
Crymych
Mathry
PRESELY HILLS
Greenway
St. David's
Hd.
487
Letterston
Rosebush
W. Cleddau
4329
478
Tal
St. David's
Solva
Wolf's Castle
Llys-y-Fran
Res.
Ramsey
I.
Treffgarne
E. Cleddau
Llandissilio
Newgale
Roch
St. Brides
Bay
487
Wiston
Llawhaden
Whitland
St.
Clear
Haverfordwest
40
Broad Haven
Canaston
Bridge
Narberth
Llanddowror
St. Brides
4076
Templeton
477
Laugha
Skomer I.
St.
Ishmael's
Milford
Haven
4075
Amroth
Marros
Marloes
Kilgetty
Pendir
477
Neyland
Pendi
Sane
Dale
478
Saundersfoot
Skokholm I.
Milford Haven
Carew
Angle
Pembroke
Dock
Pembroke
St.
Florence
Tenby
Carmar
Bay
Rhoscrowther
Lamphey
Castlemartin
4139
Caldy I.
Stackpole
Lydstep
Bosherston
Manorbier
St. Govan's
Chapel
St. Govan's
Head

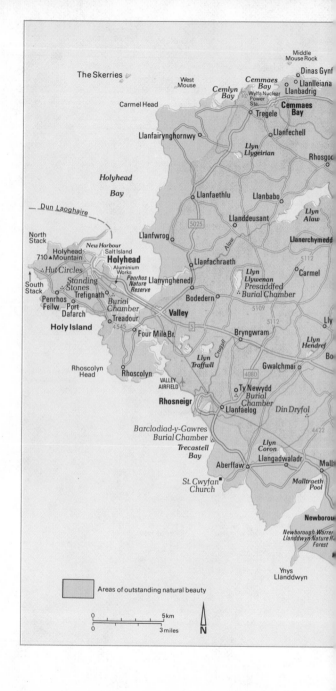

The Skerries

Middle Mouse Rock

Dinas Gynf

West Mouse

Cemmaes Bay

Llanlleiana

Llanbadrig

Cemlyn Bay

Wylfa Nuclear Power Sta.

Cemmaes Bay

Carmel Head

Tregele

Llanfechell

Llanfairynghornwy

Llyn Llygeirian

Rhosgoc

Holyhead

Llanfaethlu

Llanbabo

Bay

Llanddeusant

Llyn Alaw

Dun Laoghaire

Llanfwrog

Llanerchymedd

North Stack

710 ▲ Holyhead Mountain

New Harbour Salt Island

Holyhead

Llanfachraeth

5112

Carmel

Hut Circles

Aluminium Works

Penrhos Nature Reserve

Llanynghenedl

Llyn Llywenan Presaddfed :: Burial Chamber

South Stack

Standing Stones

Trefignath

Burial Chamber

Bodedern

5109

Lly

5112

Penrhos Feilw

Port

Dafarch

Treadour

4545

Valley

Bryngwran

Llyn Hendref

Bo

Holy Island

Four Mile Br.

5

Llyn Traffwll

Craigyll

Gwalchmai

Rhoscolyn Head

Rhoscolyn

VALLEY AIRFIELD

4080

Rhosneigr

Ty Newydd :: Burial Chamber

Llanfaelog

Din Dryfol

4422

Barclodiad-y-Gawres Burial Chamber

Trecastell Bay

Llyn Coron

Llangadwaladr

Mall

Aberffaw

Malltraeth Pool

St. Cwyfan Church

Newborou

Newborough Warren Llanddwyn Nature R Forest

Ynys Llanddwyn

Areas of outstanding natural beauty

0 ————— 5km

0 ————— 3 miles

N

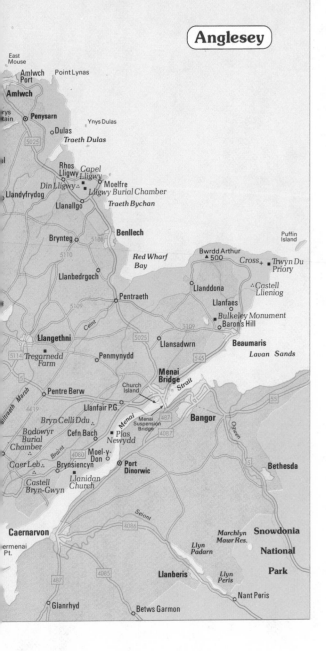

Anglesey

East Mouse
Amlwch Port
Point Lynas
Amlwch
rys tain
Penysarn
Ynys Dulas
Dulas
Traeth Dulas
B5025
al
Rhos Lligwy
Capel Lligwy
Din Lligwy
Moelfre
Lligwy Burial Chamber
Llandyfrydog
Llanallgo
Traeth Bychan
Benllech
Puffin Island
Brynteg
B5108
B5110
Red Wharf Bay
Bwrdd Arthur
▲500
Cross +
Twyn Du Priory
Llanbedrgoch
Pentraeth
B5109
Llanddona
∴*Castell Llieniog*
Llanfaes
Bulkeley Monument
Baron's Hill
B5109
Llangefni
B5025
Llansadwrn
Beaumaris
Lavan Sands
B5114
Tregarnedd Farm
Penmynydd
A545
Menai Bridge
A5
altraeth Marsh
Pentre Berw
Church Island
Menai Strait
A55
Llanfair P.G.
A4419
Bryn Celli Ddu
Menai Suspension Bridge
A487
Bangor
Ogwen
A4087
Bodowyr Burial Chamber
Cefn Bach
Plas Newydd
Caer Leb
Braint
Moel-y-Don
A4060
Bethesda
Brynsiencyn
Port Dinorwic
A5
Castell Bryn-Gwyn
Llanidan Church
ermenai Pt.
Seiont
Caernarvon
Marchlyn Mawr Res.
Snowdonia
Llyn Padarn
A4086
National
Llanberis
Llyn Peris
Park
Nant Peris
A487
A4085
Glanrhyd
Betws Garmon